SOCIAL PSYCHOLOGY

Under the General Editorship of

Jerome Kagan

Harvard University

SOCIAL PSYCHOLOGY

Kenneth J. Gergen

Mary M. Gergen

Swarthmore College

Harcourt Brace Jovanovich, Inc.

New York / San Diego / Chicago / San Francisco / Atlanta

London / Sydney / Toronto

ISBN: 0-15-581562-8

Library of Congress Catalog Card Number: 80-85167

Printed in the United States of America

Cover art: Joan Miró, *The Poetess*, 1940. Gouache and oil wash on paper, 15″ × 18⅛″.
Collection: Mr. and Mrs. Ralph F. Colin, New York.

Original cartoons by Tony Hall.

Charts by Fred Haynes.

Copyrights and Acknowledgments begin on page 546, which constitutes a continuation
of the copyright page.

For the future—

to Laura, Lisa, Stan, and Michael

PREFACE

The course of our lives is powerfully influenced by our experiences with others—in private relationships, small groups, and the larger institutions of society. Social psychology is chiefly concerned with understanding the character of those relationships. It is the discipline that focuses most sharply on people's thoughts about themselves and others, their passions and fears, their sense of right and wrong, their attempts to help and hinder each other, and their accomplishments and failures. In fact, no other field of psychology cuts common experience so close to the bone. In the present volume we wish to share what we believe are some of the most significant and stimulating insights to emerge from theory and research in social psychology. We also hope to show how the knowledge generated by social psychology contributes to self-understanding and to an understanding of broader social issues.

More specifically, the central concern of this book is the psychological basis of people's interaction with one another. Social psychology has traditionally tried to explain such behaviors as attraction, discrimination, aggression, and leadership in terms of the thoughts and feelings of the individuals involved. In treating these and other topics, our aims have been (1) to provide a coherent sense of theoretical ideas central to the field, (2) to demonstrate the significance of empirical research, (3) to make clear the real-world implications of social psychological scholarship, and (4) to do all of this in a form that will be most interesting and useful for the student reader.

Theoretical coherence. The emphasis on theoretical ideas begins in the first chapter of the book. There we compare the behaviorist, cognitive, and rule-role orientations. We believe that these viewpoints form the generating context for many of the more specific ideas in the volume. In later chapters we show how these orientations have influenced the questions that have been asked and the explanations that have been offered for various kinds of social behavior. In our discussion of attitude change in Chapter 5, for example, we distinguish between the behaviorists' focus on outward influences on attitudes—the characteristics of the audience, message, and the like—and the cognitivists' focus on inner processes—memory, attention, and thinking. In the discussion of morality in Chapter 6, we highlight the behaviorists' focus on moral action and the cognitivists' concern with moral thinking.

Research importance. In each chapter we have tried to create a framework that gives structure to the wide range of data that has been amassed by researchers in the field. Research findings are essential, we believe, in lending strength to theoretical insights. And the student should gain from the book a basic understanding of the place of research both in social psychology and in society. In each chapter we discuss representative studies in enough detail to stimulate classroom discussion.

Broad implications. Throughout the book we have tried to make clear that social psychology is a discipline with significant application to major areas of social life. We emphasize the contributions that social psychology can make to the way in which people manage their lives and to the solution of such problems as race and sex discrimination, crime, poverty, and international conflict.

Clarity of presentation. For a textbook to be useful, it must engage the reader. We hope that our writing style, including our use of anecdotes and examples, will draw the reader in and maintain his or her interest. For the sake of clarity we have minimized jargon and offered in-text definitions of technical terms. We pause often to review and at the end of each chapter present point-by-point summaries.

A specific logic underlies the organization of the book. We start by introducing the student to the field, discussing the nature of theory and research as well as specific theories and methods. In the next four chapters we focus on the individual, looking at the processes of thought and feeling that are of greatest consequence in relationships with others. In their concern with psychological process, these chapters on social perception, attraction, prejudice, and attitude change form the building blocks for the remainder of the volume. We then begin to shift emphasis outward toward social conduct. In chapters on morality, positive social action, and aggression we explore the relationship between psychological processes on the one hand and social action on the other. The next three chapters shift the balance more strongly in the direction of social action. In these discussions of social influence, power, and social exchange our central concern is with the interdependency of people's actions—how each person's behavior depends on the actions of others. The chapter on small group psychology extends this concern to special problems that result from increasing the numbers of persons in a relationship. The final chapter, dealing with the application of social psychology to problems of the physical and social environment, complements the introductory chapter. Whereas we first channeled interest inward toward the subject of social psychology, we end by turning the student's interest again toward problems in the society more generally.

The within-chapter presentation has its own organization as well. We begin each section with major ideas and findings. At the close of these discussions we often suggest possible qualification of the major arguments. Students learn best when discussions are clear-cut and simple. Nevertheless, social psychology is anything but simple-minded, and its conclusions are anything but final. We feel that it would be a disservice to the student and the profession to omit indications of the continuous questioning and creating that are central to scholarly life.

All of the above considerations—from logic of the organization to strategies of presentation—have influenced our choice of materials. We have tried to choose work that has interest and relevance as well as scholarly merit. We give full attention to the classic work, to the theory and research that form the foundation of the discipline. We also explore the more exciting areas of contemporary research. And for those concerned with the discipline's future, we include discussions of new departures in thinking and research.

The book is intended for introductory courses in social psychology. We have tried to write in a clear and concise way that can be appreciated by students of wide-ranging abilities. Each chapter begins with an outline of major headings and subheadings. To increase the impact of the verbal material we have included many figures, tables, and photographs. Each has a caption designed to draw the reader's attention to the significance of the material and to underscore points made in the text. Important issues are further underscored in a series of cartoons drawn for us by the British artist Tony Hall. No words can rise to the level of his puckish imagination, and we offer his drawings without captions, leaving the reader the fun of puzzling out their meaning. Boxes in each chapter complement the text; these typically explore innovative research topics and applications. As an invitation to the student who wishes to read further, we have included a list of suggested readings at the end of each chapter and an extensive list of references at the end of the book. A glossary of key terms is also found at the end of the book.

For whatever virtues one may find in the volume, we can hardly take full credit. This book is truly the result of a collective effort. In part, such efforts have been indirect. Our students have taught us much; these lessons are reflected on every page. Similarly, past teachers and colleagues such as Kurt W. Back, Raymond Bauer, Arthur R. Cohen, Edward E. Jones, David Riesman, and John Thibaut have furnished unstinting inspiration to the senior author. The junior author wishes to thank her teachers at Temple University, particularly Louise H. Kidder, Ralph Rosnow, and Willis F. Overton, as well as her first mentor in social psychology, Kenneth Gergen.

Many others have had a direct impact on the volume. Without the unceasing enthusiasm and infectious stimulation of Judith Greissman, Psychology Editor at Harcourt Brace Jovanovich, this book would never have been completed. Phyllis Fisher, our editor at HBJ, has contributed so much in the way of intelligence, sensitivity, and verbal fluency to the present manuscript that we hesitate to claim sole authorship. Didi Beebe of Swarthmore College has been a pillar of strength throughout; she has patiently typed and retyped the half-dozen revisions of each chapter, while simultaneously furnishing insightful opinion and psychological support. Sue Santa Maria contributed additional invaluable secretarial and organizational help along with much supportive concern. Elizabeth Albrecht of Swarthmore College has not only served as author of the glossary, but with tenacity and self-sacrifice successfully juggled thousands of details under impossible deadlines. Jill Morawski of Wesleyan University has given generously to this endeavor, developing the index and lifting our spirits throughout. The book has also profited from the work of other staff members at Harcourt Brace Jovanovich. We especially want to thank Marilyn Marcus, who designed the book; Dodie Shaw, who researched the photographs; Abigail Winograd and Carolyn Viola-John, who copy edited the manuscript; and Tracy Cabanis, who managed the in-house course of production. They have not only contributed their considerable skills, but they have made us aware that we were working with one of the finest publishing teams in the world.

We wish also to thank our colleagues in the field who have made an inestimable contribution to the book through their critical reviews. We owe a particular debt of gratitude to Ellen Berscheid of the University of Minnesota, who reviewed the first draft of the manuscript in detail and made a close appraisal of the third revision. Her imagination, creativity, and commitment have been so vast that thanks are really inadequate. Her knowledge and insights will be found throughout the book. We also want to thank Jerome Kagan of Harvard University, our General Editor, for his careful readings of each chapter. In addition, the volume has been improved inestimably by the careful and sophisticated chapter reviews furnished by:

Richard D. Ashmore, Rutgers University

Jim Bryan, Research and Education Consultants, Evanston, Illinois

Robert B. Cialdini, Arizona State University

Ed Donnerstein, University of Wisconsin

Alice H. Eagly, University of Massachusetts

Jeffrey David Fisher, University of Connecticut

Russell G. Geen, University of Missouri

George T. Goethals, Williams College

Martin S. Greenberg, University of Pittsburgh

Karl L. Hakmiller, University of Connecticut

David Kipnis, Temple University

George Levinger, University of Massachusetts

Darwyn E. Linder, Arizona State University

Daniel McGillis, Harvard University

Norman Miller, University of Southern California

Walter S. Neff, East Hampton, New York

Harry Reis, University of Rochester

Kelly G. Shaver, College of William and Mary

Harold Sigall, University of Maryland

Ivan D. Steiner, University of Massachusetts

Abraham Tesser, University of Georgia

Ladd Wheeler, University of Rochester

Russell H. Wiegel, Amherst College

Lauren Wispé, University of Oklahoma

Finally, we wish to thank those family members, friends, and acquaintances who have brought many of the ideas in the book vividly to life, whose enthusiasm has been essential to us, and whose experiences will be found throughout these pages.

Kenneth J. Gergen
Mary M. Gergen

CONTENTS

SOCIAL PERCEPTION 38

INTERPERSONAL ATTRACTION 80

PREJUDICE AND DISCRIMINATION 118

ATTITUDE CHANGE 160

MORALITY IN THOUGHT AND ACTION 200

POSITIVE SOCIAL ACTION 240

AGGRESSION 276

POWER, LEADERSHIP, AND CONTROL   310

SOCIAL INFLUENCE 346

EXCHANGE AND STRATEGY 382

INTERACTION IN GROUPS 418

THE PHYSICAL AND SOCIAL ENVIRONMENT 454

SOCIAL PSYCHOLOGY

THEORY AND RESEARCH IN SOCIAL PSYCHOLOGY

■ *Stephen, a promising young architect, won a coveted award that enabled him to travel for six months and see the world's architectural treasures. Stephen set out in September, leaving his wife and their two school-aged children behind. He returned in mid-October, in a state of emotional turmoil. He had discovered that he could not survive emotionally without his family. Since they could not afford to travel together, Stephen gave up the remaining months of travel.*

■ *For the fourth year in a row Donna has devoted herself tirelessly to her studies. She seldom attends campus social events and she doesn't participate in any activities that would interfere with her work. The results of her devotion have paid off: she has been accepted by one of the top medical schools in the country. Most importantly, she has lived up to the wishes of her father, who died prematurely just before she entered college. Before her father died, Donna solemnly promised him that she would take his place in the medical profession.*

■ *Rich was fired recently from his job with a construction company. For many months he had been a cement-truck driver. However, when making a delivery early one morning he passed his girlfriend's apartment and saw his best friend's convertible parked in front. Rich deposited the entire load of cement into the car.*

What do these three dramas of daily life have in common? Each of them highlights the enormous significance of personal relationships in people's lives. Stephen gave up a coveted award because of his deep attachment to his family. Donna made a promise to her father that has dictated the course of her life. Rich's anger over his friends' deceit moved him to make a dramatic but costly action. Whether developing friendships, sustaining love, protecting life and limb, or simply trying to live in harmony with modern social institutions, relationships with others dominate most people's lives and influence their plans and goals.

These dramas of daily life also have in common the puzzlement that they create in the observer. Stephen, Donna, and Rich seem to have allowed their emotions to interfere with their reason. Stephen returned to his family too quickly. Would most people be so attached? Donna's obligation to her father seems to be too intense. Why would a person keep a promise for a lifetime when others break promises in a moment? And Rich's behavior could end only in punishment. Why did he dump the cement into his friend's car when he could have found many less costly ways of getting even? The world of daily relationships abounds in questions like these, and the search for answers consumes much time and energy.

The issues raised by these stories are precisely those that interest social psychologists. Because relationships are critically important to people and often are hard to understand, they deserve careful study and thoughtful explanation. The social psychologist attempts to carry out such study, to develop explanations, and to demonstrate how the explanations relate to daily life. Most social psychologists hope to improve the human condition through their work—furnishing insights and answers that will enable people to lead more fulfilling lives. As this book will demonstrate, social psychology spans an immense range of concerns. Topics of interest include how people perceive or think about each other, why people develop feelings of attraction and hostility, how people's attitudes develop and change, why people hurt one another, how they select leaders, and why they rebel against them.

What Is Social Psychology?

In formal terms, *social psychology* is a discipline devoted to the *systematic study of human interaction and its psychological basis.* Systematic study usually includes the following three major components:

1. *The development of theory.* The social psychologist tries to *describe* and *explain* aspects of social life, using clear and logically connected statements. These theoretical statements not only allow people to understand the world in an orderly way, but they also explain why things happen as they do. The explanations typically rely on psychological concepts, such as thought, affect, attitude, expectancy, or rule.

2. *The documentation of theory.* Not only does the psychologist describe and explain, but he or she attempts to *document the theoretical ideas* with carefully collected data. To facilitate this effort, a variety of research techniques—experiments, field observations, and analyses of historical documents—may be used to demonstrate the strength and importance of the theory.

3. *The encouragement of action.* Many, but not all, social psychologists believe that systematic study is not complete unless it leads to *social action.* The results of theory and research should be made available to other social psychologists and to the public. Theoretical ideas should be put into use—whether in relationships with family members, with friends and people in the community, or when making public policy. When ideas are put into action, evaluation can take place, weaknesses can be found, and the ideas can be revised.

No precise boundary exists between social psychology and other domains of psychology, such as learning, development, and personality. Although specialists in these other areas do not focus their attention on social interaction, they share with social psychologists many areas of common interest. Thus, for example, you will find that concepts of the learning psychologist are employed in this volume to explain human aggression (Chapter 8); developmental concepts are used to explain morality (Chapter 6); and personality concepts are used to explain prejudice (Chapter 4) and power (Chapter 9).

The social psychologist's concern with human interaction also is shared with sociologists, political scientists, and anthropologists. How, then, does social psychology differ from these disciplines? Again, boundaries among disciplines are not clearly defined. However, two key differences distinguish much work in sociology and political science from that in social psychology. They are as follows:

1. *The unit of analysis.* The entity selected for study in social psychology is the *individual actor.* The major question in social psychology is how the individual person carries out relationships with other people. In contrast, the usual focus of study in both sociology and political science is the large institution or group (for example, the Senate, the Republican party, the medical profession, or the educational system).

2. *The base of explanation.* The focus of interest in social psychology is the *internal processes of the individual.* Psychologists explain people's action in terms of thoughts, emotions, attitudes, and other inner processes. Sociologists and political

scientists generally do not use psychological concepts such as these to explain group behavior. Sociologists and political scientists explain the actions of institutions or groups in terms of the organizational divisions, the distribution of power, the rigidity of the hierarchy, and similar external processes. In effect, they explain group action on the basis of group properties.

Social psychologists share many interests with social anthropologists. Indeed, many social psychologists are deeply engaged in the comparison of social patterns across cultures (Segall, 1979; Triandis and Brislin, 1980). Both disciplines tend to use the individual as the principal unit of analysis, and they tend to use psychological concepts to explain behavior. However, one major difference separates most social psychologists from their colleagues in anthropology. The social psychologist searches for *similarities among people across cultures.* In contrast, the social anthropologist is interested primarily in the way *cultures differ from one another.* Anthropologists usually try to understand the patterns of human relationships *within* distinct cultures. They seek answers to such questions as what characterizes the typical behavior of the Japanese, the Trobriand Islanders, or the Ik? And, how do these patterns differ from one another and from those in Western culture?

In this chapter we will introduce some of the basic assumptions of the discipline of social psychology. We will look at the ways in which social psychologists deal with problems of human action, and we will examine the problems and pitfalls of such work. First we present a brief history of the shaping of modern social psychology: we describe how the field developed from social philosophy and what new ingredients have been added to it. We then consider the two major products of social psychology: theory and research. We consider what social psychologists hope to accomplish in their theory and data gathering, and why. We describe the major theoretical orientations of contemporary social psychology: the behaviorist, the cognitive, and the rule-role. Strong competition exists among these views, even though this competition is not always obvious to the student. Finally we turn to the methods of research and look at the major research methods, their advantages, and their shortcomings.

The Shaping of Modern Social Psychology

Interest in the problems of human interaction is not new. Theories about social behavior predate systematic thinking about the physical world. In fact, many of the basic concepts that were used in the first formal studies of physical phenomena were drawn from earlier theories of social life (Durkheim, 1895). Scholars such as Plato, Aristotle, Kant, Hegel, Locke, Bentham, Mill, Hobbes, and Rousseau thought deeply and creatively about how people come to act as they do, and their work set the stage for modern social psychology.

Yet, if over the centuries such serious scholarly attention has been given to understanding human relations, what more does modern social psychology have to offer? In what sense does modern social psychology differ from previous forms of inquiry? This question has two major answers: the first is concerned with theory, and the second with method.

Theory in the Development of a Scholarly Profession

A century ago there was virtually no recognizable profession of social psychology. Social thought was confined largely to a small segment in the study of philosophy. Today approximately five thousand psychologists in the United States and Canada devote their professional lives to the systematic study of social behavior. The rate of growth in the field of social psychology has been phenomenal. Over 90 percent of all investigation in social psychology has been conducted within the last twenty-five years (Shaver, 1977). The first North American textbook in social psychology, written by William McDougall, was published in 1908. This text is concerned almost wholly with the power of biological instincts in controlling social life. It refers to the works of fewer than one hundred fifty scholars, more than two-thirds of whom were not psychologists. In contrast, this textbook treats twelve major topics, including social perception, attraction, prejudice, attitude change, aggression, altruism, and group processes. The influence of instincts now is a relatively minor issue. Our own reference list, not an unusual one, includes the names of over three thousand scholars. Most of these individuals are professional social psychologists. Social psychology now is an identifiable profession.

The development of social psychology has had two notable effects on social theory. First, advances have taken place in the richness or complexity of social thought. Early theoretical formulations tended to be *simple* and *sovereign* (Allport, 1968). That is, the formulations often relied on a single guiding principle, and all answers to the complex questions of social life were derived from this unifying principle. For example, philosophers such as Jeremy Bentham and John Stuart Mill developed the doctrine of *hedonism,* which proposes that people's actions are driven by the search for pleasure and the avoidance of pain. In contrast, Thomas Hobbes believed that the central motivating force is *power.* As he maintained, people possess "a desire for power after power that ceaseth only in death" (1651, p. 63). And according to the French theorist Gabriel Tarde, people's innate tendency to *imitate* each other furnishes the "key to the social mystery." For Tarde, "society is imitation" (1903, p. 74).

As you will see, each of these motives—pleasure, power, and imitation—continues to be of critical interest to social psychologists. However, simple and sovereign formulations have largely withered as the profession has grown, and multiple views of social issues have been developed. Social psychologists now see a wide range of factors motivating people's behavior, and they try to understand and take account of these factors in all of their complexity. Thus, for example, virtually no contemporary social psychologist would suggest that power is the only factor of importance in social life. Investigators who are concerned with power have tried to differentiate among various kinds of power and understand their advantages and limitations (see Chapter 9).

In addition to advancing the richness or complexity of social theory, the development of social psychology also has been accompanied by an increased concern for application. Most early social thinkers were philosophers; they were less concerned than are today's psychologists with how theory can help solve the *concrete problems* that face the society. This concern with application developed in part in response to the problems that arose when a large number of people immigrated to the North American continent (Apfelbaum, 1978; Samelson, 1980) and in part in response to the needs of industrialists, who believed that workers might be engineered in the way that machines are (Baritz, 1980; Schwartz, Lacey, and Schuldenfrei, 1978; Sokal, 1980). Perhaps the most important stimulant to theoretical application, however, was the Second World War. Psychologists pitched in to help in the war effort. In 1939 the American Psychological Association announced:

> Be it resolved that the American Psychological Association, believing democratic institutions to be the indispensable foundation of free scientific inquiry into human behavior, record its conviction that earnest efforts should be

made by American psychologists to study all those phases of American life and opinion which bear on the safeguarding of our fundamental liberties and peaceful way of life.

The outcome of the close connections between the profession of social psychology and the remainder of society is best reflected in theories of prejudice (Chapter 4), attitude change (Chapter 5), conformity (Chapter 10), and group productivity (Chapter 12).

Thus we see that with the development of a scholarly profession two major changes took place in the character of social theory. First, as compared with the simple and sovereign theories of the past, social psychological theory has become both richer and more complex. Second, because of the intimate connections between social psychology and such institutions as government and industry, much social psychological theory has been directed toward the solution of social problems.

The Development of Observational Skills

We now have seen how modern social theory differs from the work that was done by social thinkers of the past. Another important difference is in the arsenal of observational methods that psychologists now have at their disposal. As you would expect, advances in natural science were largely responsible for the development of social science. The most outstanding feature of natural science is its emphasis on rigorous observation. Social scientists began to realize that they must adopt similar procedures if their studies of human behavior were to yield substantial gains.

In this atmosphere Norman Triplett set out in 1897 to conduct one of the first systematic studies of social activity. Triplett was interested in finding what effects the social environment had on human performance. Would people perform various tasks more effectively if other people were present or if they were absent? And how would competition with other people affect a person's performance? Triplett first explored these questions by scanning the records of bicyclists who had completed a twenty-five-mile course under one of three conditions: (1) competing against a clock, (2) riding with a companion who paced them, and (3) competing with other riders. Under which condition would the cyclist perform with the greatest speed? The results showed that the presence of another person facilitated performance greatly. When riding alone against the clock, the cyclists averaged approximately twenty-four miles per hour. However, when a pacer was present the average speed was thirty-one miles per hour. Competition failed to improve this speed very much (the average was about thirty-two and a half miles per hour). Triplett continued his work by demonstrating that similar effects occurred when subjects in the laboratory carried out such tasks as counting, jumping up and down, or winding fishing reels. In Chapter 12, in a discussion of *social facilitation*, we will deal more extensively with such effects.

The emphasis on observation has increased dramatically since the turn of the century. Research methodology has become highly sophisticated over the years. Methods of electronic observation now enable psychologists to make precise records of behavior in social settings, and by using survey procedures scientists are able to sample from the population at large. Statistical procedures that enable investigators to make sound estimates of the *reliability* or repeatability of their findings have been developed. Human social behavior now is far better documented than ever before. Research reports currently represent one of the chief products of the discipline. Some 90 percent of all articles that appear in the field's most prestigious journal, *The Journal of Personality and Social Psychology*, report the results of experimental studies.

Purposes of Theory

Social psychologists are concerned with theories and with precise observation of interpersonal behavior. With these products they attempt to help the society better its condition. But how are theories and research used to accomplish these aims? How can they be of help to people? Let us turn first to theory. What is a theory, and what purposes does it serve?

A *theory* may be defined as a set of logically related propositions that describe and explain a domain of observation. Everyone constructs informal theories about social behavior. Some people may believe, for example, that as people get wealthier they begin to resist social change. They also may believe that as a person's love for someone increases, his or her love for other people will decrease. Consider an additional example. You probably would accept the proposition that people who dress the way you dress would be more likely than people who dress differently to come to your aid. This proposition probably *describes* your general experience with some accuracy. You also might accept the additional formulation that people who dress the way you dress would be more likely than people who dress differently to do a favor for you, because they would feel that you are one of them and not likely to bring harm. This is a *proposition*, or statement, that *explains* why there is a relationship between similar dress and doing favors. When a theoretical proposition is used to predict behavior that as yet is unobserved, we generally refer to it as a *hypothesis*. Thus, if you were in a strange city and your wallet was stolen, you might use the similar-dress hypothesis when choosing a person to ask to help you.

How do social psychologists' theories differ from the theories used on an informal basis? First, social psychologists attempt to make their theories *public*, or *explicit*. Even though the proposition about the relationship between similar dress and doing favors may not be a surprise to you, most people have probably never stated this idea in so many words—it has remained implicit, or unstated. The social psychologist makes such statements public so that they can be critically examined and so their strengths and weaknesses can be made clear. Would the similar-dress proposition always stand up under critical scrutiny? Probably not. For example, would a woman in an evening dress be likely to receive help changing a flat tire from another woman dressed in an evening dress? As the theory becomes explicit and criticisms are encountered, it can be developed and enriched.

In addition to making their theories public, social psychologists also attempt to formulate *general propositions*—that is, nonspecific statements of explanation. Most of the theories people develop in their daily relationships apply to very specific aspects of their lives. You may have implicit theories about how your parents will react to your school performance or how your friends will respond to your taste in music. In contrast, social psychologists try to formulate propositions that are relevant to most people's lives. For instance, rather than focusing attention on similarity in clothing styles, social psychologists have tried to understand how people react to other people whose opinions, styles of relating, and a variety of other general characteristics are similar to theirs (see Chapter 3). Propositions about similarity in clothing style would be considered a minor aspect of the more general problem. Social psychologists often want their theories to speak to people everywhere and for all times.

Finally, social psychologists make a special attempt to develop theories that are *logically coherent*. Most implicit theories are filled with contradictions. Someone may believe that people really need security and stability in their lives, and at the same time he or she may believe that people need growth

*Gestures
across Space
and Time*

How would you react if a male friend made a gesture by poking his thumb through his clenched fist? Chances are you would find the gesture to be meaningless; it would communicate nothing, and you might disregard it. In fact, according to Desmond Morris and his colleagues (1979), if you lived in twelfth-century Italy you might have responded to the gesture with hurt feelings or hostility. As is indicated by Morris's study of gestures across history and culture, medieval Italians used this particular gesture as an insult. And although most North Americans would find the gesture to be meaningless, it has continued to have important significance in many European communities. Interestingly, however, the gesture is no longer viewed as an insult, but rather, as a signal of sexual arousal. The thumb symbolizes the male genital, and the bent fingers symbolize the genitals of the female. The sexual meaning of the gesture predates its insulting implications and can be traced to pre-Christian Greece, where small carvings of the gesture were worn as good-luck tokens. The evil spirits, it was believed, would be so fascinated by the female genitals that they would be distracted from their purposes.

Consider the gesture shown on the next page—the middle finger bent across the index finger. If a friend made this gesture in your presence, you might think that he or she was wishing you good luck. In using this gesture, North Americans can communicate quite well with Europeans. Both communities use the symbol for luck and as a protective signal. The gesture says, in effect, "I hope all goes well." According to Morris and his colleagues, this particular meaning originated with the early Christians.

and change. Or someone may believe that people want love more than anything else, and at the same time he or she may believe that people today try to avoid deep relationships. In constructing theories, the social psychologist makes a strong effort to avoid these kinds of contradictions. When contradictions are discovered the theorist often is motivated to revise the theory or develop it in greater detail.

Given these special characteristics of social psychological theory, we may now ask more directly, what do social psychologists hope to accomplish with their theories? Let us consider three major goals: increased un-

derstanding, increased sensitivity, and access to new ways of behaving.

The Organization and Communication of Experience

To appreciate the social theorist's first major aim, you might consider the interesting fact that, for the most part, people's actions—talking, smiling, sitting, walking down the street, holding hands—make sense to you. You recognize the meaning of these activities because of your previous learning. Other people's behavior doesn't come prepackaged in organized and comprehensible units. Rather,

Instead of publicly making the sign of the cross, they used this gesture to express in an obscure and less noticeable way the wish that the Holy Spirit would go with a departing person. Yet this meaning is not shared around the world. In many communities the gesture is used to undo a falsehood. Children will cross their fingers while telling a lie. In modern Turkey the gesture symbolizes neither luck nor the wish to undo a lie. Instead, the sign indicates deep friendship. The two fingers in this case appear to signal intertwined persons—two persons being one.

Thus, whether a word or a gesture is recognized as having meaning and whatever meaning it possesses may change across time and across cultures.

each member of a culture must learn to recognize that certain patterns of behavior form distinct units (talking, sitting, smiling). And the individual must refer to these units in order to communicate with others successfully. American children learn, for example, that certain patterns of behavior are signals of hostility (for example, thumb to the nose or middle finger raised) and that these patterns must be distinguished from signals of affection (a hug or a kiss, for example). The particular patterns singled out for attention will vary from one culture to another and across history. Many insulting gestures in contemporary North America probably would not have been recognized as meaningful actions in eighth-century Persia.

Over time the members of a culture also learn to attach verbal labels to these various units of behavior. Certain actions are labeled *insults*, and others are called *compliments*. Once verbal labels have been assigned, large amounts of information about the world can be transmitted from one person to another. People can discuss their common problems and develop solutions together. And so, whether the newcomer is a growing infant or a foreign visitor, acquiring the language of a culture means developing a way of understanding the world and learning a way of effectively communicating about it. Social psychological theorists work in a similar way. They try to discern patterns of social life and develop words that will enable people to communicate about those patterns. Their theories furnish a means of understanding and the means to communicate this understanding to others. For example, many social psychologists are concerned about the quality of urban life. Understanding urban life requires making distinctions and developing terms to represent these distinctions. One interesting distinction that has emerged from this work is the *friendly stranger* (Milgram, 1977). The friendly stranger is a person whom one sees often enough to recognize, but with whom one has no relationship. Because friendly strangers exist, life in large cities may not be as impersonal and anonymous as it often is thought to be. People frequently may feel as if they are in the company of others whom they "know," even if they don't actually communicate with those individuals. Yet if the theorist had not developed the concept of the friendly stranger, recognition of and communication about this kind of silent social support would have remained unknown.

Theory as a Sensitizing Device

Prediction of ongoing events also has been an aim of social theorists. Following in the footsteps of the natural scientists, social theorists have hoped that their theories could ultimately be used to make sound predictions of such issues as divorce, personal success, racial tension, or who would become President. Although many persons in the field still hope that such predictions will be possible one day, mounting opinion suggests that this view is overly optimistic. There are two major reasons for such doubts. First, the facts of social life undergo frequent change. People's desires, beliefs, wants, needs, and hopes change as time goes by, and there is little reason to suspect that today's accurate account of behavior

will serve as an adequate basis for predictions for a later period (Cronbach, 1975; Gergen, 1973). Second, accurate prediction is threatened by *enlightenment effects.* That is, people may be enlightened by theory and change their activities as a result, so the theory no longer can be used to make successful predictions (Scheibe, 1979). If you were aware of a theory that predicted you would get divorced, you might try especially hard to maintain a good marital relationship. The theory then would fail to predict your behavior.

Because of these problems, many social psychologists no longer believe that firm prediction should be a chief purpose of theory. Rather, theories may best serve as *sensitizers,* pointing to possible factors that influence people's daily lives and calling attention to possible consequences of their actions. While theories may not offer precise predictions, they can be extremely useful in suggesting what might happen and why. Armed with such suggestions, people may better prepare themselves for the future.

Theory as a Liberating Agent

For many women who feel or have felt confined by the role of homemaker, the women's movement has had a liberating effect. Women increasingly have come to realize that their traditional role is the result of cultural myths about male-female differences, and because of this realization they have begun to seek alternative lifestyles. Social psychologists also attempt to develop theories that will both increase people's awareness of the shortcomings that exist in their present activities and guide them to more fruitful alternatives. Theories used in this way may liberate people from existing constraints of everyday life.

These theoretical aspirations were developed initially in the 1920s by a group of social scientists at the Institute of Social Research, in Frankfurt, Germany. This group, often called the Frankfurt School (Jay, 1973), was

influenced strongly by Karl Marx's writings and was especially disturbed by the great social inequalities that had been produced by the capitalist system in which they lived. They argued that the capitalist system continued to thrive in part because people had ceased questioning its basic assumptions. What was needed, then, was critical theorizing, theorizing that would point to the shortcomings in people's basic assumptions. This, they felt, would open people's minds to the possibilities of a Marxist system.

Many contemporary social psychologists believe that their profession should continue to raise questions concerning the basic assumptions or beliefs about *social life.* They hope to open people's minds to new ideas by designing theories that suggest alternatives to the *status quo.* A theory that creates such alternatives may be termed a *generative theory* (Gergen, 1978). Such theories challenge the assumptions that are common to a culture, giving people a chance to question what previously they believed to be true, and in the

process of creating this challenge they offer choice in place of dogmatic or unquestioned beliefs. Consider, for example, a typical "truth." Most people's theories about child rearing include the assumption that a harmonious relationship between parents is essential if children are to grow up happily. Parents who believe this may try hard to make their relationship seem to be amicable, at least on the surface. This fundamental assumption thus determines their actions. Yet one might pose a contrary theory, arguing that parents should be emotionally open: they should air their disagreements and vent their hostilities so that the child will learn to confront a world of real, as opposed to artificial, people. This kind of theory, which is contrary to widely accepted beliefs, is generative. It challenges people to try other alternatives.

In summary, then, theories of social behavior may be useful in making the social world understandable, in increasing sensitivity to factors that influence people's lives, and in helping people find new ways of behaving.

Now we will turn to research and see what important purposes it serves.

The Fruits of Research

Few social psychologists are content with theorizing alone. They typically try to link their theories to research in order to provide information about past and present patterns of social behavior, in order to help forecast coming events, and in order to increase the impact of theory through demonstration. In this section we will discuss these central goals of research. And later in this chapter we will explore the principal research methods that are used.

The Documentation of Social Life

Have you ever wondered about the proportion of the population that uses marijuana, the amount of prejudice that is directed against Jews and Catholics, or the size of the gay community in contemporary society? These are important questions. Their answers can influence people's actions—their votes, their choice of career, their choice of residence, and so forth.

Often the task of describing social life is left to the social critic, the news commentator, or the politician. However most of their accounts rely on the personal and possibly biased views of people who have gathered little systematic information and who are not concerned with the adequacy of their population samples or the reliability of their observations. In contrast, social psychologists are quite concerned with such matters and have developed a systematic battery of methods that can yield highly reliable information about social life.

To illustrate the kind of insights that systematic research can offer, consider the problem of police brutality. In 1968, millions of people watched Chicago police on television

Do you approve of the police officer's behavior? Survey research has shown that punitive action is strongly supported by a large percentage of white, middle-aged men and women. Young people and black men and women—who may be hurt in encounters with the police—are likely to oppose police violence.

as they used dogs, clubs, and tear gas to attack demonstrators at the Democratic national convention. This was not a unique occurrence. The police sometimes appear to abuse their position, harassing, physically attacking, and even killing people who are relatively helpless. But what is the public's reaction to police brutality? Do people care? And if they care, why don't they collectively do something about it?

To explore these issues investigators surveyed a sample of over eleven hundred individuals who had been selected randomly from the national population (Gamson and McEvoy, 1970). Respondents were asked, among other things, whether they believed that (1) the police were wrong to beat up unarmed protesters, even if the protesters called them names, (2) the police often used more force than was really needed, and (3) a man who insults a policeman has reason for complaint if he gets beaten up. In analyzing the data, the researchers categorized people into two groups: those who tended to agree or strongly agree that police violence was wrong and those who were not opposed to police violence.

The results of this study proved to be both surprising and disappointing to the researchers. Among white citizens of the United States, only 27 percent were opposed to police violence. Among citizens over 50 years of age who were financially well satisfied and who were Republicans, there was almost no opposition to police violence. But what about black Americans, the people who most often suffer from police violence? The data showed that a full 69 percent of this group opposed police violence in all of the above cases. They were joined in their sentiments by young, educated, white citizens.

These results provide new information about social behavior in that they suggest that one of the major reasons for police brutality in America is that it is approved of by the majority. The police really don't have to worry too much if they abuse the rights of those persons who are slightly out of line. The results also provide fuel for social change. Living in a democracy need not mean that the majority has the right to tyrannize the minority. And if the minority is the major target of police brutality, legal and political action may be taken. Finally, it appears that the young and the educated could play a special role in changing the situation.

Social Prediction

In addition to its role in documenting social life, research can play an important role in aiding prediction. Society faces an immense number of problems for which reliable predictions would be valuable. For example,

many lives would be improved if schools could predict which students would make good doctors, if young couples could predict which marriages were likely to end in divorce, or if legislators could predict how their constituents would react to a new piece of legislation. Social forecasting is always hazardous; it is far more difficult than is predicting the weather. Social events are always in flux, and new incidents are taking place that may upset the forecasts. Forecasting the stock market, for example, is seldom successful, primarily because market prices can be influenced by almost anything—from today's presidential announcement to tomorrow's snowfall in Manhattan. Yet with proper methods limited predictions about social life are possible, and these predictions can be more successful than is impulsive guesswork.

To illustrate, consider the problem of energy. There are many powerful reasons why people should reduce their consumption of energy, and yet it is not at all clear that people will change their ways. Similarly, good arguments can be made against smoking, and millions of people continue to smoke. In both cases, programs and policies are needed to convince people to change their ways. But what kinds of policies or programs are required? Testing every program that comes to mind would be too costly a process. Can predictions be made about what kinds of programs will work best?

One way to improve prediction is to find out why people continue to use energy, even though there seems to be a crisis. Is it because they don't believe in the crisis, or is it not worth the extra money they would save, or are they simply unwilling to give up their comforts? To explore these possibilities, researchers asked over one hundred adult couples to complete a questionnaire regarding their use of energy (Seligman et al., 1979). Questions were concerned with the respondents' beliefs in the energy crisis, their efforts to save money, and their desire for comfort.

Permission was obtained to take readings from the respondents' electric meters during the hot summer months when air conditioners might be in use.

Armed with these data, the researchers were able to examine the relationship between attitudes toward the crisis, as expressed in the subjects' answers to the various questions, and energy use. The results indicated that the most significant factor in accounting for energy use was comfort. People who said that comfort was important used great amounts of electricity. Those who felt that comfort was less important used very little energy. Belief in the energy crisis or attitudes toward saving money made little difference in energy use.

More extensive research would be required before national programs could be set up to encourage saving energy. Clearly, however, one could predict that a program designed to deal with people's feelings about comfort would be far more effective in reducing energy consumption than would a program designed to convince people of the reality of the crisis or the benefits of saving money. With research results such as these, one can formulate plans that are far better than are those that rely on guesswork.

Demonstration of Theory

We have seen that theory can do much to make events understandable, to call attention

Will Americans accept the wind car? Rapidly rising fuel prices have encouraged inventive people like James L. Amich of Ann Arbor, Michigan, to create vehicles powered by alternative sources of energy. What policies would you choose to increase public acceptance of such a vehicle? Experimental research could help you determine in advance whether your policy choices would be effective.

to possible consequences of action, and to create alternatives to the *status quo*. Yet very often theories need illustration: they need some concrete evidence to show that what the theorist says is relevant. Does the theory really isolate factors or processes that influence our daily lives, or is it merely armchair speculation? The theorist cannot actually *prove* that his or her vision is accurate. Theories operate as lenses, helping people see things a little differently. No theory can account for everything. However, the theorist can be expected to furnish research evidence that demonstrates a theory's relevance to daily life.

To appreciate this argument more fully, let us consider a study of self-handicapping strategies (Berglas and Jones, 1978). Theorists have suggested that people often are unsure of their exact capabilities. Sometimes people succeed, and sometimes they fail, and therefore they seldom can be certain of their true strengths. Uncertainty can lead people to handicap themselves when put to the test—that is, they may do something to make good performance more difficult. Then, if they fail, they don't have to face the possibility that they really aren't capable. And if they succeed, they have proof that they are truly skilled. For example, a student who gets drunk the night before a big exam may be engaging in self-handicapping. Failure the following morning can be blamed on the alcohol, not on low intelligence. If the student passes the exam with flying colors, he or she can feel superior, having overcome the handicap of the evening's drinking.

Do people really engage in self-handicapping of this sort, or is this reasoning mere speculation? Research data is helpful at this point. Berglas and Jones told undergraduates who had volunteered for drug research that they were participating in a study that was meant to ascertain the effects of various drugs on problem-solving abilities. The subjects

first were given a preliminary exercise in problem-solving, which the investigators set up in such a way that half of the students felt confident about their abilities and the other half felt insecure. Then, before taking the crucial test of their abilities, all the students were asked to choose one of two drugs: Actavil, which was said to improve performance, or Pandocin, which was said to have harmful effects on performance. The investigators reasoned that people who are insecure

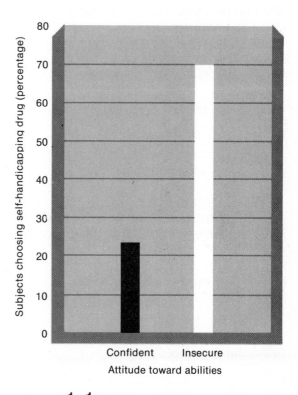

FIGURE **1-1**

Do insecure people fear success?

An overwhelming percentage of subjects who believed that they were poor at problem-solving chose a drug that was supposed to hinder performance on a test. (Adapted from Berglas and Jones, 1978)

in their abilities are especially likely to adopt self-handicapping strategies, which shield them from seeing themselves as being incapable. Thus, it was reasoned, self-handicapping would be demonstrated if subjects who had been made to feel insecure showed a preference for Pandocin and subjects who had been made to feel confident preferred Actavil.

Did the research demonstration prove to be effective? As you can see in Figure 1-1, the results do lend support to the self-handicapping argument. In a seeming attempt to handicap themselves, insecure students selected the drug that was likely to reduce their performance. Those who knew they were good didn't handicap themselves in this way. While the results don't prove the theory of self-handicapping, they do suggest that self-handicapping is a strategy that often is adopted by people who are dealing with threatening evaluations. This demonstration thus causes us to pay greater attention to the theorists' argument and to place greater trust in the idea that self-handicapping is a common occurrence.

In summary, careful research can provide reliable information about society, make limited predictions possible, and illustrate theories of social interaction. Now that we have explored the major uses of theory and research, we can examine specific theories and research methods in social psychology.

Major Theoretical Orientations in Social Psychology

Among those theoretical positions of central importance in modern social psychology are the behaviorist, the cognitive, and the rule-role orientations. You will learn a good deal about the impact of these points of view as you proceed through this book. Here we will describe basic assumptions of each position and discuss important ways in which they differ.

Behaviorist Theory: A Living Tradition

From the 1920s to the 1950s American psychology was dominated largely by *behaviorist theory*, which is based on the assumption that human action is governed primarily by external events. Ivan Pavlov's famous conditioning experiments with dogs furnished some of the first impressive support for this position. As Pavlov (1927) showed, if an investigator manipulates incoming stimuli in a systematic fashion, dogs can reliably be taught new patterns of response. The outspoken behaviorist John B. Watson (1919) argued that with proper use of environmental reward and punishment, children's behavior could be shaped and formed in any way that society required. For social psychologists, Floyd Allport's 1924 text *Social Psychology* most forcefully expressed this emphasis on the environment's power to shape behavior. Allport's book also expressed the optimistic view that psychologists could discover behavior-environment laws—that is, specific formulations of the conditions under which environment would affect behavior.

A theorist who argues that human behavior can be understood entirely in terms of the environment is called a *radical behaviorist*. The best known contemporary radical behaviorist is B. F. Skinner. Skinner maintains that all behavior patterns are created, sustained, or abandoned as a result of environmental rewards and punishments (1948, 1971). Most social psychologists are not content with the radical form of behaviorism. Rather, they believe that psychological processes must be taken into account—processes like thought, motivation, and feeling. Thus radical behaviorism has been largely replaced by *neobehaviorism*. The neobehaviorist continues to place great importance on environmental events. However, such events are significant because they influence psychological states, which then are responsible for behavior. Thus, while the radical behaviorist is concerned with the direct effects of reward and punishment on behavior, the neobehaviorist might argue that reward and punishment affect a person's attitudes, or internal feelings, and that these attitudes in turn influence the person's actions.

As you will discover in later chapters, the neobehaviorist position has stimulated a great deal of thought and research in social psychology. For example, the discussions of attitude change (Chapter 5), positive social action (Chapter 7), conformity and obedience (Chapter 10), and behavior exchange (Chapter 11), all are indebted to behaviorist thought. The behaviorist approach has been especially useful in stimulating investigators to search for environmental events that are reliably related to people's actions. People often are content to believe that they do things simply because they feel like doing them. Clearly, however, "feeling like it" may depend on the specific situation. Behaviorists argue that an increased understanding of the effect of environmental events may make possible the anticipation of their influence (the sensitizing function of theory discussed previously). Gaining control over events might then be possible, so that people can be influenced to feel like acting in one way as opposed to another way.

To appreciate the behaviorist orientation in action, consider a classic study, carried out by William Verplanck and his students (1955). They were interested in finding out whether people could control the course of conversation through the subtle use of reward and punishment. To explore this possibility, each student in Verplanck's class sought out situations in which he or she was alone with a person, could observe a clock unobtrusively, and could make doodles on a piece of paper. The conversations took place in dormitory rooms, restaurants, lounges, and even over the telephone. The student first engaged the friend in ten minutes of polite conversation, trying not to support or reject anything that was said. At the same time, using a series of coded doodles, the student carefully noted the number of opinions that the friend expressed. After ten minutes of this procedure, which was designed to establish the friend's basic rate of offering opinions, the student went to work. The point of the experiment was to use social approval as a reward and thereby increase the number of opinions that the friend expressed. Thus each time the friend voiced any opinion, the student would respond with such comments as "You're right," or "I agree," or the student would smile and nod in approval. The doodles again were used to record the number of opinions expressed by the friend. After an additional ten minutes the student stopped furnishing rewards. Rather, he or she either failed to respond to statements of opinion or disagreed subtly with everything the friend said. The results of this procedure proved to be striking. All twenty-four people who were tested increased their rate of expressing opinions during the reward period. Then twenty-one of the twenty-four reduced their rate of expressing opinions during the disagreement (punishment) period.

In summary, behaviorist theory assumes that human action is governed primarily by external events. For the social psychologist with this orientation, the focus of interest is the power of the environment to influence human interaction. Radical behaviorism, which emphasizes the power of environmental reward and punishment, is less influential in social psychology than is neobehaviorism, which takes psychological processes into account. In Verplanck's opinion-shaping experiment, behaviorist theory stimulated investigators to explore how social approval and disapproval (that is, social reward and punishment) could be used to shape the number of opinions one person shares with another.

The roots of modern social psychology are often traced to the works of two nineteenth-century thinkers, one French and one German. The Frenchman, Auguste Comte (1798–1857), was deeply impressed with the progress that was taking place in the natural sciences and with the possibilities that scientific knowledge offered for improving the human condition. Comte hoped to be able to classify all the various bodies of scientific thought and show how these various classes of knowledge were related. Specifically, he believed that knowledge progresses through stages, so that knowledge in certain disciplines is necessary for the later growth of other disciplines (Allport, 1968). Mathematics, for example, was viewed as a primary scientific discipline, since no other science could make progress until measuring, counting, and a variety of other mathematical operations could be carried out. The culmination of all the sciences, Comte believed, would be a discipline called *la morale*—the study of the individual in his or her social surroundings. The growth of this discipline, he argued, depends on established knowledge of biology and sociology: biology would furnish knowledge of the human organism—the nervous system, the hormones, and the like—while sociology would provide basic knowledge about societies as a whole. La morale would be concerned with the actions of individuals to the extent that these actions depend on both biology and society. The new science would recognize both the internal workings of the body and the external characteristics of the society. La morale also would have important applications: it would help solve the moral problems faced by society. In la morale, science and religion would become one (Samelson, 1974).

Aspects of Comte's formulation still permeate social psychology. Although most modern social psychologists do not base their work on either biology or sociology, an active interchange with these disciplines remains (Boutilier, Reed, and Svendsen, 1980; Evans, 1980; Stroebe et al., 1981). Contemporary social psychologists generally do not believe that the science can solve moral questions or that it should become a religion. Following the Comtian tradition, however, a strong commitment to using

Cognitive Theory: Turning Inward

Many people reject the behaviorists' focus on environmental influences and prefer a perspective that puts more emphasis on inner processes. Cognitive theorists are influential proponents of this point of view. *Cognitive theory* stresses the effect of people's thoughts and interpretations on social activity. Just as Pavlov's experiments with dogs stimulated early behavioral theorists, cognitive theorists found inspiration in the work of the Gestalt psychologists. *Gestalt* is a German word meaning "form." Gestalt psychologists such as Wolfgang Köhler (1947) and Kurt Koffka (1935) were particularly interested in the way in which people's internal processes impose form on the external world. To illustrate, you probably do not see the dots on page 21 as six isolated points; rather, in your mind you see

social psychological knowledge for improving the human condition still is made. The implications that social psychological findings have for moral purposes will be evident as we discuss prejudice (Chapter 4), positive social action (Chapter 7), aggression (Chapter 8), and environmental application (Chapter 13).

In contrast to Comte's theories were the views of the German psychologist Wilhelm Wundt (1832–1920), the founder of the first psychology laboratory. Wundt believed that the understanding of social behavior does not require a knowledge of natural sciences, such as biology (Blumenthal, 1975, 1977). People's actions, maintained Wundt, are based on their ideas or thoughts. Ideas are not natural substances about which biology can provide information, but are social creations. People develop and change ideas over time as they carry on relationships with each other. Thus the roots of such ideas as honor, duty, friendship, and the like cannot be illuminated by studies of human physiology. These notions are created by *people* during *specific times* in history for particular purposes. For Wundt, the purpose of the new discipline, called *Volkerpsychologie* ("cultural psychology"), was to study the origin and change of thinking in society. We can understand the present, argued Wundt, by looking back to see how it developed.

Although Wundt's concern with the development and change in people's psychological condition has generated active interest in modern social psychology (Martindale, 1975; Morawski, 1979; Simonton, 1980), most social psychologists are concerned not with the past, but with present-day behavior, and they try to understand this behavior on its own terms. Wundt's concern with the function of ideas or the function of thinking in social life remains as a focus of interest, however. The issue of thinking, or *cognition,* is a central concern in discussions of social perception (Chapter 2), prejudice (Chapter 4), and morality (Chapter 6).

We see, then, that modern psychology has not followed the precise lines laid out by these early thinkers. However, both Comte and Wundt have had an important influence on the field.

them as two groups, each group forming a triangle. Groups of dots and triangles are

.   .

.   .   .   .

not actual objects sitting out there in the world, waiting to be seen. These patterns are imposed on the world by internal mental processes. Knowing this, you can understand the bitter battles that have been waged between the behaviorists and the cognitivists (Gergen, 1979). While the behaviorists believe that environmental events influence people, the cognitivists believe that people's perception of environmental events is the key influence on their behavior.

The work of Kurt Lewin (1890–1947) was most influential in developing the cognitive

Fritz Heider, Adelbert Ames, and Kurt Lewin. Lewin visited Dartmouth College in the summer of 1946 along with his friend Fritz Heider, whose work is discussed in Chapters 2 and 5. They went to Dartmouth to see the visual demonstrations of psychologist Adelbert Ames. In this photograph from Heider's personal collection, Lewin is on the right, Ames is in the middle, and Heider is on the left.

orientation in social psychology. Many psychologists consider Lewin to be the father of modern social psychology. In 1945, after escaping from Nazi Germany and teaching at Cornell and Iowa universities, Lewin established the Research Center for Group Dynamics at Massachusetts Institute of Technology. His theoretical skills, combined with his deep interest in solving practical social problems and his ability to stimulate research, had profound effects on the development of social psychology. Many of his students became leaders of the discipline.

Lewin was the first social psychologist to develop a general theory of human social behavior. Central to his *field theory* (1935) was the view that the psychological way in which people represent their world is the primary determinant of their actions. Borrowing from his experiences in the trenches in the First World War (Marrow, 1969), Lewin argued that the physical landscape—the hills, gulleys, trees, and thickets—appears to be entirely different to a soldier looking for a place to defend himself than it does to a person who is enjoying its beauty while taking a peaceful country walk. Lewin was proposing, in effect, that an individual's psychological construction of the world may vary according to internal needs or goals. He went on to offer a solution to the difficult task of portraying the psychological world. Influenced by theoretical physics, he proposed that the psychological world be viewed as a *field.* In effect, this field consists of all of the related influences that affect a given behavior when it takes place. The field is composed of interdependent regions: the principal components are the *life space (L),* the *person (P),* and the *environment (E).* Lewin maintained that a person's life space is usually quite complex. People differentiate among various aspects of the self *(P)*—for example, between their physical assets and their shortcomings. They also distinguish various properties of the environment *(E).* Depending on one's needs or wants *at any given mo-*

ment, the person region or the environment region may be separated into segments.

Figure 1-2 offers an example of the way in which Lewin might have diagramed the life spaces of a soldier engaged in battle and a person strolling in a park on a beautiful Sunday afternoon. You can see that the soldier, who is thinking primarily of the enemy, does not have many divisions in the *P* region of his life space. The Sunday stroller who is musing about his or her personality might make a variety of distinctions. In the same way, the soldier in the front lines might distinguish among many different features of the landscape, while the Sunday stroller might see just a pleasant, relatively undifferentiated terrain.

Although Lewin's field theory currently is used by only a few psychologists (Hornstein, 1976), it drew social psychologists' attention

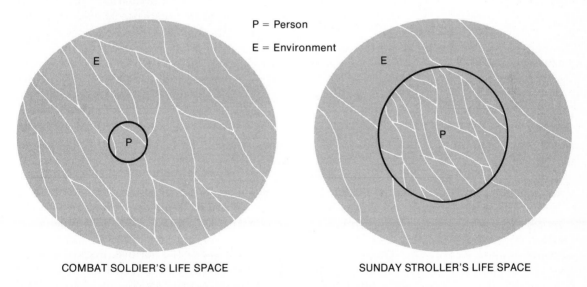

P = Person

E = Environment

COMBAT SOLDIER'S LIFE SPACE

SUNDAY STROLLER'S LIFE SPACE

FIGURE 1-2 **Life space: the individual and the psychological environment**

Lewin's field theory takes account of the actor's characteristics (*P*) and the situation in which the action takes place (*E*). Lewin liked to define his concepts spatially. In this illustration of his model, the psychological reality of the frightened soldier is clearly different from that of the relaxed and expansive Sunday stroller.

to the mental constructions that influence behavior. Cognitive processes have become central to contemporary social psychology. Most social psychologists now are committed to the view that (1) people construct their worlds in different ways, and that (2) these psychological constructions are critical to the individual's actions. The cognitive orientation will be most clearly represented in discussions of social perception (Chapter 2), prejudice (Chapter 4), cognitive consistency (Chapter 5), and moral development (Chapter 6).

Thus we see that cognitive theory stresses inner mental processes. For the social psychologist with this orientation, the focus of interest is the effect of people's thoughts and interpretations on social activity. In the chapters that follow, the discussions of social perception and prejudice will show that people's positive and negative cognitions can have a major impact on social relationships.

Rule-Role Theory: The Guiding Hand

The behaviorist and cognitive orientations are immensely important in modern social psychology. Both positions also have close connections with other areas of psychology, such as learning, development, and cognition. However, there is a third point of view, which has its roots in sociology. This approach, the rule-role orientation, has emerged from sociologists' concern with the broad patterns of social activity that exist in society. Sociologists typically explore such questions as how large numbers of people can live together in relative harmony. In order to explain these patterns of adaptive behavior, some sociologists have argued that people share *rules* for guiding their conduct over time. When these rules are adopted widely and people agree to obey them, even the most complex relationships may run smoothly. The concept of *role* can be substituted for that of rule. Theorists who believe that roles are important in determining behavior find that people may be looked on as actors in a play, each person playing a particular part. In this case a harmonious society is possible if people all play their prescribed roles.

The rule-role orientation differs in important ways from both the behaviorist and cognitive positions. As we saw, behaviorist theory emphasizes the relationship between external events, such as rewards and punishments, and behavior. Rule-role theorists are far less concerned with external inputs. They focus on the way internal rules guide conduct. Given this emphasis on rules and conduct, the rule-role theorist, unlike the cognitive theorist, does not typically explore the way in which a person interprets or perceives information from the external world.

The rule-role approach is particularly useful in understanding behavior sequences of extended duration. Behaviorists tend to focus on the momentary relationship between the stimulus and an immediate behavioral response. Cognitive theorists usually are concerned with the immediate perception of a stimulus and what the perceiver thinks. In contrast, the rule-role theorist often is concerned with rules that may govern relationships across extended periods, such as rules of courtship, rules for giving a dinner party, or rules for ending a relationship. The rule-role approach will play a part in our later discussions of social attraction (Chapter 3), the giving of help (Chapter 7), and self-presentation strategies (Chapter 11).

Let us see how the rule-role theory might be used in the service of liberating people—that is, in helping people see the world in a way that frees them from old patterns of action and encourages them to try new ways of behaving. Consider the behavior of Ilie Nastase, one of the world's most gifted tennis players. Nastase often has been banned from major tournaments because of his terrible temper. He frequently curses referees, shouts abuse at fans, and even smashes balls into the stands. When interviewed about his antics,

Nastase has said, "There is nothing I can do about it. I don't think anyone will change me. Even if they fine me a million dollars, that is the way I am . . . no one can change my personality." Nastase is voicing a belief, widely held in modern society, that each of us is possessed with a style of behaving, a set of deep-seated dispositions that constitutes our *personality*. Personality is formed early in life, and after it is established only the most powerful retraining experiences can change it.

Rule-role theorists offer a critical challenge to this traditional view. From their perspective personality is little more than the set of roles adopted by an individual for a given audience. Personalities are "creations of the moment, called forth by the recognition of situations" (DeWaele and Harré, 1976, p. 194). New roles can be located if the individual is willing to set aside old patterns and stop making the excuse that "I just can't help it, it's my personality."

The concept of mental illness can be reevaluated from the rule-role point of view. Typically in our society mental illness is seen as the product of a defective personality. Mentally ill individuals are believed to be people with deep-seated and lasting problems who can't help what they do. Yet, from the rule-role perspective, mental illness often is governed by certain rules and learned in much the same way that one might learn a part in a play. As Thomas Szasz (1960) has argued, many mentally ill persons act as they do in order to create particular effects according to the unwritten rules of our social institutions. A person entering a mental hospital learns what rules govern a mental patient's behavior and how to play the role of a mentally ill person. The patient who does not learn these rules is punished by the institution. Thus hospital staff members are not merely caretakers: in their specialized treatment of the patient they teach him or her the advantages of acting in a crippled fashion (Goffman, 1961).

To demonstrate this line of thinking, investigators have shown that mental patients are quite capable of altering their behavior in order to appear more or less ill (Braginsky, Braginsky, and Ring, 1969). When they are interviewed by the professional staff they are capable of increasing or decreasing the apparent seriousness of their symptoms, depending on whether they wish to be released or whether they wish to remain in the hospital. In the past ten years the rule-role approach has meant true liberation for many mental patients. Largely through the efforts of Szasz and others like him, asylum doors have been opened and laws have been established to prevent involuntary confinement to mental hospitals.

To summarize, we can say that the *rule-role orientation* explains people's behavior in terms of the internalized rules that people follow or in terms of the roles they play in daily life. Orderly social behavior results when people follow the proper rules or roles in various social situations. We have seen how the rule-role orientation can be used as a liberating agent. It was used to challenge the traditional assumption that people's actions are determined by their personalities, from which there is no escape. Rule-role theory suggests that changes in lifestyle can be made at any time. Research on mental patients has been used to illustrate the point that even mental illness has rules and roles.

Theoretical Perspectives and Human Values

The three major theoretical perspectives in social psychology—the behaviorist, the cognitive, and the rule-role—have stimulated much thinking and research about social behavior. At this point you might well ask which of these perspectives is the most promising? Is it possible to choose among them? One way to answer this question is by finding out which viewpoint is the most accurate—

BOX
1-3

A Comparison of Theoretical Orientations

Radical behaviorist orientation
This approach focuses on the stimulus and on the behavioral response of the organism. No attention is paid to the internal workings of the person.

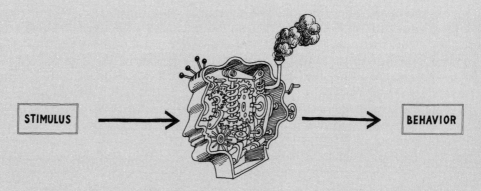

Neobehaviorist orientation
This approach recognizes the psychological properties of the organism that are important in determining the relationship between the stimulus and the behavioral response. Internal mechanisms are typically seen as being triggered by events in the world.

that is, by finding out which agrees most with the facts of social life. However, the perspectives cannot be compared on factual grounds, for two reasons. First, researchers who have been influenced by each perspective focus on different phenomena. The behavioral theorist looks at the relations between observable stimuli and behavioral responses, while the cognitive theorist is concerned with perceptual transformation of observable stimuli. In contrast, the rule-role theorist is interested in the way a person constructs long sequences of activity in order to reach certain goals. Second, when behaviorists, cognitivists, and rule-role theorists consider the same phenomena, they do not necessarily disagree

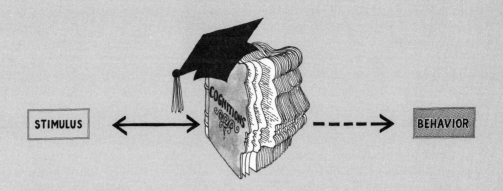

Cognitive orientation
This approach emphasizes the importance of those thought processes within the person that organize and interpret the stimulus properties of the environment. Behavioral consequences usually are deemphasized.

Rule-role orientation
This approach emphasizes the internal rules or role prescriptions that are available for the individual in any situation. The focus of study is on defining these rules and roles and relating them to social conduct. The stimulus properties of the environment are deemphasized.

about the facts; they simply may interpret them differently. A cry for help may be viewed by the behavioral theorist as a learned response; it may be viewed by the cognitive theorist as the result of the individual's perception of danger, and it may be viewed by the rule-role theorist as part of the role sequence that a person acts out when help is needed. Thus each theory offers a different way of describing and explaining human action. Each offers a different view of the world.

Are there other means of comparing the theoretical perspectives? One possibility is to evaluate the theories in terms of the fresh or useful insights they furnish about human activity. This task sometimes is complicated by the tendency of many investigators to blend elements of the various perspectives when designing their research. Recently a number of commentators have argued that theories should be judged in terms of human values (Gergen, 1978; Sampson, 1977; Shotter, 1977). How do human values enter the picture? Each theoretical perspective makes certain assumptions about human nature, and these assumptions have implications for how people should treat each other and what sort of society is favored in the future. Thus a theoretical perspective may operate subtly, advocating certain forms of social life and discouraging others. As a result, argue the critics, the perspectives should be evaluated in terms of the way of life they seem to favor, and these judgments can and should reflect one's own values.

Consider the behaviorist perspective. Behaviorists view human action largely as the product of heredity and environment. Individual action is subject to deterministic laws of the same kind as those that govern the movement of the stars or the ocean tides. To its credit, then, behaviorist theory furnishes the individual with a sense of an orderly social world—one that is knowable and predictable. Yet critics argue that if behavior is determined by rewards and punishments, the concepts of freedom and human dignity are destroyed. The individual could not take pride in his or her good works and would not feel guilt for misdeeds. And if people held no responsibility for their actions, the rules of right and wrong would no longer apply. If these rules do not operate, then what holds organized society together (Shotter, 1980)? In addition, the theory suggests that people have no control over their actions. But people who believe that they just are pushed along by life's events often become depressed: they feel helpless and without control. (For additional discussion of this point, see Chapter 9.)

The cognitive orientation also has both positive and negative implications for society.

Many supporters credit the orientation for its celebration of the autonomous individual. The cognitivist believes that individual thought processes play a critical function in social life. If society is to progress, it must encourage individual creativity. However, critics of the cognitivists suggest that the orientation places too much emphasis on the individual (Sampson, 1980). If people think of society as being composed of a collection of autonomous individuals, the sense of group membership is lost. If people think in terms of *I* rather than *we*, there can be little loyalty to another person, to families, to communities, and so on.

Finally, the rule-role orientation has been praised by many persons who attack the behaviorist position (Emmet, 1966; Hollis, 1977). Rule-role theory does endow people with freedom and responsibility. If people act according to rules or roles, it is argued, they also can choose to break the rules or act another role. Critics suggest, however, that the rule-role orientation undermines people's sense of trust. If people believe that everyone is merely playing games or acting out roles on the stage of life, then how can anyone really believe in anyone else? Relationships may seem shallow and fragile. Anyone may choose at any moment to leave the game or take up another part elsewhere.

In summary, we see that each theoretical perspective interprets social life in a different way. The perspectives cannot be easily compared on objective grounds. Each perspective favors certain forms of social activity and discourages others. Thus, personal values are crucial in evaluating each of the perspectives. The debate over value implications undoubtedly will continue.

Research Methods in Social Psychology

In our discussion thus far we have explored some of the goals of social psychological investigation. Our remaining task in this chapter is to describe the major research methods used to carry out these investigations. Four methods will occupy our attention: the archival study, the field study, the interview, and the experiment. We will consider each in turn, paying particular attention to their advantages and shortcomings, and examining some ethical issues that are of special concern to the discipline.

The Archival Study: Adventure into the Past

If you wanted to know what life was like under the reign of Napoleon how would you go about finding out? One possibility would be to examine the newspapers, autobiographies, and official records of that period. Such documents and records form the *archives* of the period. Archives can be extremely useful to the social psychologist who is interested in social patterns that unfold over long periods of time or those that depend on particular historical conditions (Gergen, 1973; Rosnow, 1978). For example, patterns of interaction within families have changed greatly over the past century (Gadlin, 1978), as have life patterns of the elderly and women (Ruddick and Daniels, 1977). Archival research furnishes one of the best means of exploring such changes.

Let us see how the archival study operates in practice. One investigator (Simonton, 1977) was curious to know why certain periods in history were marked by bursts of creative energy while other periods seemed to contribute so little of lasting consequence. For example, during the Italian Renaissance the arts flourished as never before. In contrast, the Dark Ages of Europe produced little in the way of art or scientific advances. What factors led people to create in one period but not in another? To explore this question, Simonton developed a list of some five thousand highly creative individuals who lived

between 700 B.C. and A.D. 1840. Knowing the approximate birthday of each individual, Simonton was able to identify certain periods when creativity flourished. Next, Simonton examined historical documents to identify specific ways in which these historical periods differed. He was particularly interested in the relationship between political strife and creativity. As he reasoned, strong political or ideological differences in a nation often set people to thinking, motivate them to take sides, and bring them into contact with differing ideas. Thus political strife or fragmentation might favor creativity in the arts, letters, and sciences.

After Simonton obtained reliable ratings of the political instability of each period he compared highly creative periods with periods low in creativity. The results suggested that so long as a nation was not actively engaged in war or revolution a fragmented political climate was highly characteristic of the more creative periods. Thus Simonton's careful examination of archives provides new information about the past: social upheaval, not tranquillity, proved to be beneficial to creative work.

The Field Study

Although archival research can be illuminating, most social psychologists are interested in the present. Perhaps the most direct means of learning about contemporary life is through *field research*. The field researcher attempts to record in precise and systematic fashion the ongoing activities of people in their normal environment. The researcher may take notes or use a tape recorder or film. Such research has been conducted in the classroom, at social gatherings, on street corners, in businesses, in private homes, and even in public lavatories.

When a field study is limited to a single person, group, or occasion, it usually is called a *case study*. Because of the small number of persons or occasions observed and because of the small number of observations, one cannot confidently draw broad generalizations from case findings. However, the case study can be an excellent vehicle for developing ideas for more thorough study, since firsthand experience in a given setting frequently provides the investigator with much interesting information. In a classic study of this kind, a researcher joined a gang of Italian adolescents who hung out on a city street corner (Whyte, 1943). The investigator was most concerned with people's tendency to see ghetto youths as being disorganized, lawless, and without character. He was able to show that the gang was highly organized according to informal rules, that there were strong loyalties and ethics within the group, and that close ties existed between the group and the neighborhood. When an outsider sees a given activity as a "senseless crime," he or she may be failing to understand the organization of a ghetto.

Field research need not be confined to a single person, group, or occasion. Modern electronic devices make possible the recording of activities of large numbers of people (Ginsburg, 1979). For example, by analyzing dozens of telephone calls, investigators have been able to identify a widely shared ritual that is used to end conversations (Albert and Kessler, 1978). This ritual has four parts: Almost invariably one person will summarize (for example, "I'm glad you will be able to go with me on Saturday"). Next, a justification is made for terminating the call ("I really have to hit the books now"). Then, perhaps to insure that the reason for terminating the call doesn't seem to be unfriendly, something positive will be said ("I really look forward to seeing you on Saturday"). Finally some indication of continuity in the relationship will be expressed ("I'll try to call you again before then"). See if you participate in this ritual the next time you are talking on the phone with a friend.

Field research furnishes the best method for documenting people's daily activities. When effective, it calls attention to patterns of behavior that were not noticed previously. However, subjects in such research sometimes know that they are being observed and do not act as they would normally. When people change their behavior because they are under observation, they are said to be *responding reactively* (Selltiz, Wrightsman, and Cook, 1976). To combat reactive responding, psychologists have developed unobtrusive measures that document people's behavior without their awareness (Webb et al., 1966). For example, the names on routing envelopes might provide an unobtrusive measure of the flow of communication within a large organization. Hidden cameras also may be used to film the activities of crowds, children at play, or pedestrians.

The field researcher faces other problems as well. The method of observation is time-consuming, and people's ideas or feelings often cannot be explored. In addition, the method raises ethical questions: is it right to study people without their consent—to breach the barriers of their privacy? The issue of ethics in social psychology will be explored in the last section of this chapter.

The Interview

Many social psychologists use interviewing procedures in which people are asked questions about their behavior, motives, ideas, and preferences. In the *questionnaire* form of interview, individuals usually respond in writing to printed questions. Many investigators believe that the single best way to find out about the psychological underpinnings of people's actions is to ask them directly (Allport, 1935; Harré and Secord, 1972). The *public opinion survey* is perhaps the most widely used form of interview research. With this method, large representative samples of peo-

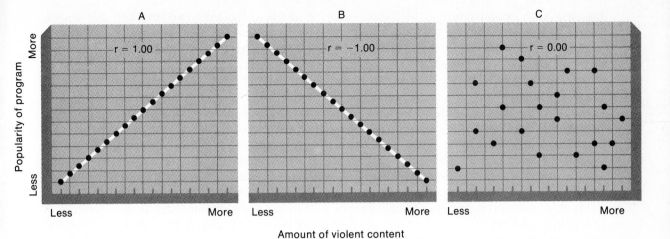

FIGURE 1-3 **Correlations of +1, −1, and 0**

A is an example of a perfect positive correlation between the amount of violence and the popularity of the TV show. B shows a perfect negative relationship between the two variables (that is, the more violence the less popular the show). C illustrates no relationship between the two variables.

ple are questioned, either in person or by telephone. The survey interview is perhaps the best available method for documenting the broad characteristics of a culture at any given time: reliable information may be obtained on almost any topic about which people feel free to talk.

In a recent public opinion survey, researchers who were interested in the issue of television violence explored the relationship between program popularity and violence. Many social critics have argued that television violence has harmful effects on society. The networks have responded to these arguments by pointing out that a certain amount of violence is necessary because that is what people want to watch. Does violence make shows popular? To explore the question, researchers used results of Nielson surveys in which people were asked about programs they watch (Diener and Defour, 1978). They used the survey results to gauge the popularity of

many different episodes of "Hawaii Five-O," "Adam 12", "The Untouchables," and other programs that feature violence. The investigators asked independent observers to assess the amount of violence that occurred in sixty-two episodes of eleven different programs. They then examined the correlation between the popularity of each episode and the amount of violence that occurred in it.

A *correlation* is essentially a measure of the relationship between two different factors. In this case it furnishes an indication of whether variations in program popularity are associated with variations in the amount of violence. You may recall from earlier psychology courses that the *correlation coefficient* is the numerical indicator of the degree of relationship. The coefficient may vary from +1 for a perfect positive correlation, to −1 for a perfect negative correlation. Three examples of correlations are shown above. If every increase in program popularity were associated with an increase in violence, +1 would be achieved (see Figure 1-3). A perfect negative correlation (−1) would emerge if every increase in popularity were associated with a decrease in violence. If there were no relationship between the two measures, the correlation coefficient would be close to zero. In fact, this latter result emerged from Diener and Defour's investigation. The correlation coefficient for the relationship between program popularity and violent content was only .05. This low coefficient indicates that no reliable relationship exists between the ratings of violence and popularity.

As indicated earlier, interview research can be extremely valuable in probing people's thoughts and feelings and can be used to gain information about a culture. Yet the above study also illustrates one of the chief shortcomings of interview research. Generally such research employs the correlational method of analysis; it provides evidence of the existence of a relationship between two factors, such as a program's popularity and the amount of violence in it. However, correlations do *not* indicate whether the first factor alone is responsible for variations in the second. For example, Diener and Defour were asking whether program violence alone is responsible for variations in popularity. A valid study of the programming and popularity of violence thus would have to insure that (1) the violent nature of a program preceded its popularity and (2) no other factors were responsible for the observed popularity. Is the present investigation valid according to these demands? This is not an easy question to answer. Think it over.

First, is it clear that program violence always preceded the popularity ratings? Certainly this was the case for any given episode: the viewers' reactions could not change the content of the program they were watching at the time. However, ratings of many different episodes of the same program were made.

Perhaps a violent program that was shown one week caused people to watch a later program that was less violent. This might explain the low correlation between violence and popularity on a given night. Or perhaps some other sequence of factors was responsible for the pattern of the results. As violence varies in a program, many other factors may change as well. Violent programs often are about police work, feature more actors than actresses, and depict situations that are more or less real to the viewer. All of these factors could be responsible for the fluctuations in popularity ratings; none of them is ruled out by the analysis. Thus, it is not certain that violence and popularity are unrelated, as the low correlation suggests. Such an inability to specify sequences is a shortcoming that is characteristic of most interview studies.

Experimental Research

Because correlation does not guarantee *causation*, as it is said, many investigators prefer to use the experimental method. The experimentalist tries to gain precise control over the sequences of behavior he or she is studying. In the violence example, an experimentalist would want to ensure that violence was the only factor that preceded program choice. Thus the experimenter would try to vary the amount of violence in a given program while holding all other factors constant. Then he or she might measure how much people like the programs that have a high amount of violence as opposed to how much they like those that have a low amount. When experimental research is conducted the factor that is varied systematically by the experimenter is termed the *independent variable*. The behavior that results from the experimental manipulation is termed the *dependent variable*. Thus the amount of violence in a program would be the independent variable, and the resulting popularity would be the dependent variable.

In order to gain complete control over the independent variable the researcher often must work in a laboratory. For example, in order to control the amount of violence in a program and keep all other factors constant, two films would have to be constructed, and all of the films' events would have to be precisely the same except for a single act of violence. Arranging to have such films shown on television would be difficult, so the laboratory is the obvious location for the experiment.

Laboratory experiments may be contrasted with *field experiments* in which the researcher tries to control the independent variable while working in the normal realm of daily life. Field experiments are sometimes difficult to arrange. However, researchers actually have been able to convince a television network to broadcast a prime-time drama with two different endings—one version was shown in some cities and the second version was shown in other cities (Milgram and Shotland, 1973). Viewers in some cities witnessed a robbery, while viewers in other cities saw a program without a robbery. The researchers then measured differences in the dependent variable—the amount of petty theft that was committed in the differing cities. In this case no important effects were discovered.

Several of the experiments described in this chapter were laboratory experiments. In the study of self-handicapping strategies, the researchers wanted to know whether threats to the subjects' self-confidence (the independent variable) influenced the subjects to engage in self-handicapping (the dependent variable). (You may want to look again at Figure 1-1.) As it happens, the great bulk of research in social psychology is experimental. Experimentation is the best method for the precise tracing of sequences of events. In addition, the experiment allows a researcher to arrange the necessary conditions and thus produce powerful illustrations of his or her theory.

The experimentalist does not need to wait for an illustration to present itself in nature. Rather, he or she can use the laboratory like a canvas and carefully paint the illustration that is necessary to give life to an interesting idea.

Because experiments are used widely in social psychology, their shortcomings must be stressed. Experiments can be immensely powerful instruments when conducted properly. However, they may be accompanied by a number of special problems.

Experimenter bias

In a typical experiment the investigator and the subjects communicate with one another, and the investigator may sometimes use this communication inadvertently to give subjects cues as to how they should behave. Thus the results of the experiment may not be due to the variations that the investigator claims. Such experimental results are said to reflect experimenter bias. In dozens of studies Robert Rosenthal (1966) and others have shown how experimenters can influence the behavior of subjects, be they laboratory rats or college students. Apparently investigators are not fully aware of their influence over subjects and do not intend to produce the effects that they produce. However, through very subtle changes in their tone of voice, in their smiles and body gestures, and so forth investigators can furnish clues that tell subjects how they ought to behave. Clues that place social demands on a subject—so that the subject is influenced to behave in ways that conform to the investigator's expectations—are called *demand characteristics* (Orne, 1962). Thus the results of such research are biased.

Experimenters have developed a variety of safeguards against experimenter bias. For example, an assistant often is employed to conduct the experiment but is not told of the hypothesis. Because they are unaware of the expected results, such assistants are less likely than an informed experimenter to bias subjects in the hoped-for direction. Another safeguard is writing or tape recording instructions for the subjects. In this way interaction between experimenter and subject is reduced, and in turn the potential effects of subtle cues are reduced.

Subject selection

In comparison with public opinion surveys, which may question several hundred respondents, experiments usually are limited to a small sample—often between thirty and fifty people. Further, the survey researcher usually will take elaborate pains to select respondents randomly from the entire population. In contrast, the experimenter typically must choose his or her subjects from the local population—often from the university population. The experimentalist wishes to draw conclusions that may be generalized throughout society. Yet if the samples used in the experiment are quite different from the culture at large, the generalizations will be unwarranted. For these reasons experimenters have become increasingly worried about the possibility that subject selection may bias results, and they have attempted to develop a variety of means for combating such bias.

One means of reducing selection bias is to explore the ways in which different segments of a population respond to being experimental subjects. Perhaps men and women respond to experiments differently or the young and the aged respond differently (Back and Gergen, 1963). Researchers have been particularly interested in the volunteer subject (Rosenthal and Rosnow, 1969). One cannot choose people at random and make them participate in experiments. Most often the experimenter must ask for volunteers. Yet volunteer subjects often are more sensitive to demand characteristics than are nonvolunteers: they often are more likely to detect the subtle cues that

show them what is expected by the experimenter. Special safeguards must be used, then, when volunteer subjects are obtained.

Another major way to reduce selection bias is to *replicate*—that is, to repeat an experiment using widely diverse populations. Stable results across experiments suggest that selection bias has not influenced findings. In recent years many experimentalists have collaborated with foreign scholars to pursue cross-cultural replication (Triandis and Brislin, 1980), and an international society has been established to encourage such cross-cultural work.

Ethical issues in experimentation

A final problem in social psychological experiments is ethical in character, and two major concerns have emerged. First is the *infliction of pain*. Social psychologists are interested in the effects that pain, stress, fear, low self-esteem, and a host of other unpleasant psychological states have on social relationships. To study these states in an experimental setting, the experimental conditions almost always must be manipulated so that some subjects experience pain and others do not, or so that some undergo stress and others remain neutral, and so forth. Many critics believe that experimenters have no right to inflict such states on other persons (Kelman, 1977; Smith, 1974). They suggest that the rights of subjects should be protected more adequately.

Ethical issues, such as the infliction of pain, have aroused vigorous debate in social psychology (Baumrind, 1964, 1979; Kelman, 1977; Milgram, 1964). In response to this criticism, many social psychologists argue that the discomfort experienced by subjects usually is minor. When subjects are *debriefed* after the experiment—that is, when they are informed of the complete design and purpose of the experiment—any remaining discomfort usually vanishes. Further, it is argued, since the ultimate aim of research usually is to help society, people should make small sacrifices. Yet critics point out that debriefing is not always effective (Ross, 1978), even when experimenters think that it is. And the social benefit of research is not always apparent.

The second important ethical problem is *deception*, and the problem has come about because experimenters need to have subjects remain unaware of the true purpose of their studies. If subjects are aware of the question that is being studied, the results of the research may be distorted by experimenter bias. In order to reduce subject awareness, experimenters often mislead subjects: they deliberately present misinformation about the aims of the research or the events to which the subjects will be exposed. Recall the research on self-handicapping strategies (see Figure 1-1). Subjects were caused to succeed or fail and were led to believe that their success or failure was due to their own abilities. Without this deception the study could not have been conducted. Yet many people believe that deception is fundamentally immoral and should not be allowed in the research process. They believe that psychologists have no right to deceive people.

In response, social psychologists argue that deception is a common part of social life. People select clothing to hide physical shortcomings; they wear makeup to appear more beautiful than they really are; and they seldom disclose all of their purposes to other people. Why, then, should the social psychologist be prevented from engaging in what essentially is a common social practice? And

since the psychologist's ultimate aims are to help the society, a small amount of deception should be tolerated. Yet the critics respond that deception is bad in principle and that the use of deception only contributes to the decay of social trust.

Many social psychologists have searched for alternative research methods in order to resolve these issues. For example, *role playing* has been proposed as a major alternative to the common experiment (Kelman, 1968; Mixon, 1972). Subjects in a role-playing study are asked to describe the way in which they would respond to a given situation, rather than being confronted with the situation directly. Thus in a role-playing study of self-handicapping strategies, subjects might be asked how they would respond to success or failure. They are not actually made to succeed or fail. Critics of this method point out that the way people imagine they would behave is different from their actual behavior. And so the search for alternative methods continues.

A second important way in which the ethical problem has been reduced is by establishing ethical standards for research. These standards are used by review boards within various institutions to evaluate all experimental designs before they are carried out. At present the entire field of psychology, as well as most areas of research that involve human subjects, is guided by a code of research ethics (American Psychological Association, 1973). In addition, internal review boards carefully evaluate most research proposals to ensure subjects' safety and the significance of the proposed research.

SUMMARY

1 Social psychology is a discipline that is devoted to the systematic study of human interaction and its psychological basis. The social psychologist attempts to generate theories that describe and explain various aspects of social life, document these ideas through observation, and, ultimately, see that these ideas are used for human betterment.

2　As the profession of social psychology has developed, early philosophical accounts of social behavior have been largely cast aside. In contrast with these early accounts, modern social psychological theory is richly complex and more concerned with real-world application. Unlike the early thinkers, social psychologists use a range of highly developed research methods to obtain reliable data about social life.

3　Social psychological theories differ from theories used informally by people in daily life. In formal theory assumptions are made explicit, the focus of interest is general rather than specific, and logical coherence is stressed. Social psychologists' theories furnish people with a means to understand and communicate about social life, a device for becoming sensitive to various processes that affect their lives, and an opportunity to consider alternative forms of action.

4　Through observational research the social psychologist provides reliable information about aspects of social life, aids in the process of social prediction, and demonstrates the importance of various theoretical insights.

5　The three major theoretical orientations in modern social psychology are the behaviorist, the cognitive, and the rule-role. The behaviorist orientation places primary emphasis on exploring reliable relationships between environmental conditions and behavior. The cognitive orientation emphasizes the ways in which people's thought processes organize their experience of the world. The rule-role orientation emphasizes the way shared rules or role prescriptions influence patterns of conduct across time. Each orientation interprets social life in a different way. Each favors certain forms of social activity and discourages others.

6　Four major research methods are used to carry out social psychological investigations. The archival study, which makes use of documents and records from the past, is an especially useful method for exploring social patterns across historical periods. In field research the investigator makes a record of people's ongoing activities in their normal environment. Field studies are especially useful in documenting people's daily activities. The interview method is used most commonly to tap the opinions or attitudes of large numbers of persons and to document particular characteristics of a culture at a given time. In the experimental method, subjects are exposed to various carefully controlled conditions and the experimenter observes the resulting behavior patterns. The experiment is the best method for tracing the sequence between various social conditions and people's reactions to them.

7　Although most research in modern social psychology is experimental, the experimenter confronts important problems. He or she must avoid biasing experimental results by unintentionally informing subjects about the goals of the research. The experimenter also must try to obtain population samples that are representative enough so that generalizations can be drawn from the experiment. Finally, the experimenter must take pains to treat subjects in an ethical manner.

SUGGESTED READINGS

Allport, G. W. *The historical background of modern social psychology.* In G. Lindzey & E. Aronson, (Eds.), *The handbook of social psychology* (Vol. 1), (2nd ed.). Reading, Mass.: Addison-Wesley, 1968.

Lana, R. E. *Assumptions of social psychology.* New York: Appleton-Century Crofts, 1969.

Lewin, M. *Understanding psychological research.* New York: John Wiley, 1979.

2: SOCIAL PERCEPTION

■ *Michael just phoned us from Chicago. His warm and reassuring voice closed the gap of six months' silence. His wife had given birth to a baby girl, and Michael had devoted himself so steadfastly to home that he had little time left for his friends. He seems happy and energetic now, and he wants his friends to share in his experiences.*

Let us pause for a moment to reflect on this account of our friend. It seems normal enough, the kind of description of friends many people would make. Yet, consider again what we have said. Michael talked for about twenty minutes. His tone of voice, vocabulary, and manner of relating were continuously changing during this period. We as listeners were faced with an immensely complex and ever-shifting pattern of verbal stimulation. Yet, our description of Michael has reduced everything to a few simple terms. Michael was warm, reassuring, happy, energetic, and expansive. In an important sense our description created Michael; it carved him from the complexity of the telephonic impulses.

How will we react to Michael's next phone call? Probably we will be warm and responsive, delighted to hear from him. Why? Because of the conception of him we created and continue to carry with us. In the same way all people create conceptions of others and of themselves. These conceptions are immensely important in guiding behavior. For example, people who feel that their parents are old-fashioned and conservative may avoid talking to them about things that really matter. People who perceive themselves as being insecure in groups may never speak out, even when they have something important to say. The United States may never trust Russia as long as Russia is seen as being unscrupulous and competitive. In all of these cases an immensely complex range of experience has been transformed into a few simple concepts, and these concepts have become guides to conduct.

In this chapter we will look at how people develop and use their perceptions of others and themselves. A great deal of the work that has been done on social perception derives from the cognitive orientation, discussed in Chapter 1. In this chapter we will first look at the advantages of transforming the social world into understandable units. We also will discuss some of the limitations built into this kind of transformation. In the remainder of the chapter we will examine the ways in which people form conceptions or impressions of other people and themselves. In particular, we will be concerned with what factors influence the impressions of others that people form, how individuals organize these impressions, and how they go about deciding on the causes of people's behavior. Finally, we will turn to the issue of self-perception. Special problems await persons who try to define who they are or what they feel.

Foundations of Social Perception

In perceiving or having thoughts about another person, the perceiver must *conceptualize* the behavior he or she observes. To conceptualize is to treat separate stimuli as being equivalent or as forming a unit. For example, out of the complex world of experience certain observations can be grouped together and perceived as smiles, while others can be classed as frowns. Even though each smile is different from all others, the single idea, or concept, of a smile is used by many people. In the same way, certain features, movements, and sounds can be classified as John, while other groups of stimuli are classed as Lisa or as Rick. John will not remain quite the same from one moment to the next, but he remains the same person at the conceptual level.

Concepts: Sources of Survival

Being able to group together experiences in various ways is an immensely valuable skill (Eiser and Stroebe, 1972). First, grouping simplifies the world, makes it manageable, and thus improves the capacity to adapt. The world is alive with constant change and movement. A crowd of people at a street corner is a kaleidoscope: continuously changing variations in color and sound. Organizing this vast quantity of information into meaningful units reduces the confusion. Concepts are the essential vehicles for this simplification. Classifying some stimuli as being equivalent and others as being different also is the first step toward adaptation. A child who can classify certain stimuli as being harmful and others as being pleasureful, for example, has begun to gain control of the environment. Successful action depends on the ability to separate the stimuli into separate classes.

Simplifying the world into conceptual units also aids both memory and clarity of thought. People remember more when they organize information into chunks (Markus, 1977). Think of how you might go about memorizing a long-distance phone number. You probably would divide the numbers into groups of three or four digits—remembering far more in that way than you would if you considered each number separately. Verbal statements may be especially useful for recalling information about oneself (Lord, 1980). For example, statements along a good–bad dimension ("I am a good basketball player") may be useful in recalling past actions (Judd and Kulik, 1980). People think more clearly when they use concepts. In planning a political campaign, for example, strategists translate the world into conceptual units, such as the union vote, the black vote,

the youth vote, and so on. Their planning wouldn't get far if they thought vaguely about "all those folk out there."

Concepts also help people communicate. The verbal labels attached to concepts allow people to talk about smiles and frowns, John and Lisa. Experiences that people cannot easily divide into simplified units are hard to talk about. Thus, a beautiful sunset or the incoming tide is the domain of the artist and is simply admired silently by the average person.

Finally, concepts may help reduce anxiety. Until a person knows what's out there in the world, he or she can't begin to know how to react to what takes place. Thus, a world that can't be defined using concepts is potentially dangerous. Having a category may reduce the experience of fear. For example, waking up with a stomach pain may be an extremely frightening experience. Having a label, even an unpleasant one (like, an ulcer), can reduce fears and actually alleviate pain. Often there is comfort in classification.

In summary, then, the ability to use concepts is an immensely useful human attribute. Concepts help people (1) simplify the world and thus act more adaptively, (2) think and remember more effectively, (3) communicate with one another more effectively, and (4) master anxiety.

Conceptual Biases: Sources of Dismay

Given the complexity of the social world, the adaptive value of conceptualization is readily apparent. Indeed, many people claim that the human species is superior to all other species because of the human capacity to think and speak in terms of concepts. But categorization can have negative consequences. The overuse of categories can limit one's experiences. Categorization can obscure subtle differences among individuals. Let us explore these shortcomings.

Who is a grown-up? Western culture provides a number of handy categories for sorting people according to age including *babies, little children, older children, teen-agers, grown-ups,* and *old people.* While people tend to think of these categories as real, they are in fact imposed upon the world to give it order. To illustrate: if asked to select a cut-off point for *grown-ups* in the photographs above, you would probably consider the man and the women starting with number 7 to be adults. However, according to research being carried out by Carolyn Pope Edwards of the University of Massachusetts and Michael Lewis of the Educational Testing Service, this conception is not shared by young children. When six-year-olds are asked to sort pictures of this type, they set the beginning of being grown-up at about the age of sixteen (photo 5). And six-year-olds do not agree with three-year-olds. For the latter, adulthood starts at about thirteen (photo 4).

Concepts and the lost person

The newspaper columnist Russell Baker once poked fun at America's exploration of Mars by writing a fictitious story about an alien power's probe of Earth. The aliens landed a machine in Times Square. The machine, programmed only to search for the presence of gin, scurried down the streets and examined policemen, dogs, fireplugs, and debris. Finally it relayed to its source the message, "Yes, there are traces of a low grade gin on the planet Earth." All other details about Manhattan and about Earth and its people were never revealed because the "right" questions never had been asked. Concepts may operate in much the same way as did the alien machine—they draw our attention to certain characteristics while blinding us to others.

One of the most important kinds of social blindness results from the tendency to see people in one category as being totally different from people in other categories. When this happens, many similarities may be overlooked. The conflict between Catholics and Protestants in Northern Ireland is an example of this kind of problem. Vast differences exist within both religious groups. In fact, many Catholics have more in common with certain Protestants than with other Catholics. When any group acts as if everyone in the opposing camp is the same, the chance for valuable dialogue is lost. Because neither group can break through its single-minded outlook, both groups continue to suffer. In the same way, labels like feminist, professor, jock, and gay obscure the many important differences that exist among the members of groups.

The same argument holds for the perception of single individuals. Conceptualizing Lisa as being aggressive or John as being easygoing draws attention to a few of Lisa's or John's characteristics and disregards many others. Few individuals are always aggressive or always easygoing. Labels gloss over the varied character of the other person's behavior.

In the moment of labeling, individuality may be lost.

Concepts and leftover reality

Consider the oil painting by Jackson Pollack, shown on page 44. If you were trying to describe the painting to someone who never had seen it, what would you say? You might say that the painting looks as if someone had dripped paint on the canvas, that it contains both light and dark shades, and that it is extremely complex. However, you would not be able to capture in words the painting's rich variations of tone and design. The failure of words to do justice to the painting derives from the nature of verbal concepts. Concepts most adequately represent distinct classes of similar events. When patterns are complex and unique, concepts do not adequately represent them. In the same sense, concepts like black and white, rich and poor, and fat and thin may not be good representations of the social world. Skin shades, income, and weight vary greatly, and where a distinction between groups should be drawn is never clear.

Concepts do not adequately describe continuous change across time. If events are in motion so that each moment is different from the one that preceded it, conceptual distinctions are hard to make. For example, clear distinctions among the various movements that are made as a football player kicks a punt or as an ice skater leaps through the air are simply not possible. As a result, the kicking of a football or a skater's movements cannot be described in such a way that anyone ignorant of these activities could repeat them.

Because of these various difficulties, some critics have questioned the adequacy of social knowledge that is based on concepts alone. When people analyze or discuss other people, they rely on a limited kind of knowledge. A baseball player learning to pitch doesn't read books about pitching or talk about it. The experience is what counts, with its ongoing flow of action. In the same way, learning how

Jackson Pollack: *Number 29,* 1950. When the forty-four-year-old Pollack died in a car crash in 1956, he was one of America's most innovative artists. He created his colorful paintings by spreading canvas on the floor and dribbling paint from cans and buckets. Concepts cannot capture the rich complexity of his work. Are concepts adequate to capture human action?

to get on with other people is a matter of experience. No book can explain how to carry on a friendly conversation. Some aspects of what people know are based on concepts— that is, on *explicit* knowledge. Other learning is based on continuing experience, or *implicit* knowledge (Polanyi, 1967). In this chapter we are mainly concerned with explicit, or conceptual, knowledge. We will deal with implicit knowledge in a later discussion of encounter groups (Chapter 12). Thus we now will turn to the problem of acquiring and organizing concepts.

The Development of Concepts

How does the perceiver come to divide the world into perceptual units? How are concepts developed? Both social and physiological processes seem to be involved in concept formation.

Natural categories

Certain basic concepts may result from the natural world's impact on the eyes, ears, and skin. Bright light produces a physiological response different from that produced by dark, and heat and cold also differ in their effects on the nervous system. Thus, concepts of light and dark or heat and cold may reflect basic biological reactions. The term *natural category* refers to this biologically based organization of experience (Rosch, 1978). Does such categorization occur in the perception of people? Research by Darren Newtson and his colleagues suggests that it does (Newtson, 1973; Newtson, Enquist, and Boris, 1977). As they argue, the perceiver does not always see a continuous stream of action, but rather, often breaks the stream into segments. A person walks by a shop window *and then* pauses to gaze into it *and then* turns to look at a bus. The perception of separate bits of action occurs primarily when there is a *distinctive change* in the movement of the body being observed. If a person moves and then pauses, for example, the perceiver doesn't see a smooth flow of uninterrupted activity, but sees two separate actions, the move and the pause.

Concept learning

Although some concepts may be favored by biological makeup, most of the concepts used in social relations are not simple reflections of real-world differences. People generally are in motion, changing from moment to moment, furnishing the perceiver with an immense amount of information. Distinctions between black and white or big and small are too simple to be helpful in sorting out the complexity of social relationships. More useful are such concepts as loving, aggressive, helpful, boring, and so forth. These concepts are tied closely to the current state of society. Not too many years ago, people frequently asked themselves whether they were frigid, sinful, noble-minded, chivalrous, or square. Today such concepts seem old-fashioned and irrelevant.

The process of acquiring society's concepts begins in infancy. Psychologists often account for this learning as a process of *hypothesis testing* (Bourne, Donmowski, and Loftus, 1979; Levine, 1975). That is, in trying to gain their ends, people formulate tentative concepts and then test these concepts against their experiences. Concepts that are rewarded are retained, while those that are punished are pushed aside. Thus, if a child realizes that Daddy sometimes plays, the child may begin to formulate various concepts of what kind of activity might produce Daddy-play. He or she then tests to see if any of the hypothesized concepts meets with success. Is smiling a class of activity that produces Daddy-play? Is crying, running, or yelling? By testing various concepts to see if Daddy plays, the child may come to realize that smiling is a different class of activity from crying. Smiling as an activity seems to encourage Daddy to play while crying may not.

Lighting a fire with language

The words people use when communicating with others are closely tied to concepts. Spoken language is not a perfect map of the concept system. There are concepts for which no words exist (artists may recognize a certain shade of color but have no word for it). And there are words for which no concepts exist (the nonsense syllables used in psychological research are good examples). However, most concepts are represented by words, and this close association makes possible the communication of ideas. Many psychologists believe that most concepts are acquired as speech is learned. In the initial stages of what has been called the "original word game" (R. Brown, 1958), the child learns to use words to label classes of events. The mother points to a cow and says, "cow," and if the child happens to utter a resembling sound, he or she may bask in the mother's praise. As the child learns such verbal labels, however, he or she also learns to place similar-looking creatures into this special class, or category.

Additional concepts are learned as the child masters the logic underlying the language. For example, new words often alert the child to conceptual distinctions. The child may overhear a parent say, "What a shame! Portuguese have moved onto our block." Because of the child's linguistic knowledge, this simple sentence may first inform the child of the existence of a class of people labeled Portuguese—after all, only *people* move onto the block. Second, the term *Portuguese* must refer to a different kind of people, for the child realizes that he or she has never been given this label. Third, the negative exclamation also informs the child that the event is an unwelcome one—that is, Portuguese must be bad. From these simple remarks, then, a new concept suddenly has sprung to life. From the family's point of view the child has learned to think "properly."

In summary, we can say that the individual acquires a set of basic concepts for understanding the world and that these concepts are acquired through exposure to the natural world, by testing ideas against experience, and by learning language. The physiological makeup of human beings, as well as their membership in the culture, demands that they master a set of basic concepts about what exists in the world. And the knowledge that is contained in the shared concepts serves as a basis for social life. A person would not get far if he or she talked about someone as being weak-haired, searchless, or edible. The acceptance of shared concepts can limit the perception of alternatives, however. The distinction between such concepts as mine and yours, old and young, or homosexual and heterosexual, for example, is not based on natural law. These concepts are cultural hand-me-downs. The more open people are to the ideas of other cultures and other times, the more flexible and enriched their own concept systems can become. And with the development of new concepts, new ways of living become available.

Forming Impressions: The Laying on of Labels

As we have seen, social perception is essentially the process of forming concepts of others. Having looked at the ways in which these various concepts are acquired, we now can consider some cultural and personal influences on conceptualization. Sally, Al, and Rob don't come with labels attached to their sleeves. They are moving, constantly changing, offering countless images and bits of information. Somehow the perceiver cuts through all of the information and concludes that Sally is smart, Al is dishonest, and Rob is a lady's man. How are such labels selected? Let us consider three important influences: social rules, motivation, and immediate context.

Following the Rules of Perception

The first basis for assigning labels to other persons follows directly from the preceding discussion. As described, concepts are primarily learned through social interchange. Through such interchange people learn that others can be viewed as being aggressive, friendly, sad, and so forth. In addition to learning the culture's basic concepts, people also learn the conditions under which various concepts should be applied. They learn what actions or what people should be labeled aggressive, friendly, or sad. Thus, much social labeling is simply a matter of following rules that already have been mastered. Although this process seems clear enough, its implications are dramatic.

Once the rules for "how things are to be called" become commonly accepted, an important transformation usually occurs. The rules become *objectified*—that is, what started out as rules of social agreement come to be descriptions of objective reality. Blacks, whites, and Chinese are no longer convenient categories, but are real groups in the social world. Friendship and hostility are no longer helpful classifications, but are real acts. Labels are transformed into "things." When this transformation occurs, people acquire the *natural attitude*—that is, the common-sense view of what makes up the social world (Garfinkel, 1967). That there are blacks, whites, and Chinese becomes common-sense reality. The possibility of there being a society in which these particular distinctions were not made would seem peculiar.

To illustrate the transformation from labeling to objective reality, let us consider that part of the natural attitude in Western culture holding that there are two genders. People come in two categories: male and female. This knowledge is common sense. And yet, as research demonstrates, not all cultures share the rules on which this common sense is based (Kessler and McKenna, 1979). Some cultures have three genders, including one that falls between man and woman. Further, in our society, a variety of rules determines who is male and who is female. Most people use the genitals as the determining factor for gender. Yet, medical examiners at the Olympic games don't agree that genitals determine gender. They use chromosomes as the basis of distinction, and thus individuals who always have believed themselves to be women have been prevented from Olympic participation. Transsexuals consider neither genitals nor chromosomes in determining what sex they really are; instead they consider their own personal feelings. Children use entirely different criteria, including size and strength. Thus, while common sense leads you to believe you must be either a man or a woman, we see that this assumption rests on rules of agreement—rules that could be changed (Unger, 1979).

Motivated Perception: Desire on the Loose

We have seen that the perceiver is influenced by social rules. When people adapt to these rules, they become better able to get along in society. However, people also must get along with themselves. At some point social adaptation may be pushed aside and *self-gratifying* labeling may take place—labeling that favors the perceiver's purposes. Later in this chapter we will have more to say about this process. For now, let us consider some of the first research that demonstrated this argument.

Pepitone (1949) was interested in finding out whether an individual's wanting something badly would influence his or her view of another person. He offered high-school boys an opportunity to win free tickets to a basketball game, and he caused desire for the tickets to be varied by informing one group of boys that the tickets were for a high-school game that was of little interest and informing the other boys that the tickets were for an important college game. To obtain the tickets, each student had to answer a number of questions put to him by a visiting panel of three "coaches." If the panel found a boy's opinions to be of high quality, the boy would win the tickets. The coaches were specially trained accomplices of the experimenter. One (Mr. Friendly) was instructed to respond in a friendly manner to everything a student said. A second (Mr. Neutral) was instructed to be more neutral in his reactions, and the third (Mr. Negative) was trained to act in a highly critical fashion. After the interview each student rated the panel members on how *approving* each was toward him and how *influential* each was in determining whether the tickets would be granted.

The results supported the idea of motivated perception. Although Mr. Friendly maintained the same role throughout the study, students with a strong desire for the tickets were more likely to rate him as being

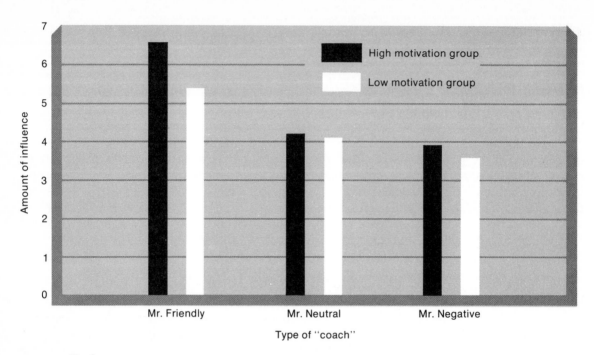

FIGURE 2-1 **The influence of motivation on social perception**

Note that students who were told that they might receive free tickets to an important basketball game were more likely to rate the favorable "coach" as being influential in awarding the tickets than were their less motivated fellow students. When the "coach" was friendly, both groups considered him to be most influential. (Adapted from Pepitone, 1949)

approving and influential than were students who had little interest in the tickets (see Figure 2-1). Further, students generally tended to rate Mr. Friendly as being more influential than either Mr. Neutral or Mr. Negative. All students, then, gave themselves a psychological boost by perceiving the most approving individual as having more influence over the outcome. It appears, then, that people often perceive the social world in ways that are personally gratifying.

The Context and the Base Rate

Our discussion thus far has stressed the influence of both social rules and motivation on the way others are perceived. However, social perception also is influenced by the *context* in which a person's actions are encountered— the range of surrounding circumstances, both social and physical. Demonstrations of this point were first made in studies of how people judge facial expressions. Researchers have long been interested in how people know that an action is hostile, for example, as opposed to intense or worried. Context often is the basis for such judgments (Frijda, 1958; Landis, 1929).

Consider the faces depicted in the following photos. What kind of emotions are being expressed here? Is the man experiencing pleasure or pain? Does the woman's face express joy or sorrow? People often are confused in their judgments about such expressions

What kinds of feelings are being expressed here? Before turning to the next page, try to guess. You probably will not be sure about your interpretation of either the woman's or man's facial expression.

(Munn, 1940). Now consider the same faces embedded within the context in which they were photographed (see page 50). Suddenly you are relatively sure of your judgments. When you see that the man's face is that of a victor in a race, you are relatively sure he is feeling intense joy. When you see that the woman is looking at a baseball game, you might well view her emotion as great excitement.

Context usually affects judgment by providing cues to expected behavior. Members of a given culture learn what is supposed to occur in various contexts. For example, people expect affection to be expressed on a date but not in the classroom or during a job interview (Price and Bouffard, 1974). Thus, the smile that on a date is perceived as being affectionate may be categorized as friendly in the classroom and good-natured in the interview. Similarly, people know from experience which actions are supposed to follow other actions (Peabody, 1968). If a person says something generous, gratitude is the expected response. There is thus a bias toward interpreting a subsequent smile as expressing gratitude rather than self-satisfaction. Several

investigators argue that features of the immediate situation can engulf the observer (Taylor and Fiske, 1975; Taylor et al., 1979). The person may fasten onto the immediate situation so intently that important information is overlooked. Let us consider one important aspect of this problem: the tendency to ignore information about probabilities.

Consider the following situation: you are trying to decide whether someone is warm and accepting. You see that the individual responds sympathetically to another person's problems, and you conclude that the individual is probably warm and accepting. Your judgment is reasonable in light of what you know. But it would be improved if you could observe the person's actions over a long period and if you could discover whether the reaction you observed is typical or unusual. In other words, your judgment would be improved by knowledge of the *base rate,* or general probability, of the event over time. Al-

Suddenly the feelings are clear. Context is an important key to understanding others' facial expressions. The woman is excited. The man is joyful. The context—a race and a baseball game—make the emotions immediately obvious.

though people don't always have access to base-rate information, theorists Amos Tversky and Daniel Kahneman (1980) argue that even when it is available, it often is not taken into account.

In a demonstration of their argument, they gave problems like the following one to adult subjects:

> A panel of psychologists interviewed a sample of 70 engineers and 30 lawyers, and summarized their impressions in thumbnail descriptions of those individuals. The following description has been drawn at random from the sample of 70 engineers and 30 lawyers.

"John is a 39-year-old man. He is married and has two children. He is active in local politics. The hobby that he most enjoys is a rare book collection. He is competitive, argumentative, and articulate."

Question: What is the probability that John is a lawyer rather than an engineer? (Kahneman and Tversky, 1973, p. 61)

In response to this problem, people typically say that there is a 95-percent probability rate of John's being a lawyer. This answer seems to be quite reasonable in terms of the single description of John: he sounds like a lawyer. Yet, in paying attention to the description alone, the respondents disregarded the fact that the base rate for lawyers in the sample is only 30 percent. Given the base rate, they would have been on safer ground if they had classified John as an engineer.

This is not to say that people always avoid base-rate information in making judgments. Reliance on base-rate information may increase if the information is seen as being *causal* (Ajzen, 1977; Manis et al., 1980). If earlier events are believed to cause the event in question, the earlier events may be given special attention. In the above case, the percentage of lawyers and engineers in the sample is unrelated to the habits and interests of the person described. If, however, the subjects had been told that the engineers in the sample had received special training in the liberal arts, estimates of whether John is a lawyer surely would have been lower. In this case, the special training would be assumed to produce a lifestyle unlike that of the stereotypical engineer.

Reliance on base-rate information may also depend on the *concreteness* of the information at hand (Nisbett et al., 1976). Cancer statistics may make little impression: they are very abstract. However, if a family member contracts cancer, his or her relatives may soon begin to have regular checkups. The illness is a concrete event. Similarly, in shopping for college courses, a student may pay little attention to the statistical evaluations of various courses but be very much swayed by a friend's experiences. When immediate events are highly concrete, they may be especially potent in their influence. When the past is summarized in a brief abstraction, it may be far more reliable but far less salient (Borgida and Nisbett, 1977).

In summary, forming impressions of others is a complex cognitive process that is subject to a variety of cultural and psychological influences. People follow their culture's rules about what labels or concepts apply to various people or actions. The observer's wants and needs also may bias what is seen. Finally, social perception can be affected by context— by culturally based expectations as to what ought to happen in a given situation. Concentration on the immediate context may lead to a disregard of important information.

The Organization of Perception: Putting It All Together

Although placing people in categories is fundamental to most social relationships, such labeling is not enough. Typically people also try to *organize* their perceptions into a coherent whole so that a series of observations make sense. People are said to carry with them *implicit theories of others' personalities* (Schneider, Hastorf, and Ellsworth, 1979). A fruitful line of inquiry in social psychology has emerged from attempts to understand such principles of organization. We now will look at attempts that have been made to understand this mental organization.

The Whole Is Greater than the Sum: The Asch Attempt

Solomon Asch was one of the first psychologists to explore the problem of how we organize our perceptions of people. Asch was much influenced by the Gestalt theory of perception, which emphasizes the way in which the human being shapes his or her perceptions from within (see Chapter 1). Asch (1946) attempted to apply this line of thinking to social perception. In particular, he felt that the total perception of another person is not a simple sum of the individual concepts used in labeling the person. Rather, the perceiver attempts to organize the traits into a whole and, in so doing, attempts to create a perception of the other person that is qualitatively different from the simple sum of the parts. To take a simple case, if someone is described

BOX
2-1

*The Perils
of the
Intuitive
Scientist*

Why are people's thinking and reasoning so often faulty? Many theorists believe that emotions or motives cloud people's thoughts. Freud, for example, believed that sexual motives bend and shape people's thinking. This line of argument is represented in this chapter in the discussion of motivated perception. Psychologists in recent years have changed the focus of their attention from motives to faults in the actual process of thinking. They maintain that lack of training in clear thinking, rather than emotions, is what hinders thinking. As Richard Nisbett and Lee Ross (1980) argue, people must continuously make judgments about each other: they must make decisions about others' characteristics—gender, age, occupation, personality, and so forth. In thinking through such judgments people ideally ought to use the same rigorous standards that are used by scientists. However, because people can't make exact tests and carry out complex statistical procedures on an intuitive level, they often make errors in thinking. As intuitive scientists, people make judgments that often are incorrect.

Let us consider two strategies that people use in making social judgments. First is *the availability bias.* People generally rely on their immediately available memories in making judgments. They don't take careful account of all instances, as a scientist might, but instead simply rely on what at the time is available in memory. More formally, they use an *availability heuristic,* or habit of solving problems (Kahneman and Tversky, 1973), and often the results are poor. To illustrate, suppose you were asked whether your mother is a nurturant person. To answer this question as a scientist you would want an accurate record of all your mother's actions over time. This information would enable you to make a precise statement about your mother's character. Of course, no one has such records. All that usually is available are scattered memories, and these may change with circumstance. Thus, if you were asked about your mother's nurturance on a day that happened to be your birthday and your mother had forgotten your birthday, your available memories probably would be unfavorable to your mother. On another day, when she was more motherly, your memories might be different and you might give a much different answer. The availability bias would have caused you to make errors in judgment.

as being friendly, this concept or trait has quite different meanings if the person also is perceived as being trustworthy as opposed to untrustworthy. If a person is untrustworthy, his or her friendliness may be a con game—it may be superficial and possibly threatening. Friendship has a deeper meaning if the other person seems trustworthy. Thus, the meaning of a trait is not given in the term itself: much depends on its surrounding context.

A second faulty strategy of thinking is *false consensus bias* (Ross, 1977). People tend to see their own actions as being relatively normal, appropriate, and in consensus with others, while viewing others who behave differently as being odd or deviant. For example, parents who batter their children may be more likely than parents who don't rely on physical force to see such action as being normal. Neither group has an accurate and reliable count of the incidence of child abuse in the society. However, for a variety of reasons, including their belief that they are normal people and the fact that they associate with people who are similar to them, they tend to assume that "most people" are like themselves.

In one demonstration of the false consensus bias in action, investigators asked students who had volunteered as research subjects to walk around their campus for thirty minutes while wearing a large sign that said "EAT AT JOE'S" (Ross, Greene, and House, 1977). The subjects were told that they did not have to participate in the research but that if they did they might "learn something interesting." After indicating whether they would participate, the subjects were asked to estimate the proportion of students who also would agree to wear the sign. As you can see from the table below, subjects who agreed to wear the sign estimated that the vast majority of their peers also would do so. Similarly, those students who refused to wear the sign also assumed that they were in consensus with others: they strongly believed that other students would refuse.

People can get through life quite successfully despite these faulty patterns of thought. However, a person who knows about them may be somewhat cautious in making social judgments.

Type of subject	Estimated commonness of agreement	Estimated commonness of refusal
Subjects who agreed to wear sign	62%	38%
Subjects who refused to wear sign	33	67

To explore these issues further, Asch gave undergraduate students a list of seven traits said to be characteristic of a hypothetical individual. The students were asked to write a general description of the individual and judge the person on a variety of dimensions. To one group of students Asch gave the adjectives intelligent, industrious, skillful, determined, practical, cautious, and warm. The second group received the same list, but with

**BOX
2-2**

*Warm versus
Cold: Trait
Descriptions
Make a
Difference*

Solomon Asch has found that *warm* and *cold* are extremely important concepts around which people can weave complex descriptions of other people's personalities. Asch's subjects viewed the warm person much more positively than they viewed the cold person. Social psychologist Harold Kelley (1950) took the logical next step and asked: do people act differently when they interact with a *real* person who has been described as *warm* as opposed to one who has been described as *cold*? He wondered whether two descriptions of an individual identical in all respects except these trait dimensions would influence people's behavior. Would people be distant and critical when interacting with the person if they thought the person was cold? Would they be friendly and accepting if they thought the person was warm? If their behavior was different, then the power of a single word placed in a conversation could have profound effects on social relations.

To explore this possibility, Kelley provided university students with a description of a visiting instructor. Two forms of the description were distributed at random. The forms were identical except that the phrase "very warm" was used to describe the instructor in half of the cases and "rather cold" was used in the other half of the cases. The note read:

Mr. ——— is a graduate student in the Department of Economics and Social Science here at M. I. T. He has had three semesters of teaching experience in psychology at another college. This is his first semester teaching Ec. 70. He is 26 years old, a veteran, and married. People who know him consider him to be a rather cold [or, "very warm"] person, industrious, critical, practical, and determined. (p. 433)

Students were unaware that the notes differed.

a single change: the trait *warm* was replaced by *cold*. Three findings emerged from this inquiry. First, the students experienced almost no difficulty in weaving the various traits into a coherent whole: the students were able to organize the traits into a larger and more logically connected scheme. Second, substituting the term *cold* for *warm* produced a striking difference in the overall picture developed by the students. When the term *warm* was included in the list, the students typically went on to describe the individual as being successful, popular, happy, humorous, and so forth. If, however, *cold* appeared in the list, the individual was described as being stingy, unsuccessful, unpopular, and unhappy. The single trait seemed to color the entire characterization of the individual. The third major finding was that the terms *warm* and *cold* seemed to be particularly potent in coloring overall perception. For example, if the terms *polite* and *blunt* were inserted instead of *warm* and *cold*, the effects were far less striking. Asch concluded that

After the students had read the description the instructor arrived to take over the class. He led the group in a twenty-minute discussion, and during this period the experimenter recorded the amount of student participation. After the instructor departed Kelley asked the class for anonymous evaluations of him.

The results of the warm–cold variation were potent. Both the evaluations of the instructor and student interactions with him were affected by the single piece of information. The table below presents the students' average ratings of the instructor on a series of other traits. The higher the mean score, the more of the trait was attributed to the instructor.

The warm–cold variation also affected participation in the class discussion. Among the students who had been told that the leader was warm, 56 percent participated in class discussion, while only 32 percent of the subjects who had been told that he was cold did so.

| Trait | Mean score received by instructor | |
	"Warm" group	"Cold" group
Self-centered	6.3	9.6
Formal	6.3	9.6
Unsociable	5.6	10.4
Unpopular	4.0	7.4
Irritable	9.4	12.0
Humorless	8.3	11.7
Ruthless	8.6	11.0

certain traits, such as warm and cold, act as central organizing traits, while others are of secondary importance.

Organization by Association:
An Answer to Asch

Although Asch's findings triggered a long line of research (Anderson, 1966; Kaplan, 1971; Livesley and Bromley, 1973), his Gestalt interpretation now commands less attention. Why? The answer lies partly in the failure of this approach to explain (1) how the various trait terms are organized and (2) why certain traits are central and others secondary. What principle did people use to form coherent accounts of the fictitious person, and why was the warm–cold dimension central?

Many investigators believe that a good answer to such knotty questions can be furnished by the idea of *learned associations*. You may recall from introductory psychology that when two events frequently occur in temporal proximity, the presence of one may stimulate an individual to think of the other. To illustrate, if you were asked to name the first word that pops into your head when you hear the word *father,* you probably would respond quickly with the word *mother, Dad,* or *heavenly.* All of these words frequently occur in temporal proximity to the word *father* in everyday speech. Association learning suggests that through frequent pairing, various traits come to be related to each other. A coherent account of a person's personality, then, could be based on clusters of associated concepts. Association learning thus answers the first question raised by the Asch research: namely, how various trait terms are organized.

The process of association also can answer the centrality question (Wishner, 1960; Zanna and Hamilton, 1972). For example, if you are trying to decide whether a person is popular, chances are your decision would be strongly influenced if you learned that the person is happy. This is because popularity and happiness frequently are associated in our culture—both in terms of our language use and in fact (Shweder, 1977). In effect, happiness is central to your judgments of popularity. In contrast, if you learned that the person is brown-eyed, your ratings of his or her popularity would not be affected. Eye color and popularity are little associated in present-day American culture. Eye color thus would be noncentral to your impression of the person's popularity. In general, then, any trait can play a central role in determining impressions. Centrality will depend on the degree to which the trait is associated with the dimension about which the impression is being formed (Schneider, 1978).

This analysis has led others to explore the ways in which people organize their associations. The researchers start with the assumption that people have certain ways of clustering various traits—they assume that honesty is associated with kindness, sincerity, and dependability, for example, but not with popu-

larity or stoutness. An individual's particular clustering preferences may be said to form his or her *implicit theory of personality* (Schneider, 1973).

In one of the earliest demonstrations of implicit personality theory, the learning theorist Edward Thorndike (1920) showed that people frequently tend to see others as possessing all good *or* all bad traits. When people judge a person as being kind, for example, they also may see him or her as being happy, popular, and intelligent, but not moody, insincere, or lazy. The tendency to see individuals as possessing all positive characteristics and none that are negative is termed the *halo effect.* We will shortly consider several reasons for the existence of this effect.

Additional research on the clustering tendencies of college students reveals that not one, but two positive–negative dimensions are often used (Rosenberg, Nelson, and Vivekanathan, 1968). As you can see in Figure 2-2, one of these dimensions seems to be related to social life and the other to intellectual abilities. Thus, if you were told that Lisa is scientific, you would be inclined to believe that she also is determined, skillful, industrious, and intelligent, but not naive or frivolous. If you were told that she is helpful, you might also see her as being sincere, happy, and sociable, but not moody or pessimistic. You would come to this conclusion without any direct behavioral evidence that the person really is happy, sociable, or sincere. The strength of the association would be sufficient "evidence" (Ebbeson and Allen, 1979; Shweder, 1975).

If you look again at the traits clustering around the ends of the dimensions, you will begin to see that as a group the traits suggest types of personalities: the unsociable grind, the brainless popularity seeker, and so forth. These clusterings have been termed *prototypes* (Cantor and Mischel, 1979) and often may be used in daily relations as convenient ways of sorting people. One student described

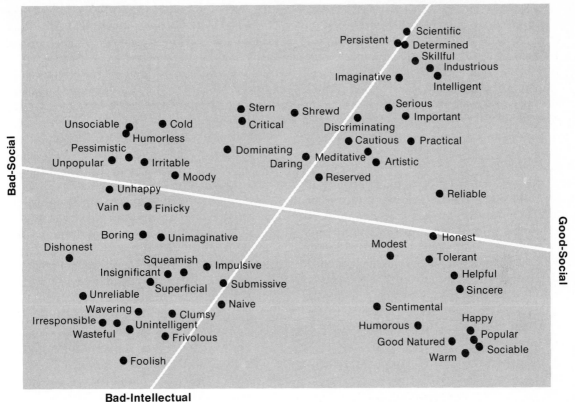

FIGURE **2-2** **How college students cluster the personality traits of their peers**

Fellow students are rated along social and intellectual dimensions. In interpreting this figure, assume that placement of a trait at an extreme means it is strongly desirable or undesirable. Centrality means that the trait is relatively neutral. Thus, *scientific* is a very important positive intellectual trait and is not relevant in terms of the social dimension. (From Rosenberg, Nelson, and Vivekanathan, 1968)

his prototype of a door-to-door salesman as wearing a cheap leisure suit (polyester wardrobe), being short and chubby, having a grin on his all-American face, having neatly trimmed hair, and talking fast. People also may cluster prototypes into more general categories. Thus, they may see door-to-door salesmen, campaign managers, and press agents as examples of a more general or abstract prototype: the public relations person. You may find it interesting to assess your own typology for sorting friends and acquaintances.

Consistency and Integration of Information

If you asked people to share their impressions of former President Richard Nixon, you might receive a very critical appraisal: "He lied to the American people" or "He didn't use wisdom in selecting the people he worked with."

If you then asked whether Nixon had any virtues, the answer might well be no. Yet, on further inquiry, these same people will recall that Nixon was instrumental in opening communications with China, that the Vietnam War did come to an end while he was in office, and that he was popular enough to have been reelected in 1972 by the greatest margin of votes in American history. In spite of such facts, many people can scarcely list any of Nixon's virtues.

This kind of reaction indicates the perceiver's failure to use all of the information available in forming an impression, and social psychologists have been interested in why this happens. Investigators believe that the tendency reflects one of the major principles underlying perceptual organization: *consistency*. People often organize their perceptions of others so that all of the elements fit together into a coherent, logical pattern (Mar-

kus, 1977; Rogers, 1978; Wyer, 1974). At times the need for consistency may blind the observer to various facts or events. For example, in one early study (Gollin, 1954) subjects were shown a movie of a young woman who was behaving in seemingly contradictory ways from one scene to another. In some scenes she appeared kindly and helpful. She was shown assisting an elderly person in distress. In other scenes she seemed to be hard and promiscuous: she might have been a prostitute walking the streets. Just as in the Asch study, subjects were asked to write an overall description of the woman. The majority of the subjects (58 percent) ignored various scenes in the film in order to form a consistent whole. If their descriptions were positive in character, they left out the scenes in which the woman's character was questionable. If they condemned the woman, they failed to mention her more admirable behavior.

Other investigators believe that in addition to striving for *logical consistency*, people also try to maintain *emotional consistency* in their impressions of others. As Norman Anderson (1978) maintains, people typically integrate diverse pieces of information to reach an overall preference. They don't like to have mixed feelings. Consider a concrete case. You are planning to live in a double room next year and two friends have asked to room with you. You can select only one. The first possibility is lively and physically attractive but uses more drugs than you think desirable. The other is friendly, has varied interests, but is extremely messy. How would you reach an overall conclusion in this situation? Which roommate would you select?

You might make your decision by simply *adding up* your reactions to each of the separate pieces of information (see Table 2-1). Thus, in the above situation you have two positive facts and one negative fact for each candidate. Therefore, your attraction for each should outweigh your negative feelings, but you still would have to flip a coin to decide who would be the more attractive roommate. Do people actually use this simple process of adding the amounts of positive and negative information? Research findings support such a possibility. Research indicates that overall attraction to a person can often be predicted on the basis of the proportion of positive as opposed to negative traits the person possesses (Byrne and Rhamey, 1965; Clore and Byrne, 1974). The greater the proportion of the good things in comparison with the bad, the more general feelings of regard there are.

Apparently people don't always stop with simple addition in reaching an overall preference. They may ask themselves not only how many pieces of positive or negative information there are, but *how* positive or negative the information is. For example, you learn three new facts about candidate A: he or she is good at playing Monopoly, marbles, and hearts. However, you also learn a new

fact about B: he or she is a very caring person. You have three positive facts about A and only one positive fact about B. Yet, you probably would select the second of the two. Why? Because being very caring is a far more positive characteristic than is being a good player of three childish games. In this case overall feelings would represent not a simple sum of the facts, but the *average value* of the available information.

This logic is also illustrated in Table 2-1, where we have assigned a value of +1 to each of candidate A's game-playing abilities, and a value of +3 to candidate B's single trait of caring. If the values are added together, they both yield a sum of +3. Indeed this is a good argument, and at times people may simply add information in this way. However, most research on this topic indicates that people typically use the *average value* of the available pieces of information rather than the sum of the values (Anderson, 1965; Kaplan, 1974; Leon, Oden, and Anderson, 1973). In the present case the average for candidate A is only +1, and the average for candidate B is +3.

Yet, people may not always stop with simple averaging. After all, much also depends on the importance attached to various pieces of information. Each candidate for roommate has a single bad trait: one uses drugs excessively, and the other is very messy. Both traits may seem to you to be equally negative, but in selecting a roommate one of these pieces of information may be far more important than the other. The drug abuser may create more difficult problems for you. Thus, in reaching an overall preference you may also *multiply* each fact by its *importance* (Anderson, 1978; Clore and Byrne, 1974). Look again at Table 2-1. Each potential roommate has two positive characteristics and one negative. Let us suppose that the two positive characteristics are equally positive (+5 on a scale ranging from −10 to +10) and equally important (rated +3 on a scale ranging from 0

TABLE 2-1   **Choosing a roommate**

A comparison of the averaging and adding models of decision making. Note that in the adding model the amount of information counts, in the averaging model the value of information is considered, and in the weighted averaging model the importance attached to the information is also taken into account.

Adding model			
Candidate A		Candidate B	
Characteristics	Value	Characteristics	Value
Lively	+1	Friendly	+1
Attractive	+1	Varied interests	+1
Drug-abuser	−1	Messy	−1
TOTAL VALUE	+1	TOTAL VALUE	+1
	A = B		

Averaging model			
Candidate A		Candidate B	
Characteristics	Value	Characteristics	Value
Plays Monopoly	+1	Very caring	+3
Plays marbles	+1		+3
Plays hearts	+1		
	+3		
AVERAGE VALUE = 3 ÷ 3 =	+1	AVERAGE VALUE = 3 ÷ 1 =	+3
	B is preferred		

Weighted averaging model			
Candidate A		Candidate B	
Characteristics	Value × weight	Characteristics	Value × weight
Lively	+5 × 3 = 15	Friendly	+5 × 3 = 15
Attractive	+5 × 3 = 15	Varied interests	+5 × 3 = 15
Drug-abuser	−3 × 5 = −15	Messy	−3 × 2 = −6
	15		24
WEIGHTED AVERAGE VALUE 15 ÷ 3 = 5		WEIGHTED AVERAGE VALUE 24 ÷ 3 = 8	
	B is preferred		

for no importance to $+5$ for highly important). Drug abuse and messiness are each evaluated at -3. Yet, the importance of drug abuse is 5 on a five-point scale, while messiness is 2. If you multiply each characteristic by its importance, you will decide that the messy roommate is much more preferable.

Recency, Primacy, and Person Memory

From the standpoint of needs for consistency, people ought to develop a coherent view of each person they meet and discount all subsequent contradictory information. In other words, there should be a *primacy effect* in which information received first is more important in determining an impression than is information received later. But no one is always consistent. If people continue to remain open to new facts, a *recency effect* may occur; that is, recent information will be more important in shaping an overall impression than is early information. Which of these effects do you think is more common? If people seek to remain consistent, then primacy effects should dominate. If they try to be open-minded and flexible, then recency effects may be more frequent.

Much early research suggested that primacy was the rule in forming impressions of others. In Asch's (1946) classic study, college students were asked to form an overall impression of a person who was "intelligent, industrious, impulsive, critical, stubborn, and envious." As you can see, the list begins with very positive traits and moves to more negative traits. A second group of students received the same list, but the order of the traits was reversed: the negative traits preceded the positive ones. As Asch found, the impressions formed by the students were greatly influenced by the order of presentation. Subjects who first were exposed to positive traits formed more positive overall impressions than did those who first were exposed to neg-

ative traits. In other words, initial impressions seemed to persist regardless of later information. The subjects may have discounted the later information, as described in our discussion of consistency. Or the meaning of later information might have been altered in light of the students' initial impression (Ostrom, 1977). To illustrate, if you think a person is dependent and you learn *later* that he or she is generous, you may see the generosity as a way of establishing a relationship in which the individual can be dependent. If the person is first perceived as being *independent*, the generosity could be seen as an expression of that trait (Kaplan, 1975; Zanna and Hamilton, 1972). In other words, the meaning of generosity changes depending on the context in which the trait is encountered. Primacy effects have been demonstrated in dozens of carefully controlled studies (Jones and Goethals, 1972; also see Lana's 1964 review). As it is said, people often seem to be cognitively conservative—that is, they resist changing their impressions (Greenwald, 1980).

Such results imply that people generally stick to an impression and close themselves off from new information. Because this is a disturbing possibility, researchers have continued to pursue the issues of primacy and recency. They have tried to destroy or reverse the primacy effect through the use of special instructions. For example, the primacy effect may disappear when subjects are asked to reformulate their impressions each time they are presented with a new trait (Stewart, 1965). When subjects pay close attention to each new piece of information, primacy does not seem to prevail. Similarly, when the experimental instructions discourage discounting (Kaplan, 1973) or when subjects are given a simple warning as to the dangers of premature impressions (Luchins, 1957), the primacy effect can be destroyed effectively. And when subjects are asked to recall all the traits that have been presented to them before they form

their overall impression, the primacy effect may be neutralized (Anderson and Hubert, 1963).

So far we have limited our discussion of the recency and primacy effects to periods of short duration. Researchers typically have confined their interest in this issue to the problem of how people form and maintain judgments within a single hour. However, in normal life the time during which new things are learned about a person may stretch over many years. Under these conditions, old information may be forgotten. And as earlier experiences with a person are lost from memory, there is a decline in the effects of primacy (Miller and Campbell, 1959). When recall becomes too difficult, people may rely on the immediate situation. In this case recent information may exert a bias on impression formation.

The fact that information can be lost from memory has challenged researchers to explore memory processes in their own right. Apparently memories are frequently organized around a central theme or concept (Lingle et al., 1979). If memories are not organized in

this way, very little may be remembered (Hamilton, Katz, and Leirer, 1980). Thus, if people conceptualize Jane as being a helpful sort of person, they later remember events or traits that are consistent with this theme and forget those that are inconsistent. In fact, people frequently will retain the theme in memory and forget the events on which it was based (Ross, Greene, and House, 1977; Wyer and Srull, 1980). Because memory can be vague and poorly organized, investigators have become intrigued with the possibility that recent events can alter older memories. In one study, for example, students were given a detailed case history of a woman (Snyder and Uranowitz, 1978). They were supplied with many facts about her relationships with friends, lovers, family, and others. Later the students learned either that the woman was currently living as a heterosexual or as a lesbian. Then they were tested on what they remembered of the woman's early history. The results showed that the recent information strongly influenced what was remembered. Students who learned that the woman was heterosexual remembered facts that were consistent with this lifestyle, while students who learned that she was a lesbian remembered more facts that were consistent with this outcome. When the students made errors, the errors tended to support the recent information on lifestyle.

We see, then, that primacy effects are not all-powerful. First, a variety of simple instructions may destroy or reverse them. Second, people often seem to forget their first impressions, or these impressions become less important in organizing later information. When recency effects occur, memory of early information may be altered to fit the existing impression.

To summarize our discussion more generally, we find that people often organize information about others in two important ways: (1) they often may cluster various traits according to their learned associations and (2) they form theories that possess both logical and emotional consistency. People may vary a great deal in such tendencies (Peever and Secord, 1973; Streufert and Streufert, 1978). Everyone's way of putting information together is unique to some degree (Rosenberg and Sedlak, 1972).

Attribution of Causality

Tom, a friend of ours, was walking recently in the city when a boy of fourteen darted up behind him, plunged a knife into his back, and ran down a nearby alley. Fortunately a hospital was close by and Tom's life was saved. As Tom's friends, we were deeply upset and anxious to see the youth caught and punished. In fact, the boy was found, but our desire for punishment began to wane as his story unfolded. The stabbing proved to be an initiation rite for a neighborhood gang, and if the youth had not given in to gang pressure, his own life would have been endangered. What else could he do?

Why should this explanation be so effective in reducing our desire for revenge? How had our perception of the youth changed? As the theorist Fritz Heider (1958) suggests, our desire for revenge changed because our perception of the *causal source* of the stabbing was altered. Originally we saw the boy as the causal source, and we held him responsible. However, as we learned more about the case, we began to perceive the gang as the source of his actions. In formal terms, we first made an *internal attribution* of causality—to the actor himself; this was replaced by an *external attribution*—to the situation in which the boy lived. And as our perception of causality changed, so did our blame and corresponding desire to see the boy punished.

From Heider's standpoint the perception of personal causality plays a critical role in social life. Not only does blame depend on the perception of causality, but reward does so as well. If a person does a good deed and the action seems to have been voluntary, or self-caused, the person will receive far more rewards from others than would be the case if he or she had been paid to do the deed. If the person had been paid, the causal source would be external (Gross and Latané, 1974). Given the importance of causal attribution in social life, the first question we must ask is how do people go about deciding who has caused an action? Are there any particular rules they follow in reaching such judgments? And if there are rules, how widely are they used? Are there cases in which they are abandoned? Finally, how do we know when we have made a correct judgment of causal source? We now will consider each of these issues.

Scientists in Miniature: The Kelley Model

Harold Kelley has developed one of the most useful accounts of the common rules of causal attribution (Kelley, 1973; Kelley and Michela, 1980). Kelley suggests that people use roughly the same set of rules in their daily affairs as a scientist in the laboratory might use to sift through evidence and locate the cause of a disease. However, the scientist usually tries to follow the rules with care and precision, while the pressing and haphazard circumstances of daily life may make such procedures difficult for the average individual to follow. What are the rules? Kelley believes there are three rules, each of which is derived from the same general principle—that of *covariation*. Specifically, Kelley says, "an effect is attributed to that condition which is present when the effect is present and absent when the effect is absent" (1967, p. 194). In other words, if a condition is evident to the perceiver *when* an event occurs and is *not* evident when the event *does not* occur, people will conclude that the condition caused the event. The three rules that are derived from this tendency are described here.

The rule of distinctiveness

Let us say that you have just given an important talk to your class. You aren't really sure if it was any good, but Ron comes to you after class and compliments your presentation. You want very much to know whether it was your talk (an external source) that produced the compliment or something peculiar within Ron (an internal source), such as his generally positive disposition. One of the first factors you might take into account is whether Ron's compliment is *distinctive* to you. Does Ron compliment everyone who gives an oral report? Is he generally complimentary in his daily relationships? If the compliment is distinctive to you, you may well conclude that your talk produced the compliment. In keeping with the covariation principle, the talk was present when the compliment occurred, and there was no compliment at other times. Thus, you attribute cause to the talk.

In one illustration of this principle, students were asked to judge a series of fictitious situations (McArthur, 1972). For example, some students were told that John laughs in response to a particular comedian and that he doesn't laugh at other comedians. As you can see, John's laughter in this case is distinctive to this comedian. Other students were told that John laughs in response to almost all other comedians. Clearly his laughter is not distinctive to the particular comedian. Both groups then were asked to judge whether something about the comedian (an external source) caused John to laugh or whether something about John (an internal source) caused him to laugh. In general, subjects were far more likely to view the external source as being responsible if John's reaction was distinctive—that is, if John laughed only at the particular comedian.

The rule of consensus

In judging whether your talk caused Ron's compliment, you also may be concerned about whether other students agree with Ron. Thus, if many others congratulated you, you might feel more sure that your talk produced Ron's compliment. In short, the greater the consensus in people's response to a given stimulus, the greater the attribution of causality to the stimulus.

Some researchers have argued that people don't always apply the consensus rule. They often are so involved in their own actions that they don't take into account other people's responses to a stimulus (Nisbett et al., 1976). As you can see, not paying attention to consensus is similar to overlooking the base rate, as described earlier. However, when consensus is easily evident, people frequently take it into account (Ruble and Feldman, 1976; Wells and Harvey, 1978; Zuckerman, 1978). In fact, by overestimating the amount of consensus, people may come to feel more secure in their judgments (Goethals, Allison, and Frost, 1979). For example, at one university students who supported the women's liberation movement estimated that 57 percent of the student body shared their views. Fellow students who did not support the movement believed that 67 percent of the students shared their opinion (Ross, Greene, and House, 1977). Both groups clearly were inflating their estimates.

Consensus also influences one's judgments of others' personality. Imagine, for example, that you decide to wear blue jeans to class because you feel that any other clothing is too dressy. If all of your classmates also wear jeans, people probably will not look at your wearing jeans as being especially expressive of your own personality (internal cause). Instead, the jeans are likely to be seen as a response to the demands of an external source, the peer group (Jones and Davis, 1965). This reaction may occur even if you feel that the jeans do express something important about you. Thus, when an action is socially desirable, so that most everyone does it, the action is more likely to be seen as being externally, rather than internally, caused. In fact, if you always do what is socially desirable, you may be seen as not having any personality.

The rule of consistency

In judging the adequacy of your class presentation, you also would be concerned with the consistency of responses over time or across situations. For example, if you typed your talk and gave it to the teacher, would it receive a good grade? If you took the central arguments and put them into a paper to be used in another class, would the arguments still receive approval? If you see that the reaction is consistent across time and situations, you may be more confident that your work, rather than some other factor, is the causal source of the compliment. In general, the greater the consistency of a stimulus in producing a response, the greater the attribution of causality to that stimulus.

Choice of rules and the number of these rules used may depend on the circumstances (Ferguson and Wells, 1980). People may use certain of these rules to judge the cause of crime, for example, and other rules to decide what they should do to protect themselves from criminals (Kidder and Cohn, 1979). Kelley argues that sometimes people use all three rules at once. He has been especially interested in the question of how people decide between two or more competing causes. In such cases, argues Kelley (1972), positive evidence for one cause usually ends the decision-making process. Other competitors are discounted. Imagine, for example, that your younger brother took your radio and that you weren't sure whether he took it because his radio was broken or because he was angry with you. The hint that he might have been angry would probably be sufficient for you to discount wholly the possibility that his radio was broken. This tendency to discount all other causes when there is support for any given cause is called the *discounting principle*.

Achievement and Attribution: Looking Inward

Let us say that in applying Kelley's attribution rules you concluded that your talk was, indeed, responsible for Ron's compliment. Ron did not compliment anyone else (the compliment was *distinctive*), many other people complimented you (there was high *consensus*), and you found that your teacher liked the typed draft of the talk (there was *consistency*). Would you necessarily feel pleased with yourself? Not according to Bernard Weiner and his colleagues (Meyer et al., 1980; Weiner, 1979; Weiner et al., 1979). As they argue, determining whether you yourself have caused the outcome in matters of success and failure is not enough. You also may want to identify whether the outcome was due to *effort* or *ability*. For example, if you receive a low mark on a math test, your subsequent feelings may be affected by your

The Fundamental Attribution Error and Judging the Poor

The tendency to disregard the effects of situations on people's actions while focusing on their personal dispositions has been called the *fundamental attribution error* (Ross, 1977). The development of national policies for aiding the poor is one concrete situation in which the fundamental attribution error may have profound implications for action. Should the nation help the poor by providing such benefits as welfare checks, food stamps, special tax-reductions, job programs, and similar policies? Or should the poor be left to help themselves? The answer to these questions depends in part on whether the poor person is viewed as being responsible for his or her own poverty or whether the poverty is seen as being *situationally determined*. Is poverty a reflection of the individual's lack of motivation, sense of responsibility, or character, or is it the result of poor governmental policies, inflation, or capitalistic economics?

Opinion surveys have explored the way in which American citizens view the plight of the poor. In particular, the public has been asked whether poor people can be blamed for their economic condition or whether their poverty is due to circumstances beyond their control (Schiltz, 1970). As you can see in the table below, in four of five periods during which such surveys have been conducted, the larger percentage of respondents attributed poverty to an individual's lack of effort rather than to the general social or economic circumstances. In 1967 the percentage of respondents blaming the poor person exceeded those blaming the situation by more than two to one. The fact that these results were obtained in four different time periods suggests that the tendency to blame a person as opposed to a

causal analysis. Did you fail because you are lacking in math aptitude (ability) or because you just didn't try (effort)? If you attribute failure to low ability, you might feel that you were destined to fail the course (Bar-Tal, 1979). If you think your failure was due to poor effort, you might study a lot harder the next time.

But how do you decide whether to attribute your performance to ability or to effort? It is not always so easy to know. According to Weiner, your attention would be drawn to the stability of your performance. Most people assume that ability is a stable feature of their makeup, while they expect their effort to change frequently from one situation to

another. Thus, if you always fail math tests, you would most likely conclude that you lacked ability. If you always received high scores, you might perceive yourself as being highly able. However, if you sometimes fail and at other times succeed, you would be more apt to conclude that your failure was because of effort.

To demonstrate this line of reasoning, students were given information about the task performance of a hypothetical individual (Frieze and Weiner, 1971). The results showed that inconsistent performance was attributed to the individual's effort. Success on a task that the individual previously had failed was attributed to trying harder. Failure on a task

situation continues even as wide variations take place in social and economic circumstances. The results of these surveys appear to reflect the fundamental attribution error. The question of whether these views of the poor ought to influence national spending on poverty is well worth debate. As we will discover later in this chapter, discerning the difference between situationally produced behavior and behavior produced by personal dispositions is no easy matter. In effect, whether the so-called attribution error really is an error is not clear.

QUESTION: In your opinion, which is more often to blame if a person is poor: lack of effort on his own part, or circumstances beyond his control?

Response	March 1964	November 1964	October 1965	December 1965	June 1967
Lack of effort	33%	30%	40%	40%	42%
Circumstances beyond control	29	31	27	29	19
Both	32	34	27	28	*
No opinion	6	5	6	3	*
TOTAL	100	100	100	100	*

* Data not available

previously completed successfully was due to not trying. On the other hand, an individual who was consistently successful was seen as having great ability. And an individual who always failed was judged as lacking in ability.

The Differing Perspectives of Actor and Audience

In our discussion thus far we have suggested that people often follow three common rules for deciding whether the causal source of an action lies within the person or is part of the situation. However, we also have stressed people's inconsistency. No one always follows such rules. Whether an individual

chooses to do so may depend on a good many factors. One major disruptive influence is the person's perspective in the situation. Perspective varies depending on whether the individual is an actor in the situation or an observer. Return to the example of the ghetto youth who stabbed our friend. As observers we saw the youth as the cause of his own behavior and thus we wanted him to be punished. Yet, from his viewpoint he didn't have any choice. We thus looked at the same event from different perspectives.

As attribution theorists Jones and Nisbett (1971) have argued, people commonly see others as the source of their actions, while they see themselves as acting according to environmental constraints. Why should actor and observer differ in their attributions of causality? First, different quantities of information are available to each of them. Usually actors have much more information about the situation surrounding the action than do observers. Actors know about factors in their past that may propel them toward action; they can identify the specific aspects of a situation that have powerful effects on them. Observers are less knowledgeable in all these respects and thus tend to see actors as deciding for themselves. The second reason that actor and observer differ in their viewpoints is related to their focus of attention. Actors primarily focus their attention outward, toward the environment's obstacles, potentials, and so forth. Observers mainly focus on the actor. Other aspects of the situation—those which constrain the actor's choices—may go unnoticed by the observer. The observer simply sees the actor act. For these reasons, observers often tend to see people as being responsible for their own behavior, while actors see themselves as responding to the situation.

In one ethically controversial demonstration of this argument, investigators attempted to recreate the experience of the participants in the Watergate incident (West, Gunn, and Chernicky, 1975). They gave a group of students an elaborate rationale for burglarizing a local advertising firm, and they were able to secure agreement from the students that the break-in had merit. A second group (observers) simply read about the events and the subjects' agreement. When asked later about responsibility for the burglary, the subjects who had faced the facts from the actors' standpoint tended to see the burglary as being justifiably necessary. Subjects who only read about the case (observers) placed blame on the actors themselves. Thus, differences in perspective would explain both a plea by Nixon's men that their actions were demanded by the situation and the public's view that the Watergate incident was the re-

sult of poor character. Many other studies reveal similar patterns (Miller and Ross, 1975; Sicoly and Ross, 1977; Zuckerman, 1979).

Again, we must make clear that we are speaking of tendencies, not absolute laws of behavior. For example, many people tend to attribute causality to themselves regardless of circumstance. As we shall discuss in Chapter 9, some people generally see their actions as being under internal control, while others view their actions as being controlled by circumstances. Providing more information can also reduce the differences between actors and observers. Observers who have enough information about a situation come to resemble actors in their tendency to attribute cause to the situation (Eisen, 1979). Finally, personal goals can also change the way both actors and observers attribute causality (Jones and Thibaut, 1958).

Self-serving Bias in Causal Attribution

As we frequently have stressed in this chapter, interpreting human interaction can be an extremely difficult matter. People are in constant motion and one can never be too certain of the meaning of any given action. This ambiguity leaves room for many different interpretations of causality. As we have just seen, the actor and observer may come to different conclusions because they have different perspectives. We now must consider the influence of people's motives and personal goals on causal attribution. Investigators have been particularly concerned with *self-serving bias*—that is, the tendency to see oneself as the cause of one's successes but to attribute failure to external sources (Bradley, 1978).

In one early attempt to demonstrate self-serving bias, experimenters arranged for teams of students to work together for many hours in a game situation (Streufert and Streufert, 1969). Each team was given responsibility for governing a fictitious nation torn by revolution. At various intervals each team received information about the state of its nation's economy, the revolutionary force, its people's attitudes, and so forth. Many decisions were required, and their outcome was uncertain. However, the experimenters arranged matters so that during one designated period the teams consistently met with disaster. Every decision seemed to make matters worse. During a second period the experimenters caused the teams to experience consistent success. After each of these periods, members of the teams were asked to evaluate privately the causes of their success or failure. The results were clear-cut. When the team failed consistently, students placed the blame on the situation. However, when their actions met with success, they rated themselves as being highly responsible for the various outcomes. The cause of success was internal.

If such laboratory results seem remote, consider some evidence from the educational world. Who should receive credit for a student's successful performance, the teacher who uses excellent teaching methods or the student who puts in devoted effort? In one study of this issue (Johnson, Feigenbaum, and Weiby, 1964), teachers rated children in terms of whether level of performance was due primarily to the children's abilities and efforts or to their own teaching skill. The children performed in various ways—sometimes well and at other times poorly. When a child turned in a poor performance, the teachers tended to blame the child's poor ability on effort. When the child succeeded, the teachers were far more likely to take the credit themselves. We should be charitable in our judgments of the teachers, however, since students also are likely to see their successes as being their own responsibility while considering their failures to be due to circumstance (Bernstein, Stephan, and Davis, 1979). And psychotherapists have been found to demonstrate similar patterns of self-serving attribution (Weary, 1980). Although people often avoid publicly boasting that they are responsible for their successes but not their failures (Arkin, Appelman, and Burger, 1980), the private expression of self-serving biases has been demonstrated in numerous studies (Schopler and Layton, 1972; Snyder, Stephan, and Rosenfield, 1976; Wortman, Costanza, and Witt, 1973). Is taking credit for one's success always self-serving? Many studies suggest that people tend to see *every* individual's successes as being due to the individual's own efforts (Cooper and Lowe, 1977; Kelley and Michela, 1980). Most people just don't believe that anyone would try to fail.

In Search of True Cause

The preceding discussion indicates that people frequently use rules of distinctiveness, consensus, and consistency in deciding on the causal source of a given action. People's causal attributions also may shift depending on whether the persons are actors or observers and on what may benefit them in a situation. As you can see, wide disagreement is possible in tracing the responsibility for an action— that is, in deciding whether the individual should be blamed (or praised). The resolution of such disagreements sometimes can have life-or-death consequences. Consider the situation of jury members who must decide whether a murder was voluntary (internally caused) or provoked (externally caused). How can one decide about the true cause of people's actions?

From the present standpoint, one must face the possibility that true cause is a kind of social myth—never to be located on an objective basis (Gergen and Gergen, 1979). True cause is difficult to determine because decisions about cause depend primarily on where people direct their attention (Taylor and Fiske, 1975). We have already seen how actor and observer may disagree on causal attribution. They disagree not because one of them is more objective than the other, but because one attends to the actor in motion and the other to the situational demands. The point is made with even greater clarity in research on *causal chains*—that is, series of events that may be causally linked (Brickman, Ryan, and Wortman, 1975). Consider a rape case in which the act seems to have been premeditated and thus can be attributed to internal causes. The defendant may be blamed for the action. But if the external situation preceding the rape is considered, then blame is not so certain. The defendant may have been at the mercy of an uncontrollable urge. He may have been upset because his mother and older sisters beat him during his childhood and because a month before the rape his wife left him without warning. Now it appears that the social situation should be blamed. However, looking backward once more to consider the reason for the mother's, sisters', and wife's actions, the blame may again fall on the defendant. Perhaps he provoked the women in his life. But then again, we could consider the circumstances that caused him to provoke their attack, and so on, without objective end. How much responsibility one assigns to the defendant thus depends on what point in the causal chain is being considered.

In opposition to this line of argument, some critics maintain that people know when their actions are voluntary. That is, people can distinguish between their voluntary and involuntary actions (Steiner, 1980). But can people be accurate in such assessments? If success and failure can bias causal attributions, then we may well wonder whether people can ever judge their own motives adequately. A series of studies by Richard Nisbett and his colleagues (Nisbett and Bellows, 1977; Nisbett and Wilson, 1977) demonstrate that people are generally not aware of the cognitive processes underlying their conscious decisions. If asked to give your mother's maiden name, you may quickly produce a response, but you cannot identify the particular memory processes that produced

the response. Or, as the poet Howard Nemerov has revealed in conversation, "I don't know why I write what I do. My words tumble out on the page and I wait to see what they say."

Yet, even though true cause may be beyond knowledge, it is nevertheless an extremely valuable concept for society. If people are not seen as the originators of their actions, no way exists to hold them accountable or responsible. And without a concept of social responsibility, trust in human relations may disappear. Further, the system of laws and courts would have no place in a world where people were not viewed as the originators of their actions. For the good of society, then, people must continue to negotiate the causes of one another's actions (Scott and Lyman, 1968; Shotter, 1980).

Self-perception

Social perception is not just a matter of observing others and trying to understand their behavior. People also try to understand themselves—to be aware of what they really feel, what they truly are. People question their own motives, ask why they are attracted to a given person, why they are afraid to break certain social rules, and so forth. People wonder about their values and attitudes, and they seek to define what it is they really believe about the world. They try to understand their emotions and discover their true feelings about various people and situations. Most people seem to agree with the early Greeks' belief that to "know thyself" is extremely important.

Let us examine the question of self-knowledge in light of what we have said so far in this chapter. We have argued that the perception of others is based primarily on a set of preestablished concepts or explanations that are popular within a culture. From this perspective, to understand or to perceive others properly is to apply the concept or explanation that is required to get along successfully in the culture. There is every reason to believe that people also rely on these rules of description when they try to understand their own actions. The culture furnishes labels that define action for the *actor* as well as for the *observer*. For example, if you verbally criticize your friends at a party, chances are you will be seen as having been aggressive. If you said your behavior at the party was really affectionate, your friends probably would laugh, *even if* your verbal attacks were your own particular way of expressing affectionate respect. In this light, we will explore the problem of personal identity.

The Social Construction of Self-concept

Young people often go to great lengths to discover their true or basic selves. They talk endlessly with close friends, drop out of school for a year, join the army, see a psychotherapist, and so forth. However, the preceding discussion suggests that knowing oneself

Who am I? Establishing a sense of self is part of growing up. This boy seems to be working hard at finding his identity, which may reside more within the social sphere than within the self.

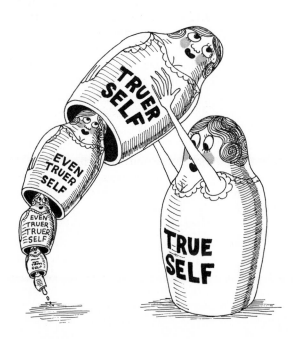

is primarily a matter of applying social labels. If feelings of personal identity are created by the choice of labels, then a person's self-concept may depend on the social situation. Thus let us examine three social processes that may influence a person's concept of self.

The looking-glass self

Suppose you want to know whether you are truly warm and loving or basically alienated from others. Sometimes you seem loving enough, but you also are aware that at times being so is an effort. You wish to know what kind of person you *really* are. From the present standpoint, the answer to this question lies in the definitions supplied by the social environment. The most direct solution to the problem is simply to rely on others' opinions of you. Indeed, the early social theorist George Herbert Mead (1934) reasoned that one's concept of self is altogether a reflection of the opinions communicated by significant others. Society provides a *looking glass* in which people discover their image, or self-label.

Let us see how the social looking glass can shape a particular aspect of self-concept, namely, *self-esteem.* Self-esteem refers to an individual's perceptions of his or her own adequacy, competence, or goodness as a person. In one experiment, female undergraduates were interviewed by an attractive female graduate student whose field was clinical psychology (Gergen, 1965). During the interview the undergraduates were asked to evaluate themselves as honestly as possible. Each student rated her own personality, looks, social abilities, and so forth. The graduate student showed subtle signs of agreement each time the subject rated herself positively and disagreement each time the subject criticized herself. To show agreement the graduate student would smile, nod approvingly, or murmur, "Yes, I think so too." Disagreement was evidenced by silence, a frown, or an occasional disagreement with the subjects' self-doubts. The effects that this communication had on the expressions of self-esteem demonstrated by the undergraduates during the interview are shown in Figure 2-3. Compare the amount of positive self-evaluation evidenced by the subjects with that expressed by a control group that received no such regard from the interviewer. As you can see, the graduate student's approval produced a steady increase in the subject's self-regard. The research also revealed that the undergraduate's new definition of self continued even after the interview was completed. Approximately twenty minutes after the interview, subjects were asked

to give an honest and anonymous self-appraisal. As shown in the figure, the graduate student's high opinion of the subjects carried over to this occasion. As one student later said, "I don't know why, I just felt great the whole day."

Students in this experiment allowed themselves to accept the views of the graduate student. However, people can be very selective in their choice of a looking glass. Certain people's opinions may be welcomed and others' opinions may be rejected. For example, if others' estimates disagree greatly with one's own self-estimates, they may be discredited (Bergin, 1962). In addition, people may discredit others who evaluate them unfavorably. A study of 1,500 adolescents showed that the more favorable another person's opinion was, the greater was the importance of the opinion to the individual (Rosenberg, 1979). Apparently, people bolster their self-esteem by placing greater trust in the opinions of people who evaluate them favorably.

Social comparison effects

People also discover the "proper" labels for themselves through *social comparison*—that is, by estimating how they stack up in comparison with those around them. For example, a friend may be considered by everyone to be a warm and loving person. If you find yourself behaving just like the friend, you may conclude that you too are warm and loving. The influential theorist Leon Festinger (1954) has proposed that the process of social comparison is perhaps the major vehicle through which people determine what is true and false about social life. We will say more about the process in Chapter 10. However, in one dramatic demonstration of the comparison process, a summer job was offered to a group of male college students (Morse and Gergen, 1970). When each applicant arrived for an interview, he was seated

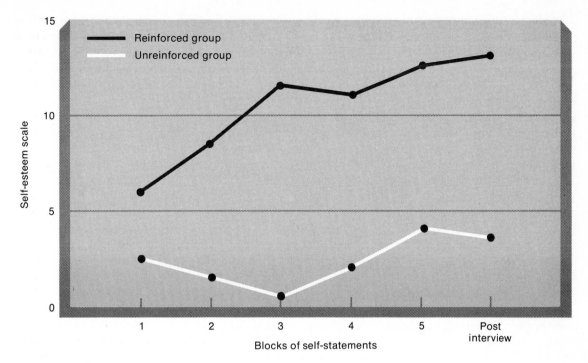

FIGURE **2-3** **The effect of social reinforcement on self-esteem**

Note the increase in self-esteem in the group that received support from the graduate student. Increased self-esteem persisted in a different setting. (Adapted from Gergen, 1965)

alone and given a number of forms to fill out. Among the forms was a standardized test of self-esteem. When the applicant had completed half of the self-esteem test, a secretary brought a second applicant into the room. This individual, an accomplice of the experimenters, appeared in either one of two guises. For half of the subjects, he cut an impressive figure. He wore a beautiful suit and carried an attaché case. As soon as he was seated across the table from the subject, he opened his case to reveal sharpened pencils, a philosophy book, and a slide rule. We privately labeled this applicant Mr. Clean. For the remaining subjects, the same collaborator appeared, but dressed in a smelly sweat shirt, torn pants, and several days' growth of whisk-

ers. He looked dazed, and as he slumped into his seat he threw a dogeared copy of a cheap sex novel onto the table. He was privately knighted Mr. Dirty. No words were exchanged between the accomplice and the subject. After the accomplice was seated, the original applicant went on to complete the second half of the self-esteem test.

An examination of the self-esteem scores revealed a striking effect. In the presence of Mr. Clean, applicants showed a marked *decline* in good feelings about themselves. The ratings were far more negative than they had been before Mr. Clean arrived. Precisely the opposite effect occurred when applicants were exposed to Mr. Dirty. When they compared themselves with him, they showed a marked *increase* in self-esteem. Self-concept often may depend, then, on comparison—on who happens to be present.

Social distinctiveness: "How do I differ?"

If you were asked to talk about yourself, chances are you would not mention that you are a person with two feet, two eyes, or a nose. Yet, if you lacked a foot, an eye, or a nose, you probably would think of this as an important aspect of yourself—perhaps an essential one in understanding who you are. Apparently people also develop a sense of self by observing the ways in which they differ from others. Observing a difference seems to increase consciousness of a particular characteristic. The characteristic then becomes a means of personal identification.

In one study of distinctiveness effects, investigators interviewed more than five hundred high-school students, asking them to talk about themselves for five minutes and to say anything that came to mind (McGuire et al., 1978). Approximately 82 percent of the students were English-speaking whites, while 9 percent were black and 8 percent were Hispanic. The black and Hispanic students were more distinctive than were the white students in this environment. As the self-descriptions revealed, very few (1 percent) of the white students spontaneously mentioned their racial identity—their being white simply was not on their minds. In contrast, 17 percent of the blacks and 14 percent of the Hispanics mentioned their race or ethnic background. Similar results were obtained in an analysis of whether students mentioned their gender (McGuire, McGuire, and Winton, 1979). Whether students identified themselves as male or female depended on how many males or females were in their household. If a male lived with a mother and three sisters, for example, his maleness became an important part of the way he saw himself.

In summary, we find that the way people define themselves at any particular time seems to depend on the responses and the presence of others. People come to know themselves by observing the way others react to their behavior, by comparing themselves with those around them, and by focusing on the aspects of the self that are different from other people's. In a sense, an individual is defined by the company he or she keeps.

Understanding Emotions

Now that we have seen how self-identity may be molded by a social situation, we can turn to a second important aspect of self-perception: the emotions. To what extent does an individual's emotional life depend on the application of labels? You may believe that your emotions are not up for social grabs. After all, you may feel that you *know* when you are angry or sad or fearful. And besides, don't emotions reflect underlying physiological differences? In discovering feelings, aren't people primarily registering the state of the nervous system at the moment? The body provides different messages for elation, hate, love, anger, and so forth. Although these arguments sound plausible enough, let us reconsider.

First, let us examine more carefully the physiological basis of emotions. As it happens, research in this area indicates that few emotions can be clearly differentiated on a physiological basis. Thus, some physiological differences do exist between generalized positive or negative feelings (Lazarus, Kanner, and Folkman, 1980) and between extreme states of rage and fear (Ax, 1953). However, beyond very gross differences, telling one emotion from another is difficult (Holmes and Masuda, 1974; Selye, 1976). Physiology does little to discriminate, for example, among love, admiration, infatuation, sympathy, affectionate regard, or friendliness. Nor have physiological differences that distinguish among hate, envy, jealousy, spite, or anger been discovered. Instead, many different feelings seem to be accompanied by a state of *generalized physiological arousal.* But if there is little emotional discrimination on the physiological level, why are so many distinct emotions represented in language?

An intriguing answer to this puzzle is furnished by Stanley Schachter's (1964) *two-factor theory of emotions.* Schachter suggests that our emotional experience requires first *generalized arousal* and then a *cognitive label* for the arousal. Since the arousal doesn't come with a label attached, people must necessarily turn outward to their social surroundings. Social rules determine what label applies in a given situation. The rules specify, for example, that if you are aroused by a member of the opposite sex, you should call the feeling *love, infatuation,* or *sexual attraction.* If the other person is of the same sex, the arousal should be labeled *friendship.* If the person is much older, you might label the arousal *admiration.* What we think we feel thus depends importantly on the social rules governing what we are *supposed* to feel under varying circumstances (Averill, 1980).

The classic demonstration of this argument was provided by Schachter and his colleague Jerome Singer (1962). In their experiment subjects were injected with a substance they were told was a vitamin supplement. The substance was, in fact, *epinephrine,* a sympathetic nervous system stimulant. One group of participants was then told that the "vitamin supplement" would produce flushing, tremor, an increase in heart rate, and so forth. These subjects thus knew what effects the drug actually would produce. A second group of subjects remained uninformed. They were told nothing of the drug's effects. Once they received the shot, both groups of subjects experienced physiological arousal, but the subjects in one group had a label that would enable them to understand their arousal, and the second group did not. As the investigators reasoned, the second group would be more open to environmental cues suggesting how

to define their feelings than would the first group. A third group, injected with a nonarousing solution, was not expected to be much aroused (placebo condition).

After the injection each subject was sent to a room to wait for an experiment in vision. A confederate of the experimenters, posing as another subject, was already in the waiting room. He set the stage for emotional labeling. For half of the subjects in each of the above conditions, the confederate tried to produce *euphoria.* He happily threw paper planes, tossed wads of paper into a waste basket, and played with a hula hoop. For the other subjects the confederate tried to produce *anger.* As he filled out a questionnaire, he became angry and made increasingly critical remarks about the questionnaire and its originators. Finally, in a fit of rage he crushed the form into a ball and threw it into a waste basket.

After exposure to the confederate, subjects rated their emotional state. As you can see in Figure 2-4, subjects who had no label for their arousal (who were uninformed about the drug's effects) were more likely to feel euphoric or angry than were informed subjects. In other words, subjects who had no way to interpret their arousal except by using social cues were most influenced by the social circumstances. In addition, subjects who received the placebo were also less euphoric and less angry than were subjects who were aroused and uninformed. As the investigators reasoned, both arousal and a search for cues are essential for identifying emotions.

In Schachter and Singer's experiment the subjects were aroused artificially. This procedure was necessary because the investigators wanted to manipulate arousal while holding other factors constant. In daily life the sequence of events is seldom so clear. As Arlie Hochschild (1979) has argued, people often are confronted with rules about what they *ought* to feel *before* they are aroused. People expect to feel sad at a funeral, enthusiastic at a sports contest, or grateful when

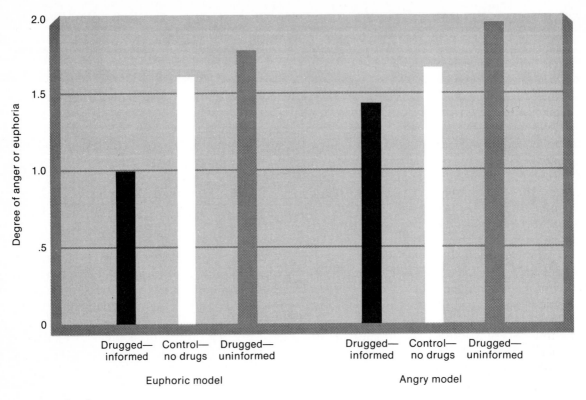

FIGURE 2-4 **How do people know what they feel?**

In this demonstration of Schachter's two-factor theory of emotion, note that uninformed subjects tended to give their unexplained arousal the same label as that for the behavior they were observing. (Adapted from Schachter and Singer, 1962)

receiving a gift—and yet often these feelings are absent. At such times, observes Hochschild, people carry out *emotional work* in order to have the experience that is demanded by the occasion. That is, they try through various psychological mechanisms to align their experienced feelings with the situational requirements. These psychological mechanisms can be cognitive, physiological, or expressive. For example, in order to feel grief at a funeral one might bring to mind fond memories of the deceased (cognitive), breath more deeply in order to increase heart rate and thus produce the experience of hav-

ing an emotion (physiological), and adopt a posture of sadness (expressive). This emotional work helps to bring on the required state of feeling.

Although Schachter's research suggests that emotional labeling is highly dependent on social circumstances, his work has not been without criticism. Some critics have pointed out important flaws in the experimental methodology (Leventhal, 1974; Plutchik and Ax, 1962), and others have not been able to repeat the experiment successfully. For example, it has been found that most people don't like to experience unexplained arousal (Marshall, 1976; Maslach, 1979). If the dose of epinephrine is strong, for example, the subject will feel uncomfortable regardless of the information provided by the environment. Many theorists continue to believe in a limited number of fundamental emotions (Ekman, Friesen, and Ellsworth, 1972; Izard, 1977). Yet, even though Schachter's work has its critics, it has stimulated much fascinating research.

Research on the *reattribution of emotional states* deserves special attention. If emotional feelings are as ambiguous as Schachter maintains them to be, then label selection can be rather arbitrary—people need only agree that a label is appropriate. Therefore, giving people different kinds of information should produce a reattribution of their emotional state—a shift from one label to another. This set of assumptions offers exciting possibilities for workers in the fields of mental health and medicine. Think about using reattribution to reduce pain. Can it be done? The fact that people can walk on hot coals or lie on a bed of nails suggests that cognitive factors can be important in determining how much pain a person feels. To explore this possibility more directly, the Schachter group gave subjects a "drug"—a harmless substance that had no effect (Nisbett and Schachter, 1966). Half of the subjects were told that the drug would cause an arousal reaction similar to that produced by electric shock, while the others were informed that it would have few or no side effects. Later the subjects were given a test of pain tolerance. They received increasingly high dosages of electric shock and were told they could terminate the ex-periment whenever the shocks became too painful. The two groups differed markedly in the amount of shock they could tolerate. Individuals in the group that had been told that the drug had shocklike effects were able to withstand more shock than were those who had not received this information. Seemingly, those who thought that the drug had side effects attributed the effects of the shock to the "drug" and did not label the shock as pain. Thus, through reattribution the experience of pain was reduced greatly.

What are the limits of reattribution techniques? Are psychological anesthetics feasible? Are there more effective means for reducing anxiety or depression in therapy patients? Some steps have been taken toward developing such techniques. Research has shown, for example, that altering people's attributions can reduce insomnia (Storms et al., 1979), rid people of snake phobias (Dienstbier, 1972), increase sexual satisfaction (Morris and O'Neal, 1974), reduce fear (Ross, Rodin, and Zimbardo, 1969), and reduce the pain of giving up cigarettes (Barefoot and Girodo, 1972). Other researchers are exploring the possibility that menstrual pain is dependent on conceptual labeling (Koeske and Koeske, 1975). At this point it is too early to know how effective relabeling of emotional states can be. Some investigators feel that long-established habits of labeling can be altered and that new habits can be established (Loftis and Ross, 1974). However, other investigators have discovered defects in the early studies (Calvert-Bozanowsky, and Leventhal, 1975; Kellog and Baron, 1975). Clearly, reattribution has interesting and important potential.

SUMMARY

1 To conceptualize is to treat separate entities or stimuli as equivalent or as forming a unit. By grouping stimuli together into concepts, people simplify the world and make it manageable. This simplification helps people adapt to a complex world, aids memory and clarity of thought, and enables people to communicate.

2   Because concepts simplify, they cause people to overlook differences among persons classified as belonging to the same group. And because concepts fragment the world into different units, dealing with continuous, qualitative changes in experience is difficult for people.

3   Certain concepts may have their basis in the impact of the world on the senses. These concepts are called natural categories. However, most concepts are acquired through social learning. This learning may take place as an individual formulates a concept tentatively and tests it in subsequent interaction. Thus social learning expands markedly with the acquisition of language.

4   In forming impressions of other people, the perceiver applies concepts or labels. The concepts reflect cultural rules of usage, the motives of the perceiver, and the context in which the action takes place—that is, the range of surrounding circumstances, both physical and social. Because immediate experience often engulfs people's attention, people tend to make conceptual errors. For example, they often disregard the base rate, or probability of occurrence, of a given phenomenon.

5   Solomon Asch was one of the first social psychologists concerned with the organization of impressions. He argued that overall impressions often are organized around a central trait, or concept. More recent research indicates that the centrality of a trait is related to its close association in the perceiver's mind with many other traits. A cluster of associated traits is often described as an implicit personality theory.

6   People generally strive for logical consistency in their overall impressions of others, a striving that may result in overlooking contradictory facts. People also try to maintain an emotional order in organizing their impressions of others. They integrate various pieces of information by adding them, averaging them, and weighing the information in terms of its importance.

7   A primacy effect occurs when information that is received first is more important in determining a person's impressions than is information received later. If later information is more important, a recency effect has occurred. Primacy effects are typical in the short run. As information is lost from memory, recency effects may dominate. Recent events also can alter what is remembered about the past.

8   The theorist Fritz Heider maintains that people tend to see others' actions as being caused either by themselves (internally caused) or the environment (externally caused). Most people tend to hold others responsible for actions perceived as having been internally caused. Harold Kelley theorized that we use three rules in determining the cause of an action: the rule of distinctiveness, the rule of consensus, and the rule of consistency. People also try to determine whether their success

or failure is due to effort or ability. If performance is stable, they often assume that the outcome is a reflection of skill.

9   Attributions tend to shift depending on who is doing the observing. Actors often see their actions as having been caused by the environment (external), while observers see the same actions as having been caused by the actor (internal). Attribution can also be biased by inner motives. People see themselves as the cause of their successes, but they attribute their failures to external sources.

10   The impression of themselves that people form is termed self-concept. People's self-concept can be influenced by observing the way others react to them, by comparing themselves to others, and by focusing on those aspects of the self that the individual considers to be distinctive.

11   Stanley Schachter has argued that in trying to understand their own emotions, people first experience a generalized state of physiological arousal and then use the social environment to suggest a label for the emotion. People can be influenced to shift the labels they use to categorize what they feel. This shifting is termed reattribution, and it has many clinical uses.

SUGGESTED READINGS

Eiser, J. R. *Cognitive social psychology.* London: McGraw-Hill, 1980.

Schneider, D. J., Hastorf, A. H., & Ellsworth, P. C. *Person perception* (2d ed.). Reading, Mass.: Addison-Wesley, 1979.

Shaver, K. G. *An introduction to attribution processes.* Cambridge, Mass.: Winthrop, 1975.

Wegner, D. M., & Vallacher, R. R. *The self in social psychology.* New York: Oxford University Press, 1980.

3:

INTERPERSONAL ATTRACTION

■ *All of us have our seasons of unreason. Recently a student friend of ours was selected for a desirable work-study position in a day school for underprivileged youngsters. She returned to college after only three days of work. One of the most brilliant students we ever taught recently quit his position in a top New York law firm to come to Philadelphia. He doesn't intend to practice law any longer. Last year a neighbor, who had a fine job and a lovely daughter, turned on the gas and killed himself. What do all of these cases have in common? Each of these "unreasonable" actions was based on strong feelings of attraction. The college student gave up her job because she was lonely for her boyfriend of eight months. The lawyer left New York because he couldn't stand being away from his lover. He doesn't want to practice law any longer because he wants to devote himself fully to the relationship. The suicide victim had been asked to leave his home; his wife had tired of him.*

To be sure, rash actions are not the only behaviors that can be motivated by strong feelings of attraction. Many social theorists argue that positive feelings are the glue that holds society together (Durkheim, 1949; Tönnies, 1957). Positive sentiment motivates men and women to seek the company of others, raise children, join organizations, or live in a particular community. Because attraction has an immensely powerful effect on people's lives, understanding what draws people together has become a major challenge to social psychologists. Among the questions of interest are what do people seek from their friends or loved ones, what differentiates liking and loving, and what makes close relationships difficult to maintain. These issues and others related to interpersonal attraction are the topic of this chapter.

As you can see, we have shifted our concerns from *cognition*, or thoughts of others, as discussed in Chapter 2, to *affect*, or how we feel about others. In Chapters 4 and 5, when we discuss attitude formation and change, we will deal with thoughts *and* feelings. In this chapter we will focus on positive feelings in relationships. First we will explore the question of how attraction develops. We will discuss five factors that can play an important role in developing relationships: physical proximity, physical appearance, interpersonal similarity, positive regard, and in-

formation. We then direct our attention to deep relationships. We will consider how close relationships develop and the factors that cause them to dissolve. Special attention will be given to our culture's norms, or rules, of intimacy.

No, this discussion will not solve your problems with friends, lovers, or members of your family. Indeed, as this chapter will show, problems are an inherent part of such relationships. But the discussion should furnish some fresh ways of thinking. With new ideas often come new alternatives.

The Creation of Attraction

Answering the question of what creates attraction is no simple matter. One person may like another person for a multitude of reasons. Also, relationships with friends seem very different from relationships with family members or lovers. Do all such feelings spring from the same sources? To help understand this question, ask yourself first what the people whom you like, respect, or love have in common. At the most general level your answer may be that they *reward* you in some way; they make you feel good, happy, satisfied, or even ecstatic. Of course, relationships usually are more complicated, offering various combinations of good and bad experiences. Love often causes pain.

The theorist George Homans (1974) has proposed that people view their feelings for others in terms of *profit*—that is, in terms of the amount of reward obtained from the relationship minus the cost. The greater the reward and the less the cost, the greater the attraction. In this way Homans suggests a common feature that all attraction—friendship, family relationships, or romance—may share. All of these relationships are based on being rewarded in some way. Homans's formulation also suggests that attraction is not mystical and fathomless. Love is not only a matter for poets and songwriters, but it may be traced to observable rewards and costs—to what people *do* for each other. Any reward may create attraction at some time or place. Love is not necessarily sustained by caresses and fond words, for example. It may thrive on a full stomach, beautiful clothes, or increased social status. And, by implication, what produces attraction may change with time and circumstance. If you are feeling bad about yourself, you may be attracted to a person

Attraction and dislike: a precarious balance. A special celebration, a warm and happy group, and suddenly the balance tips and feelings change. We will pay special attention in this chapter to this paradox: any source of attraction can also produce dislike.

who is complimentary and supportive. If you are feeling bored with daily events, you may be attracted to someone who promises change and excitement. Attraction has no single cause.

This last conclusion raises an extremely interesting possibility—one that will be of continuing concern to us in our discussion. If attraction depends on the value placed on another person's behavior and if this value can change from one situation to another, then the same behavior may sometimes create attraction and at other times create dislike. You may, for example, appreciate someone who is openly expressive. Such a person helps you to be open and helps to reduce your loneliness. But sometimes you may want to be alone and think things through for yourself. Suddenly, the other person's open expressiveness seems to be intrusive and irritating. What produced attraction now produces irritation. In the same way, gentleness, rationality, predictability, perseverance, and passion all have the capacity to produce attraction *or* dislike—depending on the situation.

Because any reward is potentially a cost, most relationships exist in a *precarious balance*. What once was attracting may also prove to be alienating. We will pay special attention to this balance as our discussion proceeds.

With these thoughts in mind, let us turn our attention to sources of attraction. First, we will consider two sources that are usually most powerful at the more superficial level of first acquaintanceship: physical proximity and personal appearance. We then move to two sources of attraction that seem to be more important as a relationship progresses: personal similarity and positive regard. Finally, we look at the special case of information and attraction. As will be shown, each of these five sources of attraction also can produce dislike.

The Power of Proximity

A frequent finding in sociological studies of marriage is that geographic proximity reliably predicts choice of marriage partner (Katz and Hill, 1958; Kerckhoff, 1974). The closer the residence, the greater the likelihood of meeting and marrying. Thus a person who wants to marry someone who is wealthy or artistic or a surfing enthusiast probably should move to Park Avenue or to Soho in New York City or to Malibu Beach. The fact that as geographic distance decreases, attraction-based relationships are likely to increase is termed the *propinquity effect*. Yet, if such findings simply mean that strangers don't get married, the point would hardly be worth discussing. Some social psychologists are more interested in the processes underlying the propinquity effect. Distance may influence attraction for a variety of subtle reasons.

The effects of accessibility

In one of the first attempts to study the effects of physical proximity on attraction, researchers investigated friendship patterns within a residential housing area (Festinger, Schachter, and Back, 1950). Although a person's general location within a city or state may restrict friendship choices, whether the distance between apartments in the same housing complex should make a difference is not clear. After all, it's easy to walk a block or two or take an elevator to see a friend. Yet, the investigators found that even within the same housing complex the effects of physical proximity were strong. The closer any two families lived, the greater the likelihood of their being friends. And families were more likely to become friends with the people next door than with people whose entrances were only one door removed. Further, people who lived next to staircases had more friends than did people who lived at the ends of the hallways. If you live in a dormitory or an apartment building, you might try to see if such effects operate in your own life. Your popularity may depend on the particular room you occupy.

The effects of familiarity

In addition to allowing for accessibility, physical proximity also increases people's opportunities to get used to one another. Consider the following situation: during the first few days of a new class, you, as students, often may experience an anxiety similar to ours, as teachers. Somehow all those strange faces are unsettling. However, as the semester progresses the tension usually disappears: you feel more comfortable with classmates whom you have seen day after day. Sometimes you may even feel a slight thrill at seeing a classmate outside of the confines of the classroom. A special bond has developed between the two of you. Does spending time with someone create attraction?

The most systematic investigation of the relationship between opportunities for contact and attraction was carried out by Robert Zajonc and his colleagues (Zajonc et al., 1971, 1974). Zajonc argues that mere exposure to a person, or to any stimulus, is in itself sufficient to increase attraction. Seeing people results in liking them more (or disliking them less). Zajonc demonstrated his point by asking students to evaluate photographs of strangers. Those faces that appeared most frequently in the evaluation exercise were rated more positively than were those seen less frequently. Much the same finding emerged when subjects were asked to rate familiar versus novel paintings (Zajonc et al., 1972), Pakistani music (Heingartner and Hall, 1974), and political candidates (Stang, 1974). In the case of politics, researchers have found that the amount of media exposure given to political candidates predicted 83 percent of the winners in political primaries (Grush, McKeough, and Ahlering, 1978). Even animals show an

increased acceptance of the familiar (Zajonc, Markus, and Wilson, 1974). By increasing amounts of exposure, experimenters have increased rats' preferences for selections by Mozart (Cross, Halcomb, and Matter, 1967).

The effects of exposure can even overcome the ill effects of an unpleasant environment. As one study showed, when groups of subjects were required to sip unpleasant-tasting laboratory solutions, ratings obtained after the experiment indicated that no matter how unpleasant the shared experiences, those participants who met together frequently were more attracted to each other than were those who shared the experience only once (Saegert, Swap, and Zajonc, 1973).

The more frequently people see a stimulus, the more likely they are to feel positively about it, even if they are unaware that the stimulus is familiar. Thus, you might become better friends with your next-door neighbor without knowing that the only reason for the increase in friendship is greater frequency of contact. To demonstrate this growth of attraction without awareness William Wilson (1979) exposed subjects to various ten-second sound sequences that approximated brief melodies. Some sequences were presented five times during the experiment; others were presented only once. Subjects were asked to indicate how much they liked the various sequences and whether they had heard them before. The ratings for the sequences are shown in Table 3-1. You can see that subjects showed greater liking for the sequences that they recognized than they did for those they identified as being novel. Subjects frequently could not accurately identify whether they previously had heard a tone sequence. However, as the table shows, actual exposure frequencies had an effect on liking even when subjects were not aware that they had already heard the sequence before. These data suggest that people come to like other people without knowing why they do so. The reasons for the

TABLE **3-1**   **Familiarity breeds content**

Subjects preferred melodies that they had heard before, even if they didn't recall them.

Actual exposure	Subjects' recall of melody	
	Recalled	Not recalled
5 times	4.22*	4.00
0 times	3.77	3.04

* Responses on the liking scale ranged from 0 to 6, with 6 indicating the most liking.

Source: Adapted from Wilson, 1979.

attraction are developed afterward (Carducci, Cozby, and Ward, 1978, Zajonc, 1980a).

Although exposure effects are found in a variety of circumstances, the reasons for them continue to be debated (Birnbaum and Mullers, 1979; Harrison, 1977; Moreland and Zajonc, 1979). One possible explanation is that the continued appearance of the other person operates as a *drive reducer*. Specifically, an encounter with a stranger alerts and arouses the physical system. This state of arousal is unpleasant. The individual must deal with fear and uncertainty and is too tense to feel attraction. However, over time the other person begins to seem safe and predictable. Arousal is lessened, and as feelings of relief become associated with the presence of the other person, attraction grows. In other words, just as people come to like foods that satisfy their hunger or a job that satisfies their needs for growth, they learn to appreciate a person who produces a decrease in negative arousal. This explanation does seem to be plausible, and research has shown that if you are highly anxious, the presence of a friend (but not the presence of a stranger) can reduce this state of arousal (Kissel, 1965). However, as extensive review of the findings reveals, other explanations cannot be ruled out (Harrison, 1977).

Yet, like most social phenomena these effects are not always reliable (Burgess and Sales, 1971; Stang, 1974). People do not always welcome the reappearance of the same stimulus. They go to different movies; they buy different things to eat. Repetition can produce boredom. It has also been argued that in social groups agreements develop among group members about how attractive each person is (Newcomb, 1979). Once these agreements are reached, attraction may cease to increase—regardless of the amount of additional exposure. Apparently, increased exposure is most likely to increase attraction in ambiguous situations—when the individual is in doubt about other people's actions. When people are very certain of the attributes of a stimulus, increasing exposure can *reduce* attraction (Smith and Dorfman, 1975). When uncertainty is high, exposure often *increases* liking.

Rules of distance: it's not who you are but where you are

We have seen that living near someone or seeing someone frequently can encourage attraction by increasing accessibility and reducing anxiety. However, in neither of these cases is physical distance itself the critical factor. One can be close at hand without being accessible or reducing anxiety. Can distance itself have effects on attraction? One intriguing answer to this question has been proposed by Edward Hall (1959, 1966). As Hall argues, people seem to carry with them *proxemic rules*—that is, rules that specify (1) the amount of physical distance that is appropriate in daily relationships and (2) the kinds of situations in which closeness or distance is proper. Hall believes that people's feelings for others may depend on whether these culturally determined rules are followed.

According to Hall, the rules governing physical distance vary with the nature of a relationship. Intimate friends are allowed to make closer approaches than are acquaintances. A good friend may be allowed to walk with his or her arm around your shoulder. If he or she chose to walk at a distance of four feet, you might become irritated. You probably expect strangers to maintain a greater distance, and you may be resentful if a stranger comes too close. Specifically, Hall believes, people distinguish among four zones:

1. *The zone of intimacy* ranges from actual body contact to a distance of about eighteen inches from the body. This zone is primarily for an individual's most intimate acquaintances. If strangers enter this zone, suspicion or irritability is a typical response.

2. *Personal distance* extends from approximately one-and-a-half to four feet. This zone is allotted for close friends, trusted acquaintances, and persons who share special interests.

3. *Social distance* includes an area approximately four to twelve feet from the body. This space is appropriate for impersonal relationships, work settings, or casual greetings.

4. *The public zone* consists of all space beyond twelve feet. This zone is appropriate for formal meetings, passing strangers, and meetings with high-ranking persons.

Perhaps the best demonstrations of such zonal preferences have been furnished by Robert Sommer and his colleagues (1969). To explore the question of what happens when a stranger enters the zone reserved for personal acquaintances or intimates, Sommer

The public zone. People carry with them rules that specify the physical distance that is appropriate in any situation. Given a large number of benches and a small number of people, twelve feet is about the right distance between strangers in a city park.

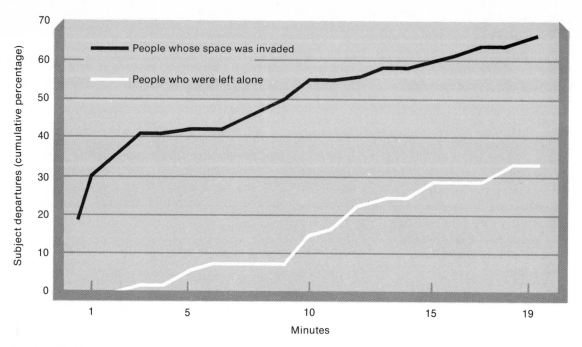

FIGURE **3-1** **How people react to invasions of their privacy**

Often people cope with the violation of personal space by leaving the invaded area as soon as possible. Can you think of conditions or cultures in which this would not happen? (Adapted from Sommers, 1969)

seated himself six inches from individuals who happened to be sitting alone on a park bench. He then assessed the amount of time the stranger remained seated after he arrived. The results of this study are depicted in Figure 3-1. As you can see, people don't seem to like a stranger to invade space reserved for personal acquaintances or intimates. Compared with a control group that was left alone, the longer the intruder sat the more likely was departure of the "victim"—probably in search of another bench.

Other investigators argue that successful friendships may *require* an initial establishment of boundary understandings (Altman and Haythorn, 1967; Altman and Taylor, 1973). That is, people may have to be certain that the other person recognizes and respects boundary rules before they can develop close relationships. To illustrate this point, pairs of sailors who volunteered to be subjects were isolated in a small chamber for ten days (Altman, Taylor, and Wheeler, 1971). Cots and tables were placed in the chamber, along with toilet facilities and means for obtaining food and water. During the ten-day period, video recordings of the sailors' behavior were made. The investigators wanted to know how well the pairs of sailors would get along. Would two individuals become close buddies, would they become withdrawn, or would they even refuse to continue the experiment?

The behavior of the men under these isolated conditions confirmed the importance of boundary understandings. Although many pairs were able to establish friendly relationships, others did not. Most critical for our purposes is the finding that friendly relationships generally developed between partners who established strong territorial divisions at the very outset. When a pair decided quickly who would sleep in which bed or sit in which chair and on which side of the table, for example, cordial relationships were apt to develop. In contrast, if they failed to set up these territorial boundaries, friendship was not likely to develop. A significant number of the unfriendly pairs attempted to quit the experiment before its conclusion.

In summary, we find that physical proximity increases the likelihood of contact. People often seem to select as friends those persons who may be visited with the least amount of effort. Moreover, physical proximity also can increase exposure, and the resulting familiarity seems to create attraction. Commonly shared rules govern the amount of distance that is considered to be proper in various relationships. Obeying these rules may be very important in generating friendship.

Physical Beauty

Different cultures have different conceptions of physical beauty. In some cultures a woman who weighs less than 140 pounds is ugly, while in other cultures a woman may threaten her own happiness if she weighs more than 100 pounds. In some cultures pale skin is vastly preferred, while in others it is considered to be sickly. And within a given society styles of beauty come and go from year to year. Muscular men may be preferred in one era and viewed with suspicion in the next. Carefully groomed hair is stylish one year, while the natural look is a hit the next. There also are people who are ugly by popular standards but whose faces have "character," and there are people who are so "pretty" that they seem to be unreal. Nevertheless, popular

standards are powerful. Within a given culture there usually are persistent and widely shared standards of physical attractiveness. People respond to one another in terms of these standards. Physical beauty can be a key factor in initial attraction, but it also can create problems. Let us first consider the question of how physical beauty increases attraction.

Initial attraction: fair faces make unfair races

How important is physical beauty in creating attraction? Must one person match another person's conceptions of what is beautiful? In exploring this issue, we will focus on heterosexual attraction. We will do so not be-

Changing styles of beauty. When Peter Paul Rubens painted *The Three Graces* in 1639, fleshiness was greatly admired. The slenderness idealized in today's society would merely have seemed ill-nourished to Rubens and his contemporaries.

cause the effects of beauty are limited to this area, but because heterosexual attraction has been of central interest in research.

In one of the more provocative studies of the importance of physical beauty in heterosexual attraction, researchers arranged a computer dance during the freshman orientation week at a large state university (Walster et al., 1966). Each student who attended the dance was randomly assigned a date for the evening. Unknown to the students, the investigators had gained access to their scholastic records and personality-test data. In addition, a panel of judges had independently rated the physical attractiveness of each student. The researchers wanted to know how important the factors of scholastic achievement, personality, and physical attractiveness would be in predicting a couple's attraction to each other during the evening. Would appearance, intelligence, or personality be primary? To find out, the researchers asked each student to privately rate his or her date. The evaluations took place during the dance and again some weeks later. For both men and women, personality and intelligence proved to be of trivial significance. Physical attractiveness was central in predicting personal attraction. A person who the panel had rated as being physically attractive usually was well liked and could expect to see his or her date again. Perhaps the music and dancing prevented anything but trivial conversation. In any case, under these circumstances the cover of the book was all that mattered.

Does this mean that most people chase madly after the most beautiful creature they can find? It does not appear so. Rather, theorists believe, a *matching process* often occurs (Berscheid and Walster, 1969). Although people may long for a partner who is beautiful, they also take into account their own prospects for attainment (Shanteau and Nagy, 1979). People who doubt their own self-worth may not anticipate success in courting a beautiful person. Afraid of the competition,

expecting rejection, lacking in self-confidence, the doubting individual may think, what chance is there? And, who needs the pain of trying and failing? Such thinking apparently leads people to avoid the most beautiful person they can find and instead leads them to select someone who matches their own estimate of themselves.

In one clever demonstration of the matching process, investigators arranged an experiment in which male undergraduates were given a bogus intelligence test (Kiesler and Baral, 1970). In order to temporarily raise or lower the students' self-estimates, the investigators told half of the students that they had done very well on the test, and they told the others that they had done poorly. After each student received his scores he was invited to join the experimenter in a snack bar, where a female accomplice of the experimenter joined the pair. The accomplice's appearance was especially prepared for the occasion: half of the subjects saw her looking attractive; the others saw her as an unattractive woman—she was dressed in a formless lab coat, had a severe hair style, and wore no makeup. After introductions the experimenter excused herself to make a phone call. The investigators' major question was how much romantic behavior would the subject then demonstrate toward the accomplice. To measure the behavior, the accomplice took careful note of any actions with obvious romantic implications, such as whether the subject offered to pay for her drink, complimented her, asked for her telephone number, or asked to see her again.

Figure 3-2 presents the results of the study. You can see that subjects who had been made to feel good about themselves were likely to act romantically toward the woman in her attractive guise. Apparently, success on the test boosted these subjects' anticipation of success in flirting with the attractive assistant. In dramatic contrast, subjects who believed that they had failed the test didn't try

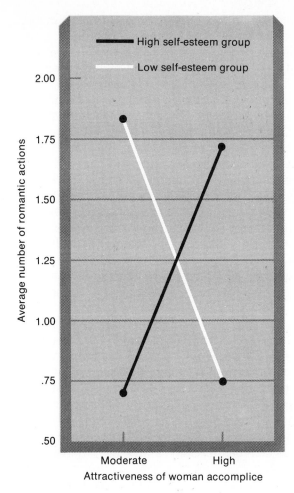

FIGURE **3-2**

Does self-esteem influence romantic behavior?

Men whose self-esteem had been boosted made more romantic advances toward an attractive woman than they did toward an unattractive woman. The opposite was true for men who had suffered a blow to their self-esteem. (Adapted from Kiesler and Baral, 1970)

as hard to obtain the woman's regard when she looked attractive. Instead, they showed more attention when she looked unattractive. Consistent with this finding is the report that physically attractive men have a higher ex-

pectation of acceptance by an attractive female than do less attractive men. However, if it is clear that a woman will accept them, men generally select a physically attractive woman regardless of their own level of physical beauty (Huston, 1973).

The sexes are not equally swayed by physical beauty, however. In general, men seem to be more responsive to beauty than woman seem to be. For example, males generally seem to prefer an attractive woman for purposes of working, dating, or marriage. In contrast, females generally consider similarity of interests to be equal to or more important than physical appearance (Stroebe et al., 1971). Physically attractive women have significantly more frequent dates than do women who are less attractive. Men's dating frequency is unrelated to physical attractiveness (Krebs and Adinolfi, 1975). And after a dance, males are more likely than females to report feelings of attraction based on physical appearance (Berscheid and Walster, 1974).

Such sex differences may stem from the traditional sex-role positions. If a female is viewed primarily as being a male's possession, a plaything who doesn't have the capacity for such serious concerns as making a living, then her looks become one of her most important assets. Her appearance gives the male increased public status and private pleasure. Research shows that males can use attractive females to boost other people's respect for them (Sigall and Landy, 1973). A man can "own" an attractive woman in the same way he owns an expensive automobile. In contrast, females don't seem to gain public esteem by marrying a physically attractive male (Bar-Tal and Saxe, 1976). Apparently men can bargain in the heterosexual market with a wide range of assets, including their economic capabilities, worldly experience, and social importance. A man's looks are not so important. If the women's liberation movement can achieve its goals of increasing women's power, then physical appearance

**What Makes
a Person
Beautiful?**

Many studies described in this chapter demonstrate that physical beauty has a strong influence on people. However, what makes a person look beautiful to others? Why are some people seen as being beautiful, while others are not? We have seen that cultures develop various standards of beauty, but these standards change across time and within various segments of the culture. Thus, there can be broad disagreement as to who is beautiful, and a great many factors can influence judgments of a particular person's beauty. In addition, the same person may seem to be physically attractive at one moment and unattractive the next. For example, if you are engaged in a heated discussion, you probably will see a person who agrees with you as being more physically attractive than someone who disagrees with you. In fact, the person who disagrees with you may suddenly lose his or her physical appeal (Walster, 1971). Further, people make constant comparisons: you may find a person to be gorgeous in one social setting and rather plain in another. One study showed that after male college students watched "Charlie's Angels," a television program featuring beautiful women, they evaluated a coed as being less attractive than she had otherwise seemed to be (Kendrick and Gutierres, 1980).

People's personality also may make a difference in whether they seem to be beautiful (Felson and Bohrnstedt, 1979). If you hear that a person has been described as "friendly, energetic, helpful, considerate, and thoughtful," your rating of that person's physical attractiveness may be increased. In one study, college students were given either unfavorable, average, or highly favorable personality descriptions of women, and they were asked to judge the women's attractiveness, as depicted in photographs (Gross and Crofton, 1977). The photographs had been rated previously by other students as being either unattractive, average, or

may become less important for women in determining their heterosexual relationships.

*After the ball is over:
the social effects of beauty*

Although physical appearance may be a powerful source of heterosexual attraction, an important question remains. That is, does beauty operate as anything more than an initial magnet for bringing people into range? What effect does it have on the later development of the relationship?

Many investigators believe that physical features have an impact far beyond that of simply bringing people together (Adams, 1977; Dion, Berscheid, and Walster, 1972). One person's entire impression of another person's personality, capabilities, skills, and so on may be influenced subtly by the latter's appearance. As you will recall from the discussion in Chapter 2 of Asch's research, one's overall impression of another person may be influenced vitally by a single piece of information. The insertion of a single word, such as *warm* or *cold,* into a lengthy personality description may modify the entire conception

attractive. As the table below illustrates, the more favorable the personal description, the higher the ratings of physical attractiveness. In fact, the woman rated most physically attractive received only average ratings from those who were unaware of the personality ratings. Her beauty was clearly a function of the positive description of her personality.

Over time the appearance of another person's face or body may change. Thus, if you get along well with someone, you may come to see him or her as increasingly attractive over a period of time (Cavior, 1970). In modern culture, wearing glasses may reduce an individual's attractiveness—but not for long. As research shows, a person may react immediately more negatively to a person wearing glasses than to someone who isn't wearing glasses. However, the negative effects of glasses disappear in about five minutes (Argyle and McHenry, 1971). In this case people quickly learn to look beyond a superficial characteristic.

We see then that beauty is not like a birthmark. A person's physical attractiveness can be a sometime thing—waxing or waning with the social circumstances.

Previous classification of photographs	Mean physical attractiveness rating with personality description		
	Unfavorable	Average	Favorable
Unattractive	2.78	3.47	4.80
Average	4.50	4.91	6.04
Attractive	5.13	5.73	5.90

Source: Adapted from Gross and Crafton, 1977.

of an individual. Physical beauty can have the same effect. Apparently many people agree with the German poet Schiller that "Physical beauty is the sign of an interior beauty, a spiritual and moral beauty . . ."

To demonstrate the influence of beauty on people's impressions of one another, researchers asked male college students to evaluate essays that supposedly were written by female students (Landy and Sigall, 1974). A photograph of the author was attached. One group of students read an essay and saw a picture of a very attractive woman, while another group read the same essay but saw a picture of a very unattractive woman. Half of the essays in each group were well written and half were poorly written. Although the students did evaluate the good essays more positively than they evaluated the poor ones, the essays that were supposed to have been the work of an attractive woman were evaluated more much positively that were those supposedly written by an unattractive woman. This effect was particularly noticeable when the essay was poor.

Further studies have shown that people

believe that individuals who are especially attractive physically have more desirable personality traits, are more successful personally and professionally, and are more socially adept than are people who are less attractive physically (Berscheid and Walster, 1974; Dion, 1977; Dion, Berscheid, and Walster, 1972). The social effects of physical attractiveness have been found to affect the lives of children as young as elementary school age (Dion, 1973). Adults who were asked to rate the academic achievement of children and the seriousness of their misbehavior were far more inclined to reward achievement and forgive the misbehavior if the child was physically attractive. Children also are attuned to physical beauty. Physically attractive elementary school children are generally more popular with their peers than are less attractive children (Dion and Berscheid, 1974). The special treatment received by physically attractive persons may also affect their personal traits or styles. The physically attractive person may acquire such valued traits as friendliness and self-confidence (Adams, 1977; Snyder, Tanke, and Berscheid, 1977). And having such traits seems to increase the attractive person's capacity to influence members of the opposite sex. This power over others holds true for adults who are attractive (Chaiken, 1979) and for attractive elementary school children as well (Dion and Stein, 1978).

Beauty reexamined

In spite of the benefits of being physically attractive, beauty also can have negative consequences. The attractive person may be desirable, but his or her appearance may cause envy and resentment. For example, researchers have found that physically attractive people often are seen as being vain, egocentric, materialistic, snobbish, unsympathetic to oppressed people, and likely to have an extramarital affair or to want a divorce (Dermer and Thiel, 1975). Further, an attractive criminal who commits an offense in which suc-

cess may depend on physical appearance (swindling, for example) is more likely to be given a harsh sentence than is an ugly criminal (Sigall and Ostrove, 1975). When the offense doesn't depend on tricking the victim, however, the unattractive offender is likely to get the harsher sentence. Apparently people are deeply offended when an attractive person uses his or her endowments to exploit others.

Attractiveness also can interfere with popularity. In a study of university freshmen, researchers found that the most attractive students were often the *least* liked students. Students who were attractive but were not the *most* attractive were the most popular (Krebs and Adinolfi, 1975). Similarly, research suggests that physically attractive males may be avoided by other males and that moderately attractive females are more likely to be satisfied with their social relationships than are their less or more attractive peers (Reis, Nezlek, and Wheeler, 1980). And among sixth-graders, less attractive boys had more influence over their peers than did attractive boys (Dion and Stein, 1978). In other words, moderate amounts of physical beauty may increase one's social position, but great physical beauty may kindle resentment and hostility.

Why are beautiful people resented? One reason may be that their simple presence makes others feel inferior. As a female friend said after sitting across the dinner table from a spectacular blond woman, "Generally I feel pretty good about myself, but last night I had to keep checking to make sure I was really an OK person." Perhaps such feelings explain the finding that physically attractive people often are unable to influence those of their own sex (Dion and Stein, 1978). In fact, a physically unattractive male may be more successful than an attractive male in influencing his peers. Attractive people also may create resentment because of their unavailability. That is, in dealing with the failure to gain the love of an attractive person, an individual

must face up to his or her own inferiorities. The conflicts created by unavailability also are demonstrated in research that shows that men generally are not attracted to women who play hard-to-get. The common folk wisdom that unavailability is appealing is correct only if the woman is hard to get for everyone else *but you* (Walster et al., 1973).

In summary, then, we can say that physical beauty may attract and repel. Good looks may make life more pleasant and successful for the attractive person. At the same time, however, beauty also may generate suffering and hidden resentment. The beautiful person walks a special tightrope.

Personal Similarity

Once proximity and beauty have brought people together, what happens? What sources of attraction are likely to sustain a relationship or bring it to an end? One very important factor is interpersonal similarity—the sharing of opinions, likes and dislikes, styles of relating, energy levels, and so forth. Clearly, if no similarity exists, continuing a relationship will be difficult. However, similarity doesn't always generate liking. Sometimes people look for companions who complement their own strengths and weaknesses. Let us consider first the positive aspects of similarity.

The joys of similarity

The most extensive investigations of the effects of similarity on attraction have been undertaken by Donn Byrne and his colleagues (Byrne and Clore, 1970; Byrne and Griffitt, 1973; Byrne and Lamberth, 1971). In this research, college students typically learn about the opinions of a fellow student. The opinions vary in the extent to which they match those of the subject. In some cases a subject may find that there is agreement on such topics as politics, religion, and university life. In other cases the subject may find few areas of agreement.

In virtually all of their studies Byrne and his colleagues have found that increasing similarity of opinion has a strong positive effect on attraction. The greater the number of areas in which the other person's attitudes seem similar to the subject's, the greater the subject's attraction. In one field experiment, thirteen previously unacquainted male volunteers were paid to spend ten days together in a cramped fallout shelter, where their diet was limited to water, crackers, and candy (Griffitt and Veitch, 1974). Before entering the shelter each volunteer had completed a forty-four-item opinion scale. Then several times during the days of participation the volunteers were asked to indicate which two members of the group they would most prefer to keep in the group and which they would most prefer to exclude. An analysis of their preferences indicated a strong relationship between opinion agreement and whom they liked. Most-liked companions shared 70-percent attitude agreement, while least-liked companions shared only 59-percent agreement. The best-liked subjects were those whose opinions were most similar. The least-liked were those whose opinions were most different.

In extensions of this work, attraction also has been found to be generated by similarities in abilities (Zander and Havelin, 1960), emotional states (Zimbardo and Formica, 1963), conceptual systems (Craig and Duck, 1977), social or economic status (Mehrabian and Ksionsky, 1971), and preferred activities (Werner and Parmalee, 1979). In addition, married couples who share similar attitudes toward pornography are likely to be happier with each other than are couples whose attitudes toward pornography are dissimilar (Byrne et al., 1973). And adolescents who use drugs are likely to seek other drug users, rather than abstainers, as friends (Kandel, 1978).

Why are people attracted to others like

themselves? First, similarity may boost people's *self-esteem* by making them feel that their opinions or lifestyle are well chosen (Arrowood and Short, 1973; Hensley and Duval, 1976). When a person has feelings of self-doubt, someone whose opinions are similar to his or hers is especially likely to become a friend (Gormly, 1974). A second reason for attraction is that people anticipate a more *positive relationship* with someone similar to themselves. The similarity suggests that good things will come of the relationship and that the other person will be helpful and friendly (Karylowski, 1976; Sussman and Davis, 1975). Third, similarity of opinion often seems to imply that the other person has likable traits (Ajzen, 1977). For example, you might be hostile toward someone who expresses racist views, because these attitudes suggest that the other person may be bigoted and narrow-minded. Perhaps you can think of additional reasons for liking someone who is similar to you.

Similarity versus complementarity

Despite the considerable amount of evidence indicating that people like those people who are similar, many investigators have not been content with the assumption that similarity *always* breeds attraction (Grush and Yel, 1979; Russ, Gold, and Stone, 1979). Like other sources of attraction, similarity may be two-edged, sometimes producing attraction and at other times producing dislike. For example, people often desire to see themselves as being unique, unlike other people. Under such circumstances, other people who are highly similar may be disliked (Snyder and Fromkin, 1980). Consider how you would feel, for example, if you believed that you had discovered a unique topic for a term paper, and six of your classmates all decided to write on the same topic. If another person is too similar, opportunities for personal growth may also be limited (Grush, Clore, and Costin, 1975), you may be bored with that person,

or you may find that you have to compete harder for limited resources.

One of the most serious questions concerning the power of similarity has been raised by theorists who believe that good relations depend on how people's traits or abilities complement each other. This argument deserves close attention. Have you ever gone out with someone who was extremely uninhibited and adventuresome? If so, you may have found yourself becoming cautious—furnishing the voice of reason so you could have fun but avoid trouble. In this situation the two of you were acting in a *complementary* fashion. You each furnished a behavioral resource that, when added together, yielded gratification for both of you. You appreciated the spontaneous enthusiasm of your friend, and he or she needed your help to channel the enthusiasm so that it paid off. In a similar fashion, people who want to be taken care of may get along best with people who like to give nurturance, and an incessant talker may be most compatible with someone who likes to listen. In each case the difference, rather than the similarity, creates the positive relationship.

The classic statement of this position is Robert Winch's (1958) theory of complementarity in mate selection. Winch was particularly interested in finding the ingredients that go into making happy marriages. As he and his colleagues found, happy marriages often were based on the abilities of each person to fulfill the needs of the other (Winch, 1958; Winch, Ktsanes, and Ktsanes, 1954). Thus, if one partner liked being dominant, he or she was happiest when the mate was submissive. If one partner was a leader, the other was best as a follower. The effects of complementarity are not limited to heterosexual relationships. Camp counselors of the same sex form the strongest friendships when one partner is nurturant and the other needs nurturance, or when one is exhibitionistic and the other more deferent, or when one is aggressive and the other self-punishing (Wagner, 1975). Complementarity may be especially important as a relationship grows deeper. People may initially be attracted by similarity of opinion, but complementarity may become more powerful as people's styles of relating become more obvious (Kerckhoff and Davis, 1962).

As you might imagine, similarity theorists have carried on a heated debate with theorists who advocate complementarity. The former have been able to show that similarity can be important in determining marital happiness (Burgess and Wallin, 1953; Cattell and Nesselroade, 1967) and that complementarity studies have various methodological flaws (Huston and Levinger, 1978). At the same time, other researchers have collected data that lend support to the arguments against similarity (Centers, 1975) and have found shortcomings in the methods for demonstrating similarity effects (Gergen, 1978b).

Who is correct? In the final analysis, probably both the similarity and the complementarity theorists are right. The theory that proves to be the strongest in predicting attraction or marital happiness may depend on a number of factors, such as the following.

1. *The personal characteristics selected.* If you are an active person, you might well be happiest with someone who is similar to you. A passive stay-at-home would be a burden. Here similarity would favor attraction. Yet, if you are a dominating person, you might be especially attracted to someone who likes to have another person take over. In this case complementarity would lend itself to attraction (Lipetz et al., 1970).

2. *The nature of the situation.* In a classroom, for example, students typically like an instructor whose knowledge is superior to their own, rather than one whose expertise is at a level similar to theirs (Grush, Clore, and Costin, 1975). Further, breaking through and communicating

with a dissimilar other may produce an especially close relationship (Brink, 1977; Lombardo, Weiss, and Stich, 1973). Persons who travel abroad often find this to be true. On the other hand, in a stressful situation, as in the fallout shelter study discussed previously (Griffitt and Veitch, 1974), similarity produces closeness.

3. *The manner in which the individual is defined by the similarity.* People are apt to dislike or avoid a person who is similar to themselves if the person is a mental patient (Novak and Lerner, 1968), a drug addict (Lerner and Agar, 1972), a poor performer (Senn, 1971), or otherwise obnoxious (Taylor and Mettee, 1971). Others who share poorly valued traits bring one's own shortcomings into the public eye. They may be avoided or disliked as a result (Leonard, 1975).

4. *One's motives or goals in the situation.* On a fishing trip you may enjoy a companion who is just as lazy as you are. When the time comes to clean the fish and put away the gear, you may appreciate someone whose energy complements your laziness. Among a group of midwestern college women, similar religious attitudes were important indicators of attraction to males—that is, the women looked for men who shared their religious beliefs. In contrast, religious similarity was not especially important to their male classmates. The men were more attracted to women who agreed with their sexual attitudes (Touhey, 1972).

Thus we see that although similarity often may generate attraction, it sometimes may lead to dislike. People often search for persons who are different from themselves or who complement them in some way. Whether similarity or complementarity will prove to be more powerful may depend on a variety of factors, such as the kind of traits one is considering, the nature of the situation, a person's motives, and so forth. Again we find relationships in a precarious balance. A factor may promote harmony sometimes and foster antagonism at other times.

Positive Regard:
All You Need Is Love

No one disputes the power of a warm smile, an embrace, an attentive gaze, or words of support in generating feelings of attraction. Most people would agree that such behaviors are important because, in one way or another, they express positive regard. Many theorists believe that positive regard is one of the most significant sources of attraction in human affairs (Becker, 1968; Rogers, 1961). Psychological research lends strong support to this belief. Numerous experiments have shown that attraction toward another person can be increased by the expression of even minimal positive regard (Aronson and Worchel, 1966; Backman and Secord, 1959; Bleda, 1974; Jones and Panitch, 1971). We seem to bask in other people's esteem for us.

Why does positive regard have such strong and pervasive effects? Many theorists agree with the noted psychotherapist Carl Rogers that people learn to need other people's regard and that these needs develop early in life. As a child comes to see that rewards are associated with parental regard and that punishment reflects parental disfavor, regard comes to have its own value. Without others' regard, most people feel insecure. Someone who is ignored for even a few minutes may begin to feel dull, shy, and uninteresting (Geller et al., 1974). Other people's regard makes people feel happy and secure and thus more attracted to the giver.

In an extension of this argument, Elaine Walster (1965) reasoned that people whose needs for regard are especially great often may be *most* receptive to another person's liking. Thus, for example, if you feel miserable about

yourself because you failed an exam, your needs for regard may be especially high and you may be especially attracted to someone who puts a friendly arm around you. To demonstrate this possibility, Walster arranged for female subjects to either succeed in a test of social sensitivity or do poorly. As each of the women was considering her success or failure, an attractive male accomplice of the experimenter entered the room "by accident" and struck up a conversation. As the accomplice was leaving, he indicated an interest in going out with the subject. Later, each woman was required to evaluate a number of persons, including the male stranger. The ratings demonstrated that the women whose feelings of self-regard were lowered because of failure were far more attracted to the stranger than were the successful women.

People's need for positive regard raises a profound social dilemma: the problem of ingratiation. People *want* to believe in the sincerity of another person's positive expressions, but no one can ever be totally sure whether the sentiments are a form of flattery or are true feelings. If the regard is primarily manipulation, if it is based on a wish to gain something, the other person may be employing an *ingratiation strategy* (Jones and Pittman, in press). That is, he or she may be engaging in an activity that is designed to create attraction. Positive regard is not the only possible ingratiation tactic. People also will change their style of self-presentation—the way they define themselves to others—in order to gain the favor of a powerful person (Jones, Gergen, and Davis, 1962). And people will change their opinions frequently to agree with persons from whom they need favors (Jones et al., 1965).

What is the appropriate reaction to the ingratiation dilemma? Given a basic desire to be loved or praised and a desire not to be manipulated, most people simply look for cues that indicate whether other persons really mean what they say. And so, sometimes a person may be pleased by another person's praise or indications that his or her own choices are good ones (Thelan, Dollinger, and Roberts, 1975). However, if an ulterior motive is perceived, reaction may be cool (Jones, Jones, and Gergen, 1963). A person who possesses power is in a difficult position. He or she may feel especially cautious about accepting friendship or praise from persons who are junior or who have less power (Jones, Gergen, and Davis, 1962). As a result, persons in senior positions may be intensely lonely— they don't know whom to trust. Perhaps the beautiful and the wealthy suffer the same isolation. Yet people may not always try to look for cues regarding sincerity. As needs for regard are increased, people may come to accept any signal that can be construed as regard. When the need is great, sincerity may be unimportant.

Information Please: Affiliation for a Purpose

Any discussion of sources of attraction would be incomplete without considering the influence of accurate information. You may wonder how the exchange of information could possibly affect attraction. After all, information comes from books, the mass media, public officials, and similar sources. The possibility of a relationship between information and attraction first occurred to us when we began to study the close relationships that often develop between students and teachers. As one anonymous student wrote, "He [the teacher] opened our eyes to a kind of education different from anything we'd ever had in that very conservative school. He taught us to experiment and think for ourselves. He made us visit college libraries, do outside reading and be original. . . . We all still love him." This girl's comments and dozens much like them strongly suggest that information can generate attraction.

To explore the matter more fully, consider a classic series of studies carried out by Stanley Schachter (1959) and his colleagues. The researchers set out to investigate the influence of fear arousal on people's desire to affiliate. Groups of female subjects were confronted by an experimenter, who was dressed in a white lab coat. Dr. Zilstein, as he was called, told the subjects in one group that they were part of an experiment concerning reactions to electric shock and that each subject would be tested. They were told that they shouldn't be frightened since the shock, while painful, would "inflict no *permanent* damage." Dr. Zilstein's voice and manner were ominous. Other groups of students encountered a more reasonable Dr. Zilstein who told them that they would experience very mild, almost imperceptible, amounts of shock. Subjects in all groups were then asked to indicate on a sheet of paper whether they wished to wait for the shock alone or with others. In fact, the students never received the shock. The investigators' sole interest was in the effects of fear arousal on preferences for affiliation. The findings were clear. In the high-fear condition most students expressed a desire to be with others. In the low-fear condition, far fewer subjects wished to wait with their peers.

What motivates this desire for affiliation? One possibility is that people learn at an early age to seek the company of others when they are fearful. Other persons can be reassuring and can defend a person against danger. In other words, waiting with others may reduce fear. To support this position, Schachter used an interesting argument. That is, when they are anxious, some people may be especially in need of the presence of other people. In particular, since parents usually are extremely nurturant with their first child, firstborn and only children may learn to associate the relief of discomfort with the presence of others. With later-born children, parents may be relatively casual and likely to leave the child to comfort himself or herself. Firstborn and only children thus should be more likely to affiliate with other people when anxious. To support this reasoning, Schachter drew on earlier studies that showed that firstborn and only children are more likely than later-borns to seek psychotherapy when they are experiencing difficulty, and that they are less likely than later-borns to become effective fighter pilots (an ability that tends to be found in persons who can work alone under conditions of fear). Later research also tends to support Schachter's argument (Altus, 1966; Breland, 1973; Vockell, Felker, and Miley, 1973). As you can see in Table 3-2, within fifteen minutes after an earthquake, firstborn women talked with twice as many people as did later-born women (Hoyt and Raven, 1973). How did birth order relate to affiliation preferences in Schachter's research? When threatened with shock, firstborns twice as often chose to wait with others as opposed to waiting alone. For later-borns, the preference is reversed: they strongly preferred to wait alone. When not threatened by shock, firstborns and only children no longer differ from later-borns.

Most investigators believe that reduction of fear is only one reason people seek the company of others when they are anxious (Buck and Parke, 1972; Epley, 1974; Mac-Donald, 1970). It is at this point that the quest for information is relevant. As Schachter reasoned, the high-fear condition also created a great deal of ambiguity. The subjects didn't know how they were supposed to react when their cooperative behavior—volunteering to be in an experiment—was "rewarded" with painful shock. Should they be fearful or resentful? Should they revolt or resign from the experiment? What was happening to them? In order to reduce this ambiguity, they wanted to compare their views with those of others. (In Chapter 2, see the discussion of the effects of social comparison.) The subjects wanted information from others as to how they should react. Support for Schachter's view comes first from the study in which

Schachter demonstrated that anxious subjects strongly preferred to be with other subjects in the same experiment—they didn't want to wait with just anyone (Schachter, 1959). The assumption, then, is that the subjects were eager to exchange views about the experiment with other persons undergoing the same experience. In addition, experiments that have placed fearful subjects together generally indicate that the subjects do trade information with each other and that, as a result, they come to share the same feelings (Ring, Lipinski, and Braginsky, 1965; Wrightsman, 1960).

Much research has been stimulated by Schachter's work, and almost without exception it adds weight to his arguments (see Morris et al., 1976). For example, when students are uncertain of their opinions, they are likely to join others in discussions (Radloff, 1961). And when people have physiological information that gives them a definite indication of their emotional state, they are not likely to affiliate with others (Gerard and Rabbie, 1961). Members of discussion groups often seem to want others to agree with their opinions, especially when the issues are ambiguous (Shrauger and Jones, 1968).

Yet, you may still question the initial thesis that information can produce attraction. After all, the evidence thus far has suggested that information produces affiliation. In a

TABLE **3-2** **Look who's talking**

Firstborn females were more likely to turn to others for support in the aftermath of an earthquake than were later-borns.

	Birth order	
Sex of person	Firstborns	Later-borns
Male	3.58*	2.80
Female	3.97	1.67
* Average number of persons spoken to.		

Source: Adapted from Hoyt and Raven, 1973.

BOX 3-2

Loneliness

People affiliate with others for many reasons. One of the chief reasons may be to avoid loneliness. Loneliness is said to exist when the individual's network of social relationships is smaller or less satisfying than the individual desires it to be (Perlman and Peplau, in press). Thus loneliness does not necessarily mean that other people are physically absent. Loneliness exists whenever others fail to furnish needed psychological resources (Shaver and Rubenstein, 1979). Some people may feel lonely in the midst of a crowd or in the presence of their families. Other people may live alone and be perfectly content. Generally, however, other people are necessary in order to reduce loneliness.

Two types of loneliness are often distinguished: one is accompanied by emotional isolation and the second by social isolation (Weiss, 1973). In the case of emotional isolation, the individual lacks a single, intense emotional relationship. Some form of exclusive intimacy is required; the presence of family or friends may not be sufficient. This form of loneliness has been found to be prevalent among members of Parents Without Partners, an organization of divorced people who are raising their children alone (Weiss, 1973). Loneliness produced by social isolation results when supportive friends and community are unavailable. Nonworking wives and wives who have just moved to a new place of residence often suffer from this form of loneliness.

Some psychologists believe that loneliness is a major problem in modern society (Greydanus, 1976; Sermat, 1974). Studies have shown that almost all people experience loneliness at one point or another (Sermat, 1974). One study of calls made to a distress center found that 80 percent of the 16,000 callers complained about a sense of extreme loneliness (Sermat, 1972). Similarly, over 80 percent of a group of psychiatric patients stated that loneliness was their chief reason for seeking help (Graham, 1969).

Is loneliness a problem for the population in general? One public opinion survey asked people in a cross section of the nation's population to indicate whether they recently had felt "very lonely or remote from other people." Among the respondents, 26 percent said that they had. Many of them indicated that they also felt very depressed and unhappy (Bradburn, 1969). Other investigators, noting the sense of depression that often accompanies loneliness, have suggested that lonely people feel that they have failed in some important way (Gordon, 1976). These people apparently believe that they have not measured up in terms of the accomplishments usually required of the normal adult. The depression may be particularly intense if the individual traces the causal source for loneliness to himself or herself (Weiner, Russell, and Lerman, 1978). To select one's own shortcomings as the major source of loneliness is to make a self-defeating attribution (see Chapter 2). The individual is saying,

"I'm too uninteresting and unattractive for anyone to care about." To blame oneself for loneliness also may begin a vicious and self-defeating cycle in which the individual blames his or her loneliness on personal shortcomings, which in turn leads to depression and inactivity (Rubenstein and Shaver, 1980). The depression and inactivity then reduce the likelihood of the individual seeking new relationships. Loneliness increases.

What are some of the major sources of loneliness in modern society? Two major influences seem to create feelings of loneliness: one has its roots in the social context and the other comes from within the individual. In the social realm, loss of family may be a powerful contributor to loneliness. In one survey, over 50 percent of widowed men and 29 percent of widowed women said that they had been extremely lonely during the past week (Maisel, 1969). Since the work place also is a context in which people find close companionship, joblessness can contribute to loneliness (Seeman, 1971). As one unemployed man wrote, "You have no friends when you're unemployed. They think it's a disease that is contagious and might jump on them" (quoted in Braginsky and Braginsky, 1975). Retirement can have the same consequences, and housewives who remain at home during the day can manifest particularly high levels of loneliness. One study of a sample of housewives who had a low number of social contacts per week found that 81 percent of the women expressed emotional dissatisfaction. In a comparison group of housewives who had a high degree of social contact, the figure dropped to 46 percent (Oakley, 1974).

Not all loneliness can be traced to the social environment. Some people may be prone to feel lonely. That is, they may be more likely than other people to experience loneliness in a given setting. Lonely people, according to Shaver and Rubenstein (1981) often are those who have suffered from some form of *anxious attachment* as children. That is, they have grown up uncertain that they can receive the gratification that they need from other people, and they often are uncertain as to whether they are worthy of support and love. Early childhood episodes have left them feeling low in self-esteem. Some psychologists have argued that children of divorced parents may be especially vulnerable to this problem. Support for this reasoning comes from studies of adults whose parents were divorced (Rubenstein, Shaver, and Peplau, 1979). Those adults who were children when their parents were divorced report more loneliness in adulthood than do people who experienced their parents' divorce as adolescents. Although other studies have shown similar effects of divorce (Kukla and Weingarten, 1979), the unhappy but unbroken home has been found to be even worse for the child. Later psychological adjustment for these individuals may be most difficult.

sense affiliation takes place any time someone provides a service: a bank teller, a weather forecaster, and a clerk in a department store form brief affiliations with the persons they are helping. But is attraction increased as a result? In what kinds of situations does information-giving actually foster liking? Two conditions especially seem to favor the development of attraction: the need for information must be great, and the information-seeker must trust and value the information-giver.

Consider, for example, the following situation. You play shortstop for a softball team. Your team has had a winning season but it is beginning to slump. You realize that your fielding has not been up to par, and in fact, several losses are due directly to your errors. After a loss in which you have made two important errors, the second baseman tells you that you really played your best. Later, however, your catcher wants to talk with you about your fielding. The two of you discuss how you might change your fielding strategy. For which of your teammates would you feel more warmth? Very probably you would prefer your catcher. The second baseman's comments are positive but seem superficial and untrustworthy. Perhaps they even were intended to cut you down. On the other hand, the catcher seems to have sized up the situation quite accurately and is willing to explore your problems in detail. You would probably feel that the catcher was the kind of person who could become your close friend—a person in whom you could place a great deal of confidence.

In this kind of a situation you are faced with two kinds of information: positive but possibly false and negative but probably accurate. The former may build your self-esteem temporarily. The latter may hurt momentarily but help in the long run. Do people actually respond with warmth to candid information from others? In one of the first demonstrations of this possibility, students participating in a cooperative task were made to feel that they either had contributed a great deal to the group's success or had turned in the worst performance in the group (Deutsch and Solomon, 1959). Subsequently each subject received from another group member a message that was either very accepting or somewhat critical. The subjects then were asked to indicate their feelings toward the person who had evaluated them. In general, all subjects, regardless of their performance, were most attracted to the person whose evaluation seemed to be honest. Thus, if they believed that they had hurt the group, they expressed more liking for the critical group member than for one who responded positively. If they succeeded, they preferred the evaluator who responded in a positive, as opposed to a critical, manner. As later research indicates, a critical but honest evaluator may be especially well liked if he or she is in a position to gain through flattery (Drachman, de Carofel, and Insko, 1978). The evaluator gains extra credit by telling the truth when truthfulness might be costly. Good information, then, can build attraction in a relationship (see also Backman and Secord, 1959; Newcomb, 1961).

Accurate feedback at times can be too painful to build attraction (Jones, 1973). Honesty may be highly valued, but sometimes the need for positive regard may exceed the value placed on honesty. After an especially bitter failure, an individual may want just loving acceptance, even if the support is not merited (Friedman, 1976; Jones and Regan, 1974). An accurate appraisal after a dismal performance simply adds to one's misery. As we saw in our discussion of flattery, people may put such high value on others' regard that they will drink in praise even when they suspect that it is false. Flattery may be apppreciated more than the candid truth is.

In summary, we again discover a precarious balance. On the one hand, people value accurate information about themselves, and they value the persons who provide the information. Yet people also want to be regarded highly by others, and accurate information sometimes reflects criticism. Particularly after failure, a person may be more attracted to a potential flatterer than to someone who has offered an accurate appraisal of his or her weaknesses. As we now see, this particular quest is only one of a larger group of contradictions that are found in most significant relationships. Not only do people want candid opinions and complete acceptance, but they also ask for security and growth, stability and stimulation, devotion and the absence of limits on freedom, the free expression of feelings, and not too much emotionality. Perhaps this is too much to ask from one relationship (Gadlin, 1977). However, to expect relationships to be different from this may require going beyond common cultural norms—striking out in new and different directions. With these thoughts in mind, we turn our attention from the factors that create attraction to the realm of deep relationships.

Deep Relations

You chat with a stranger at the bus stop one morning. The stranger seems to be both pleasant and interesting, but the two of you never meet again. If you were asked to describe your relationship with this person, you might say that it was casual or superficial. You might add, however, that had you seen the person again the relationship might have developed into something. Let us stop to consider this choice of words. The relationship was "superficial"; it could have "developed." These words strongly suggest that people carry with them a concept of relationships as growing in *depth*. Consider the possibility that you and the stranger did meet again and that you became friends. At that point you might be inclined to say that the relationship had become

closer. If eventually you lived together happily for a number of years, you most likely would describe the relationship as being deep and important. The conception that relationships vary in depth—that is, in closeness, intimacy, intensity, or caring—has been documented in a variety of careful studies (Marwell and Hage, 1970; Triandis, 1976; Wish, Deutsch, and Kaplan, 1976). Variations in depth seem to characterize a wide range of relationships: heterosexual romance, relationships between parents and children, homosexual relationships, and so forth. All can vary from superficial to very deep.

In the remainder of this chapter we will examine the development of deep relationships. Once again, the heterosexual relationship will be our main focus of interest, although much that we say applies to other kinds of relationships. We will look first at a common course of development as a relationship deepens. We will consider why a common path of development exists, whether the same path always has been followed, and how it varies from one culture or historical period to another. Of special concern here will be the function of social norms in channeling people's actions and possibly even in influencing the extent of their passion. Finally, we will look at the future of deep relationships. Once intimacy is attained in a relationship, how can it be sustained?

The Course of Intimacy

That people often search out deep relationships is hardly in question. The search may begin at an early age and continue throughout a person's life. For many people a deep relationship gives meaning to life. This seems particularly true of young and elderly people. Research suggests that for people in these categories, having close relationships is central to feelings of personal well-being (Campbell, Converse, and Rodgers, 1976). Yet in spite of the intensity of passionate feelings, most contemporary research indicates that the path to intimacy is not irrational and chaotic. People don't rush about frantically grasping for what they want. Rather, increasing intimacy in relationships seems to often follow a common path (Altman and Taylor, 1973; Levinger and Snoek, 1972). This path is a kind of continuum divided into more or less discrete levels of intimacy. People may move along the path as long as the relationship continues to be rewarding. They will break off when rewards are diminished (Levinger and Huesman, 1980). To explore this continuum, let us con-sider two persons, P and O, represented in Figure 3-3 by circles. At first there is *zero contact*—the two individuals exist in mutual ignorance of each other. Whether the two move to *mutual awareness* depends primarily on physical distance. Thus our earlier discussion of the effects of propinquity on attraction may be most relevant at this juncture.

As the couple moves to the level of *surface contact*, a variety of factors often affect the relationship. At the outset, physical attractiveness may play a role in bringing people into contact. With increased contact, personal

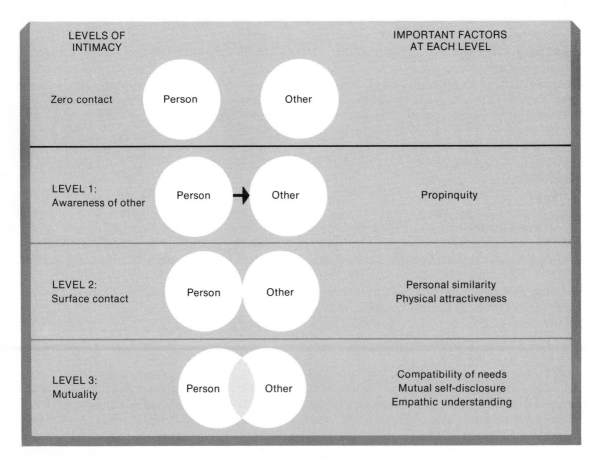

FIGURE 3-3 **Levels of intimacy**

Interpersonal relationships often pass through three levels of intimacy. At each level people emphasize different criteria for attraction. (Adapted from Levinger and Snoek, 1972)

similarity may gain in importance. The couple may spend time exploring a variety of interests and attitudes. Often such explorations may be somewhat narrow and superficial (Altman and Taylor, 1973). Common acquaintances, movies, music, and so forth are more likely to be topics of discussion than are such issues as fears about the future and feelings about having children. In fact, if a person reveals deep secrets too early in a relationship, the other member of the pair may withdraw (Archer and Burleson, 1980; Wortman et al., 1976). Although the surface-contact stage may be superficial, the events of this period may have important effects on the unfolding of the relationship. Just as first impressions often play a part in ongoing relationships (see Chapter 2), the ways two people come to think of each other and themselves as a couple also may continue to exert effects on the deep relationship (Berscheid and Graziano, 1979).

If exchanges are rewarding during the surface-contact stage and a similarity of interests is found, the couple may move on to the level of *mutuality*. The degree of mutuality may vary, however, from a *minor intersection* of the circles to *total unity*. A minor intersection is represented in Figure 3-3. This degree of mutuality might be typified by two briefly acquainted persons who want to explore the good feelings they have for one another. A major intersection might characterize a long-term intimate relationship, such as marriage. Total unity might be reserved for the type of deep union described by the ninth-century mystic Sari-al-Skadi, in which each partner addresses his or her love as "O Myself" (Levinger, 1974). Compatibility of needs may be the central factor in attachment during the mutuality stage. The couple may increasingly come to rely on each other, and the feeling of interdependence may begin to emerge (Huston and Burgess, 1979; Scanzoni, 1979).

The partners typically disclose increasing amounts of information about themselves. If

each rewards the other by accepting and empathizing with the disclosures, the relationship is likely to deepen (Altman and Taylor, 1973). As each individual comes to feel that the partner accepts the entire range of behavior, from good to bad, he or she is likely to feel increasing love for the partner. You will recognize here, of course, the importance of positive regard, discussed earlier. The deepest relationship is achieved, it is said, when two people can reveal the full range of self with full depth of emotions. The most intimate relationship thus features self-revealingness in *breadth* and *depth*.

The importance of self-revelation in establishing deep relationships has been demonstrated in a variety of studies. Such research generally shows a high correlation between how much two people reveal and their attraction toward each other (Jourard, 1959; Worthy, Gary, and Kahn, 1969). The more that is revealed the greater the attraction. And the longer people know one another, the more they reveal. Roommates in college, for example, often proceed from superficial disclosures during the early part of a semester to more intimate disclosures as the year proceeds (Taylor, 1968). The likelihood of self-disclosure may be especially high when people feel that they form a unit around which there is a boundary—that is, when they think that the other person will not break the trust that together they have established (Derlega and Chaikin, 1977; Taylor, DeSoto, and Lieb, 1979). When such boundaries are established, it is said that the partners have developed a communion (Schwartz and Merten, 1980). Laboratory demonstrations also show that people who disclose privileged information about themselves frequently gain others' liking by doing so (Certner, 1973; Daher and Banikiotes, 1976). Liking is further increased if the revelation is related in some way to the things the listener has revealed about himself or herself (Davis and Perkowitz, 1979). Liking may decrease, however, if the disclosure takes place too early in the relationship or is otherwise inappropriate (Derlega and Grzelak, 1979; Kleinke, 1979).

To illustrate the changes that occur as a relationship deepens, consider what a sample of eighty people said about the kinds of activities that typify relationships of various depths (Rands and Levinger, 1978). The students were asked to estimate the probable occurrence of each of the following kinds of behavior: self-disclosure (openness about feelings, for example), social activity (outings, games, working together), praise (regard, affection), criticism (disagreement, irritation), physical contact (holding hands, sexual intimacy), and norm regulation (giving up friends the other doesn't like, not asking permission to use the other person's belongings). The subjects rated the likelihood of each kind of behavior being found in relationships of the following levels of increasing intimacy: casual acquaintanceship, good friendship, close relationship (for example, two people care about each other very much and have no other equally intimate relationship), and marriage (defined in the same way as the close relationship but with the added assumption of permanence).

The results of Marylyn Rands and George Levinger's study are summarized in Table 3-3. As the depth of the relationship increases, so does the likelihood that each of the classes of behavior will occur. First, as suggested earlier, both social and physical contact are increased, along with the amount of disclosure. And as you might expect from our discussion of positive regard, praise increases as the relationship grows more intimate. More unexpected is the finding that criticism and control also increase as the relationship deepens.

TABLE **3-3**   **The influence of intimacy on behavior**

People believe that in all areas of life the probability of mutual activity increases as relationships become more intimate. Marriage offers the most involvement and the greatest opportunity for negative as well as positive behavior.

Type of relationship	Likelihood that mutual activity will occur					
	Social activity	Physical contact	Self-disclosure	Praise	Criticism	Norm regulation
Casual acquaintances	49%	23%	22%	35%	23%	17%
Good friends	71	39	47	58	37	36
Close relationships	81	57	67	73	48	53
Marriage	87	90	83	86	61	68

Source: Adapted from Rands and Levinger, 1979.

Apparently, as rewards increase, so does the punishing capacity of the relationship. People experience greater amounts of criticism and are pressured to shape themselves to the other person's specifications. The result may be conflict or antagonism. But as research indicates, even the best of relationships can be full of conflict (Braiker and Kelley, 1979; Burgess, 1979; Norton and Glick, 1976). Again we find evidence for a precarious balance in attraction-based relationships.

We can say, then, that most relationships vary along a dimension that people think of as depth. Casual relationships differ from deep relationships in a variety of orderly and reliable ways. As a relationship develops, there is an increase in the amount of interaction, physical contact, and self-disclosure and in the communication of regard and criticism. But why should relationships unfold in this manner? Human beings are not programmed like robots are. What accounts for the orderly pattern of behavior in deepening relationships?

Intimacy Norms in Cultural and Historical Perspective

How would you feel if your twelve-year-old brother decided it was time he married, if your father decided to keep several wives, or if a stranger approached you on the street and proposed sexual intimacy? Chances are that each of these experiences would upset you in some way. You might be angry, irritated, or resentful. Such reactions underscore the fact that people generally share rather well-defined expectations about what is appropriate in various kinds of relationships. Further, these expectations are particular to present-day, mainstream America (Rands and Levinger, 1979). In many cultures twelve years of age has been considered an appropriate age for marriage. Polygamy, too, has had its day in many cultures. In fact, polygamy has been the custom more often than not, and its decline can be traced to the spread of Western culture (Ford and Beach, 1951). Further, a proposal of sexual intimacy on chance meeting is neither uncommon nor unexpected in many parts of society. In the gay sections of large cities some young males might feel slighted if they didn't receive such proposals. In both Rome and Paris males can build satisfactory sex lives around casual proposals to women tourists. Clearly, appropriate behavior on the path to intimacy is highly dependent on time and circumstance. This analysis of the development of deep relationships is relevant primarily to twentieth-century American society.

In a more formal sense, widely shared ideas about what is appropriate may be termed *normative expectations*. Such expectations not only apply to others, but also may play an important role in guiding an individual's own behavior. Behavior that is consistent with normative expectations constitutes the *norm for the culture*. Such expectations typically emerge from widely shared views of social life, views that form part of the natural attitude (see Chapter 2). Present-day society frowns on childhood marriages because children are seen as being immature, not experienced enough to make wise choices about marriage, and unable to earn a living. Most members of the society accept these views as common sense. The natural attitude also is closely connected to systems of *normative*, or commonly accepted, *values* concerning what is good or right in society. The rationale for not marrying at the age of twelve is supported by the positive value placed on long-lasting marriages, on education, and on financial success.

As you can see, failure to behave according to the normative expectations makes behavior seem unintelligible. For example, a twelve-year-old bridegroom would seem nonsensical in our culture. If people cannot make sense of someone's actions, they may think the behavior is crazy (Garfinkel, 1967; Schutz,

How Do I Know I'm in Love?

Major life decisions often are based on whether or not people believe that they are in love. A couple may hesitate to share deep secrets, permit themselves to become physically intimate, or get married until they are certain that they are in love. However, people often are not sure whether "real love" or simply deep friendship is being experienced. How can one tell the difference? To explore these issues more carefully, Zick Rubin (1970, 1973) set out to develop both a measure of one person's love for another and a measure of liking or friendship. Rubin reasoned that people who are in love (1) depend on each other, (2) want very much to help each other, and (3) want an exclusive relationship. Thus items on the love measure ask, for example, whether a person would be miserable if he or she could not be with his or her partner, whether the person would forgive his or her partner for practically anything, and whether the person felt a strong duty to cheer up the partner. In contrast, Rubin reasoned, people who like each other (1) see each other as being similar and (2) possess a high regard for each other. Items used to measure liking asked, for example, whether the person thought that the partner seemed to be unusually well adjusted, had sound judgment, and was the sort of person one would like to be.

The two scales were then given to 158 college students who were dating but were not engaged. Each subject evaluated his or her feelings toward the dating partner and toward another person of the same sex whom they considered a good friend. The mean scores for these assessments are found in the table below. As you can see, the dating partner received a much higher rating on the love scale than did the good friend of the opposite sex. This finding is true for both women and men. Apparently, loving is reserved for a romantic partner and is less likely to be experienced for a friend. However, Rubin also found that the students were more likely to rate the romantic partner than the good friend higher on the liking scale. Apparently romantic partners may be loved and can be good friends at the same time. Additional support for the idea that loving and liking are two separate processes was revealed when the students were

1962). Because the norms are often wedded to values, the person flouting them suffers social disapproval. If deviations from the norm are too great, imprisonment and even execution are possible. In effect, norms operate as rules. Norms specify the behavior that is appropriate in various kinds of relationships as well as at various levels of intimacy.

Many investigators have been interested in finding out how the norms for close relationships have changed over time (Brain, 1976; Hunt, 1959). Such work generally suggests that different cultures and historical periods have had different norms. Contemporary Western patterns of intimacy are quite different from customs in other parts of the world or across recorded history. Even within recent history, for example, the norms gov-

asked to estimate the probability that they would marry their current dating partner. The love-scale scores were highly correlated (+.59) with probability of marriage, while the liking-scale scores were correlated only moderately with such estimates (+.35 for men and +.32 for women). (You may wish to look again at Figure 1-3.)

Rubin wondered whether scores on the scales would be related to the couples' behavior in daily life. To find out, he restudied two groups of couples from his original sample: one group composed of dating pairs who had high love-scale scores and a second group of dating pairs who had low love-scale scores. The partners were invited to the laboratory, and each couple was permitted several minutes of free time while they were waiting for the experiment to begin. During this period observers rated the amount of time each member of the pair gazed at the other. The results showed that couples who loved each other greatly, according to their scale scores, spent more time looking at one another than did couples who were less strongly in love.

Loving and liking do seem to be separate processes. If you want to know whether you are in love, at least in Rubin's terms, ask yourself about feelings of dependency, helpfulness, and exclusiveness. An important question for future research is whether love or liking is the better predictor of happiness. Can love continue to remain strong if the partners do not strongly like one another?

Feeling for other	Mean love or liking rating	
	Women	Men
Love for dating partner	89.46	89.37
Love for friend	65.27	55.07
Liking for dating partner	88.48	84.65
Liking for friend	80.47	79.10

erning sexual intimacy have undergone marked changes (Gagnon and Simon, 1976). Sexual intimacy now appears to be far less tied to criteria of love than in previous periods (D'Augelli and D'Augelli, 1979). Other scholars have been concerned with the *functional value*, or utility, of various rules of intimacy. In what ways are such arrangements useful to people? In what ways are they detrimental?

For example, does the set of norms governing deep relationships in our society serve our needs adequately? Many scholars believe that men and women differ in this respect, and that current norms favor the woman. Women often have more emotionally intense relationships with other women than men have with other men (Rubin, 1973). Women talk more freely and reveal more about themselves to one another (Aebischer, 1979; Jourard, 1971). Women's relationships last longer (Wheeler and Nezlek, 1977). And women are more likely than men to do things together spontaneously, to be warmly supportive of one another (Weiss and Lowenthal, 1975), and to have physical contact with one another (Rands and Levinger, 1979). These findings suggest that current norms for male behavior limit men's options in intimate relationships: men less often can choose another man, while women more often can achieve intimacy with either sex. The basis for these differences and the desirability of maintaining them are topics that have generated much debate.

Are deep relationships also affected by normative expectations? Let us turn to two aspects of this question. First, to what extent are deep feelings of passionate love dependent on a series of normative expectancies? Second, do Western society's current norms for intimacy serve common needs? Do they offer happiness and fulfillment? And if not, can anything be done about it?

Of passionate love: the rules of labeling

In addition to a culture's widely shared assumptions about what *activities* should occur as relationships deepen, people share certain norms for describing *feelings*. For example, if a friend told you that he or she had truly fallen in love on first meeting someone, you might be skeptical. Nor are you likely to expect that two people who have lived together for years will still be infatuated with each other. In effect, your reactions reflect a normative vocabulary of emotional terms—a set of expectations about the feelings that are appropriate at a given depth in a relationship. This vocabulary of emotion may provide a key to answering the question of how norms and passions are related.

As Ellen Berscheid and Elaine Walster (1973) have argued, the normative vocabulary of emotion may be critical in determining

when people believe that they are in love. People don't simply fall in love. Rather, they experience a generalized emotional arousal that may be defined in any number of ways. How it is defined depends strongly on the labels favored by the culture—that is, on the normative vocabulary relevant to the stage of the relationship. If this argument seems strange, think back to the discussion of understanding emotions and emotional labeling, in Chapter 2. Recall the work by Stanley Schachter and others on the two components of emotional experience: the vague and amorphous feeling of arousal and the socially based label for this arousal. By following this theory we can see that the same generalized state of arousal may be defined as being gratitude, admiration, affection, sympathy, friendliness, or love—depending on the individual's assumption of what label is appropriate. Early in a relationship attraction or possibly infatuation would be the socially prescribed label. Six months later the same arousal might be labeled passionate love. And at a later stage of the relationship the very same arousal might be attributed to deep friendship.

Does this view still seem unconvincing? Perhaps some empirical demonstrations will help to clarify it. Consider first a study of the effects of fear arousal on feelings of romantic attraction (Brehm et al., 1970). The investigators hoped to show that arousal that is caused by an irrelevant event could be relabeled romantic attraction. A group of men were led to believe that they would receive severe electric shocks. While the men were waiting for this fear-inducing experience, an attractive woman joined them. After having talked with her, the men were asked to indicate privately their liking for her. These ratings then were compared with ratings made by a control group, consisting of men who had not been told that they would be shocked. If Berscheid and Walster's theory is right, the arousal produced by the threat of shock should be vague and amorphous and therefore could be reattributed to attraction. That is precisely what happened. Men who were anticipating shock indicated greater feelings of attraction toward the woman than did the men in the control group.

As part of a similar study, an attractive female research assistant interviewed male pedestrians who were crossing a dangerously high suspension bridge, and she interviewed other men who were walking across a low, safe bridge (Dutton and Aron, 1974). The researchers reasoned that the suspension bridge would create greater arousal than the low bridge would, and the presence of the attractive interviewer might cause the men to label the arousal as having been sexual. Indeed, stories written by the passersbys on the high bridge revealed significantly more sexual content than did stories written by the men on the safe bridge. Further, the high-bridge subjects made more attempts to contact the interviewer for a rendezvous than did the low bridge subjects.

The view that feelings of passionate love depend on rules of emotional labeling suggests that romantic love may be a product of culture and not simply the eternal truth of poetry and song. Labeling theory does offer a plausible explanation of how people come to describe their feelings of arousal. However, the theory does not explain why certain people cause other people to feel aroused. In studying passionate love, then, the most important question to be explained is the original source of the arousal.

Long-term relationships: is there hope?

We now have seen that the norms, or rules, for developing relationships may influence both the way people behave and the way they define what they are feeling. We now must ask whether the particular norms of intimacy in our culture furnish happiness or fulfillment. The history of a love affair is in some sense the drama of its fight against time. Somehow, love affairs have an unfor-

tunate way of dying—some very rapidly. Increasingly, married couples' relationships also seem to be breaking down. How do common conceptions of what is acceptable and proper influence the quality of married life?

One answer to this question has been provided by an extensive investigation of the romantic relationships of married couples over time (Blood, 1967). Blood was particularly interested in comparing the fate of marriages based on love with the fate of marriages that had been arranged by the couples' families. In North America most people assume that love is the firmest foundation on which a marriage can be built. However, in many countries, including Japan, marriages often are based on a family decision concerning the most fitting and appropriate mate. Love rarely is a consideration. Which system is more successful in terms of the long-term happiness of the pair? To answer this question, Blood compared Japanese marriages based on romantic love and Japanese arranged marriages.

Couples in the study were interviewed about their feelings of well-being, the extent of their self-revelation, their sexual interaction, and so forth. Figure 3-4 presents a comparison of expressions of affection in the two groups—that is, the frequency with which the husband expressed (verbally or otherwise) his love for his wife. As you can see, no important differences exist between the two groups in the first two years of marriage. Men whose marriages are arranged are as emotionally expressive as are men who marry for love. Between the second and fourth year of marriage, however, the amount of affection declines dramatically, particularly for the arranged-marriage male. Yet by the ninth year of marriage both groups are similar, and the amount of affection expressed by the husbands is approximately a third of what it had been during the initial phase of marriage. This general decline in expression of affection is paralleled by declines in sexuality, self-revealingness, and general marital satisfaction (Blood and

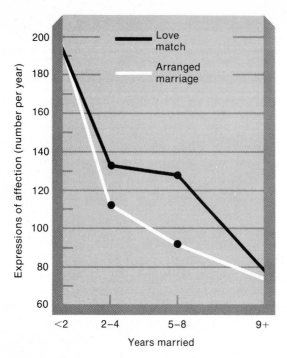

FIGURE **3-4** **The decline of love**

Expressions of love decline more rapidly in arranged marriages than in marriages based on love, but after ten years the difference disappears. (Adapted from Blood, 1967)

Wolfe, 1960; Pineo, 1961). Regardless of initial feelings then, the future of marriage relationship appears grim.

These results do not mean that married couples face some sort of law of failure, however. Blood's findings are averages, and variations always surround an average. Some couples had gratifying marriages; others experienced failure. Blood questioned the successful couples to find out what made them exceptional. The following factors were found to be particularly important.

1. *Communication.* Couples who were open about their emotions and who communicated freely with each other were more likely to feel satisfaction over time with their marriages than were couples who were not open and communicative. This finding gains support from an extensive series of experimental studies designed to ascertain how couples resolve their conflicts. In this work, distressed couples were found to suffer from a *communication deficit*—they didn't seem to adequately send or perceive signals from their mates (Gottman, 1979). Thus the capacity to communicate skillfully may be a major force in sustaining a relationship.

2. *Equitable division of labor.* Couples who shared in equitable ways the labor of living together were also more likely to remain close. Other investigators believe that good relationships demand equity in every domain, not just in the division of labor. The partners must feel that they are getting as much from the relationship as they are putting into it (Hatfield, Utne, and Traupmann, 1979; Wish et al., 1976). They must feel that the tasks are equally divided and that each member is accepting responsibility for his or her tasks (Kelley, 1979). As one study indicated, both husbands and wives who feel that their relationship is inequitable are more likely than those who believe they have an equitable relationship to develop extramarital affairs (Berscheid, Walster, and Bohrnstedt, 1973). The noted feminist Jesse Bernard (1972) has proposed that in today's marriages men generally stand to gain far more and lose less than do women. The typical marriage may be stacked against the female's gaining personal fulfillment. Thus, as women become sensitized to their condition, they may frequently be responsible for breaking the traditional marital relationship. As research indicates, the greater the earnings of a wife, the greater the likelihood she will want a divorce (Cherlin, 1979).

What is unique about this young woman? Only the woman circled remains with her first husband. All nine of the other young women, smiling happily at their high school homecoming celebration, have been divorced. Research indicates that expressions of love decline over the course of a marriage. The rising divorce rate may indicate that people today are unwilling to remain in loveless marriages.

3. *Equality of decision-making power.* The happiest marriages were found to be those in which both members shared in decision making. If the power of decision making seemed to be split unevenly, deterioration in the relationship was likely. This finding is supported by research on the power needs of American couples (Stewart and Rubin, 1976). Investigators found that males who are very high in power needs are more likely to report a history of broken relationships than are those who are low in such needs. Undoubtedly many other factors contribute to the longevity of a satisfying relationship (Levinger, 1976; Hatfield and Traupmann, 1981). As a study of 231 college couples showed, most breakups occurred because of boredom, desire for independence, the development of different interests, and conflicting sexual needs (Hill, Rubin, and Peplau, 1976). Interpersonal trust is often a critical factor in the longevity of relationships (Leik and Leik, 1977). As you can see, the problem of how close relationships can be maintained still is far from solved. And as norms and values change, it may have to be solved again and again.

SUMMARY

1 Personal attraction is defined as a positive sentiment or emotional feeling toward another person. Attraction is generated when another person furnishes rewards, and it decreases as one is punished. As George Homans has theorized, attraction thus depends on profit—that is, the rewards derived from the relationship minus the costs of the relationship. Because an action sometimes can produce reward and at other times cost, most relationships exist in a precarious balance. Any given source of attraction can produce both positive and negative feelings.

2 The likelihood that any two people will become attracted to each other increases as the geographic distance between them decreases. This is called the propinquity effect. One result of the propinquity effect is evident in housing projects and dormitories, where architectural design may influence friendship choices. Physical proximity also means that there is continued exposure to another person, and the resulting familiarity may increase attraction. This effect may occur because the presence of the other person is drive-reducing, and it may occur without a person's being conscious of the amount of exposure.

3 Personal distance rules, often called proxemic rules, typically regulate the amount of physical distance maintained between people. According to Edward Hall, contemporary Western society differentiates among four distance zones: the intimacy zone, for those who share the deepest relationships; the personal zone, for friends and close acquaintances; the social zone, for casual acquaintances and work settings; and the public zone, for strangers in formal meetings. Obeying the rules of distance may enable close relationships to develop. Gross violations of the rules may produce hostility.

4 Physical beauty often is a powerful factor in producing heterosexual attraction. People don't always search for someone who is outstandingly attractive, but rather for someone whose attractiveness matches their own. People often use physical beauty as a factor in judging a person's personality. The beautiful person may be assigned both positive and negative traits.

5 People are frequently attracted to others whose opinions, values, social background, and other characteristics are similiar to their own. However, people also seek others whose traits and capacities complement their own and enable them to increase their rewards together. Whether similarity or complementarity is more important in producing and maintaining attraction depends on such factors as the personal characteristics at stake, the nature of the situation, the meaning of the similarity, and the individual's motives in the situation.

6 People also need other people's positive regard, and they may be strongly attracted to people from whom such regard is received. Giving positive regard also may be used as an ingratiation strategy—that is, as an illicit device to gain one's personal ends.

7 Studies of affiliation indicate that attraction often is influenced by people's need for information when in ambiguous situations. An honest appraisal is usually appreciated. However, after an especially bitter failure an individual may be attracted to someone who provides loving acceptance, even if it is not merited.

8 Deep relationships between people in Western culture usually progress through a regular series of stages. Starting with zero contact, mutual awareness develops as a result of proximity, repeated exposure, or a positive response to physical appearance. At the next level, that of surface contact, mutual interests and attitudes may be explored. If relations continue to be rewarding, a couple may move to the level of mutuality. Mutuality increases to the extent that the participants reveal themselves to one another, accept each other, and complement each other's needs.

9 The path to deep relationships is based on the shared norms, or rules, of a given society. These norms may be responsible for the experience of passionate love. Although love seems to decline steadily over the course of most marriages, some couples find continuing gratification together. Qualities that may contribute to a successful marriage are open communication between the pair, equitable division of labor, and equal power in decision making.

SUGGESTED READINGS

Berscheid, E., & Walster, E. H. *Interpersonal attraction* (2nd ed.). Reading, Mass.: Addison-Wesley, 1978.

Huston, T. L. (Ed.). *Foundations of interpersonal attraction.* New York: Academic Press, 1974.

Rubin, Z. *Liking and loving: An invitation to social psychology.* New York: Holt, Rinehart & Winston, 1973.

4: PREJUDICE AND DISCRIMINATION

■ *At dinner recently a friend argued forcefully that prejudice is outmoded. The extermination of the Jews by the Nazis, he argued, was so terrifying that modern society has learned its lesson and racial and ethnic slurs that were common before the Second World War are no longer permissible. Our friend's argument was interesting, but not convincing. It seemed to us that people simply may be hiding their prejudices more skillfully. Perhaps prejudice is no longer centered on a few groups (such as blacks or Jews) but is more generalized. To explore such matters we asked our students to write anonymously about prejudices they thought they might have. Although we expected them to express some intolerance of other groups, we were not entirely prepared for the intensity of their replies. Let us share a few of them:*

"Despite sincere desires not to be so, I am a sexist. I assume those in power are male, and want men to take the positions of leadership and authority. I am distrustful of dominant women and paternalistic toward those who are not."

"One prejudice which I hold and have held for as long as I can remember is against men. They seem petty, self-centered, and egotistical."

"After I went to prep school, high school kids seemed like a bunch of hicks who just drove around endlessly and got wasted."

"Prep school kids are generally spoiled kids who have everything given them on a silver platter and never had to face the rigors of the outside world."

"Cheerleaders, homecoming queens and pretty girls in general seem so superficial; they live off the level of their physical appearance."

"Fraternity men are vain, macho, beer-guzzling football player types, lacking in any sensitivity or common sense."

"Fat people are disgusting. They deliberately continue their misery by eating."

Clearly, prejudice is very much alive, and it affects virtually all of us in one way or another. Most people evaluate certain groups negatively, while at the same time they are members of groups that are the target of other people's animosity. Such prejudices have consequences. The slaughter of six million Jews by Nazi Germany is perhaps the most blatant example in recent history. However, almost any American black, Indian, or Chicano can talk at length about the suffering and hardship that pervade daily life when one is a victim of the social and economic discrimination that results from majority prejudice.

Given the prevalence of prejudice and its devastating consequences, a reasonable question is, what can be done about it? Unfortunately the question is easier to ask than it is to answer. Solutions depend on what is being discussed. Is the focus of concern *prejudice*—a type of attitude—or is it *discrimination*—a type of behavior? Although these words often are used interchangeably, social psychologists consider the attitude-behavior distinction to be an important one (see Chapter 5). People don't always act the way they feel. Situational constraints may prevent a prejudiced person from behaving in a discriminatory manner. And some acts of discrimination may be so ingrained in a culture that the sexist or racist individual may be unaware of his or her feelings of prejudice. Therefore attempts to reduce prejudice may sometimes be quite different from attempts to reduce discrimination. There is a real question about whether all negative attitudes can be overcome. But many means, including legal and economic, are available to those who would reduce discrimination.

As a theoretical and research issue, prejudiced attitudes, rather than discriminatory behavior, have claimed more attention in social psychology. In this chapter we will maintain this tradition, focusing mainly on prejudice. After considering prejudice as a type of attitude and looking at several psychological consequences of discrimination, we will examine the broad question of how prejudice develops and is maintained. How is it acquired in childhood and later in life? How is it supported in day-to-day experience? We then will conclude the chapter by returning to our original question: what can be done about prejudice.

Prejudice and Discrimination: What Are They?

An *attitude* may be defined as a readiness to respond in a favorable or an unfavorable manner to a particular object or class of objects (Oskamp, 1977). In other words, attitudes (1) have a *topic* (the object), (2) are *judgmental*, or evaluative (favorable or unfavorable), and (3) are relatively *long-lasting* (thus the readiness to respond). People can have attitudes about almost anything, from apple pie to the legalization of marijuana, from social psychology to Chinese Communists. In each instance the individual is predisposed to respond to the object, issue, or group in a way that varies from positive (for example, liking or supporting) to negative (for example, disliking or despising). Prejudice has these characteristics and therefore is an attitude.

This definition is quite general, and social psychologists who are interested in attitudes have tried to refine and focus the concept. Three components of attitudes have been distinguished. Two components will be quite familiar, since they were discussed in previous chapters; the third component is new to this chapter.

1. *The cognitive component.* This component consists of the concepts and perceptions the individual has about the object or class of objects. For example, having an attitude about the Moonies requires that someone have a concept of the group—he or she must be able to distinguish it from other groups. As we saw in Chapter 2, people tend to cluster concepts. Concepts like religious, zealous, and proselytizing might be associated with the word Moonie and thus make up an implicit theory about the group. Connections between the words *spoiled* and *preppies* and between the words *superficial* and *pretty* in our students' essays demonstrate a similar kind of association.

2. *The affective component.* This component consists of the feelings that the individual has about the object or class of objects. The spectrum of feelings discussed in Chapter 3—ranging from liking to loving—forms the basis of positive attitudes. Prejudice is a negative attitude. A person who feels all Moonies are bad would be harboring a prejudice. The dislike of women that was expressed by one of our students is another example of this phenomenon.

3. *The conative component.* This component consists of one's action orientation toward the object or class of objects. Thus, the belief that the Moonies should be forbidden to appear on the streets or that the group should be outlawed would be the conative component of his or her attitude. If our student had said that fraternities should be abolished, she would have been expressing the conative component of her attitude.

Prejudice, then, is a readiness to respond to a person in an unfavorable manner on the basis of his or her class or category membership. The words that were selected by our students for their essays illustrate both the affec-

Genocide. In this chapter we will focus primarily on the psychological effects of discrimination, but we must not overlook its actual and devastating toll in terms of lives lost. We do not know whether this German-Jewish family, seen fleeing their home in 1939, survived the holocaust. Six million Jews did not survive.

tive and cognitive components of prejudice. In using words like *hicks, egotistical,* and *vain,* the students were not only placing people into conceptual categories, but they also were indicating their dislike. For many of our students, these various beliefs and feelings also are reflected on the behavioral level. The student who was prejudiced against fat people, for example, told us later that he avoids them at school and could never have a friend who

was fat. We may speak of prejudice at the behavioral level as being *discrimination.*

If you accept this broad definition, then prejudice is universal. Some theorists prefer to reserve the term *prejudice* for an *unjustified dislike* of a group or its members. They would be inclined to view hostility toward minority groups as prejudice because such feelings are unjustified. Negative feelings toward drug addicts, for example, wouldn't be classified as prejudice because these feelings might be justified by the damage that drug addicts do to others and to themselves. In our view, people probably are capable of justifying almost all of their negative feelings—whether about drug addicts or any other group—and making an objective appraisal of whether their assessment is correct is virtually impossible. What some people see as being justifiable others see as being absurd, and there is no objective yardstick to tell us who is correct. Nevertheless, justified or not, some unfavorable attitudes are more likely than others to have devastating consequences for society. And those attitudes—racism, sexism, and religious prejudice—that create unhappiness for multitudes and devisiveness in society will be the focus of concern in this chapter.

The Effects of Discrimination

Consider the following facts:

> Although slavery was abolished more than a century ago, the average income of the American black remains only half that of the American white ("Income of Blacks Remains Half of Whites," 1978).

> The average life expectancy of the North American Indian is forty-four years, almost thirty years less than that of the American white. The average Indian receives less than six years of education (Trimble, 1972).

In California some 53 percent of the Spanish-speaking population is employed as domestic servants; the average salary for the Chicano woman who works forty hours a week is little above the poverty line (Hepburn, Gonzales, and deBurciaga, 1977).

If a woman earns a Ph.D., she is significantly more likely to be lower than her male contemporary in academic rank and to receive a salary that is 20 percent lower than his (National Center for Educational Statistics, 1975).

Such facts have furnished the basis for powerful social movements over the past decade. And this kind of unequal opportunity is among the more obvious effects of discrimination. However, social psychologists have been interested in less obvious effects. In particular, their major concern has been the *psychological effects* of social, educational, and economic deprivation. Although less apparent, such effects are no less painful or harmful. Society may seem to be quite peaceful on the surface, while many of its members are living a private hell. Let us explore the effects of discrimination on people's feelings about themselves and on their expectations for success and failure.

Target: Self-esteem

The person who is a target of discrimination frequently may carry a heavy psychological burden. In particular, he or she may come to feel worthless or inferior (see the Chapter 2 discussion of self-perception). Such effects were first brought to light by social scientists who were themselves members of minority groups. For example, Kenneth Clark, a past president of the American Psychological Association, spoke of the "pernicious self and group hatred, the Negro's complex debilitating prejudice against himself" (1965). And Kurt Lewin (1941) made a similar case regard-ing the Jews, suggesting that because Jews so often were targets of discrimination, they became hostile. However, rather than turn their hostility directly on the aggressor, they have directed it inward toward themselves (Lewin, 1941; Sarnoff, 1951). Women also have been found to have self-critical tendencies (Herzberg, 1977).

Original investigation of the problem of self-hatred was carried out in 1947 by Kenneth and Mamie Clark. They showed pairs of dolls to black children who were between the ages of three and seven. One of the dolls in each pair was dark brown, and the other was lighter in skin tone. The children were asked to compare the dolls in a number of ways: they were asked which doll they preferred to play with, which doll was nicer, which doll looked bad, and so forth. The Clarks found that two-thirds of the children favored the doll with the lighter skin. The black children seemed to dislike the dolls that most resembled them in appearance. Similar results have been obtained in numerous extensions of this early study (Asher and Allen, 1969; Brody, 1964; Landreth and Johnson, 1953; Radke and Trager, 1950; Stevenson and Stewart, 1958). Careful clinical analysis of blacks undergoing psychiatric treatment also has revealed feelings of self-hatred (Kardiner and Ovesey, 1951). No wonder the Supreme Court judges noted such findings in their 1954 opinion that outlawed segregation.

Similar findings have emerged in research on American women (Fernberger, 1948; Lynne, 1959). In one extensive series of studies, researchers asked more than one thousand adults their opinion of the average male and female (Rosenkrantz et al., 1968). They found that both sexes rated men as being more independent, objective, active, logical, leading, ambitious, and knowledgeable about the world than women. Women were assigned a few positive attributes. They were seen as being more tactful, tender, and sensitive to others' feelings than men. However, when

Sticks and Stones and Names that Hurt

Nicknames can make life a nightmare. The derision that lies behind such names as "Stink Weed," "Hollow Head," "Liver Lips," or "Flea Brain" can mark an individual for life, creating a permanent loss of self-esteem. An individual may cut himself or herself off from social activities because of the risk of being humiliated. In effect, nicknames can represent a form of social discrimination. Studies by Harré, Morgan, and O'Neill (1979) indicate, however, that nicknames are not simple expressions of prejudice. Nicknames have important social functions in special circumstances.

The investigators have found that nicknames are far more common in certain segments of society than in others. In particular, most nicknaming occurs in the adolescent subculture. The investigators speculate that young people use nicknaming to experiment with taking control. By changing the names dictated by adults, they are remaking the social world for themselves. While adults may call them "Freddie" and "Chrissie," the young people have created the names "Meatloaf" and "Jugs." Further, the nicknames create a new status structure, since the names usually carry value connotations. Not all nicknames are negative: names like "Wizard," "Chief," "Iron Man," "Whizzer," and "Foxy" carry highly positive implications. The nicknames, then, create a reality that is different from that furnished by the adult world.

Consistent with this line of argument, Harré, Morgan, and O'Neill find that the tendency to give nicknames often is more marked in situations in which the adult world is particularly oppressive to the young. Under such conditions the young may be especially motivated to rebel against adult interpretations. Thus children in English boarding schools, which are extremely strict and demanding, have many nicknames for one another and for the schools' authorities. In more permissive schools, such as suburban American high schools, fewer nicknames are found. The oppression effect also accounts for the other situations in which nicknames flourish. In both the lower ranks of military organizations and in prisons, nicknaming is a frequent occurrence.

people were asked to rate the desirability of the various traits, over three-quarters of the traits typically assigned to men were felt to be more desirable than those attributed to women (see Table 4-1).

Are these attitudes adopted by women themselves? Often they are. For example, when boys and girls between six and ten years of age were asked to indicate their preferences for activities and objects, both sexes preferred those that traditionally are male (D. Brown, 1958). From five to twelve times as many women as men recall wishing that they were members of the opposite sex (Gallup, 1955; Terman, 1938). Given a set of negative traits that frequently are assigned to women (for

Nicknames also are used to distinguish friendship groups. For example, members of certain subgroups may create nicknames for their own and each other's groups and guard the names from anyone who is defined as being outside the group. Some people will permit only their friends to call them by a given nickname. Its use by anyone else implies hostility or the taking of liberties that the outsider does not deserve. Thus, for example, the black comedian Richard Pryor can use the word *nigger* in his comedy routines to describe his friends. However, his use of the word implies a deep and friendly bond. Use of the same term by someone else would generate intense conflict. Because nicknames can imply friendship, the investigators argue, having a nickname—even a negative one—often is better than not having one at all. As they maintain, people who have no nicknames are nonpeople—they are not attached to any status structure or friendship group. It may be better to be called "Sewage" than merely to be called John.

Yet persons who are stuck with negative nicknames remain disadvantaged. A derisive name, like "Fatso" or "Stinko," may serve to warn other members of a subculture of the appropriate standards of acceptability. Of course, the victim of the name does not have to be ostracized for good. One may reform—by forswearing fattening food or by washing regularly. Indirect methods sometimes overcome the derision behind the name. Most important, the victim sometimes can change the name's meaning. A boy called "Dino" because his gigantic size reminded his peers of a dinosaur later joined a football team. In this context his size was a valuable asset, and his name slowly became a term of glowing regard.

Thus nicknames serve a function far more complex than that of reflecting prejudice. Despite the pain they may cause, they can play a variety of important functions in social groups, the most important of which may be that of creating and maintaining an autonomous social order.

example, complaining, frivolous, fussy, and prudish), female respondents are more likely than male respondents to agree that the descriptions are appropriate (Williams and Bennet, 1975). Men often are less prejudiced toward women than women are toward themselves (Linsenmeir and Wortman, 1979). For equal work they may pay themselves and each other less than men will pay themselves (Callahan-Levy and Messé, 1979).

Not only do women often possess a negative self-image, but people generally believe that women *should* feel negatively about themselves. College males think that possession of traits usually considered to be male is more desirable for men than for women

Stereotypic traits valued by men and women
Male sex-role traits

Aggressive
Independent
Unemotional
Hides emotions
Objective
Not easily influenced
Dominant
Likes math and science
Not excitable in a minor crisis
Active
Competitive
Logical
Worldly
Skilled in business
Direct
Knows the way of the world
Feelings not easily hurt
Adventurous
Makes decisions easily
Never cries
Acts as a leader
Self-confident
Not uncomfortable about being aggressive
Ambitious
Able to separate feelings from ideas
Not dependent
Not conceited about appearance
Thinks men are superior to women
Talks freely about sex with men

Female sex-role traits

Does not use harsh language
Talkative
Tactful
Gentle
Aware of feelings of others
Religious
Interested in own appearance
Neat in habits
Quiet
Strong need for security
Appreciates art and literature
Expresses tender feelings

Source: From Rosenkrantz et al., 1968

TABLE **4-1**

Sex-role stereotypes and self-esteem

Note the discrepancy between the large number of male traits that were highly valued by both men and women and the relatively few female traits that were highly valued by both men and women.

(Broverman et al., 1972). Thus they felt that women should be less independent, less rational, and less ambitious than men. Further research has shown that both males *and* females feel that the ideal woman is significantly less independent, dominant, and active and more emotional than the ideal man (Elman et al., 1970). Such biases also are shared by male and female psychologists, psychiatrists, and social workers. In one study, seventy-nine mental health clinicians were asked to give ratings of the "mature, healthy, socially competent" man and woman (Broverman et al., 1970). Both sexes agreed that the healthy woman differs from the healthy man by being more submissive, less independent, less adventurous, more easily influenced, less objective, less competitive, more excitable in minor crises, more emotional, and more conceited about appearance. The researchers conclude that both sexes incorporate positive and negative sex-role traits into their self-concepts. Since feminine traits are likely to have negative connotations, women are more likely than men to have negative self-concepts. Probably all targets of discrimination in society suffer the same problem at some time. Such suffering also may be related to a second major effect of prejudice: willingness to fail.

The Will to Fail

If people believe that doors to success are closed to them, how do they react? One possibility is that they give up trying. As the theorist Julian Rotter (1966) has argued, efforts at success depend largely on the perception of the *probability of success.* If one feels there is no chance of success, there is little reason to try. People may even find comfort in not trying. As one of our students once remarked, "If I don't try, then I never have to face the possibility that I might not have any ability." There is good reason to believe, then, that the victim of discrimination may develop a self-defeating pattern of behavior.

Research on the psychology of women has been especially concerned with the issue of self-defeating attitudes. Matina Horner (1972) reasoned that women are anxious about achieving success because they expect negative consequences if they succeed. They often fear rejection from both males and females and anticipate feeling unfeminine. To explore these ideas, Horner (1970) asked men and women to write a story in response to the following situation: "After the first term finals, Anne finds herself at the top of her medical school class." (For men, the hero was John.) Horner reasoned that in the fantasized stories the subjects would reveal their own underlying fears and motives. She found that 65 percent of the women wrote stories in which images suggested that they feared success. A common theme was social rejection. In one story, for example, Anne deliberately lowered her academic standing during the next term and did all she could to help her boyfriend Carl achieve better grades. Anne then dropped out of medical school, married Carl, and raised their children, while he went on to become a doctor. In writing about John, only 10 percent of the males wrote stories in which John did not succeed. The remaining 90 percent showed strong positive feelings, indicated increased striving and confidence in the future, and demonstrated a belief that John's success would lead to many other successes.

Research also has shown that a steady increase takes place with age in such negative reactions to success. Only 47 percent of a sample of junior high school girls showed such reactions, while 60 percent of eleventh-graders felt this way. This figure leaped to 81 percent for college undergraduates (Horner and Rhoem, 1968). Additional research suggests that anxiety about success actually makes a difference in how successful women become in their work (Schwenn, 1970). Moreover, anxious women come to experience less professional success.

Because of doubts about Horner's method and interpretations (Condry and Dyer, 1976; Shaver, 1976), other investigators have tried to approach the problem in different ways. Instead of asking about the consequences of success, investigators have studied women's expectations of success. Apparently, women's expectations of success are lower than men's on a wide range of tasks (Frieze, 1976). These differences are found even among kindergarten children. Further, when women succeed, they may attribute their success to luck. When they fail they frequently blame themselves (Bar-Tal and Frieze, 1977; Simon and Feather, 1973). We will return to this topic shortly, but first let us consider another major result of discrimination.

Discrimination Is Self-fulfilling: The Pygmalion Effect

People who discriminate against others often may produce in the target the behavior that justifies their discrimination. Prejudice operates as a form of expectancy. If your prejudicial view of members of a group is that they are "unable to take care of themselves," for example, you may expect this behavior from them and you may act toward them in a nurturant way and create their dependency. In the schoolroom these expectations may come to be *self-fulfilling.* That is, a teacher's assumption that the students are unable to take care of themselves may produce the helpless behavior that the teacher expects (Cooper and Fazio, 1979).

Since demonstrating the negative effects of prejudicial expectancies would be unethical, researchers have furnished a dramatic illustration of positive effects. The researchers (Rosenthal and Jacobson, 1968) gave students who were enrolling in fall classes of an elementary school system a disguised IQ test that was supposed to measure the likelihood that a child would show a rapid intellectual spurt in the near future. The children's teachers were told that the test scores indicated that certain selected students could be expected to bloom within the coming year. In fact, the bloomers were chosen *at random*. The researchers simply selected about 20 percent of the students in each class and gave their names to the teachers. The researchers thus created positive expectations toward one group of students in each class and no expectations for the remainder of the students in each class. The question being asked was whether these expectations would cause teachers to discriminate in such a way that the students' classroom performance would be affected.

To test for effects of discrimination, the investigators readministered the disguised IQ test four, eight, and twenty months after the expectations had been implanted. In addition, they obtained grades and teacher ratings for each child. Four months after the false expectations were created the children who had been expected to bloom began to demonstrate increased IQ scores. The difference between the two groups continued to increase, and by the end of the year it truly was impressive (see Figure 4-1). Children who were in the first and second grades and for whom expectations were high showed increases in IQ levels that were an average of ten to fifteen points greater than the increases in the control group. It was further found that the increased IQ scores tended to persist through the *following* year.

The improved test scores were paralleled by increases in marks that were given to the students by the teachers. Particularly in the lower grades, students from whom good things were expected received higher grades and higher personal ratings from the teachers. Low-expectation children were rated as being less curious, less interesting, less happy, and less likely to be successful in the future. In effect, the teacher had created what he or she had expected to find. Certain students gained, not because they were inherently more intelligent or more skilled, but because teachers expected them to do better. When someone creates in others what he or she expects to find, this behavior is called the *Pygmalion effect*, after the Greek sculptor, Pygmalion, who created a statue of such great beauty that he fell in love with it and it came alive.

Although Rosenthal and Jacobson's findings were much disputed at the time (Snow, 1969; Thorndike, 1966), many similar demonstrations of the Pygmalion effect have left little doubt about the power of social expectations in shaping behavior (Jones, 1977; Rosenthal, 1973). Rosenthal believes that four major sources of social influence operate in the classroom. First, teachers create an *emotional climate* by showing warmth and positive regard to some students but not to others. The teachers smile and nod at, lean toward, and maintain more eye contact with favored students (Chaiken, Sigler, and Derlega, 1974). Second, teachers vary in how much *informational input* they provide for various students. They try to teach more material of greater difficulty to students they favor (Taylor, 1979). Third, teachers vary in how much *student output* they encourage. Favored students are allowed more chances to talk, are asked harder questions, and are shown more patience. Finally, teachers vary in how much *feedback* about schoolwork they give students. Clearer and more constant feedback often is given to more favored students. As related research has shown, white interviewers in a job setting often position themselves further from black job applicants than from

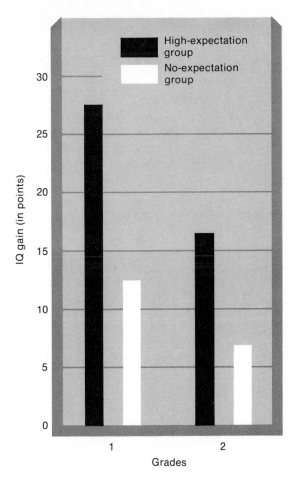

FIGURE **4-1**

Teachers and the Pygmalion effect

Gains in intelligence were shown by children who were expected by their teachers to show intellectual growth. In fact, the children's names were chosen randomly. Children of whom nothing was expected showed lesser gains. (Adapted from Rosenthal and Jacobson, 1968)

white job applicants; when interviewing blacks they make more speech errors than they do when interviewing whites; and they conclude interviews with blacks more rapidly than they conclude them with whites. All of these circumstances lead to blacks making a poorer showing in the interview (Word, Zanna, and Cooper, 1974).

When educational institutions expect members of minority groups to fail, social, educational, and economic advancement may be systematically hindered. When white teachers interact with black students who are labeled as being gifted, such students often are given little positive feedback. At times they are ignored altogether (Rubovitz and Maehr, 1971). White teachers often expect less of lower-class children than they do of middle-class children (Deutsch, 1963; Wilson, 1963), and black students frequently believe that their white teachers have low estimates of their ability (Brown, 1968). Because of subtle discrimination, minority members have the cards stacked against them in school (Ashmore, 1970).

How can we escape these effects of *institutional discrimination*? Some theorists believe that individual minority group members must take more active steps to combat discrimination. When such persons give in to teacher expectations, they are cooperating with the opposition (Bunker and Seashore, 1977). Other theorists believe that school systems, in particular, must be decentralized (Aberback and Walker, 1970). When local neighborhoods are given the authority to direct school policies, discrimination may be reduced.

Protest against the Liberal Line

We have just examined three attempts to document effects of discrimination. We have cited evidence to illustrate that targets of discrimination frequently experience a loss of self-esteem, a willingness or desire to fail, and a tendency to fulfill negative expectations. Many psychologists have a deep investment in such work. They feel that their studies (1) sensitize people to the subtle ways in which discrimination brings harm to others, (2) make people more aware of underlying forces that affect their lives, and (3) create motivation for social change. However, critics suggest that this type of research tends to paint an almost pathological picture of the victim of discrimination. For example, research findings often make black Americans seem to be pitiful, while in comparison whites appear to be adjusted and healthy (Jennings, 1972). Further, since most studies are designed to demonstrate the negative effects of discrimination and since the investigators want to prick the public conscience, findings that don't support the liberal cause may not be published. The investigators simply keep looking until they find what they want. Arguments such as these have led researchers to take a second and more careful look at the psychological effects of discrimination. Two major conclusions may be drawn from this reanalysis:

1. *All people are not equally affected.* Most studies of the injurious effects of discrimination draw generalized conclusions, implying that the effects are equal for all targets. Yet not all victims of discrimination are psychologically wounded. In one demonstration of this point, almost two thousand Baltimore public school students from the third to the twelfth grades were given a test of self-esteem (Rosenberg and Simmons, 1971). The pupils were asked, for example, whether they ever felt like there was "a lot wrong with me" or "I'm not much good at anything." The researchers found *no difference* in the feelings of self-esteem between blacks and whites in this racially heterogeneous city. Further, blacks generally rated blacks as (1) contributing greatly to the culture, (2) being as physically attractive as whites, and (3) being as high in social status as whites. Fatherless black children with the darkest skin, the least intelligence, and the lowest socioeconomic status did not demonstrate lower self-esteem than did the *average*

white. In fact, the lowest self-esteem in the study was found in white students who were from low socioeconomic statuses and from broken homes. One is tempted to conclude from this research that the high level of black self-esteem was due to the greater proportion of blacks in the school system. When more blacks are present, less discrimination occurs, as do fewer negative effects on self-esteem. However, extended research indicates that a black minority in an integrated school system also can maintain a high level of self-esteem (Epps, 1975).

2. *The effects of discrimination depend on historical conditions.* Much of the research on discrimination was carried out years ago. Today, black cultural consciousness is high, issues of women's rights are central, and barriers to social and economic mobility have been reduced. Therefore, many of the earlier findings may no longer be valid (Gerard and Miller, in press). Some research tends to show that differences between self-esteem in black and white children may have been erased for the most part, if not reversed (Edwards, 1974; Hraba and Grant, 1970; Katz and Zalk, 1974). Research on black performance (Sappington and Grizzard, 1975) suggests that black students sometimes perform better in the presence of whites. Similarly, studies of participants in the black power movement show that black activists value whites less highly than they value blacks (Lessing and Zagorin, 1972). And as women's status in society changes, biased judgment may be reduced (Deaux and Taylor, 1973). The belief that women fear success more than men do may be much less true today than it was when Horner carried out her original research (Robbins and Robbins, 1973). Generalizations across time must be made

with caution. Discrimination can have devastating psychological effects on self-esteem and expectations. Nevertheless, social change is taking place continuously.

Roots of Prejudice

Prejudice pervades society. Everyone has harbored some prejudice and at some time has been the victim of prejudice. Given the social problems prejudice creates, we must ask how it begins. For countermeasures to be effective, there must be an understanding of the roots of prejudice. Two major sources of prejudice demand particular attention: early socialization and the rewards and punishments of adult life.

Early Socialization: Setting the Stage

Many people believe that the foundation of most attitudes toward other people is established in the early years of life and that prejudice begins during these so-called formative years. Research tends to support this view. Racial prejudice, for example, has been detected in white American children as young as three years of age (Goodman, 1952; Vaughan, 1964), and such attitudes are found to increase in intensity until late adolescence, when they become stabilized (Horowitz, 1936; Mayo and Kinzer, 1950; Wilson, 1963). However, these findings vary with time and place. In New Zealand, for example, racial discrimination is not evident until about the age of seven (Vaughan, 1963). White children in the American South recently have been found to reach a peak in racial prejudice during the second grade and subsequently to experience a decline in such prejudice (Williams, Best, and Boswell, 1975). These latter studies suggest that whether prejudice is learned as a child, at what age it is learned, and whether it increases or decreases over time are quite dependent on the historical circumstances. The learning of prejudice may begin as soon as a child is capable of learning concepts, or it may be postponed indefinitely. How, then, do children learn prejudiced attitudes? Let us consider two possible sources: parental modeling, and the mass media.

Parental modeling: the case of authoritarianism

Parents can have a powerful influence on their children's patterns of action. Children observe what their parents do, and they copy their actions. This attempt to repeat the actions of others is termed *modeling*. In our discussions of altruism (Chapter 7) and aggression (Chapter 8) we will have much more to say about factors that influence modeling. For now, modeling is important in that it is a process by which children can acquire their parents' attitudes—especially their parents' prejudices.

One of the first sets of findings to draw attention to the relationship between modeling and prejudice emerged from research on the authoritarian personality. In the 1940s a team of investigators—including Adorno and Frenkel-Brunswik, both of whom had fled Nazi Germany, and Levinson and Sanford, both of whom were from the United States—set out to explore the roots of anti-Semitism. Dismayed by the vicious treatment of Jews in Nazi Germany, these investigators wanted to find out what kinds of people hated Jews. As their work proceeded they came to believe that the problem encompassed more than anti-Semitism. They suggested that a special personality type exists, one that not only dislikes Jews, but tends to dislike all minority groups (Adorno et al., 1950). The term *authoritarian* was chosen to describe this type of personality because people with such personalities seemed to follow leaders uncritically. Authoritarians were found to cling to the kinds of conventional values and ways of life that often are endorsed by religious and

Like parent, like child. Children learn social behavior by modeling—that is, by watching others and copying what they do. Sometimes modeling has positive effects. This father's calm mastery of the woodworking task is reflected in the child's identical posture. However, modeling sometimes has negative effects as we will see in the discussion of prejudice and violence (Chapter 8).

others' behavior or to facts that do not confirm their biased view of others. They are less able than nonauthoritarians to shift from one mode of problem solving to another (Rokeach, 1948). Under conditions of great ambiguity, they seem to fasten on to a norm more rapidly than do nonauthoritarians (Milton, 1957). Unlike nonauthoritarians, authoritarians see realistic images when they are exposed to ambiguous stimuli, and they continue to see these images when it is inappropriate (Harvey, 1963). They tend to have positive biases toward the police (Larsen, 1968; Mitchell, 1973) and negative biases toward pornography (Byrne et al., 1973; Griffitt, 1973). Authoritarians also are highly susceptible to social influence—particularly when the agent of influence is higher in social status than they (Crutchfield, 1955; Nadler, 1959). Further, when they serve on juries, authoritarians are more likely than nonauthoritarians to give guilty verdicts and to recommend long sentences (Bray and Noble, 1978). They seem to let their emotions guide their view of the defendant's guilt or innocence (Mitchell and Byrne, 1973).

When the researchers looked at the question of how people came to be authoritarian, modeling effects became apparent. Interview data suggested that children learn their basic attitudes toward authority and toward minority groups from their parents (Frenkel-Brunswik, 1954). Correspondingly, other investigators have found that college students with high F scores tend to have parents who also scored high on the F-Scale (Byrne, 1965). Authoritarian parents also are more likely than nonauthoritarian parents to emphasize discipline, conventionalism, and submission to authority in their child-rearing habits (Levinson and Huffman, 1955). All of this evidence suggests that authoritarianism is self-perpetuating. Authoritarian parents tend to raise authoritarian children, and authoritarian children are likely to have prejudiced attitudes. This does not mean that a child

political leaders, and they seemed to condemn unconventionality. Because minorities are typically unconventional, they also are scorned by authoritarians.

The major measure of authoritarianism is termed the *F-Scale*—for fascist—and it has been used by hundreds of investigators since the 1950s (Cherry and Byrne, 1977). Authoritarians have been found to have rigid styles of thought: they seem blind to variations in

HE'S DEFINITELY GOT HIS FATHER'S NOSE.....

who has modeled his or her authoritarian parents will necessarily remain authoritarian throughout life. As research shows, if one's later social group punishes authoritarian tendencies, these tendencies may be reduced greatly (Griffitt and Garcia, 1979).

The media and prejudice

Children in our culture typically are exposed to television, children's books, magazines, and the like. Many psychologists believe that these sources of information have strong formative influences on children's ideas and behavior. Children may spend many hours watching television. By the age of twelve most children have spent more hours in front of the television than in school (Gerbner and Gross, 1976). Children's books and television programs often are planned to have maximal impact and strong appeal. Of course, few writers or producers of media materials want to teach prejudice. Nevertheless, close

analyses of the contents of books and television programs suggest that unplanned and inadvertent messages often contribute to patterns of prejudice and discrimination.

Some of the most dramatic findings come from studies of sex bias. What do the media tell young boys and girls about themselves? How are the two sexes depicted? One massive study of 2,750 children's stories (Women on Words and Images, 1972) found the following sex-bias ratios:

Boy-centered to girl-centered stories	5:2
Adult male to adult female main characters	3:1
Male biographies to female biographies	6:1

The researchers believe that this lack of balance teaches children that men are more important and more central to the culture than are women. The study also found that the stories typically endowed male characters with such traits as bravery, achievement striving, sportsmanship, curiosity, cleverness, and adventuresomeness. In contrast, females often were portrayed as being incompetent, fearful, dependent, and concerned with their appearance.

This same study revealed that children's stories describe more possible careers for boys than for girls. The books depicted 147 separate occupations for boys (including astronaut, architect, and professor), but only 26 occupations for girls (including a fat lady in the circus and a witch). Only three working mothers were portrayed. In one prize-winning textbook for grammar school students, an illustration showed the Nobel prize-winner Marie Curie peering from behind her husband's shoulder, while he and a colleague conferred (U'Ren, 1971).

Studies of the content of television programs reveal a similar pattern of sex bias (McArthur and Resko, 1975; Tuchman, 1978). For example, the men portrayed on ten popular children's programs tended to be constructive, helpful, and aggressive and frequently were rewarded for their actions (Sternglanz and Serbin, 1974). In contrast, females were portrayed as being deferential and passive and frequently were punished for their activities. Females also had less impact over the course of events in the television stories, unless they resorted to magic. In commercials, neither sex is portrayed as being very competent or admirable. In commercials about cleaning products, women speak far more than men do. Yet when the voice of authority is heard to speak about the benefits of the product, 95 percent of the time the voice is male (Women on Words and Images, 1975).

Apparently, in fostering prejudice toward various groups, the media also produce a drop in esteem for those within the target group. If the media continually suggest that a group is inferior, members of the group eventually may come to accept this idea. As one experimental study has shown, randomly selected women who were exposed to male-centered commercials behaved differently from women who were shown the same commercials but with females taking the lead parts (Jennings [Walstead], Geis, and Brown, 1980). Women who had been shown the male-centered commercials later showed less independence of opinion in a group situation than did those who had seen the female-centered commercials. Further, when the self-confidence of members of the two groups was measured, the women who had seen the female-centered commercials showed more self-confidence than did those who had seen the male-centered commercials. In Chapter 8 we will consider some additional effects that television has on social activity.

In summary, we can see that experiences during the early years may be responsible for much of the prejudice that is experienced in daily life. Children often learn to think as their elders think and they learn from the media a variety of negative attitudes. Some early experiences may have lifelong impact; other experiences may not. Attitudes are being learned and unlearned continuously. Prejudice may rise or fall at any point in a person's life. Thus the processes that we have described may operate in the lives of some adults, just as processes of learning that affect adults sometimes may occur during the early years.

We now will examine several sources of the prejudice that arises in many adults' daily lives.

Prejudice and Payoff

In Chapter 3 we argued that people often are attracted to those people who furnish them with rewards. We now extend this argument to say that when people are punished they frequently develop prejudice against the persons who cause the pain. That is, punishment creates hostility toward the agent of punishment. The hostility may be expressed by tagging the agent with negative labels, by feeling dislike or revulsion, or by trying to punish the agent. For example, if your car were stolen, you might curse the thief angrily and seek ways of revenging the act. If someone else's car were stolen, you might not feel anger: you might view the theft as a retaliation by the poor against the rich, and you might think about ways of changing society, rather than thinking about ways of punishing the thief.

Punishment also may produce other reactions that poison the relations between people. First, the injured person may become less discerning or less sensitive and look only at the specific attributes of the person who caused the pain, failing to take into account any positive qualities (Brigham, 1971; Secord and Backman, 1964). The car thief may be seen as a mischief-maker in need of punishment. The car-owner cares nothing about the thief's total life situation. Further, the injured person often may *accentuate differences* (Tajfel, 1973): the car thief and his or her kind come to be seen as an entirely different culture—one that is immoral, evil, and untrustworthy.

Many studies lend support to the link between punishment and prejudice. For example, some three hundred non-Jewish-Americans were asked about their satisfaction with their financial situation and with the national political scene, and they then were asked about their attitudes toward Jews (Campbell, 1947). Results of this analysis appear in Table 4-2. As you can see, a strong relationship exists between dissatisfaction and anti-Semitism. People who expressed general dissatisfaction also evidenced far more prejudice than did people who did not express such dissatisfaction. Of those who were generally satisfied, only 22 percent indicated any form of prejudice. Among those who were dissatisfied, 62 percent viewed Jews in a prejudiced way. Those people who were experiencing intermediate satisfaction fell between the two extremes. For the dissatisfied, then, the Jews served as *scapegoats*—that is, as socially acceptable targets of the hostility that was generated by political and economic frustration.

Of course, such correlational findings can be interpreted in many ways, but they are consistent with many other studies that show how judgments become biased against persons who are perceived as being harmful or threatening (Konečni, 1979). For example, many studies indicate high levels of racism among lower-class whites, who may feel that blacks will take away their jobs (Maykovich,

TABLE 4-2 Are Jews economic scapegoats?

In this study, respondents who were dissatisfied with their economic and political situation were more likely than those who were satisfied to express negative attitudes toward Jews. This finding supports the idea that dissatisfaction breeds prejudice.

Type of response	Level of economic and political satisfaction	
	Satisfied or moderately satisfied	Dissatisfied or moderately dissatisfied
Expresses liking for Jews	12.0%	3.8%
Shows no dislike of Jews	65.8	34.0
Expresses dislike for Jews, avoids them, or shows active hostility	22.2	62.2

Source: Adapted from Campbell, 1947

1975; Selznick and Steinberg, 1969). Whites who feel threatened by the black power movement are more likely than those who support it to be biased against blacks who are involved in judicial proceedings (Ashmore and Butsch, 1972). Blacks who feel harassed by the police may become particularly hostile toward white society and are more likely than other blacks to participate in violent disruption (Sears and McConahay, 1972). Yet various kinds of punishment raise different issues of far-reaching significance. It is useful to examine in greater detail the effects of two forms of punishment: intergroup competition and dissimilarity.

Intergroup competition: in-group versus out-group

One of the most dramatic and controversial findings to emerge from early work on race relations was the relationship between lynchings of blacks and the level of economic prosperity in the South. As prosperity declined during the period between 1880 and 1930, the number of lynchings of blacks in the South increased. During the prosperous years the number of lynchings decreased (Hovland and Sears, 1940). Although many possible interpretations can be drawn from these findings, they are highly consistent with data from many other nations and from other times in history. The indication is that the greater the competition for scarce resources, the greater the hostility among various ethnic groups (Brewer, 1979; Gurr, 1968; Lane, 1976). To cite but one other example, investigators have tried to locate reasons for bloody and brutal feuding among clans in Morocco. One explanation was that "the most common causes for clan feuding involved disputations over water rights in lands parched as a result of inadequate rainfall, [and] soil to be employed for pasturage of trees whose fruit lay in dispute" (Lewis, 1961, p. 44). Intergroup competition, then, may play

an important role in producing prejudice and discrimination.

Although this line of argument seems simple enough, explorations into group competition reveal a number of significant subtleties. In ground-breaking work on this problem, Muzafer Sherif and his colleagues (Sherif and Sherif, 1953; Sherif, White, and Harvey, 1955; Sherif et al., 1961) carried out a series of studies of group competition in boys' summer camps. In one of these studies, two isolated groups of boys were observed first as they went hiking, swam, played baseball, and participated in other camp activities. During this period each group developed its own unwritten rules, informal leaders, group name, and other earmarks of group organization. The investigators, posing as camp counselors, then brought the groups together for a competition. They arranged a tournament that pitted the groups against each other in tug of war, football, baseball, and other games. As a result of the competition, the boys began to make clear distinctions between "we" and "they." Their own group was seen as an *in-group*—that is, a group that was believed to be superior. The opposition became an *out-group*, seemingly made up of undesirables. With help from the investigators, the groups were evenly matched for the various competitive games. However, as the games went on, good sportsmanship gradually gave way to accusations and name calling. By the end of the tournament fights were breaking out between the two groups.

The investigators then tried to improve relations between the groups—they tried to bring them together again. Arrangements were made for members of the groups to eat together. The researchers hoped that hostilities might be reduced by increased contact. However, one group succeeded in arriving at the site before the other, and its members consumed most of the food. When members of the second group arrived they became furious. A food fight broke out, and the social event had to be terminated.

Based on these and many additional studies of group conflict, investigators have drawn several major conclusions:

1. When groups are engaged in frustrating competition, unfavorable or prejudicial attitudes toward the competitors will develop within each group (Sherif and Sherif, 1979). These prejudices will become incorporated into the group norms, so that acting positively toward a member of an opposing group results in punishment from one's own group. Criticizing or cursing the opposing group may increase one's favor with one's peers (Ferguson and Kelley, 1964). Prejudice may develop toward the outgroup even when its members possess the same physical and personal characteristics as the in-group. As one cross-cultural study showed, there is a strong general tendency in seventeen different societies to evaluate one's own culture more positively than other cultures on a variety of traits (Brewer, 1974). As we saw in Chapter 2, once a prejudiced view has developed, it may be extremely difficult to change. People see primarily what they want to see. One study has demonstrated that in watching films of a college football game, students from the opposing schools tend to notice when the "other" team violates the rules and to overlook their own team's violations (Hastorf and Cantril, 1954). Given the opposing prejudices, two groups of college students didn't seem to be watching the same game.

2. As prejudice toward members of an out-group develops, members of the in-group will develop self-glorifying attitudes toward themselves. This practice may be sustained whether the group is succeeding or failing (Hinkle and Schopler, 1979; Worchel et al., 1975). First, by reminding themselves of their good qualities, the group members come to feel more secure. They believe that their group is strong and can win out over all others and that there is nothing to fear. Second, in thinking about their group's good qualities, the members gain esteem for themselves (Tajfel and Turner, 1979). Because they are members of the group, they feel that they possess all of the strengths that the group as a whole possesses. These self-glorifying attitudes can be useful in building team spirit or pride in one's organization. They also can be dangerous, as when nationalistic fervor leads to attacks on neighboring countries.

3. As each in-group comes to congratulate itself and as group members come to rely on each other for security and self-esteem, members of the out-group may come to see the in-group as being snobbish, arrogant, and the like (Campbell, 1967). In effect, the in-group can be viewed as *ethnocentric*—that is, as having a pervasive feeling that it is superior (Brewer, 1979). Its group members see themselves as being loyal, while the out-group sees them as being clannish. They see themselves as a loving community of fast friends, while the out-group sees them as a closed community or as being stuck-up. To members of the out-group, the in-group members' views of themselves seem to be designed to exclude outsiders. In fact, if you are outside the group and an in-group member treats you nicely, you may feel that the action doesn't represent the in-group member's true feelings. You may think that he or she

is being nice merely because the situation demands it (Regan, Straus, and Fazio, 1974).

Dissimilarity breeds discontent

How would you feel about someone who believes that having sexual relations with as many partners as possible is the only worthwhile goal in life? Your reaction to him or her probably would be negative, and you would exclude such a person from your social group. The main reason for this prejudicial reaction is the difference in your points of view. People tend to dislike those people who are different, and this dislike can form a basis for prejudice. Early support for this position came from a study indicating that the most racial prejudice is found among whites who believe that blacks' views are different from their own (Byrne and Wong, 1962). At times even the slightest indication that another person is different may be enough to produce prejudice and discrimination (Brewer, 1979; Tajfel and Turner, 1979). In one study, people were placed into one of two groups and were told that the placement was random (Billig and Tajfel, 1973). This one piece of information was sufficient to produce favoritism when the subjects later were asked to split rewards between their group and the other group. Subjects gave more to members of their own group. Additional research shows that members of juries are more likely to find a defendant guilty when the defendant differs from them in race than when their race is the same (Davis, Bray, and Holt, in press). This is true for both whites and blacks (Ugwaegbu, 1979). Why do people have such discriminatory reactions? One reason is that a dissimilar person can be a threat to one's self-esteem. The difference in beliefs calls an individual's own beliefs into question. People also may feel that others who are like themselves are likely to be accepting and supportive.

The similarity factor also may be more important to a person than are racial differences. In one study, black and white job applicants in two mental institutions were observed in order to demonstrate the relative importance of race and similarity (Rokeach and Mezei, 1966). Each applicant was taken to a room to wait for his job interview. Four confederates of the experimenters were already seated in the waiting room, and each was looking intently at an article entitled, "Problems of Working with Mental Patients." Two of the confederates were black, and two were white. When the applicant was seated, one of the confederates began what appeared to be a spontaneous conversation about how one ought to deal with mental patients. Gradually the subject was drawn into the conversation. Regardless of the subject's point of view, two of the confederates (one white, one black) systematically agreed with him and the other two disagreed. Thus each subject found himself in an argument in which a black and a white shared his beliefs and a black and a white opposed him. When the experimenter returned he asked each applicant to select privately the two men in the group he would most like to work with, if hired.

Thirty of the fifty subjects preferred the two men who *agreed* with them. Only three subjects chose the two men who disagreed with their views. Opinion agreement, then, proved to be such a strong determinant of choice that it overcame racial preferences. Both whites and blacks tended to choose the men who agreed with them, regardless of race. The finding that similarity can overcome the effects of racial differences has been reported in a number of studies (Goldstein and Davis, 1972; Robinson and Insko, 1969) and has wide application in efforts to reduce prejudice. Some psychologists believe that many attitudes that look like racial prejudice really are prejudice against economic groups that are different from one's own (Bayton, McAlister, and Hamer, 1956; Smedley and Bayton, 1978). Other psychologists believe that emphasizing similarities among people—

whether in the high-school setting, the armed services, or an executive training program in business—may make it possible for people to work together more comfortably. However, the emphasis on similarity will not always be effective in creating accord (Goldstein and Davis, 1972). And even when beliefs are similar, prejudice still may be a barrier in close relationships or in marriage (Triandis and Davis, 1965).

We see, then, that prejudice has its roots in the parental and cultural influences of childhood and in some of the negative experiences of adult life. When people find themselves to be frustrated in some way, they may turn their hostility toward a socially acceptable substitute—a minority group. Competition between groups and simply finding members of another group to be different also may contribute to the development of prejudice.

The Maintenance of Prejudice

As we have seen, prejudice may develop at any point in life and toward members of almost any group. Because prejudice may be in a continuous state of change, a good deal of inconsistency may exist in people's prejudices. We cannot be certain that today's liberal won't be tomorrow's racist or that the equal rights policy that was supported one year won't be a set of empty promises by the next year. Do people actually display such inconsistencies in their prejudices? Let us consider the results of several investigations.

In the early 1930s Richard LaPiere took a Chinese couple on a ten-thousand-mile automobile trip through the United States. During the trip the trio ate or slept in 251 hotels, motels, and restaurants. After the trip LaPiere wrote to each establishment and asked whether they accepted "members of the Chinese race as guests." Only 1 of the 128

answers to his letters was affirmative.

A field study of coal miners in West Virginia found that while in the mines over 80 percent of the white miners showed friendliness toward and solidarity with the black miners. However, when they were not working in the mines, only 20 percent of the white miners maintained friendly relationships with their black fellow workers (Minard, 1952).

Respondents to a public opinion survey were asked their opinions about Jews. When the interviewer looked Jewish and used a Jewish name, anti-Semitic attitudes were almost nonexistent. However, when the interviewer had no apparent Jewish characteristics, anti-Semitic responses increased dramatically (Robinson and Rhode, 1946).

In spite of such findings, you still may question the assumption that people's prejudices are inconsistent (Dillehay, 1973). For example, the hotel and restaurant managers who wrote letters to LaPiere saying that they would refuse to admit members of racial minorities probably were not the same individuals who gladly received the Chinese couple when they arrived at the establishment. In addition, common experience suggests that people's prejudices tend to remain stable over time. The conflicts between Catholics and Protestants in Northern Ireland, between blacks and whites in South Africa, and between Arabs and Israelis have continued for years. Is prejudice changeable, as the above arguments indicate, or is it stable over time? Research suggests that prejudice persists and is expressed if *sustaining mechanisms* are present to support and maintain it from one situation to the next. Without sustaining mechanisms an individual's attitudes and actions may change as circumstances change. In the presence of sustaining mechanisms, prejudice may endure for a lifetime. Let us consider three important influences that maintain prejudice within social groups: shared values, awareness of group membership, and shared labels.

**BOX
4-2**

*Homophobia:
Hatred of
Homosexuals*

Deviating from a community's sexual norms often has resulted in punishment for those persons who so deviate and who are discovered. Homosexuals, especially males, have been subject to ridicule, exclusion, and physical abuse over the years. Because many people's reactions to homosexuals have been so extreme, psychologists suspect that these reactions are *phobic*—that is, that they are based on a fear beyond the realm of the rational. The term *homophobia* often is used to denote the irrational and persistent hatred of homosexuals (Lehne, 1976; MacDonald, 1976). Many heterosexuals characterize homosexuals as being "sick and dangerous" (Pattison, 1975; Steffensmeier and Steffensmeier, 1976) and accentuate the differences between homosexuals and themselves (Krulewitz and Nash, 1980). When someone is identified as a homosexual, people often avoid being near him or her (Wolfgang and Wolfgang, 1971). When a group is told that a male group member is homosexual, that individual often becomes one of the least popular members of the group—even if he had been one of the most popular group members before being labeled. Further, a man who is said to be homosexual is usually rated as being more tense, shallow, yielding, impulsive, passive, and quiet than a man who is labeled heterosexual. He also is evaluated as being less honest, fair, healthy, valuable, stable, intellectual, friendly, and clean as a result of his "homosexuality" (Karr, 1975, 1978).

Investigators studying the origins of homophobia have offered a variety of explanations for it. Sex-role training that places a strong emphasis on being *either* male *or* female is one possible causal factor. Boys learn at an early age, for example, that displaying feminine characteristics exposes them to ridicule (Lehne, 1976) and that being called "sissy" is a slap in the face. Supporting research indicates that males who have a constricted attitude about what behavior is appropriate for men tend to score higher on measures of homophobia than do males with less restricted attitudes. The restricted men also tend to believe that males who have "feminine characteristics" are harboring homosexual tendencies (Dunbar, Brown, and Amoroso, 1973). Additional support for the view that homophobia results from sex-role training comes from a cross-cultural study of attitudes toward homosexuals (Brown and Amoroso, 1975). The study, undertaken in Brazil, the West Indies, and Canada, revealed that of the three cultures, Brazilians have the most rigid rules for differentiating male and female behaviors and the most negative attitudes toward homosexuals. Canadians were found to be least rigid in the rules of sex-appropriate behavior, and they were the least homophobic of the three cultures. The West Indians achieved moderate scores on both scales.

Other investigators believe that homophobia may have its origins in people's doubts about their own sexual preferences (MacDonald, 1976). By directing hostility toward homosexuals, people may convince themselves that they are not homosexual. Research indicates that heterosexual males who find that they may have characteristics similar to those of homosexuals become particularly negative in their evaluations of homosexuals (San Miguel and Milham, 1976). If they begin to think that they may be homosexual, their denial takes the form of homophobia. Further, males who are most negative toward their own sexuality seem more likely than other men to despise and fear sexuality in others (Churchill, 1967).

Over the past several decades homophobic reactions seem to have declined in North America. In a 1970 survey, for example, 84 percent of the respondents agreed that homosexuality is a "social corruption that can cause the downfall of civilization" (Levitt and Klassen, 1974, p. 35). By 1977, however, 56 percent of those responding believed that homosexuals should have equal job opportunities (Gallup, 1977). Despite the lessening of hostility, a liberal attitude does not yet prevail. Most Americans do not believe that homosexuals should be elementary school teachers (65 percent) or members of the clergy (54 percent), and many people believe that homosexuals should not be allowed to practice medicine (44 percent) or to serve in the armed forces (38 percent). And 43 percent of the population would deny consenting adults the freedom to engage in homosexual acts (Gallup, 1977). Individuals with the most negative attitudes toward homosexuals are white, male, and live in the Midwest or in the South (Levitt and Klassen, 1974). These individuals possess highly traditional views about family, women, and religion (MacDonald and Games, 1974). They believe that families should have a dominant father, a submissive wife, and obedient children, and they often are fundamentalist in their religious beliefs (Krulewitz and Nash, 1980; Levitt and Klassen, 1974). They tend to believe that a woman's place is in the home, and they are against the feminist movement (Minnigerode, 1976).

Some social psychologists have explored means of reducing homophobia. For example, a single college course on homosexuality yielded a dramatic reduction in prejudice toward homosexuals (Morin, 1974). Visiting gay bars also reduced homophobic reactions among groups of graduate students (Morin and Garfinkle, 1978). Members of men's groups that concentrate on problems of intimacy, communication, and friendship also have become accepting of homosexuality (Pleck, 1975). Finally, long-term associations with individual homosexuals also dispel myths about homosexuals and increase accepting attitudes toward them (McConaghy, 1970).

Social Support: Gaining Praise and Avoiding Punishment

In response to our classroom query about prejudice, one of our students wrote the following:

> I grew up in Minnesota where there is a whole lot of prejudice against Indians. A lot of people see them as just a bunch of no-good drunks. And, I must admit, for a long time I felt that way myself. After I came here to college and got to thinking about the Indian situation out there, I began to see that the popular attitudes back home are very prejudicial. But the terrible thing is that every time I go home for awhile I find myself slipping right back into the old ways, cracking jokes about the Indians, agreeing with people that it's their own fault, etc. It's really hard for me to tell my friends they are a bunch of bigots.

This student may be putting his finger on the single most powerful sustaining mechanism of prejudice: social support. Apparently, the persistence of prejudices depends largely on the amount of social support that the prejudices receive (Murphy and Likert, 1938). If expressing prejudices elicits acts of friendship, then prejudiced attitudes are hard to give up. If the prejudice elicits punishment, it may disappear very rapidly. Thomas Pettigrew (1969) believes that social support is primarily responsible for the persistence of racism in certain sectors of the South. As Pettigrew says:

> It is the path of least resistance in most Southern circles to favor white supremacy. When an individual's parents and his peers are racially prejudiced, when his limited world accepts racial discrimination as a given way of life, when his deviance means certain ostracism, then his anti-Negro attitudes are not so much expressive as they are socially adjusting. (p.109)

And it is for this reason that Martin Luther King, Jr. (1968) advocated an "association of maladjusted people—that is, an association of people who refuse to abide by the racist norms of the surrounding society."

Social support may be responsible for the inconsistent responses just described. The social costs of expressing prejudice may have been so high that prejudice could not be sustained (Wicker, 1969). Thus, if faced with the Chinese couple, the hotel and restaurant managers might not have wanted to experience the embarrassment of turning them away. When the couple was not present the managers did not have to confront this situation and were able to sustain their prejudice. The same kinds of fears may have enabled the white and black miners to get along in public and may have caused the survey respondents to hide their anti-Semitism when a seemingly Jewish interviewer was present. When the social costs of retaining and expressing prejudice are too severe, the prejudice may be denied temporarily or abandoned permanently. The social support that parents give their children may be especially important. For example, while school desegregation can do much to decrease racial prejudice (Silverman and Shaw, 1973; Webster, 1961), it does not always do so (Armor, 1972). One of the most significant reasons for the failure of school desegregation may be parents. When parents oppose integration their children are likely to remain prejudiced (Stephan and Rosenfield, 1978).

Attitudinal Salience: What's up Front Counts

Our discussion has assumed that the hotel and restaurant managers, the miners, and the survey respondents were prejudiced and simply didn't want to express their prejudices in front of their victims (Campbell, 1963). Social punishment often operates as a barrier against attitude expression, a fact that has led many researchers to worry about how prejudice can be measured. For example, investigators have used a *bogus pipeline* procedure to measure

Internment camps: U.S.A. During World War II Europe was not the only place where prejudice was expressed against minority group members. Soon after the bombing of Pearl Harbor Americans of Japanese ancestry were "evacuated" from their homes and sent to War Location Authority centers "for the duration." Pictured here are members of the Mochida family waiting for a bus to take them to a camp. The camp at Manzana, California is also shown during a dust storm, July 1942.

prejudice. Subjects are told that the electrical equipment to which they are attached will indicate whether they are lying (Jones and Sigall, 1971; Quigley-Fernandez and Tedeschi, 1978). Under these conditions subjects will usually reveal more negative attitudes toward other groups. But how can we be certain that any individual who expresses prejudice is basically prejudiced?

The question of true prejudice is complicated by the structure of people's attitudes. People usually possess more than one kind of attitude toward another person or group. When you think of teachers, for example, chances are you can recall some times when your attitudes were highly positive and other times when they were quite hostile. And most of us have had both good and bad experiences with many other groups. In fact, most learning experiences are inconsistent (see Wicker, 1969), and as a result, people's attitudes are inconsistent. The most ardent member of the Ku Klux Klan has been taught lessons of human brotherhood, and the most vicious anti-Catholic may respect the Catholic church's work for famine relief. A person who seems to be a bigot may have some humanistic attitudes, and an apparent humanist may be a potential bigot.

From this perspective, maintaining an attitude requires that the attitude be made *salient*—that is, it must be made prominent by calling attention to it. If people are reminded continuously of the way they are supposed to feel, then attitudes will be sustained for long periods. Governments try to sustain interest in war by publicizing constantly their nation's needs and by encouraging hostile attitudes toward the enemy. News, public speeches, billboards, bumper stickers, parades, and so forth may be used to increase attitudinal salience.

In a classic experiment demonstrating effects of salience, groups of Catholic students were queried about their religious beliefs (Charters and Newcomb, 1952). Subjects in the experimental group were reminded of their Catholicism and were told that they would be discussing religious fundamentals. Thus their identity as Catholics was made highly salient. Subjects in the control group were not reminded in any way of their religious affiliation. Later all subjects were asked for their "own personal opinions" on various aspects of religious belief, and anonymity was guaranteed.

Figure 4-2 compares the views of the two groups on issues related to the Catholic church (questions dealt with the Pope, the Holy Writ, and so forth). Beliefs expressed by non-Catholic students at the same university also are represented. As you can see, students whose religious affiliation was made salient held private opinions that were similar to the church's position. In contrast, the beliefs of the Catholic students who were not reminded of their religion more nearly resembled the beliefs expressed by the non-Catholics. Thus a simple reminder of their Catholic identity moved the students to express attitudes that were in keeping with more orthodox beliefs. What the students earnestly believed depended on the circumstances.

Usually people are unaware that they harbor diverse attitudes. At any given moment they may be aware of only a single attitude, and that attitude at that moment may seem to be real and authentic—a reflection of true self (Gergen, in press). Investigators have been interested in finding out what happens when an individual realizes that he or she is ambivalent—that is, that he or she possesses both positive and negative attitudes. As Katz and Glass (1979) have reasoned, people generally find the state of ambivalence to be uncomfortable. In Western culture one should not be mixed up, as it is said, but should be clear about one's feelings (recall our Chapter 2 discussion of consistency in impressions). Thus to avoid an uncomfortable threat to self-es-

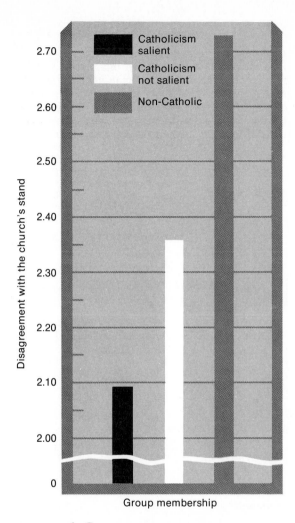

FIGURE 4-2 **The salience effect**

This study showed that reminders are helpful in maintaining one's religious convictions. Note the low level of disagreement with the church's position on important matters of faith among students who were reminded of their Catholicism. (Adapted from Charters and Newcomb, 1958)

teem, people who are faced with possible ambivalence will respond more extremely than will other people. To show that they are not wishy-washy they will demonstrate either an extremely positive or an extremely negative

attitude, depending on the circumstances. To illustrate this position, Katz and Glass presented subjects with information about the pros and cons of increasing the number of handicapped students attending their university. Ambivalence was stimulated by presenting both sides of the argument. The subjects later read one of two transcripts of an interview with a handicapped person: one transcript was favorable to the handicapped person, the other unfavorable. They then rated the handicapped person. Exposure to the ambivalent information was found to have pushed the ratings in extreme directions. Compared with a control group that had not been exposed to ambivalent information, the subjects showed either markedly positive or markedly negative feelings. Ambivalence thus appears to be an uncomfortable state; it often may be relieved by taking an extreme stand.

From this discussion we can see that for a prejudicial attitude to be sustained, its salience may have to be ensured: people may have to be reminded of their attitudes. Yet if people are reminded of their ambivalence, they may display an extremely negative or an extremely positive attitude.

Stereotypes: Convenient Quicksand

Dyke; pig; honkey; WASP; MCP—all of these terms are used in our culture to convey animosity toward particular groups. However, people's thoughts about such groups are seldom limited to the simple act of naming (in Chapter 2, see the discussion of organized impressions). Rather, when a group is named, numerous additional concepts come to mind quickly. The concept of "WASP" may call forth other concepts, including snobbish, self-satisfied, or tight. The ease with which such associations are made was demonstrated as early as 1933, when Katz and Braly asked one hundred undergraduates at an Ivy League college to pick from a series of eighty-four attributes five that they thought were most characteristic of various ethnic groups. The students showed considerable consensus in their views. Over 75 percent agreed that Negroes are lazy and superstitious, Jews are shrewd, and Germans scientifically minded. Approximately half of the students saw Americans as being intelligent, Italians as impulsive, Irish as pugnacious, and Turks as cruel (see Table 4-3).

These characterizations often were made without firsthand knowledge. For example, most students had never met a Turk and yet were quite willing to describe Turks in general. Other research shows that students were quite willing to describe fictitious people, such as the "Wallonians" and the "Pirenians" (Hartley, 1946). Typically these strange folks are described in unflattering terms. Are results such as these simply a reflection of the lack of liberal sophistication that existed at an Ivy League college in the 1930s? When the study was replicated at the same university in 1969, students still exhibited stereotyped reactions. As you can see in Table 4-3, however, the present-day students were less willing than were their predecessors to apply negative labels to entire groups of people.

A cognitive base for stereotypes

These oversimplified descriptions of groups of people are called *stereotypes*, a name taken from Walter Lippmann's early discussion of public opinion. To Lippmann (1922), stereotypes are the "pictures in our heads." Social scientists today talk about stereotypes as concepts or categories into which we place other people (Taylor, in press). A category is a stereotype when the members of a culture or a subculture unquestioningly believe that a particular concept characterizes *all members* of a group. Thus to say that the Japanese are industrious or that Jews are clannish is to agree to a common social stereo-

TABLE 4-3 Stereotyping, past and present

A series of studies have shown a decline in college students' willingness to use either complementary or disparaging labels to describe various ethnic groups. While the use of negative labels has shown the most marked decline, stereotyping clearly has not disappeared entirely, even among a group of highly educated young people.

Ethnic group	Students checking trait	
and trait	1933	1967
Americans		
Industrious	48%	23%
Intelligent	47	20
Materialistic	33	67
Ambitious	33	42
Progressive	27	17
Pleasure loving	26	28
Negroes		
Superstitious	84	13
Lazy	75	26
Happy-go-lucky	38	27
Ignorant	38	11
Musical	26	47
Ostentatious	26	25
Jews		
Shrewd	79	30
Mercenary	49	15
Industrious	48	33
Grasping	34	17
Intelligent	29	37
Ambitious	21	48
Turks		
Cruel	47	9
Religious	26	7
Treacherous	21	13
Sensual	20	9
Ignorant	15	13
Physically dirty	15	14

Source: Adapted from Karlins, Coffman, and Walters, 1969

type, and to do so without careful thought. Stereotypes are a major mechanism in sustaining prejudice. Once people agree on prejudicial labels, such labeling becomes resistant to change. Members of the labeling group have a shared reality that helps them communicate with each other (Berger and Luckman, 1966).

Stereotypes influence many daily actions. Consider the simple matter of clothing. People apparently monitor continuously the clothing that others wear, and in deciding how to react they fall back on stereotyped ideas about the characteristics of the people who wear particular kinds of clothing. For example, when women were shown a series of photographs of fashion models who were wearing different dresses, the women immediately were willing to provide extensive accounts of each model's personality, level of education, morality, hobbies, and so forth (Gibbins, 1969). A model who was wearing a

particular type of dress was described as being snobbish, fun-loving, assertive, rebellious and gay, with easy-going morals. Do clothing stereotypes guide people's actions? Apparently they do. Research has shown that success in collecting signatures on a petition may be influenced more by the clothes worn by the petitioner than by the petitioner's cause. On an ordinary street corner a conventionally dressed individual usually will collect more signatures than will a person who looks hip or bohemian (Keasey and Tomlinson-Keasey, 1973). At a rally for a liberal cause, such as the promotion of peace or women's rights, exactly the reverse may be true (Suedfeld, Bochner, and Matas, 1971). Apparently people with a stereotyped view of individuals in hip clothing assume that such people are committed to liberal or radical causes.

People may hold stereotypes about their own group as well as about other groups. However, the results of stereotyping may be

She was in surgery this morning. If you are like most people, you may wonder how this woman could look so fresh and healthy only a few hours after an operation. However, your response illustrates the power of stereotypes. This woman was not a patient. She is a practicing surgeon. Our stereotype of surgeons as males allows our thoughts to move along rapidly—but insensitively.

1. *Overgeneralizations.* In dealing with out-groups rather than in-groups, people may be far more willing to generalize from the behavior of a single individual to a whole group (Quattrone and Jones, 1980). Thus if a German visitor acts rudely, an American might be willing to conclude that Germans are rude. If the same behavior were displayed by an American, chances are that no conclusion would be drawn about Americans in general.

2. *Negative-memory bias.* Stereotypes of the outgroup also may create a negative-memory bias. As research has shown, people often remember better those facts that support their stereotypes (Rothbart, Evans, and Fulero, 1979). More importantly, people tend to have better recall of facts that are critical of the out-group than they have of facts that are positive (Howard and Rothbart, 1980). Thus, over time the existence of the out-group stereotype may ensure that one remains prejudiced.

3. *Polarized judgments.* Appraisals of members of out-groups may vary widely from one situation to another (Linville and Jones, 1980). With little detailed knowledge of what the out-group really is like, an individual is vulnerable to polarized shifts in judgment. To illustrate, investigators asked white subjects to read applications to a law school. One group of subjects was told that one particularly impressive application was from a black person; another group was told that the same application had been sent by a white person. Subjects judged the black applicant far more positively than they judged the white applicant. Subjects then were asked to judge an unimpressive application. Again, some subjects were told that the applicant was black; others were told that the applicant was white. This time the subjects judged the black applicant far

different in the two cases. The stereotypes of one's own group usually are complex and highly differentiated. In contrast, lack of experience with members of an out-group may mean that one's stereotypes of the out-group reflect a simple set of ideas about what its members are like (Wilder, 1978). This difference in the complexity of stereotyping may have a variety of important effects:

more harshly than they judged the white applicant. In effect, their judgments of the out-group members were polarized—the black applicants were either very good or very bad. The subjects were far more cautious in judging members of their own racial group. Interestingly, the same kind of polarization was found when males judged female applicants (Linville and Jones, 1980). Even though the women were white, they nevertheless were members of an out-group.

Stereotypes: pro and con

Because stereotypes tend to sustain prejudice, we usually think of them as a social evil. Yet stereotypes may be both an inevitable and a functionally valuable by-product of social interaction. If there were no shared-but-partially-inaccurate understandings about individuals or groups, social life would be filled with chaos and conflict. Stereotypes are useful for smooth and cooperative interaction (see the Chapter 2 discussion of the advantages of social concepts). For example, most people share the stereotyped belief that other people are not dangerous. While generally true, this view is not always justified. Yet, if this belief were not available in every new encounter and if other people's intentions had to be checked and rechecked every few minutes, positive relations soon would disintegrate. Satisfying relationships often require that the participants share a wide number of partial truths.

This last statement hints at a second important value in stereotyping. Most stereotypes appear to contain what Gordon Allport (1954), in his innovative work on prejudice, called the "grain of truth." Stereotypes often are based on just enough fact for them to be useful in predicting other people's actions. At times the amount of factual support may be considerable. For example, the stereotypic view of French Canadians being hostile and

rebellious is based on the strong French separatist movement that exists in Canada. Obviously not all French Canadians fit this description, but the politician who disregards the stereotype may be in for a rough time.

Even people who are the targets of stereotypes may agree with the facts upon which they are based. For example, when people in six different countries judged the national character of the English, Russians, Germans, Americans, French, and Italians (Peabody, 1980), they showed almost unanimous agreement in judging their own and others' national character. And people from the nations being judged generally agreed with the raters from other nations. However, the terms that were selected to characterize the nations depended on positive or negative feelings toward the nation. As you can see in Table 4-4, there was general agreement that the English, Germans, and Russians have a tight style of relating. The choice of a positive word, like *thrifty*, or a negative word, like *stingy*, depended on whether the nationality was liked or disliked. Americans, French, and Italians were seen as being loose in style, but a positive judgment, like *spontaneous*, as opposed to a negative judgment, like *impulsive*, for example, also depended on the feelings of the judges.

Despite their usefulness and partial accuracy, stereotypes can create major social problems. As the theorist Donald Campbell (1967) has argued, stereotypes can lead to important errors that maintain biased and brutalizing behavior in society. Some of these biases follow:

1. *Overestimation of differences between groups.* The placing of people in one category or another tends to accentuate the differences between groups. Assigning people to such groups as *children, adolescents, adults,* and *aged* accentuates the differences between these groups. The val-

TABLE **4-4**   **Stereotypes: not always false**

When individuals in different countries were asked to describe their own and each others' national character, a high level of agreement was found. French, Italians, and Americans generally were seen as being easygoing, while English, Russians, and Germans were described as being just the opposite. Respondents who liked a country tended to give positive labels to those traits that had been labeled negatively by respondents who disliked the country.

Nationality grouping and type of stereotyped trait chosen			
English, Russians, and Germans		French, Italians, and Americans	
Positive	Negative	Positive	Negative
Thrifty	Stingy	Generous	Extravagant
Serious	Grim	Gay	Frivolous
Skeptical	Distrustful	Trusting	Gullible
Cautious	Timid	Bold	Rash
Selective	Choosy	Broad-minded	Undiscriminating

Source: Adapted from Peabody, 1980

ues, needs, and other characteristics of such groups may vary to a small degree, yet their being stereotyped results in their seeming to be vastly different.

2. *Underestimation of the variations within a group.* Stereotypes assume that large groups of people are wholly similar. However, within any group there always are individuals whose life patterns are unlike those of other group members. For example, there may be adolescents who are more similar to children or to old people than to their peers. Yet because of the stereotype, people tend to see all adolescents as being alike.

3. *Distortions of reality.* The clusters of overgeneralizations that make up a stereotype usually are treated as gospel truth. The assumption that, for example, old people are conservative usually is offered without qualification, when in fact there may be little basis for such a statement.

4. *Justification of hostility or oppression.* As long as a stereotype is in the forefront of consciousness, an individual never is forced to examine the reasons underlying it. For example, an adolescent male who is unsure of his sexuality may find homosexuals to be personally threatening. He becomes hostile and begins to stereotype homosexual behavior as sick or perverted. Thereafter he can discriminate against homosexuals because of the stereotype; it can be used as an excuse to continue hostility.

In summary, we find that once a prejudicial attitude has been acquired it may be sustained in a variety of ways. Whether or not an attitude persists and is expressed may depend on social support for the attitude and on its salience in a given situation. The common use of stereotypes may ensure that the prejudicial attitude remains robust.

Having explored the way in which attitudes develop and are sustained, we turn now to the important problem of how prejudice may be reduced.

Reduction of Prejudice

As should be clear, many paths lead toward prejudice, and they all are easily taken. Some prejudice probably is inevitable in a multi-group, competitive society. To acknowledge its universality is not to accept it, however. Some prejudices present real social dangers, feeding bitter struggles between races, economic groups, sexes, and religions. And so social scientists have tried to find ways to reduce prejudice. One obvious possibility is by reducing discrimination—that is, by changing people's actions. Some possible means for effecting this kind of change are clearly implied in our earlier discussion. For example, parents can reduce discrimination in their children by not showing discriminatory behavior. Negative stereotypes in books and in television programming can be eliminated. Racist and sexist policies in the schools can be overcome. Dealing with prejudice as it develops in daily relations is more difficult, since it often is supported by peer groups and common custom. Specialized programs or policies may be needed to combat these more informal sources of prejudice. We now will explore three specialized attempts to reduce prejudice: increased contact, education, and consciousness raising.

Contact: When Does Getting Together Help?

Many psychologists believe that the best means by which to reduce prejudice between groups is bringing the groups together and putting them in situations where each group can learn more about the other and the two can develop lasting relations. In this way,

communication barriers, which seem to be a primary source of conflict between people, can be overcome (Newcomb, 1947). When people are separated, the stage is set for *autistic hostility*. That is, when people lack information about others, they fail to understand the reasoning behind their actions. Thus when someone finds another person's actions to be frustrating and does not understand the other person's reasoning, he or she develops hostility in private, without its being checked against the other person's point of view. If people are in touch, they cannot blame each other as easily as they can if they are out of touch. If members of separate groups develop autistic hostility, the stage is then set for what is termed the *mirror-image phenomenon* (Bronfenbrenner, 1960). That is, both sides come to see themselves as being well-intentioned and right thinking, and they come to see their enemy as being mistaken and threatening.

By increasing contact, the out-group loses its strangeness and seems to be more differentiated. The out-group is no longer a single set of equivalent people, but comes to be seen as a collection of unique individuals. As the out-group becomes differentiated, discrimination may be reduced (Wilder, 1978). In addition, with contact one begins to see similarities between oneself and members of the out-group. In fact, when groups spend time together, differences sometimes disappear as the groups begin to imitate each other (Eaton and Clore, 1975). In an integrated society there is less opportunity for unrealistic beliefs to develop about "them," and placing people in simple, stereotyped categories becomes difficult. Problem-solving workshops, in which leading members of hostile groups are brought together to discuss their problems with each other, have been a fruitful form of contact (Kelman and Cohen, 1979). However, many social psychologists have been concerned with contact on the grass-roots level.

Race prejudice is not inevitable. School desegregation has meant increased contact between children of different racial and ethnic backgrounds. Simply bringing people together is not enough to reduce prejudice, however, as the accompanying discussion will show.

A study of interracial housing provides strong support for the contact hypothesis (Deutsch and Collins, 1951). Two different kinds of housing projects were compared: one in which blacks and whites were assigned homes without regard to race, and one in which whites were separated from blacks. Intensive interviews that were carried out with the residents of both kinds of projects re- vealed that both casual and neighborly inter- racial contact was greater in the integrated projects than in the segregated projects (see Table 4-5). Most important for the present argument, people in the integrated projects were more likely than those in the segregated projects to report friendly relationships with people of the other race. For example, white residents of the integrated units showed sig-

TABLE 4-5 **The effect of integration on interracial contacts**

Note that dwellers in the integrated projects meet their neighbors informally on home ground, while contact in segregated projects is more likely to be at formal meetings or at locations outside the projects.

	Type of project			
	Integrated interracial		Segregated biracial	
Meeting place	Koaltown*	Sacktown*	Bakerville*	Frankville*
In the building	60%†	53%	0%	0%
Laundry facilities in or near building	13	17	0	0
Outdoor benches	46	64	7	21
Office, and so forth	2	1	7	17
Tenant meetings	2	17	28	28
Store near the project	12	13	81	60
Children's schools	1	3	14	0

* The project names are pseudonyms.

† Only the whites who responded "yes" or "uncertain" to the question of how they got to know blacks are included. The percentage figures add up to more than one hundred because many people named more than one meeting place.

Source: Adapted from Deutsch and Collins, 1951

nificantly more positive feelings toward blacks than did whites in the segregated units.

Similar findings have emerged from studies carried out in a variety of other settings. Living in integrated housing has been found to reduce the tendency to stereotype minority group members (Kramer, 1950). Apprehension about integration of suburban neighborhoods has been found to decline within a year after integration has occurred (Hamilton and Bishop, 1976). After an elementary school has been integrated, the social distance that black and white pupils experience seems to decline, while the children's desire for relationships with people of different races increases (Koslin et al., 1969). Integrated job situations may increase an employee's willingness to work on an equal basis with members of another race (Harding and Hogrefe, 1952). Integrated

summer camps can reduce campers' prejudice (Clore et al, 1978). Bringing members of different college groups together can decrease their prejudice; keeping them separate has the opposite effect (Wilder and Thompson, 1980). Even contact with a single person who contradicts previous stereotypes may reduce prejudice (Gurwitz and Dodge, 1977).

Yet we cannot conclude that simply putting people together will reduce prejudice (Amir, 1976). For each of the positive results just cited a case exists in which contact has backfired, making relations worse. Several additional factors must be taken into account.

1. *Equality of status.* The long history of contact between males and females has had no apparent effects on the rights of women throughout the world. In part the failure of contact in reducing prejudice may be

traced to the inequality in the roles that have been assigned to each sex. The servant role that traditionally has been adopted by women often ensures their continued devaluation (Tavris and Offir, 1977). As research shows, special attention should be given to ensuring that members of different groups have equal status—from their own perspective—in order for contact to be successful (Cohen and Roper, 1972). To reduce prejudice through increased contact, individuals should enter a situation on equal terms (Pettigrew, 1969), and there should be social support for the equitable role relationships (Campbell, 1958; Foley, 1976).

2. *Common goals.* For contact to have beneficial effects, individuals may need to share common goals—they should feel they are working together toward similar ends (Weigel, Wiser, and Cook, 1975). As Muzafer Sherif (1979) has put it, they require *superordinate goals,* goals that can be achieved only by working together. In an attempt to illustrate these arguments, a work situation was arranged in which blacks and whites were assigned equal status and common goals (Cook, 1971). Southern white women who were particularly racist in their attitudes were selected to work with black women in a business management game. The experiment required the interracial teams to operate a simulated railroad. The team members worked together for more than an hour a day for approximately three weeks. In this situation the racist women almost invariably developed close friendships with their black teammates. In addition, on general measures of prejudice taken outside the working context, these subjects showed a decrease in prejudice. Reduction of prejudice was not found in a control group of racist women who did not participate on the teams.

3. *Success.* Another factor that contributes to the reduction of prejudice when people work together closely is the group's ability to reach its goals (Blanchard and Cook, 1976; Worchel, 1979). When a work group or an athletic team performs successfully, prejudices break down and frequently strong friendships develop. If cooperating groups experience failure, each may come to blame the other group (Worchel et al., 1977). A group's history of hostility makes the opposing group an easy scapegoat for failure.

4. *Participation in decision making.* Prejudice is more likely to be reduced when all members of a group are given a chance to express their opinions, rather than when only a few persons have a say (Weigel and Cook, 1975).

Now that we have seen how intergroup contact can be used to reduce prejudice, let us examine the effects of education on attitudes toward others.

Education and the Reduction of Prejudice

Education is considered to be a principal means by which prejudice can be reduced. Education can offer information about groups of people, the historical background of present-day problems, and so forth. As a result of exposure to such information, people should become more accepting of others. Education should be liberating. But is it, in fact? Is there evidence to show that education makes a difference? One answer to this question was furnished in an interview study of whites' attitudes toward blacks. Some twenty-six hundred whites who were living in urban centers in the United States were interviewed (Campbell, 1971). Respondents were asked a number of questions that dealt with attitudes toward interracial contact. They were asked, for example, to what extent they would like to see their children have black friends; to what extent they would mind if their supervisor were a qualified black; and if they would mind a black family moving next door. Other questions dealt with sympathy for the black power movement—were they in favor of nonviolent marches, and did they feel that blacks were pushing too fast for what they wanted?

Figure 4-3 presents the major findings that relate education with prejudice. As you can see, a strong relationship exists between education and attitudes toward interracial contact and the black power movement. As the amount of education increases, positive attitudes toward interracial contact and sympa-

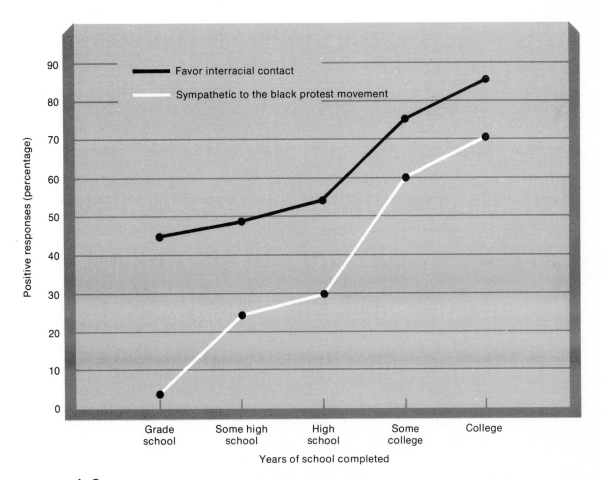

FIGURE 4-3   **Are racial attitudes affected by education?**

Education seemed to encourage support for interracial contact and black power in this sample of people under forty years of age. Note that the sympathy for black power is virtually absent in subjects who attended only grade school. Perhaps less educated people would have most to lose if the power structure were altered. (Adapted from Campbell, 1971)

thy for black power also increase. Men and women with a high-school education show less prejudice than do those without a high-school education. Those with a college education constitute the least prejudiced group. Additional research indicates that education works in much the same way for blacks. Among blacks with at least some college education, prejudice against whites is half as prevalent as it is among blacks with only a ninth-grade education (Marx, 1969). Increased education also leads to less prejudice toward Jews (Selznick and Steinberg, 1969).

Although such results are encouraging, caution is necessary in interpreting them. For example, education may simply increase people's sophistication about survey interviews. Educated people may be no less prejudiced but may be considerably more guarded during an interview. Also, the results may be less a reflection of education than of some other factor, such as intelligence. If people with greater intelligence are less likely to be prej-

udiced and also are more likely to work toward a college degree, then the results may be due to intelligence. Education may only *appear* to be reducing prejudice. Clearly, more research must be conducted.

Consciousness Raising

In recent years consciousness-raising techniques have been employed increasingly by a variety of groups, most notably those attempting to change the traditional sex-role structure (Kravetz and Sargent, 1977). Often the aims of such efforts are sensitizing group members to oppressive influences on their lives and developing a sense of solidarity and collective power and a means of collective defense. Martha Mednick (1975) has formalized the process of consciousness raising as follows: At the outset individuals feel dissatisfied with their condition. For example, women may find their traditional homemaking tasks to be unfulfilling, and they may feel depressed and unhappy.

They may come to blame themselves for their misery and feel that they have no control over their lives. The time is right for use of direct consciousness-raising techniques when individual women begin to think of themselves as members of an oppressed group. Rather than seeing their problem as a product of their own family or mental condition, they recognize that their problems are common to women as a group. At this point the consciousness-raiser attempts to furnish an ideology behind which the women can unite—showing them that the social system controls the individual and is to blame for their dissatisfaction. As a member of a group, the woman comes to perceive herself as having increased control, and the group then can direct action against the system (see Figure 4-4).

An additional benefit derived from consciousness-raising activity is the creation of alternative realities. To the extent that members of oppressed groups accept the dominant view of reality, they are prevented from developing an *alternative* framework for understanding. Consciousness raising gives the oppressed person another way of evaluating his or her position and thereby may offer freedom from the shackles of majority reality.

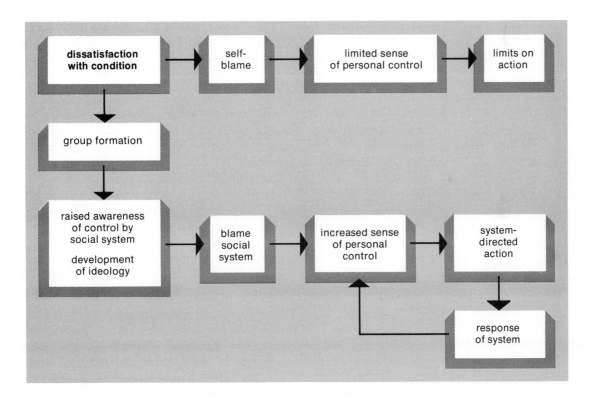

FIGURE 4-4   **An outline of the consciousness-raising process**

At first people are dissatisfied with the condition of their lives. They may blame themselves for these conditions or come to see themselves as members of an oppressed group. If consciousness of group membership increases, changes may take place in the individual and in society. (Adapted from Mednick, 1975)

Do consciousness-raising endeavors produce significant change? All of them probably do not. However, they frequently may make an important difference. Research shows that participants often develop "an active outgoing approach to the world . . . accompanied by a high degree of achievement striving and a strong valuation of autonomy and independence" (Cherniss, 1972, pp. 113–14). Other research has found that participants in consciousness-raising groups may gain in self-esteem, self-insight, feelings of competence, comfort with their bodies, and concern with equality (Eastman, 1973; Newton and Walton, 1974). Clearly, consciousness-raising techniques have significant potential.

SUMMARY

1 Prejudice is an attitude. An attitude may be defined as a readiness to respond in a favorable or unfavorable manner to a particular object or to class of objects. Attitudes have a cognitive, an affective, and a conative component. On the cognitive level the individual possesses a concept or perception of the object or class. On the affective level he or she possesses a feeling that varies from positive to negative. On the conative level he or she has an action orientation toward the object. When these components are expressed in behavior, the behavior is termed discrimination.

2 One result of discriminatory practices is that persons toward whom the discrimination is directed may come to experience lowered self-esteem or a sense of inferiority. Such effects of discrimination have been demonstrated in the cases of blacks and women in American society. People who experience discrimination also may develop a will to fail—that is, they may avoid the possibility of success in competition. Also, they may come to behave in ways that justify the discrimination. When someone creates in others what he or she expects to find, it is called a Pygmalion effect. This effect has been demonstrated most forcefully in studies of teacher-student relations. Not all targets of discrimination necessarily experience these effects, however. The results of discrimination depend on the group involved and the prevailing historical conditions.

3 Prejudice may begin in the early years of life. Often it is acquired when a child models his or her parents. The authoritarian personality has been analyzed closely because of the strong link between authoritarianism and prejudice against minorities. Studies show that authoritarians resemble their parents in personality. The communications media, including television programs and children's books, also promote prejudice in children. Studies of these media have revealed a variety of ways in which prejudice against women is encouraged.

4 Prejudice may be acquired throughout the life span. Much prejudice is generated when an adult is punished in some way by other people. When people unfairly blame another group for its problems, the blam-

ing is termed scapegoating. Intergroup competition may frequently generate prejudice. And in the same way that similarity may encourage the development of attraction, dissimilarity may help to generate prejudice.

5 Prejudice often is sustained through social support. One's prejudices may secure friendship in certain social groups. Whether a given attitude is sustained also will depend on its salience—that is, on whether it is recalled to attention at the time. Stereotypes, or concepts shared by a given group without question, also help to sustain prejudice across time. Stereotypes are essential in social life but have many unfortunate side effects, including the overemphasis of group differences, distortions of reality, and justification for hostility.

6 Prejudice can be reduced in society by increasing social contact among alien groups. However, for contact to reduce prejudice there must be an equality of status among the group members, and they should participate equally in working together toward common goals. Increased education is thought to reduce prejudice, but this finding needs further study. Consciousness-raising techniques can be used by targets of discrimination in order to reduce the effects of discrimination on them and to change society.

SUGGESTED READINGS

Austin, W. G. & Worchel, S. *The social psychology of intergroup relations.* Monterey, Calif.: Brooks/Cole, 1979.

Katz, P. A. (Ed.). *Towards the elimination of racism.* Elmsford, N. Y.: Pergamon Press, 1976.

Kidder, L. H. & Stewart, V. M. *The psychology of intergroup relations: Conflict and consciousness.* New York: McGraw-Hill, 1975.

ATTITUDE CHANGE

■ *As an undergraduate Charles spent most of his spare time working for the Democratic party. He involved himself most intensely with programs for minorities and the poor. His attitude toward Republicans was hostile. After law school Charles was offered a job with high pay and considerable status, which he accepted with reluctance, as it required working with Republican politicians. As time went on Charles became increasingly involved in party affairs. At the present time he is employed by the Republican party. His attitude toward Democrats is hostile. He has experienced a dramatic shift in his attitudes over a span of five years, and this shift has had important consequences for his way of life.*

Attitude change is a central feature of social life. People are under constant pressure to change their attitudes, and in turn they put pressure on others to change. People differ in their attitudes toward political candidates, consumer products, friends, and strangers. No matter what the topic, the quality of social life may depend on whether or not people are willing to change their attitudes. In 1935 the distinguished theorist Gordon Allport wrote that the concept of attitude was "the keystone in the edifice of American social psychology" (p. 798). Almost forty years later his successor at Harvard, Herbert Kelman, wrote, "In the years since publication of Allport's paper, attitudes have, if anything, become even more central in social psychology" (1974, p. 310). Social psychologists are concerned with attitudes because of the close connection between attitudes and people's actions. The conduct of human beings is influenced strongly by underlying thoughts and feelings—that is, people often act on what they believe and feel about others, themselves, and the world around them. Anyone who wants to improve the conditions of social life usually will face the problem of changing others' attitudes. This task presents itself in every area of social life—from close relationships to psychotherapy or political campaigns.

In our discussions of attraction and prejudice we looked at the development of attitudes. We asked how people come to have positive or negative feelings toward one another. In this chapter we will look at the way in which attitudes are changed in society. In particular we will focus on processes that can produce such change. We will contrast two key approaches to understanding attitude change. The first approach emerges from the behaviorist tradition and emphasizes the effects of the external world on attitudes (for example, the physical or personal characteristics of the persuader). The second approach is related closely to the cognitive orientation and emphasizes the thought processes that affect attitude change. (You may wish to review the theoretical viewpoints, discussed in Chapter 1.) After considering these approaches in some detail, we will explore the relationship between attitudes and behavior. The two are not always tied together tightly. The connection is complex and deserves close attention.

Communication and Persuasion

If you were trying to figure out how to change someone's attitudes, how would you begin? One thing probably would occur to you immediately: most attitudes are changed when one person communicates with another. Social communication produces most attitude change. If you take this point of view, the logical first step in your analysis would be to find out what factors in the communication process can produce attitude change. What is it about the person who is delivering the communication, or what is it about the communication itself, for example, that produces change? This line of questioning has formed the basis for an immense research effort that began in the 1940s and is continuing today. During the 1940s the U.S. government wanted to mobilize support for the war effort and persuade people to make the personal sacrifices necessary for victory. Social psychologists joined the effort by developing and testing theories that might help the government influence public attitudes. The work was guided by attitude specialist Carl Hovland and his colleagues at the Yale Attitude Change Center, and it followed the stimulus-response orientation of the behaviorists. Their theories paid special attention to the stimulus characteristics of the persuasion process—that is, how each stimulus characteristic increases or decreases the effects of persuasion on attitudes. The key characteristics to emerge from this work fall conveniently into five classes:

1. *The communicator.* The personality, style, and other characteristics of the person who makes the influence attempt.

2. *The message.* The content, style, and other characteristics of the communication.

3. *The channel.* The medium through which the communication is presented—for example, television, radio, or a pamphlet.

4. *The audience.* The feelings and personality of the individual or individuals to whom the communication is addressed.

5. *The communication environment.* The social and physical characteristics of the communication setting—that is, who is present and in what environment.

Research continues on each of these classes. Let us consider them in turn.

The Communicator

People are bombarded with many persuasive messages each day. Regardless of the merit of the message, research indicates that the reaction to the message often depends on the characteristics of the person doing the persuading. Three characteristics that have interested social psychologists are the credibility, physical attractiveness, and perceived intentions of the communicator.

Communicator credibility and the sleeper effect

An important question people ask themselves when receiving a persuasive message is whether the communicator is credible— that is, whether he or she is a trustworthy, informed, and unbiased source of information (Birnbaum and Stegner, 1979). If the source is credible, the listener may be moved by a message that otherwise would leave him or her cold. In a classic study supporting this position, students were exposed to four different communications on such matters as the feasibility of atomic submarines, the effects of television on the movie business, and the steel shortage (Hovland and Weiss, 1951). Two of the communications were attributed to a high-credibility source, the respected physicist J. Robert Oppenheimer. The two other communications were attributed to a source with low credibility, the Russian newspaper *Pravda*. Attitudes toward the issues were assessed by questionnaire before and after the subjects read the persuasive communications.

The findings were clear-cut: subjects who were exposed to the arguments of the high-credibility source were significantly more influenced than were subjects who believed that the *same* arguments were the opinion of a low-credibility source. Evaluations of the fairness of the arguments paralleled the attitude-change pattern. For example, 96 percent of the subjects considered Oppenheimer's argument to be fair, while only 69 percent considered the same arguments to be fair when they were attributed to *Pravda*. Similar effects have been found when the communicator is said to have *expertise* relevant to the persuasive message (Horai, Naccari, and Fatoullah, 1974). Further, these effects have been found in many different cultures (McGinnies and Ward, 1974).

How long do credibility effects last, and do they persist longer when the source has high rather than low credibility? To explore these questions, Hovland and Weiss assessed their subjects' attitudes four weeks after the experiment. Both messages proved to have a long-term effect. However, contrary to expectation, the impact of the high-credibility message *decreased* over the period, while the effects of the low-credibility message *increased* and were *more powerful* after four weeks than they had been immediately after the message was heard. You can see from Figure 5-1 that after four weeks both groups' attitudes were quite similar. The *sleeper effect* is a term used to describe the delayed effect that a low-credibility source has on attitudes, an effect that is muted at the outset but increases in impact over time. This effect is often, but not always, found in attitude-change research (Cook et al., 1979; Gillig and Greenwald, 1974).

Why should there be a sleeper effect, and why did the message from a high-credibility source lose its impact? The investigators reasoned that over time the message and the source become *dissociated*. The person remembers the message but not its source, and the effect of source credibility wears off. To demonstrate this reasoning, the investigators showed that if people are *reminded* of the communicator's identity, the sleeper effect doesn't occur and the power of the communicator remains about as it was when the message first was heard (Kelman and Hovland, 1953). In other words, by *reinstating the communicator*, the effects of credibility are renewed.

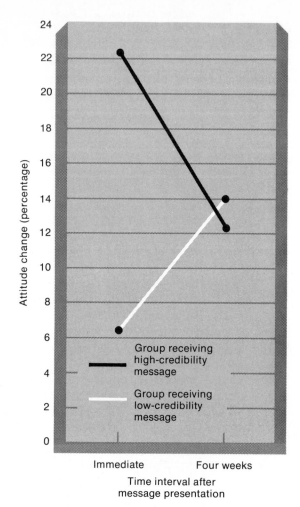

FIGURE 5-1 **The sleeper effect**

In this demonstration of the delayed persuasive power of a low-credibility communicator, note the disappearance of differences in attitudes held by the two groups of subjects. (Adapted from Hovland and Weiss, 1951)

Additional research has tried to explore the limits of the communicator's credibility. For example, the impact of a message may increase if an audience learns that a persuasive message is not in the communicator's best interests (Eagly, Wood, and Chaiken,

1978). Thus public figures, such as generals or civil rights leaders, may be regarded as being more credible when their arguments are opposite of what would be expected (Koeske and Crano, 1968). To reduce the impact of a credible communicator, fighting fire with fire seems to be the best tactic—that is, presenting *another* credible communicator who disagrees with the first (Ference, 1971). Many trial lawyers use this principle to their advantage. Showing how the source is biased also may be possible, in which case his or her expertise may come under suspicion (Birnbaum and Stegner, 1979).

Communicator attractiveness

In present-day America, movie stars, astronauts, preachers, and the like—persons with no specialized training in government—often gain political office. Could their political appeal be a product of their personal attractiveness, and might someone accept their political opinions primarily because they are beautiful, brave, or humorous? As attitude

The added punch. Jane Fonda has been a persuasive force on a variety of social issues. Here she is addressing demonstrators at the May 6, 1979 anti-nuclear rally in Washington, D.C. Researchers have found that the persuasiveness of a message is often increased by the attractiveness of the communicator. Jane Fonda's speeches may gain additional power through this means.

specialist Herbert Kelman (1968) has argued, personal attractiveness may affect the listener because the listener wishes to be like, or *identifies* with, the communicator. An attractive communicator may engage the listener's attention more easily than an unattractive communicator will, since looking at and listening to him or her is enjoyable. The listener also may have the fantasy that the attractive communicator would like a person who agrees with his or her position.

In one demonstration of the relationship between attractiveness and attitude change, male students were asked about various educational reforms (Mills and Aronson, 1965). Two months later the students met in large groups and were exposed to a classmate's opinions on one of the issues. One group heard a very attractive female student speak on the issue of general versus specialized education. A second group heard the same views from the same woman, but she had changed her clothing and hair style to make herself appear to be unattractive. Attitude measures later showed that in her attractive guise the woman was far more effective in her attempts to persuade than she was when she looked unattractive. Research also has shown that the communicator's appearance may have a particularly powerful effect when the message is *unpopular*. If the message is likely to be well received in any case, the appearance of the source may make little difference (Eagly and Chaikin, 1975).

Expressed intention: the effects of forewarning

If we had begun this book by saying that we are going to try to change your beliefs, you might have closed the book and read no further. Most people dislike being told that other people intend to convince them of something, and they may resist (Allyn and Festinger, 1961; Hass, 1975). One reason for the resistance is that if we were to say that you *will* be convinced, we would be implying that you are gullible or possess inferior opinions. In response, you probably would prepare to defend yourselves (Petty and Cacioppo, 1979). Similarly, the statement of intent may imply competition—you may feel that we are against you. You thus may try hard to find flaws in our arguments. The statement of intent also suggests that our opinions will be biased. If our primary aim is to convince, how can you be sure that a truthful case will be presented? One study of the effect of forewarning found that people began to tense their bodies as soon as they learned that someone was going to disagree with them (Cacioppo and Petty, 1979). Observers even detected subtle changes in facial muscles as the resistant subjects began to develop counterarguments.

Forewarning may be especially powerful in producing resistance to persuasion if the audience already is committed to a particular position (Freedman and Sears, 1965; Kiesler, 1971). In fact, if an individual is committed to a position, the mere mention that debate may take place can harden resistance (Sears, Freedman, and O'Connor, 1964). The committed person may develop counterarguments to prepare for the meeting. However, all of this preparation may not be effective in the long run. Once the opponent has been heard, his or her message may sink in. And like the sleeper effect, once the forewarning is forgotten the message may begin to alter attitudes (Watts and Holt, 1979).

Yet in spite of all of these reasons for rejecting the ideas of the announced persuader, people do not always do so. If there is no implied threat, suggestion of inferiority, or competition, the communicator's views may be welcome. Fundamentalist preachers often tell their listeners of their intentions to persuade, and the response generally is enthusiastic. The listeners want to be persuaded. People who know that someone is going to try to persuade them may even change their attitudes to agree with those of the persuader *without hearing* any supporting arguments (Hass, 1975).

We see that the credibility, physical attractiveness, and expressed intent of the communicator can make an important difference in the persuasiveness of a message. Other factors also can affect persuasiveness. For example, if the communicator is perceived as being similar to the target, the impact of the message sometimes can be increased (Goethals and Nelson, 1973; Hendrick and Bukoff, 1976). People tend to be influenced by and more trusting of opinions that are expressed by those who are just like themselves. Persuasion also may be increased by perceived similarity in life styles (Dabbs, 1964; Leventhal and Perloe, 1962; Mills and Jellison, 1967), attitudes (Berscheid, 1966), past experience (Brock, 1965), and race (Aronson and Golden, 1962; Mazen and Leventhal, 1972). However, the similarity must be seen as being true, and not as having been adopted for the occasion. For example, political candidates who shift their opinions to accommodate various groups often are disliked as a result (Allegeir et al., 1979).

We now will consider the characteristics of persuasive messages.

The Message

My case rests on the following evidence.

If you truly love God you will know in your heart that . . .

The argument is best made in an old Will Rogers story.

The rhetoric goes on and on, and some of it sinks in. Messages can change lives. The question for the psychologist, of course, is what makes a message powerful? First, the message must be understandable. If people don't *comprehend* a message, then little attitude change can occur (Eagly and Chaiken, 1975). In fact, if a message confuses an audience, it even can cause active resentment (Eagly, 1974). Once comprehension has taken place, additional factors may be important. Let us consider two of them: one-sidedness versus two-sidedness and fear arousal.

One side, two sides, and a conclusion

In trying to persuade another person, is giving only arguments that support the position better than also taking into account opposition arguments? Is giving a balanced picture better than giving an unbalanced one? The classic study of this problem was carried out by Hovland and his colleagues during the Second World War. Late in the war the U.S. government began to worry that troops might build up false hopes of an early Japanese surrender and that their disappointment might cause morale to suffer and the war effort to be reduced. To counteract this possibility, an effort was made to persuade the troops that war with the Japanese might be prolonged. In helping with the effort, Hovland, Lumsdaine, and Sheffield (1949) prepared two different persuasive messages. The first was a *one-sided* argument in which the strength of the Japanese forces, the difficulties in fighting a war in the Pacific, and other factors likely to prolong the war were stressed. The second message was *two-sided:* it presented the same arguments as the first message did, but also included several opposing facts (for example, U.S. military superiority and Japan's tactical problems). Each message was presented to more than two hundred men, and their estimates of the war's probable length were assessed both before and after receiving the communications.

The results showed that *neither* message was generally superior. Whether a message was effective depended on the characteristics of the listener. One characteristic of special importance was the listener's education. Among the more educated, the two-sided communication proved to be more effective. For the less educated, the one-sided message was more influential. Perhaps education in-

creases sensitivity to a well-rounded message. People with less education may be less likely then people with more education to question what they hear—they may fail to raise questions about what is left out. When people believe that they are being shielded from the second side of an argument, suspicious resistance may develop, and the communicator may be less effective (Jones and Brehm, 1970). A sophisticated audience may need to know early in the communication that another side exists and what it is (Hass and Linder, 1972).

Revealing both sides of an argument often makes the argument more complicated. Then the question is whether the audience should be presented with a conclusion. Seemingly, the force of the arguments would be stronger if the conclusions were very clear to the audience. An early study of this issue found that drawing conclusions about the devaluation of the American dollar was far more effective in changing attitudes than was leaving the con-

clusion to the audience (Hovland and Mandell, 1952). Perhaps the arguments in this case were so complex that drawing conclusions was a valuable help. Yet many people resent being "led by the hand" to an obvious conclusion. A study of prejudice found that for an intelligent audience an antiprejudice film that did *not* draw a conclusion was more effective than one that did draw a conclusion (Cooper and Dinerman, 1951). Perhaps this group resented a conclusion that was too apparent.

The wages of fear

The Surgeon General of the United States has declared that cigarette smoking is dangerous to one's health. However, smoking cigarettes is child's play in comparison with smoking marijuana. Inhaling the smoke of a single marijuana cigarette has the same effect on the lungs as does fourteen cigarettes. Marijuana smoke is full of impurities that no tobacco company would tolerate. And the physical and mental effects of marijuana present considerable danger. Numerous auto fatalities, drownings, and even a rail collision have been traced to use of the drug.

What you have just read is a message specially designed to create fear. The message-maker hoped that fear would increase the attention paid to the argument and at the same time cause marijuana and fear to become linked psychologically. The fear then would change the reader's attitude toward marijuana. A large number of studies illustrate that the more fear-inducing the message, the more potent it is in changing both attitudes and behavior. Fear-arousing messages have altered people's attitudes about smoking and have reduced their actual consumption of cigarettes (Insko, Arkoff, and Insko, 1965; Leventhal, Watts, and Pagano, 1967). Fear also has motivated people to get tetanus shots (Dabbs and Leventhal, 1966), take better care of their teeth (Halfner, 1965; Leventhal and Singer, 1966), use seat belts (Leventhal and Niles, 1965), and change their attitudes toward Communist China, fallout shelters, atom-bomb testing, and capital punishment (see Leventhal's 1970 review).

Handling serpents. A persuasive message can arouse people's fear, and it can also enable them to conquer very basic anxieties. These believers in the gospel of the Pentacostal Church of God are convinced that the snake will not harm them. The power of persuasion is well demonstrated in their actions.

Nevertheless, we can't assume that fear-arousing messages always are effective. In one of the earliest explorations of this question, investigators found that fear actually inhibited attitude change (Janis and Feshbach, 1953). In an attempt to change attitudes toward brushing teeth, the investigators used appeals of varying strength: A high-fear lecture stressed the painful consequences of tooth decay and presented slides of badly decayed teeth and serious mouth infections. A low-fear lecture made little mention of the ill effects of poor dental hygiene and presented nonthreatening slides. A week later the investigators found that only 8 percent of the subjects who heard the high-fear lecture had followed the recommendations. But 36 percent of the low-fear group indicated that they had complied with the message.

Such results are not unique (Dembroski, Lasater, and Ramirez, 1978; Krisher, Darley, and Darley, 1973), and the circumstances under which fear produces more rather than less attitude change have been of great interest to social psychologists. Perhaps the most important factor in determining reactions to fear arousal is the presence or absence of *effective means of coping* (Janis and Feshbach, 1953). Studies of messages about driver safety, cigarette smoking, and venereal disease have found that if the persuasive appeal shows how the dangers can be avoided, then increasing the amount of fear arousal can result in greater attitude change. However, if no effective remedies are mentioned in the communication, then people may engage in *defensive avoidance* (Rogers and Mewborn, 1976). As the fear is increased, resistance to the persuasive appeal also is increased. Apparently, if fear-arousing messages do not offer clear strategies for avoiding dreadful consequences, the communication may *boomerang*. That is, it actually may strengthen the audience's initial position, rather than undermining it.

In summarizing the characteristics of a persuasive message, we see that the balance or lack of balance in a message and the amount of fear it arouses can increase or decrease a message's impact. Other factors also are relevant. For example, if a communicator uses *rhetorical questions*—such as "Don't you think so?" or "Isn't that right?"—he or she often can increase the message's effectiveness (Zillmann, 1972). *Recency* and *primacy* effects also affect attitude change, and you may wish to refer to our discussion in Chapter 2 for a review of these processes.

The Communications Channel

How to present a message most effectively is a key question for anyone who is trying to change attitudes. What communications media should be used? Should the message be delivered in person, or should newspapers, the mail, or magazines be used? When media are chosen well, changes can be produced in people's racial attitudes (Peterson and Thurstone, 1933), consumer purchases (Bauer, 1964), voting preferences (Grush, 1980), and identification with various heroes (Zajonc, 1954). Shifting the roles assigned to men and women in television commercials can increase women's self-confidence and independence of judgment (Jennings [Walstedt], Geis, and Brown, 1980). Poor media choices can result in no change in attitudes or action (Berelson, Lazarsfeld, and McPee, 1954; Campbell, Gurin, and Miller, 1954).

Broad generalizations about the best medium to use in any situation are extremely difficult to make. Choice of medium must be tailored to time and circumstances. For example, newspapers and television advertising generally reach different audiences, and these audiences may shift significantly over the years. Research does suggest that the more closely a medium resembles face-to-face interaction, the more persuasive is its message. Communicators in person thus may be more persuasive than those on television; television may be more effective than radio; and radio may be more powerful than newspapers (Frandsen, 1963; Williams, 1975). In face-to-face relations the audience's opportunities for tuning out by walking away or changing channels are diminished, and an audience may be prevented by norms of courtesy from showing strong disagreement. Yet this advantage may be lost at times. If the contents of the messages are complex, people may not always understand what is being presented in the face-to-face situation (Chaiken and Eagly, 1976). When the material is available in written form, it may be studied more carefully and its contents can be digested.

The Audience

Thus far in our discussion we have considered the target of persuasion to be a rather passive individual who sits around being manipulated. We now must adjust this picture by examining ways in which the audience determines its own fate. People don't just absorb the views of others: they *act on* the infor-

mation they receive. Their own dispositions can have a great impact on whether their attitudes change. Let us look at three lines of research that demonstrate audience effects. This research deals with people's desire to achieve harmony, their need for insulation against attack, and their personalities.

Positive bias: agreement at any cost

A variety of studies suggest that many people carry with them a *positive bias* toward persuasion attempts—that is, a tendency to agree with any persuasive message (Sears and Whitney, 1973). For example, results of public opinion polls suggest that political figures tend to be evaluated positively regardless of party and that such evaluations tend to persist over long periods (Lane, 1965). With few exceptions, candidates for president of the United States have tended to receive positive ratings in polls. Civil rights groups and black leaders also have been evaluated positively (Sears and Riley, 1969). In black communities that were recovering from major riots, both

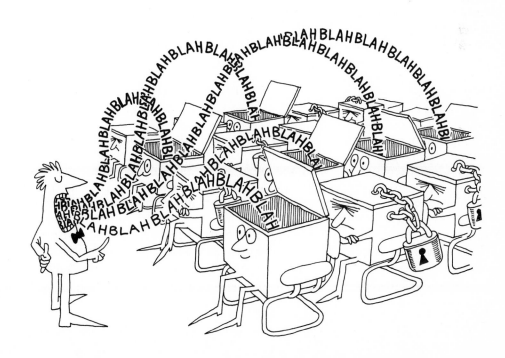

An important question for any audience is whether a persuasive message agrees or disagrees with what one already believes. The question is complicated by the fact that people seldom have a single belief about a subject. Rather, most people hold a variety of related beliefs. To explore the way in which a person makes judgments about incoming messages, theorists Muzafer Sherif and Carl Hovland (1961) have proposed that people order their beliefs about a given position along a continuum, from positive to negative. For example, in the case of the new draft laws, the statement "Everyone should be willing to help his or her country by serving in the military" would be on the positive end of the continuum, while the statement "The draft simply gives the Pentagon more power" would be placed toward the negative end of the continuum. Regardless of a person's stated position on the draft, a number of statements that the person would be willing to endorse and others that he or she would find disagreeable are likely to exist along the continuum. Sherif and Hovland use the term *latitude of acceptance* to refer to the range of statements that the person would agree with and *latitude of rejection* to denote the range of statements that the person would reject.

Latitudes of acceptance and rejection may be crucial in determining a person's reaction to persuasive messages. Messages that barely fall into one's latitude of acceptance often are judged as being *more supportive* of one's position than they actually are. This type of distortion is termed *assimilation*. Messages that barely fall into the latitude of rejection are distorted in the opposite direction. They are seen as being *less supportive* of one's position than they actually are, and this type of distortion is termed *contrast*. Processes of assimilation and contrast enable individuals to simplify the world—they allow the world to be perceived in the simple terms of black and white.

ordinary citizens and those who were arrested during the riots gave positive evaluations of all leaders except those with the most extreme views. At times people may shift their attitudes so that they agree with people they are soon to meet (Cialdini et al., 1976). They may wish to avoid any antagonisms that might arise in the interchange (Hass and Mann, 1976).

Research suggests that the positive bias may be especially characteristic of Americans (Almond and Verba, 1963). Samples of English, Germans, Italians, and Mexicans have been found to be much more critical of opposition party leaders than are Americans. Schools in the United States may be responsible for the positive bias. For example, many grade-school instructors teach their pupils to dislike political conflict (Hess and Torney, 1976). The suppression of controversy appears to be most characteristic of teachers who have been in the profession for many years and teach in small towns, especially in the South and Midwest (Jennings and Zeigler, 1968). These findings raise a question about Americans' political judgment. One wonders how discerning a

To demonstrate assimilation and contrast, Hovland, Harvey, and Sherif (1957) carried out a field study in a community that was divided on the issue of whether the sale of alcoholic beverages should be restricted. They presented a moderately proregulation message to three distinct groups of subjects: *Wets*, who were in favor of abolishing controls on the sale and use of alcohol; *Drys*, who supported prohibition; and *Moderates*, who wanted regulation and control of liquor sales. Subjects in each group listened to the fifteen-minute message and then judged how positive or negative they thought it to be. Subjects with extreme views—the Wets and the Drys—saw the message as being *less supportive* than it really was. The message did not fall within their latitudes of acceptance, and therefore a contrast effect occurred. The Moderates showed the reverse tendency. They saw the message as being *more supportive* of their position than it actually was. Since the message fell within their latitude of acceptance, an assimilation effect took place.

Many additional studies have revealed assimilation and contrast effects in many situations (Judd and Harackiewicz, 1980; Ward, 1966; Zavalloni and Cook, 1965). Researchers have shown that these effects can have an important influence on people's actions—for example, they may affect their participating in energy conservation programs (Sherman et al., 1978). Such effects also have stimulated theorists to consider the processes of assimilation and contrast more carefully (Eiser and Stroebe, 1972; Tajfel, 1957; Upshaw, 1969). Additional research has asked what factors influence these biases. This work suggests that *involvement in an issue* may play a very important role in whether a person turns the world into black and white. People who feel strongly about an issue are more likely than others to engage in assimilation and contrast (Sherif, Sherif, and Nebergall, 1965).

people can be if they can't tolerate controversy. Under some circumstances, however, education can be as important in reducing positive bias as it can be in creating it. When education encourages dispute, positive bias can be negated (Sears and Riley, 1969).

Inoculation against persuasion

Despite positive bias, people often are quite closed to other people's views—they may fight against or turn away from unacceptable opinions. Why are people sometimes inoculated against persuasion and sometimes vulnerable to it? The most interesting work on this question has been carried out by William McGuire and his colleagues (1961). These investigators have been concerned particularly with both the vulnerability of attitudes about which there is unquestioned agreement in society and how that vulnerability can be reduced. For example, almost everyone agrees that brushing one's teeth at least once a day is desirable, that having a physical examination at least once a year is wise, and that eating vegetables every day promotes good health. Such statements are *cultural truisms:* people in present-day Western society have been socialized to accept them without question. Cultural truisms such as these are especially interesting because they may be essential in holding together a society. They represent areas of common agreement that enable people to see essential similarities between themselves and others, make people intelligible to one another, and provide common ground on which relationships may be established (see Chapter 2). However, as McGuire has argued, it is just such truisms that are most vulnerable to attack. Because the truisms have never been questioned or criticized, people aren't equipped to defend them. These agreements, which are of central value to social solidarity, may be extremely vulnerable to attack.

McGuire argues that people can be inoculated against persuasion if they are exposed beforehand to (1) arguments against the truisms that are combined with (2) arguments showing how the counterarguments are incorrect. By working through the pros and cons of an issue, one can form a *refutational defense.* People will know what attacks to expect and why they are wrong. And those who are supplied with a refutational defense should be more resistant to influence than are those who receive a *supportive defense*—that is, a series of arguments that support only what they already believe. However, having the supportive defense should be better than having *no defense at all.*

To demonstrate these ideas, college students were presented with a series of truisms and were asked to indicate their degree of agreement or disagreement with each (McGuire and Papageorgis, 1961). Then each subject received a refutational defense for one randomly selected truism and a supportive defense for another. Two days later each subject was exposed to three attacks: one against the truism for which a refutational defense had been given, a second against the truism for which a supportive defense had been

given, and a third against a truism for which no defense had been given. After the students heard the attacks, their agreement with the truisms was tested.

Subjects' final agreement with the truisms is presented in Figure 5-2. You can see that the attack against the truisms had little influence when the subjects had a refutational defense—when they were inoculated against attack. In contrast, the subjects were vulnerable to attack on those issues for which they had been supplied with a supportive defense. The supportive defense proved only slightly superior to having no defense at all. Later research has shown that resistance to a persuasive attack can be increased further by raising people's heart rate (Cacioppo, 1979). When people are aroused, even if artificially, they think up more arguments against the persuader. Apparently, resisting influence requires that an individual know how to defend his or her beliefs. The ornery person often may just be better prepared.

Personality and persuasibility

Everyone has preferred styles or ways of dealing with other people, and often these preferences affect openness or resistance to persuasion. One of the best-developed areas of research on this issue centers on the effects of self-esteem on persuasibility. As we saw in Chapter 3, people who lack self-esteem often depend on others for approval. If they need such regard, they may be especially inclined to adopt other people's opinions and doubt the validity of their own opinions. Since they hold themselves in low regard, they do not trust themselves, and other people's opinions may seem more valid than their own. Similarly, people who think very highly of themselves may not want to change their ideas about anything.

A variety of studies support this general line of reasoning. Hovland and his colleagues (Hovland and Janis, 1959) have carried out the most extensive research on the topic. Using a battery of tests they first isolated a group of people who were very persuadable and a group of people who were very independent in their attitudes. Then the researchers tried to find out how the two groups differed in personality and in self-esteem. Feelings of personal inadequacy were found to be significantly stronger in the highly persuadable group (Janis and Field, 1959). Further, when working on a task in pairs, people who had high scores on a self-esteem test were more likely than those with low scores to try to change their partners' opinions, and they also were less likely to have their own opinions changed (Cohen, 1959). This finding also is typical of children. One study found that children who were judged as being popular and attractive were less persuadable than those who scored low in popularity and attractiveness (Lesser and Abelson, 1959).

It would be simple-minded to conclude from this research that all people who suffer

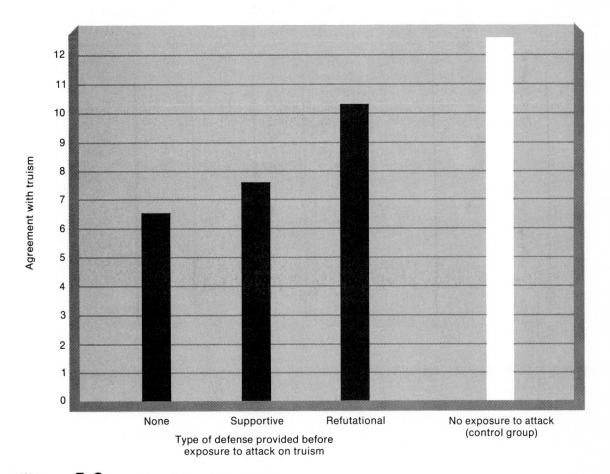

FIGURE 5-2 Immunity against persuasion

People who have facts about both sides of an issue can *refute* arguments and resist persuasion. People who only can *support* what they already believe are more likely than others to give in to a contrary persuasive argument. (Adapted from McGuire and Papageorgis, 1961)

from self-doubts are persuadable (McGuire, 1961). Self-doubts can make people hostile toward others. "What makes those wise guys think they know so much?" may be a common reaction. All people with low self-esteem do not act the same way. Self-esteem is only one of the many different motives that enter into people's reactions to social influence (Katz and Stotland, 1959). For example, research shows that there are at least two distinct groups who are persuaded to join the women's liberation movement: those who desire to achieve cooperative equality between the sexes, and those who are hostile toward men (Taleporos, 1977). A message based on cooperative equality might succeed for one group but not for the other.

We now have examined three ways in which an audience acts on the information it receives and thus determines the amount of attitude change. First, *positive bias* may predispose an audience toward accepting any persuasive communication. Second, *familiarity* with the counterarguments and the shortcomings of those arguments may inoculate an audience against persuasion. Finally, *personal styles*, or dispositions—including differences in self-esteem—may influence both openness and resistance to persuasion attempts. Let us now turn from consideration of the audience to a discussion of the final set of factors that affect attitude change: the context of the communication.

The Communications Environment

Communication takes place in various social and physical environments, and these surroundings can have a marked impact on whether attitudes are changed. Although many factors in the environment can influence the success or failure of persuasive appeals, two that have been of interest to researchers are distraction and learned associations.

Distraction: is it always distracting?

When noise disrupts a conversation or when the television picture does flip-flops, people usually stop paying attention to the communicator. Although such distraction can reduce the effectiveness of the communication (Vohs and Garrett, 1968), it does not always do so (Festinger and Maccoby, 1964; Insko, Turnbull, and Yandell, 1975). In particular, a *minor* distraction sometimes can have a strengthening effect. For example, distraction may cause people to *increase* their efforts at listening to a speaker (Dorris, 1967). Further, as efforts to comprehend are increased, the time spent thinking of counterarguments may decrease (Baron, Baron, and Miller, 1973; Insko et al., 1975), and the persuasiveness of the communicator may thus be increased—just when it's least wanted (Petty, Wells, and Brock, 1976).

Of course, many kinds of distractions exist and each raises slightly different issues. Consider the effects of a heckler on the impact of a political speech. Heckling can lower people's evaluation of a speaker's credibility and can decrease the persuasiveness of the speech. Even those people who initially agree with a speaker can lose confidence in their position when hecklers are present (Sloan, Love, and Ostrom, 1974). Yet heckling also can increase the persuasiveness of the communicator. If the heckler arouses antagonism, the audience may unite in defense of the speaker. And if the speaker reacts with calmness and deals with the relevant issues, he or she can totally wipe away any negative effects of heckling (Petty, Wells, and Brock, 1976).

Person-environment association: influential accidents

People often speak of a restaurant as having atmosphere or of a particular neighborhood as being safe or dangerous. Such feelings about an environment can affect people's reactions to others who are encountered in the environment. In particular, feelings about the place may come to be associated with feelings about the person (including his or her message). Thus responsiveness to a communication may depend on where it is encountered (Zanna, Kiesler, and Pilkonis, 1970).

To demonstrate the effects of learned associations on persuasiveness, researchers presented persuasive communications to two groups of college students (Janis, Kaye, and Kirschner, 1965). Subjects in one group were offered peanuts and a soft drink, which the experimenter was consuming as they arrived. Subjects in a second group were not offered any food. The researchers found that the pleasant act of eating while reading persuasive communications increased the likelihood of attitude change. The implications of such research are unsettling. Can people's attitudes toward other people be influenced by feelings about where the others live, for example, rather than by their actual characteristics? Does the sight of rows of unimaginatively designed suburban houses color attitudes toward the people who live in the houses? Do the dirt and decay of a slum make people feel less positive about its inhabitants? Such possibilities are worth exploring. To be sure, other environmental factors can influence the amount of attitude change. As one study of the social environment showed, when people are in groups they often assume that others in the group will take the responsibility for examining the issues (Petty, Harkins, and Williams, 1980). In failing to give thought to the issues, they often show less attitude change than they would if they were alone. Thus, everyone in a family may disregard a political speech assuming that at least one family member will keep informed. The speech then falls on deaf ears.

Our discussion of understanding attitude change from the behaviorist orientation now is complete. With its special concentration on characteristics of the environment, the behaviorist tradition is a rich one, offering much insight into factors that can influence attitudes. For politicians, social activists, and other individuals engaged in attitude change, this tradition pinpoints a variety of factors that should be taken into account in planning strategies. It tells the agent of change that he or she ought to pay attention to specific characteristics of the communicator, the message, the medium, the recipient, and the communications environment.

But does this approach tell people all they need to know about attitude change? Do you harbor any doubts about this orientation? Perhaps the discussion seemed like a laundry list of unrelated factors. You may have wondered why there were no unifying principles. In fact, many social psychologists also are bothered by this lack of coherence, and the search for single principles to unify and focus this research continues. Increasingly, researchers have focused on cognitive processes. Attitude change, they reason, may depend on the way in which people process information. These researchers have provided many new insights into the process of attitude change. Let us now consider in more detail the fruits of the cognitive approach.

Cognition and Attitude Change

The cognitive orientation in social psychology was first introduced in Chapter 1. We saw that much insight into human relations can be gained by exploring people's manner of thinking. This approach dominated our discussion of social perception (Chapter 2) as we looked at the ways in which people conceptualize their own and others' actions. How can this concentration on thought processes help us understand attitude change? The remainder of this chapter will be devoted to this question. First, we will look at the individual's need for cognitive consistency and the way this need influences attitude change. Second, we will consider how attitudes may be affected by the way people use information. In particular, we will be concerned with three sources on which people draw when they process information: the environment, their own actions, and their memories. Finally, we will focus on cognitive models that attempt to predict people's behavior on the basis of their attitudes.

Cognitive Dissonance and Attitude Change

If you want to lose weight, you wouldn't plan to double your consumption of dessert. If you believed in air purity, you might try to think of ways to control air pollution. These choices seem quite logical: they make good sense. Many psychologists believe that such decisions reflect a fundamental motive for *cognitive consistency*—that is, for consistency among one's thoughts about the world (see the Chapter 2 discussion of consistency in impressions). The assumption is that most people want their ideas to be related logically—it doesn't make sense to believe something is true, desirable, or necessary and simultaneously believe its opposite (see Abelson et al., 1968). The most celebrated formulation of this position is Leon Festinger's theory of cognitive dissonance (1957). As Festinger reasoned, when a person holds two cognitions (ideas about the world) that are consistent with each other, he or she experiences a satisfying state of *consonance*. However, two (or more) cognitions that are inconsistent (one cognition implies the opposite of another) result in *dissonance*, an unpleasant state of arousal (Higgins, Rhodewalt, and Zanna, 1979; Kiesler and Pallak, 1976; Waterman and Katkin, 1967). Festinger argued that people are motivated to reduce the unsettling state of cognitive dissonance.

Dissonance becomes increasingly painful as the cognitions increase in importance. Taking an aspirin may be dissonant with your opinion that you are not a drug taker. However, the dissonance is probably meager, since taking an aspirin is a trivial event. However, for many people, taking drugs such as mescaline or cocaine might arouse a great deal of dissonance, since drug taking can be inconsistent with thoughts about one's health or legal status, and such matters are very important. Thus, *as the cognitions increase in importance, so does the magnitude of the dissonance.* And *the greater the dissonance, the greater the motivation for dissonance reduction.*

People can reduce dissonance in a number of ways. Consider, for example, the dissonant cognitions, "I despise bicycle theft" and "I am buying a stolen bicycle." The dissonance between these cognitions can be reduced by *changing behavior*—by not going through with the purchase. However, dissonance also can be reduced by *changing cognition*—by shifting ideas about bicycle theft. A person could think again and conclude that bicycles are largely stolen from the wealthy, who don't have any financial worries, and it's not so bad for a struggling student to get a bike cut-rate. Both kinds of change achieve consonance.

You now can begin to see how the motive to achieve cognitive consistency is related to attitude change. Many cognitions, or thoughts, are evaluative and thus fall within the definition of attitudes. "I despise bicycle theft" is an obvious example. The change from "I oppose bicycle theft" to "bicycle theft isn't always so bad" is an attitude change. Thus cognitive consistency often means attitude consistency.

Let us now explore two attempts to use dissonance reduction to change attitudes.

Changing attitudes through changing behavior

Often people find themselves acting without having thought carefully: they may defend a position before their thoughts are formulated fully, or they may join an enthusiastic crowd at a political rally or at an athletic contest without really caring about what's going on. However, if people do strive for consistency among their cognitions, then these surface behaviors ought to have significant effects on attitudes. Consider the following situation. You find yourself acting in a way that gives rise to one cognition—"I am acting friendly toward Nick"—while you simultaneously hold a second but inconsistent cognition—"I don't like Nick." As a result of the inconsistency, you may experience dissonance. One way to reduce this dissonance is to change your thoughts about Nick. You might achieve consonance by becoming more positive toward him ("He's not such a bad guy after all"). Or you might change your behavior—that is, act in an unfriendly way. However, because behavior already has occurred ("I have acted friendly toward Nick"), a change in action may be impossible. Further, changing your ideas may be easier than changing your action (Brehm, 1960). No one may be able to tell that your attitude has changed, but unfriendly behavior toward Nick may get you into trouble. Thus, the dissonance that results from inconsistency between attitudes and behavior may be most easily resolved by changing the attitude.

Most research demonstrations of the effects of behavior on attitudes have used methods of *role playing* in which people are asked to deliver a speech or act in a certain way. As dissonance theory suggests, people may come to change their attitudes simply because they have played a certain role. Attitudes thus follow behavior. In one classic experiment on role playing and attitude change, subjects were asked to present a speech from a prepared outline while other subjects simply listened (Janis and King, 1954). Each speech supported a position that was more extreme than the one that the subject had held privately (according to earlier measures). After the role

playing, assessments of the subjects' attitudes were made. The speaker's beliefs showed significant change in the direction of the attitudes expressed in the speech; the listeners' attitudes were affected very little. This role-playing method also has been used to reduce race prejudice. In one study, whites who were prejudiced against blacks were asked to either act the part of a black moving into an all-white neighborhood or watch others in the role (Culbertson, 1957). Later measures revealed that the actors showed a greater reduction in prejudice than the watchers. By inducing people to act out particular roles, researchers have been able to change attitudes toward intercollegiate athletics (Rabbie, Brehm, and Cohen, 1959), create hostility toward another person (Jones and Davis, 1965), and reduce cigarette smoking (Janis and Mann, 1965).

Additional research indicates that the greater the effort expended in the role playing, the greater its effects. Why should this be? Here it is argued that the expenditure of a great deal of effort on behalf of something an individual doesn't believe privately arouses greater dissonance than does the expenditure of a little effort. If you went out of your way to do a favor for the disliked acquaintance Nick, more dissonance should be created than if you simply said hello to him and smiled. The greater the dissonance, the greater the attitude change. Investigators have employed a clever means of demonstrating this idea (Zimbardo and Ebbeson, 1969). While subjects were presenting a speech that disagreed with their private opinion, they listened simultaneously—through earphones—to their own voice. To make the task especially difficult, the sound of the speaker's voice was delayed by a fraction of a second. If you have ever heard the sound of your voice moments after you have spoken, you can appreciate the difficulty that the subjects faced in paying attention to what they were saying. Subjects in a control group did not face this difficult task.

**BOX
5-2**

*When
Prophecy
Fails*

Although much of the research on dissonance theory has been conducted in the laboratory, one of the first and most fascinating dissonance studies looked at a real-life event: a prophecy that the world was going to end. Festinger, along with his colleagues Schachter and Riecken (1956) noticed a newspaper story about a housewife, Marian Keech, who said she had received messages from outer space. Mrs. Keech said that superior beings from the planet Clarion had warned her of the earth's destruction. The beings had visited earth in flying saucers and had observed fault lines in the earth's crust. They predicted that an earthquake would be followed by a flood and that water would cover the land from the Arctic Circle to the Gulf of Mexico. The event was supposed to take place on December 21. Mrs. Keech attracted a small group of followers. They formed a group called *The Seekers* and met for several months to discuss spiritual issues and cosmology. Many of the followers terminated their normal lives: they quit their jobs and gave away their possessions. The group interested Festinger and his colleagues because of the intense dissonance that the group was going to encounter when catastrophe failed to take place. The knowledge that the world had not ended would stand in direct contradiction to their belief in Mrs. Keech's prophecy. How would the group members reduce the dissonance that would be produced by these contradictory cognitions? To find out, the researchers joined the group of believers.

On the morning of December 20, Mrs. Keech reported that she had received a message instructing the group to be prepared to flee at midnight in a flying saucer. A few minutes before midnight the group assembled in the living room of Mrs. Keech's home. With their coats in their hands they sat listening to the clock. As midnight came and went they sat in silence. Gradually they began to talk, review their beliefs, and express pain and despair. Mrs. Keech began to cry and prayed that the faithful would shed their light on others.

Subjects exposed to the *delayed auditory feedback* were more than twice as likely to be convinced by their own presentation than were those who presented the argument without distraction.

Later work has shown that enjoyable role playing may have no effects on attitudes (Cooper, Zanna, and Goethals, 1974; Hoyt, Henley, and Collins, 1972). Enjoyable role playing takes no effort and creates little dissonance. Similarly, if people are told that the

disagreeable feelings they experience during role playing are produced by a pill they have taken, their attitudes won't change (Zanna, Higgins, and Taves, 1976). In other words, attitudes are changed when people can't explain away their feelings of dissonance.

Forced compliance: when rewards fail

Does the role-playing research mean that if people are *forced* to behave in a certain way, their private attitudes will shift in the direc-

At 4:45 A.M. Mrs. Keech suddenly announced that she had received a message informing the group that the power of their faith had saved the earth. This message was received with great rejoicing by the group. Their faith was restored. They sought out the news media and began to proselytize among those who expressed any interest in the event. The group members reduced dissonance not by painfully admitting they were wrong, but by increasing the intensity of their initial belief.

A later study in a real-life setting concentrated on a religious sect led by a prophet who believed that a nuclear disaster was imminent (Hardyck and Braden, 1962). The group of 103 men, women, and children huddled in an underground shelter for forty-two days awaiting the event. When they finally received word to come out of the shelter, they held a joyous reunion during which the pastor asked, "Did you have victory?" In unison the group replied, "Yes, praise the Lord." They later told interviewers that their faith had been increased by the experience. They did not try to proselytize. The investigators believe that the group members kept to themselves because their group already was quite large and because they had good reason to expect public ridicule.

Similar expressions of increased faith in response to catastrophe were reported recently when a dam broke in Toccoa, Georgia. The flood killed thirty-eight persons on the campus of a Bible college. Again, students and faculty gave no indication of a decline in the belief that they were loved by God. They praised God. They said that those who had gone to join God were fortunate and that those who had been saved by God had reason for thanks. As one student remarked, "We'd been praying that God would come down and touch our campus in His special way."

Festinger and his colleagues propose that a bolstering of beliefs in the face of disconfirming events is especially likely to occur when people have strong social support from other believers. Together people can find a means of renewing their faith. Alone they might not be able to sustain their faith.

tion of their behavior? Will students who are forced to go to integrated schools come to like their fellow students? Will conquered peoples give up their love of country if they are forced to submit to their conquerors? Will someone who is forced to perform a sexual act come to like the partner more as a result? The intuitive answer to these questions is no, and Festinger (1957) was able to supply a theoretical reason why. Specifically, the cognition "I am being forced to do X" is *not* inconsistent, or dissonant, with the cognition "I do not like X." With no dissonance arousal, there is little reason to expect attitude change. In general, argued Festinger, the *greater the pressure placed on a person to perform an action, the less the dissonance arousal.*

This line of reasoning seems simple enough, but the research supporting it has produced a storm of controversy. At issue is the kind of pressure placed on the performer of the action. Most people would agree that

Their faith renewed. These women escaped injury in the Toccoa Falls disaster. Here they are shown embracing and praying. Their renewed faith confirms the research finding that committed believers whose faith is challenged often reduce the resulting dissonance by becoming more faithful.

if the pressure involved *punishment,* there would be little increase in liking for the disagreeable activity. All of the above examples are of this variety. But what if the performer is *rewarded* for engaging in a disagreeable action? After all, reward also is a useful source of pressure. It is on the question of reward that many psychologists part company with the dissonance theorists. The dissonance theorist suggests that rewards should have the same effects as punishment. Both reward and punishment *force* the performer to act and thus should not cause liking of the activity. Yet common observation and elementary principles of learning (see Chapter 3) strongly suggest that people come to *like* those actions for which they are rewarded. The critics of dissonance theory might say that if you reward people for going to integrated schools,

obeying conquerors, or engaging in forced sex, they will develop positive attitudes. The two views thus compete.

A number of research demonstrations support the dissonance position. Festinger and Carlsmith (1959) reasoned, for example, that if people were paid enough for telling a lie, they should feel no dissonance, but would tell themselves that they had been *forced* by the size of the reward to engage in deceit. However, if people were paid only a small amount for telling the same lie, they would be unable to explain away their behavior and thus would be faced with painful dissonance, which they might reduce by coming to believe the lie. The investigators paid one group of students $20 for telling a classmate that an extremely boring task was actually very interesting. Students in another group were paid only $1 to tell the same lie. Later tests showed that the poorly paid students were more convinced that the task wasn't so bad after all than were the well-paid students.

In other research, hungry subjects were asked to agree to additional hours of fasting (Brehm and Crocker, 1962). Some were offered $5 if they would continue to fast, while subjects in another group were offered nothing. When the subjects later were asked to rate their hunger, those who were offered no reward for fasting reported significantly less hunger than did those who were paid. Other studies have shown that when people are persuaded by an unattractive person (low reward) to behave in a way that contradicts their private attitudes, they may come to change their attitudes in the direction of their behavior. People coaxed into the same action by an attractive person (high reward) change very little (Kiesler and DeSalvo, 1967; Weick, 1964).

While these various findings suggest that high reward for an action often may produce less attitude change than low reward, some theorists continue to resist this interpretation of the findings, and we will explore their views later in this chapter. Other critics believe that the most important task is identifying the conditions under which rewards are effective in changing attitudes and the conditions under which they are ineffective. This problem remains to be solved.

We have seen that when people are persuaded but not forced into a course of conduct, they may change their attitudes to make them consistent with their conduct. However, people often choose their actions without being coaxed or persuaded. Thus we now will consider how dissonance reduction may affect attitude change under free-choice conditions.

Changing attitudes through decisions

Students often face difficult choices: which college to attend, what major to select,

what summer job to take. Such choices depend in part on attitudes, but often the attitudes are mixed. College X is in a good location but costs too much. College Y has an excellent academic reputation but a dull social life. With such mixed attitudes how should people make decisions? From the standpoint of the dissonance theorist the answer is simple: people should make a choice—either choice—and dissonance reduction usually takes care of the rest. Once the decision is made, attitudes tend to move in a direction that justifies the decision. It works this way: the cognition "I have chosen X" is dissonant with the cognition that "Y could be better." To reduce this dissonance the individual may develop: (1) a more positive attitude toward the chosen alternative or (2) a more negative attitude toward the rejected alternative. Either alternative is likely to result in happier feelings about the decision.

In one early demonstration of this position, two hundred women, participating in what appeared to be a market research project, were asked to rate various products (Brehm, 1956). After making the ratings, they were allowed to choose between two products to keep as their own. Women in one group were allowed to choose between products that were *similar in value* (for example, an automatic toaster and an automatic sandwich grill). This choice, it was reasoned, would create especially high dissonance because the rejected alternative would be as attractive as the chosen one. Women in another group were given a choice between products of *very different value*. The researchers assumed that this choice would produce less dissonance, since one object was obviously more desirable than the other. After making the initial ratings and choosing between the products, the women were asked to rate the products a second time ("now that you have had more time to think about them"). The researchers wanted to know whether the women would shift their attitudes and come to see the chosen item as being more attractive and the rejected alternative as being less attractive.

The women's changes in attitude toward the products are presented in Figure 5-3. You can see that in the low-dissonance condition, in which the products were *not* difficult to compare, very little change took place in their attitudes. In the high-dissonance condition, in which the products were almost indistin-guishable, substantial attitude change occurred. The chosen product was rated as being significantly more attractive, and the rejected alternative was seen as being less attractive. Such results also have been obtained by many other investigators (Deutsch, Krauss, and Rosenau, 1962; Walster, 1964).

Under what conditions is this tidying up of attitudes likely to take place? Such effects depend importantly on the extent to which

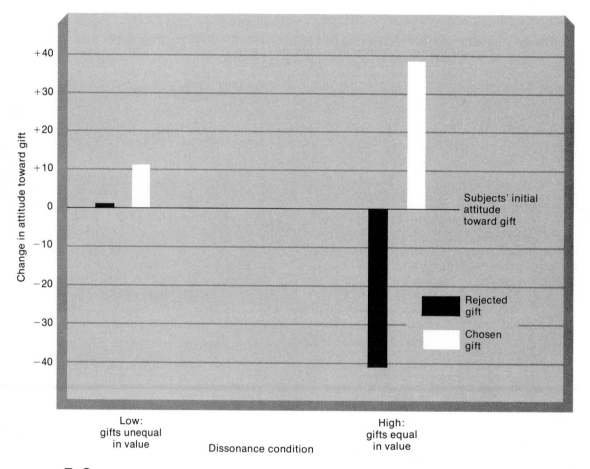

FIGURE 5-3 **Dissonance and attitude change**

Given a choice between products of unequal value, no justification of choice is necessary. But when the choice is not clear-cut, people come to value the chosen item and devalue the rejected one, thus reducing cognitive dissonance. (Adapted from Brehm, 1956)

the individual sees himself or herself as being *personally responsible* for the choice (Wicklund and Brehm, 1976). That is, the individual must experience a sense of freedom of choice and be able to anticipate the outcomes of the choice (Cooper, 1971; Goethals, Cooper, and Naficy, 1979). Apparently, people also must have a sense of *commitment* to their choice in order for such effects to occur. If they feel that they can reverse the choice later on (take it back), little attitude change takes place (Allen, 1964; Davidson and Kiesler, 1964). Marriage is such a commitment. The partners may need to reduce dissonance by convincing themselves that each is the one and only and that all other choices are inferior. A lesser commitment, like spending a few days together, would not be likely to set the dissonance processes in motion. But let us look more closely at the process of dissonance reduction after decision making. Precisely how does an individual go about bolstering his or her decision? The answer to this question has broad implications.

Selectivity in exposure, learning, and memory

How do people convince themselves that their choice was the better one after all? Sometimes they search for information that supports their choice and ignore information that doesn't support it. This technique of *selective exposure* would be illustrated in the product-choice study if the women had looked over the products again and noticed the good features of the chosen item and the unattractive features of the rejected alternative. This kind of selective exposure has long been noted in investigations of the mass media. People do not notice all billboards or listen to all radio appeals and all television commercials. Rather, they tend to be selective, and their selectivity often is biased in favor of their *preexisting attitudes.* Communications specialist Joseph Klapper has noted that

"every product of the mass media (1) attracts an audience which already prefers that particular type of material, and (2) fails to attract any significant number of persons who are either of contrary inclination or have been hitherto uninterested" (1949, pp. 16–17). Klapper's position is somewhat overstated (Freedman and Sears, 1965). Research has demonstrated a number of exceptions to the selectivity rule. For example, when people are very *confident* in their attitudes they may be quite willing to examine opposition arguments (Rosnow, Gitler, and Holz, 1969). They also may pay attention to opposition arguments out of *fairness* (Sears, 1965) or because the message may prove *useful* to them (Canon, 1964). Nevertheless, demonstrations of selective exposure remain quite numerous (see Wicklund and Brehm's 1976 summary), and the implications are significant. For example, one study found that people on opposing sides of an issue may become only more extreme in their positions as increasing information becomes available (Lord, Ross, and Lepper, 1979). Each side tends to select from the available information exactly those portions that are consistent with their existing attitudes. More and better information does not necessarily bring people into closer agreement.

Not only do people avoid messages that don't support their preexisting attitudes, but they often have a difficult time making sense of or remembering opposition material. A variety of studies have shown that people tend to learn better and remember longer those arguments that are consistent with their preexisting attitudes. For example, anti-Communists tend to learn anti-Communist arguments faster than they learn pro-Communist arguments, and the anti-Communist arguments are remembered longer. For pro-Communists, exactly the reverse holds true (Levine and Murphy, 1943). When exposed to both favorable and unfavorable facts about a black

Selective exposure. The message is clear: stop working and have fun. Will the busy, well-dressed man be receptive to the message? Research suggests that people tend to avoid messages that do not support their preexisting opinions.

baseball player, black youths recall more of the favorable facts than do white youths (Taft, 1954). And females are more likely than males to remember facts that are anti-male (Alper and Korchin, 1952).

To summarize our discussion of cognitive dissonance, we can say that people often are motivated to achieve consistency among their thoughts. When they find themselves holding a position and its opposite simultaneously, they may experience the uncomfortable psychological state of dissonance. One way in which people reduce dissonance is by changing their attitudes. When behavior contradicts attitudes, people frequently modify

their attitudes to agree with their behavior. If they are *forced* into the behavior, attitude change generally does not take place. However, *voluntary* behavior does increase the likelihood of dissonance reduction. After making a free choice, people frequently develop a more positive attitude toward the chosen alternative and a more negative attitude toward the rejected alternative. Such attitude change reduces dissonance. In the process of dissonance reduction the individual often attends and remembers selectively.

Information Processing and Attitude Change

Principles of cognitive consistency have a central position in social psychologists' studies of attitude change. Not only does the theory seem to unify understanding, but it also offers insights into certain aspects of human behavior that seem irrational. In striving for consistency, people rationalize their actions and their choices simply because they made them. However, many social psychologists feel that the focus on consistency is too narrow and that other cognitive processes must be considered. As it is argued, people often try to take account of many sources of information and integrate this information in order to reach decisions about the positive or negative qualities of the object of an attitude. If someone is intensely interested in an issue, he or she may engage in a great deal of cognitive work in order to reach a "best solution" (Romer, 1979). We now will consider some research on how people use information from various sources in making evaluative decisions.

Environmental information

People look to the environment for the information that they need in forming their attitudes. The information can be acquired from friends, the media, and many other sources (Ostrom, 1977). In deciding, for example, whether to support a presidential candidate, people generally acquaint themselves with the candidate's views on equal rights, the draft, atomic power, and other issues. But how much information is crucial in deciding to vote for a given candidate? Is one strong piece of information as influential as a dozen lesser arguments in generating support?

In one study of this issue, more than seven hundred students listened to testimony on both sides of a court case (Calder, Insko, and Yandell, 1974). The students were exposed to varying amounts of information in support of either the prosecution's or the defense's position. Some students were exposed only to a single argument favoring a verdict of guilt or innocence. Others were exposed to four arguments on one side or the other, and additional groups heard seven different pieces of testimony. After reading the evidence, the students rated the extent of the defendant's guilt or innocence.

The effects of the prosecution's arguments are shown in Figure 5-4. Note that the more arguments the students were given, the more extreme were their ratings of the defendant's guilt. A similar curve describes the responses of the students who were exposed to the defense's arguments. Although these findings seem to be straightforward enough, note one additional feature of the graph. As more information was received, proportionately less change in the ratings of guilt (or innocence) took place. Thus moving from a single argument to four arguments resulted in greater change in ratings of guilt (or innocence) than did moving from four to seven arguments. In more formal terms, the slope that relates amount of information to persuasion is accelerated negatively. After eleven arguments had been presented on one side or the other, the increase in ratings was scarcely noticeable. Perhaps the initial arguments create the basic attitude and the remaining arguments can effect little change (see the Chapter 2 discussion of primacy effects).

Self-perception: "to be is to do"

People not only scan the environment for useful information, but they look to their own behavior as a powerful source of information on which to base their attitudes. Attitudes about one's self, for example, often develop out of a person's perception of his or her performance. If your performance in tennis is outstanding, you probably have a positive attitude toward your ability to play tennis. If you began to lose consistently, your attitude probably would shift in a negative

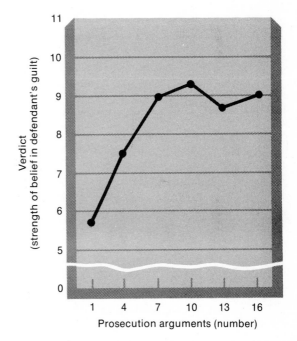

FIGURE **5-4**

Guilty versus innocent: how many arguments are effective?

In this simulation of the experience of jury members, the more arguments the prosecuting attorney put forth, the more strongly the jurors believed in the defendant's guilt. This tendency peaked at about ten arguments. Additional arguments added proportionately less weight. (Adapted from Calder, Insko, and Yandell, 1974)

Cognitive Balance: Keeping One's Attitudes in Order

One of the most interesting aspects of the cognitivists' approach to attitudes lies in their view of the relationship between thought and feelings. Theorists, beginning with Freud, have maintained that thoughts are a victim of emotions—that one's wants and needs fashion one's thoughts. Cognitive theorists suggest that the opposite may be true—habits of thinking may influence feelings. One of the most intriguing of these arguments is balance theory. Originally proposed by Fritz Heider (1946), who is pictured with his friend Kurt Lewin in Chapter 1, the theory has been modified and extended (Cartwright and Harary, 1956; Newcomb, 1953; Osgood and Tannenbaum, 1955; Rosenberg and Abelson, 1960).

As Heider (1946) argued, people tend to organize their perceptions of objects and other people into units. People are seen as belonging in families, for example, or as forming couples or cliques. They also are seen as forming units with the objects they own—the objects "belong" to them. This kind of mental clustering, argued Heider, has a strong influence on feelings, or attitudes. People want to see objects or other people in the cognitive unit as having a positive relationship with each other. The people who make up a unit should be related to one another through positive feelings. They also should be bound to the objects they own by positive attitudes. When elements within a unit are bound by positive sentiments, or attitudes, *cognitive balance* is said to exist. When imbalance is present, maintains Heider, the tendency will be to bring relationships into a state of balance.

Let us see how balance theory might work in the case of a person (P), another person (O), and an object (X). In this example the object, X, is the poetry that P has written. As you can see in the accompanying diagram, P has a positive attitude toward X. Positive feelings also connect P and O. P and O are good friends. If P wants to know how O feels about the poetry and wants O to remain in the unit with P, only one answer to this question is possible: a positive attitude must be expressed. If you were O, wouldn't you feel strong pressure to respond positively?

Look at the other P-O-X diagrams. As you can see, if P and O are good friends and they both have a negative attitude toward a particular movie star, their relationship would be in balance. Their unit remains in a positive state, and the movie star is separated from both of them. If P and O are enemies and P dislikes mathematics, P may hope that O will have a positive attitude toward the subject. In this way P would have no basis for forming a unit with O. As a general rule, one can determine whether balance exists in a P-O-X triad by multiplying the three sentiment signs. If the result is positive, there is balance. In the original example of P as the writer of poetry, $(+) \times (+) \times (+) = +$.

When various balanced and imbalanced relationships are described,

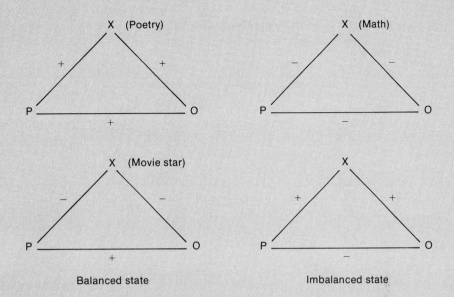

X (Poetry)

+   +

P _____ O
          +

X (Math)

−   −

P _____ O
          −

X (Movie star)

−   −

P _____ O
          +

Balanced state

X

+   +

P _____ O
          −

Imbalanced state

people generally believe that balanced relationships are more acceptable, harmonious, or preferable than imbalanced ones (Jordan, 1953; Rodrigues, 1968; Rossman and Gollob, 1976). And if people are told about two of the three relationships in a triad—such as P's feelings about his or her poetry and P's feelings toward O—predictions about the third relationship (O's feelings about the poetry) generally support balance theory (Burnstein, 1967; Wellens and Thistlethwaite, 1971). In one study of developing relationships among college students, Newcomb (1961) found that knowing how students felt about various issues before college made possible successful prediction of their choice of friends at college. The students chose friends who permitted balance—friends with whom they shared likes and dislikes.

Recent research suggests that additional biases sometimes may interfere with or accentuate balance effects (Gollob, 1974). For example, the *agreement bias* refers to people's general tendency to prefer positive relationships and oppose negative ones (Whitney, 1971). Thus a triad that consists of three positive sentiments would be preferred to one in which two sentiments were negative and one positive. The *justice bias* refers to the tendency to prefer units in which punishments of various kinds form a unit with people who are disliked (Eiser, 1980; Gollob, 1974). However, despite these subtle additional factors, the general preference for overall balance remains the most robust influence on attitudes (Thompson, Gard, and Phillips, 1980).

direction. In this sense, self-esteem often depends on the success of an individual's performance (Diggory, 1966).

Yet a more challenging argument can be made about the effects of self-perception. As Daryl Bem (1972) reasons, people do not always know how they feel or think about an issue. When asked about their thoughts or feelings, they may not be sure of what exactly they believe. Looking inward and being certain of one's attitudes is not easy (Nisbett and Wilson, 1977). When attitudes aren't clear, people may use their own behavior as a source of information about their feelings. If you were asked whether you like your social psychology professor, for example, you might scan your activities. Do you always attend class? Do you criticize him or her when you are with your friends? Do you act cordially in a conversation with him or her? By scanning behaviors such as these, Bem argues, people identify their attitudes.

As you may realize, Bem's arguments can be used to interpret the role-playing effects described by dissonance researchers. You will recall that from the standpoint of dissonance theory, when a person takes a given stand and it is in disagreement with private attitudes, dissonance is created. To reduce dissonance, the individual may change the private attitudes so that they agree with the public stand. However, from Bem's standpoint, dissonance is irrelevant. People simply observe their own behavior, and on the basis of their behavior alone they figure out how they must be feeling.

To demonstrate his point, Bem made use of a well-known dissonance study. In the original study (Cohen, 1962), students were interviewed just after a major riot in which fellow-students allegedly had been brutalized by the police. Hostility toward the police was running high on the campus. Individual students were asked if they would, for money, write a brief essay in support of the action by the police. Subjects in one group were offered 50¢ for their effort, while those in another group were promised $1 for writing the same essay. As we saw, dissonance theory would predict that writing the speech for the smaller amount of money would create more dissonance with internal beliefs than would accepting the larger amount for the same action. Thus dissonance theory would predict more positive attitude change toward the police in the 50¢ condition than in the $1 condition. And the study did reveal exactly this pattern of results.

Bem added extra conditions to Cohen's study. Subjects *were told* all the circumstances and procedures of the original experiment and were asked what they thought the resulting attitudes of the subjects would be. As Bem reasoned, people ordinarily observe behavior and use their observation to decide what the actor's attitude must be. Thus, if they see that a student is willing to write the essay for 50¢, they may conclude that his or her attitude is more favorable toward the topic than is the attitude of a student who demands $1. Dissonance is irrelevant to this process of judging attitudes from behavior. Bem's subjects were able to predict perfectly the pattern of findings that was obtained in the original experiment. His findings raise the possibility that the original subjects were simply judging their attitudes on the basis of their behavior.

Of course, the findings are hardly conclusive, and as you can imagine, Bem has been attacked for his views (Jones et al., 1968; Schaffer, 1975). However, through clever reasoning and countercritique, Bem (1978) has managed to maintain his position, and dissonance researchers have not been able to demonstrate that Bem's interpretation of their results is necessarily wrong (Wicklund and Brehm, 1976). Self-perception theory thus remains a plausible and provocative alternative to dissonance theory.

Memory scanning:
self-generated attitude change

Memory is another information source that is very useful in generating attitude change. For example, if you were asked about your attitude toward Joseph Stalin, you might try to recall information you had learned in courses in modern history. If you recalled Stalin's murderous purging of his government and the thousands of people who were imprisoned, you might conclude that your attitude toward Stalin is negative.

The first significant work on memory and attitudes was carried out by Hovland and his associates (Hovland, Janis, and Kelley, 1953). They were trying to account theoretically for the observation that when people act out a given position, they come to believe in the position. Hovland and his colleagues reasoned that accepting the task of making a speech or playing a role motivates an actor to think of good arguments in support of the position and suppress or actively avoid opposing arguments. In effect, the actor engages in *biased scanning* of his or her memory. With all the supporting arguments in mind, a person might reasonably be expected to change his or her attitudes in the direction of the public presentation. To demonstrate their position, the researchers compared attitude change in two groups of students who had read a speech silently: students in one group were then required to *read* the speech aloud, and those in another group had to *improvise* a version of the speech (King and Janis, 1956). The investigators reasoned that the students who improvised would be forced to scan their memory for arguments to support their public position. Thus the improvisers would be more likely than the readers to experience attitude change. The results supported this reasoning. In addition, later research confirmed the effects of biased scanning. If people are encouraged to think over the pros and cons of a position before they realize they must defend it, they do not scan memory in a biased way, and role-playing effects are not found (Greenwald, 1970).

As you may see, this line of thinking poses another threat to dissonance researchers. The effects of role playing on attitudes may be examples of biased scanning rather than examples of dissonance reduction. This argument has not been viewed kindly by dissonance researchers, and over the years dissonance advocates and memory-scanning advocates have engaged in fierce debate (Elms and Janis, 1965; Janis and Gilmore, 1965). Other researchers have tried to combine the two explanations into a single theory (Gerard, Conolley, and Wilhelmy, 1974) or compare their strengths (Wicklund and Brehm, 1976). Given the desirability of multiple theories, excluding either position would seem to be unwise. Different theories direct attention to different aspects of behavior.

This emphasis on memory processes and their influence on attitudes has been extended in one additional direction. Abraham Tesser (1978) has proposed that as people think back on an experience, they tend to *simplify* it. That is, human beings try to organize memory in a coherent fashion, rapidly forgetting inconsistent or irrelevant images (see Chapter 2). As a result of this tendency, memories of past experiences may become condensed and intensified. In calling forth memories of an attractive person you met last summer, you probably will think of images that support the concept of attractiveness and forget disagreeable images. You thus may develop a more positive attitude in the other person's absence than you would in his or her presence. As the saying goes, absence makes the heart grow fonder.

Tesser's reasoning suggests that over time positive feelings should become more positive and negative feelings more negative. In other words, the more deeply a person reflects on a given memory, the more his or her attitudes will polarize. To demonstrate this position, researchers asked subjects how they felt about various issues, such as the legalization of prostitution and political revolution (Tesser and Conlee, 1975). Then the subjects were asked to give the issues further thought and again indicate their attitudes. Reflection time varied from thirty seconds to three minutes. The investigators reasoned that as more thought was given to an issue, the attitude would *polarize* (become more positive if initially positive and more negative if initially negative). As you can see in Figure 5-5, attitudes did become more polarized as increasing thought was given to any issue. When people draw on their store of memories, then, their attitudes often become more extreme.

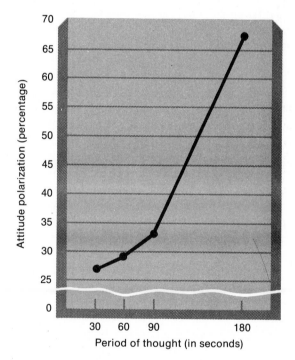

FIGURE 5-5 **The polarizing effect of memory**

The more people think about a set of issues, the more they simplify and intensify their attitude—that is, the more extreme their point of view becomes. (Adapted from Tesser and Conlee, 1975)

We now have explored two arguments concerning the function of cognition in attitude change. They are that (1) motivation for consistency among cognitions may lead to change and that (2) the processing of information from the environment, from people's own behavior, and from memory may lead to change. To complete our discussion of cognition and attitudes, we turn to one of the most important questions facing attitude investigators, the question of how attitudes are related to behavior.

Attitudes and Behavior: The Critical Question

In the introduction to this chapter we pointed out that the study of attitudes holds a central place in social psychology because attitudes are so closely related to actions. Thus, knowing a person's attitude toward another person, group, or object should make possible the prediction of that person's behavior. This assumption makes good intuitive sense. For example, people tend to vote for candidates toward whom they have positive attitudes, and they tend to avoid living in places they don't like. In each of these situations, attitudes seem to be fairly accurate predictors of action.

Yet we saw in Chapter 4 that prejudiced attitudes are not always related to discriminatory behavior. People may have prejudicial attitudes but may fail to express them; they also may engage in institutionalized discrimination without having any underlying negative attitudes. A major attack on the assumption that attitudes are good predictors of behavior was made in 1969 by Allen Wicker. After an extensive review of the vast literature relating attitudes to action, Wicker concluded that "taken as a whole, these studies suggest that it is considerably more likely that attitudes will be unrelated or only slightly related to overt behaviors than that

Does behavior depend on attitudes? People who earn their living manufacturing cars would probably say yes. As attitudes about fuel conservation have changed, the market for large American cars has diminished and the U.S has faced a virtual invasion by small, fuel-efficient foreign cars.

attitudes will be closely related to actions" (p. 65). In effect, the existing research revealed only the weakest relationship between attitudes and behavior. It seemed that a person's behavior seldom could be predicted on the basis of his or her attitudes. Other researchers have since joined Wicker's challenge to the traditional assumption that attitudes and actions are related closely (Calder and Ross, 1973; Deutscher, 1973; McClelland and Winter, 1969). To illustrate Wicker's position, consider a study in which some five hundred people were interviewed regarding their attitudes toward picking up litter (Bickman, 1972). Approximately 94 percent of the sample indicated strong feelings of personal responsibility for picking up litter. Yet after the respondents left the interview, less than 2 percent bothered to pick up a piece of litter planted by the investigator in an obvious place.

Three Possible Answers to the Attitudes-Behavior Question

The line of questioning that was outlined by Wicker has had a powerful effect on attitude research over the past decade. Investigators have been energetic in seeking ways to combat the growing doubt about the relationship between attitudes and behavior. One approach assumes that Wicker's conclusion was based on a poor sample of studies, and it searches for counterexamples in which attitudes are related clearly to action (Kahle and Berman, 1979). A typical counterexample is a large-scale survey of attitudes toward open housing; in this survey, initial attitudes were found to be correlated highly with people's later willingness to sign and publicize petitions favoring open housing (Brannon et al., 1973). Similarly, a large-scale study of women's support for the women's liberation movement found that attitudes toward women's liberation were a strong predictor of who would join the movement (Goldschmidt et al., 1974). While attitudes toward women's liberation were the strongest predictor, twenty other variables predicted less well. Studies of attitudes toward rape also are enlightening (Brownmiller, 1975). People vary in their attitudes toward rapists, and these attitudes have been found to influence (1) willingness of victims to report rape (Schwendinger and Schwendinger, 1974), (2) the treatment of rape victims by judges and juries (Bohmer and Blumberg, 1975; Scroggs, 1976), and (3) the thoroughness of police investigation (Galton, 1976; Keefe and O'Reilly, 1976).

Alarmingly, research shows that the police and the rapists themselves share many attitudes toward rape (Feild, 1978). In any case, these findings suggest that attitudes may not *always* predict behavior, but saying that they *never* do is misleading.

A second approach to answering the questions raised by Wicker and others has been to identify various research procedures that can improve the chances of making good predictions. For example, investigators have noted that the behavioral expression of an attitude can take many different forms. Correlating an attitude measure with a *single* action may result in a low coefficient of correlation. However, when taking account of the *overall pattern* of a person's behavior—that is, of a variety of his or her actions—the attitude measure may predict well (Fishbein and Ajzen, 1974; Schwartz and Tessler, 1972; Werner, 1978). To illustrate, investigators have developed a general measure of attitudes toward protecting the quality of the environment (Weigel and Newman, 1976). This measure was not a very good predictor of whether a person would sign either a petition against nuclear power *or* a petition in favor of increased auto-exhaust regulations, nor was it a very good predictor of whether a person would either pick up litter *or* gather paper and glass for recycling. However, when the researchers developed a comprehensive behavioral measure that included the person's petition signing, willingness to pick up litter, and willingness to recycle wastes, the general attitude measure proved to be a powerful predictor of the overall pattern of behavior. The higher a person's score on the attitude measure, the greater the number of proenvironmental actions. More formally, we can say that the likelihood of predicting action from attitudes may be increased by using *multiple measures of action*.

Investigators also have shown that much of the earlier work yielded poor results because of the *lack of correspondence between the measure of attitudes and the relevant behavior* (Ajzen and Fishbein, 1977; Weigel, Vernon, and Tognacci, 1974). For example, if the measure of attitudes taps *generalized* feelings toward any group—blacks or whites, Arabs or Israelis—there is little reason to expect that the measure will be a good predictor of generosity toward a *single* member of one of the groups. The attitude measures assess general feelings; the behavior is a special type of action directed toward a single individual. Correspondence between the two measures might well be lacking. However, an investigator who measures attitudes toward birth control methods and then measures actual birth control practices is likely to find a high correlation (Kothandapani, 1971). Here the measures correspond more closely.

A third important answer to the attack on the link between attitudes and behavior has been in locating various factors that may strengthen or weaken the link (Wicker, 1971). For example, an individual may have a positive attitude toward the environmental movement, but signing a petition or participating in the movement's activities may depend on many other factors, such as time, other responsibilities, or opportunities to participate.

Formal study of a variety of factors that strengthen or weaken the attitude-behavior link has been made. First, whether attitudes predict behavior depends on the *time interval* separating the attitude assessment and the relevant behavior (Schwartz, 1978). Changing people's attitudes in a given situation is not difficult, but such change does not always persist (Cook and Flay, 1978). Many investigators feel that attitudes are highly elastic and subject to immediate and dramatic change (Cialdini et al., 1976; Hass and Mann, 1976). Thus months before voting occurs, little relationship exists between attitudes toward a political candidate and later voting behavior. If the attitude were measured on the day before the election, a high attitude-

behavior relationship might be found (Davidson and Jaccard, 1979). Whether attitudes predict behavior also depends on the *certainty* with which the attitude is held (Fazio and Zanna, 1979). Attitudes that emerge from a great deal of previous experience are more likely to predict behavior than are attitudes that don't have much basis in experience. And if people have little confidence in their attitudes, their attitudes may be unrelated to their behavior. Finally, some people maintain closer correspondence between behavior and attitudes than do others. In particular, people who don't attempt to fit into or adapt to social situations often are more likely to act according to their attitudes than are more socially flexible people (Snyder and Tanke, 1976; Zanna, Olson, and Fazio, 1980).

These defenses against Wicker's arguments make sense, but investigators have not been entirely content. The problem is similar to the one encountered by supporters of the persuasion approach to attitude change: the solution is not aesthetically pleasing. Too many factors must be taken into account, and often the factors seem to be unrelated. Again, cognitive theory plays a special role in solving the problem of integration. Many social psychologists feel that the cognitive approach can help clarify and create needed unity. One important attempt to create a unified explanation is Fishbein's expectancy-value formulation.

The Fishbein Model
for Behavioral Prediction

Martin Fishbein proposes that people act primarily according to their *intentions* (Fishbein, 1967, 1972; Fishbein and Ajzen, 1975). To find out whether someone will join in a protest against nuclear power plants, simply ask the person what he or she intends to do. If the response is honest and nothing intervenes, behavior will be highly correlated with intentions. However, intentions are influenced by several factors: *attitudes, normative beliefs,* and *motivation.*

1. *Attitudes.* What people intend to do depends on their relevant attitudes. Thus an individual who has a negative attitude toward demonstrations against nuclear power plants probably will not intend to protest; one whose attitude toward participation is positive may well intend to protest. However, attitudes also depend on other factors, one of which is *expectation of outcome.* The potential protester probably would think about the result of an anti–nuclear energy demonstration before

deciding to demonstrate. Will the protest halt construction of a plant or only lead to disappointment? A second factor that contributes to the person's attitude is the *value of the expected outcome.* If the protester expects that demonstrations will lead to a halting of the plant's construction and if he or she places a high value on this outcome, a very positive attitude toward demonstrating would be expected. This attitude probably would lead to an increase in the intention to participate. Of course, most people have a variety of expectations, each of which is valued to a different degree. The overall attitude thus

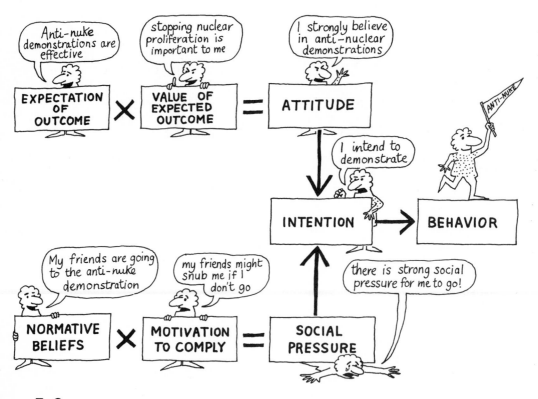

FIGURE 5-6   The Fishbein model

This model makes possible the prediction of a person's behavior from a knowledge of his or her attitudes.

would consist of the sum of each expectation weighted by its value.

2. *Normative beliefs.* What people intend to do also depends on their beliefs about what other people think they *should* do in the particular case. For example, if friends and relatives are opposed to demonstrations, the potential protester may feel pressure to avoid participating in demonstrations against nuclear power.

3. *Motivation to comply.* Intention also is influenced by the degree to which the individual is motivated to comply with other people's feelings. The protester may be aware of the negative feelings toward demonstrations that are held by family and friends but may or may not be motivated to comply with those views.

Fishbein's formulation suggests that the intention to participate depends on attitude plus the sum of a person's beliefs about others' expectancies, weighted by the individual's motivation to comply. In other words, how people will act in a given situation depends on attitudes and social pressure. To predict behavior from attitudes, one needs to know a good deal about how people perceive and evaluate the results of their actions, including other people's responses to them (see Figure 5-6).

Fishbein's model has elicited much attention because it is coherent, integrated, and pleasing and because it can be used to make reliable predictions about people's activities. In one early study, Fishbein (1966) tried to predict whether university students would engage in premarital sex. At the beginning of the semester he assessed their attitudes toward premarital sex, their beliefs concerning what others felt they should do, and their motivation to comply with others' expectancies. At the close of the semester he asked the students whether they actually had engaged in sexual intercourse during the semester. The results showed that the initial measures were excellent predictors of the students' intentions and that intentions successfully predicted sexual activity. Other researchers have been able to use attitude assessment to successfully predict such behavior as women's use of oral contraceptives (Werner and Middlestadt, 1979), reactions to nuclear-energy proposals (Bowman and Fishbein, 1978), altruistic acts (Pomazal and Jaccard, 1976), and church attendance (Brinberg, 1979). We find, then, that when used with care and sophistication, attitude measures can help in making accurate behavioral predictions.

SUMMARY

1 Attitude change is a central feature of social life. Research on this topic reflects two key theoretical orientations: the behaviorist and the cognitive. The behaviorist approach to attitude change emphasizes various stimulus factors—the communicator, the message, the channel, audience characteristics, and the communications environment—that increase or decrease the effect of persuasion on attitudes.

2 The communicator's credibility often increases the impact of a message. As time passes, however, a message that was delivered by a low-credibility source may have increasing impact. This delayed phenomenon, called the sleeper effect, seems to occur because the message is dissociated from its particular source. The persuasiveness of a message

also is increased by the personal attractiveness of the communicator. If the communicator forewarns an audience of a persuasive appeal, the audience may mobilize to resist persuasion. However, if the audience does not feel threatened by the forewarning, the forewarning may increase the audience's persuasibility.

3   To be persuasive a message first must be understood. How much information the message should contain depends on the characteristics of the audience. Presenting all sides of an issue and drawing no clear conclusions may be ineffective with a poorly educated audience but quite persuasive with more educated people. The threat of fearful effects can increase the impact of a message. However, if the message fails to offer strategies for avoiding the effects, persuasion may be diminished.

4   Which medium for communication is most effective depends on time and circumstances. When simple material is being presented, the more closely a medium approximates face-to-face interaction, the more persuasive it may be.

5   The audience participates actively in attitude change. People often demonstrate a positive bias toward communicators—that is, a tendency to agree with any message. This bias may be encouraged by the schools. People also resist persuasion. One effective inoculation against persuasion is learning the opposition's arguments and the weakness of those arguments. In this way a refutational defense is formed. People who are low in self-esteem are often found to be more persuadable than those who are self-confident.

6   The actual environment and people's associations to it can influence the success or failure of a message. Intense distraction can be disruptive, while minor distraction can increase attention and thus can increase persuasion effects. Because of learned associations, communicators often may be more effective if they are encountered in pleasant environments.

7   The cognitive approach to attitude change focuses on the thought processes of the audience and especially on the need for cognitive consistency. Festinger's theory of cognitive dissonance suggests that when two or more cognitions are inconsistent, the individual may experience the pain of cognitive dissonance and will attempt to reduce the pain by changing behavior or changing cognition. When people publicly act out a role that is discrepant with their private attitudes, dissonance may result. The dissonance may be resolved by changing the private attitude in the direction of the publicly advocated position. When an individual is pressured to engage in behavior contrary to his or her private attitudes, less dissonance is created and less attitude change takes place. When given an opportunity to make a free choice,

people later change their attitudes to support the choice. This effect may be especially strong when they feel personal responsibility for the choice. In the process of dissonance reduction, people often attend and remember selectively.

8 People process information in reaching decisions about the goodness or badness of attitude objects. They may work hard to reach judgments on the basis of information that is available in the environment. However, as more information is received, the information may have less impact. People often scan their own behavior to gather information about their attitudes, and they may judge their own attitudes on the basis of observations of their own behavior. People also scan their memories for information relevant to their attitudes. However, this information scanning often may be biased in the direction of a favored outcome.

9 The assumption that attitudes predict behavior holds a central place in social psychology. Wicker and others have suggested, however, that attitudes often fail to predict behavior. In their counterarguments supporters of the attitude-behavior link have cited studies in which prediction did occur. They also have suggested that failure to find a link reflects poor research methods rather than the absence of a relationship between attitudes and behavior.

10 Fishbein has proposed a model that makes possible the prediction of behavior from attitudes. The model takes into account the person's expectation of outcomes, the value placed on the outcomes, the perception of what is normative or proper, and the motivation to comply with normative standards.

SUGGESTED READINGS

Ajzen, I., & Fishbein, M. *Understanding attitudes and predicting social behavior.* Englewood Cliffs, N.J.: Prentice-Hall, 1980.

Dawes, R.M. *Fundamentals of attitude measurement.* New York: John Wiley, 1972.

Greenwald, A.G., Ostrom, T., & Brock, T. (Eds.). *Psychological foundations of attitudes.* New York: Academic Press, 1968.

Oskamp, S. *Attitudes and opinions.* Englewood Cliffs, N.J.: Prentice-Hall, 1977.

Rokeach, M. *Beliefs, attitudes, and values: A theory of organization and change.* San Francisco: Jossey-Bass, 1968.

Triandis, H.C. *Attitude and attitude change.* New York: John Wiley, 1971.

6:
MORALITY IN THOUGHT AND ACTION

■ *In Cyra McFadden's* The Serial, *a humorous novel about life with the "beautiful people" who live in California's Marin County, there is a description of the activities of a group of neighborhood children as their parents sit and try to talk to each other. A child named John-John is swinging on his neighbor Martha's drapes. His mother, Naomi, says, "John-John, I shouldn't engage in that form of activity if I were you. Your actions might be subject to misinterpretation, don't you agree?" John-John stares at his mother and responds, "I don't give a s———." Then he picks up a tool and begins to beat Martha's daughter over the head. Naomi doesn't stop him. She feels that expressing his natural instincts may be good for him. A few moments later John-John pours a cup of scalding coffee down his father's leg. His father, writhing in agony, responds, "John, I can only surmise that your impulsive gesture, in pouring hot coffee on your father, was the result of some instinctual aversion to the use of stimulants . . . I feel we should discuss the question of how one chooses the form of protest he employs as a vehicle for his convictions. . . ." John-John gives his father the finger, snatches Martha's food from her plate, and pulls Martha's son's hair.*

This painful little scene raises one of the most profound questions facing society: what can parents do to nurture in their children forms of conduct that ensure society's continued survival—that is, the kind of conduct that usually is called *moral*? Many individuals who are concerned with morality might say that John-John typifies humans in their natural state, for he seeks to avoid pain and to gain pleasure for himself. Many Christians believe that humans are born in sin and achieve grace through God. The seventeenth-century philosopher Thomas Hobbes argued that without intervention people in their natural state would conduct a "war of all against all." The view that humans in their natural state are bent only on self-gratification was first elaborated in psychology by Sigmund Freud. According to Freud there are no innate safeguards to inhibit a man from murdering his father, raping his mother, or destroying his brothers and taking their goods. Donald Campbell (1978), a past president of the American Psychological Association, has argued that to be adaptive a society must foster a sense of guilt in its members. If people were not inhibited by guilt, their natural instincts might have full expression. The re-

sults would be catastrophic. These views are not merely academic; they have many real-world consequences. As research indicates, people who believe in inherent evil prefer strong social restraints, such as strict laws and a powerful police force (Hogan and Dickstein, 1972). If we believe that people basically are bad, we often seek ways by which to control them.

Still, social life is not just a war of all against all. Few sons murder their fathers, and few mothers need to be protected from their sons. Most people observe a good deal of social restraint, giving resources as well as taking and sharing them. Of course, Hobbes and Freud were aware of the generally restrained nature of human relations, and a major part of their work attempted to solve what they considered to be one of humankind's master riddles. That is, if human beings are born in a brutish state, how can they live in relative harmony? For Hobbes (1651) the answer lay in the creation of the state, or the *Leviathan*. If people can agree to a common rule, Hobbes believed, then their natural immorality can be curtailed and order may reign.

For Freud (1933), the basis for people's good acts was their superego, the self-critical part of a person's personality that maintains his or her ethics and standards. Freud believed that superego develops during a child's association with significant caretakers, especially with the child's parents. Freud's view has an advantage over the theories of the social philosophers since it offers an explanation of the *mechanisms* through which moral socialization takes place. For Freud, the superego is acquired through fear of parental punishment. Although this theory is no longer favored by social and developmental psychologists, the concern with parent-child relationships continues to be focal. The reader who would like more information on the psychoanalytic approach to moral development may want to review Maccoby (1980). In this chapter we will explore two modern and now-familiar approaches to understanding moral development: the behaviorist orientation and the cognitive orientation.

Our chief concern is the question of how morality develops (or fails to develop) in an individual. Although every society *socializes,* or shapes, most of its members' behavior with some success, finding out exactly how the socialization is managed presents a perplexing problem. The fact that socialization so often fails, and does so with such shattering consequences for so many people, lends additional urgency to the issue. As Eleanor Maccoby (1980) points out, most societies develop rules that are meant to control aggression, prevent people from endangering each other, ensure that work is carried out, and ensure that people are reliable. In the *process of learning the rules that are established by the culture to ensure its continuation,* the individual develops *morality.* Of course, cultures differ greatly in their required rules. There also is considerable conflict within cultures concerning what rules are needed: consider the issues of the draft and homosexuality in North American society. In this discussion we will not evaluate any particular set of rules. We accept as given the general need for

some system of rules in a culture, and we simply ask how the rules are acquired by the individual.

As indicated, our discussion will emphasize the behaviorist and cognitive orientations: for the former we will focus on the impact of the external environment, and for the latter we will focus on the cognitive processes of the individual. Thus we first will consider the shaping of moral behavior through external patterns of reward and punishment. This approach will highlight specific ways in which parents and others influence children's moral actions. When we turn to the cognitive approach to moral development we will see that in a significant sense children are active participants in their own socialization. That is, to understand children's development one also must understand their cognitive capacities. Finally we will consider the important question of whether a child's early shaping is likely to have long-term consequences. Does early socialization implant long-lasting moral dispositions, or does the social milieu continue to influence an individual's moral activity?

The Behaviorist Approach: Morality through Reinforcement

North America generally is considered to be a no-nonsense culture in which people believe what they can see. People in our society seem to distrust fancy ideas or too much talk and no action. This emphasis on the observable has been carried to beliefs about teaching people to be moral. Punishment is considered to be a prerequisite for morality. The old aphorism "spare the rod and spoil the child" and the modern belief that abandoning the death penalty will encourage crime both exemplify this orientation. And this point of view also is represented in the behaviorist approach to morality. The behaviorist generally believes that whether or not a person obeys the culture's moral rules depends on the consequences of doing so—that is, on the rewards and punishments that will be received from others. Further, the behaviorist generally is interested less in what people think about morality than in how they act. The behaviorist emphasis, then, is on the effects of reward and punishment on moral behavior. Here we will explore two offshoots of this position: (1) the classical behaviorist approach, which considers the way in which people use rewards and punishments of various magnitudes in various ways to shape other people's moral development and (2) the social learning approach, which takes account of internal processes, particularly the learning that takes place through observation of other people's actions.

Shaping Moral Behavior:
From Pigeons to Prisons

In a series of challenging books, Harvard psychologist B. F. Skinner has argued that virtually all human behavior is shaped by *reinforcement*—that is, by reward and punishment. Many psychologists, philosophers, legislators, and members of the clergy, as well as teeming numbers of students, have found Skinner's views to be disagreeable. It is said that Skinner's position robs people of their capacity for free decision-making, their dignity as human beings, and all responsibility for their behavior. While the merits of Skinner's position are a legitimate matter for debate, the controversy should not be allowed to obscure the valuable insights that can be gained from the study of reinforcement.

The behaviorist premise is a simple one: behaviors that provide reward for a person in a given situation will be more likely than other behaviors to recur in that situation, and behaviors that are punished will be less likely to recur. Behaviorists generally refer to reward as *positive reinforcement* and punishment as *negative reinforcement*. This premise has been demonstrated frequently and powerfully in the animal laboratory. With the judicious use of food pellets and electric shock, for example, some animals—including pigeons, rats, and monkeys—have been taught to carry out an impressive range of behaviors, from playing complicated games to guiding a bomb to its target. Using rewards and punishments to mold such behavior is termed *operant conditioning*, a process well detailed in any introductory psychology book. You easily can see how principles of operant conditioning might apply to the shaping of moral behavior. If a child clears the table after dinner and the mother rewards the effort with hugs and kisses, her reaction should serve as a positive reinforcement of the child's behavior. Thereafter the child should be increasingly disposed to help with the household chores. Punishment should operate in an opposite fashion. If a child steals a friend's toys and the father responds by spanking the child, the likelihood of the child's stealing again should be reduced.

Experiments illustrate nicely the power of these simple ideas. For example, in the case of reward, researchers have given one group of children bubble gum or praise for sharing marbles with other children (Fischer, 1963). Later these children proved to be more likely to give additional marbles to other children than did a group that had not been rewarded previously. Similarly, the generosity of children has been increased by hugging them whenever they gave sweets to needy children (Midlarsky and Bryan, 1967) or by praising them (Gelfand et al., 1975). Further, children who were given praise for cooperating were more likely to increase their cooperative behavior than were a group that had not been rewarded (Serbin, Tonnick, and Sternglanz, 1977). Clearly, reward often can have immediate effects on an individual's behavior toward others.

Numerous research illustrations also have demonstrated the effects of punishment on

The power of positive reinforcement. What can parents do to encourage good habits, values, and goals in their children? The behaviorist's answer to this question emphasizes the shaping power of reward such as the loving affection this child is enjoying.

behavior. Aggressive play with dolls has been reduced by punishment (Hollenberg and Sperry, 1951), children's tendencies to dominate other children have been reduced by withholding candy (Blum and Kennedy, 1967), and children's sharing has been increased by giving punishment for not sharing (Hartman et al., 1976). Punishment also has been used to increase children's resistance to temptation (Aronfreed and Reber, 1965).

We suspect that most people don't need to be presented with research evidence in order for their beliefs in the effects of reward and punishment to be bolstered. For example, no matter how much you may disagree with the basic behaviorist position, chances are that the first time your child throws a glass of milk on the floor you will respond with punishment, and the first time you hear your child say "please" or "thank you" you will respond with praise. For good or ill most of us are behaviorists at heart. However, as children grow up few of them fit their parents' images of what they should be like, and almost all parents have been frustrated occasionally by seeming to have no influence over their children. Reward and punishment clearly must be considered in greater detail. Let us discuss three major factors that may increase or reduce the effects of reward and

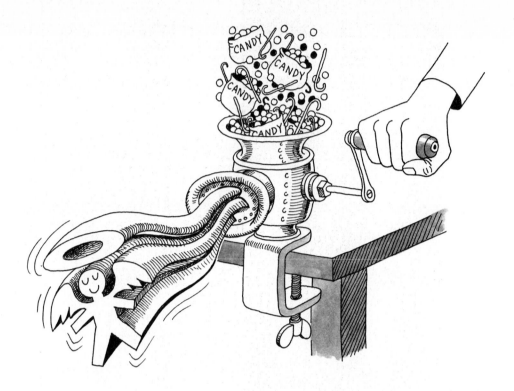

punishment on behavior: magnitude, scheduling, and timing.

Reinforcement magnitude: is the more the mightier?

How much reward or punishment to give is a frequent quandary faced by parents. A reasonable assumption is that a greater reward will increase the likelihood of the recurrence of a given behavior and that increased punishment will have the reverse effect. Research does illustrate this position. For example, investigators have shown that the greater the amount of praise given by parents to a child who shows initiative and independence, the greater the child's desire for achievement (Crandall, Preston, and Rabson, 1960; Rosen and D'Andrade, 1959). And a child who receives severe punishment for an action is more likely than a lightly punished child to show resistance to later temptation

(Aronfreed and Leff, 1963). The increased punishment seems to insulate the child from later invitations to disobey.

Yet increasing the amount of reward or punishment does not always increase the strength of moral actions. In particular, if the magnitude of the reinforcement is *extreme*, the praise or punishment may produce disbelief or disregard. One study found that threat of *strong punishment* was less powerful in causing children to resist a temptation than was either a *mild threat* or *no threat* at all (Lepper, Greene, and Nisbett, 1973). Children were more likely to cheat when threatened with strong punishment for cheating than when not threatened. Perhaps they disbelieved the threat. Moderate increases in reward and punishment may produce immediate effects on moral behavior. However, when increases are extreme, reinforcement may lose its effect altogether.

Reinforcement scheduling:
is constancy its own reward?

Must a child constantly be rewarded or punished in order for moral behavior to be ensured? Are well-learned lessons of morality simply left behind if they are not reinforced continuously? Answers to such questions are furnished by research into *schedules of reinforcement*—that is, research that varies the frequency with which a given action is reinforced. Such work suggests that reinforcement requirements are different during the period of *learning* a response and during the period of *maintaining* it (Reese, 1978). Research suggests that when a child is learning to carry out a moral action, such as sharing, helping, or being responsible, the act should be rewarded each time it is performed. When the reinforcement is continuous, the child is likely to learn rapidly the desired behavior.

When the goal is maintaining moral actions, however, intermittent reinforcement may be far more efficient. In fact, if a slow transition is made and behavior that once was reinforced continuously is reinforced only periodically, the desired behavior may be maintained for long periods without reinforcement. Clear demonstrations of such effects with humans are unavailable. However, in one dramatic study of chimpanzees, researchers succeeded in eliciting as many as four thousand rapid-fire lever presses for a single food reinforcement (Findley and Brady, 1965). Intermittent reinforcement is thought to be effective because an individual cannot be certain when reinforcement will occur. Witness the person who endlessly inserts coins into a slot machine. Usually he or she receives nothing, but there always is the possibility that on the next try . . . The same kind of reasoning may apply to some patterns of moral behavior. People continue to engage in moral behavior even though they receive no immediate rewards. After all, one can never be certain that reinforcement won't occur, even if the activity must be continued until Judgment Day.

Reinforcement timing:
the fatal moment

Common wisdom tells us that when housebreaking pets, punishment must follow the act rapidly or the transgression will happen again. This principle ought to apply in the socialization of children. Yet many mothers wait until daddy gets home and expect him to deliver punishment for serious misbehavior. When this happens, the reinforcement is separated in time from the transgression. Does the timing of reward or punishment matter? Is immediate reinforcement more effective than delayed reinforcement in shaping moral dispositions?

Research suggests that parents who do not deliver punishment until *after* a transgression has occurred miss the most effective opportunity for the punishment. In one study that explored the effects of the timing of punishment, young boys in one group were punished verbally for touching attractive toys while they were in the act of reaching—as the transgression was about to occur (Aronfreed, 1963). Boys in another group were punished a few moments after they had picked up the attractive toys. The boys then were left alone in a room with the toys and told not to touch them. The boys' resistance to this temptation was influenced greatly by the timing of the earlier reinforcement. The children whose punishment preceded touching the forbidden toys were less likely to transgress than were those whose punishment followed touching. Early punishment possibly creates an active fear that is associated with the first steps that are involved in the behavior. Thus this fear of punishment serves as a deterrent *before* the "crime" is committed.

We have seen that factors such as the magnitude, scheduling, and the timing of reward and punishment play a significant role in

Punishment power. Negative reinforcement can be as powerful as positive reinforcement in shaping moral behavior. Research suggests, however, that punishment is most effective in cutting off *undesirable* behavior, while reward encourages *desirable* actions.

shaping moral action. To complete our discussion of reinforcement effects we will consider the relative effectiveness of reward and punishment. Which kind of reinforcement is more useful in shaping moral behavior?

Reward versus punishment:
a parent's quandary

With which of the following statements do you most agree?

The most significant effects on a child's moral behavior are produced through punishment. By using physical force, by withdrawing love, or by reducing privileges you can go a long way toward shaping a child's respect for principles of right and wrong.

The most significant effects on a child's moral behavior are produced through reward. By offering positive incentives, such as food or money, by providing loving attention, or by offering special favors you can go a long way toward shaping a child's devotion to moral principles.

Perhaps you found this dilemma difficult to solve. However, you shouldn't cast the issue aside—it is more than just an intellectual game. If you ever attempt to rear a child, you will run headlong into this dilemma the first time your child misbehaves. Should you punish the child for the transgression or reward him or her for some alternate behavior? Psychologists have tussled with the problem since the early 1900s. In 1932 the influential learning theorist E. L. Thorndike reached a solution that gained widespread acceptance. Specifically, reward was considered to be preferable to punishment in teaching children because punishment was thought to merely *suppress* immediate behavior and not produce any long-term change in inner control. Strong punishment for committing crimes, for example, would not reduce the occurrence of crimes but simply would cause the would-be criminal to become craftier or more careful. If reward were used to reinforce resistance to temptation, the person might come to like this state—he or she might feel much happier and more secure when acting morally.

Although this position seems to account for many failures in our prison system, closer examination indicates that the issue is far more complex than simply being a question of reward or punishment. First, research has shown that when used properly, punishment can produce long-term effects on moral behavior (see Walters and Grusec's 1977 review). Second, just because one type of reward is more potent than one type of punishment, all rewards are not necessarily more effective than all punishments. Thus, praise may be more effective than a whipping in encouraging kindness in children, but withdrawing favorite toys may be more effective than a pleasant smile. A final difficulty is that reward and punishment are partially defined by each other. Reward can be considered the absence of punishment; punishment can be considered the withdrawal of reward. Thus the child can see the failure to reward as a punishment and the failure to punish as a reward. Simply failing to give a reward of love can be more punishing than a spanking.

Clearly the question of reward versus punishment is too complex to be answered directly. What are the special assets and liabilities associated with both types of reinforcement. What characteristics make each valuable for certain purposes and harmful for others? First, the assets. Reward has the special virtue of providing information about which of the thousands of alternatives for action are likely to bring happiness. Punishment does not tell people what they should do; it simply tells them what they shouldn't do. From this standpoint, reward may be especially useful in producing moral action—honesty, cooperation, and helping behavior—while punishment may create fear of undesirable action. Reward also may be especially useful in *creating high morale* or a joyous sense of life. Knowing that certain actions will definitely bring pleasure may create optimism. As we shall see, such positive feelings about life often motivate people to help others. As far as the liabilities are concerned, rewards generally *do not suppress undesirable behavior*. They do not inform people of what they ought *not* to do. And punishment often creates hostility toward the punishing agent. The individual who is being punished may seek ways of breaking off a relationship or quietly rebelling against the punishing agent (Walters and Grusec, 1977).

The hostility created by punishment has been of special concern to social psychologists. As research shows, people who wish to deter unwanted behavior by others often use punishment to gain this end. For example, judges who wish to halt the occurrence of a particular kind of crime may use stiff penalties to deter the criminal (McFatter, 1978). Are these tactics likely to be effective? It appears that they are not. Research into criminal decision-making shows, for example, that the size of the penalty is only a secondary concern when a crime is being contemplated (Carroll, 1978). Of primary concern is the amount of reward that can be reaped for the criminal act. Further, if the penalties are raised, certain groups may come to feel they are being treated unjustly and may increase

**The Hidden
Cost
of Reward**

One of the oldest principles of psychology is that if a response is rewarded, it probably will recur. We devote a considerable amount of attention in this chapter to the various ways in which reward can be used to shape moral behavior. Interestingly, however, reward does not always have such positive effects. Recently social psychologists have begun to consider the circumstances under which reward has the opposite effect—that is, when it *decreases* the probability of behavior.

Most of the research that demonstrates the positive effects of reward has focused on *extrinsic* reward—reward received as a result of action. In the case of a racing-car driver, for example, trophies, prize money, and the crowd's cheers are extrinsic rewards. To understand the negative effects of reward, extrinsic rewards must be contrasted with *intrinsic* rewards. An intrinsic reward is derived from the process of carrying out the action. For example, a racing-car driver may experience the intrinsic reward of mastering the movements of the automobile, speeding around curves with precision, or sensing and solving problems in controlling the car. People often experience intrinsic rewards when they conquer challenges that are optimal for their capacities (Deci, 1975; Deci and Porac, 1978).

The negative effect of reward seems to occur when *extrinsic rewards are offered for activities that already are providing intrinsic reward.* For example, if the racing-car driver races for the thrill of it, then offering prize money may later reduce the driver's ability to obtain these thrills. One explanation of this effect draws on the self-perception theory, discussed in Chapter 2. People try to make sense of both the world and their own actions. They try to explain to themselves why they act as they do. When they find themselves carrying out an action for which no extrinsic rewards are offered, they may conclude that they *like* what they are doing. If extrinsic rewards, such as pay or praise, are offered, people's explanations for their own behavior may change. They may conclude that they were motivated by the desire for extrinsic rewards (Bem, 1972; Lepper and Greene, 1978). If the extrinsic reward is then withdrawn, they may decide that the activity no longer is worth doing.

In one demonstration of these ideas, investigators compared preschool-aged children's responses to extrinsic rewards with their responses to intrinsic rewards (Lepper, Greene, and Nisbett, 1973). The investigators arranged for an art project to be presented to a class, along with a number of attractive alternatives. Children who demonstrated a great deal of intrinsic interest in the drawing exercise were taken to a new setting and exposed to one of three conditions. Children in one group were told that if they carried out the drawing task, they would receive a "good player" certificate—an extrinsic award. Children in a second group were not told of the award, but after they had participated in the drawing task they were given the "good player" certificate unexpectedly. Those in the third group continued to engage in the drawing activity without promise of extrinsic reward and without receiving any reward at the end of the period. Two weeks later the experimenters again offered the children the opportunity to engage in the drawing activity. No rewards were offered, and a record was made of the length of time the children spent on the activity.

The researchers found that children who had been given the extrinsic reward spent less time on the activity than did children in either of the other two groups. Since all of the children originally had greatly enjoyed drawing, the experimenters concluded that the reward changed the children's understanding of their own behavior. Thus, to the children who had received the extrinsic reward, the activity became less worthwhile. Numerous studies of adults and children have demonstrated a similar decline in interest in a variety of tasks (Anderson et al., 1976; Calder and Staw, 1975; Deci, 1975; Dollinger and Thelen, 1978; Harackiewicz, 1979; Pittman, Cooper, and Smith, 1977; Smith, 1976). The reduction in activity is termed the *overjustification effect,* referring to the fact that when external reasons for doing something can be found, the individual ceases to believe that the activity is justified in itself.

Apparently, overjustification effects can even cast a pall on romance. The argument is as follows: awareness of the extrinsic reasons for loving someone causes the lover to attribute his or her feelings to extrinsic rewards, rather than to the intrinsic reward of satisfaction in the partner's presence. Thus, if you know your partner may inherit a million dollars, your faith in your love might be upset. You might not be able to shake off the suspicion that you were after your partner's money. Research has confirmed this possibility. Dating couples in one group were asked to think of the extrinsic rewards obtained from going out with their partners (Seligman, Fazio, and Zanna, 1980). Couples in a second group were asked to think of intrinsic rewards. When later asked to evaluate their feelings, the couples who had thought about the extrinsic rewards evaluated themselves as being less "in love" than did those who had thought about intrinsic rewards.

Research on the overjustification effect has many implications. First, giving rewards for good performance often may rob people of the pleasure of doing things for their own sake. Second, if people are rewarded for moral actions that they otherwise would find to be intrinsically satisfying, the reward ultimately may destroy their internal motivation for being moral. A society that provides no opportunities for intrinsic satisfactions may create the kind of people who respond only to external reward and punishment (Schwartz, Lacey, and Schuldenfrei, 1978).

their unlawfulness in retaliation. For example, attempts by the United States Army to stop crime in its ranks by increasing punishment appear to have had the reverse effect (Hart, 1978). Lawlessness increased after the strict punishments went into effect, seemingly as a sign of resentment toward the harsh treatment. Finally, when a criminal is apprehended and faces a jury, he or she is likely to find the jury to be relatively more lenient if the punishment for the crime is very high. As punishments for crimes are increased, juries are found to convict less often (Kerr, 1978). Thus, using strong punishment—such as the death penalty—to stop crime would not appear to be very effective. Increasing rewards for positive behavior or decreasing the reward for criminal activity would appear to be a more promising approach.

In summary, the behaviorist approach to understanding moral action suggests that people frequently are responsive to reward and punishment and that such factors as magnitude, continuity, and timing may be important in determining the effectiveness of reinforcement. Reinforcement cannot be applied mechanically. For example, if a parent is not warmly attached to a child, reinforcement may be of little consequence in altering the child's behavior (Garbarino and Bronfenbrenner, 1976; Staub, 1975; Weissbrod, 1976). If parents want to encourage moral behavior in their children, the behaviorist approach suggests that attention must be paid to the kinds of rewards and punishment to which the children are exposed from day to day. The approach also has implications for the creation of a moral society. Americans think a great deal about punishment and have developed elaborate penal systems for punishing people who exploit or injure others. Rewarding people for their good works is comparatively rare. The Nobel Peace Prize is virtually unique. The creation of many more means of rewarding those persons who benefit the so-ciety might make the world a better place in which to live.

The Social Learning Approach: Learning without Reinforcement

In our discussion so far we have examined ways in which people can *act on* others to shape their moral behavior. This emphasis is in keeping with the traditional behaviorist approach, as described in Chapter 1. However, more recent neobehaviorist formulations have not placed such a strong emphasis on external reinforcement. These formulations take account of internal processes and the way in which these processes relate stimuli and responses. One of the most significant neobehaviorist formulations has been developed by Albert Bandura and his colleagues and is called *social learning theory*. This theory offers a range of interesting insights about the development of morality.

As Bandura (1977) reasons, much learning about moral rules does not depend at all on direct exposure to reward and punishment. Rather, people learn by observing others. Observation clearly is a valuable tool for the young child. It offers opportunities to discover the consequences of certain actions and the behavior that is appropriate or rewarding in a situation. In this sense learning occurs even when the child does not intend to use the information for any special purpose (Rosenthal and Zimmerman, 1977).

When the behavior patterns observed in other people are adopted by the child, the others are serving as *models*. Research clearly illustrates that models affect moral behavior. In one study, boys were given a difficult vigilance task; at the same time, an interesting movie was being shown in the next room (Stein, 1967). Following instructions thus required *resisting the temptation* of watching the movie. Some children saw an adult working on the task, and the adult announced, "I

Preparation for later life. Some people believe that the taking of a life is an immoral act—even in self-defense or war. From this perspective, children who imitate the warlike ways of adults are being prepared for immoral action in later life.

sure wish I could watch the movie." Soon the adult left the vigilance task to see the film. Children who saw the model give in to temptation were far more likely to be distracted by the movie than were those who saw the same model remain at the task. Interestingly, children who saw no model at all were as likely to resist temptation as were those who saw the steadfast model. Does this mean that models can encourage self-indulgence but not resistance to temptation? Additional research suggests that the answer is no. Several studies have successfully demonstrated that models can increase children's resistance to temptation (Rosenkoetter, 1973; Ross, 1971). In one

study resistance to the temptation of playing with a forbidden toy remained a reliable response for a month (Wolf and Cheyne, 1972).

Who is the effective model?

In the same way that traditional behaviorists have explored the kinds of reinforcement that are most powerful, social learning specialists have been concerned with the sorts of models that people are most likely to copy. What kinds of characteristics favor strong modeling effects? Let us consider two important factors.

First, it appears that people often are likely to choose as models those who are most *at-*

tractive. Advertisers are fully aware of this fact and use it to increase purchases of cigarettes, beer, clothing, automobiles, and other products. The assumption is that in buying these items people feel that they are acquiring the characteristics of the model. The effect of the model's attractiveness on moral behavior is illustrated in a clever study of jaywalking (Lefkowitz, Blake, and Mouton, 1955). Jaywalking is an illegal act that not only interrupts the traffic flow in urban areas, but also contributes to the death toll. A major reason why people jaywalk, reasoned the investigators, is modeling. People see others do it and assume that it must be safe for themselves. In particular, they may imitate the attractive person in their midst. To demonstrate this possibility, an accomplice of the investigators was stationed at a street corner. When pedestrians had gathered to wait for the light and no cars were in sight, he crossed the street illegally. Half of the time he dressed as a well-to-do business executive; the rest of the time he wore tattered clothing. An observer, counting the number of people who followed the model's example, found that the pedestrians were more likely to follow the attractive model than the unattractive model.

A second factor that may influence modeling effects is the *consistency* of the model. Many adults wonder why their children do not adopt the standards set for them at home. They feel that the honesty, the self-sacrifice, and the loving behavior that they display should rub off on the child. Yet in spite of the desire to set a good example, few adults can maintain such standards on a consistent basis. Parents frequently are selfish and dishonest, in spite of their wishes to be otherwise, and loving behavior often is interspersed with fits of temper. Research suggests that these inconsistencies may have a strong influence

on the young observer. In one study, children were exposed to models who varied the rewards they gave themselves and others (Rosenhan, Frederick, and Burrowes, 1968). When the model was good to herself *and* to others, the children were very likely to adopt her behavior. Her consistency was apparently important. The children were much less likely to copy her behavior when she was good to herself and punished others or when she was kind to others and punished herself. Further research on model consistency shows that observing two models carrying out the same activity has a more powerful effect than does watching the same model twice (Fehrenbach, Miller, and Thelen, 1979).

Concern with consistency also has prompted investigators to ask what happens to children's moral development when parents don't practice what they preach. Is talking about the difference between right and wrong enough, or must words be backed by action? Apparently talking is not enough; children tend to model adults exactly (Bryan and Walbek, 1970). The parents' demand that the child "do as I say, not as I do" is translated into "I'll say as you say, and do as you do." If parents preach charity, children echo these sentiments. However, if the adults' behavior is at odds with their preaching, children's behavior copies this inconsistency.

Self-reinforcement: the pellet machines in our heads

Earlier we said that neobehaviorist theories emphasize internal, or psychological, processes. Bandura (1977) maintains that these processes are of chief importance in understanding how learned behavior is maintained across time. As he points out, if what people learn didn't persist over time, they would act "like segregationists with a racial bigot, like John Birchers with a zealous Bircher, like Communists with a devoted Communist, like Republicans with a staunch conservative" (1977, p. 734). For Bandura, inner processes promote behavioral consistency, and the key process by which consistency is maintained is *self-reinforcement.* That is, Bandura is suggesting that people evaluate their actions as the actions are about to occur, and they reward or punish themselves psychologically. These self-evaluative reactions sometimes can be more powerful than the most dramatic forms of external reward and punishment. For example, the martyr may accept death because martyrdom furnishes a psychological reward to self that is more potent than is the punishment of death.

Bandura believes that self-reinforcement is learned through two forms of modeling. First, *people treat themselves as the model has treated them.* When other people react positively or negatively toward them, the others are serving as models for how they should treat themselves. In one demonstration of this process, researchers gave either lavish praise or rather limited and unrewarding feedback to groups of adults who were carrying out a task (Kanfer and Marston, 1963). Subjects in each of two groups were subsequently left alone and allowed to reward their own performance. The experimenters had rigged the task so that all subjects would perform equally. Nevertheless, subjects who had been indulged by the experimenters gave themselves far more rewards for their efforts than did those who had been treated strictly.

Not only do people imitate the behavior that another person shows toward them, argues Bandura, but they also adopt the *model's form of self-treatment.* Football players who score touchdowns often reward themselves by heaving the ball to the ground, a signal of their success. Such behavior is repeated in thousands of sandlots across the nation. To illustrate this point, Bandura and Kupers (1964) arranged for children to observe models who set differing standards of reward for themselves. One group saw a model who rewarded himself very sparingly and only when he had performed outstandingly. A second group saw a model who rewarded himself generously for poor performance. Each child subsequently carried out the task that the model had performed and was allowed to reward himself or herself as desired. The effects of the model proved to be quite potent. The children who had been exposed to the model with high standards rewarded their own good performance sparingly; those who had observed the self-indulgent model rewarded themselves quite handsomely—even for poor performance. In effect, the children set standards for themselves that copied the model's standards.

Several investigators believe that habits of self-reinforcement may have especially powerful effects on moral action if people's attention is turned toward the self instead of toward the environment (Diener and Srull, 1979). The assumption is that self-awareness results in more thought being given to moral standards and to deciding whether to meet the standards. In support of this argument, investigators have shown that when college students sit in front of a mirror and listen to tape recordings of their own voices, their cheating on tests is reduced (Vallacher and Solodky, 1979). The mirror and the recording are assumed to have increased the subjects' awareness of their own standards of right and wrong. Similarly, Halloween trick-or-treaters were found to take less candy when a mirror was placed behind the bowl, so that the takers could see themselves as they reached for the candy (Beaman et al., 1979).

Does the behavior of models have lasting effects on children? The question of the power of early experience in shaping adult character is both important and controversial. We will deal with this issue more generally in a later section of this chapter. In the case of modeling, however, no convincing evidence exists to show that models have a long-term influence on behavior. One study has demonstrated that male children from homes in which the father is deviant and the parents are both aggressive and argumentative are more likely to become criminals as adults than are children from homes in which the parents' behavior is less abnormal (McCord, 1979). However, children from such homes differ from other children in many ways, and parental modeling therefore may not be the major cause of their criminality.

In summarizing we can say that social learning theory emphasizes the learning that takes place through observation. Children may learn patterns of morality by modeling their behavior on others. Modeling effects may be especially likely to occur if the model is attractive and if his or her actions are consistent. The effects of modeling may persist over time if the individual learns how to reinforce himself or herself psychologically. And children may learn self-reinforcement by watching others reward and punish themselves.

Social learning: an assessment

As we have seen, reinforcement theorists who are interested in moral behavior concentrate on the use of reward and punishment by parents and others. Social learning theorists have focused their attention on children's learning by observation and self-reinforcement. Do these formulations offer a fully satisfactory explanation for the development of moral behavior? Many critics do not think so. In particular, behaviorist theories are said to be too mechanical. The person is viewed primarily as a product of the forces to which he or she is exposed. The theories imply that unless people are exposed either to reinforcement or to models, morality cannot exist. The behaviorist orientation does not take account of an individual's ability to think things out for himself or herself. Many observers believe that children do not require direct observation or reinforcement in order to acquire moral tendencies (Hoffman, 1977). Children can learn through explanation. Thus being told of the socially harmful effects of a given action may be enough to create moral action. In one demonstration of this argument, investigators looked at the relationship between techniques of parental discipline and various indicators of the morality of seventh-grade children (Hoffman and Saltzstein, 1967). Three different discipline techniques were measured: (1) the use of power (ordering the child and threatening him or her with punishment), (2) love withdrawal (taking support and affection from the child for disobedience), and (3) induction (explaining to the child the consequences of his or her actions—how others will be hurt by them). The children's moral dispositions also were assessed. These dispositions included the capacity for guilt, reliance on moral principles, incidence of confession (as indicated by the mother), acceptance of responsibility (as indicated by teachers), consideration for others (as rated by peers), and identification (the child's desire to be like his or her parents). Correlations then were computed between each of the parental tactics and each of the indicators of the children's morality.

The results of this study are shown in Table 6-1. You can see that the mothers' use of power is related *negatively* to almost all indicators of their children's moral dispositions. The mother who relies exclusively on power tactics may be creating, rather than solving, problems for her children. Love withdrawal has almost no effect on children's morality. In bold contrast, however, the mothers' use of induction or explanation has a high correlation with children's morality. On five of the six measures, the use of induction is correlated positively with the child's moral dispositions. Although the fathers' use of power was found to be slightly more effective than the mothers', in general the fathers' tactics were not correlated with their children's moral dispositions.

The behaviorist views the child as a blank slate on which society inscribes its directions for morality. Depending on reinforcement and models, moral activities may be pushed in any direction. Yet, critics argue, many cultures have highly similar moral codes. If people's moral dispositions can be bent in any

TABLE **6-1**   **Disciplinary techniques and morality**

Note the negative relationship between mothers' assertion of power and their children's moral dispositions and the positive correlations between the mothers' use of induction and their children's morality.

Morality index	Mothers' disciplinary technique		
	Power assertion	Love withdrawal	Induction
Guilt	N		P
Moral principles	N	N	
Confession	N		P
Accepts responsibility	N		P
Consideration of others			P
Identification	N		P

N = significant negative correlation.

Blank = no significant relationship.

P = significant positive correlation.

Source: Hoffman and Saltzstein, 1967

direction, what explains the similarities across cultures? In an effort to answer these questions, we turn now to another approach to moral development, one that places more emphasis on people's thinking or understanding: the cognitive orientation.

The Cognitive Orientation to Morality

One of the century's most challenging approaches to understanding child development has been formulated by the eminent Swiss psychologist Jean Piaget (1965; Piaget and Inhelder, 1958). Through many years of careful observation, experimentation, and theorizing, Piaget and his colleagues have unsettled a number of widely shared assumptions about children's development and have opened the way to new and exciting areas of inquiry. As a result of Piaget's work on moral development, the old notion that children are adults in miniature—entirely capable of proper moral conduct once they are trained properly—must be questioned. Piaget argues that children and adults differ in their patterns of thought and therefore in the kinds of moral decisions that they can make. His work has made clear that there is *no* single best way to teach moral dispositions, no ideal set of child-rearing patterns that parents *always* should use. Children may change in their vulnerability to certain kinds of teaching or training methods. Children can no longer be blamed and punished for every bad behavior. Piaget has shown that taking careful account of a child's age and ability to understand his or her own actions is essential.

Piaget and the Development of Moral Thought

Piaget believes that just as children require time to develop bones, teeth, and secondary sex characteristics, they also require time for the character of their thought patterns to mature. The change is not merely *quantitative*: the child does not simply remember more or solve increasingly difficult problems. Rather, through increased experience the *qualitative* style of thinking undergoes change. A brief account of Piaget's analysis will be useful at this point.

Piagetian theory suggests that until approximately the second year of life the child's reactions to the world are based primarily on immediate sensory experience. The effects of immediate physical reward and punishment dominate. Smiling and crying depend directly on the experience of pleasure or pain. This stage of cognitive development is termed the *sensorimotor stage.* Sometime during the second year of life the child begins to represent the external world through internal symbols or thoughts. Stimuli are grouped together into concepts (see Chapter 2). This stage is termed the *preoperational stage.* From about seven years until approximately the age of twelve, the ability to carry out symbolic operations develops. The child begins to think about the incoming sensory data. Children in this stage, for example, can spend their allowance many times over in their imagination before actually buying something. This is termed the stage of *concrete operations.* After the age of twelve or so, the child's characteristic style of thinking again undergoes change. The child begins to manipulate the concepts he or she has developed: increasingly more reliance is placed on the formation and testing of abstract propositions. At this point the child might be able to contrast democratic versus autocratic ideas of government or perhaps solve complex mathematical equations. Piaget considers thinking at this stage of *formal operations* to be quite advanced. Table 6-2 presents an outline of the stages of cognitive development.

In his book *The Moral Judgment of the Child* (1965) Piaget theorizes extensively on the connections between a child's general

TABLE 6-2 **Piaget's stages of cognitive development**

This is a general description of the sequence of stages that Piaget believes characterizes children's intellectual growth. Note that the ages are approximate. Different children progress through the stages at different rates.

Stage	Approximate age	Description
Sensorimotor	Birth–2 years	Infant moves about, observes things, and learns that self is different from environment and that objects exist even if out of sight. Concepts of time, space, and cause and effect are grasped.
Preoperational	2–7 years	Child can represent things mentally as images and as words and is able to copy, talk, and take perspective from his or her own.
Concrete operational	7–12 years	Child becomes capable of logical thought, can classify objects and manipulate them mentally (for example, add, subtract, reverse), and has greater understanding of space, time, and causality.
Formal operational	12 years and up	Child can think in abstract terms, perform scientific experiments, construct a belief system, and think about himself or herself.

Source: Based on Piaget and Inhelder, 1969

style of thinking and his or her notions of right and wrong. In particular, argues Piaget, the very young child, who simply attends to incoming stimuli, will use concrete or observable standards of right or wrong. In contrast, older children, who are capable of thinking more abstractly, will tend to rely on more general principles. For example, they may use standards involving the concept of intention, and they are able to forgive bad actions if they were not intended.

Piaget explored these ideas by telling children stories that were similar to the following two and then asking the children questions.

1. John was in his room when his mother called him to dinner. John went downstairs and opened the door to the dining room. But behind the door was a chair, and on the chair was a tray with fifteen cups on it. John did not know that the cups were behind the door. He opened the door, the door hit the tray, bang went the fifteen cups, and they all got broken.

2. One day when Henry's mother was out, Henry tried to get some cookies out of the cupboard. He climbed up on a chair, but the cookie jar was still too high, and he couldn't reach it. But while he was trying to get the cookie jar, he knocked over a cup. The cup fell down and broke.

After Piaget judged that the child could understand the stories, he asked which boy is the naughtier and why. Although most adults probably would answer that Henry is the greater culprit, an interesting diversity of opinion was found on this issue. Children who are in the concrete operational stage of development judge that John is naughtier than Henry. After all, John broke fifteen cups in comparison with Henry's one. The fact that John's intentions are noble and Henry's are not matters little to the younger children. They are concerned primarily with the concrete issue of how much damage has occurred. Quantity is everything. Among children in the stage of formal operations, however, Henry's intentions are considered more important. The older children are able to make judgments based on their conception of inner and unseen motives. More careful research indicates that very young children do have a concept of intention (Karnoil, 1978), but as Piaget maintained, the concept tends to play a more central role in thinking as the child grows older (Costanzo et al., 1973; Flapan, 1968).

You can see that Piaget's theory has important implications for understanding moral decision-making. Children who are concerned primarily with immediate reward and punishment are likely to have different standards of right and wrong than are those who are concerned with such abstract qualities as intention or motivation.

Fairness, Trust, and Seeing the World as Others See It

Piaget's ideas have stimulated a wide range of studies of children's moral thinking. Many investigators feel that the concept of intention is only one aspect of moral thinking that changes as the child grows older. Concepts of fairness and lying also may change with time. Fairness, for example, is a highly abstract concept that people use when judging whether events are consistent with rules. A child in the sensorimotor or preoperational stage of thought should have little capability for thinking in terms of what is fair or just. To demonstrate, four- to eight-year-olds were asked what they would consider to be a fair division of candy, money, or toys among several children (Damon, 1977). Younger children saw little difference between what they wanted and what was fair. Often they simply failed to comprehend or answer the question. With increasing age, children began to consider equality as a criterion for distributing the goodies. By the age of eight they had started to think beyond equality and were considering differences in various children's needs.

Similar patterns of development have been discovered in children's understanding of trust. Again, the concept of trust is not like the concept of a flower or the rain. Trust is not visible; it develops from people's mutual understanding. In one illustrative study, children were presented in story form with various dilemmas involving promises (Selman, 1976). For example, in one story the father of a girl named Holly is worried that Holly might get hurt climbing trees. Holly loves to climb trees but promises she will not climb them anymore. Later, however, a friend's kitten is found stuck in the high branches of a tree. Holly is the only child who can climb well enough to rescue the kitten. What should she do? Six-year-old children tend to solve the dilemma hedonistically. Holly should do what she wants as long as she can avoid trouble. Older children experience a real conflict. Their sympathy with the kitten is at odds with their sense that rescuing the kitten may endanger the father's trust. Older children often resolve the dilemma by thinking of ways in which Holly can explain her actions to her father so that he will see her point of view.

As argued by developmentalist John Flavell and others (1968), concepts such as fairness, justice, and trust demand not only that the individual conceptualize the unseen, but also that he or she take *the perspective of another*. That is, the individual must place himself or herself mentally in the position of another person. This kind of advanced cognitive activity is critical to a vast range of

moral thinking. Mercy, forgiveness, and sympathy rely on such capacities. To appreciate someone's pain, personal needs, and reasons for acting in ways that would otherwise be annoying, an individual must be able to see the world from the other's point of view.

Do such skills change as the child moves from the stage of sensorimotor activity to the stage of formal operations? Very young children do seem to have limited capacities for taking the perspective of others (Huttenlocher and Presson, 1973; Shantz and Watson, 1971), but these capacities improve substantially as the children grow older (Nahir and Yussen, 1977; Rubin and Schneider, 1973; Shantz, 1975). In one clever demonstration of changes in perspective taking, children of various ages were asked to explain the rules of a game to a person who either was blindfolded or could see (Flavell et al., 1968). The game required that a player match the colors on a cube with colors on a playing board. Younger children generally had a more difficult time

explaining the game. More relevant, however, was the great difficulty they encountered in taking account of the blindfolded listener's lack of vision. They would talk about the colors as if the listener could see, and sometimes they gestured toward the cube or the squares as if the listener could follow the gestures. Older children were far more successful in taking the perspective of the listener who could not see. By mid-high-school-age the subjects were able to give equally clear instructions to blindfolded and sighted listeners.

The Kohlberg Variations: Toward Natural Morality

We see that children experience developmental changes in the quality of their thinking and that these cognitive changes are closely connected to the ability to make moral decisions. For Harvard education specialist Lawrence Kohlberg such developmental changes pose a special challenge.

Kohlberg (1968) reasons that if cognitive development in human beings has a natural and normal developmental course, then moral reasoning also may demonstrate a normal pattern of development. And if moral reasoning shows a standard, or universal, form of development with increasing maturity, then the mature form of moral thinking can be considered to be *better or more desirable* than the earlier forms of moral thought (Kohlberg, 1969).

At this point you may begin to sense the immense social implications of research on cognitive development. For example, if people everywhere move in the same direction in their moral thinking, the possibility of a community of all people begins to seem reasonable. Perhaps underneath superficial differences there are universal similarities that may bind human beings together. A world of individuals who think alike ought to be able to set aside differences and form universal codes of right and wrong. World law should be an inevitable outcome of thoughtful negotiation, and reduction of tension among competing religious groups should be a real possibility. Finally, if moral systems can be judged in terms of their maturity, then perhaps objective standards of good can be developed for society, if not for the world. Kohlberg's viewpoint offers a possible answer to the moral relativists who argue that morality is largely a matter of personal taste.

In his research, Kohlberg first set for himself the task of describing precisely the development of moral thought. Piaget was interested in the more general development of thinking; his concern with moral thinking was only one small stream fed by his larger concern. Kohlberg's goal was to describe systematically the changes in children's moral thinking that occur with development. To explore these changes Kohlberg presented his subjects with various moral dilemmas in story form. The Heinz story is the most famous. It concerns a poor man, Heinz, whose wife is sick with an incurable disease. A druggist in the town has invented a new medicine but will not give it to Heinz free of charge. The medicine is extremely expensive. Heinz borrows some money and offers to pay the rest later, but the druggist refuses. Heinz breaks into the store and steals the drug. Should Heinz have done that? Why or why not?

How would you answer these questions? Try to match your answer as closely as possible to the following possible solutions:

1. He should not have done it; he is bound to be caught and will probably wind up in jail.

2. He should have stolen the medicine. If his wife lives she will do many more good things for him because of it. He will be a happier man.

3. He was right to help his wife because that is a kind thing to do; his wife and his friends would think more highly of him for doing it.

4. The man should obey the law even if it causes a personal hardship. The law is the law.

5. He was right to do it because the druggist was unjust in preventing him from taking care of his wife. He was not obliged to obey an unfair rule.

6. The life of his wife is more important than the right of the druggist to his property. He should have stolen the drug.

As it happens, each of these statements is an example of a stage of moral development in Kohlberg's theory of the growth in moral thought. These stages may be outlined as follows:

LEVEL ONE: PRECONVENTIONAL MORALITY
As you would expect since you know about Piaget's influence on Kohlberg's thinking,

children at the earliest level are primarily concerned with concrete, observable events. Rules are followed because of fear of punishment or expectation of reward. This level has two stages:

STAGE ONE: PUNISHMENT AND OBEDIENCE ORIENTATION

Initially the child is most concerned about getting caught and being punished. Thus young children don't consider good and bad as abstract ideas, but believe that they should do whatever they can get away with. The first response to the moral dilemma posed above is a good example of this kind of thinking. The drug should not have been stolen because Heinz might go to jail as a result.

STAGE TWO: HEDONISTIC ORIENTATION

The concern with the concrete consequences of a given action also may center on rewards. Particularly, the individual may judge the right or wrong of a given action in terms of what may be gained from it. The second of the above responses is illustrative. The medicine should have been stolen, it is reasoned, because Heinz may hope to gain future rewards from his wife.

Should I or shouldn't I? The electric outlet is forbidden. The child finds it enticing and will probably touch it if her caretaker is out of sight. At this first (preconventional) level of moral development, rules are followed out of fear of punishment or promise of reward.

LEVEL TWO: CONVENTIONAL MORALITY

As the child grows older and becomes increasingly able to conceptualize his or her actions, matters of immediate consequence become less important. Instead, the individual begins to attend to social rules and expectations supported by social convention. This level has two stages:

STAGE THREE: GOOD-BOY/NICE-GIRL ORIENTATION

During this stage the individual is particularly concerned with the approval of others. Thus he or she may display great conformity to what appear to be the normal standards of morality or good conduct. In the example above, the explanation that Heinz should help because others would think more highly of him illustrates this line of reasoning.

STAGE FOUR: LAW-AND-ORDER ORIENTATION

At this stage the individual is most concerned with the established rules or laws of the society. To be moral is to do one's duty, to show respect for authority, or to uphold the law except when it conflicts with clear social duty. To argue that the drug should not be stolen because "the law is the law" is to adopt this orientation.

LEVEL THREE: POSTCONVENTIONAL, OR PRINCIPLED, MORALITY

With increased experience the individual becomes able to separate himself or herself from the particular consequences of a given act and from the concrete reactions of others. Increasing reliance is placed, instead, on one's conceptual or symbolic understanding of morality. When social rules conflict with personal principles, the principles tend to win out. This level also has two stages:

STAGE FIVE: SOCIAL-CONTRACT, OR LEGALISTIC, ORIENTATION

An individual reaching this stage begins to think in terms of what kinds of rules, laws, or social obligations will lead to the general welfare of society. Particular attention may be paid to individual rights and how these are reflected in the existing standards of society. While the individual at stage four might not question the existing laws of the land, the person at stage five might think about how to improve the system. The response to the Heinz dilemma that argues for theft because a person is not obliged to obey "an unfair rule" is an example of stage-five thinking.

STAGE SIX: ORIENTATION OF UNIVERSAL ETHICAL PRINCIPLES

Kohlberg considers thinking at this stage to be the most advanced. The individual is not concerned with existing laws and rules, but with generating for himself or herself a set of principles of right and wrong. These principles might be very abstract ones, covering many cases, and might even aspire to be universal. The individual has a sense of personal commitment to the principles. Considering the possibility that human life is more important than personal property, as in the last of the responses to the Heinz dilemma, would exemplify this kind of thinking.

A variety of research studies illustrate the strength of Kohlberg's ideas. First, many investigators have been able to show a progression in children's moral-reasoning abilities from early childhood to late adolescence (Kohlberg and Kramer, 1969; Kuhn et al., 1977; Rest et al., 1974). These changes in the character of moral thought are reflected in the individual's developing ideas about the need for law and order, rules, and justice (Tapp and Kohlberg, 1971). In one study, for example, the investigator looked at the relationship between children's stages of moral development and their understanding of thinking at more advanced stages (Turiel, 1966). The investigator reasoned that if development takes place in a stagelike fashion, children at any given stage should be more influenced by solutions close to their actual stage than solutions that are far more advanced. Thus, a stage-one child who is simply trying to avoid being punished should have an easier time comprehending and discussing those arguments that support morality for social approval's sake (stage three) rather than those that support the ideal of fairness (stage five). To demonstrate this position, children at various stages of moral development were exposed to arguments that were one or two stages removed from the stage at which they were when they entered the experiment. Tests were given to measure their ability to understand arguments at both stages. The results indicated that children show better understanding of arguments that are one level, as opposed to two levels, in advance of the stage at which they were when they entered the experiment.

Differences in moral thought also have been related to behavior under a variety of social conditions. Kohlberg (1969) reports, for example, that people who have attained a high level on the scale are less likely than those who are lower to obey an experimenter who orders them to deliver intense shocks to another person. Similarly, stage-three children (those seeking social approval in their moral choice) are more likely than are children at lower stages to give way to group pressure (Saltzstein, Diamond, and Belenky, 1972), and persons at stages five and six are less likely to cheat than are those at stages three or four (Grim, Kohlberg, and White, 1968). Stage of moral development also is correlated with the way in which rewards are distributed among a group of co-workers (Gunzberger, Wegner, and Anooshin, 1977). Adolescents at stage three generally fail to take account of the helpful intentions of group members in giving out rewards, whereas those at stages five and six reward individuals who want to help but cannot.

Significant links have been found between moral stages and the political ideology of students at eight major universities (Fishkin, Keniston, and MacKinnan, 1973). Students at the conventional level were found to be politically conservative. In contrast, those at the preconventional level tended to favor radical political action, if not violence. Students at the postconventional levels might be classified as political liberals—they rejected conservatism but did not embrace radical activity. Interestingly, these various orientations also are found among the faculty members. Natural science faculty members employ far more law-and-order reasoning than do those in the social sciences and the humanities (Fontana and Noel, 1973). The natural scientists are joined by university administrators in this law-and-order orientation.

Other investigators have carried their studies across cultural boundaries to preliterate societies in Africa and Asia, looking for universal similarities in the ethics of mature individuals (Kohlberg and Turiel, 1971; White, Bushnell, and Regnemer, 1978). These studies suggest that people in different cultures do undergo similar changes in the development of moral thought. However, cultures differ in the level of moral maturity achieved. Adults in preliterate cultures tend to prefer solutions that fall at the preconventional and early conventional stages of development. In the Bahamas, for example, researchers had difficulty locating adults who had achieved more than stage-three moral reasoning (White, 1975). In contrast, adults in more technically advanced cultures tend to prefer solutions at more "morally advanced" stages. In dealing with such results, Kohlberg has argued that preliterate peoples do not emphasize abstract thought because they have little written language. As a result, individuals in these societies are stabilized at early stages of moral development. The more technologically advanced societies of the Western world, however, utilize a written language, employ a great deal of symbolic thinking, and are exposed to rapid change. Thus, people in

Dialectic Thinking: A Step beyond Moral Principles?

Kohlberg argues that young children make moral decisions on the basis of what will hurt and what will give immediate pleasure. As an individual's cognitive capacities mature, Kohlberg believes, he or she begins to think in terms of principles of right and wrong. At the most advanced moral stage, people try to develop their own abstract principles of right and wrong.

Although Kohlberg's argument has many supporters, other theorists have not been content to view abstract principles as the most mature, or advanced, form of thought. Critics suggest that abstract principles are best adapted to a world that is stable and unchanging. For example, abstract formulations about the state of the physical world are possible. One can state with assurance that pineapples grow only where the climate is hot and moist. This principle reflects stable fact and can be applied successfully throughout the world and across history. In the case of human action, however, change is frequent. People may decide at one time that they like to vacation in hot, moist climates, and at another time they may prefer cold, dry regions. While people continue to change, general principles about people's actions remain dangerously static. This problem applies to the use of abstract principles of morality: fixed moral principles also do not take account of continuously changing social conditions.

In light of the shortcomings of abstract principles, many social psychologists have come to believe that *dialectic thinking* is equipped to deal with change in a way that principled thinking is not (Altman and Gauvain, in press; Buss, 1979; Cvetkovich, 1977; Gadlin, 1978; Rappoport, 1975; Ziller, 1977). In the process of dialectic thinking, an individual considers conflicting forces and the change that is produced by the conflict. The dialectic thinker assumes that conflicting forces are at work at any moment. The result of the conflict is continuous change. Because people always face conflicting forces, both internal and environmental, their behavior changes over time.

How would a person who uses abstract principles to solve a moral problem differ from someone who uses dialectic thinking? Consider the case of the young woman who finds herself pregnant and considers having an abortion. The woman could adopt a clear moral principle, such as "Abortion is bad because it means taking a life. I do not believe in taking lives, and thus I will not have an abortion." For the dialectic thinker, however, this moral principle would not be the end point of moral reasoning. Instead it would be the beginning. The dialectic thinker would try to take account of opposing facts or ideas. Thus the woman might consider the possibility that having a child would prevent her from making a major career investment and that a career is important not only for a personal sense of fulfillment, but also as a contribution to society. With these opposing ideas in mind, the woman might then begin to search for a synthesis. She might decide to look for a career that would not be threatened by the presence of the child. She might think about changing society's institutions so that women are allowed to be professionals and mothers at the same time.

To explore the possibility that dialectic thinking is more advanced than principled, or formal, reasoning, Michael Basseches (in press) interviewed three groups of individuals at different stages of adolescence and adulthood: freshmen at a liberal arts college, seniors at the same college, and faculty at the college. The subjects were asked about the nature of the educational process at the college and what might be done to improve it. Basseches identified twenty-four aspects of dialectic thought, and his major question was how many of these aspects would be expressed by each group. For example, would respondents show a recognition of change, or would they talk about opposing forces—both indicators of dialectic thinking? As you can see in the accompanying figure, the average number of elements of dialectic thinking increased with age and education. Freshmen used only five of the elements of dialectic thought that were identified by Basseches. This figure jumps to almost nine among the seniors and thirteen in the faculty group. These data suggest that the use of the components of dialectic thinking increases with cognitive maturity.

We see, then, that many theorists are not content with the view that formal, or principled, thought is the most mature form. As they argue, dialectic thought may be a superior method of solving problems of human activity and problems of moral significance.

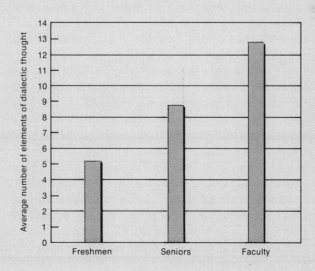

Western society are capable of reaching more mature levels of moral development.

Universal Ethics, or Ethical Imperialism?

Kohlberg's variations on the Piagetian theme have made an important contribution to psychologists' understanding of the development of moral thought. Kohlberg's work also has aroused considerable criticism. One line of opposition has originated in the camp of the social learning theorists. They question the assumption of a moral ethic that is independent of the social environment. From the social learning point of view, once a child has acquired the ability necessary to communicate, he or she can be taught virtually any system of right and wrong. The developmental progression is not predetermined. The social environment can shift the person's moral dispositions in any direction.

In an attempt to demonstrate this argument, children between the ages of five and eleven first were asked to solve a series of moral dilemmas; this was done to tap their preferred styles of moral thought (Bandura and McDonald, 1963). Later certain children heard an adult model give her answers to similar dilemmas. For one group the model always chose solutions that emphasized *objective* features of the situation. An objective criterion, for example, would be used if a child is judged to be naughtier when accidently breaking fifteen cups as opposed to breaking three. According to Piaget and Kohlberg, such responses should be preferred by younger children, who think concretely. Other children were exposed to a model who consistently chose *subjective* answers to the problems, answers that emphasized intentions or motives. According to cognitive developmental theory, such answers should be preferred by older children, who think more abstractly. As the children listened to the model's responses, they expressed their preferences. A third measure of the children's

moral preferences was taken later in another room with neither the experimenter nor the model being present. This final test was used to tap each child's capacity to use the model's choices in her absence.

The results of this experiment are featured in Figure 6-1. As you can see, when children were exposed to the objective model they began to shift their preferences in the direction of her solutions—an effect that continued into the post-test phase. Similarly, if the model preferred subjective solutions, the children began to express subjective preferences. These preferences also continued into the third testing period. Children who were in a control group, which was exposed to no models at all, remained relatively unchanged in their preferences. The slight changes that did occur can be attributed to the behavior of the experimenter, who expressed approval for both the model's and the children's responses, which were objective in the one condition and subjective in the other. In short, the children's level of moral thought came to match that of the adult model.

Although compelling, these results do not conclusively rule out cognitive theories stressing an ordered sequence of moral thought. The children in Bandura and McDonald's experiment simply may have been adopting superficial behavior patterns that did not reflect changes in basic dispositions. They may have mimicked well, but with little understanding of or commitment to what they said. However, this kind of demonstration has succeeded in provoking widespread doubt about the adequacy of Kohlberg's ideas.

Inspired by the debate, many other investigators have challenged Kohlberg's notion of an inflexible upward progression in the development of moral thought. For example, attempts to accelerate progress through the sequence by special education or training generally do not show lasting effects (Keasey, 1973). People may show the advances that are stressed by Kohlberg, but soon they will slip

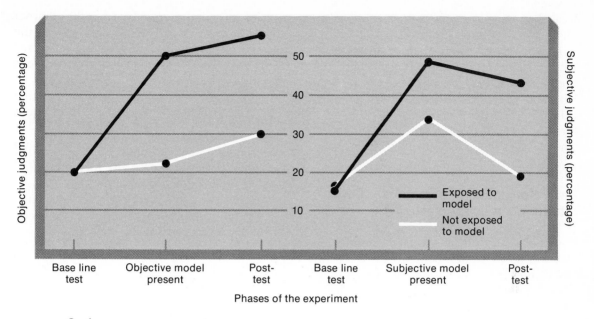

FIGURE 6-1 **The influence of models on moral decision**

Children exposed to a model who preferred objective solutions to moral dilemmas demonstrated a preference for objective solutions; those exposed to a model who preferred subjective solutions chose subjective solutions. Both kinds of preferences were retained in the post-test period. (Adapted from Bandura and McDonald, 1963)

back to earlier levels in their thinking (Holstein, 1976; O'Connor, 1971)—a phenomenon that according to the Kohlberg formulation should not take place. Other researchers have found that five-year-olds are capable of using many different levels of thought in solving moral dilemmas (Gottlieb, Taylor, and Ruderman, 1977). Adolescents also can shift developmental levels at will, sometimes relying on abstract principles and other times relying on social agreement (Haan, 1978). Finally, people shift their levels of moral thinking as the characters in the moral dilemmas are changed—level of thought seems to depend on the persons being thought about (Levine, 1976). Kohlberg may be correct in suggesting that moral thought follows a fairly predictable developmental course as a child grows older, but the pattern of change probably is

not as rigid or predetermined as he proposed. Children may learn new ways of thinking, but the old ways are not necessarily discarded.

Finally, Kohlberg's assumption of a universal ethic has been questioned on value grounds (Sampson, 1977; Sullivan, 1977). It is dangerous business to posit a hierarchy of moral dispositions when that hierarchy allows the highly educated adult male a disproportionate likelihood of being on top. In effect, Kohlberg's theory places the men of Western society in a position of moral superiority. By implication, others are placed in inferior positions—a point of view that may have unfortunate consequences. Consider, for example, some research on women's decisions about abortion (Gilligan, 1979, 1980). The researcher concludes that women often base their decisions to have an abortion not on abstract principles, but rather on feelings of responsibility toward the real people about whom they care. Kohlberg views such thinking as being less advanced (stage three) (Kohlberg and Kramer, 1979). Gilligan challenges this view, arguing that Kohlberg's theory caters to male tastes for abstract principles. These issues demand continued debate.

Early Socialization and the Situationism Controversy

In this chapter thus far we have explored two views of how children come to adopt various moral rules in their relationships with others. We must now confront a question that is critical for theorists, parents, and others interested in moral action. Do the lessons of early socialization persist and guide the individual's conduct through adulthood? Many theorists believe that early experience stamps in various dispositions—moral and otherwise. Most parents hope that once a child is launched from the home, the "twig will be bent" for life. Indeed, one good reason that many women give up professional life is to ensure that their children will be well reared and thus will lead successful adult lives.

The assumption that early experience guides adult life is open to question. As we saw in previous chapters, social perception, attraction, prejudice, and other attitudes change frequently. People often shift dramatically in their perceptions and feelings about others and themselves and in their attitudes about major issues. Why should moral rule-following be any different? To deal with this issue, let us first examine several kinds of evidence that often are used to support the assumption that early socialization stamps in various dispositions. Then we will consider the opposite possibility—that people are creatures of the situations in which they find themselves. By looking at the extremes we

may be able to draw more reasonable conclusions about the effects of socialization.

The Case Study: Psychiatric Evidence

Perhaps the largest reservoir of evidence stressing the importance of early socialization comes from the annals of psychiatry and psychoanalysis. Following Freud's path, the typical therapist spends hundreds of hours with the adult patient, attempting to unravel the reasons underlying his or her distress. Almost invariably the roots of the adult disturbance are located in experiences of the early years. Yet such evidence must be viewed with caution. Life histories are rich and complex. Everyone has experienced hard emotional knocks at some point in childhood, along with many highly satisfying experiences. These positive and negative experiences can be used to explain virtually any failure in adult life, as well as any success. However, the critical test of whether an early experience has long-term effects is in its usefulness in prediction. Can adult behavior be predicted on the basis of the early life-history material? Do the facts enable one to tell whether a child is likely to grow up to be a criminal, a minister, a psychotic, or an average person? If accurate predictions are not possible, then the assumption that early socialization has a strong effect on adult character is called into question.

Perhaps you would like to try your hand at predicting from some actual case material. Consider the following account given by a man of some note:

> My father [was] a conscientious employee of the [government], my mother was occupied with the household, and above all was devoted to us children with loving care. . . . How it happened, I cannot now say, but one day it was clear to me that I would be a painter, an artist. . . . The only curious thing was that, as I grew older, I took an increasing interest in architecture. . . . Along with music, I thought architecture the queen of the arts. . . .

Surely this sounds like a reasonable, if not promising, boyhood. Yet this budding young lover of the arts later became perhaps the most despised human being of the century, Adolf Hitler (1943, p. 4). Alongside this account, we must consider a few details from the life of Charles Watson:

> Watson was a big, handsome boy who grew up in a small Texas town. He starred in football, basketball, and track, and managed, at the

What is the effect of early socialization? Charles "Tex" Watson, murderer and key member of the Manson cult, is shown in a chapel at the California state prison where his prison job includes assisting the pastor. Watson's socialization seems contradicted by his criminal activity, while his pastorship seems consistent with his early experiences. Can we be certain that early socialization has long-term effects?

same time, to achieve high grades in school. He attended a Methodist church near his father's small grocery store and gas station. In his junior year in high school he was voted outstanding member of his class.

Only a few years after he left home to attend college, Watson became a central member of the Charles Manson cult. He and his friends slaughtered almost a dozen persons without provocation. On the chest of one victim, Watson carved his initials.

Let us consider another case. In this autobiography we find:

> With a friend, I stole money to buy cigarettes. . . . I recollect having been put to school. It was with some difficulty that I got through the multiplication tables. The incident [of encouraging students to cheat on a standardized exam] did not in the least diminish my respect for my teacher. I was, by nature, blind to the faults of elders. . . .

Most parents would wince at the thought of having such a son. Most people would never suspect that this boy of little promise grew up to be India's greatest leader, Mahatma Ghandi (quoted in Erikson, 1969, p. 117).

These various cases do not *prove* anything; after all, we preselected them. But the many case studies that are used to support the importance of early socialization don't prove anything either. Such cases also are preselected.

Longitudinal Research: Predicting Adult Behavior from Childhood Observations

Far more reliable information on the long-term effects of early socialization can be obtained through longitudinal research. In this case the investigator follows the development of individuals from an early age into adulthood, making possible an examination of the relationship between each individual's childhood and adult behaviors. Is the six-year-old bully aggressive at the age of twenty-six?

**BOX
6-3**

*Informal
Rules and
the Morality
of
Subordination*

In Chapter 1 we presented three major orientations to the understanding of social life: the behaviorist, the cognitive, and the rule-role. In this chapter we consider moral development from the behaviorist and the cognitive points of view. Although rule-role theorists offer a less-developed account of moral behavior, the relevance of the rule-role orientation was made clear as early as 1934, when theorist George Herbert Mead pointed out that "Manners in their best sense . . . cannot be distinguished from morals, and are nothing but the expression of the courtesy of an individual toward people about him" (p. 263). In extending this view, Robert Hogan (1973, 1975) argues that moral behavior is essentially a matter of carrying out the rules that apply in various social situations. From this standpoint, one does not have to be reinforced to learn morality. One can learn rules through instruction or observation, just as rules are learned in games or athletics.

One of the most interesting implications of the rule-role perspective for understanding morality is suggested by the quote from Mead. Social manners, Mead argues, are patterns of moral action. Thus morality is not an occasional matter, and moral judgment need not be reserved for circumstances in which crime is considered or humanitarian dilemmas are faced. Moral choices are being made at every moment, as the individual decides whether or not to comply with informal social rules (see Chapters 2 and 3). As Erving Goffman (1959) points out, each individual's social life is a kind of *moral career*—that is, the individual's behavior is judged constantly by others as being proper or improper. Judgments about a person's moral career may be based on minute details of conduct, including what a person wears, how he or she speaks, and what kind of work he or she chooses to do.

Goffman believes that in contemporary society advertising plays a major role as moral adviser. Ads serve a kind of priestly function in small

Does the shy nursery school child avoid social gatherings at the age of thirty-six? Is the child who shares candy with first-grade classmates the same adult who sets aside money for charity? The most exhaustive study of this kind followed a sample of some eighty men and women from early infancy to adulthood, some thirty years later (Kagan and Moss, 1962). At various intervals during the observation period, over one hundred objective assessments of such personal characteristics as aggressiveness, passivity, dependency,

achievement motivation, and sexual interest were made. Correlations then were performed to assess the degree of relationship between scores during the early period and scores achieved during adulthood. The investigators were interested in finding out whether the personality dispositions of childhood predict adult dispositions. Additional correlations were computed between adult scores and scores obtained when the subjects were between three and six years of age and between six and ten years of age. Thus characteristics

matters of daily life (Goffman, 1979). People look to advertising to set standards for proper buying. Ads tell people what to wear, what automobiles to drive, what to drink on various occasions, and so forth. In addition, Goffman maintains, ads not only offer messages about various products or services, but they also subtly tell people how a moral person should behave. Goffman is particularly concerned with the message about power that is transmitted by advertising: who should be treated with respect and who should be considered a subordinate. Goffman demonstrates that ads are consistent in teaching that the man should have senior status in male-female relationships.

Advertisements frequently show men in directing roles. The man is teaching the woman to play tennis or ride a horse, or he is giving her medical advice or explaining a product. While such ads are numerous and the sexist message is clear, other ads are more subtle. A recent ad for women's shoes, for example, contains a hidden message about male direction and control. A male arm holds a starting pistol; the woman is the one who has to run—in high-heeled shoes. The man stands over her; she is bent low with her buttocks raised. If the moral message here is not female subordination, try to imagine this advertisement with roles reversed.

Subordination signals also are supplied in the bodily postures or gestures adopted by the people in the ads. Men frequently stand in front of groups. Women often are depicted in a lounging position, presumably waiting for the man to free himself for leisure activities. Or the posture of the woman may express dependency, while the man's posture seems to be more autonomous.

We see, then, that the informal rules of society can have moral significance. Advertising may often teach people both rules and roles, and in contemporary society it may teach women to adopt a position that is subordinate to the man's position.

at different stages of development could be related to adult traits.

Although Kagan and Moss report that a number of measures that were taken during the early periods successfully predict adult behavior, a close look at the analysis raises serious questions (Gergen, 1977). First, in order to demonstrate continuity of traits over the thirty-year period, the investigators had to select from a great mass of data just those correlations that support this conclusion (see Chapter 1 for a discussion of correlation). In other words, many of the correlations showed no relationship between the characteristics of childhood and those of adulthood, and these negative findings had to be discarded in order for the investigators to make their case. Close analysis indicates that correlations between measures that were taken between the years of three and six and during adulthood are *all within chance expectancy*. Second, although there are significant correlations between measures taken in late childhood and in adulthood, the magnitude of these correlations is very low. Thus, even when childhood dispositions are found to be related to the same dispositions in adulthood, *the strength of the relationship is weak.* Longitudinal research thus seems to provide only trivial support for the assumption that early socialization affects adult behavior. Neither case study nor longitudinal research evidence provides support for the notion that what happens during childhood necessarily has lasting effects.

Transsituational Consistency: The Search for Character

Another way of asking about the effects of early learning on adult behavior is in terms of consistency in behavior across situations. Rather than comparing behavior during childhood with behavior during adulthood, we can question whether people who demonstrate certain characteristics in one situation behave in similar fashion in other situations.

For example, are men who are honest in their business dealings also honest with their wives and children, with their neighbors, and with the Internal Revenue Service? Finding a high degree of consistency in behavior across situations would suggest that adults do possess stable clusters of personality traits that are recognizable across diverse circumstances.

The classic study on the question of a stable disposition toward being moral, or honest, was carried out in 1928 by Hartshorne and May. Some six thousand children were given a variety of tests, all of which allowed the children the opportunity to cheat. Cheating could be detected by the investigators without a child knowing he or she had been caught. Among the assessments were (1) a *copying test,* in which children were allowed to score their own tests, with a subsequent check being made to ascertain how many answers had been changed; (2) a *speed test,* in which cheating was measured by the differ-

TABLE 6-3 **Honesty may depend on opportunity**

These coefficients of correlation suggest that little correspondence exists between behaviors on each pair of tasks. Note, for example, that there is absolutely no relationship between the children's tendency to lie and their tendency to cheat on an athletic task.

	Correlations between measures of cheating				
	Copying	*Speed*	*Peeping*	*Faking*	*Athletic*
Copying	—				
Speed	0.29	—			
Peeping	0.28	0.22	—		
Faking	0.29	0.26	0.20	—	
Athletic	0.20	0.19	0.06	0.18	—
Lying	0.31	0.25	0.16	0.21	0.00

Source: Adapted from Hartshorne and May, 1928

ence between practice-test scores and a score obtained when cheating was possible; (3) a *peeping test*, in which deception was measured in terms of the closeness of the child's solution to the one that could be reached only through cheating; (4) a *lying test*, in which the score was based on the difference between parents' reports of their child's behavior and the child's report; and (5) an *athletic test*, in which deceit was assessed in terms of the difference between a score kept by the child and one kept by the teacher.

The correlations among the various scores are presented in Table 6-3. As you will recall from Chapter 1, the higher the correlation the stronger the association between performance on the two measures. There clearly is little relationship between the various measures of the children's honesty on the various tests. Resistance to the temptation to cheat does not seem to be a stable characteristic of this population. No correlation exceeds 0.31, and the average correlation is only 0.21 (maximum correlation is 1.00). Thus, knowing an individual's score on one measure gives practically no information about whether he or she might cheat in another situation. Inconsistency across situations seems to be the norm.

Similar findings have emerged in other studies of morality (Kurdek, 1978), as well as in studies of punctuality (Dudycha, 1936) and sociability (Newcomb, 1929). In each case, predicting behavior across situations is difficult. This is not to say that *no* continuity across situations exists: a low degree of correlation often can be discerned (Burton, 1963; Koretzky, Kohn, and Jaeger, 1978; Nelson, Grinder, and Mutterer, 1969). However, as Walter Mischel (1968) has concluded in a lengthy review of relevant research, measures of any behavioral disposition seldom achieve a correlation of 0.30 with an action in any given situation. Thus, even though moral behavior may be found in one situation, it cannot reliably be expected in another situation.

Is Situationism the Answer?

Given the lack of powerful evidence to support the view that early socialization stamps in morality or any other behavioral disposition, we will turn our attention to the opposite possibility. Are people creatures of circumstances? Do they continuously adapt themselves to changing situations in such a way that new commitments, feelings, beliefs, and moral values arise as each new situation demands? The view that circumstances determine actions is termed *situationism* (Bowers, 1973). Although few social psychologists would subscribe to the situationist view in extreme form, situationism is central to the vast majority of experiments in social psychology. As we saw in our discussions of social perception, attraction, prejudice, and attitude change, people are influenced by situations. Experimental situations have powerful effects on people's thoughts, feelings, and actions. Yet most studies are specially designed to demonstrate the power of situational factors. The question of consistency across situations rarely is the focus of interest.

Recently researchers have begun to look more carefully at consistencies in people's personal styles and traits, or dispositions. Bem and Allen (1974) have argued, for example, that each person may have certain stable traits, or dispositions, and certain unstable ones. A person may consistently display one trait and inconsistently display another one. A person may be argumentative with everyone but may vary in self-revealingness from one situation to another. Another person may reveal himself or herself consistently but may vary in argumentativeness. Thus, in order to discover whether underlying dispositions exist, different traits for different people must be taken into account.

To illustrate their point, Bem and Allen asked college students to rate the variability of their *friendliness* from situation to situation. Some of the students indicated that the trait was very stable, and others said that it was highly variable. Bem and Allen's question was whether the students who characterized themselves as being generally friendly would actually display a great deal of consistency across situations and thus demonstrate that stable trait dispositions do exist. The students' self-ratings were correlated with impressions of their friendliness that were provided by their parents and one close friend. These correlations are presented in Table 6-4. You can see that for the students who believed that they were consistently friendly, a sizable degree of consistency exists between self-ratings and others' observations on the trait of general friendliness. In contrast, for students who said that they weren't very consistent, the correlations between the measures are much smaller. Thus these findings do suggest that each person may be highly consistent in displaying certain characteristics across situations, but inconsistent in other characteristics.

Further support for the view that people do possess stable traits comes from a study of students who kept daily records, or diaries, of their personal experiences for up to five weeks (Epstein, 1980). Special attention was paid to their ratings of the positive and negative experiences that they encountered each day. The students showed highly reliable trends in the way they rated their positive and negative feelings and actions. As the number of days on which they maintained diaries was increased, so was the consistency in their ratings. Other research indicates that self-ratings that are obtained during adolescence often show at least a moderate degree of consistency with self-ratings obtained when the same people reach their thirties (Block, 1977). And while adulthood is not necessarily a stable period (Runyon, 1980), researchers often find a high degree of stability in adult populations across time (Costa, McCrae, and Arenberg, 1980).

The Interactionist Solution

Let us try to fit into a coherent whole the seemingly conflicting evidence that we have discussed. First, there is no strong reason to believe that early socialization stamps in life-long habits—moral or otherwise. People seem

TABLE 6-4   **Consistency and inconsistency in behavior**

These findings suggest that people who think that they are consistent in their friendliness are probably right—other people who know them well agree with them. Similarly, people who do not see themselves as being consistently friendly are probably less so. Each person may be consistent in certain respects and inconsistent in other respects.

	Type of belief about self	
Pairs of reports correlated	*Consistently friendly*	*Inconsistently friendly*
Mother's and self	r = 0.61	r = 0.51
Father's and self	0.48	0.24
Peer's and self	0.62	0.56
Mother's and father's	0.75	0.28
Mother's and peer's	0.71	0.40
Father's and peer's	0.50	0.34

Source: Adapted from Bem and Allen, 1974

to be capable of changing at any point in their lives. If early dispositions persist, their persistence over time may be due to continued support from the social environment. And the existence of stable traits in adulthood does not necessarily mean that the traits were developed in childhood. For example, if a man joins the army, his life may change substantially. He may develop and sustain reliable patterns of behavior as long as he remains in the service. Yet when he returns to civilian life, many of these patterns will be dropped. People may display reliable traits or dispositions across time, but these traits may be acquired or abandoned at any point in the life cycle.

We see, then, that situations can alter or change people's dispositions, but at the same time people do bring certain traits or dispositions with them into various situations. Most social psychologists today agree that people's actions result from an *interaction* between personal dispositions and situational factors (Magnusson and Endler, 1977). Thus, for example, as a result of both early socialization and peer-group support, a person may have a personal disposition not to lie. However, when facing a situation in which a good friend is threatened and lying may protect him or her, the person's behavior ultimately will reflect the operation of both the disposition and the situational pressure.

SUMMARY

1 Morality may be viewed as behavior that is consistent with the rules that are established by a culture to ensure its continuation. The development of morality has long been an issue of concern to social philosophers and psychologists. Freud believed that morality develops in early childhood, when conscience is acquired through the child's interaction with significant caretakers.

2 The behaviorist approach focuses on moral behavior and emphasizes the shaping effects of positive and negative reinforcement on this behavior. From the behaviorist standpoint, reward can encourage moral action, and punishment can encourage resistance to temptation. Three factors may increase or reduce the effects of reward and punishment. First, the greater the magnitude of reinforcement, the more potent its capacity to shape moral behavior. However, too much praise or overly harsh punishment may be less effective than moderate amounts of reinforcement. Second, the scheduling of reinforcement also is important. Partial or inconsistent reinforcement may be more effective than continuous reinforcement in maintaining long-term moral habits. Third, the timing of reinforcement has an effect. Negative reinforcement that occurs just prior to a transgression may be more effective than reinforcement delivered after the transgression.

3 The social learning approach to moral development suggests that children can learn moral behavior by observing the actions of others and modeling themselves on this behavior. When a model is attractive and behaves in a consistent fashion, other people are likely to copy the

model's behavior. The effects of modeling may persist over time if the individual learns how to reinforce himself or herself psychologically. Children may learn self-reinforcement by observing others as they reward or punish themselves.

4   The cognitive approach to morality emphasizes the development of the individual's thought processes. People weigh the pros and cons of moral issues, it is argued, and their actions depend on their thinking. Piaget differentiated among four major stages of cognitive growth: the sensorimotor stage, in which the child is largely responding to direct pleasure or pain; the preoperational stage, in which objects can be represented with symbols and words; the stage of concrete operations, in which the child becomes capable of logical thought; and the stage of formal operations, in which the child thinks about the world in highly abstract ways.

5   Without the ability to think abstractly, the child cannot consider people's intentions in his or her moral judgments. As children grow and acquire the capacity to think abstractly, they also begin to use the concepts of fairness or trust, and in making moral decisions they gain the capacity to take the perspective of other people.

6   Based on Piaget's ideas, Kohlberg has outlined six stages of development in moral thinking, and he believes these to be universal. The stages range from the first stage, in which the child thinks only in terms of getting caught and being punished, to the most advanced stage, in which the individual seeks to generate universal ethical principles. Critics of Kohlberg argue that his system (1) disregards the influence of the social environment on children's moral development, (2) assumes a too-rigid and a predetermined pattern of growth, and (3) posits a hierarchy that places educated Western men at the top.

7   Many theorists believe that early socialization stamps in moral dispositions that may persist throughout a person's life. Neither case-study material nor longitudinal research supports this view. The situationist argues that people's conduct is determined primarily by the characteristics of the immediate situations in which people find themselves. However, this extreme view is not supported. Studies that take account of differences among people suggest that some stable individual dispositions do exist. The most widely accepted position in modern social psychology is the interactionist point of view, which assumes that people bring various dispositions with them into situations and that their behavior is the result of a combination of situational and personal factors.

SUGGESTED READINGS

Damon, W. (Ed.). *New directions for child development: Moral development.* San Francisco: Jossey-Bass, 1978.

Maccoby, E. E. *Social development: Psychological growth and the parent-child relationship.* New York: Harcourt Brace Jovanovich, 1980.

Magnusson, D., & Endler, N. S. (Eds.). *Personality at the crossroads: Current issues in interactional psychology.* Hillsdale, N.J.: Lawrence Erlbaum, 1977.

Mussen, P. H., & Eisenberg-Berg, N. *Roots of caring, sharing, and helping: The development of prosocial behavior in children.* San Francisco: W. H. Freeman, 1977.

Phillips, J. L. *The origins of the intellect: Piaget's theory.* San Francisco: W. H. Freeman, 1975.

7: POSITIVE SOCIAL ACTION

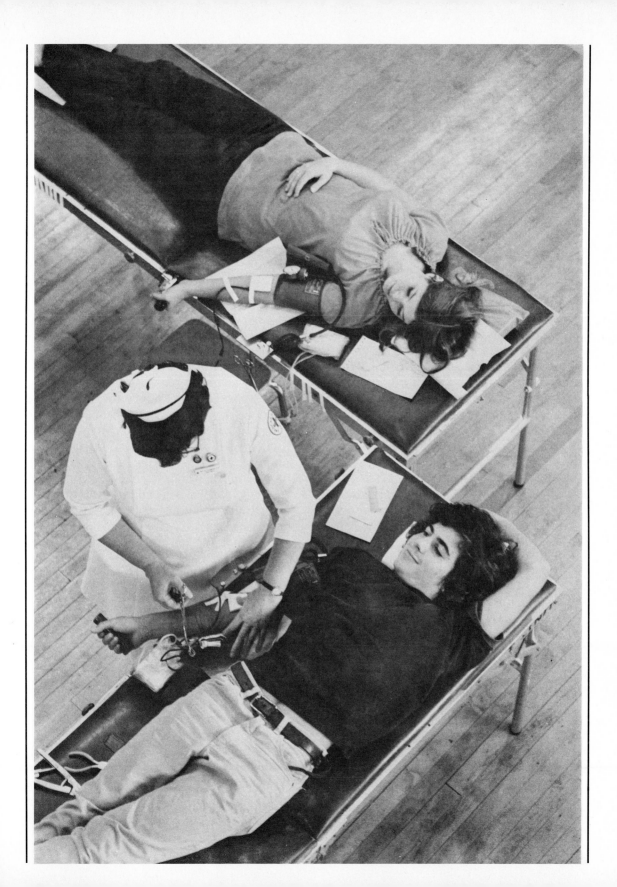

■ *A woman lawyer who was waiting for a train in an urban railway station was taken at gunpoint to the end of the platform, where she was badly beaten and raped. Not until twenty-four hours later was she discovered, by a group of people who were investigating a rape case that had occurred in the same place a year before. The woman was rushed to the hospital. She lived, but she suffered severe brain damage. Many people had seen the frightened woman being hustled through the station by a man of rough appearance. Not one bystander followed the pair, called the police, or made any attempt to inquire about what was happening. Several days later one bystander confessed that she had noticed the pair and had been upset by them. Her description of the rapist eventually led to his being captured. During the twenty-four hours that the battered victim lay on the platform, many people noticed her, but they too failed to inquire. Several railroad employees said that they simply thought she was a vagrant.*

The people in this situation were faced with an option to help someone in distress, and they did not choose to offer aid. This is a dramatic example of a situation that people face every day. An encounter with a beggar on the street, a request to give blood, or a call from a friend who is lonely or depressed—all these are situations in which someone can do something to benefit someone else. Such activity may be termed *positive social action* (Staub, 1978). Such acts as donating money or goods to charity, cooperating with others in carrying out a project, and doing favors for a person in need are typical examples of positive social action. Behavior of this kind may be contrasted with *antisocial action*, such behavior as aggression, harm, destruction, and selfishness (Bar-Tal, 1976). Some theorists use the term *prosocial behavior* in order to stress the contrast with antisocial behavior. Other theorists prefer to use the term *altruism*, to emphasize the element of self-sacrifice that exists in many positive social actions. Altruism is action that benefits other people and is carried out with no expectation of external reward. Whatever words are used and with whatever emphasis, however, positive social action is intriguing because such behavior seems morally admirable and also contributes to the survival of society (Campbell, 1978; Cohen, 1978). Most people admire the indi-vidual who makes sacrifices so that others may benefit, and most people would agree that society would be better off if everyone were less self-centered.

Many social psychologists are concerned with ways in which positive social action can be fostered in the culture—for example, how people's relations with one another can be improved and how a general concern with other people's welfare can be promoted. A first step in this endeavor is to develop an understanding of the roots of such action. Under what conditions are people most likely to help others? When are people likely to turn their backs on those in need? This chapter will be concerned with these issues. We will begin by looking at the decisions that people make when they decide whether to engage in positive social action. Particular attention will be paid to the ways in which people cal-culate (1) the benefits and costs to themselves of such action, (2) the needs and the worthi-ness of the person or group to be helped, and (3) the appropriateness of the helping action. We will argue that people calculate the ad-vantages and disadvantages of helping and that they make their decisions accordingly. We then will look at positive social action from the recipient's point of view. Sacrificing in order to help others is not always an act of kindness. Helping can create suffering for the person on the receiving end of the act. Help can put the receiver at a disadvantage in comparison with the donor.

Assessing One's Self: Personal Gain through Giving

Why do people help each other, even when helping is costly to them? Over the past several years we have asked our students to take notes on their own behavior. Whenever they found themselves doing something for someone else, they were to think about the reasons for their action. The students' accounts suggest that most seemingly selfless actions actually were self-gratifying. While making sacrifices, they felt they were gaining psychologically. Further, when confronted with a situation in which help might be needed, the students asked themselves a variety of questions. The decision to help seemed to depend on the answers to these questions. These *estimates of the gains and losses* in helping seem to characterize most people's responses to the observation of other people's need. Apparently people make use of an extensive *calculus of positive social action* (Lynch and Cohen, 1978; Piliavin, Piliavin, and Rodin, 1975). They typically ask themselves such questions as: what will I gain, what might I lose, and can I afford to help?

Does the Action Bring Pleasure?

Much positive social action only *seems* like self-sacrifice—the helper only seems to be putting others first. In fact, the helper is experiencing much private satisfaction. Positive social action can serve indirectly almost any personal need. Many people's helpfulness is inspired by hope for God's favor. For example, some of Europe's most magnificent cathedral windows were donated by individuals who felt that their path to heaven could be paved with stained glass. Some people may give to others in order to satisfy an internalized parent or peer group. "They may not be here to see me," the individual might think, "but if they were, they really would love me for doing this." Still others may help because they expect direct personal gain. Female motorists often are more successful than male motorists in obtaining help from male passersby (West, Whitney, and Schnedler, 1975). One can scarcely rule out the possibility that heterosexual interest guides such acts of good will.

To demonstrate the varied payoffs that people may obtain from giving help, the two of us and our then-student Ken Meter carried out a research project in which a large number of undergraduates were given an opportunity to help others. Tasks included assisting a researcher with a project on unusual states of consciousness, counseling troubled high-school students, and helping out in the college psychology office (Gergen, Gergen, and Meter, 1972). Subsequent tests of the students' needs revealed that most of the students chose to help on projects that would give them the greatest pleasure, however indirectly. Students who enjoyed novelty were more likely than others to volunteer to help in the research on unusual states of consciousness. Students who liked intense social relations avoided this choice and were more interested than were other students in helping troubled high-school students. Thus, the students chose to help in ways that gratified them personally.

Of course positive social activity is only one of the ways in which people might try to obtain such rewards as God's favor, love from an imagined other, or novelty. Do people ever enjoy helping for its own sake? Apparently they do. As you will recall from our discussion of moral development (Chapter 6), the normally socialized individual usually has developed a positive evaluation of moral action. He or she has learned to appreciate those persons who are self-sacrificing, generous, helpful, and charitable. Children learn such lessons very early. Even children in the primary grades believe that giving money to needy others is desirable. Young children and adolescents give positive ratings to people who help others (Bryan and Walbek, 1970). Thus people learn that altruistic action is good. And if they act altruistically, they may feel that they themselves are good. Research findings support this notion. Many civil rights workers believe that their work expresses their need to value others (Rosenhan, 1978). Similarly, many Christians who helped Jews escape from the Nazis believed that they were motivated by positive feelings of morality (London, 1970). And many kidney donors have expressed feelings of goodness and nobility after having given of themselves (Fellner and Marshall, 1970). Recalling the last chapter's discussion of self-reinforcement, we might say that people develop the capacity to reward themselves for their own good works.

Can I Avoid Pain?
The Empathic Response

If people are likely to do good when they think of the pleasure it will bring, then avoidance of pain should have an opposite effect. For example, while any bystander would be likely to help a child who is floundering in the shallow end of a swimming pool, very few people would be willing to dive alone into the surf to rescue a panicked man who was caught in an undertow. In a research demonstration of this point, investigators found that the likelihood of a person's giving blood depends on whether he or she thinks that the donation will result in pain, dizziness, or lack of energy (Pomazal and Jaccard, 1976). Indeed, by keeping away from people who ask for help, and especially by keeping away from those who usually succeed in getting it, the costs of helping can be avoided (Pancer et al., 1979). These and other demonstrations (McGovern, 1976; Penner et al., 1976; Wagner and Wheeler, 1969) are so striking that many theorists believe that people's assessment of the costs of giving aid is usually the most powerful determinant of helpfulness (Hatfield, Walster, and Piliavin, 1978).

Yet, paradoxically, pain also can motivate helpfulness. Motivation of this kind emerges from the human capacity for *empathic responses*—that is, the capacity to imagine oneself in the place of others (Hoffman, 1975). Seeing a person in distress is emotionally arousing to most people (Berger, 1962; Geer and Jamecky, 1973). This arousal may be painful and can be relieved by helping the person in distress. Giving help, it is reasoned, reduces the observer's *own pain* (Lenrow, 1965; Weiss et al., 1971). Positive social action, then, reduces the suffering of two people— the other and the self.

Helpfulness as an empathic response may be the key to a centuries-old controversy. Social thinkers have long argued that positive social action is basic to human nature. As the most intellectually advanced creatures on earth, it is argued, human beings are *instinctively* inclined to aid others. Most contemporary psychologists reject this notion. There are too many variations among cultures, too many differences among people within a culture, and too many individual exceptions to the rule of helpfulness for most contemporary theorists to accept the argument that people instinctively are bound to be altruistic (see

Empathy and altruism. Even very young children seem able to feel what others are feeling. Research has shown that when people empathize with a person in pain or in need, they may be more inclined to help.

Campbell, 1978; Cohen, 1978). However, even if people are not preprogrammed genetically to help others, genetics does appear to furnish the capacity for empathy that motivates positive social action. Thus the genetic contribution is indirect rather than direct.

Almost everyone has had the experience of feeling another person's pain. Children demonstrate this capacity as early as the second year of life (Hoffman, 1975). And this feeling of oneness with another can move an individual to act on the other person's behalf. In one study, for example, undergraduates were asked to imagine that a friend had become terminally ill, and they were instructed to think about the dying friend's feelings

(Thompson, Lowan, and Rosenhan, 1980). When the subjects later were given a chance to do an anonymous favor for someone, they were much more likely to do the favor than were subjects in another group, who simply had been asked to think about *their own*, rather than their friend's, reaction to the illness. Yet children and adults clearly do not always respond empathically. At times people enjoy another's distress. Thus we ask: what circumstances promote or reduce empathy?

One factor that may influence the amount of empathy is the *similarity of the victim to oneself* (Krebs, 1975). This possibility seems quite plausible in light of our discussion of the way in which similarity often increases one's attraction for another person (see Chapter 3). To demonstrate the effects of similarity

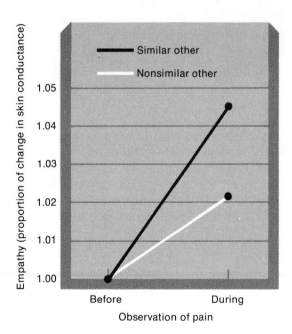

FIGURE **7-1**

The effects of similarity on empathy

Note that observing a similar other in pain produced greater arousal than did observing a nonsimilar other undergoing the same experience. (Adapted from Krebs, 1975)

on empathy, Dennis Krebs asked a group of students to observe another student (hired for the purpose) play a game of roulette. Half of the subjects were told that with each win the player would receive money and that losses would bring him a painful shock. Subjects in the other group were told simply that the player was practicing his skill; he would receive neither reward nor shock. Further, within each group, half of the subjects were told that the player was very similar to them in personality, while the other half were told that he was quite different. Krebs hoped to show that when subjects felt that the player would be shocked for his losses they would feel some of his pain themselves. Further, Krebs expected that more pain would be experienced by subjects who thought that the player was similar to them than by those who thought that he was quite different.

Krebs used the subjects' physiological arousal to measure empathy. The amount of arousal was measured by electrical conductance of the skin. In Figure 7-1 you can see that when the player was in pain *and* was thought to be similar to the subject, greater empathic arousal was produced than when the player was in pain but was thought to be dissimilar.

The next question was whether those subjects who demonstrated the greatest amount of empathic arousal also would behave altruistically. Would they be more likely than the dissimilar group to sacrifice something for the player in pain? Each subject was allowed to divide a monetary payment between himself and the other player—the more money the subject gave to the player, the less was available for the subject. Subjects who had felt more empathy—those who thought that the player had been in pain and was similar to them—also gave up more money to reward him.

Similarity is only one of the factors that may affect empathy for others. A second important factor is the *awareness of pain-pro-*

ducing conditions. Research indicates that seeing a person's pained expression is not very arousing by itself. When the same expression is believed to be a reaction to electric shock, arousal is high (Vaughan and Lanzetta, 1980). Another factor that may increase empathy is the individual's *cognitive set*—that is, the point of view he or she takes when thinking about the person in need of help (Regan and Totten, 1975). When asked, for example, to imagine oneself in the place of a victim, an individual is likely to feel empathy, be concerned with the causes of the problem, remember accurately, and—most important for our purposes—give help (Harvey et al., 1980). In contrast, when asked to observe a victim from the perspective of an objective research scientist, an individual may feel little empathic distress. Perhaps such training in objectivity enables doctors to avoid being overcome by the pain that is experienced by their patients. Many investigators believe that people can *learn* to take the perspective of others (Aronfreed, 1968; Ekstein, 1978). A variety of studies have demonstrated that children can be trained in perspective taking and that this training increases the likelihood that they will aid others in distress (Staub, 1971). Helpfulness also may be increased if feelings *are labeled* as empathic (Coke, Batson, and McDavis, 1978). As you will recall from our Chapter 2 discussion of self-labeling, emotional arousal usually is ambiguous and lends itself to many different interpretations. If you believed fear to be the bad feeling you experienced when you saw someone in pain, you might be less willing to help than if you believed you were experiencing concern for the person (Gaertner and Dovidio, 1977).

Do I Have the Resources?
The Warm-Glow Effect

In addition to asking how much pleasure or pain will result from helping, people also may ask whether they have the resources to give.

How people estimate their resources depends on a number of different factors. First, *variations exist among cultures* in terms of what constitutes adequate resources—the same objective resources may be considered to be sufficient by one group and insufficient by another (L'Armand and Pepitone, 1975). Given the very same income, for example, some people will feel that they have plenty of money while others will feel that they desperately need more.

Situational factors also may change our resource estimates from moment to moment. In one fascinating demonstration of this point, Darley and Batson (1971) evaluated the helpfulness of students who were attending a religious seminary. You might expect that seminarians would be extremely helpful to those in need. After all, they plan to devote their professional lives to the service of humanity. However, Darley and Batson reasoned that time also is a precious commodity. When people—even altruists-in-training—have a great deal of time they will engage in more socially beneficial acts than they will when time is limited. The seminary students were invited to prepare and record a professional talk. One group's topic was the Good Samaritan, a Bible story that glorifies the individual who sacrifices his resources to help a stranger. The other group's topic was unrelated to altruism. The groups were subdivided further in terms of time available for the task. Half of the subjects in each group were told that they had *plenty of time* in which to get to a nearby building to record the talk, and the other half were told that they *already were late and should hurry.* As each subject walked down a narrow street on the way to the recording session he came upon a young man who was lying in a doorway coughing and groaning. The young man of course was a confederate of the investigators. The question was: who would stop to offer help? The results were clear: of those who had time to spare, 41 percent stopped to help, while only

10 percent of those who were in a hurry stopped. The reminder that was provided by the story of the Good Samaritan made little difference. The seminarians who had been assigned this topic generally failed to help if they were late.

These results suggest that even those persons who are highly motivated toward positive social action may not stop to help someone if they are in a hurry. Yet situational factors do not always have a negative effect. *People's estimates of their own helping capacities can be increased by situational factors.* Sudden success can make people feel that they have more to give. And as Alice Isen (1970) has argued, just being made to feel good may lead to more altruistic, or generous, behavior. Good feelings not only may increase one's sense of prosperity, but they also may bring to mind positive incidents from the past (Isen et al., 1978). This increase in feelings of personal prosperity, often called the *warm-glow*, tends to increase a person's generosity. To illustrate this possibility, Isen (1970) looked at the relationship between success on a test of creativity and contributions to charity. The experimenter told a randomly selected group of junior-high-school teachers that they had done extremely well on a creativity test. Other teachers were told that they had done poorly. The experimenter then paid each teacher for her time and excused herself momentarily. While the teacher sat waiting for the experimenter to return, an accomplice entered the room carrying a collection can labeled "Junior High Air-Conditioning Fund," explained about the need for an air conditioner, put the can on a table, and departed. The teachers' success and failure experiences had striking effects on their subsequent generosity. The teachers who had succeeded on the test gave almost seven times as much money to the fund as did those who failed. (All teachers later were told about the study, and the donations were returned.)

Further research indicates that the reasons for the warm glow make little difference—feeling good about anything can increase people's helpfulness. One study showed that people who "accidentally" found a dime in the coin return of a public telephone were more likely to help a passing stranger who "accidently" dropped papers in front of them than were callers who didn't find money (Isen and Levin, 1972). And good weather can increase helpfulness. In northern climates, the amount of sunshine, the temperature, and the wind velocity can affect the amount of help that people are willing to give to others (Cunningham, 1979).

Other studies have found that (1) a gain in status can increase people's desire to help others (Midlarsky and Midlarsky, 1976), (2) succeeding in a test may increase willingness to volunteer time to the American Cancer Society (Weyant, 1978), and (3) soothing music may increase people's willingness to do favors for others (Fried and Berkowitz, 1979). Warm-glow effects also are found among children. Children are more likely to donate to charity if they succeed, rather than fail, in a game (Isen, Horn, and Rosenhan, 1973). Simply reminding children of happy events in their lives may increase their charitable behavior toward other children (Rosenhan, Underwood, and Moore, 1974). Warm-glow effects do not appear to be long-lasting. This kind of behavior reflects immediate moods that may change as the situation changes (Isen, Clark, and Schwartz, 1976; Weyant, 1978). And if the act of helping is so difficult or painful that it will interfere with one's good mood, people may prefer not to help (Isen and Simmonds, 1978).

Although positive moods can be potent sources of helping behavior, some researchers believe that negative moods can have the same effect under special conditions (Apsler, 1975; Kidd and Berkowitz, 1976; Konečni, 1972; Steele, 1975). In particular, people who are in a negative mood may help others because by giving help they may be able to relieve their discomfort. As we saw, giving help can make one feel like a better person and thus can improve one's mood. Even young children may have mastered this mechanism. In one study, children in the first to third grades were asked to imagine either a sad experience or a neutral one (Kenrick, Bauman, and Cialdini, 1979). When the children later were given an opportunity to contribute to charity, those who had thought about sad events gave more than did those who had thought about neutral events. Guilt as a negative mood can often have the same effect (Regan, 1971). In one study, subjects who were made to feel guilty about breaking a camera reacted more generously to a charity request than did those who had no reason to feel guilty (Cunningham, Steinberg, and Greu, 1980).

To summarize, we see that people who face situations in which help may be needed first make decisions about themselves. People may ask about the extent to which the act of helping will give them pleasure—either by direct reward or through indirect psychological advantage. In addition, people may assess the degree of pain involved: sometimes helpfulness may be reduced by the wish to avoid pain; sometimes helpfulness may be increased by the wish to end the empathic pain that is being experienced. People also may ask whether they have the resources to help, and a positive mood may increase the sense that resources are ample.

Assessing the Needy

We see that people often ask themselves about rewards, costs, and resources before they engage in positive social action. In addition to these inward-looking questions, however, people also ask themselves about the person in need of help: is there really a problem, is help actually needed, do I like the victim enough to help? Let us now examine in more detail issues such as these.

Is the Need Noticeable?
The Problem of Self-preoccupation

Before positive social action can occur the potential helper must realize that aid is needed. If someone clearly is dependent on another person, aid may be immediately forthcoming (Gruder, Romer, and Korth, 1978). And if someone is in danger of being harmed greatly, rescue is more likely than if the danger is slight (Austin, 1979). However, need is not always noticed (Schwartz, 1974). Many subtle factors can raise or lower attention to another person's distress. For example, a person's tone of voice may be important. Making a request in an urgent voice may increase the chances of receiving help (Langer and Abelson, 1972). And a high degree of environmental noise can distract people from noticing the needs of others (Mathews and Canon, 1975). Most important, however, may be the presence of someone who defines the situation as being one in which help is needed (Bar-Tal, 1976). Emergency situations, for example, often are ambiguous. People often don't want to believe that a crisis exists, nor do they want to look foolish by labeling the situation an emergency if it is not. People often are unwilling to take the risk of being wrong in their definition of an emergency situation. Ironically, people often will risk the lives of others rather than risk being embarrassed.

Leonard Berkowitz (1970) has argued that the value that is placed on self-concern—facing one's feelings, examining one's motives, reflecting on one's goals—may interfere with appropriate concern for an individual's fellow beings. As Berkowitz writes, "Worry about one's self, thoughts and misgivings about one's self-worth, dreams of success or fear of

"Should you ever collapse, suddenly and critically ill, somebody other than a doctor will most probably decide not only whether or not you are dead, but whether or not you live" (Simpson, 1976, p. 243).

This dire prediction reflects the results of a study of ambulance services and hospital admissions procedures, made by Michael A. Simpson of the Royal Free Hospital Medical School of London University. Simpson's research was stimulated by the work of the American sociologist David Sudnow (1973), who is interested in the social interpretation of death. When one person finds another in a state of collapse, a decision must be made as to whether the collapsed person (1) requires no help because he or she merely *seems* to be ill ("he is just drunk"), (2) needs help urgently, or (3) is dead or as good as dead. Placing a victim in the first category allows the passerby to move on without taking action. Use of this category accounts for the low level of helpfulness that is found in many of the studies reported in this chapter. The decision that medical attention is needed urgently usually means that resuscitation attempts begin immediately, that the ambulance staff continues the resuscitation attempts, and that the emergency-room staff makes preparations for the victim's arrival. If the victim is assumed to be dead or done for, resuscitation attempts are virtually nonexistent, the ambulance makes no haste, and the emergency-room staff is lethargic.

As both Simpson and Sudnow argue, the category in which the collapsed person is placed depends importantly on social factors. For example, age may have a major influence over the categorization process. As Simpson observed, the older the patient, the more likely that his or her lack of vital signs of life will be taken at face value—the person is assumed to be dead. Seven of ten older persons observed by Simpson were classified as dead and given no help in the emergency room. However, the same lack of vital signs may be viewed as "cardiac arrest" if the person is younger, and resuscitation attempts may commence immediately.

failure in important activities, all may distract the person so that (momentarily, at least) he does not think of the helping ideal" (p. 144). To demonstrate his argument, Berkowitz and his colleagues looked at the relationship between self-concern and helpfulness. Self-concern was aroused in half of the subjects by telling them that the task they were to perform—judging photographs—would serve as an indicator of their "social intelligence." The rest of the subjects believed that they were expressing simple preferences

for facial appearances. Later in the session the experimenter asked each subject to help score some data from another study. Subjects whose self-concern had been aroused did less to help the experimenter than did those who had not been stimulated to think about themselves.

Does self-concern always decrease helping behavior? Probably not. In the Berkowitz study the self-concern was a response to the threat of failure. When self-concern is *not threatening* it even may *increase* one's sense

Energetic attempts were made to save the lives of all patients between the ages of thirty and forty-three.

Another factor that may determine the category into which people are placed is presumed moral character. Alcohol use, especially by someone dressed shabbily or unwashed, leads to an assumption that the person is "merely drunk," and little help is furnished. Alcoholics also are frequently assumed to be dead or near death. Drug addicts, prostitutes, vagrants, persons injured in fights, homosexuals, and attempted suicides are less often judged as needing urgent attention. Hospital medical personnel, Simpson argues, seem to feel that such persons are less deserving of help than those of higher moral character. In the case of attempted suicides who require stomach pumping, Simpson reports: "In many instances I have observed the turgid, phallic, red rubber tubes flourished with grim zeal to the accompaniment of mutually supportive comments like 'this'll teach her a lesson,' or 'maybe now she'll think twice before doing this again'" (p. 245).

In contrast, a person who is successful according to society's standards usually receives rapid and continuous help. The *New York Times* (1963) reported a Dallas physician's comments concerning the life-giving efforts devoted to President Kennedy:

Medically, it was apparent the President was not alive when he was brought in. There was no spontaneous respiration. He had dilated, fixed pupils. It was obviously a lethal head wound. Technically, however, by using vigorous resuscitation, intravenous tubes and all the usual supportive measures we were able to raise the semblance of a heart beat (quoted in Simpson, 1976, p. 246).

As Simpson says, "How to avoid dying from a heart attack: look as young as you can, dress well, disguise your deviances, and keep your breath fresh" (p. 248).

of responsibility and desire to help. In one study, students were shown pictures of themselves and then were shown pictures of victims of venereal disease. The students were more likely to volunteer to help the victims than were students who were not given an opportunity to consider their own images (Duval, Duval, and Neely, 1979). A searching self-examination can increase awareness of mutual dependence and ultimately may prove to be valuable in fostering positive social action.

Is Help Deserved?
The Just-World Hypothesis

After noticing that help is needed, a person often asks next whether help is *deserved*. People are dying of hunger: that fact no one can deny. Yet activity designed to help starving people—or those people who are experiencing any kind of distress—may depend partially on beliefs about whether the victims deserve help. The belief that people are *responsible* for their distress (see Box 2-3) may counteract the inclination to help them. Melvin Lerner (1970) argues that such a reaction is based on widely shared beliefs in a *just world:* "It seems that many people care deeply about justice for themselves and others—not justice in the legal sense but in a more general psychological sense. They want to believe in a world where people get what they deserve, or . . . deserve what they get" (p. 207). This belief has intriguing implications. One who has a belief in a just world may come to believe that people who suffer deserve their suffering. The sight of someone suffering may cause people to think that the victim must have done something to deserve the discomfort. From this perspective, the poor are not worthy of help; they deserve their condition.

To explore this idea, Lerner (1965) asked female college students to evaluate the appearance and personality of a female "victim." The subjects believed that they were participating in a study on the perception of emotional arousal. They found themselves watching on closed-circuit television another female student (the experimenter's accomplice), who groaned and shrieked as she received "extremely painful" electric shocks. The subjects were told that when the victim signed up for the experiment she had not known that she was to receive the shocks and that she virtually was unable to leave. Actually, no pain was being experienced. The experimenter varied the instructions in order to manipulate the subjects' perception of the victim's pain. Some subjects were told that the event *soon would be terminated.* Others were told that another session would follow and that the woman would have to go through ten more minutes of the shock procedure.

To explore the relationship between observed suffering and feelings of hostility, the subjects were asked to rate the victim's attractiveness, adjustment, intelligence, and other traits. These ratings proved to be strongly influenced by the amount of pain the victim was to experience. Subjects who thought that the event was almost finished showed mild dislike for the victim. Subjects who thought that the victim was to undergo another session of shock rated the victim more negatively. She was seen as being less well adjusted, a less attractive person, and so on. The more suffering the victim was believed to experience, the less positively she was evaluated. Similar findings have emerged from other research (Apsler and Friedman, 1975; Zuckerman, 1975).

Such findings seem to contradict much of what we said earlier about the role of empathy in human affairs. We emphasized that the propensity to help is related to the experience of other people's pain. Can empathic helpfulness exist alongside the desire to blame the victim of suffering? There is no reason why opposing feelings cannot exist. Self-examination probably would reveal that most people have some hostile feelings, even toward their closest companions. However, one type of feeling—positive or negative—usually is more powerful than others. The question is, how can we reduce negative feelings and increase positive ones, thereby cutting down on people's tendency to blame victims of suffering?

One effective way to reduce the tendency to blame the victim is by increasing the available information on the cause of the suffering. Blaming the victim may not occur if the victim is seen as being totally innocent (Piliavin, Hardyck, and Vadom, 1967) or is seen as suffering because of someone else's irresponsible action (Simons and Piliavin, 1972). Thus workers often may help their mates who fall behind in a task if the mate's shortcomings seem to be the result of someone else's mismanagement (Berkowitz, 1973).

Is the Recipient Attractive?

In assessing the needy, the potential helper not only notices that help is needed and determines whether it is deserved, but, as our students have so often informed us, he or she also makes judgments about the attractiveness and likableness of the needy individual. People don't just help *anybody*—they are far more likely to help those whom they find attractive or likable. Such factors also may operate on the governmental level. The United States generally refuses to give aid to nations whose policies or leadership are at odds with its own. For example, in 1979 foreign aid to Afghanistan was stopped after the U.S. ambassador to that country was assassinated by an Afghan political activist. On the personal level, numerous demonstrations of the effects of attractiveness on helping behavior have been made. For example, workers are far more likely to help a supervisor who is seen as being likable than they are to help one who is not (Daniels and Berkowitz, 1963). A victim of a subway emergency who has an unattractive birthmark is less likely to receive help than is one who doesn't have such a mark (Piliavin, Piliavin, and Rodin, 1975). And the victim receives more help if he isn't bleeding from the mouth than if he is (Piliavin and Piliavin, 1972). Male subjects are more likely to donate money to a woman for a tetanus injection when she looks attractive than when she looks unattractive (West and Brown, 1975). Phrasing a request for help in a positive, upbeat tone may boost the chances of being helped (Kriss, Indenbaum, and Tesch, 1974); however, individuals who are too assertive may fail to secure help (Katz, Cohen, and Glass, 1975). A stranded motorist who is dressed and groomed neatly is far more likely to receive help than is one whose clothing is

casual and hair long (Graf and Riddell, 1972; Morgan, 1973). Attractiveness effects may begin very early in life. A preschool child's willingness to share playthings depends on the likability of the recipient (Staub, 1978). And although the communal life of the Israeli kibbutzim has been much celebrated, kibbutz children are far more prone to help close friends than they are to help anyone else (Sharabany, 1973, 1974).

Such results raise a distressing paradox: persons in need generally are among the most unattractive members of society, but they may be the least likely to elicit helping behavior. Survey data are relevant here (Nunnally, 1961). Four hundred respondents, representing a cross section of the United States population in terms of education, sex, income, religious affiliation, and age, were asked to rate a variety of persons on a broad number of traits. They gave higher ratings to average individuals than to people who were said to be insane or neurotic—people who are among the neediest in contemporary society. Figure 7-2 presents a comparison between the ratings given an "insane man" and those given an "average man." You can see that the insane man was labeled "foolish," "dirty," and "worthless." The average man's rating was at the opposite end of the scale: he was seen as being "wise," "clean," and "valuable." Clearly, being neurotic or insane carries a very strong stigma.

The problem of reduced aid to those peo-

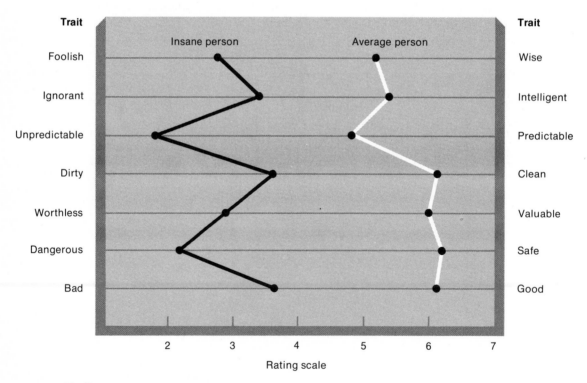

FIGURE 7-2 **The stigma of insanity**

Note the discrepancy in the ratings that were obtained by the two hypothetical individuals. People apparently feel strong dislike for those who depart from normalcy. (Adapted from Nunnally, 1961)

ple who are most in need is not simply a theoretical issue. Practitioners of general medicine and psychiatry share a distaste for treating patients from lower economic spheres. Studies in a public clinic indicate, for example, that children whose parents are unskilled laborers are far less likely to be recommended for psychotherapy than are children from professional families (de Ajuriaguerra, 1980). This bias was not based on economics—the treatment was at the state's expense. Apparently, dissimilarity is an important factor. The lower-class person is different from the practitioner in terms of verbal ability, interests, values, motivation, and so forth. Unfortunately, working with people who are alien seems to offer the upper-middle-class doctor little satisfaction. New health-care policies must take account of the needy person's attractiveness to those in a position to help.

In summary, we see that people not only assess themselves before giving help, but they also examine the characteristics of the potential recipient. People ask whether the other person really needs help. The answer to this question may depend on the cost of giving and on the helper's self-preoccupation. People also may ask whether help is deserved. Individuals who believe in a just world may decide that victims deserve their problems and that help therefore is unnecessary.

Assessing the Social Context

Positive social action is seldom just a matter between the helper and the victim. Not only do people take account of their own pleasure and pain and the victim's characteristics, but they also are influenced by their surroundings. Helping relationships take place within the context of the social and physical environment, and this environment can make an immense difference in whether or not aid is given, rescue is attempted, or sacrifices are made. Once again the potential helper asks himself or herself certain questions, in this case about the situation: if something is wrong, why doesn't someone else help, is help appropriate in these circumstances, how are others behaving?

Are Other Helpers Available? Bystander Intervention

Social psychologists have been keenly interested in the effects of others' presence on people's tendencies to help one another. The question gained special significance in 1964 when a woman named Kitty Genovese was attacked one evening outside her apartment building in a New York City housing complex. Her screams of pain and cries for help drew at least thirty-nine neighbors to their windows. These people watched from the safety of their apartments as the attacker fought with Kitty Genovese for over thirty minutes and stabbed her numerous times. *Not one* of the bystanders came to her defense. No one even picked up the phone to notify the police. The question that was raised by this and similar incidents is: why didn't anyone help?

The most extensive attempt to answer this question was made by Bibb Latané and John Darley (1970). Latané and Darley argue against personally blaming Genovese's neighbors for cruelty. They suggest that most people would act as the neighbors did—that their inaction grew out of a typical question that people ask themselves about the social environment when they are confronted with a situation in which help is needed. Before considering this question, put yourself in the place of one of Latané and Darley's subjects in an experiment designed to demonstrate their ideas: You report to a psychology laboratory to take part in a study on student problems, and you are placed in one of several rooms leading off a long corridor. In order to protect anonymity and enhance openness, the

BOX 7-2

Crime and the Not-So-Innocent Bystander

One of the most frightening aspects of urban life is the knowledge that if you are singled out for a mugging, the chances of anyone helping you are small. Burglaries, car thefts, and purse snatchings seem to take place without anyone lifting a finger. Most people wonder whether the outcome would be different if they were bystanders to such happenings.

Social psychologist Harold Takooshian has tried to bring this collective inaction to public attention (McCall, 1980). To shock and edify, Takooshian has used mock crimes that demonstrate people's indifference to other people's difficulties. In one extreme example, a man carried a seemingly unconscious woman from an apartment building, threw her into the trunk of a car, slammed the lid, and drove off. Although many bystanders were present in twenty replications of this scene, few witnesses stopped the man, wrote down the car's license number, or called the police.

To explore whether the failure to respond was based on a fear for personal safety, Takooshian arranged for a "policeman," armed with a gun, a nightstick, and handcuffs, to be on the scene as a "thief" jimmied open a car door and walked off with fur coats and cameras. Not a single witness spoke to the policeman. However, five witnesses warned the thief to look out for the cop. In one case researchers interviewed a street vendor who said, "I saw it, but I don't give a ——. Take the whole block. It's not mine" (p.71). Takooshian believes that bystander apathy is responsible for much of today's street crime. If bystanders contributed even minimal support to victims, he believes, street crime would decrease.

Studies by other investigators offer additional explanations for people's failure to intervene:

1. *The difficulty of identifying a crime.* Even when the crime is carried out openly, people often fail to define the event as a crime (Gelfand et al., 1973). Even the most blatant acts of shoplifting and theft can be defined by bystanders in alternative ways.

2. *Lack of motivation.* Once a crime is identified, the bystander must want to intervene. For example, research suggests that females may be motivated by feelings of empathy with the victim, while males tend to be sensitive to the crime's magnitude (Austin, 1979). Males are more likely to intervene if the crime is serious than if it is inconsequential. Being asked to guard someone's property also may motivate a bystander to intervene. In one study, a group of sunbathers asked nearby people to watch their radio while they were

discussion in which you are to participate will take place over an intercom system. You are provided with a microphone and earphones and are told that since the experimenter will not take part in or listen to the initial discussion (again to facilitate openness), each person will take turns giving his or her opinions. Each person's microphone is

away. These bystanders were much more likely to intervene when a "thief" stole the radio than were bystanders from whom no commitment had been obtained (Moriarty, 1975).

3. *The presence of others.* Bystanders who are alone are more likely to take action than are those who are in a group (Shaffer, Rogel, and Hendrick, 1975). Apparently, responsibility for reporting the crime is diffused among group members. However, if a group of bystanders is urged to help, intervention is more likely to take place than it would be if members of the group were left to make their own decisions.

Why does a victim of a crime fail to report the incident? Apparently many victims feel that the police will not take action or will be unable to apprehend the criminal. In addition, the victim may want to avoid the emotional stress of reliving the unpleasant experience. To explore the possibility that people would rather forget a crime than do something about it, Martin Greenberg and his colleagues developed laboratory experiments in which subjects were victims of a minor theft (Greenberg et al., 1979, 1980; Greenberg, Wilson, and Mills, in press). Eight hundred volunteers for a study of industrial work efficiency were solicited through newspaper advertisements. During the course of these studies, one volunteer (a confederate of the experimenters) cheated each subject of his or her rightful earnings and left with the money. Following discovery of the theft, a bystander (also hired by the experimenters) urged some subjects to do something about the theft, told some subjects to do nothing about it, and said nothing to others. The question was whether subjects in the various conditions would call the police, an obvious alternative under the circumstances. Few subjects bothered to report the crime. However, those who were encouraged to do nothing were less likely to call the police than were those who were encouraged in vague terms "to do something" and those who were given no advice. In later studies, the bystander specifically suggested that the police be called. Under these conditions the subject's willingness to report the crime increased markedly.

Survey research shows that most victims of crime confer with at least one person before deciding what to do (Van Kirk, 1978). Clearly, those who are in a position to give advice may have an important influence on whether a crime is reported by a victim. And reporting is certainly worthwhile. Even if the criminal is not apprehended, the accumulation of reports may lead to an ultimate improvement in systems of public protection.

to be activated electronically for approximately two minutes, during which time the person can deliver initial feelings about his or her problems. During the second phase each person is to have an additional two minutes to comment on what the others have said. During the two-minute period only the person whose microphone is activated can speak;

See no evil. A hidden camera filmed one of Harold Takooshian's confederates robbing a car. Of approximately thirty-five hundred witnesses to this and similar mock crimes, only nine said anything to the thief. Only one witness, a visitor to New York City, chased the man. For further discussion of the not-so-innocent bystander, see Box 7-2.

begins to talk calmly, but then his voice becomes more incoherent. You hear him say:

> I-er-it somebody could help me out it would-it would er-er s-s-sure be-sure be good . . . because er-the-er-er-a cause I-er-I-uh-I've got a-a-one of the-er-sei- - - - -er-er-things coming on and-and-and I could really-er-use some help so if somebody would-er-give me a little h-help-un-er-er-er-er-er c-could somebody er-er-help-er-uh-uh-uh- (choking sounds). . . . I'm gonna die-er-er-I'm . . . gonna die-er-er-seizure-er (chokes, then quiet). (Latané and Darley, 1970, pp. 95–96).

You might not hear the student's final words because you, like many other participants, might go for help before he lapsed into silence. Or you might wait until the final choking, think for a minute, and then seek help. Or you might not move at all.

Latané and Darley were interested in the subjects' helping behavior in this "emergency." In their series of experiments no emergency existed: the subjects were listening to other persons' prerecorded voices. The question was, what effect does the *number of other bystanders present* have on an individual's helpfulness? How fast would the subjects respond to the emergency, and how many participants would leave the experimental chamber to seek help if there were *five* potential helpers (as in the situation just described) as opposed to *one* or *two?* The question of number is important because when many other people are present in a potential emergency, one's tendencies to help may be reduced by the others' presence. This reduced tendency to help can be traced to three sources:

no interruptions are permitted by the electronic circuitry, nor can anyone speak over his or her microphone to anyone in any of the other rooms.

You find that there are six of you in the discussion and that your turn is last. The first student talks about the difficulties of adjusting to the city and to his studies. With embarrassment he mentions also that he is prone to seizures, particularly when studying or taking exams. The other students speak of their lives and problems, and you volunteer your opinions, thus finishing the first round of talks. The second round begins, and the student who had mentioned having seizures

1. *Responsibility for the action is diffused.* The more bystanders present, the less personal responsibility for helping one may feel (Berkowitz, 1978). The individual may reason, "I shouldn't be the only one to help; everybody else should be responsible, too." Or he or she may feel that someone else already has taken care of the

problem. The tendency to diffuse responsibility may be especially strong *when helping is costly* (Morgan, 1978). If one risks injury in helping another, the reasons why helping is someone else's responsibility may come to mind. If a member of another racial group needs aid, potential helpers may fear that they will be misunderstood and possibly held responsible for the emergency. Diffusing responsibility is easier than helping a stranger (Gaertner and Dovidio, 1977).

2. *The possible shame of a mistaken definition is increased.* As we have seen, determining when help is needed sometimes is difficult. Misinterpretation of a situation may lead to ridicule. If no one is present to laugh at a mistake, an individual may feel less inhibited about taking a chance and may check to see if help truly is needed. When many people are present, the risk of embarrassment is greater.

3. *The collective definition of the situation may encourage inaction.* As each person sees others who are watching and not helping he or she may conclude that the situation is not an emergency, that help isn't needed, or that it isn't safe to give it. As a result, members of an entire group may influence one another to remain in collective ignorance (Howard and Crano, 1974).

Do people really think in these ways? Let us look at the results of Latané and Darley's study.

Figure 7-3 shows the percentage of subjects who sought help during a period that started with the confederate's first cry for help and ended four minutes later. As the graph shows, if you had been in the six-person group, the chances were about 30 percent that you would have raced to the door by the end of the four-minute period. In marked contrast, if you had been in a three-person group, there is a 62-percent chance that you would have

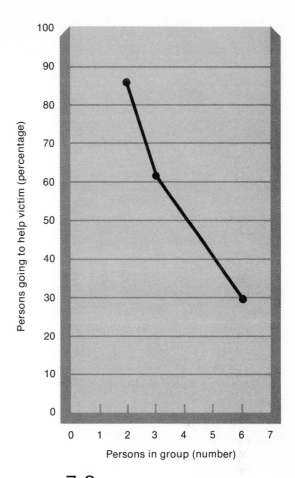

FIGURE **7-3**

The effect of group size on helpfulness

The more members there are in a group, the less likely it is that any member will react in an emergency. (Adapted from Latané and Darley, 1970)

helped within this time period. If you and the victim had been talking alone with each other, the chance of your giving help would be 85 percent. In fact, at any point during the four-minute period, proportionately more subjects from the two-person groups responded than did subjects from the three-person groups, and more subjects from the latter groups than from the six-person groups responded.

The relationship between number of persons present and amount of helping behavior has been demonstrated in many other studies. For example, Latané and Darley (1968) arranged for college students to fill out questionnaires while in a room with various numbers of experimental confederates. At a certain point, smoke was forced into the room through a wall vent. The smoke entered in irregular puffs, but gradually it began to fill the room and obscure the occupants' vision. Of the students working alone in the room, 75 percent reported the emergency to authorities. When three people were present the percentage of students who reported the smoke dropped to 38 percent. In a further study of the bystander effect (Latané and Rodin, 1969), male undergraduates, seated in a waiting room either alone or with others, heard a female "market researcher" in an adjoining room say that she was going to climb up on a chair to reach a stack of papers on the bookcase. A loud crash followed, and then a scream. Then the woman cried out, "Oh, my God! My foot . . . I . . . I . . . can't move it." Over 70 percent of the subjects who were waiting alone went to her aid, while only 40 percent of those who were waiting with oth-

The bystander effect. If you have ever visited a large city, like the persons shown here, you probably walked right by a prostrate form stretched out on the pavement. Your behavior typifies the bystander effect: as the number of witnesses in an emergency situation increases, the time required before help is given also increases.

ers did so. The effects of groups on helping behavior also have been demonstrated in real-life settings. For example, researchers have found that if you ever are alone in a city and need a favor, your request is far more likely to be successful if you ask a lone individual than if you approach a group of people who are walking and talking together (Latané, 1970; Levy et al., 1972).

The results of Latané and Darley's studies seem to be counterintuitive. Usually the greater the number of persons available in an emergency, the more rapidly and the more effectively one would expect to receive help. If there isn't always safety in numbers, then under what conditions does the size of a group increase, rather than decrease, the chances of being helped? Two factors seem to be espe-

cially likely to influence the probability of positive social action:

1. *The possibility for communication.* If bystanders communicate with each other and can discuss who should take responsibility, aid often is likely to be given. In the studies just described, the subjects were not always able to discuss the emergency with the experimenters' confederates, and therefore they may have assumed that someone else was taking care of it. The fact that helping depends on personal responsibility has implications for public appeals from such organizations as the Kidney Fund. The Kidney Fund's drives for donations probably would be more successful if they informed people about the

small percentage of persons who actually make contributions. This type of appeal would make it hard for people to assume that others are contributing needed funds. Increased communication also should break the seal of collective ignorance— that is, people will be less likely to assume that others' silence means no emergency exists or that nothing needs to be done.

2. *The provision of numerous help-giving roles.* When a situation requires help from many people, many different helping tasks are available and the more who contribute the better the aid (Latané and Dabbs, 1975). People are more likely to help in a crisis that claims many victims than they are when the number of victims is few (Wegner and Schaefer, 1978). Save-the-environment appeals seem to attract volunteers on this basis; almost everyone can contribute something.

Returning to the studies of bystander intervention, we see that responsibility often was diffused by lack of communication and that the number of possible help-giving roles usually was limited. In effect, increases in group size thus operated to decrease the potential for individual responsibility and the likelihood that helping roles would be available. In light of the factors discussed above, consider a study of positive social behavior in a metropolitan subway (Piliavin, Rodin, and Piliavin, 1969). Student-confederates of the researchers created two different emergency situations. In half of the cases, one of the student-confederates, smelling of liquor and carrying a liquor bottle in a brown paper bag, posed as a drunk. In the remaining cases, the student-confederate, dressed in an identical manner and carrying a black cane, showed no evidence of alcohol. Drunk or lame, the student-confederate stood quietly until the train passed the first station, and then he staggered forward and collapsed onto the floor of the car. A second student-confederate sat unob-

trusively in another section of the car and recorded the riders' attempts to provide help to the prostrate victim. If no help was provided in a standard amount of time, the observer helped the victim to his feet and escorted him off the train. How much help would you imagine the victim received as the number of riders varied?

The passengers could hardly avoid communication—they were able to talk to one another. They also could see whether the victim received help, and they were aware that more than one helping role was available. People were needed to carry the victim, to stay with him while others sought help of various kinds, and to keep curious people from crowding too close. The results of the experiment seemed to reflect these factors. Contrary to the laboratory studies, the larger the group of bystanders, the *more rapidly* help was given. Regardless of whether the victim seemed drunk or was carrying a cane, help was offered more quickly when seven or more bystanders were present than when four to six bystanders were present. And in the case of the drunk, when only one to three bystanders were present help came twice as slowly as when four to six bystanders were present. Such results also have been found in other research (Clark and Word, 1974; Schwartz and Clausen, 1970; Staub, 1970), making clear that safety in numbers really does exist.

What Is the Norm?

The potential helper may not only ask how many people are available to help, but also whether action is appropriate in the situation. In other words, before helping, most people ask themselves what is the *norm*? Norms are patterns of behavior that are shared by large numbers of people. People usually obey norms because often they are punished when they do not obey them. Neglecting standards of common decency, for example, makes people vulnerable to severe criticism. As we pointed out in Chapter 2, failing to act properly and reasonably—like a "normal" human being—can turn an individual into a moral outcast. Thus, passing the salt at dinner when someone requests it and providing one's children with food are examples of normative behavior. In American society there are strong norms for giving support to people who have been innocently victimized (Harris and Meyer, 1973; Konečni, 1972) and to people who are greatly in need of help (Gruder, Romer, and Korth, 1978).

The most intensive study of the relationship between norms and positive social action has centered on *reciprocity*, the norm that good, and not harm, will be returned to those who have been helpful. Harming someone who has given help is despised almost universally. Alvin Gouldner (1960) has argued that the reciprocity norm may be essential to society. If people did not expect that others would return kindness with kindness, then social relationships would be filled with doubt and suspicion. Yet people seldom stop to think about returning good for good in these terms. They simply help those who have helped them because doing so feels right. When asked, people generally express the belief that this norm influences many of their positive acts toward others (Muir and Weinstein, 1962), and many researchers have tried to illustrate the reciprocity norm in action. For example, researchers have found that the more help an individual has received from another person in the past, the greater the likelihood of his or her helping if the benefactor is in need (Pruitt, 1968; Wilke and Lanzetta, 1970). Further, a person who hurts someone accidentally and cannot right the wrong by doing something nice for the hurt person may find someone else to help (Rawlings, 1970). The need for reciprocity may persist until the person who has inflicted the injury finds someone to help. Such tendencies can begin at an early age. Nursery school children are more likely to share crayons with a child who previously has given them candy than with one who has not (Staub and Sherk, 1970).

Yet the reciprocity norm is not *always* obeyed. For example, if people feel that another's favor is not *voluntary*, they may feel very little responsibility for returning the favor (Goranson and Berkowitz, 1966). Apparently the other's favor must appear to be a true indication of his or her liking, and not a forced action (see Chapter 2), in order for the reciprocity norm to apply. This principle may explain why little satisfaction is obtained from love that is *owed* an individual. Such love may be expressed *only* because the lover is obliged. Further, if a favor is *inappropriate*, the recipient may not bother to reciprocate (Schopler and Thompson, 1968). Norms govern the kinds of exchanges that are appropriate in given circumstances—when and where they are to occur (Foa and Foa, 1974). If these norms are not obeyed, reciprocity becomes irrelevant. For example, we once arranged a study in a little town in Denmark. In the study, a female co-worker carried a basket of coins and tried to give the coins to strangers on the street. "Free money" read the sign on the basket. Yet almost no one would accept the coins; giving away money just wasn't part of the culture's normative system. In fact, almost as many people responded by putting money *into* the basket as by taking it out. Norms existed for giving to charity, but not for accepting free money.

Although many broad cultural norms specify how much help one should give to others, Shalom Schwartz (1977) has argued that people also possess *personal norms*, which can be extremely important in influencing actions. As Schwartz points out, most people feel personally obligated to give help in various situations, and they experience distress if they don't act according to these feelings. Thus, for example, people who feel personally obligated to donate blood are more likely to do so than are those who don't feel such

obligation (Pomazal, 1974; Zuckerman and Reis, 1978). If people feel that helping their country by buying lead-free gas rather than leaded gas is a duty, they are more likely than others to buy the lead-free gas (Hebelein and Black, 1976). And people who feel responsible for the public good in general or for welfare recipients in particular are more willing to donate resources for such causes than are people who do not feel such responsibility (Fleishman, 1980; Schwartz and Fleishman, 1978). Feelings of momentary guilt over failure to act according to principles also can increase helpfulness, as people try to reduce these feelings by helping others. Thus, when people have failed to meet their own personal standards (Weyant, 1978), have been induced to lie (Kidd and Berkowitz, 1976), or seem to have ruined a psychological experiment (Cunningham, Steinberg, and Greu, 1980), they may go out of their way to help others.

We cannot always depend on personal norms to produce helping actions. As Schwartz (1977) has shown, people some-

times forget the norm, don't see that it is relevant, or don't want to believe that it applies, especially in a situation where helping is costly. In such instances the norm may have to be *activated* by reminding people about what is proper or right. One experiment showed that simply overhearing a short newscast that featured stories about altruism was enough to increase people's cooperation in a later game situation (Hornstein et al., 1976). In other research, people have been made aware of themselves, either by seeing themselves in a mirror or by filling out a biographical sketch (Duval, Duval, and Neely, 1979). Causing people to feel self-conscious increased their subsequent feelings of responsibility and their willingness to help the poor.

Who Is Helping? The Effects of Models

Although norms can be powerful, situations in which norms have yet to be established often develop. What is the norm, for example, for providing your younger sister with birth control information? In cases where norms are ambiguous, people may look for guidance to the behavior of models—those who already have committed themselves in spite of the ambiguity (Staub, 1978). As we saw in our discussion of moral development (Chapter 6), models can be influential in demonstrating right and wrong to children. And models are no less helpful in showing adolescents and adults how to give help, be generous, or benefit others. Models may influence people to join a search party (Ross, 1970), fix a flat tire (Bryan and Test, 1967), or donate to charity (Rushton, 1975). Models are so effective that investigators have wondered whether they influence actions *even when they aren't physically present.* That is, do people imagine a model's presence or behavior and behave accordingly? Supporting this view is the finding that college students believe strongly that altruistic behavior by their parents serves as an important source of their own altruistic actions (Rettig, 1956). Further, people who are most generous in making sacrifices for the civil rights movement see their parents as people who are more socially concerned than the average person is. People who are less committed to civil rights are far less likely to see their parents in this way (Rosenhan, 1970). And young girls who are rated by their classmates as being altruistic tend to have mothers who value altruism (Hoffman, 1975).

Can any model influence positive social behavior? Apparently not. As you might expect from our Chapter 6 discussion of models and morality, people are more likely to follow a model who is *similar* to themselves than to follow one who is different. In one fascinating demonstration of the effect of similarity on a model's effectiveness, investigators left on the streets of New York City open envelopes from which a wallet protruded (Hornstein, Fisch, and Holmes, 1968). Money was in the wallet, and a letter was in the envelope. One version of the letter indicated in ordinary English that the wallet was being returned.

Another version said the same thing, but in foreign-sounding English. The researchers wanted to know if finders would mail the envelope and return the money. Most important for the present discussion: would similarity between the finder and the letter-writer (the model) influence the likelihood of the money's being returned?

Half of the finders read a letter that said, "I found your wallet which I am returning. Everything is here just as I found it." The rest of the finders read a letter that said, "I am visit your country finding your ways not familiar and strange. But I find your wallet which I here return. Everything is here just as I find it." The researchers assumed that if similarity has an effect, the note in ordinary English would produce more returns of the wallet and the money than would the foreign-sounding note. And in fact, more finders of the normal-English letter followed the model's lead than did not. In contrast, more finders of the foreign-sounding letter stole, rather than returned, the money and the wallet.

Similarity is not the only characteristic of models to which people may be attuned. People may prefer to imitate the model who is in a position to give *rewards* (Hartup and Coates, 1967). Modeling effects are likely if the model has been very *nurturant* in the past (Weissbrod, 1975) or if the model appears to be *morally consistent*—matching words with deeds (Midlarsky, Bryan, and Brickman, 1973). Finally, signs that the model experiences *personal pleasure* after helping someone also may increase modeling effects (Bryan, 1971).

In summary, we see that people ask themselves questions about the social context when they are deciding whether to give aid. A key question is whether action really needs to be taken. If others are present, the individual's sense of responsibility may be diffused, or the individual may avoid action out of a fear of misinterpreting the situation. Other

Marta goes to bed hungry every night.

When Marta goes to bed hungry, there's not much hope she can forget all the bad things that have happened to her.

But with your help, there is hope.

Through our "adoption" program, you can help provide a hungry child with nourishing food, clothing, medical attention and schooling. And all it costs is just $15 a month.

And remember, when you help you'll be doing more than nourishing a frail little body. You'll also be nourishing a mind.

Inspiration for the giver. The framers of this advertisement seem to have taken account of key factors in the calculus of positive social action. Note the clear statement of positive outcomes and the attractiveness of the needy child.

people's inaction also may make aid seem to be unnecessary. And the potential helper may be influenced by norms that apply in the situation and by observation of helpful models.

The Calculus of Positive Social Action

Our analysis thus far does not leave much room for romanticizing about positive social behavior. Apparently most people don't sacrifice themselves unthinkingly for others. Most positive social acts seem to provide pleasure to the giver or help him or her avoid pain. A good deal of calculation, conscious or not, seems to precede positive action. That people evaluate costs and benefits before acting does not lessen the value that is placed on positive social acts. However, for social psychologists the issue is not the value of positive action—that is accepted as given—but rather how one can use what has been learned in order to *increase* positive social action. Can social psychological analysis be used to solve problems of daily life?

Research on positive social behavior suggests that people cannot be counted on to be naturally good and helpful to each other. Knowing the value of altruism may be important, but as a principle altruism is not likely to inspire charitable acts. If you were in charge of increasing charity donations, for example, this analysis indicates that you not only should seek means of making people feel good about themselves through giving (taking advantage of learned values), but that you also should emphasize other positive outcomes. The United Fund is successful partly because its campaigns make people aware of other payoffs. For example, the United Fund often works through places of business, and the donors' names and amounts of contributions often are maintained there. Other persons on the job, including one's employer, may therefore be aware of one's contribution—a social reward or punishment that can increase the force of the request.

The present analysis also suggests that giving to charity should increase if people know more about the need—but at the same time the needy individual should not seem to be too unattractive. For example, the photographs used by relief organizations often depict destitute *but charming* children. Thus the prospective donor is made aware of the need, but is not made uncomfortable by the children's poverty. As is also indicated, people need to feel that their donations have an effect and that their particular donation is as important as another person's. Thus, when a relief agency publicizes the number of starving people who already have been aided by small donations, a donor's sense of making a unique and effective contribution is increased. Finally, indicating that helping is a norm and using the behavior of models to demonstrate this fact can be beneficial. For example, the United Fund is effective in establishing norms for giving. When collections are made at places of business, many employees receive an indication of the amount of money that is an appropriate contribution for persons at their income level. And the television marathons that raise money for muscular dystrophy are among the best examples of effective modeling: people may be moved to donate partly because they see that others are doing so. Of course, these sorts of maneuvers may themselves seem to be calculated and may appear to take the heart out of giving. However, as our analysis makes clear, if all giving depended on heart, there might be very little charity.

Reactions to Help: When Gifts Prove Unkind

What is the position of the one who receives all of this kindness? Most people assume that help always is appreciated, that aid just naturally will breed good will. When an individual stops to help someone change a tire, volunteers time to tutor a slow reader, or sends a gift to a charity, the assumption is that the recipient will be happy, appreciative, and perhaps even moved to help others in return. Certainly much of our earlier discussion suggests that this is a reasonable view. We have said that social attraction increases as one receives benefit from another person (Chapter 3). And as we have just seen, the reciprocity norm strongly urges the return of good for good.

A concrete problem is created by helpfulness, however. In the words of a foreign aid official, "One of the over-riding problems of our times is the yawning gap between rich and poor, between the haves and have-nots of our global society. This gap is not only a moral outrage, it constitutes a threat to world peace" (Sommer, 1979). Almost all of the powerful nations of the world have responded to this problem by developing programs of foreign aid. Yet the history of such programs is flawed by many failures. Programs have been resisted by the recipients; donor nations have been expelled from recipient nations; aid supplies have been stolen or burned; and in some cases givers of aid have been murdered by the very people they were trying to help. Clearly we cannot assume that good works are always appreciated (Fisher, Nadler, and Whitcher, 1980).

The recipient's position often is difficult. The saying that "it is more blessed to give than to receive" may be true in more than one way. Some social critics have argued that aid to needy groups actually is beneficial to those in power (Guttentag, 1973; Ryan, 1971). Giving help to the needy, the critics suggest, makes the needy appear to be incompetent and hides the major problem—the society's failure to provide meaningful roles and a respectable wage (Lenrow, 1978). The person who receives help faces four major problems: the donor may try to manipulate the recipi-

No help wanted here. This destitute woman, her possessions at her side, seems to be warning passersby to keep their distance. Shopping-bag ladies are an increasingly familiar part of the urban scene. They treasure their independence and react with hostility to offers of aid.

ent, and the recipient may feel inferior, obligated, or simply hostile to the donor.

As we consider the recipient's problems, let us also broaden our perspective. Most of the research that is discussed in this book has focused on the behavior of North Americans. We have said little about whether their the-ories and research apply to other cultures. Research on reactions to aid, however, has included observations of the behavior of people in other cultures. The goal of this work has been to improve international relations through providing aid. Researchers often have been able to gather data in several countries, thus offering an opportunity to discover whether people in different cultures share tendencies and responses. Let us now consider the problems that are created by receiving aid.

Aid as Manipulation

We once had the opportunity to interview a Tunisian cabinet minister on the subject of his views of American aid to his country. *Interview* probably is not the best word to use in describing our experience. The minister spent two hours burying American aid under a torrent of abuse. His major complaint was the way in which the aid was used to manipulate his nation's policies. Tunisia was in great need, but instead of giving for humane reasons, he argued, the United States government used aid to advance its own interests. He said that Tunisia was being forced to support U.S. policies in the United Nations, represent U.S. views in the Arab bloc, build an educational system that reflected U.S. educational philosophies, and so on. This concern with the manipulative character of aid is echoed worldwide. As the old Eskimo saying goes, "with gifts you make slaves, just as with whips you make dogs" (quoted in Farb, 1968). If aid is seen as being manipulative, people may fail to accept it (Gergen and Gergen, 1972), and if they accept it, they may not feel gratitude or an obligation to return it (Greenberg, 1980).

The view that aid is manipulative means that the wealthy international donor—or any gift-giver who seems to have great wealth—may suffer a disadvantage. The recipient can never be certain that the gift is not of trivial concern to the donor or that it was given casually. In one demonstration of this point, pairs of undergraduates played games in which they could earn money (Pruitt, 1968). At the end of the first game one student was allowed to divide the winnings. He was instructed privately to behave generously, giving his partner a full 80 percent of the $1 they had won. In a contrasting condition the giver was told to share only 20 percent of the winnings with his partner. However, because these subjects had won $4, the partner received *precisely the same* amount of money as in the first condition. The difference was in the *percentage* of the money shared. The partner who shared $1 gave little, but he seemed to be sacrificing much. The partner in the $4 condition gave the same amount, but the sacrifice seemed to be trivial. The variation in self-sacrifice proved to be very influential when the second subject took a turn at dividing the winnings. The subjects who had received 80 percent of the giver's resources were far more generous than were those who had received 20 percent. Similar demonstrations have confirmed that this reaction is typical in both Europe and Asia (Fisher and Nadler, 1976; Gergen et al., 1975; Pruitt, 1968). Perhaps American aid never will be very successful in building friendly relations abroad. The resources of the United States are so great in comparison with those of needy nations that whatever Americans give may seem to be trivial.

Aid as Debasement

Have you ever wondered what a beggar is thinking as he or she stands with hand outstretched? Most people can't imagine being so open to public scorn. To some degree, however, most people who turn to others for help are in such a position. In the request for help often lies the admission that one is not self-sufficient and that the other is superior in some respect. Thus needy nations, welfare recipients, beggars, and others who require aid must face the touchy problem of seeming to be weak or inferior. Also, an offer of help suggests that the needy person is unable to help himself or herself (Brickman et al., 1979).

The recipient of aid thus may come to feel a lowered sense of self-esteem (Andreas, 1969; Nadler, Altman, and Fisher, 1979). Or the offer of help may produce intense resentment.

An illustration of resentment that is produced by aid has been provided by an experiment in which Italian university students were asked to solve a difficult puzzle (Morse, 1972). The importance of succeeding at the task was varied systematically. Some subjects were told that the puzzle was a measure of intelligence, thus making the task important to their sense of self-esteem. For a second group, no personal importance was attached to doing well; the subjects simply were told that the puzzle was being pretested for later work. As each subject was working on the puzzle the experimenter "happened by" and looked at the subject's work. The experimenter then mumbled that the subject didn't seem to be doing very well, and he gave the subject a key that would allow easy completion of the puzzle. Subjects then indicated privately their feelings toward the experimenter. Subjects who thought that the test was an indicator of their intelligence were quite angry about the experimenter's help. Even though the experimenter gave precisely the same amount of help to all subjects, when the help implied that the subject was unintelligent, the reaction was hostility.

Additional research indicates that needy people in society often avoid seeking help for reasons of self-esteem (Broll, Gross, and Piliavin, 1974). Many individuals don't wish to acknowledge inferiority in any respect; their pride stands in the way of asking for help. In addition, they may believe that the help-giver will see them as being incompetent (DePaulo and Fisher, 1980). The implications of this work are far-reaching. Even though help is available, many impoverished people may suffer for years because of their need to retain self-esteem. Help for them may be possible, however. If people are not *required* to ask for

help, but instead are offered help without implications for their self-esteem, they may accept it more gladly (Broll, Gross, and Piliavin, 1974). Second, if the needy believe that the help is not costly to the donor, they may be more willing to seek help than they otherwise would be (DePaulo and Fisher, 1980). Third, if the needy can be convinced that their problems are the result of factors in the environment and are not due to their inadequate skills or motives, the help may be more welcome than it otherwise might be (Worchel and Andreoli, 1974; Morris and Rosen, 1973). And finally, if the person who needs help can remain relatively anonymous, he or she may be more willing to seek or accept help than otherwise would be the case (Nadler and Porat, 1978).

Aid as Obligation

Have you ever bought a present for a friend and, instead of being thanked, found yourself the object of the friend's anger? Perhaps the friend could not afford to give you a present and thus did not want one from you. Accepting a gift without giving one in return may burden the recipient with obligation that has no end. And as Demosthanes said, "To remind a man of a good turn you have done him is very much like a reproach." George Homans (1974) has termed this feeling the *tension of obligation*. Homans believes that people feel such tension whenever someone benefits them. This uncomfortable tension may be experienced as indebtedness (Greenberg, 1980). Such reasoning is quite consistent, of course, with our earlier discussion of the reciprocity norm. If you receive benefits, the norm demands that you give something in return.

Does the tension of obligation really interfere with relationships? Robert Dillon (1968), an investigator of world affairs, believes so. After the Second World War the

United States provided billions of dollars to western European countries to aid their reconstruction. Yet soon afterwards, European feelings toward the United States cooled. From his study of this situation Dillon concludes that the major problem with the American aid program was that it created a tension of obligation, and there was no way to relieve the tension. The European nations still were too poor to right the balance and come to feel equal.

In order to explore the tension of obligation on an individual level, we arranged a laboratory study in Japan, Sweden, and the United States (Gergen et al., 1975). University men were asked to play a wagering game that might enable them to win a handsome sum of money. By design, the subjects lost their bets until they reached a point where one more unlucky throw of the dice would exhaust their stake. At this point each subject received from another "participant" (a confederate), a gift of additional money that allowed him to continue in the game. For one group of subjects the gift was accompanied by a note that said that they were to keep the money and that nothing was wanted in return. In effect, the subjects received a gift *without relief of obligation*. A comparison group received a note asking that the money be returned at the close of the game. The subject thus had an *opportunity for relief of obligation*. All subjects later had an opportunity to evaluate the donor anonymously.

The evaluations of the donor prove quite interesting. As you can see in Figure 7-4, the students from all three nations had more favorable feelings toward someone who essentially gave them less—that is, someone who lent, rather than gave, the money. They liked the donor who wanted his gift returned more than they liked the one who gave something for nothing. Similarly, people often avoid asking for help if they can't repay it (Greenberg and Shapiro, 1971). And if aid is received from

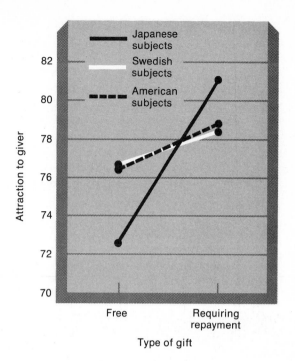

FIGURE 7-4 **When giving hurts the giver**

In this cross-cultural study subjects from three countries were more attracted to a donor who demanded repayment than they were to an overly generous person. (Adapted from Gergen et al., 1975)

someone who cannot be repaid, the donor may be disliked (Castro, 1974; Gross and Latané, 1973). This dislike may be especially strong if the donor is very similar to the recipient (Clark, Gotay, and Mills, 1974). Give a friend a gift that he or she can't reciprocate, and you may threaten your friendship.

Aid as a Creator of Undesirable Alliances

If you suddenly received a gift from someone you didn't respect, you might feel resentful. Your resentment might stem in part from the implication that the giver and you are close or similar in some way. As Fritz Heider (1958) has proposed, receiving a benefit from someone establishes a *unit relationship* in which the giver and the receiver are seen as being locked together in a positive bond. Interviews with foreign aid officials reveal that governments are especially sensitive to such bonds (Gergen and Gergen, 1972). National pride suffers if aid is accepted from a nation whose policies or character is disliked by the receiving nation's government. Communist nations are sensitive about aid from capitalist countries, and vice versa. The Greeks are not happy with aid from nations that are friends with the Turks. Similar problems exist between other countries. People seem to want aid primarily from those whom they would like to call their friends.

Are such feelings shared widely by the world's populations? To explore this issue we examined survey research in which people from developing nations were asked about the

TABLE **7-1** **Aid isn't always helpful**

Foreign aid may improve relations between countries when the recipient's attitude is positive in the first place. Aid from an enemy seems to increase hostility.

Recipient's country of origin	Attitude toward donor	Reaction to aid
Brazil	Family ties are close in the United States	U.S. aid is more effective
India	The United States has made a positive impression	U.S. aid will be more effective
Iran	The United States is domineering	Iran should not receive U.S. aid
Nigeria	The Soviet Union gives a fairer share of wealth to its citizens	The Soviet Union helps Nigeria more than the United States does
Senegal	The United States treats blacks badly	The United States is greedy for African wealth
Turkey	The United States is boastful	U.S. aid does not help Turkey's standard of living

Source: Adapted from Gergen and Gergen, 1974

characteristics of the countries giving aid to their nation (Gergen and Gergen, 1974). They were asked if they thought that the giver was aggressive, peace loving, or dominating. They were also questioned about the kinds of family ties that they thought the people in the rich nations had and how they thought minorities were treated in those nations. In each case the respondents also were asked about their attitudes toward receiving aid from these nations: did they approve of the aid these nations gave, and was it effective in producing social change? Thus the donor's evaluation could be correlated with reactions to aid from the same nation. Knowing how the citizens of Kenya feel about American imperialism or race relations in the United States, for example, should make possible the prediction of their feelings toward American aid to Kenya. Table 7-1 summarizes a sample of statistically reliable findings from the study. You can see that the recipients' views of the donor are related consistently to their reactions to aid. If a nation seems to be pushy, imperialistic, unfair to minorities, and boastful, its aid is seen as being less desirable or less effective than that of an admired nation.

These negative reactions raise special problems for foreign policy. A nation that is disliked and wishes to improve relations by giving aid may find its overtures unwelcome—even if they are well-intentioned. To illustrate this problem, researchers arranged a strategy game in which teams of subjects acted the part of decision-makers in a revolution-torn nation (Nadler, Fisher, and Streufert, 1974). At one point the players learned that their people had suffered an epidemic of a dangerous disease. Some subjects learned that an ally, and others learned that an enemy, had drugs with which to combat the disease and was willing to provide them to help protect the lives of the innocent. After the offer was made, team members rated the donor. An offer of aid by an ally was viewed as having more value and as having required a greater sacrifice than was the same aid from the enemy. Further, the ally was liked more as a result of the offer, while the enemy did not gain at all in the decision-makers' esteem. Offers of aid, even if well-intentioned, may not be enough to reduce animosity toward an enemy.

In summary, we see that positive social actions may not always be positive in their consequences. The wise giver will take care that his or her actions do not appear to be manipulative or self-interested, that the aid doesn't threaten the recipient's self-regard, and that the help doesn't leave the recipient obligated. Finally, the giver may wish to ask whether he or she will be considered a friend to the recipient. As the French playwright Pierre Corneille wrote, "The manner of giving is worth more than the gift" (*Le Menteur*, 1642, act 1, scene 1). We now can see what some of the major components of that manner may be.

SUMMARY

1 When a person does something to benefit another person, the behavior is termed positive social action. Altruism is similar to positive social action, but the term implies that the act or benefit is carried out without expectation of reward for one's self.

2 Before giving help, people usually assess themselves. Typically they weigh the rewards and the costs of the proposed positive action. They first may ask whether the action will bring pleasure. Giving help to

others can yield a wide variety of rewards. People act positively to reduce pain. When an individual empathizes with—imagines himself or herself in the place of—a person in pain, the inclination to help may increase. By helping, both the victim's pain and the observer's pain may be reduced. People also take account of their own resources when deciding whether to help. A positive mood—the warm glow of success—may cause people to increase the estimate of their resources and be more inclined to benefit others.

3   People also assess the one in need. Benefits to others usually do not take place unless the other's need is perceived. Excessive preoccupation with one's self may interfere with the awareness of that need. The prospective helper also may ask whether help seems to be deserved. Those who believe in a just world often think that the needy deserve their condition and may thus fail to offer help. Increased information about people's suffering may reduce this bias. If the needy person seems to be attractive, aid is more likely to be given than if he or she seems to be unattractive.

4   Before helping, people assess the social context. As the number of bystanders in an emergency situation increases, the amount of time that passes before help is given also may increase. The failure of individuals in larger groups to respond may be related to diffusion of responsibility for helping. And as group size increases, the possibility of experiencing shame for making a mistake increases. Finally, the inactivity of other bystanders may make intervention seem to be unnecessary. The tendency for decreased responsiveness in large groups may be reversed, however, if people communicate with one another and if the number of help-giving roles is large.

5   In deciding to help, people may take account of the society's common norms. Failing to follow norms may bring social punishment. The norm of reciprocity demands that people return good with good and that they not harm those who have benefited them. The reciprocity norm—along with personal norms, which encourage positive social action—may contribute to people's help giving in many situations. People also take account of the behavior of models who benefit the needy. When the model is similar to the observer, the positive effects of giving help may be especially potent.

6   Being the recipient of aid may be a mixed blessing. Aid may create considerable agony for the needy. The recipient may feel resentment if he or she believes that the benefit is being used to manipulate. Offers of aid also can be resented when they imply that the recipient is inferior to the donor.

7 Aid often carries with it a *tension of obligation,* which requires that the recipient return the benefit to the donor. Under some conditions people may prefer a loan to an outright gift, as the latter creates a tension that is difficult to relieve. Receiving benefit from someone implies that the receiver shares characteristics with the donor. Thus receiving help from someone who is believed to be undesirable may make the recipient angry. As a result, using aid to reduce animosity between people may not be successful.

SUGGESTED READINGS

Bar-Tal, D. *Prosocial behavior: Theory and research.* New York: John Wiley, 1976.

Staub, E. (Ed.). *Positive social behavior and morality* (Vols. 1 & 2). New York: Academic Press, 1978, 1979.

Wispé, L. G. (Ed.). *Altruism, sympathy, and helping: Psychological and sociological principles.* New York: Academic Press, 1978.

AGGRESSION

■ *In San Francisco three youths were arrested as they were assaulting an elderly man. The youths said that they belonged to a gang and that attacking strangers without provocation is the major requirement for membership. Each attack earns a prospective gang member ten points. One hundred points are required for full membership.*

■ *The Philadelphia newspapers recently reported that two brothers—accused leaders of an interstate burglary ring—made jokes about having killed three young members of their gang. As they led one victim to a grave that they had dug in the woods, they said, the young man noticed the hole and ran two feet closer to it before he was shot. According to one of the killers, the brothers laughed about the fact that they didn't have to carry the victim so far in order to bury him.*

■ *In Wilmington, Delaware, a woman was shot to death and her husband was critically wounded by the couple's son-in-law, who forced their car off the highway and opened fire.*

Similar reports of violence appear in each day's newspapers. While the use of guns is a fairly recent development in human history, violence is not new on the human scene. The pre-Christian Romans eradicated the populations of entire cities. Medieval religious leaders used poison to remove their undesirable acquaintances. And more recently, over six million Jews were exterminated by the Nazi regime. Western civilization's vast experience with aggression has done little to reduce violence. Judging by the number of people who meet violent death, human beings seem to be using their accumulated wisdom not to control or reduce aggression, but rather to perfect the tools of violence.

The central role that aggression has continued to play in human conduct presents a profound puzzle. Consider your own reaction to the incidents we have described. Your response probably was similar to ours—a mixture of revulsion and dismay. You may have asked yourself how people can treat one another so cruelly, or you may have asked what kind of person would casually destroy the life of another. Aggression on a minor scale also is distressing. Seeing a person verbally attack another person or associating with an argumentative person can be unpleasant. Negative reactions such as these undoubtedly have been typical of previous generations. Throughout human history most people probably would have preferred a society in which aggression did not prevail. The puzzling questions, then, are these: (1) if aggression is condemned widely, what explains its robust continuation, (2) why do people find controlling aggression to be so hard, and (3) is aggression inevitable in human society?

In exploring these questions we first will examine two competing orientations to aggression: one emphasizes the hereditary basis of aggression, and the other focuses on the learned character of aggression. Although human beings may be born with biological predispositions toward aggression, social learning appears to be more important in determining when and where aggression takes place. We will examine the role of emotion in aggressive action, and we will see that aggression is not always the rational process that is implied by theories of learning. Emotional states such as frustration, anger, and hostility also contribute to aggressive activity. After considering the roles of learning and emotion in the production of aggressive behavior, we will turn to the impact of social situations. Whether or not aggression occurs often depends on the social and physical environment—on factors such as the presence of others and the presence of weapons. An exploration of these topics should provide insight into why aggression continues to be prominent in social life and what might be done about it.

Defining Aggression

Although we all can agree that *aggression* is an important issue, people disagree on the meaning of the term. Some people consider hunting and fishing to be forms of aggression; others do not. Similar disagreement exists about whether the term applies to accidental injury, theft, cursing, and simply *hoping* that another person will suffer. No single definition really does justice to the entire range of thinking and research in this area. However, most social psychologists define *aggression* as *behavior that is designed to deliver negative outcomes (such as pain, sorrow, or death) to another person or persons* (Bandura, 1973; Baron, 1977). Several distinctions among different kinds of aggression may be useful. For example, *direct aggression,* in which the aggressive act is an end in itself, can be distinguished from *indirect aggression,* in which the infliction of pain or suffering is a means to some other end. To insult someone who has been rude to you is a form of direct aggression since the insult is designed specifically to hurt the person. To strike a child for playing in the street is a form of indirect aggression since the pain is a means of teaching the child to stay out of the street. In addition, *active aggression,* in which harm is delivered through an activity such as striking a blow or criticizing, can be distinguished from *passive aggression,* in which inactivity may cause harm (for example, by failing to help someone reduce his or her pain). Finally, important differences can be found in the processes that underlie *physical aggression* and *verbal aggression.*

You may have noticed that our definition of aggression says nothing about underlying *feelings*—the anger and hostility that usually are associated with aggression. This omission reflects the generally accepted view that aggressive behavior often is independent of emotions. After all, much aggression seems to occur without anger. Push-button warfare may be conducted with calm calculation. Further, people who are angry or hostile do not always behave aggressively; they often grin and bear it. Thus the connection between strong emotion and aggressive behavior does not seem to be close enough to *require* the inclusion of emotion in the basic definition. However, aggression and emotion are intertwined in most people's experiences. The topic has received much attention from researchers and will be discussed in detail later in this chapter.

Readers also should realize that the definition of aggression emphasizes the aggressor's viewpoint. When aggression is defined as action that is designed by the aggressor to hurt or punish someone, the target's or the outside observer's views are de-emphasized (Kane, Joseph, and Tedeschi, 1976). In judging what is aggressive and what is not, the observer may use standards that are quite different from those of the aggressor. For example, if you are hurt by another person, you may assume that the person's action was deliberate even if this is denied strongly. "What do you *mean* you didn't think I'd be hurt?" you might exclaim. You are telling your attacker that you define a particular action as being aggressive even if he or she does not. Such differences in viewpoint must be kept in mind as we review research in which experimenters decide what counts as aggression (Rajecki et al., 1979). Finally, a value bias is inherent in the definition of aggression. Aggression is presented as a negative form of behavior that should be reduced or controlled. Yet some people, particularly those who are oppressed in their society, may use aggression to call attention to their condition (Lubek, 1980). The 1956 Hungarian uprising against the Soviet Union stirred the sympathies of people throughout the world. And riots in South Africa and in ghettos in the United States are other good examples of aggressive activities that have gained international attention and support. Thus we can see that the automatic assumption that aggression should be reduced or controlled overlooks the potentially useful social functions of aggression. At times peace simply may mean that oppression is perfect.

The Biological Basis of Aggression

Having tangled with the problem of definition, we can turn our attention to sources of aggression. In trying to answer the question of why aggression occurs, we first will consider an approach that stresses nature.

The Instinct to Aggress

The course of human behavior over the centuries, across cultures, or during early periods of child development almost always has included aggression. "History reveals a long and uninterrupted record of war, invasion, torture and destruction stretching back to the shadowy beginnings of organized society" (Baron, 1977, p. 1). During the past three decades, for example, violent conflicts have taken place in 114 of the world's 121 largest nations (Gurr, 1970). And aggressive behavior is found among every age group. With little cause for provocation, even very young children will hurt each other. The range and persistence of aggressive behavior suggest that aggression is part of human nature—people seem to inherit a disposition to behave aggressively.

The early psychologist William MacDougall (1908) termed this disposition an "instinct of pugnacity." Freud also believed that aggression is instinctive. In 1932 the League of Nations arranged for an exchange between Albert Einstein and Freud, and Einstein queried Freud on the causes of war. Central to Freud's reply was his notion that the human is born with two primary motives, one directed toward pleasure (Eros) and the other toward death and destruction (Thanatos). War, Freud believed, primarily was the result of the individual's attempt to gratify his or her destructive impulses: "This instinct functions in every living being, striving to work its ruin and reduce life to its primal state of inert matter" (1964, p. 77).

Similar conclusions about an inborn disposition to aggress have been reached by *ethologists*—biologists whose major concern is with the instinctive patterns of behavior that are common to various animal species. The Nobel Prize winning ethologist Konrad Lorenz (1966, 1970) has investigated aggression in a wide range of species. He is convinced that both human beings and lower animals are naturally aggressive. However, through natural selection most animal species have developed genetically based means of controlling and limiting aggression within their species. Common among animal species, for instance, are sham fights, in which the contenders threaten, push, or scratch, but never kill one another—even when they easily could do so. The animals *instinctively* stop short of destroying one another. In Lorenz's view such innate inhibitions require centuries in which to develop. Lorenz argues that humans have failed to develop these means of control. Instead, according to Lorenz, humans' advanced mental capabilities have allowed them to create a highly sophisticated technology of destruction. The instinct to control within-species aggression has not had time to develop. Thus humans stand at the edge of a precipice: they possess the means with which to destroy their own species and have little instinctive inhibition against doing so.

Lorenz's and Freud's arguments suggest that little can be done to prevent human aggression and that humans are bound by genetics to act self-destructively. As Freud said, "there is no likelihood of our being able to suppress humanity's aggressive tendencies" (1964, p. 77). Lorenz has suggested that the human species' chances for survival would be increased if aggression were channeled into competitive athletics. However, cross-cultural research indicates that competitive sports are most well developed in the most warlike cultures (Sipes, 1973). Studies of athletes' personalities also indicate that athletes, as a group, are higher in aggressive tendencies than are other people (Gaskell and Pearton, 1979).

Does Biology Dictate Destiny?

Do Lorenz's and Freud's arguments spell disaster for the future of the human species? There is good reason to think that the answer is that they don't. A portion of the animal aggressiveness that has been observed by ethologists can be traced to the activation of the male sex hormones, the *androgens* (Brown, 1976). Hormonal activation of aggression is much less powerful in human beings (Ehrenkranz, Bliss, and Sheard, 1974). In animals the injection of androgens into males or females of various species increases aggressiveness, and castration often reduces aggressiveness (Conner, 1972). In humans the injection or stimulation of male sex hormones appears to have little *direct* or consistent relationship to aggression (Leshner, 1978). However, hormones may contribute to individual differences in emotional arousal or activity level. And people who are highly emotional or active may become aggressive under certain conditions (Widom, 1978). Yet the effects of these hormones on humans is *indirect*. Hor-

monal secretion does not *make* people more aggressive; it only makes them more aroused or generally active.

Although in lower animals some aggression is hormonal, other aggressive patterns are *situationally specific*—that is, aggression usually takes place under specialized conditions and is not generalized or indiscriminate. Animals engage in (1) *territorial aggression*, in which they defend their home territories, (2) *predatory aggression*, in which they kill for purposes of eating, (3) *maternal aggression*, in which mothers will attack those who threaten their offspring, and (4) *fear-induced aggression*, in which the threatened animal may lash out against another (Moyer, 1971). Thus special circumstances favor aggression among lower animals. If situationally specific aggression occurs in humans as well, then altering the circumstances that trigger violence should reduce the amount of human aggressiveness. If threats are not made, for example, then fear-induced aggression may not occur. In effect, the presence of a biological potential for aggression does not mean that the expression of the aggression is inevitable. Environmental conditions can be altered, and the aggression thus can be controlled.

The most important evidence against instinctive human aggression comes from research on *cross-cultural differences*. All people seem to have similar basic needs for food, oxygen, water, and so forth. In these simple requirements, common biological makeup seems to be the determining factor. Yet cross-cultural studies demonstrate that all people do *not* have similar dispositions to aggress. In a number of societies, war is virtually absent. As the anthropologist Margaret Mead has noted, "neither the Eskimos nor the Lepchas in the Himalayan mountains understand war, not even defensive warfare. The idea of warfare is lacking, and this idea is as essential to really carrying on a war as an alphabet . . . is to writing" (1940, p. 403). And, too, societies don't seem to show any periodic rhythms of aggression like those that govern hunger, sleep, and so on. Rather, the amount of aggression they display depends on historical circumstance. A culture that has been pacifistic for generations may be moved to mayhem if conditions are changed, and long-hostile cultures can experience centuries of harmony. The Semar tribe of Malaysia, long pacifistic in temperament and knowing little about war, was pressed into combat in the 1950s during a Malaysian civil war: "Taken out of their nonviolent society and ordered to kill, they seem to have been swept up in a sort of insanity which they called blood drunkenness . . . they thought only of killing" (Dentan, 1968, p. 142). In contrast, the warring tribes of tenth-century Japan were brought under a peaceful rule that lasted almost nine hundred years.

We see, then, that although all people share a certain degree of biological makeup and although a biological predisposition for arousal and activity may exist in humans, aggressiveness differs considerably from individual to individual. Being human does not guarantee aggressiveness or pacifism. As the noted sociobiologist E. O. Wilson has said, "human aggression cannot be explained as either a dark angelic flow or a bestial instinct" (1978, p. 119). Biology may set the stage for aggression, but its influence is indirect.

In order to understand the prevalence of aggression among humans, we must look at the way aggression develops in the course of daily life.

Learning to Be Aggressive

If aggression is not demanded by biological makeup, then why is it so persistent in human affairs? As Dolf Zillmann (1978) argues, aggression persists because it pays. That is, to gain one's ends in modern society, one often must choose to behave aggressively. From this point of view, people would seem to learn to be aggressive in much the same way that they learn to be moral. In our discussion of morality (Chapter 6) we showed how various learning experiences contribute to the development of moral dispositions. Particular attention was given to (1) reward and punishment and (2) modeling. Both of these processes also are key factors in the development of patterns of aggressive behavior. We will illustrate the way in which each process influences the learning of aggression. We then will consider two ways in which cultures teach violence: through television and through cultural norms, or rules.

Reward and Punishment in Action

In Chapter 6 we suggested that reward could encourage moral behavior and punishment could inhibit immoral behavior. This behaviorist point of view also is relevant to the learning of aggression. People will behave aggressively in order to achieve rewards or avoid punishment. Let us see how this view applies to an example of extreme aggressiveness: the race riots that occurred in the Watts section of Los Angeles in 1968. The riots were violent. Buildings were burned, stores looted, and over a dozen deaths resulted from armed battles between the police and the rioters. Eventually National Guard units were called in to stop the rioting with force of arms.

Shortly after the riots ended, three hundred black males who lived in Watts were interviewed (Ransford, 1968). A key question was whether the rioting had any reward value—that is, did the respondents think that it was a useful means to some desired end, such as equal rights? The investigator also was interested in the relationship between dissatisfaction and the approval of rioting as a means of gaining satisfaction. Each respondent thus was asked whether he would be "willing to use violence to get Negro rights."

The respondents also were asked how much dissatisfaction they as blacks felt with their treatment in Los Angeles and whether they believed that they had any power to influence government policy. Almost two-thirds of the respondents who experienced high racial dissatisfaction and also felt thwarted by the normal channels of government condoned the use of violence to gain equal rights. In striking contrast, less than 15 percent of those who were only mildly dissatisfied and didn't feel powerless felt that violence was justified. In effect the riots appeared to be a means of gaining a desired end.

Does this finding suggest that a redistribution of rewards might change the amount of aggression that exists in society? If aggression did not serve a function and if other options were more rewarding, would the amount of aggression decrease? Research supports this notion. Consider a study that attempted to modify the aggressiveness of male nursery school children (Brown and Elliot, 1965). Nursery school teachers often are plagued by the bickering and fighting of their young students. In an attempt to reduce such activity, the investigators instructed the teachers to reward all of the cooperative or positive social behavior that the children showed and disregard all of the aggressive behavior. The investigators reasoned that a

naughty child might consider attention to be rewarding. The results of the teachers' tactics after two weeks are shown in Table 8-1. You can see that both physical and verbal aggression were reduced substantially.

When additional observations were made a few weeks after the reward tactics had been discontinued, physical aggression had increased, while verbal aggression continued to decrease. The teachers then were asked to repeat the rewards for cooperative behavior and again disregard aggressive activity. The results of this renewed effort also are shown in Table 8-1. Physical aggression again had decreased, and verbal aggression was reduced to less than a fifth of what it had been at the outset of the experiment. The teachers were especially surprised that the most violent boys in the class became friendly and cooperative during the second reinforcement period. Apparently the careful use of reward can have strong effects on the aggressiveness of nursery school children.

Is punishment also effective in shaping aggressive behavior? As the developmental psychologist Richard Walters wrote in one of his more skeptical moments, "It is only the continual expectation of retaliation . . . that prevents many individuals from more freely expressing aggression" (1966, p. 69). In fact, much research has demonstrated successfully

TABLE 8-1   **The effect of praise on children's aggression**

Ignoring aggression and praising good actions had powerful effects on nursery school boys. Physical abusiveness was particularly affected by whether or not it was overlooked.

Time of observation	Average number of aggressive acts		
	Physical	Verbal	Total
Before treatment	41.2	22.8	64.0
After two weeks of treatment	26.0	17.4	43.4
Post-treatment follow-up	37.8	13.8	51.6
After second treatment	21.0	4.6	25.6

Source: Adapted from Brown and Elliot, 1965

Violence has long been a part of family life: an individual stands a greater chance of being struck and/or killed by a family member in the home than by anyone else in any other place (Gelles and Straus, 1979). Nearly one of every four murder victims in the United States and Great Britain is killed by a family member. Yet perhaps the most frequent form of violence in the home remains relatively hidden from public scrutiny—that is, the battering of a child by his or her parents. One national survey indicated that as many as 4 million people know a child who has been battered (Gil, 1970). In one survey, 82 percent of a group of three- and four-year-olds indicated that they had been struck by a parent within the year, and three children in one hundred indicated that their parents had threatened them with a gun or a knife (Gelles and Straus, 1979). Estimates of the number of children who die each year from parental beatings vary from one per day to five thousand per year (U.S. Senate, 1973).

What are the origins of such violence? At least three major factors seem to be involved:

1. *Stress and displacement.* Many researchers believe that common stress is an important source of child abuse (Justice and Duncan, 1976). Stress from a great many sources piles up during the day, and people often can do little to alleviate it. A worker cannot express anger against an employer easily, for fear of being fired. Traffic snarls allow drivers little in the way of retaliation. As a result, an exhausted and angry adult may engage in *displacement of aggression*—that is, he or she may attack some target other than the one that is producing the stress. Often children are the target of displacement, not only because they are available, but because they are defenseless against attack. Studies have found reliable statistical associations between various indicators of stress and child abuse. For example, income is an excellent predictor of violence toward children—the less income, the more violence (Gil, 1971; Sattin and Miller, 1971). One researcher found that a large proportion of mothers who abused their children were experiencing economic stress and were without supportive resources (Garbarino, 1976).

that aggression can be reduced by means of punishment. For example, punishing a child for aggressive play with a doll may reduce the **roughness** of such play (Hollenberg and Sperry, 1951). The repeated sound of an annoying buzzer can cause a child to give up thrashing a life-size doll (Deur and Parke, 1970). Adults will reduce the amount of electric shock they are giving to one another when delivery of the shock results in countershock (Donnerstein and Donnerstein, 1976; Wilson and Rogers, 1975).

Yet despite such demonstrations, punishment also may *encourage* aggression. Nations

2. *Cultural sanctions.* Even when they are experiencing great stress, most adults probably would not batter their children unless there were cultural sanctions for this kind of behavior. Adults do not, for example, attack their neighbors' children or pets. Strong informal rules prohibit such actions. However, beating one's own children is an action that has long been sanctioned in the society (Gil, 1975). As we already have seen, most parents in the United States use some form of physical punishment on their children (Erlanger, 1974; Gelles and Straus, 1979; Stark and McEvoy, 1970). Given the cultural view of the male as being more aggressive than the female and thus responsible for punishing family members, it is no surprise to find that when a father or stepfather is in the home, he is responsible for 66 percent of the cases of child abuse (Gil, 1971).

3. *The aggressive parent.* All people face a certain amount of stress and are aware of the cultural support for physical punishment. Yet most people do not batter their children. Apparently certain people are more likely to react to stress by battering their children than are others. In some cases the aggressive parent may be imitating models in his or her own family. A number of studies show that many parents who abuse their children were themselves abused in childhood (Zalba, 1967) or observed violent adult models (Green, Gaines, and Sandgrund, 1974). One investigator found a family in which five generations of children had been maltreated (Silver, Dublin, and Lourie, 1969). However, modeling may not account for all incidents of child beating. Apparently many child-abusers suffer from severe emotional problems or have other problems. Many studies show that parents of battered children are social isolates (Helfer and Kempe, 1972; Maden and Wrench, 1977; Smith, 1973) and have other social and emotional problems.

If child battering is to be reduced, one approach might be to attack the cultural rules that sanction it. If physical punishment becomes socially unacceptable, it is more likely to be monitored in the community and reduced through shame.

at war invariably resort to punishment to enforce their rules in occupied territories, and usually it doesn't work. The British in eighteenth-century America, the Nazis in twentieth-century Norway, the Americans in Vietnam, or the Russians in present-day Afghanistan used or are using inhumane punishments in an attempt at "stabilizing" otherwise hostile populations. Elementary principles of reinforcement would suggest that such punishment should discourage resistance. Yet in each of these cases resistance continued, and the aggressor's brutal treatment seemed to create counteraggression.

Displaced aggression. The deflection of aggression has considerable adaptive value if the original target is strong or powerful, and if the new target is an inanimate object. Unfortunately, however, aggression is rarely displaced by kicking a can. More often it is directed toward the weak and powerless. See the accompanying box on the battered child.

Apparently, then, punishment has limits as an aggression-reducer (Walters and Grusec, 1977). As we saw in Chapter 6, one reason for the failure of punishment is that the punish-

ing agent may anger the recipient, and he or she may try to get even. Thus the mother who strikes her child for pushing a friend may halt her child's aggression toward the friend. At the same time the child may search for a way to retaliate against the mother.

Modeling: Seeing Is Being

Aggression is taught not only by direct rewards and punishments, but also by the models that are observed. Models provide information about what pays off, what is appropriate, and how one can be a good person. As social learning theorist Albert Bandura argues, "Some of the elementary forms of physical aggression can be perfected with minimal guidance, but most aggressive activities—dueling with switchblade knives, sparring with opponents, engaging in military combat, or indulging in vengeful ridicule—entail intricate skills that require extensive social learning" (1973, p. 61). Models not only show the individual how to be aggressive, but also weaken inhibitions against aggression by demonstrating the desirability or effectiveness of a given action. Models also can show people how to use nonaggressive means in solving problems (Resick and Sweet, 1979; Tracy and Clark, 1974).

Many studies illustrate the effects that models have on aggressive behavior. In one early investigation, two groups of nursery school children were exposed for approximately two minutes to the behavior of an adult model (Bandura, Ross, and Ross, 1961). Children in one group saw the adult physically and verbally attack a large doll. The model sat on the doll, punched it in the nose, hit it in the head with a mallet, and kicked it about the room while saying such things as "sock him in the nose," "hit him down," and so on. Children in a control group saw the model play peacefully with a Tinkertoy set. Subsequently the children were allowed to

play with a variety of toys, and observers recorded their actions. The observations showed that the children who were exposed to the aggressive model were much more physically and verbally aggressive in their play than were the children who had seen the more pacifistic model.

Do models also influence adult aggression? Let us return to the example of the Watts riot. Earlier we saw that rioting had positive reward value for some people. It also may have played a powerful role in generating the rioters' aggressiveness, as the following description suggests:

> Without conscious thought of his action, he darted into the street and hurled the empty pop bottle in his hand toward the last of the department's black-and-white cars. Striking the rear fender of Sgt. Rankin's car, it shattered, and it was as if in that shattering the thousand people lining the street found their own release. It was as if in one violent contortion the bonds of restraint were snapped. Rocks, bottles, pieces of wood and iron—whatever missiles came to hand—were projected against the sides and windows of the bus and automobiles that,

halted for the past 20 minutes by the jammed street, unwittingly started through the gauntlet. . . . It was 7:45 P.M. Amidst the rending sounds of tearing metal, splintering glass, cries of bewilderment and shouts of triumph, the Los Angeles uprising had begun (Conot, 1967, p. 29).

Models also can reduce aggression among people. The Indian leader Mahatma Ghandi used pacifistic strategies against the British colonialists. Ghandi's behavior served as a model for people throughout India and the world. And in a laboratory demonstration of the aggression-reducing effects of models, male college students who were participating in an experiment that required them to deliver electric shocks to fellow students were shown a video tape in which a student delivered shocks to a victim (Donnerstein and Donnerstein, 1977). Subjects in one group saw the student select options that would hurt the victim least. Subjects in a second group were not able to tell how much shock was being delivered to the victim. As you can see in Figure 8-1, the nonaggressive model did

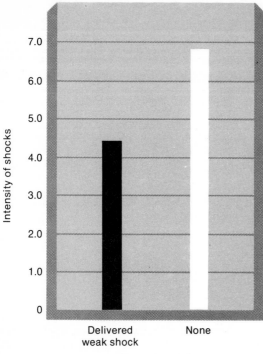

FIGURE 8-1 **Nonviolence can be taught**

Students who observed a nonaggressive model were less likely to subject a "victim" to high doses of shock than were those who had no model to observe. (Adapted from Donnerstein and Donnerstein, 1977)

have an effect. Students who witnessed his actions were significantly less aggressive than those who had no model for their behavior.

The Plight of the Punishing Model

Common-sense notions suggest that children who are punished severely for their transgressions will become respectful, obedient, and less aggressive as they grow older. Yet research findings provide little support for this notion. In fact, most evidence indicates that severe punishment makes children *more* ag-

gressive. In one study, for example, mothers who reported that they routinely use severe punishment described their children as being especially aggressive (Sears, Maccoby, and Levin, 1957). Another study found that primary school children who were rated by their schoolmates as being highly aggressive were more likely than their nonaggressive peers to have parents who used physical punishment (Bandura, 1960). Similarly, studies have found that adolescent boys who are known to be high in aggression (delinquents on probation) frequently come from homes in which physical punishment is common, while boys who are low in aggression often grow up in peaceful homes (Allinsmith, 1960; Bandura and Walters, 1963).

The aggressiveness that is displayed by children who are subject to frequent punishment may be strongly influenced by modeling. Although the children may be subdued temporarily by punishing parents, the parents are serving as models of aggression for the child. Later the child may use the parents' tactics with his or her parents as well as with other people (Anderson and Burgess, 1977). In fact, when parents use aggression they actually may be encouraging the very behavior that they are trying to eradicate.

Aggression also can be encouraged by cultural models. The present-day concept of masculinity includes aggressiveness. Femininity is less associated with aggression than is masculinity (Bem, 1974), although women can be violent if they see aggression as being justified or useful for their purposes (Frodi, Macaulay, and Thome, 1977). Males in Western culture often are more physically aggressive than are females (Gaebelein, 1977; Quay, 1965). For example, males are more likely than females to engage in armed robberies, murders, public brawls, and competitive sports, and they also are more likely than females to view military solutions to world problems more favorably (Eysenck, 1950). A male child may adopt this model in play and carry it into later life.

The Effects of Television Violence

Between his or her third and sixteenth birthdays the average child spends more time watching television than engaging in any other single activity except sleeping. A child spends approximately five hours a day in front of a television set, and during that time he or she is exposed to an overwhelming amount of aggression. During an average week, approximately eighty-four violent deaths may be witnessed between the hours of 7:30 and 9:00 P.M., when almost 30 million young viewers are glued to their sets. By the time the normal American child reaches the age of sixteen, he or she has seen an estimated twenty thousand homicides. In addition, many of the "good guys"—the intelligent and altruistic characters—are as aggressive as the bad guys. Many children actively model their television heroes, and the behavior they copy usually is aggressive.

The informal evidence that television violence encourages aggressive behavior is impressive. In Boston several years ago a gang of youths forced a woman to douse herself with gasoline, and then they set her on fire. This unusual murder was almost identical to one that occurred in a television drama that had been shown two nights earlier. A man in Baltimore went on a shooting spree in a factory only a few hours after a similar event had been shown on a popular television drama. And in Florida an adolescent who murdered an elderly widow was defended in court by lawyers who argued that the boy was a victim of televised violence.

A large number of laboratory studies also demonstrate that watching violence can increase aggression in the observer (Comstock et al., 1978; Geen, 1978). The studies we have described on modeling and aggression in children are among these demonstrations. In one

experiment, subjects were given an opportunity to give an electric shock to another person as part of a laboratory game (Berkowitz and Geen, 1967). First, however, some of the subjects were shown a film in which a victim of aggression resembled the individual they were going to shock. The subjects who saw the film administered a greater amount of shock than did those who did not view it. Research also indicates that the effects of watching violence may be detected for as long as five months after the original observation is made (Kniveton, 1973).

Many investigators have turned to real-life settings to gather evidence on the effect of television violence. In the most extensive study of this type, information on the television-viewing habits of third-graders was obtained, along with ratings of each child's general aggressiveness (Eron, 1980). Further measures of aggressiveness were obtained some ten years later, when the youngsters were approximately eighteen years old. Classmates were asked to rate each other on such questions as "who started fights for nothing?" and "who used to say mean things?" As shown in Figure 8-2, aggressive tendencies during the early years did not correlate with television preferences at the age of eighteen. The amount of television violence that was watched during the early years, however, was significantly correlated with later aggression.

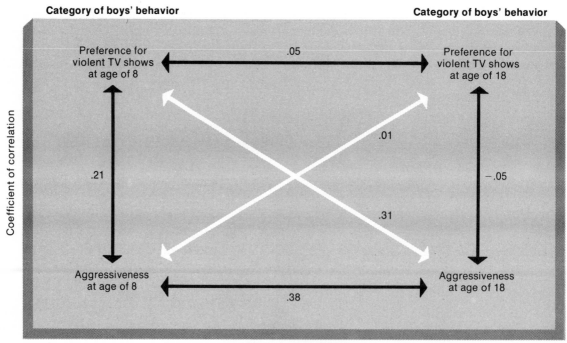

FIGURE **8-2** **Does television really encourage violence?**

The results of this longitudinal study suggest that for boys the answer is that television does encourage violence. Note the significant correlation between early exposure to television violence and later aggressiveness. (Adapted from Eron, 1980)

This relationship holds true only for the male population, however. Early exposure to television violence was unrelated to older girls' aggressiveness. Eron (1980) argues that females in our culture are not trained to be as aggressive as males. If males were trained to be more tender, cooperative, nurturant, and sensitive, television violence might have less impact on them.

Other critics argue that the negative effects of television violence go beyond action: people actually become accustomed to violence when they watch it all the time. That is, they accept violence as a common way of life (Thomas and Drabman, 1978). The lowered arousal that is produced by frequent exposure is termed *desensitization* (Comstock et al., 1978). To illustrate effects of desensitization, primary school children were given responsibility for monitoring the play of two younger children, who eventually became destructive and started to fight (Drabman and Thomas, 1974, 1976). First, half of the monitors were shown a violent film; the other monitors did not see a film. The investigators wanted to know if watching the film would influence the monitors' tolerance for fighting. They found that the monitors who watched the violent film were much slower in reporting the younger children's aggression than were monitors in the group that did not see the film, and those who watched the film also seemed to be less disturbed by the children's fight. Similarly, when children who watch many hours of television each week are compared with children who seldom watch television, the former show far less physiological arousal when watching a violent boxing match than do the latter. When watching nonviolent films, however, the groups do not differ in arousal (Cline, Croft, and Courrier, 1973). And adults who have a long history of watching violent television fare show similar effects (Thomas et al., 1977).

Yet in spite of these many demonstrations that television violence is related to aggression, we must consider one opposing view. Seymour Feshbach (1976) argues that if people approach television as imaginative play—as an exercise in fantasy—viewing violence actually may *reduce* aggressive actions. Indulging one's aggressive tendencies in fantasy may reduce the need to be aggressive in real life. To support this position an elaborate field experiment was conducted in which boys between the ages of nine and fifteen were placed on an aggressive or on a nonaggressive television diet (Feshbach and Singer, 1971). Either they watched such programs as "The FBI," "Gunsmoke," and "Have Gun, Will Travel," or they watched such programs as "The Ed Sullivan Show," "Lassie," and "Gidget." Boys who watched the nonviolent programs engaged in twice as many fights as did the boys who watched the violent programs. They also engaged in more than twice the number of loud arguments, and they insulted each other more than the boys in the other group did. More closely controlled studies in laboratories also support Feshbach's position (Berkowitz and Alioto, 1973; Noble, 1973). These findings suggest that the television violence-aggression relationship may not be as simple as it appeared to be at first. Perhaps some people are more likely than others to be influenced by televised violence. For some people television may remove the day's frustration, while for others the programs may suggest real-life plans of action. Persons in the latter group may be influenced because they don't or can't distinguish between fantasy and reality.

Many critics have used the Feshbach findings to argue that television programming should not be censored. Others have pointed to various methodological flaws that call into question the early work on televised violence (Armour, 1976; Kaplan and Singer, 1976). One argument, for example, holds that violent television doesn't produce aggression, but rather that people who are aggressively motivated may choose violent television (Fenigstein,

Batman: fantasy or reality? When the program is over, will the child run outside to join a violent game or will watching the program prove to be a sufficient outlet for his aggressive feelings? Research suggests that either outcome is possible. Television may inspire violent behavior if the action on the screen is perceived as a plan for action rather than as a fantasy.

1979). Still others feel that only the negative effects of television have been explored and that television's positive effects still need to be studied (Rubenstein, 1976). Thus it seems that the effects of television violence are uncertain enough for many critics to feel that regulation of violent programming is not merited. However, violence still remains a major theme of television programs (Gerbner, 1976), and continued attention to its effects is needed.

The Unwritten Rules of Violence

You ought to punch him in the mouth.

You can't say that to me.

She deserved what she got.

How much aggression is justified in various situations? As we mentioned in our discussion of positive social action, questions about what particular action is appropriate usually are answered by considering cultural *norms,* or rules. Most people would say that retreating from an insult is cowardly and that using physical force to punish a child is proper. Although these common norms are unwritten, members of the culture seem to learn them effortlessly. They are reinforced directly ("You were a coward not to hit him"). They are endlessly portrayed in the mass media ("Now, Son, you can't let them get away with that"). They often are expressed in our daily conversations about other people ("Jeff really shouldn't have hit her"). Aggression that seems to be aimless and spontaneous also may be governed by unseen rules such as these. A study of rowdiness at British football matches found that the drunken brawls that certain fans participated in fit a common pattern (Marsh, Rosser, and Harré, 1978). Certain individuals were "supposed" to begin the brawls at certain times. Disobeying these informal rules would bring scorn from others in the group.

The rules that govern violence in American culture give the police considerable leeway in acting aggressively. In one large survey, respondents were asked how the police should handle crimes in which property is damaged but no personal injury results (Blumenthal et al., 1972). The "villains" of the cases were of three types: a gang of hoodlums, blacks engaging in a ghetto riot, or white college students. Each respondent was asked whether the police should (1) do nothing, (2) make arrests without using clubs or guns, (3) use clubs but not guns, (4) shoot, but not to kill, or (5) shoot to kill. Two-thirds of the respondents felt that the police should shoot the hoodlums and the rioters but that they should not kill them, while half of the respondents felt that the police should open fire on the college students, but again, not to kill. A considerable percentage of the sample held even more extreme views. Almost one-third felt the police should shoot to kill the hoodlums and the ghetto rioters. One-fifth approved of shooting to kill the college students. The belief in violence is even stronger in older and less well-educated sectors of the population (Blumenthal et al., 1975). Such attitudes may explain why police forces in urban areas are found to fire an average of two bullets a month at unarmed suspects (Inn, Wheeler, and Sparling, 1977). The rules of justified violence in American culture seem to us to be extraordinarily lax and a matter for needed social change.

In the beginning of this chapter we asked why aggression continues to be a mainstay of social life. Although people generally dislike aggression, it persists. Our initial attempt at solving this problem led us to consider a genetic, or biological, basis of aggression. We found that although biological factors may play some part in human aggression, human beings' genetic makeup does not make aggression inevitable. Rather, whether or not one is aggressive depends on social experiences that take place throughout the life span. Aggression can increase or decrease, depending on an individual's learning experiences. Aggression sometimes may be chosen because it is rewarding or because it helps the individual to avoid punishment. It also may be learned or unlearned by watching aggressive models. One of the most pervasive sources of aggressive models in contemporary culture is television. Another source from which aggression is learned is the norms of the culture. People unthinkingly subscribe to norms of violence and often pass these norms on to their children because they think that the norms are "right."

Emotion and Aggression

Our discussion of aggression thus far has taken little account of feelings. We've presented aggression as a learned strategy that an individual adopts in order to reach various

**When Is
Aggression
Condemned?**

As we make clear in this chapter, certain forms of aggression are widely supported in society. For example, many social groups condone the use of violence by the police. Yet, people's acceptance or rejection of aggression in individual cases can be influenced by a variety of factors, and investigators have been interested in identifying these influences and charting their effects. Particular attention has been given to the way in which characteristics of both the aggressor and the victim can modify people's reactions to an aggressive act.

Let us first consider the aggressor—a person who has committed a murder or hurt someone seriously. Whether the aggressor will be forgiven or judged harshly may depend on how he or she is perceived. As the famous trial lawyer Clarence Darrow observed, "Jurymen seldom convict a person they like or acquit one they dislike. The main work of the trial lawyer is to make a jury like his client, or at least feel sympathy for him; facts regarding the case are relatively unimportant" (quoted in Sutherland, 1966, p. 442). Research supports Darrow's beliefs. Studies of mock juries, for example, have found that an unlikable person who has been convicted of an aggressive act is more likely to receive a stiff sentence than is a person who is perceived as being likable (Rule et al., 1975; Shepherd and Bagley, 1970). Similarly, the convicted person who is physically unattractive may be judged more harshly than one who is attractive (Dion, 1972). People also take account of the aggressor's apparent motives. The

ends. Although this view is helpful in understanding the pervasiveness of aggression in human society, it overlooks the fact that anger or rage often seems to dominate a person's aggressive experiences. Aggressive acts are not always carried out with cool rationality. An individual's most dramatic experiences with aggression usually take place when he or she loses control and is swept away in the lust for action. Does the emotional nature of human beings make aggression inevitable? When a person is angry is aggression a natural response? Can strong emotions overturn all of our attempts at teaching nonaggressive means of solving problems? In order to answer these questions we will consider the relationship between emotional states and aggression.

Frustration and Aggression

From 1940 to 1960 aggression research conducted by American psychologists was dominated by the ideas put forth in Dollard, Doob, Miller, Mowrer, and Sears's classic volume *Frustration and Aggression* (1939). The thesis of their work was bold: "the occurrence of aggressive behavior always presupposes the existence of frustration and contrawise . . . the existence of frustration always leads to some form of aggression" (p. 1). In other words, these theorists were suggesting that whenever people experience frustration, which is defined as the blocking of their goals, aggression will be a certain outcome. That is, whenever aggression occurs, one need only look for the frustration that caused the

amount of harm that was inflicted on another may be the same in two instances; but if the aggressor's motive is acceptable, he or she may be praised, while an unacceptable motive may lead to punishment. In one illustration of this point, subjects were told about two people who found a lost wallet and came to blows over who should take possession of it (Rule et al., 1975; Nesdale and Rule, 1974). Subjects condoned the aggression when they believed that the motive was to ensure the wallet's return. They condemned the aggression that was motivated by the aggressor's wanting to keep the wallet.

What about characteristics of the victim? Does forgiveness or punishment depend on the victim's identity? Again, we find useful hints from the courtroom. As legal expert Percy Foreman notes, "The best defense in a murder case is the fact that the deceased should have been killed regardless of how it happened" (quoted in Smith, 1966, p. 96). In support of this observation, research with mock juries has shown that much longer sentences are recommended for a murderer who has killed a likable, as opposed to an unlikable, person (Landy and Aronson, 1969). Similarly, if someone has raped a "respectable" woman, he will be given a stiffer sentence than if he has raped a woman who is not "respectable" (Jones and Aronson, 1973). You may want to review our discussion of how people justify aggression against others (the just-world hypothesis) in Chapter 7.

aggression to understand it. As you can imagine, a statement of this generality and simplicity proposed by such outstanding investigators demanded wide attention (Berkowitz, 1969).

Yet in spite of the attractive simplicity of the frustration-aggression hypothesis, critics have suggested that the proposal may be too broad. First, the experience of *frustration doesn't seem to always produce aggressive behavior.* For example, as we will explore in Chapter 9, some people become depressed and inactive when they are frustrated or unable to take effective action (Seligman, 1975). Frustration *sometimes* may precede aggression, but frustration also can produce other reactions. Second, *aggression often may occur without prior frustration.* For example, sol-

diers may fire on enemy troops because they have been ordered to do so or they may do so out of a sense of patriotism, but not because they are feeling frustrated. In view of these contradictions, the early theorists revised their formulation and argued that frustration *could* precede some forms of aggression and that aggression *sometimes* was produced by frustration (Miller, 1941). As aggression theorist Leonard Berkowitz (1969) concluded, this revised position seems to be quite reasonable and worth pursuing. The question then becomes, under what conditions will frustration precede aggression?

One condition that may increase aggression is *an increase in the amount of frustration that an individual experiences.* That is, the more something is desired, the greater the

The frustration-aggression hypothesis in action. Frustration may not always lead to aggression in the research laboratory, at home, or on the job, but on the road it's a different matter. The frustration of a traffic jam or a minor collision is sometimes sufficient to trigger verbal abuse or physical violence, even in relatively well-controlled people.

frustration and the greater the likelihood of aggression when the desire is thwarted. In one demonstration of this idea an experimenter arranged for either male or female confederates to break into lines of people waiting to enter restaurants, theaters, and grocery checkout counters (Harris, 1974). Half of the time the confederates cut in front of the second person in line. The rest of the time they pushed in front of the twelfth person. The researcher reasoned that people who are closer to their goal will experience greater frustration when the goal is blocked than will people farther from their goal. Thus the second person in line should react to the line-breaker with more aggression than the twelfth person would. Aggression was measured by noting the reactions of the person in line. As you can see in Figure 8-3, people at the front of the line were far more vocal in their reaction to the line-breaker than were those farther back. The amount of aggression also varied with the sex of the intruder. Female offenders were treated more nicely than were males. Perhaps people feel that in order to affect the behavior of a male, one must treat him more aggressively than one would treat a female.

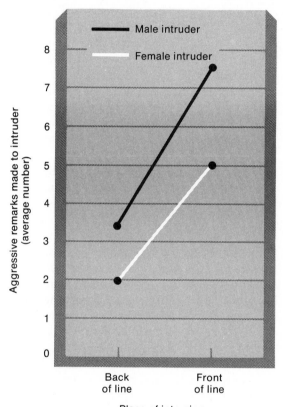

FIGURE 8-3

The relationship between frustration and aggression

Cutting into the front of a line will create a greater outburst of verbal abuse than will cutting into the rear of the line. Women who engage in this kind of aggressive behavior seem to have an easier time of it than men, however. (Adapted from Harris, 1974)

A second condition that may strengthen the link between frustration and aggression is *arbitrariness. The more arbitrary the frustrating agent, the more aggressive the reaction.* Thus, if you were hurrying to dinner and someone grabbed your arm, you well might become frustrated. If the person who grabbed you had no good reason to do so, you might respond aggressively. In contrast, if the person who grabbed you said "come quickly, your roommate is very sick," aggression would be far from your mind. Under these circumstances frustration would not seem to be arbitrary, but it would make sense in common cultural terms. In one demonstration of this point a researcher compared subjects' reactions to a frustration that only some of the subjects perceived as being arbitrary (Worchel, 1974). Some students were led to believe that they could choose either credit toward their psychology course, $5, or a bottle of men's cologne as a reward for participating in the experiment. Other students were told that they would be rewarded but that the reward would be selected by the experimenter's assistant. At the end of the experiment each student received the least attractive reward. Thus all of them were frustrated, but only the students who thought that they would be able to choose were frustrated *arbitrarily.* When later given a chance to rate the assistant and thereby express aggression, the arbitrarily frustrated subjects were much more hostile. We see, then, that the conditions under which aggression is most likely to follow frustration can be identified.

In addition to magnitude and arbitrariness of frustration, other factors can influence the frustration-aggression relationship. If you are frustrated by another person, for example, you might be more likely to react aggressively if the other person is *less* powerful than you are or has *no capacity to retaliate* (Berkowitz, 1969). Despite the power of some of these findings, social psychologists' attention has shifted away from the effects of frustration in recent years. Currently, the focus of research is the influence of generalized arousal on aggression.

Generalized Arousal and Aggression

As you will recall from Chapter 2, people often have difficulty identifying their feelings. People experience states of generalized emotional arousal, and they can label the arousal in many different ways. Thus you might experience a considerable amount of arousal if someone took $20 from your wallet. You might label the feeling *anger* if the culprit were a petty thief, and you probably would call it *disappointment* if the guilty party were your favorite roommate. This kind of reasoning has caused investigators to put aside much of their concern with frustration. After all, frustration is only another label for the generalized arousal that people feel when their goals are thwarted. The early findings on frustration and aggression may really have reflected increases in generalized arousal and not increases in the specific emotional state called *frustration*. The concern of modern research, then, is understanding how generalized emotional arousal is related to aggression.

In studying generalized arousal, investigators first tried to establish that virtually any kind of strong arousal can increase the likelihood that aggressive acts will occur (see Rule and Nesdale's 1976 review). That is, the feeling doesn't need to be labeled anger, irritation, or frustration for aggressive activity to be probable. In support of this point, researchers have shown that a person's tendencies to aggress may be increased through taking part in vigorous exercise (Zillmann, Katcher, and Milavsky, 1972), competitive activity (Christy, Gelfand, and Hartmann, 1971), and the injection of stimulating drugs (O'Neal and Kaufman, 1972).

Interestingly, these studies indicate that arousal created by one form of activity—like riding a bicycle, for example—may carry over into a different setting—let's say a conversation following the ride. Arousal that is generated in one situation and activates behavior in an entirely different situation is termed *excitation transfer* (Zillmann, 1978). Excitation transfer is believed to account for the close association that often is found between love and aggression. Episodes of intense aggression often take place in the home and involve blood relatives (Geller, 1974). Spouses, lovers, and other intimates are among the most frequent targets of assault and murder. Perhaps the arousal that intimacy can create intensifies any existing aggressive feelings. Arousal may be dangerous.

Contemporary investigators do not argue that *all* arousal produces aggression. Rather, they are searching for special conditions that may increase or decrease the likelihood that aggression will follow arousal—that is, when and where arousal is most dangerous (Rule and Nesdale, 1976). Researchers have found that arousal tends to trigger aggression *if aggression is a dominant response tendency* in a situation (Donnerstein and Wilson, 1976; Konečni, 1975). Thus, arousal becomes dangerous in the midst of a heated argument because aggression often is a dominant response tendency in this type of situation.

In one attempt to illustrate the influence of response tendencies, male college students in one group were insulted by a confederate of the experimenters, while those in a control group were treated more politely (Zillmann, Katcher, and Milavsky, 1972). Students in both groups then engaged in two-and-a-half minutes of vigorous exercise. The exercise, it was reasoned, would increase the arousal of both groups equally. However, the insult should cause aggression to be the dominant response tendency only among students in the experimental group. When both groups were given a chance to deliver electric shock to the confederate, the students who had been

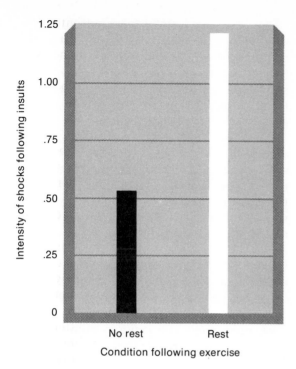

FIGURE **8-4**

Do people know when they're angry?

Subjects who interpreted their state of physiological arousal as exertion were less likely than subjects who interpreted their arousal as anger to express aggression toward an insulting person. (Adapted from Zillmann, Johnson, and Day, 1974)

for a minute and a half, but the exercise was *either preceded or followed by* six minutes of sitting quietly. The investigators reasoned that if the students exercised *and then* sat quietly, they would be likely to view their residual arousal as being due to anger. After all, they couldn't be aroused from the exercise because they had an opportunity to relax. In the contrasting condition, where rest preceded exercise, the students would be likely to view their arousal as being due to the exercise. After all, they didn't have a chance to rest. All of the students then were given a chance to shock the insulting confederate. As you can see in Figure 8-4, students who should have attributed their arousal to exercise were far less aggressive than were those who seemed to view their feelings as being caused by anger. Both groups had been insulted, and both had been aroused through exercise. Nevertheless, the students who actually were *more* aroused due to the timing of the exercise behaved *less* aggressively than did the students who were *less* aroused but who labeled their arousal as anger. Thus arousal seems to be a key factor in aggression, while frustration may be viewed as a special case of arousal. People who are emotionally aroused often become behaviorally active. If aggression is a dominant response in the situation in which people find themselves and if they label their feelings as anger, irritation, or frustration, then the arousal may well lead to aggressive behavior.

Sex, Drugs, and Aggression

Interest in the findings on general arousal and aggressive impulses lead social psychologists to ask whether other kinds of arousal—sexual arousal and drugs such as alcohol or marijuana, for example—can increase aggressive tendencies. The relationship between sex and aggression has long been a focus of interest in the arts as well as in the sciences. In the works of the Norwegian painter Edvard

insulted delivered more shocks than did those who had been treated politely.

A second factor that may influence whether or not arousal leads to aggression is *the manner in which the arousal is labeled.* When engaged in a heated argument, people are likely to label their arousal as anger. Given this label, aggressive behavior is likely to follow. This reasoning has also been illustrated by a study in which male college students were to deliver electric shock to an insulting male confederate of the experimenters (Zillmann, Johnson, and Day, 1974). These students also engaged in strenuous exercise

Munch, for example, the sexual woman often is portrayed as a vampire who kills her lover. Studies of animals also suggest a strong link between sexual and aggressive drives (Barash, 1977). If you ever have watched the courting of household cats you can appreciate the point. Nevertheless, research findings on the effects of sexual arousal on aggression are somewhat contradictory. Studies have shown that being exposed to sexually arousing pictures can make people more aggressive (Jaffe et al., 1974; Meyer, 1972) or actually can decrease tendencies to behave aggressively (Baron, 1978; Frodi, 1977). Although many factors undoubtedly are involved (Baron, 1977; Zillmann and Sapolsky, 1977), it appears that sexually provocative materials create arousal that can be labeled in different ways. The arousal can be labeled pleasant, or it can be taken as a sign of disgust. If the feelings are considered to be pleasant, then aggression may not be relevant. If the feelings are labeled disgust, then aggression may seem to be appropriate.

In one illustration of the sexual arousal-aggression relationship, college students once again were insulted by a confederate of an experimenter and given an opportunity to deliver shocks to the confederate (White, 1979). First, however, the students were shown sets of color slides: one group viewed scenes of sexual activities that many people find pleasant, and a second group viewed scenes of sexual activities that many people find disgusting. A third group viewed men and women engaged in nonsexual activity. Measurements of the amount of shock delivered to the confederate showed that the students who saw slides that allowed them to label their arousal as pleasure gave the least intense shocks. Their aggression was significantly less than that of the students who saw neutral slides. In contrast, students who were shown the slides that lead them to label their arousal as disgust delivered the most intense shocks.

Thus, pleasant feelings can reduce aggression—a finding that is supported by studies of humor (Baron, 1978). When people laugh they label their arousal as pleasant, and aggression also seems to be alien. Negatively labeled arousal, however, may increase the likelihood of aggression.

What are the effects on aggression of arousal-producing drugs. Particularly, what are the effects of alcohol and marijuana? Popular wisdom suggests that alcohol contributes to aggression and that marijuana leads to a mellow state of pacifism. However, alcohol also is widely believed to be a relaxant. And, as the President's Commission on Law Enforcement (1967) found, the use of marijuana often is correlated with violent crimes.

Although the findings in this area are inconsistent (Abel, 1977; Bennett, Buss, and Carpenter, 1969), the majority opinion is illustrated by a laboratory study that compared the effects of various doses of alcohol or marijuana on aggression (Taylor et al., 1976). In this research, male subjects received a special cocktail consisting of ginger ale mixed with either alcohol, THC (the active substance in marijuana), or peppermint oil (as a control substance). Subjects received either a light or a relatively heavy dose of each substance. Afterwards, they participated in a competitive game in which they were to deliver electric shocks to their opponents. The researchers wanted to know how much shock the subjects in the various conditions would deliver to their opponents. Table 8-2 shows that subjects who received the small dose of either alcohol or marijuana delivered a lower-level shock to their opponents than did those in the peppermint-oil (control) group. The low doses of both drugs seemed to have a mellowing effect. When larger doses of the drugs were consumed, a clear difference between alcohol and marijuana emerged. Subjects given a heavy dose of alcohol used the *most intense* shock of any group, while subjects given a

TABLE 8-2 Drunk and disorderly; stoned and stuporous

Both alcohol and marijuana affect aggression. Alcohol increases aggressiveness; marijuana reduces it. Note the dramatic difference in levels of aggression for the high-dose condition.

Drug	Amount of shock delivered to opponent	
	Small-dose group	Large-dose group
Alcohol	2.1	5.4
Marijuana	3.1	1.9
Peppermint oil (control group)	3.9	

Source: Adapted from Taylor et al., 1976

heavy dose of marijuana delivered the *least intense* shock. Since the subjects didn't know what drug they were receiving, labeling practices probably are not relevant here. Apparently the large doses of alcohol were temporarily arousing and contributed to the aggression, while the large doses of marijuana reduced both arousal and aggression.

Yet even though drugs may affect level of arousal, their ultimate effect on behavior will be influenced by social definition. When people believe that alcohol causes aggression, they have an excuse to aggress when they are drinking. They can blame their aggression on the consumption of alcohol and thus reduce their responsibility (Gelles, 1972). Indeed, the criminal law often is more forgiving of acts carried out under the influence of alcohol than it is of acts carried out when sober (Amir, 1971). As research on wife abuse demonstrates, when a man beats his wife, people hold him less responsible if he has been drinking than if he is sober (Richardson and Campbell, 1980). Ironically, if a wife is beaten by her husband, she receives more blame if she is drunk than if she is sober.

Reducing Aggression: The Emotional Approach

As we have said, the research described in this chapter has implications for the reduction of aggression in society. We have suggested that by altering patterns of reward and punishment and by exposing people to non-aggressive models, aggression might be reduced. Do findings on the emotional component of aggression offer possibilities for the broad-scale reduction of aggression? Let us consider two formulations: the catharsis hypothesis and the possibility of rechanneling arousal.

Catharsis: getting it off your chest

The authors of *Frustration and Aggression* believed that if a person acts aggressively, his or her subsequent motivation to aggress is reduced. Thus, for example, if you were a teacher and two of your students constantly exchanged angry remarks, the theorists believed that giving the students boxing gloves and letting them fight would rid them of the pattern of conflict. Getting the conflict off their chests would reduce their tensions and perhaps even enable them to become friends. *Catharsis* is the term for this kind of emotional release. The concept is an old one, dating from the time of Plato, but it continues to demand attention today. For example, many psychotherapists encourage their patients to express bottled-up emotions, in the belief that once the emotional volcano has exploded, a cleansing will occur. Primal screams, mimicking animal states by grunting and snarling, and encouraging physical assault are techniques used by theorists to promote catharsis (Janov, 1970). Attempts have been made to use athletic activities to reduce juvenile aggression. "If they can fight it out on the playing field, they won't be fighting it out in the alleys" is the rationale. The notion of catharsis has many supporters.

Two distinct arguments have been proposed to support the notion that catharsis reduces aggression:

1. *Arousal reduction.* This argument maintains that if an individual is tormented, aggression toward the tormentor can reduce his or her emotional arousal. After striking back, the individual no longer is aroused.

2. *Aggression reduction.* This argument maintains that after a person has aggressed against a tormentor, there is a general reduction in the probability that future aggression will occur. After striking back, the individual will not strike again. Although many theorists lump these two arguments into one, we will find that there are important reasons for considering them separately.

Investigators have been able to demonstrate that *arousal reduction* can take place as the aftermath of aggression against a tormentor (see Geen and Quanty's 1977 review). For example, in several early studies, student subjects were harassed and badgered by an experimenter (Baker and Schaie, 1969; Hokanson and Shetler, 1961). Later the subjects were given an opportunity to either deliver shock to the experimenter or rate him on a questionnaire. Students in a control group also were harassed, but they were given no opportunity to express their aggression. The students who were given opportunities to behave aggressively showed a more rapid return to normal levels of blood pressure (that is, normal arousal levels) than did those who had no chance to express their aggression. Aggressive behavior doesn't always lower arousal, however. If the tormentor is powerful and further attacks are possible, the victim may remain quite aroused and alert (Hokanson and Burgess, 1962). And if the aggressor feels guilty or believes that he or she acted foolishly or inappropriately, aggression may bring no reduction in arousal (Schill, 1972). In fact, when arousal remains high, aggression may occur again.

We see that aggression reduces *arousal*—but only under certain conditions. What about the second form of the catharsis argument? Can the *act of aggression* reduce subsequent tendencies to aggress (Konečni, 1975)? This catharsis effect seems less likely to occur. In fact, many investigations indicate that an aggressive action increases the likelihood of subsequent aggression. For example, a man accused of murdering four people was quoted by police officers as follows: "He said . . . he had a funny feeling in his stomach but after the first [killing] . . . it was easy." That one act of aggression leads to another has been shown in a variety of studies. Some researchers have argued, for example, that aggressive play increases, rather than decreases, children's subsequent tendencies to behave aggressively. If children are angered and then allowed to pound a box violently with a rubber hammer, the pounding does not decrease later aggression toward their tormentor. In fact, the pounding often increases later aggression (Hornberger, 1959; Ryan, 1970). Similarly, high-school football players appear to show an increase, rather than a decrease, in general hostility as the football season progresses (Patterson, 1974). In addition, most spectators at football games are more hostile after a game than before (Goldstein and Arms, 1971), and postgame riots are frequent—win or lose (Sloan, 1979). Finally, in various laboratory studies students have been antagonized, and then those who were allowed to administer shock to their antagonist were compared with others who were not given an opportunity to retaliate. When all of the students later evaluated the antagonist, those who aggressed were found to be more critical of him than were those who still owed him one (Berkowitz, Geen, and Macaulay, 1962; Geen, 1968).

This general pattern of findings, which suggests that aggression increases the likelihood of future aggression, doesn't mean that aggression produces no catharsis-like effects. Under certain conditions an aggressive act may reduce the likelihood of later aggression (Doob and Wood, 1972; Konečni, 1975; Konečni and Ebbeson, 1976). First, aggression may be cut off when retaliation hurts the tormentor. Apparently the *observation of pain can produce an empathic reaction* in the person who is retaliating (Baron, 1977). Second, the likelihood of subsequent aggression may be reduced when the *aggression is used to reciprocate punishment*. If retaliation settles the score, the need to aggress again may disappear. Thus, for example, although passengers who are overcharged by a taxi driver often respond by criticizing him or reducing the tip, observing someone else criticize the driver seems to be enough to right the balance. Under these conditions passengers generally don't complain about the overcharge, nor did they reduce their tips (Fromkin, Goldstein, and Brock, 1977).

The rechanneling of arousal

The early frustration-aggression theorists believed the aggressive response to be innate. Losing one's temper is a "natural" reaction to frustration. However, as we now see, frustration is only one of many possible labels for the arousal that sometimes precedes aggression; aggression is only one of many possible responses. Different cultures make different assumptions about what is *appropriate* action. In Japan, for example, a common reaction to frustration, anger, or irritation is to become very quiet; becoming violent would seem to be absurd. It is unlikely that Westerners' genetic constitution differs from that of the Japanese in this regard. Undoubtedly the link between labeling the emotion and the action itself is forged by learning what is appropriate within the culture.

The assumption that the relationship between an emotional state and a social action is primarily learned has important implications for reducing aggression in society. If people can learn that aggression is proper, necessary, or good when they feel angry, then they also should be able to learn responses other than aggression. In an optimistic demonstration of such relearning, female subjects were taught to reduce arousal in a situation where it would ordinarily be increased (Stone and Hokanson, 1969). Each subject was placed in an isolated booth that contained three response buttons and was instructed to interact with a "fellow subject" (actually the experimenter), who was in an adjacent booth, by using the buttons. Each member of the pair was to take turns in delivering either a *painful electric shock to the other* (via electrodes attached to the fingertips), a *token reward to the other* (signaled by a light in the subject's booth), or a *painful shock to themselves* (delivered by pushing the self-shock button). Thus the subject might begin the sequence by pushing the reward button. She would wait for her partner's response and then reward or shock her partner or shock herself. In a preliminary exchange in which the subjects found that their supposed partner was responding in no particular fashion, they seldom chose to shock themselves, but they often used the shock and reward buttons.

By design, at a particular point in the procedure the students discovered that if they rewarded the partner or chose to shock him, they received shock in return. If they shocked themselves, they were rewarded on the next trial. In other words, subjects were rewarded for punishing themselves and punished for any other behavior. For the remainder of the trials, self-shock increased significantly. Thus in response to the other's punishment, the students learned to punish themselves. In addition, measures of systolic blood pressure (an indication of emotional arousal), which had remained relatively high during the initial phase of the experiment, decreased as the participants learned to shock themselves. In effect, learning to shock oneself in order to avoid punishment was arousal-reducing. Self-shock brought about a reduction in the arousal that was caused by the aggressive behavior of another person.

In summary, we have seen that social psychologists believed initially that *frustration* is the principal state that precedes aggression. Later studies suggested that under certain conditions *generalized arousal* can, but does not always, increase the likelihood of aggressive responses. Excitation that is caused by sexual arousal or large doses of alcohol can increase the likelihood of aggressive behavior. If an act of aggression reduces the arousal, the likelihood of further aggression may be reduced. However, an act of aggression does not necessarily reduce subsequent tendencies to aggress, as is suggested by the concept of *catharsis*. Under some conditions acting aggressively can have an opposite effect—producing more aggression. Arousal can be channeled in

many directions. Research has shown that people who naturally might wish to relieve their anger through aggression can learn an entirely different pattern of action and simultaneously can reduce their level of arousal. Clearly people can learn nonaggressive responses to attack, frustration, or the loss of power (Worchel, Arnold, and Harrison, 1978). Reward and punishment may be helpful in learning nonaggression (Dengerink, Schnedler, and Covey, 1978). However, individuals also may be able to consciously change their own response patterns—by learning to communicate, searching for understanding, or relaxing, for example, rather than attacking. Research into such possibilities is much needed.

The Sticky Web of Situation

So far we have looked at the effects of both learning and emotional arousal on aggressive action. We will conclude this chapter by considering the effect of social and physical surroundings on aggressive behavior. Consider some examples we have observed recently. A mild-tempered and loving man discovered a stash of drugs in his son's room. Although he never had attacked anyone, he beat his son unmercifully. This threatening situation served to trigger his rage. Circumstances also can produce pacifism. A group of hostile teenagers were allowed to join a cooperatively oriented high-school class. After some weeks in this situation the hostile teenagers as a group decided to devote themselves to activities for the community good. The explanations we have considered so far cannot account easily for dramatic changes such as these. Clearly an immediate situation has enormous effects on aggressive action. Let us consider three situational factors that have captured the attention of social psychologists: the presence of people, the presence of weapons, and heat.

Presence of Others:
Identity and Deindividuation

Is a person likely to be more or less aggressive if others are present? Psychologists have been extremely interested in this question because of its broad implications for social planning. For example, individuals in urban environments are *almost always* in the presence of others. If that increases the likelihood of violence, then densely populated areas may be a breeding ground for violence. If it reduces aggressive activity, cities might be especially safe places in which to live.

Aggression ought to be reduced by the presence of others. Since aggression generally is considered to be undesirable, the presence of witnesses should reduce the likelihood of aggression. After all, identification can bring punishment. This reasoning seems to be supported by evidence that people inhibit their aggressive impulses if they believe they will be punished for them (Donnerstein and Donnerstein, 1975; Rogers, 1980; Wilson and Rogers, 1975). However, the situation is more complex in urban settings. When people are assembled in large groups identification often is difficult, no one individual stands out, and the likelihood of aggression may increase.

When markers of personal identity are reduced, the individual is said to be *deindividuated.* His or her identity is lost in the surrounding mass. When a person is deindividuated and thus no longer identifiable, fear of punishment may be lessened. Thus, the urban setting, with its dense population, offers freedom to aggress.

The effects of deindividuation have been documented frequently in the psychological laboratory. One early study found that students in groups in which personal identification was difficult expressed much more hostility toward their parents than did students in groups in which such identification was easy (Festinger, Pepitone, and Newcomb,

1952). In one of the most creative studies of deindividuation, the investigators arranged conditions so that thirteen hundred trick-or-treating children had an opportunity to steal money and candy on Halloween night (Diener et al., 1976). When the children were completely anonymous (for example, wearing costumes that obscured their identity and traveling in large groups), they were most likely to steal.

The link between deindividuation and aggression has been illustrated in an interesting study by Philip Zimbardo (1969). Female university students participated in an experiment that required them to deliver electric shock to another student in order to produce learning. Half of the subjects in the experiment were deindividuated—that is, they were clad in bulky laboratory coats and in hoods that hid their faces; they were spoken to in groups of four and never referred to by name. Students in a contrasting, individuated group were introduced to each other by name, were given large identification tags, and remained in their own clothing. During administration of the shock, the deindividuated students sat in the dark. The individuated students could see each other dimly.

The shocks, administered by a button placed in front of each subject, appeared to be painful to the student-victim who was visible through a one-way mirror. She writhed, twisted, grimaced, and finally tore her hand away from the strap that held her to the electrode. (In actuality, no shock was received, and all of the reactions were simulated.) Comparisons of the amount of shock delivered by the two groups showed that the deindividuated students delivered twice as much shock to the victim as did the individuated students. Further, deindividuated students who were led to believe that the victim was honest, sincere, and warm, did not give her any less shock than did those students who were led to see her as being conceited and critical. In contrast, the individuated students shifted in their aggression according to their knowledge of the victim's character.

We should not conclude from this series of studies that anonymous persons always are dangerous. Anonymity appears to free people from social inhibitions of many kinds. Only one of these is an inhibition against aggression. If a situation encourages aggression, as in Zimbardo's experiment, then aggression may be more likely. As we shall see in our discussion of environmental psychology (Chapter 13), anonymity can help people in certain environments to be more accepting or loving (Gergen, Gergen, and Barton, 1973; Johnson and Downing, 1979).

The Presence of Weapons

Deadly weapons are a fact of daily life. The police carry side arms. Hunters and marksmen own rifles and pistols. Many inner-city residents carry knives. Per capita firearm ownership in the United States is one of the highest in the world. Such facts have raised the question of whether this widespread availability of weapons contributes to high levels of violence. In such countries as Japan, England, and Sweden, few weapons are available, and in those countries the percentage of violent crimes is far less than in the United States.

Why should the presence of weapons increase the amount of violence? Many psychologists believe that two mechanisms operate to increase danger when weapons are present. First, *the presence of weapons may increase the salience of aggressive actions.* You will recall from our earlier discussion of salience (Chapter 4) that environmental cues often bring to mind actions that might not be considered otherwise. The presence of weapons may have the same effect—it may encourage the likelihood of aggressive options.

In one early attempt to demonstrate the

Candy, cigarettes, and guns. This display is not untypical of the range of products available in general stores around the United States. The easy availability of weapons may be responsible for the country's high level of violent crime.

influence of weapons on aggression, male college students were insulted by a confederate of the experimenter and then placed in a situation in which they could deliver shock to their attacker (Berkowitz and Lepage, 1967). In one experimental condition, however, a .38 caliber revolver and a 12-gauge shotgun were lying on a nearby table. The researchers wanted to know whether the mere presence of the weapons would influence the amount of shock delivered by the students. Those students who viewed the weapons did deliver far more shocks to their attacker than did those who saw no weapons. As Berkowitz later concluded, "The finger pulls the trigger, but the trigger may also be pulling the finger" (1969, p. 22).

The weapons effect that was demonstrated in this study stimulated both critical comments and support. Some investigators have confirmed that such effects occur (Frodi, 1975; Leyens and Parke, 1975), while others doubt that such effects are powerful (Buss, Booker, and Buss, 1972). Still other researchers feel that whether or not the effect occurs depends on how the individual interprets the presence of the weapons (Turner and Simons, 1974). A person who sees the weapons as signs of toughness or masculinity might react quite differently from one who is reminded of the bitter fruits of violence.

In addition to increasing the salience of aggressive actions, weapons also may influence aggression by *furnishing a means for reaching a goal or for solving a problem.* For example, police officers in England generally do not carry side arms. Thus they cannot easily shed blood as they solve the various problems they encounter each day. In the United States a police officer's possession of a pistol represents a constant invitation for violence.

Heat and Aggression

Common terms such as *hot-tempered, hot-under-the-collar, the heat of battle,* and *heated argument* suggest that heat and aggression are related. Do these terms actually reflect the environment's subtle influence on our actions? At least one body of decision-makers has felt that a connection between heat and aggression might exist. In the late 1960s a number of violent riots broke out in the urban ghettos of the United States. The Watts riot was one of the most severe. A national commission, appointed to determine the underlying causes of the riots, singled out temperature as a potentially important contributor (U.S. Riot Commission Report, 1968). Later research also showed that during the seven days that preceded the outbreak of 102 major riots in the United States, temperature increased significantly (Baron and Ransberger, 1979). As temperature increased, so did the probability of a riot (Carlsmith and Andersen, 1979).

Although no one believes that heat was the direct cause of the riots, it may have served to trigger violence in these economically deprived groups. Investigators have tried to demonstrate this possibility in the laboratory, but generally their demonstrations have been unsuccessful (Baron and Lawton, 1972; Baron and Bell, 1976). In fact, in some studies people even became *less* aggressive as the experimenters raised the heat of the laboratory room past the 90° mark. Subjects indicated that they felt more irritable under such conditions and less accepting of others in the setting (Baron and Lawton, 1972; Griffitt, 1970). However, these feelings infrequently were matched by aggressive behavior.

In order to explain these conflicting results investigators have proposed that heat primarily produces *negative feelings* (Bell and Baron, 1975). Up to a point this negative arousal may be channeled into aggression. Thus, as temperature rises, aggression may increase. However, as heat increases past a certain point people stop thinking about how they can act out their aggressive impulses and begin to think about how they can gain some relief from their discomfort. In fact, riots generally don't take place on the hottest days of the summer, nor are people who live in very hot climates any more aggressive than people who live in milder climates. When the temperature creates great discomfort, people are far less concerned with aggression than they are with finding ways to keep cool.

SUMMARY

1 Social psychologists define aggression as behavior designed to deliver negative outcomes to another person or to other persons. This definition places special emphasis on the intention of the potential aggressor, but it suggests that aggressive behavior may be separated from emotions.

2 Freud, Lorenz, and many other theorists maintain that people instinctively are aggressive. However, cross-cultural and individual differences in human aggression suggest that the genetic influences may be indirect.

3 Social learning appears to be a more powerful influence on people's aggressiveness than is biology. People often engage in aggression in order to achieve rewards or to avoid punishment. However, using punishment to reduce aggression may bring only a temporary reduction and may stimulate a later occurrence. Aggression also may be learned by observing aggressive models. Parents who punish their children for aggression may inadvertently serve as aggressive models·and increase aggressiveness in their children.

4 Television provides children with aggressive models to imitate. Children who watch large amounts of violent television programming are found to have aggressive tendencies in later years. Observing television violence also may desensitize people to aggression. Some critics believe that the case against televised violence is overstated. They believe that violence is encouraged among those who take the programs literally or already are prone to aggression.

5 Social norms also influence aggression. People in North America generally believe that aggressing against those who attack them is their right. Many people also believe that the police have the right to shoot at rioters.

6 An individual's emotional state can contribute to aggressive behavior. Early researchers believed that all aggression is produced by frustration. Although this view is no longer held, researchers have been successful in demonstrating various conditions under which frustration precedes aggression. For example, as frustration is increased or becomes more arbitrary, aggression increasingly becomes a probable result. Modern researchers have shifted their emphasis from frustration to the influence of generalized arousal on aggression. When arousal is generated in one situation and activates behavior in a different situation the response is called excitation transfer. The transfer of arousal to aggression may take place in situations in which aggression is an appropriate or dominant response tendency or in situations in which the excitation is labeled anger or hostility.

7   Other forms of arousal also can increase aggressiveness. Erotic stimuli often increase the likelihood of aggression when an individual feels that the stimuli are disgusting, but not when they are considered to be pleasant. In laboratory experiments, large doses of alcohol also raise aggression levels, and large doses of marijuana make people less aggressive.

8   Acting out aggressive impulses is widely believed to reduce further aggression. The reduction of an emotion through its expression is termed catharsis. Catharsis-like effects occur when aggressive activity reduces generalized arousal. However, aggressive actions in themselves can increase the probability of future aggression unless they are moderated by empathic feelings or the satisfaction of getting even. Aggression also can be reduced when people learn alternative ways of responding to arousal.

9   Factors in a situation also influence aggression. When markers of personal identity are reduced by the presence of other people, the resulting deindividuation may allow people to respond toward others more aggressively. Weapons also can increase the likelihood of aggression in a situation, as when their presence is interpreted as a sign of toughness or they can be used as means to a desired end. Increases in heat also may increase negative feelings and thus increase aggression. However, as heat becomes oppressive, people may become inactive.

SUGGESTED READINGS

Bandura, A. *Aggression: A social learning analysis.* Englewood Cliffs, N.J.: Prentice-Hall, 1973.

Geen, R. G. & O'Neal, E. C. (Eds.). *Perspectives on aggression.* New York: Academic Press, 1976.

Knutson, J. S. (Ed.). *The control of aggression: Implications from basic research.* Chicago: Beresford Book Service, 1973.

Megargee, E. I., & Hokanson, J. E. *The dynamics of aggression: Individual, group, and internal analysis.* New York: Harper & Row, 1970.

Zillmann, D. *Hostility and aggression.* New York: Halsted Press, 1979.

9:

POWER, LEADERSHIP, AND CONTROL

■ *Dick, a high-school student, left home because he no longer could tolerate living with his parents. They were happy to see Dick go. On the surface the problem was Dick's commitment to a girl. He insisted on seeing her whenever he chose and for as long as he wanted. His parents found this morally disagreeable and also felt that he was abandoning his responsibilities to his family. For months they fought bitterly, and finally Dick decided to leave. A counselor who talked with the parents and their son suggested that a deeper problem was at the root of the conflict—one of power and control. Dick felt that he was old enough to lead his own life—old enough to be autonomous. His parents felt that he still was a child and that he still had duties and obligations to them.*

Dick's story illustrates an aspect of human relations that everyone confronts from infancy to death: that of power and control. During one's infancy parents virtually have complete control. During childhood much effort is directed toward wrenching control from the parents' hands. Power is a dominant issue for students of any age who must deal with older and more powerful students, teachers, and administrators, who essentially control their fates. People who work within an organization, be it large or small, also become entangled in problems of power. The worker must cope with supervisors who give orders and subordinates who want to take his or her place. People also confront political, economic, and legal power. Those who live with another person continually face the problem of which of them will control the money, the children, and the leisure time. With aging often comes a threat to all the power that the individual has spent a lifetime accumulating. First one source of power crumbles, and then another, until the aged person is left as helpless as an infant.

In this chapter we will be concerned with the nature of power in personal relations. We first ask about the kinds of power that are available to people and how these operate. Some kinds of power are obvious, and others are scarcely noticeable. Each operates in different ways. We also will ask how power is acquired in social groups. This discussion will focus on issues of power motivation and leadership. Who gains leadership in groups, and how is power acquired? Once gained, power affects both the powerful and the persons who are subjected to the power. Those without power often are helpless, and helplessness can be debilitating. People with power also face problems—especially the possibility of corruption. We will ask why powerful people so often seem to abuse their position. Finally we will turn to the issue of opposition to the power structure: when is the existing power structure likely to be challenged?

Forms of Power

What is power? Most people tend to think of power in terms of politics or weapons. However, such images are too limited. To understand the meaning and effects of power, the term must be defined more broadly. *Power* may be defined as the *capacity to alter the actions of others* (Kelman, 1974; Thibaut and Kelley, 1959). When power is conceptualized in this way, an important question is raised: what kinds of power are available to people? By tracing the different kinds of power that people use, the many subtle and important processes by which people gain control over one another become clearer. Examining various forms of power also clarifies the advantages and liabilities of each form. A classic discussion of this issue (French and Raven, 1959), used as a model, allows us to consider five major forms of power: (1) information, (2) referent, (3) legitimate, (4) expert, and (5) reward and coercive.

Information Power

Several years ago tourists returning from Communist China often reported astonishment at the immense amount of anti-American literature that was available to the Chinese people. Billboards, books, pamphlets, and newspapers all presented Americans as dangerous creatures. Virtually all publishing in China is under government control, and government policy was anti-American, thus accounting for the flood of such literature. However, recent visitors to China have reported that anti-American sentiment seems to have disappeared. All of the anti-American books, posters, slogans, and newspaper stories were removed from circulation when the government position on the United States changed. These publications represented the Chinese government's use of *information power*. Since people often act according to their beliefs and attitudes about the world and since these beliefs and attitudes largely depend on the information that is at people's disposal, information clearly can be an important source of power. The Chinese government, by controlling the availability of information about the United States, could alter the attitudes of millions of its people.

How effective is information power? Some theorists believe that information is one of the most effective types of power that is available to people, more potent than arms or political office (Raven and Kruglanski, 1970). If people accept the information that is given to them and incorporate it into their belief systems, they will act autonomously in ways that support the powerful person or group. That is, by using information skillfully, people in power can change other individuals'

beliefs or attitudes so that they will act as desired, *without surveillance* (Raven and Rubin, 1976). A second advantage of information power is that its use does not create resentment or hostility. If information power is used skillfully, the targets may be unaware that they are being manipulated. People often appreciate receiving information and feel that the information increases their own power. American newspapers have much information power, and their readers generally accept press accounts of world events without question.

Referent Power

Psychologists often use the term *identification* to refer to an individual's desire or attempt to incorporate the characteristics of another person (or persons). Identification typically is accompanied by positive feelings for the other person. Thus, if you identify with a particular teacher, you like him or her and believe that the two of you share similar qualities. An individual also may identify with a group, such as a team, a fraternity, or a sorority. That is, the person believes that the group members share a common set of goals or characteristics. A target of identification, whether a teacher or a team, often is called a *referent* of identification. Being a referent of identification furnishes an individual or a group with a certain amount of power.

If another person identifies with you, he or she is likely to imitate your actions or preferences. As you change your behavior those who identify with you may change theirs as well (Grusec, 1971). Referent power thus can alter the opinions or attitudes of the target (Raven and Kruglanski, 1970). Like information power, referent power needs *no surveillance* and creates *no hostility or resentment* in the target. This form of power can be increased by *making shared characteristics salient*. People may be moved to act when they are reminded of their identification with

Jonestown: the potency of referent power. Bodies of the followers of religious cult leader Jim Jones lie scattered around the community's cultural center. More than nine hundred cult members followed their leader's orders and committed suicide by drinking poison. This mass suicide is a potent example of how the power of identification can influence people's action.

groups, such as fraternities, sororities, teams, and even nations (Tjosvold, 1977).

Legitimate Power

When government officials decide to increase the tax on liquor, alter defense spending, or lower the highway speed limit, most people are affected in one way or another. That is, their patterns of behavior may change. Even if people disagree with government decisions, they seldom question the officials' right to make them. Government officials have a high degree of *legitimate power*—power that rests on a set of social agreements about who has the right to direct behavior under various circumstances. In matters such as tax collection, defense spending, and setting speed limits, contemporary society places legitimate power in the hands of government officials. On such issues as what kind of music should be lis-

tened to or what hair style should be worn, the officials' range of legitimate power is restricted. In one illustration of the limits of legitimate power, a researcher asked people on the street to do things—such as pick up a paper bag, give a dime to a stranger, or move away from a bus stop (Bickman, 1974). When the researcher was dressed like an ordinary civilian or like a milkman, people seldom complied with his requests. However, when he was dressed as a guard, people frequently did as he asked. Guards have rights to demand certain behaviors; a milkman's domain of legitimate power is more restricted.

Because legitimate power rests on social agreement, its boundaries often are fuzzy and controversial. In Taiwan, government officials make rules that govern the musical tastes and the hair styles of teenagers. Although both long hair and rock music are condemned, the rules are not always obeyed in private. When American officials restrict private sexual activity or the practice of religion in public schools, considerable opposition usually follows, since many people believe that the government has no right to make such decisions. Thus legitimate power may be strong only so long as people believe that (1) users of power have the right to make decisions on a given issue and (2) the general public is obliged to accept the decisions.

Many persons who do not possess wealth, political influence, or information may possess legitimate power. In many countries even beggars have a certain degree of legitimate power. In most large cities the beggar is free to approach the average citizen and ask for money. If nothing is given, the beggar may induce guilt or even express scorn. Gypsies and Jewish beggars in prewar eastern Europe begged with pride and threatened the common stroller with their demanding attitude (Zborowski and Herzog, 1952). People in positions of dependency also have legitimate power (Schopler, 1965). Children may lack control over many decisions, but only kings

and queens equal children in the amount of attention given to their needs. Research shows that the dependent person may be especially powerful in obtaining nurturance when he or she is attractive (Berkowitz and Daniels, 1963), when the other person's responsibility is emphasized (Berkowitz, 1957), or when the nurturance doesn't cost too much to deliver (Schopler and Bateson, 1965).

Legitimate power shares with information and referent powers the *absence of a need for surveillance*. Most people obey laws and will stop at a red traffic light, for example, even when no one is in sight. However, unlike information power, legitimate power is *socially dependent*—that is, its force depends on continuing social agreement that the demands or requests are legitimate.

Expert Power

The form of power often used by the economically disadvantaged is expert power. Skills such as shooting baskets, playing the guitar, or writing computer programs offer a route to power. These forms of expertise may be used by an individual to secure money, obedience, esteem, or even love. The power of the clergy often stems from expertise in matters of the spirit or morality. The power of the husband in Western marriage often is based on expertise. In attributing power to their husbands, Western wives are more likely to attribute expert power to them than any of the other types of power we have discussed (Raven, 1974). In contrast, husbands most often believe that their wives possess referent power. The husband's expert power may stem from his being older and having more education than his wife. The more similar the wife to the husband in age, education, or occupational status, the less expert power he is believed to have. Clearly the use of expert power by the male is culture-bound. Among Guatemalan peasants, for example, the wife is more likely to possess expert power than is the husband (Raven, 1974). Expert power is much like information, referent, and legitimate powers in its capacity to motivate people *without surveillance.* It sometimes is resented privately by the subordinate person and is dependent on social agreement that the expert indeed is highly skilled.

Reward and Coercive Power

Reward and coercive power needs little introduction. A person has this kind of power to the extent that he or she has the ability to reward or punish another person's actions. We talked extensively about the effect of reward and punishment on moral behavior (Chapter 6), on positive social action (Chapter 7), and on aggression (Chapter 8). Clearly people respond to their parents' rewards and coercions, or punishments, from an early age, and as adults they may continue to be shaped by rewards—those of money or affection—or by the coercive power of social disapproval. Yet important reasons exist for distinguishing between reward and coercion as forms of power (see Chapter 6). In particular, *reward power*

Rebellion: a response to coercive power. The woman is waiting outside a Afghanistan prison where Russian soldiers are about to release a member of her family. Despite his weapon, the young soldier seems frightened of her rage. Research has found that the use of coercive power often backfires, producing powerful countercoercion.

frequently produces *psychological change* and *behavioral compliance.* In contrast, *coercive power* typically produces *compliance only.* Reward seems to produce change because it offers an opportunity for gain. Thus, for example, if a mother wants her teenage son to wash the dishes, she might promise him money as a reward. The son may thus obtain something he wants and look at the job as worth doing. In effect, the reward enables the boy to develop a positive attitude while complying with his mother's wishes. In contrast, if the mother threatened her son with "If you don't wash the dishes, you won't go out tonight," she would be using coercive power. The son would be faced with two negative alternatives: he wants neither to wash the dishes nor to lose his privileges. He may comply with his mother's wish, but he will not change his attitude toward the job (Zipf, 1960). When using coercive power, surveillance may be necessary.

Social psychologists have been particularly interested in finding out why coercive power proves to be so troublesome when it is used against groups of people. Five major reasons have been identified. First, when a group is threatened with coercion, the threat may bring the group together (Tedeschi, 1972). For example, arms used against demonstrators often galvanize resistance (Mulder and Stemerding, 1963). Second, the threatened group may respond with countercoercion. This reaction then may produce an intensifying of the initial coercion. The result may be an endless upward spiral of aggressive tactics (Holsti and North, 1965). Third, coercion may increase the value placed on the threatened activity (Turner and Wright, 1965). Saying "if you do X you will be punished" only may make X seem to be more desirable. Fourth, most coercive threats require surveillance in order to ensure that they are complied with. Finally, coercion also may produce *backlash,* an attempt by the coerced group to punish the coercing agent in revenge. The targets of coercion may feel that the coercive agents deserve unusually cruel treatment (Tedeschi, Smith, and Brown, 1974). Such backlash may be especially likely when the threatened individuals believe that their power is greater than that of the coercive agent. Believing that they have little to fear, those in the threatened group may feel that they can stamp out the aggressors once and for all.

To be sure, coercive power sometimes is the only kind of power that is available, and at times it may achieve what other kinds of power cannot. Corporations frequently use

TABLE 9-1 **Sources of power**

Various forms of power produce different types of agreement and require different forms of control.

| Type of power | Effects and requirements | | |
	Public compliance	Private agreement	Surveillance
Information	Yes	Yes	No
Referent	Yes	Yes	No
Legitimate	Yes	Yes	No
Expert	Yes	Yes	No
Reward	Yes	Variable	Yes
Coercive	Yes	No	Yes

coercive tactics when subsidiary businesses resist falling into line (Wilkinson and Kipnis, 1978). Political torturers use strong forms of coercion to get what they want.

In summary, we have surveyed five different forms of power that occur in everyday life. We see that power may reside in one's (1) possession of information, (2) ability to serve as a referent for others' identification, (3) having a legitimate position of authority, (4) degree of expertise, and (5) control of reward and punishment. Various forms of power have different effects and requirements (see Table 9-1). Clearly, everyone exercises a certain amount of power.

Routes to Power:
The Person or the Situation?

Even though most people typically exercise some power in their relationships, "real" power is widely believed to be in the hands of those who hold positions of authority or leadership in social groups. And elected officials do have access to many different sources of power. A president, for example, usually is given legitimate power by the people. In accepting the office, he or she also thereby gains access to information power and expert power, training in how to be a good referent, and command over many agents of coercion, including immense military forces. The question is, why do certain people acquire positions of power while others do not? Answers to this question have emphasized the personal qualities of leaders and the characteristics of the situation. Theorists who are concerned with personal characteristics argue that leaders are special people, different from the rest of us, with certain traits or needs that almost assure them a position on top. In contrast, proponents of the situational approach argue that being on top primarily is a matter of being in the right place at the right time.

That is, as group needs arise, people are selected to fill those needs. Let us consider both points of view.

The Will to Power:
The Trait Approach

The psychoanalyst Alfred Adler (1929) argued that everyone is motivated by desires for power. In all relationships people are trying to gain control over other people. While this analysis offers a rather pessimistic view of human relations, it does describe some people accurately. At the same time, many other people are so lacking in power needs that they make Adler's theory seem to be overstated. The wide differences among individual power needs have interested many investigators, who have tried to identify those people who most desire power. These investigators also have looked at the relationship between desire for and acquisition of power.

One interesting exploration of power needs has been undertaken by David Winter and his colleagues (Winter, 1973). Winter reasons that need for power operates much as need for achievement or affiliation does. These feelings may be aroused in almost everyone, but in some people they are generally stronger than in others. The exploration of these needs is complicated by the fact that power is an ambiguous concept in Western culture. People may seek and enjoy power, but they seldom admit that they do. When asked direct questions about the desire for power, an individual may not answer honestly. Thus, if an individual's power needs are to be measured, he or she must be unaware of what is being measured. Winter accomplished this by using the Thematic Appreciation Test (TAT), a technique developed by the pioneering personality theorist Henry Murray (1938). If a person is shown an ambiguous picture and asked to make up a story about the picture, Murray argued, he or she has an immense latitude of choice. Given the freedom to imagine anything, a storyteller frequently will *project* into the story his or her deepest or most important concerns. Thus, if a person has strong fears about the opposite sex and is asked to make up a story about a picture of a young couple, the fears probably would make their way into the story. Evidence of the fears would be available, yet the storyteller would be unaware of what was being measured or what he or she was expressing. Stories generated by TAT pictures can be used to explore virtually any need or motive.

Consider, for example, a story generated by a card depicting two trapeze artists. If a person wrote a story about a famous trapeze artist who was training a young assistant and saved her from falling to the ground, the storyteller probably would be scored relatively high in power motivation. The concern with the central figure's prestige and strength and with the assistant's dependency would be considered an indicator of the subject's power motives. On the other hand, if the story were about lovers who happened to be trapeze artists and the way in which their love helped them to trust each other in times of danger, the story would not receive a high power motivation score. There are virtually no power themes in such a story.

Using this device, Winter and Green (1971) explored the power motivation and power acquisition of black student activists. The investigators found that black college students who achieved high power-need scores also were likely to hold a political office on campus, be influential in black student organizations, and participate in black dramatic groups and black studies programs. In effect, students who seemed to be motivated by power needs more frequently occupied positions of power than did less power-oriented students. Other research indicates that athletes who are high in power motiva-

tion practice more and enjoy higher status than do athletes who are low in power motivation (Jones and Williamson, 1979). In addition, people with high power needs frequently see themselves as exerting great influence over the groups in which they participate (Fodor and Farrow, 1979).

The expression of power needs also has an effect on heterosexual relationships. In contrast with men who desire little power, men whose TAT stories express high power needs more often enjoy vicarious sexuality—that is, they read more pornographic literature, consider women to be objects of conquest, and marry noninterfering or dependent women. In a long-term dating situation, men high in power needs tend to be more dissatisfied and more often anticipate problems in their relationship than do men low in power needs (Stewart and Rubin, 1976). Those with high power needs also are more likely to split up with their girl friends and remain single than are men who are low in such needs. Other research indicates that men motivated by power respond favorably to people who are ingratiating or flattering (Foder and Farrow, 1979). In effect, the power-oriented male appears to have relative difficulty in carrying on successful long-term heterosexual relationships.

Information on the family backgrounds of Winter's male subjects provides some clues to the influence of childhood experiences on power needs. Winter (1973) reports that one of the major influences on power needs in males may be position in the family. In particular, an eldest son may be particularly high in aspirations of power. This child usually has the most experience in exercising power over his younger siblings and may identify with the father and attempt to imitate the father's manner in controlling the family. In Western culture, a later-born son typically is under less pressure than the firstborn to be like his father.

Characteristics
of Leaders

Although people who are motivated by power needs often seem to achieve their aims, not everyone who possesses power is highly motivated to achieve it. Many political leaders are recruited by other persons. Recruited leaders often are not high in power needs, but are high in *affiliation* (Rufus, 1968). Such people often owe their power to the efforts of others. In politics, business, and elsewhere, power is not always gained through a person's ambitious efforts; gaining power primarily depends on the agreement by others that one of their own should have the position of power. Awareness that social support contributes to the acquisition of power has prompted investigators to look for factors other than power needs that might contribute to a person's achieving power. The question often is framed in terms of leadership potential. What kinds of persons are likely to become leaders? Let us consider two factors that influence leadership potential: physical features and personality traits.

Physical features: measuring up

Are certain people blessed with bodies that give them an edge in the competition for power? Several studies suggest that this often is the case. As early as 1915, investigators who were looking at the relationship between social position and *height* found that male executives in insurance companies were on the average taller than policyholders, that university presidents generally were taller than presidents of small colleges, that sales managers were significantly taller than salesmen, and that railway presidents were typically taller than station agents (see Gibb, 1969). Data featured in Table 9-2 show the average salaries of a sample of seventeen thousand Air Force cadets in 1943 and their income twenty-six years later. While the

men's starting salaries were at roughly the same level, twenty-six years later their annual salaries were highly correlated with height. Every inch over 5'3" was worth approximately $370 per year. Perhaps tall men command more respect than short men. After all, others are forced to look up to them, much as parents are looked up to by their children. This possibility becomes more plausible in light of research that shows that when people are asked to estimate the height of others, they tend to *overestimate* the height of people in important positions (Keyes, 1980). For example, the height of U.S. presidents is overestimated by an average of three inches. In contrast, estimates of the height of those with lesser status are far less biased. Leaders also tend to be *larger in body weight* (Partridge, 1934) and tend to have a *physical appearance* that is especially pleasing to members of their group (see Chapter 3).

TABLE 9-2 **Walk tall and you may carry a fat wallet**

For this sample of men, height meant extra dollars of salary over the years.

Height	Mean 1943 salary	Mean 1968 salary
5′3″–5′5″	$3,500	$14,750
5′6″–5′7″	3,750	16,500
5′8″–5′9″	3,900	17,000
5′10″–5′11″	3,900	17,500
6′0″–6′1″	4,100	19,000
6′2″–6′3″	4,000	18,500
6′4″–6′6″	3,700	19,500

Source: Adapted from Keyes, 1980

Personality traits: the winning way

Although height and good looks may be helpful in gaining power, an individual's patterns of behavior also may influence his or her leadership potential. Most research on this topic suggests that personality characteristics that are attractive and invite identification help an individual gain *referent* power. What are these characteristics? Many studies indicate that people in leadership roles are more *self-confident* than other people. Leaders of boys' groups, college organizations, and military hierarchies generally tend to be more self-assured than the average member of the group (Gibb, 1969). In the courtroom, for example, investigators have identified *powerful speech styles*—that is, styles of speaking to juries so that cases are won (Erickson et al., 1978). The powerful speaker avoids hedging on arguments, does not hesitate, and avoids questioning intonations—he or she avoids all signs of a lack of confidence.

Many studies show that leaders tend to be *better adjusted* psychologically than other people are (see Mann's 1959 review). Leaders often demonstrate less anxiety and nervous tension (Cattell and Stice, 1954), and they appear to be less neurotic and introverted. They also seem to show greater *empathy* and

interpersonal sensitivity than other people do. For example, college-student leaders are far more accurate than nonleaders in estimating the opinions of other group members (Chowdhry and Newcomb, 1952). Judging from our earlier discussion of authoritarianism (see Chapter 4), you might expect that the rigid, suspicious, and dogmatic authoritarian would not be elected to leadership in a democratic society. Indeed, you are correct. In most groups that have been studied, leadership rarely is in the hands of authoritarian individuals (Bass, 1954; Hollander, 1958). However, egalitarians also rarely gain positions of leadership (Gibb, 1969). Groups seem to prefer as leaders individuals who are in the midrange in authoritarianism. Midrange levels of intelligence also seem to be favored. Intelligence often correlates with high position, but if a person's intelligence exceeds that of the average group member by a wide margin, he or she probably will not be preferred (Gibb, 1969).

In a comprehensive study of leadership traits that was carried out between 1960 and 1976, researchers gave personality tests to more than two thousand elected officials (Costantini and Craik, 1980). The officials scored higher than a group of nonleaders in self-confidence and in achievement and dom-

BOX 9-1

Power: Taken or Given?

Although power often depends on weapons, armies, or other means of coercion, people usually do not gain or lose power by such means. In daily life, personal skills or abilities are the usual keys to power (Henley, 1977). The various styles or traits mentioned in our discussion of leadership are typical of everyday means to power. In talking about acquisition of power, however, it is important to realize that whenever one person takes power, someone else gives it up. A person is powerful to the extent that another person is willing to give in to his or her influence.

Who is most likely to give away power, and under what conditions? One answer to this question suggests that people who are most sensitive to the wants, needs, or desires of others will be especially likely to give away power (Zuckerman et al., 1978). Because such individuals can detect the subtle cues that indicate what others desire, they are more likely to give in to these needs than are insensitive people. For example, the socially sensitive person is the one who often prepares for and cleans up after a party or listens while others monopolize the conversation. In both situations power is being given away to individuals who aren't sensitive enough to see what is needed.

In one demonstration of the sensitivity argument, Judith Hall (1980) used various measuring procedures (Rosenthal et al., 1979) to assess the sensitivity or insensitivity to various nonverbal forms of communication

inance needs. They scored lower than nonleaders on needs for others' nurturance and the need to defer to others. Differences also were found between Republican and Democratic leaders. Republican leaders were found to be higher than Democratic leaders in need for order, self-control, and endurance. In contrast, the Democrats were higher than the Republicans in needs for change and for others' nurturance. Apparently leaders of a given political party often possess characteristics that represent the party's beliefs about the characteristics of a good society.

The evidence that leaders have different personality traits from nonleaders must be interpreted with caution, however. First, exceptions that contradict almost all of the general trends can be found. Thus, having these traits does not guarantee that a person will have a position of power. Second, the direc-tion of influence is unclear. Does having a trait help an individual gain high rank, or does the high position help the individual develop the trait? As we discussed in Chapter 5, a person's disposition can be molded by the roles he or she plays. Thus, if you are elected to a position of power, your self-confidence may increase, you may feel better adjusted, and you also may try to be more sensitive to others.

We see, then, that studies of leadership characteristics can tell us a great deal about the kinds of people who often possess positions of power in a given culture. Leaders often have strong needs for power. However, if their position depends on others' accepting them, factors such as physical appearance and behavioral style often may be helpful in gaining position. Yet the trait approach leaves many questions unanswered. Let us turn to

(including quality and tone of voice) among a group of college students. Students in a second group were tested to determine their skills in nonverbal communication. Students who were either high or low in nonverbal communication skills were asked to make telephone calls to students who were high or low in social sensitivity. The communicators were told to say that they were working with the psychology department. Their specific task was to try to talk the listeners into spending up to twenty hours as subjects of a research project. All communicators used the same script. Thus success was assumed to depend on (1) the listeners' sensitivity and (2) the callers' ability to communicate.

As the research showed, students who were sensitive to nonverbal signals volunteered to give more hours to the research, regardless of the callers' skill in nonverbal communication. And skillful communicators were the most persuasive, regardless of the listeners' sensitivity. The skilled communicators succeeded in persuading sensitive subjects to volunteer an average of 18.4 hours, while the insensitive students volunteered only 10.6 hours. The unskilled communicators were able to persuade sensitive students to volunteer an average of 13.3 hours, while the insensitive students volunteered only, 9.5 hours.

Often power is given rather than taken, and individuals who are especially sensitive to others are likely to give power away.

the important competing position—that is, leadership is a matter of being in the right place at the right time.

The Situation Makes the Leader

Many social critics believe that if the Second World War had not taken place, Winston Churchill's name would be long-forgotten. Before the war Churchill lost several political elections, was demoted for making disastrous decisions in the Admiralty, and incited the wrath of the Labour Party. He was thought to be an impatient, unbending, opinionated, and dogmatic individual. Yet during the perilous years of the Second World War, Great Britain needed a leader with personality characteristics precisely like Churchill's. Britain needed someone whose determination and opinions would inspire the people to defend their na-

tion despite the odds against success, and the British selected an individual accordingly. In a major sense, history made the man; the man did not make history.

From this perspective, often called the *situationist* position (see Chapter 6), most people have the potential to serve as leaders if the times or conditions favor their talents. Let us consider an impressive demonstration of this optimistic position. This study is particularly dramatic because it takes shy and retiring people, who are among the least likely candidates for leadership, and it makes them into leaders. Most of us know people who don't speak out in groups, who don't seem to be involved with others, and whose presence hardly is noticeable. To explore the question of whether such persons could be shaped for leadership roles, male students were assembled in groups of four (Hastorf,

1970). During an initial ten-minute control session the four students talked over case-study materials, and from behind a one-way mirror the investigators made careful note of how much each person contributed to the discussion. The individual whose participation was next to the lowest in each group was selected as the target for the experimental phase of the procedure. During this phase subjects were told that shielded panels in front of each of them would display either a red light or a green light and that the lights would be controlled by experts on human behavior, who were in an adjoining room. The green light signaled encouragement to talk, while the red light suggested that silence might be more appropriate at that time. By using the lights the investigators were able to limit the contributions made by those who previously had been talkative and encourage the shy person to talk.

Did this procedure succeed in liberating the quiet person? As you can see in Figure 9-1, the encouragement proved to be most effective. The quiet person's contributions to the discussion increased substantially between the base-line and the experimental phases of the study. After twenty minutes of encouragement, a further test was given. A new case study was presented for discussion, and all participants were allowed to talk as much as they pleased. No signal lights were used. During this final discussion period the new leader did not relinquish his position. While his volume of talking did not reach quite the level that had been achieved in the experimental period, it did not drop to its previous low level. When later asked to rank the contributions that were made by members of the group during the session, his mates moved the "mouse" from a third-place to a second-place position.

Findings such as these suggest that everyone has leadership potential. Given the chance and the encouragement, most people probably could learn to take command, come

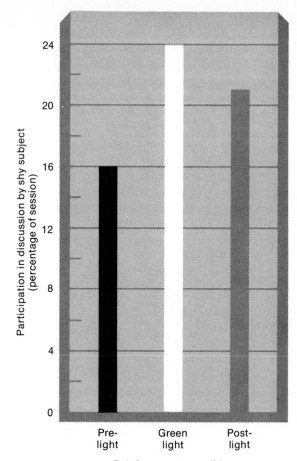

FIGURE 9-1

The mouse that roared like a lion

This demonstration shows that leadership can be shaped by social support. Note that the previously shy subject not only responded to direct encouragement to speak, but also continued to participate more freely after the green light was turned off. (adapted from Hastorf, 1965)

up with interesting ideas, and be rated highly by other group members. Common experience sometimes supports this notion. Consider, for example, the skepticism that greets many newly elected public officials—people often believe that the newcomer will make a mess of things. Later the new leader often seems to have grown into the position. He or she seems to be more mature and more capable than at first. Are we saying that a theory of leadership may disregard such personality factors as power need, gregariousness, or flexibility? Not at all. As we saw in Hastorf's study, subjects initially varied in their contributions to group discussion. Some expressed their opinions immediately and straightforwardly, and often they remained in the top ranking in the group's view. The situationist approach simply broadens the scope of understanding, suggesting that conditions can be favorable to anyone.

Interactionist Solutions to the Question of Leadership

We now have considered two contrasting approaches to understanding how people gain positions of power. The first approach emphasizes the personal characteristics of individuals, and the second focuses on the needs and demands of a situation. Each of these approaches takes account of different contributing factors, and each furnishes insights into how power is acquired. Some theorists, however, believe that these two approaches should be integrated. As we indicated in our discussion of morality (Chapter 6), many theorists believe that the *interaction* between personal characteristics and a situation best explains behavior. Let us examine the two most persuasive interactionist theories. The first centers on the match between types of people and types of situations, and the second focuses on the relationship between leaders and followers.

The Right Person for the Right Time: The Fiedler Approach

A member of a community board told us recently about the immense difficulties her board was having locating someone to head

a program designed to help ghetto children get ahead in the education system. The first leader chosen by the board was a strict disciplinarian. The children learned well but came to hate the leader so much that he had to be fired. The woman who replaced him was wonderfully close to the children but failed to inspire them to accomplish any school work. This kind of contrast in leadership styles, says group theorist Fred Fiedler (1978), is common throughout business and government. Fiedler believes that two kinds of leaders exist. Leaders who are *task-oriented*, as the disciplinarian was, are dedicated to accomplishing group goals. In terms of our earlier discussion, such people would be likely to use information, expert, and reward and coercive powers to get a job done. In contrast, leaders who are *relationship-oriented*, as the second program-leader was, are concerned with maintaining positive relationships among people. Such individuals might rely on referent power in achieving their ends. As Fiedler maintains, few people are capable of both kinds of leadership. Task-oriented leaders cannot become relationship-oriented easily, and leaders who are concerned with warm relations cannot switch suddenly to task accomplishment.

Is neither style of leadership satisfactory? Will followers always complain about what a leader cannot do? Fiedler argues that both kinds of leadership style can be quite successful. However, success depends on situational characteristics. According to Fiedler, group situations vary according to their *situational control*—that is, the degree to which the situation ensures that the individual can influence the group readily. Situations that are highly controllable possess three components: (1) the relationship between the leader and the group is positive and trusting, (2) the task is structured so that members know what to do, and (3) the leader is in a position to reward and punish the members. For example, if members of a group competing in a sailing race had just elected a captain by unanimous consent, if each member had been assigned a task, and if the captain had absolute command, these conditions would furnish high situational control for the leader. However, if the captain were unpopular, if the crew didn't know what they were supposed to do, and if the captain didn't have final authority, the conditions would be low in situational control.

Assuming that leaders vary from being task-oriented to being relationship-oriented and that situations vary from being low to being high in situational control, the major question is, how do leadership style and situation interact? Which style is effective in which situation? Fiedler's answer is shown in Figure 9-2. The diagram suggests that the task-oriented leader has most success when conditions furnish either *most* or *least* situational control. In contrast, the relationship-oriented leader experiences greatest success when conditions furnish an intermediate level of situational control.

Fiedler offers the following explanation for the style-situation interaction:

1. *Low situational control.* In this condition the task-oriented leader, who puts everything aside except group success, may produce better results than the relationship-oriented leader. He or she may take charge of an otherwise disastrous situation and lead the group to at least some accomplishment.

2. *High situational control.* Under circumstances in which group members already seem to get on well and the task is clearly structured, the task-oriented leader may be seen as doing an especially good job, and he or she may lead the group to great accomplishment.

3. *Moderate situational control.* When good relations are in question and members must work out the difficult issues of who

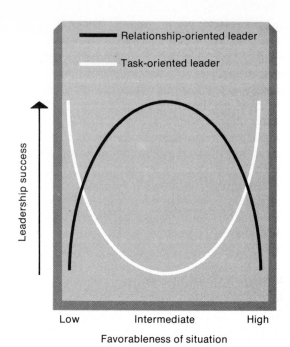

FIGURE 9-2 **What makes a good leader?**

According to Fiedler, it is the situation and the leader's style. Leaders who are concerned with positive relationships among people do well when a situation does not clearly favor success. Task-oriented leaders do well when a situation clearly favors success or appears likely to lead to failure. (Adapted from Fiedler, 1978)

should do what and with what authority, the smoothing and integrative influence of the relationship-oriented leader may be most needed, and such a person may lead this kind of group to success.

Support for this thinking has been generated by studies of high-school groups, college populations, industrial organizations, and military and civic organizations (Chemers and Skrzypek, 1972; Fiedler, O'Brien, and Ilgen, 1969; Schneider, 1977; Shiflett and Nealy, 1972; Tumes, 1972). More recently, Fiedler and his colleagues have developed programs for training people at high levels in various organizations to recognize good matches between leaders' personalities and types of situations (Fiedler, Chemers, and Mahan, 1976). Such training often has positive effects on leaders' effectiveness (Leister, Borden, and Fiedler, 1977).

Fiedler's model assumes that one style of leadership is not necessarily better than another. The task-oriented leader is not necessarily more successful than the relationship-oriented leader. Rather, whether a given style of leadership is effective depends on the circumstances. Everyone has the potential for leadership *if placed in the right situation.* Alexander the Great was only sixteen years old when he led the Macedonian cavalry to great victories, and William Pitt was Prime Minister of England at the age of twenty-four. Likewise, if a person is not a successful leader, he or she may not be right for the situation.

Interpersonal Transaction: Leadership Costs and Credits

The Fiedler approach focuses on the fit between leadership style and type of situation. Fiedler's model does not take account of either the acquisition of power or the loss of it. Leader-follower relationships seldom are stable. In order to understand leadership, the process of either gaining or losing status over time also must be considered. The key to this process, many theorists believe, is *interpersonal transactions.* That is, leadership is based on a kind of business deal in which each participant is out to gain as much as possible with the least cost (see Chapter 11). Gains may be of any kind: good policies for one's nation, victories for one's team, better pledges for one's fraternity, or a better time with one's friends. Most important for understanding leadership is the fact that members of a group will differ in how much they can contribute to the group's gain. Compared with others in a given group, certain candidates for president have more problem-solving ability, some players on a team are better

athletes, some friends are better humored. As the transaction theorists maintain, the more benefits a member contributes to a group, the more the group may reward that person in return (Hollander, 1980; Homans, 1974).

Status, or leadership, is one major reward that the group may give to the individual. Thus, if a team member does more than anyone else to boost team spirit, he or she may be elected team captain in exchange for the contribution. Or if a club member devotes more energy to the club projects than anyone else does, he or she becomes an excellent candidate for club president. As research shows, there often is a high correlation between the amount of verbal contribution a person makes to a group and the amount of leadership accorded him or her (Gintner and Lindskold, 1975; Stein and Heller, 1979). Often, then, the more an individual rewards the group in terms of achieving its goals, the more that individual in turn will be rewarded with status, position, or influence—all marks of power.

To demonstrate this process, Homans (1974) has made sensitive use of data collected in a study of leadership among female offenders who were living in a training school (Jennings, 1950). The girls were asked about a variety of matters, including the names of the other girls with whom they most would like to live and work. Using these preferences, the most central, or most popular, girls in the training school were identified. At the same time, personal evaluations of the same girls were made by the housemothers and were analyzed. The housemothers, in describing the most popular girls, focused on such characteristics as rebelliousness, reticence, and need to retaliate. Clearly the housemothers would not appreciate such characteristics. These girls, then, were *unpopular* with the housemothers because of the very characteristics that made them popular with their peers. By rebelling, retaliating, or withdrawing, the leaders were acting in ways that gratified the rebellious needs of their friends. Whether a girl was selected as leader thus seemed to depend on what she had to offer the others in her group.

In an interesting extension of this approach, Edwin Hollander and his colleagues (Hollander, 1980; Hollander and Julian, 1978) have explored one of the most interesting ironies of power: the restrictions on freedom of action that leadership may bring. We have seen that the person who furnishes a group with the greatest amount of satisfaction may gain value for the members and become the group's leader. Yet the position of power also creates expectations. Members come to rely on the leader for his or her guidance, direction, and support. If these rewards are not furnished, the group may become dissatisfied and hostile (Wahrman and Pugh, 1972, 1974). Because of the group's expectations, then, the most powerful member of the group may be least free to do as he or she wishes. Yet if this were so, would people strive as hard as they do for positions of power? Wouldn't leaders give up their positions once they learned the awful truth?

In an effort to solve this paradox, Hollander (1958) proposes that the leader is less restricted than he or she might appear to be at first. Hollander suggests that the benefits a leader provides to a group over time are much like money placed in a bank: as benefits accumulate, they establish a fund of credit on which the leader can draw when he or she wishes to. This *idiosyncrasy credit* enables the leader to deviate from expectation without fear of retaliation. At the same time, the deviancy reduces the accumulated credit. With a loss of credit, a reduction in the leader's power over the group takes place. Thus the leader is at once bound and free. He or she is bound in the sense that others continue to anticipate and depend on his or her rewards and is free in the sense that the rewards provide freedom to deviate. The free-

dom can be used up through deviation, however, and at that point power is lost.

In one experimental demonstration of this process, five-man groups were put to work on a difficult task that required a number of group decisions to be made (Hollander, 1958). The correctness of these decisions determined the amount of money that the group would receive. In this situation each member could furnish the others with two types of reward: (1) solutions that would help the group make money and (2) obedience to a set of decision-making rules that had been established by the group before the task began. A confederate of the experimenter continuously provided the first type of reward to the group, offering solutions that almost always were more accurate than anyone else's. Thus he helped the group earn money and should have gained power. Indeed, the more frequently the confederate was correct, the more the group followed his recommendations. At the same time, the confederate's behavior was not always satisfying to his colleagues. He deviated from the preestablished rules, sometimes speaking out of turn, objecting to majority rule, and being otherwise argumentative. As a result of this deviancy from group norms, the confederate's capacity to influence the group declined. Compared with situations in which he followed rules, the group was significantly less likely to agree with his argumentative or out-of-turn solutions. Deviations from the group norm, then, appear to drain one's capacity to influence a group— even though the influence would be to the group's advantage.

In summary, we have considered two interactionist solutions to the problem of how power in a group is gained. The Fiedler model sensitizes us to task-oriented and relationship-oriented leadership—two styles of leading that are often adopted. As Fiedler argues, each style is potent, but the effectiveness of a given style depends on the situation. The

relationship-oriented style is more promising when the task situation gives the leader a moderate degree of control. If the amount of control is either great or small, a task-oriented leader may be more effective. In contrast with Fiedler's approach is transactional theory, which looks at leadership as a process in continuous motion. This model suggests that an individual gains or loses power continuously by rewarding or punishing group members. From this perspective people may build their power by making contributions to group goals. Their contribution also serves to build idiosyncrasy credit, which enables the leader to depart from the group's norms in ways that would not be possible for less powerful members of the group. From this point of view, leadership is a constant process of transaction between group members and the individual who is the leader.

Power: To Have and Have Not

We have considered several types of power and alternative views as to the way in which people gain positions of power in social groups. We now will examine the effect of power on people's lives. Many social theorists believe that power differences are necessary and also inevitable in society. From small groups—families, for example—to large international alliances, effective action seems to require that some people have greater decision-making power than others. Everyone can't take on the full-time job of studying issues and making decisions for a society. Indeed, society would not exist if everyone had equal power over everyone else. Power structures are efficient and effective, and they enhance the circumstances of people's lives. Yet power has negative as well as positive consequences. And social psychologists have been especially concerned with the unseen negative consequences of being deprived of power or of having it. We will consider these two problems in turn.

Learned Helplessness: Plight of the Powerless

> The writer was witness to [a] case of death due to a loss of will within a psychiatric hospital. A female patient, who had remained in a mute state for nearly ten years, was shifted along with her floor mates to a different floor of her building while her unit was being redecorated. The psychiatric unit where the patient in question had been living was known among the patients as the "chronic hopeless" floor. In contrast, the first floor to which the patient was moved was most commonly occupied by patients who held privileges, including the freedom to come and go on the hospital grounds and the surrounding streets. Patients temporarily moved from the third floor were given medical examinations prior to the move, and the patient in question was judged to be in excellent medical health though still mute and withdrawn. Shortly after moving to the first floor, the patient surprised the ward staff by becoming socially responsive and, within a two week period, she ceased being mute and was actually becoming gregarious. As fate would have it, the redecoration of the third floor unit was soon completed, and all previous residents were returned to it. Within a week after she had been returned to the "hopeless" unit, the patient, like the legendary Snow White who had been aroused from a living torpor, collapsed and died. The subsequent autopsy revealed no pathology of note, and it was whimsically suggested at the time that the patient had died of despair (Phares, 1976, p. 2).

This case suggests that one's loss in power to control the environment, whether physical or social, can be deeply disturbing—even lethal (Schulz and Aderman, 1973). People may require a certain sense of power over their environment in order to have a sense of well-being. Major exploration of this issue has been carried out by Martin Seligman and his colleagues (Seligman, 1975; Seligman, Maier, and Solomon, 1971). The work began with a question about what happens when behavior has no effect on rewards or punishments. As we have seen, an immense amount of research has explored the effects of reward and punishment on people's actions. However, little was known about reactions to situations in which actions are *unrelated* to the amount of reward or punishment that is received. How would you respond if your grades had nothing to do with performance, if sometimes you received an A and sometimes a D, regardless of how much you studied? What if your lover sometimes embraced you and at other times cursed you, regardless of what you said or did?

To explore such reactions under extreme conditions, Seligman first studied dogs. The dogs were strapped into harnesses and given painful shocks in a random sequence. The shocks could not be avoided; the animals simply suffered this uncontrollable, unpredictable torture. Later each dog was placed in a box with a barrier that separated two compartments. The floor of the compartment that held the dog was charged electrically; the other compartment was not charged. The barrier between the compartments was low enough for the dog to jump over it to escape the shock. The dogs that had received the uncontrolled shock showed almost *no acquisition* of the vital response of jumping the barrier. Instead, they squirmed, writhed, whimpered, or cowered as the shocks continued. They seemed to have learned that they could not control their fate. In contrast, dogs that had not been exposed to the uncontrolled shock generally had little trouble learning to jump the barrier to avoid the shock. Seligman and his colleagues labeled the failure to acquire the jumping response *learned helplessness*. As their continued research indicated, animals that learn that they have no control over what happens to them often will show both a lowered level of activity and a decreased ability to learn.

The learned helplessness displayed by animals also is a human response, as more than thirty experiments have demonstrated (see Abramson, Seligman, and Teasdale's 1978 review). In fact, helplessness effects sometimes are suffered by those who simply watch others who are helpless (De Vellis, De Vellis, and McCauley, 1978). Most of this research has explored human reactions to uncontrollable situations. People have been placed in situations in which they are (1) shocked and can do nothing about it, (2) presented with a noxious noise at unexpected intervals, or (3) given unsolvable puzzles. The helplessness that is produced by these experiences affects the subjects' subsequent performance. When later presented with a situation in which they could learn to avoid shock, turn off the awful noise, or control their success in solving puzzles, they performed poorly and often showed negative mood shifts. Subjects who previously had not been exposed to an uncontrollable environment generally did not show either reductions in performance on these tasks or indications of depression. Other research in support of Seligman's position indicates that perceiving oneself as having control in the academic world is positively related to grades (Schulz and Hanusa, 1979), effectiveness of learning (Savage, Perlmutter, and Monty, 1979), speed of problem solving (Brown, 1979), and performance on measures of basic skills (De Charms, 1979).

Seligman (1975) believes that learned helplessness often is the basis for feelings of depression. People who are lethargic and sit sadly for long hours instead of striving to master their environment seem like the dogs who whined and cowered instead of learning to jump over the barrier to freedom. From this standpoint, many depressed people may not be suffering from a basic abnormality; instead they may be responding to an awareness of their lack of control (Alloy and Abramson, 1979). This thinking has practical implications for the treatment of depression. Many depressed people may not need supportive therapy; rather, they may benefit from changes in their circumstances so that their sense of control over the environment is increased. Consider the aged, for example, who often seem to be depressed and inactive. In the process of aging many individuals experience a decreasing sense of control over the environment. Indeed, society may reward the elderly for being dependent (Barton, Baltes, and Orzech, 1980). Since morale often is particularly low among persons who perceive that they are dependent on the environment, the sadness and inactivity of many old people may be not a normal consequence of growing old, but a result of the sense of losing control (M. Gergen, 1979).

Help for the Helpless

Can the negative effects of helplessness be offset? This question has received a considerable amount of attention from investigators, and a variety of promising answers have emerged (Abramson, Seligman, and Teasdale, 1978; Miller and Norman, 1979). One approach asks whether *increasing* a person's sense of control will produce reactions that are the opposite of those produced by loss of control. In a fascinating series of experiments, researchers have examined the effects that increasing people's sense of control has on physical health and mortality. Decreased control has been related to likelihood of heart failure (Krantz, Glass, and Snyder, 1974). Does health improve when control is increased? To explore this question, Richard Schulz (1976) arranged a two-month-long program of visits by undergraduates to residents in a home for the aged. Residents in a randomly selected group were told that they would have complete control over the duration and frequency

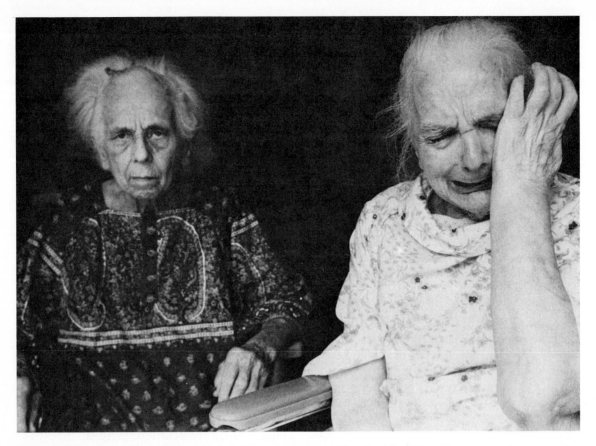

Aging and helplessness. Older people in Western society often feel that their lives are no longer under control. Sick, poor, and isolated, they can do little to improve their circumstances. Many researchers believe that the depression and inactivity that characterizes large numbers of older people is directly related to their sense of helplessness.

of the visits. If they felt lonely, they could ask the undergraduate to visit at any time. The students visited residents in a second group on a random basis. These residents had no control over the frequency or duration of visits, which otherwise were identical in frequency and duration to those that occurred on demand.

The program had an impressive effect on the residents' health. As you can see in Table 9-3, the residents who controlled the visits were later rated by an unbiased evaluator as being significantly more healthy than those

without control. These individuals also were seen as having a "zest for life" that was significantly greater than that of the low-control residents. The increases in well-being exceeded those found among residents who did not participate in the visitation program. Furnishing increased control, then, had positive effects—as long as the program continued (Schulz and Hanusa, 1978). Further research has shown that a sense of control also may increase the length of elderly people's lives. In one study, those residents of a home for the aged who simply *believed* that their en-

TABLE **9-3** **Control helps the helpless**

Residents of a home for the aged benefited both physically and emotionally from having a sense of control over the frequency with which visitors came and the length of the visitors' stay. In this table, higher scores indicate positive changes in a characteristic.

Characteristic rated	Visit by volunteer	
	Random intervals	Only when asked
Health	4.7	6.9
Zest for life	5.0	7.0
Activity level	0.0	1.0

Source: Adapted from Schulz, 1976

vironment was responsive to their actions lived longer than did those who were offered the same services but believed that they had no control over them (Rodin and Langer, 1977).

In addition to looking at the effects of an increased sense of control, investigators have asked whether *training in escape or control* can help reduce the effects of helplessness. In an early exploration of this possibility, dogs were taught to escape shock and then were made to receive shock helplessly (Seligman and Maier, 1967). The trained dogs were relatively unaffected by the helplessness experience, and they learned to escape shock as effectively as the control animals did. Perhaps human beings who can resist depression in uncontrollable situations have a history of successfully controlling their environment— or have learned a sense of control by watching others cope (Brown and Inouye, 1978).

The negative effects of helplessness may be offset also by *coping strategies*. People can be taught to react to helplessness, for example, with greater striving for achievement. As research indicates, some people respond to helplessness with an increased motivation to reestablish control over outcomes (Roth and Bootzin, 1974). Taking the blame for uncontrollable failure also produces helplessness (Diener and Dweck, 1978; Eisenberger, Kap-

lan, and Singer, 1974; Koller and Kaplan, 1978), which suggests that learning to blame the environment for failure would be a useful coping strategy. Finally, helplessness effects may be overcome by *enlightenment effects* (see Chapter 1). Research indicates that people who know about theories of learned helplessness may be insulated against helplessness effects (Schwartz, 1980). If people are told in advance that they cannot control events, a learned helplessness situation may have no effects at all (Koller and Kaplan, 1978). Awareness of what is about to happen may motivate the person to search for other possible reactions.

Internal versus External Control:
The Self-fulfilling Belief

In our discussion thus far we have focused primarily on the negative effects of immediate losses in power. But what if the state of powerlessness is prolonged? As personality theorist Julian Rotter (1966) has argued, long periods of exposure to uncontrollable reinforcement may create general expectancies that modify views of many situations. In other words, people may come to believe that they generally are helpless. Consider the following examples. One woman (we'll call her Linda) may feel depressed all day if she and her daughter have a minor argument at breakfast. The event may be small, but Linda regards it as another sign that she cannot control her life. In contrast, the other woman (Karen) continues to paint and practice ballet at a time when her husband is filing a law suit to gain custody of their children. Events may be out of Karen's control, but she sees herself as being in charge. If people believe that they have no control, they may feel continuously helpless; if they believe that they are in control, they seldom may feel helpless (Abramson, Seligman, and Teasdale, 1978). Rotter (1966) explains these differences by distinguishing between people who believe that what happens to them is largely the result of *external* occurrences (that is, events beyond their control) and people who believe that what happens to them is largely the result of *internal* circumstances (that is, their own decisions).

To explore these differing dispositions, Rotter and his colleagues designed a twenty-three item scale to measure generalized expectancies of internal versus external (I-E) control (Rotter, Liverant, and Crowne, 1961). For each item, the subject selected the statement that best reflected his or her beliefs. Here are some sample items:

1. a. Without the right breaks one cannot be an effective leader.
   b. Capable people who fail to become leaders have not taken advantage of their opportunities.
2. a. The average citizen can have an influence in government decisions.
   b. This world is run by the few people in power, and there is not much the little guy can do about it.
3. a. What happens to me is my own doing.
   b. Sometimes I feel that I don't have enough control over the direction my life is taking. (Phares, 1976, pp. 178–180)

As you might guess, if you agree that people can't lead without the right breaks, that the average citizen can't have much influence on government, and that you don't feel that you have much control over the direction your life is taking, you are making *external* choices. Consistently selecting the opposite choices in each case would suggest that you believe in *internal* control.

Responses on the I-E scale have been studied in many different settings, and the bulk of the research paints a bleak picture of individuals who believe that life events are controlled externally (Phares, 1976; Strickland, 1977). Compared with people who are more internal in their beliefs, external individuals feel more anger and perceive others as being less friendly (Holmes and Jackson, 1975), are less popular socially as children (Nowicki and Roundtree, 1971), are less persuasive (Phares, 1965), rely less on persuasion than on coercion in their personal relationships (Goodstadt and Hjelle, 1973), and are less assertive in marital conflicts (Doherty and Ryder, 1979). In the domain of task performance, externals, when compared with internals, often are less active in solving mental problems (Lefcourt, 1976), less competent in task performance (Pines and Julian, 1972), less attentive to relevant cues when skill is demanded in problem solving (Lefcourt and Wine, 1969), more likely to prefer tests of chance to tests of skill (Kahle, 1980), and likely to make lower estimates of their success even when their actual success is no less than that of internals (Benassi, Sweeney, and Drevno, 1979). With respect to their political activities, externals, when compared with internals, often express less willingness to join in civil rights work (Gore and Rotter, 1963) and participate less frequently in the women's liberation movement (Pawlicki and Almquist, 1973).

Many researchers have looked for a relationship between I-E scores and indicators of emotional and physical well-being. They reason that people who believe that their lives are controlled by external circumstances are much like subjects in learned helplessness experiments. Only people in this case carry their "helplessness" about in their heads. Research seems to support this view. In comparison with externals, internals have been shown to experience less debilitating anxiety (Strassberg, 1973), have higher morale if they are aged (Felton and Kahana, 1974), express more contentment with life (Naditch, Gargan, and Michael, 1975), experience less depression (Lefcourt, 1976; Strickland, 1974), and be less suicidal (Strickland, 1977). With respect to physical health, internals, when compared with externals, experience less illness (Kobasa, 1979) and are less likely to be cigarette-smokers (Coan, 1973). Internals engage in more physical exercise (Walker, 1973), have less coronary disease (Cromwell et al., 1977), and suffer less hypertension (Naditch, 1974) than externals do. In part, the well-being of the internals seems to be due to their use of preventive strategies. Compared with externals, internals are more likely to wear seat belts (Williams, 1972a) and engage in preventive dental care (Williams, 1972b). Finally, high-school girls with high internal scores have fewer pregnancies than do high-school girls with high external scores (Segal and DuCette, 1973).

As these many studies suggest, belief in one's own power to control situations can enrich one's life experience greatly. Yet some scholars have been concerned about the effect of believing in one's own power even when one has no power (Gregory, Chartier, and Wright, 1979). For Jews in Nazi Germany, for example, the belief that they were in control of their outcomes may have led to many deaths. Critics of this argument reply that the feeling of powerlessness is *self-fulfilling*. That is, by believing in control, one may gain control (Dweck, Goetz, and Strauss, 1980). For example, one study found that internals were more likely than externals to join politically active groups, such as the equal rights movement. By joining a movement they were able to have an impact on society. Their belief that

they had control increased their actual control over events. Findings such as these have inspired psychologists to search for ways of training people to see themselves as having control (Zuroff, 1980). Psychotherapy may be used for this purpose (Rotter, 1978), but so may experiences in successful problem solving (Dweck, 1975). Ultimately, living in a social context that is responsive to one's actions may prove to be most beneficial.

In summary, we see that when people find themselves without power to control their environment they may become listless, depressed, and closed to new experiences. With continued experiences of helplessness people may develop a general outlook about the absence of control that affects a broad range of their actions. Individuals with this outlook seem to believe that their fate depends on external circumstances. In contrast, individuals who have not experienced helplessness may believe in their own control and may strive for effective power over a wide range of situations. Both kinds of reactions can be self-fulfilling. That is, people who believe that they have control actually may achieve control, and people who see themselves as victims of fate may become helpless.

Negative Effects of Power: From Jeckyll to Hyde

Having considered the negative effects of being without power, we now will look at the negative effects of *having power*. Consider the following event: as you are walking home one evening a police car pulls sharply to the curb and two uniformed men jump out. They seize you and place you under arrest for suspicion of armed robbery. Neighbors look on while you are handcuffed, searched, and forced into the rear of the vehicle. You are not totally shaken by this experience because you know that your "arrest" is the beginning of an experiment in which you have agreed to participate for the sum of $15 per day. Along with a dozen other student-volunteers you eventually are taken to a mock jail cell in the basement of a university building. The guards, who also are volunteer subjects, strip you, spray you with a delousing fluid, take your picture, place you behind bars, and instruct you to remain silent. Suddenly you are painfully aware that you have agreed to two weeks of imprisonment.

This vignette describes the experience of volunteer subjects in an experiment that was designed to challenge traditional views about prison life (Haney, Banks, and Zimbardo, 1973). Usually prisoners' mistreatment of one another, the brutalization of prisoners by guards, and prisoners' attacks on guards are attributed to the *personal dispositions* of those involved. That is, the violence and cruelty that is displayed by both groups is assumed to result from the bad characters of the hardened criminals or from the criminals' negative influence on the guards' personality characteristics. The investigators were skeptical of this notion. Perhaps, they reasoned, the fault is not the individual's; the *prison situation* itself may be corrupting. The most humane of beings might become beasts under similar circumstances. The researchers chose students as subjects because students' life experiences differ considerably from those of

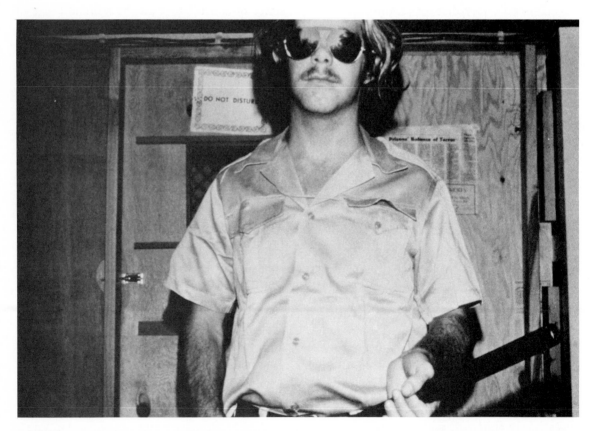

A prison guard. The young man clutching the billy club is one of the college student volunteers in Zimbardo's prison experiment. Zimbardo's experiment provides a graphic illustration of the negative effects of possessing power.

the professional criminal. The question, then, was, would ordinary college students be corrupted by a make-believe prison situation?

First, let us consider the responses of the students who were assigned the role of prisoner. Their actions are especially interesting in light of our previous discussion of learned helplessness. In general the prisoners' moods became increasingly negative with each succeeding day. They criticized themselves and their circumstances. They displayed a variety of pathological symptoms: depression, crying, rage, acute anxiety, or psychosomatic aches and pains. Almost half of the prisoners had to be released before a week had passed. Almost all of those who remained said that they would be willing to forfeit their pay if they could be released. When the experiment was terminated after six days (for humanitarian reasons), all of the prisoners expressed immense delight. The loss of control that they experienced produced severe negative consequences.

The effect of unlimited coercive power on the students who were assigned the role of guard is the question of particular interest at this point. The experiment allowed these men great freedom of choice in their methods of maintaining order in the prison. Nevertheless, the guards almost always chose to abuse the prisoners. Commands were the most frequent form of address, and verbal exchanges remained impersonal. As time passed the guards' abusive behavior intensified and often persisted even when the prisoners ceased to resist. One guard (who did not know that he was being observed) was found pacing the yard during the early morning hours while the prisoners were sleeping, vigorously pounding his night stick into his hand. Another guard placed a prisoner in solitary confinement (a small closet) and tried to keep him there all night while concealing this information from the experimenters—who he thought were too soft on the prisoners. Many guards were willing to work overtime for no

additional pay and were distressed when the experiment was terminated prematurely. Thus, given a large measure of coercive power, these otherwise decent and peaceful young men became tyrannical and inhumane—and they seemed to enjoy it.

Power Corrupts: From Acton to Kipnis

Why were the guards in the prison study so brutalized by their position? Lord Acton's well-known proclamation that "power tends to corrupt, and absolute power tends to corrupt absolutely" certainly describes the guards' behavior. But *why* does power have this effect? In a close analysis of the effects of power, David Kipnis (1977) lays out five interrelated steps by which the powerful become corrupted. Let us consider each step in turn.

1. *Access to means of power increases the probability that power will be used.* We saw in the last chapter that having implements of aggression may tempt an individual to use them. Apparently access to power produces the same kind of temptation. In one experimental demonstration of the relationship between having power and using it, Kipnis (1972) arranged for business students to supervise high-school students in an industrial game. The supervisors' power over the workers was varied. Some supervisors, those with high power, were allowed to give pay increases to the workers, transfer them to another job if they weren't doing well, give special instructions, deduct portions of their pay, and fire them. Other supervisors, those with low power, could use only their personal persuasion to influence the workers. The experimenter arranged for the productivity of the workers to be *exactly the same* in both conditions. The question was, what effects would the availability of power have on the supervisors? As you can

TABLE **9-4** **Does power corrupt?**

Note the more rapid increase in the use of influence by supervisors with power and the lesser use of influence by those without power.

Type of supervisor	Number of influence attempts		
	Period 1	Period 2	Period 3
High power	2.1	4.0	8.2
Low power	1.1	2.3	3.6

Source: Adapted from Kipnis, 1972

see in Table 9-4, those with power used their power more frequently. They seldom tried to persuade their "workers" (they used persuasion only about 16 percent of the time). Instead, they relied on threats, promises of raises, and so forth. In other words, rather than using information power, the power-holders tended to use reward and coercion.

2. *The more power used, the more likely the power-holder will believe that he or she controls the target's actions.* Recall our discussion of causal attribution (Chapter 2) in which we described how people come to decide on whether an action is controlled by the actor or the situation. Power-holders also make attributions of cause (Kaplowitz, 1978) and may use these same principles. The power-holder, who is aware of the rewards and coercions that are being used, tends to see the target's behavior as being involuntary. "The worker is doing that because I made him do it," the power-holder may think. In Kipnis's experiment, both high- and low-power-holders were asked whether their workers were self-motivated or motivated by pay. Those who had exercised more power were less likely to see their workers as being self-motivated. Rather, they attributed their workers' efforts to a desire for monetary reward. Other researchers

have found that people who have a high need for power are likely also to see themselves as agents of others' actions (Fodor and Farrow, 1979).

3. *As the power-holder comes to take credit for the target's actions, the target may seem to be less worthy.* Devaluing those who are perceived as pawns is a common response that has been demonstrated in industrial settings (Kipnis and Cosentino, 1969) and in relations among married couples (Kipnis et al., 1976). For example, if decision making in a marriage is perceived as being one-sided, the decision-maker may feel less attracted to his or her mate and less satisfied and less happy with the relationship (Alpert, 1978). This tendency by the power-holder to devalue the target is particularly high if the target seems to be acting out of fear of punishment (Wells, 1980) and may be increased by the target's tendency to be compliant or obedient. As one investigator put it, "The deference and compliance shown by the less powerful is seen by the [powerful] as a sign of weakness, if not servility" (Sampson, 1975, p. 233). These findings suggest that unless people with low power demonstrate self-motivation, the friendship of more powerful individuals may be difficult to obtain.

4. *As the target's worth is decreased, his or her social distance from the power-holder increases.* If people with high power tend to devalue those with low power, they are not likely to want to engage in close relationships or "see the world as the powerless see it" (Tjosvold and Sagaria, 1978). This point also is demonstrated in the Kipnis experiment. When high-power and low-power supervisors were asked how willing they would be to meet and talk with the workers after the experiment was completed, those with high power showed significantly less desire for contact with the workers than did those with low power.

5. *Access to and use of power may elevate the self-esteem of the powerful.* An individual who believes that others are mere pawns may come to have high self-esteem—especially if he or she believes that the implements of power are indications of self-worth. And just as the power-holder may feel like a better person because of his or her wealth or position, powerless people may come to devalue themselves. For example, people who live in nonprestigious neighborhoods may feel less self-satisfaction than those who live in better locations. People with low power may be shunned in social groups (Bales, 1970), thus adding to their lowered sense of self-esteem. A study of business managers shows a positive correlation between power and self-esteem (Kipnis, 1972). One may benefit by having high self-esteem. The problem develops when the power-holder comes to have a particularly exalted view of himself or herself or when the feelings of self-exaltation lead the power-holders to see themselves as being exempt from common standards of morality (Berle, 1967). This attitude may have led to Richard Nixon's downfall. Nixon and his associates believed that their criminal acts were excusable because they promoted the ultimate good of the country.

Kipnis's account of the steps to corruption offers a dim view of the effects of power. Must holding power *always* result in increased attempts to influence, devaluation of the less powerful, and elevation of self-esteem? The answer to this question is no—that is, not if people in organizations become aware of the possibility of corruption. In fact, the work of Kipnis and others has influenced some organizations to try rotating people in positions of power, distributing different kinds of power to different people, and offering weekend discussions in which people from all levels of the organization can talk openly about their feelings and opinions. Some investigators believe that under the right conditions the possession of power can increase compassion and deepen understanding of oneself and others (Berle, 1967; Cartwright and Zander, 1968). The challenge of identifying and establishing such conditions remains.

Recasting the Power Structure

Power will probably never be distributed equally throughout society. In fact, some theorists argue that if everyone had complete power over his or her actions, freedom would be lost (DeGré, 1970). A Hobbesian conflict of "all against all" would result. Further, in any complex society people must take different roles or carry out different responsibilities. As soon as role differentiation takes place, power differences inevitably emerge. With different people serving as—for example—armed guardians, government officials, teachers, family breadwinners, and so forth, differences in power are created. The military or the police may control coercive power, the government may have legitimate power, and

BOX 9-2

Having Your Own Way: Power Strategies in Close Relationships

The amount of power in a relationship can be measured in terms of who controls the decision making when disagreement occurs. If a couple is arguing over whether to have a second child, for example, the partner whose preference wins out can be said to be the more powerful. Psychologists Toni Falbo and Letitia Peplau have been particularly interested in the strategies that are used to control the decisions in close relationships. How do people gain power over one another? To explore this problem, undergraduates were asked to describe how they get their way (Falbo, 1977; Falbo and Peplau, 1980). Perhaps you can recognize some of your own behaviors in Falbo and Peplau's findings.

How I get my way with————

Strategy	Example
Ask	"I ask him (or her) to do what I want."
Act independently	"We do our own thing. I just do it by myself."
Bargain	"We usually negotiate something agreeable to both of us."
Act negatively	"I pout or threaten to cry if I don't get my own way."
Persist	"I remind him (or her) of what I want until he (or she) gives in."
Persuade	"I persuade him (or her) my way is right."
Act positively	"I smile a lot, and am especially affectionate."
Reason	"I reason with him (or her). I argue logically."
State importance	"I tell him (or her) how important it is to me."
Suggest	"I drop hints, make suggestions."
Talk it out	"We discuss our needs and differences."
State my goals	"I tell him (or her) what I want."
Withdrawl	"I clam up." (p.621)

Using judges' ratings, Falbo and Peplau (1980) were able to evaluate the various strategies along two dimensions. The first dimension referred

---

teachers may have information power. And because some people inevitably will be loved or admired more than others, differences in referent power always will exist.

Because power will always be distributed unequally, conflicts over power probably will always occur. Those who have nothing will press for increases in power, and those in power usually will defend what they have acquired. Because power struggles seem to be inevitable, some theorists argue that such conflict is a sign of a healthy society (Apfelbaum and Lubek, 1976; Fanon, 1965). A society with no conflict and no struggle to change the government, redistribute the

wealth, or increase freedom probably is a society in which oppression prevails.

What triggers the struggle for power? Why did militancy among blacks intensify in the mid-1950s, what brought the counterculture revolt to a height in the late 1960s, and why have the women's liberation and gay liberation movements come to play such a dominant role in recent history? Few people would accept the argument that such conflict emerged because oppression slackened just enough to allow its expression. Clearly, factors other than the amount of oppression must be taken into account. Let us consider a general approach to the question of why

to whether the strategy was *direct* or *indirect*. Bargaining and stating one's goals would be direct means of obtaining one's way, while acting in a negative or in a positive manner would be indirect means. The second dimension referred to whether the strategy was *interactive* or *solitary*. Persuading would be interactive, for example, while acting independently and withdrawing would be more solitary. Thus each strategy could be rated along both dimensions.

A major concern of the investigators was whether men and women differ in the kinds of strategies they choose. It has been argued that men and women use different power strategies in relationships—strategies that reflect their relative status in society (Johnson, 1978; Kipnis, 1976; Peplau, 1979). Thus men can afford to be more direct and interactive in relationships with women because the social system supports male dominance. In contrast, women have learned to seek more indirect and solitary means of getting their way because they lack status in heterosexual relationships. The results of Falbo and Peplau's research support this argument. Falbo and Peplau found that men were more likely than women to use direct, interactional strategies, such as persuading, reasoning, or bargaining. Women were more likely than men to employ indirect and solitary strategies, such as acting positively or negatively or just doing things on their own.

We see, then, that there are numerous means of getting one's way in a relationship, and the strategies that are selected depend in part on socially prescribed expectations. It will be interesting to note whether shifts in the choice of strategies take place as women continue to pursue equality in status.

power struggles begin: the theory of relative deprivation.

If people are unemployed, underfed, living in delapidated housing, and unheeded by governing powers, are they likely to revolt? Interestingly, the belief that people revolt because of poor circumstances is contradicted by a great deal of evidence. The French Revolution took place after almost ninety years of steadily increasing prosperity. The Russian Revolution took place during a period in which the peasants were finally beginning to achieve a decent life. The mid-1960s violence in the black ghettos occurred after ten years of increasing economic, educational, and po-

litical benefits. Poor conditions don't seem to be a critical cause of revolution. Revolutions often seem to occur during periods of relatively great prosperity.

How do we reconcile this conflict between the common-sense view that revolution is produced by poor conditions and the fact that good conditions often prevail just prior to revolution? One interesting solution has been offered by James C. Davies (1969). Davies argues that revolutionary activity is most likely to occur when an *extended period of rising expectations is followed by a reversal or leveling of outcomes.* Suddenly the gap between what is expected and what is received widens.

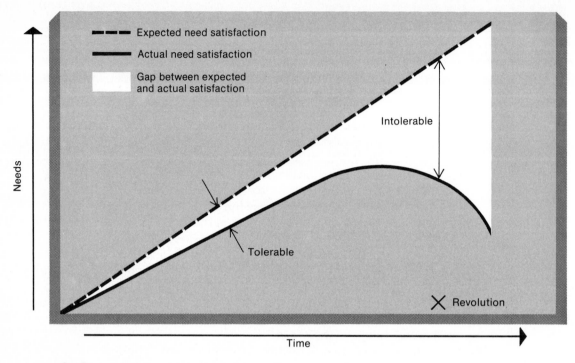

FIGURE 9-3   **A model of why revolution occurs**

Note the widening gap between expected and actual satisfaction of need. The discrepancy between what people want and what they get is believed to lead to revolution. (Adapted from Davies, 1962)

As a result, people experience intense frustration that may lead to violent action. In other words, when people are deprived relative to their expectations—that is, when they feel *relative deprivation*—they may be moved to overthrow the existing power structure (see Figure 9-3). As an illustration, prerevolutionary France experienced almost one hundred years of steady increases in prosperity. From 1700 until approximately 1780 farm and economic productivity and national power were on the rise. However, between 1788 and 1789 a severe fiscal crisis and heavy taxation were followed by a bad harvest, an unfavorable trade treaty, and a rapid increase in the price of bread. From Davies's point of view, the revolution of 1789 was a natural outgrowth of this turndown of events.

The argument that relative deprivation sets off revolutionary activity is supported by other research. In a study of civil strife in 114 different nations, short-term deprivations proved to be accurate predictors of civil strife (Gurr, 1969). Sudden famines, tax burdens, economic setbacks, and so forth preceded civil strife in almost every country. In a study of violence in 84 nations, revolutionary activity was found to be infrequent in underdeveloped or impoverished nations of the world (Feierabend, Feierabend, and Nesvold, 1969). Revolution also was infrequent in highly advanced nations. Nations at both extremes of the economic spectrum often are relatively stable. In contrast, civil violence frequently occurs in nations that are experiencing a developmental transition, where expectation and gratification may be mismatched.

In more recent work, Faye Crosby (1976) has extended the relative deprivation theory in important directions. She argues that feeling relative deprivation is just a beginning of the revolutionary process. Three other factors must be taken into account:

1. *Assignment of blame.* Do people attribute blame for their condition to themselves or to society? (See the discussion of self-perception in Chapter 2 and the discussion of consciousness raising in Chapter 4.) If people blame themselves for their condition, revolutionary activity is not likely to result. If they blame society, revolution is more likely to occur.

2. *Control over resources.* If people believe that society is at fault and if they also have the resources to produce change, the likelihood of revolution increases. If people have no control, they simply may experience stress.

3. *Absence of opportunities for change.* Means for change—elections, the development of new jobs, and changes in economic policy—must be *unavailable* if revolution is to occur. When opportunities are open, people who blame themselves may try to improve their condition. Under the same circumstances, people who believe that the society is at fault may try to find constructive ways of effecting social change. When people blame society, have the resources for change, and find no opportunities, violent revolution may be expected.

SUMMARY

1 Power may be defined as the capacity to alter the actions of others. Five types of power are distinguished: information power, which is based on the possession of useful information; referent power, which depends on one's ability to serve as a model for others; legitimate power, which rests on social agreements about who has the right to direct behavior; expert power, which is based on skill in carrying out valued activities; and reward and coercive power, which depends on the capacity to reward or punish others for their actions.

2 Answers to the question of why some people gain positions of leadership and others do not have emphasized the personal characteristics of the leader and the characteristics of the situation. Research on leadership traits indicates that many leaders are motivated by deep-seated power needs. Other research indicates that various physical features—such as height and physical appearance—along with various personal traits—such as self-confidence, adjustment, and empathic ability—often are correlated with positions of leadership. Research that emphasizes the situation suggests that as groups develop different needs, the group members select leaders who fulfill these needs.

3 Some theorists argue that in order to understand leadership, personal and situational characteristics must be considered simultaneously. Two such interactionist theories were considered. Fiedler has argued

that leaders differ in whether they are task-oriented or relationship-oriented. The task-oriented leader may be especially successful when a group shows either high or low acceptance of the leader's controlling power. When acceptance of control is at an intermediate level, the relationship-oriented leader may be most effective. A second interactionist model considers the reciprocal relationships among group members over time. To the extent that a group member rewards others, he or she may gain a position of leadership. As the leader continues to reward the group, he or she gains the right to deviate from group expectations. The more deviation, however, the less strong the position of leadership.

4 People who feel that they do not have the power to control their environment are said to be helpless. Helpless people often become inactive and depressed and demonstrate a lowered learning capacity. The effects of helplessness may be diminished by increasing the person's sense of control. Such increments may have life-saving properties. Training in escape, developing coping strategies, and making people aware of the effects of helplessness may be useful in offsetting these symptoms. Experiences of helplessness can produce a predisposition to believe that all outcomes are under the control of external circumstances. Research shows that people with an external orientation display helplessness characteristics. People who believe that they are responsible for their own outcomes (an internal orientation) generally lead more satisfying lives, accomplish more, and have better physical health than do people with an external orientation.

5 People who possess power often may be corrupted by their own power. Having power increases the likelihood that the power will be used in an attempt to influence others. As more power is exercised the power-holder becomes more likely to believe that others cannot act on their own effectively. As the power-holder comes to take credit for other people's actions, these other individuals may be devalued by the power-holder. The power-holder thus may create distance from others and come to feel an elevated sense of self-esteem. As a study of a mock prison demonstrated, the corrupting influence of power may affect virtually anyone who accepts a position of power.

6 Revolutions against power structures seem to occur not when social and economic conditions are at their worst, but when people are deprived relative to their expectations. Relative deprivation may be especially potent in inciting revolution when people attribute blame to the government rather than to themselves, when they have control over resources for revolution, and when other opportunities for social change are minimal.

SUGGESTED READINGS

Kipnis, D. *The powerholders.* Chicago: University of Chicago Press, 1976.

McClelland, D. C. *Power: The inner experience.* New York: Irvington, 1975.

Phares, E. J. *Locus of control in personality.* Morristown, N.J.: Silver Burdett/ General Learning Press, 1976.

Seligman, M. E. P. *Helplessness: On depression, development, and death.* San Francisco: W. H. Freeman, 1975.

Stogdill, R. M. *Handbook of leadership: A survey of theory and research.* New York: Free Press, 1974.

Winter, D. G. *The power motive.* New York: Free Press, 1973.

10: SOCIAL INFLUENCE

■ *A common complaint that is made about today's college students is that they are conforming. "They don't ask questions . . . they just sit and take notes . . . they don't show any individuality." Remarks like these can be heard at almost any faculty gathering. Yet in the early 1970s professors were complaining about their students' excessive individuality. "Students are too independent," they said; "they think they know everything . . . they don't trust anyone over thirty."*

The point of these observations is not that professors are fickle. Rather, the professors' remarks illustrate a central conflict that exists in our society between pressures for individuality and autonomy and pressures for fitting into existing society.

The conflict between similarity and individuality is the topic of this chapter. We will be concerned primarily with pressures for similarity—that is, *the social influences that change behavior or attitudes in the direction of patterns that prevail in the culture or subculture.* We will discuss three major forms of influence producing similarity in people's behavior: *Uniformity* is a kind of similarity that rests on an individual's acceptance of the unspoken assumption that being like others is desirable. *Conformity* is a kind of similarity that develops when an individual gives in to social pressure to be like others. And *obedience* is a kind of similarity that rests on compliance with the demands of an authority figure. All three processes can be immensely powerful, both in their immediate effects and in their social repercussions. Finally, we will consider sources of autonomy and individuality. We will look at ways in which people can break down pressures to conform and create conditions for broader flexibility of action. Although people often are under pressure to be like others, the influences can be overturned.

The Whys of Uniformity

Social thinkers have long been struck by an outstanding characteristic of social life: people in social groups tend to share many similar characteristics. Why such uniformity occurs is an intriguing and complex question. Ask yourself, for example, why a large percentage of today's students wear blue jeans. Blue jeans are not especially cheap. They are not particularly comfortable—they keep the wearer cold in the winter and warm in the summer. By traditional standards of fashion they hardly would be considered beautiful. Do students choose to wear jeans solely out of fear of social disapproval? The question of why such uniformity occurs is difficult to answer.

At the beginning of this century many social thinkers believed that uniformity is the result of *instinct*. That is, they believed that the motive to imitate other people is part of human nature. As theorist Walter Bagehot maintained, there is an "invincible attraction, the necessity of which rules all but the strongest men to imitate what is before their eyes. . ." (1875, p. 36). The developmental psychologist James Mark Baldwin (1895) believed that the individual is a "veritable copying machine" and cannot help being so. The belief that imitation is instinctive was championed also by such influential psychologists as William James and William McDougall. But this argument has not been popular since the 1920s (Bernard, 1926). To appreciate why, you may review the arguments against the aggressive instinct, discussed in Chapter 8. They parallel the case against the instinct to imitate.

Present-day social psychologists have focused their attention on four factors that influence uniformity in society: social norms, modeling, social comparison, and self-awareness. We will consider each of these influences in turn.

Following the Rules: Social Norms

The first factor that influences widespread uniformity in society will be familiar from our discussion of rules in society (Chapters 2 and 6). To facilitate the smooth running of social relations, people develop *norms*, or informal rules. Children typically learn these rules without being aware that alternatives could exist. Thus, when one family member asks another to "please pass the butter," compliance follows without a moment's hesitation. The informal rule system of dinner-table behavior demands that the butter be passed, and most people can scarcely imagine doing otherwise. In the same way, people seldom think twice about returning another person's greeting, wearing clothes in public, or waiting their turn in line. Failing to do any of these things would cause others to express dismay or hostility.

As theorist Harold Garfinkel (1967) maintains, many common patterns of action are governed by unseen rules, and people discover these rules only when they are broken. To demonstrate, Garfinkel asked students in his class to test the hidden rules that operate in their homes by acting as a boarder in the house. For fifteen minutes the students were to be polite and distant and speak formally and only when spoken to. If hidden rules specify the expected behavior of a "proper" son or daughter, being a "proper" boarder should lead to punishment. And indeed it did. The students' reports were filled with "accounts of astonishment, bewilderment, shock, anxiety, embarrassment and anger, and with charges by various family members that the student was mean, inconsiderate, selfish, nasty or impolite" (p. 47). Typical comments by family members included: "Don't bother him, he's in one of his moods again"; "pay no attention but just wait till he asks me for something"; "you're cutting me, okay I'll cut you and then some"; and "why must you

Forced compliance. Uniformity is sometimes a goal of enlightened social policy. The assumption underlying school busing programs is that social differences will be minimized in an integrated environment. The long term effects of this experiment in social influence remain to be seen. A precarious balance exists in such situations: forced compliance sometimes creates resistance to change. See the discussion of reactance later in this chapter.

always create friction in our family harmony?" Clearly, in most households very strong rules ensure that particular behavior patterns are maintained.

Following the Model: Social Contagion

A second factor that influences the development of uniform behavior patterns will be familiar from our earlier discussions of moral behavior (Chapter 6), positive social action (Chapter 7), and aggression (Chapter 8). In order to learn how to do things more effectively, people *model*, or imitate, others' actions. Thus, if an individual solves a common problem, if he or she finds a new way to save energy or a new way to secure happiness, then the solution may spread rapidly throughout society. When a model's behavior is imitated by a large number of people the phenomenon is termed *contagion*—emphasizing the tendency of the behavior pattern to spread from person to person.

In one of the most interesting studies of contagion, investigators followed up a news report of a strange set of physical symptoms that was found among workers at a fabric mill in the southern United States (Kerckhoff and Back, 1968). The plant was shut down in mid-June, a period of peak productivity, because eleven employees, suffering from severe nausea and a rash, had been admitted to the local hospital. Apparently a disease-carrying insect had entered the mill in a shipment of cloth. The number of infected employees soon increased to more than sixty, and inspectors from the U.S. Public Health Service, along with a team of biologists, engineers, and exterminators, were brought in to investigate. Their thorough investigation turned up one black ant, a housefly, two gnats, a common beetle, and a chigger. Medical examination of the patients revealed no biological basis for the malady. At that point a social basis for the epidemic had to be considered.

Kerckhoff and Back were intrigued by what they called the "June-bug epidemic," and they set out to determine whether contagion was responsible. Support for a contagion hypothesis was found. An analysis of the social relationships in the plant revealed that afflicted workers were among the most popular people in the plant. Very few social isolates were bitten by the "bug." In effect, workers who were highly visible and well liked seemed to be major sources of the effect.

In addition, the "disease" traveled primarily among groups of friends. If a worker's best friend was afflicted, that worker was more likely to be "attacked" than was a stranger. Apparently, modeling had produced a uniform set of symptoms.

Social Comparison: When in Doubt . . .

In a sequence of Allen Funt's television series, "Candid Camera," people entered a public elevator only to find all the riders (Funt's accomplices) facing the rear of the car. Soon the unsuspecting victim turned his or her back to the door in imitation of the others. This kind of uniformity in behavior cannot easily be explained in terms of social rules. Rather, as theorist Leon Festinger (1954) argues, when something causes people to doubt their own opinions or actions, they turn to others as sources of information. Specifically, people may compare their attitudes and actions with those of others and judge their correctness in terms of agreement with others. When this happens, people are engaging in a process of *social comparison* in order to gain accuracy in their perceptions of the world (Gruder, 1971). A person who enters an elevator and finds people facing backward may doubt his or her own view of what behavior is appropriate in an elevator. Since everyone in the elevator is behaving in the same way, the doubter may perceive the others as being more knowledgeable than himself or herself. Joining the others in their unusual behavior relieves the doubt. You will recall a similar line of argument in our earlier discussions of self-concept development (Chapter 2) and affiliation (Chapter 3).

One of the most dramatic demonstrations of social comparison effects was carried out in 1935 by Muzafir Sherif. To create an ambiguous situation, Sherif made use of an optical illusion: If a room is completely dark and a stationary pinpoint of light is introduced, the light often will seem to move. This apparent movement of light is termed the *autokinetic effect*. Since no objective standard exists by which an observer can judge the light's apparent movement, social comparison influences may be especially potent in this situation. Sherif placed subjects alone in a darkened chamber and allowed them to make independent decisions concerning the light's movement. He then brought the subjects together in small groups and asked them to repeat the task. As you can see in Figure 10-1, the judgments in the group situation converged on a central point, while independent judgments were more variable.

Did people really believe in these revised judgments? To find out, Sherif retested the subjects after the group session. He found that the group consensus persisted. Typically the subjects' estimates of the light's movement approximated the standard that had been acquired in the group. Later research indicates that group effects can persist for as long as a year (Rohrer et al., 1954). And participants who move to other groups may try to influence their new peers to accept the standards of the original group (Jacobs and Campbell, 1961). Provided no other influences intervene, social comparison effects can stick.

Although judgments often are based on comparison with other people, *any* other person will not do. Similarity seems to be one basis on which people choose others to compare themselves with (Castore and DiNinno, 1972). Apparently similarity increases people's confidence in the accuracy of the information they obtain. If other people are too different, believing that the others are trustworthy sources of information is difficult. Similarity also seems to increase people's confidence in their own judgment and boosts their self-esteem (Gruder, 1971).

These findings do not imply that people are influenced *only* by the opinions or abilities of those most similar to them (Mettee and Smith, 1977). For example, people who are certain of their views usually are more

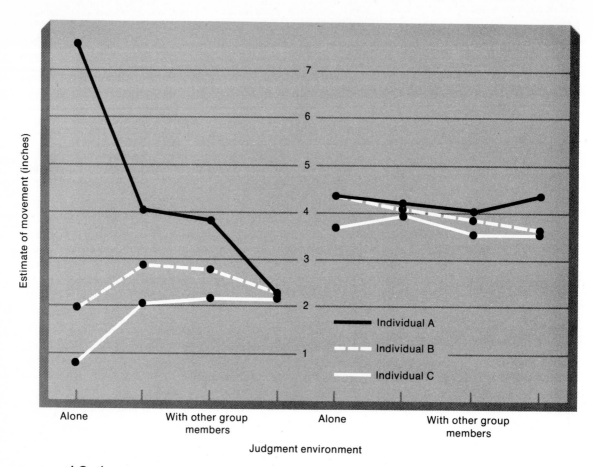

FIGURE 10-1 **Social comparison and the autokinetic effect**

When people are alone in a dark room they make diverse judgments concerning a light's apparent movement. When people make judgments in a group setting, they tend to make similar estimates of the light's movement. As the right hand figure shows, if people enter the group in agreement, they remain in agreement. (Adapted from Sherif, 1958)

open to diverse opinions than are people who are uncertain of their views. Sometimes knowing the extremes—the highest or the lowest score or the most extreme position that other people have taken—can facilitate judgments (Wheeler et al., 1969). And sometimes agreement from a person who is quite different can boost an individual's self-confidence (Goethals and Nelson, 1973). However, the major argument is this: when doubt pre-

vails and the individual is seeking accuracy, comparisons usually are made with people who seem to be similar, and uniformity usually prevails.

The Distress
of Objective Self-awareness

A final influence on uniformity rests on people's tendency to avoid feeling self-conscious.

Most people do not want to be especially noticeable. They work to achieve "normality" in their appearance, in their eating habits, in the style and decoration of their home, in their choices of furniture and car, and so forth. Being different attracts the attention of others. Being different also can cause an individual to become more conscious of himself or herself. This state of self-consciousness, also termed *objective self-awareness*, often is a negative experience, because it creates self-concern about one's failings, or shortcomings (Duval and Wicklund, 1972). By avoiding oddness, discomfort is avoided and uniformity is promoted.

In illustrating this line of argument, investigators have shown that individuals' feelings of self-satisfaction often decrease after they hear a tape recording of their own voice. Research also shows that people are far less optimistic about meeting their goals if they hear their own voice than they are if they hear a recording of another person's voice (Ickes, Wicklund, and Ferris, 1973). Self-awareness also can lead to uniformity in people's opinions. One investigator presented a group of subjects with a set of opinions while the subjects were observing their own image being flashed on a television monitor (Duval, 1972). The televised image was assumed to increase self-awareness, just as the tape recording had in the earlier research. Subjects in another group did not see their own face. The self-aware subjects were far more likely to agree with the group's opinions than were the subjects who had not seen their own face.

In summary, our discussion has touched on four sources of uniformity in society. Both rule following and modeling contribute to uniformity in people's behavior. People unthinkingly follow common-sense rules, and they often imitate other people's actions. Social comparison may play a powerful role in generating uniformity. When conditions are ambiguous people are especially likely to use the actions of others in judging their own behavior. Finally, the anxiety that accompanies self-awareness may motivate people to follow common codes of conduct.

Conformity and Obedience

We have seen that the pressure for uniformity is a fact of social life. Even though people may express a need for a greater degree of individuality, most of them automatically accept the desirability of not being different. Yet, you may argue, such pressures can't be truly powerful. We may follow rules, imitate others, compare our opinions with those of others, and try to avoid feeling self-conscious—but don't these responses take place in situations that are ambiguous or in situations that we don't care much about anyway? When people really care about an issue, don't they express their autonomy? To gain an appreciation of the effect of pressures to be like everyone else, let us consider research on conformity and destructive obedience.

The Asch Findings:
Seeing Is Not Saying

In 1946 Solomon Asch carried out a series of experiments that remain dramatic today. To better appreciate the results of Asch's work, put yourself in the place of a subject in one of the experiments. You volunteer to participate in research on perception. Seven other participants are present. All of you are seated in front of a display panel on which lines of various lengths will be placed. Your task is to compare the length of the lines. Each comparison requires that you compare a standard line that is several inches in length with three other lines. Each person will report his or her answer aloud, and you will report last. The task seems easy enough. For the first two comparisons the judgments are easy to make, and all of the participants agree. On the third

BOX 10-1

A person who enters college is doing far more than simply taking courses and having fun. A college student becomes part of a new and special social milieu. The community has its own attitudes and values concerning life goals, morality, politics, and other issues. In joining the community, students cannot easily remain insulated from the prevailing dispositions, and usually they come to embrace them. In a classic study of the influence of prevailing opinions on students' views, Theodore Newcomb and his colleagues (1943) studied political attitudes in the late 1930s at Bennington College, which at that time enrolled only women. The students came mainly from economically privileged homes where the dominant political view was conservative. In contrast, the political climate at Bennington favored strong liberal and radical views. Newcomb wanted to know how the relatively radical Bennington atmosphere would affect the students' political preferences.

Marked differences were found in the students' political attitudes. Freshmen's attitudes tended to be similar to those of their parents, while juniors and seniors were much less conservative. The percentages of students who preferred various political candidates in the 1936 presidential election are presented in the table below. The election pitted the Republican Alfred Landon against the liberal Democrat Franklin D. Roosevelt. The Socialist party candidate was Norman Thomas, and the Communist candidate was Earl Browder. As you can see, among the freshmen and their parents who were surveyed, the overwhelming choice was Landon.

Candidate	Freshmen		Sophomores		Juniors and Seniors	
	Students	Parents	Students	Parents	Students	Parents
Landon	62%	66%	43%	69%	15%	60%
Roosevelt	29	26	43	22	54	35
Thomas and Browder	9	7	15	8	30	4

By the sophomore year, students' preferences for Roosevelt, Norman, and Browder had increased, while their parents' preferences remained unchanged. The percentage of juniors and seniors who preferred Landon dropped to only 15 percent, in sharp contrast to their parents' conservative views.

Interviews with the students gave qualitative insights into the meaning of this change. As one student said: "I accepted liberal attitudes here because I had always secretly felt that my family was narrow and intolerant, and because such attitudes had prestige value. It was all part of my generally expanding personality—I had never really been part of anything before" (p. 125).

Another student indicated: "I was so anxious to be accepted that I accepted the political complexion of the community here. I just couldn't stand out against the crowd unless I had made many friends and had strong support" (p. 127).

What was the experience of students who did not change? Again, the interviews are instructive: "I'm all my mother has in the world. It's considered intellectually superior here to be a liberal or radical. This puts me on the defensive, as I refuse to consider my mother beneath me intellectually, as so many other students do" (p. 134). And as another student added: "Family against faculty has been my struggle here. As soon as I felt really secure here I decided not to let the college atmosphere affect me too much. Every time I've tried to rebel against my family I've found out how terribly wrong I am, and I've very naturally kept to my parents' attitudes" (p. 136).

What happened to the students after leaving the college environment? As they became part of different groups, which probably were more conservative than the college community, did they change once more and again reflect the dominant view in their social surroundings? A follow-up study that was conducted twenty-five years later answered this question (Newcomb et al., 1967). The graduates were polled regarding their preferences in the 1960 presidential election. A preference for Kennedy, the liberal, over Nixon, the conservative, was expressed by 60 percent. In a sample of control subjects who were matched in economic and social terms to the Bennington women, but were not graduates of that college, only 30 percent preferred Kennedy. Apparently the liberal values learned at Bennington persisted.

Why should these values persist, considering that the students had been so vulnerable to change when they arrived at college? Newcomb believes that the students were relatively unsophisticated politically when they came to Bennington. They became part of a group without being fully aware of its possible effect on them. After leaving Bennington, however, they made friends and often chose as marriage partners people who resembled them in political beliefs. Thus they were not thrust headlong into a conservative social milieu. Rather, they remained within a subculture that continued to give support to their liberal position.

Destructive obedience. The capacity of authority figures to elicit obedience is a social problem of major importance. Although most people would like to think that they would not obey a leader like Hitler, authority figures continue to exercise their influence in countries throughout the world.

round, however, you suddenly are surprised. The correct answer seems to be obvious, and yet the first member of the group makes an error. He has reported a line that obviously is a few inches shorter than the standard to be equal to it. "Silly," you think; "how could he make such a mistake?" Then the second participant agrees with him. Before you have time to think about what is happening, you find that other participants are making the same mistake. Within a minute, *all seven* of them have agreed that the obviously unequal lines are equal. It is now your turn. Will you agree with the group or not? During the next twenty minutes you will face the same dilemma six times more.

Asch found that subjects in this situation frequently gave in to the erroneous opinion of the majority (all were confederates employed by Asch). On 33.2 percent of the critical comparisons, subjects voiced agreement with the majority. Only 20 percent of the participants remained fully independent of group pressure. And 10 percent of the subjects agreed with the majority on all or on all but one of the trials. Even when a marked difference between the lines was obvious, subjects conformed to the majority to approximately the same extent. Control-group subjects, judging the lines in private, were almost entirely accurate in their assessments. Group pressure clearly had powerful effects.

Later in this chapter we will discuss conditions that lead to nonconformity. However, the question relevant here is why subjects gave in to the sense-defying majority opinion. One answer is that they were fearful of disapproval that might result if they did not go along with the group. As one participant said, "I felt disturbed, puzzled, separated, like an outcast from the rest. Every time I disagreed I was beginning to wonder if I wasn't beginning to look funny" (Asch, 1952, p. 465). The kind of social criticism that the subjects anticipated is demonstrated by a variation on the original study. Asch assembled a group of volunteers who participated with one hired confederate. The naive subjects all responded correctly. However, the lone confederate made the same errors that the group of confederates in the previous study had made. Reactions of the volunteer subjects were dramatic: sarcasm, exclamations of disbelief, and laughter were frequent. One subject wrote of the confederate, "I feel the person was attempting a stupid joke, at which I was annoyed. Then I felt sorry for a person with such poor eyesight" (Asch, 1952, p. 480). Had the hired confederates in Asch's original study behaved similarly, social pressure most certainly would have increased the amount of conformity.

Does social comparison influence conformity? Interestingly, Asch's research confirms the view that some people did use their peers in obtaining information about the correctness of their judgments. In lengthy interviews conducted after the study, Asch found that the erroneous opinions of the majority often caused subjects to doubt the validity of their own judgments. They began to wonder, for example, whether the seat had been placed so that they could not see properly or whether they might be suffering from eye strain. Further, some subjects seemed to be convinced that the erroneous majority opinion actually was correct. Comments by these individuals suggested that they were unaware of any discrepancy between the majority opinion and the actual facts of the case. They felt that they had been wholly accurate in their reports. Such results are especially interesting since they suggest that people's sense data may be shaped by social agreement.

Advances in understanding conformity

Asch is only one of many social psychologists concerned with the powerful effects of group pressures on individual decisions. In 1921 H. T. Moore showed that adults would readily change their views on what is "good" grammar or "ethical" behavior, depending on the opinions voiced by others. However, Asch's impressive research stimulated many other investigators to demonstrate compliance to group pressure. In one important methodological advance, Crutchfield (1955) streamlined Asch's procedure by having each subject sit in a separate booth from which a projection screen could be observed. As various designs were flashed on the screen, subjects flipped a switch to indicate their judgments. An electric panel in each booth informed the subjects of judgments made by other "participants." In fact, there were no other participants. The information on the panel was controlled by the experimenter, and hired confederates were not needed.

Crutchfield found that judgments could be changed readily on a wide variety of topics. For example, military officers who in private said that they were good leaders could be influenced to deny this attribute. Other investigators found that they could induce reasonably sophisticated people to agree that the average person eats six meals a day, that male babies have a life expectancy of twenty-five years, and that the United States is populated largely by old people (Tuddenham and McBride, 1959).

Additional developments in understanding conformity have taken place at the theoretical level. In particular, theorists have described important distinctions in the process of yielding to group pressure. Herbert Kelman (1958, 1961) points out that at least three separate processes may be involved, including the following:

1. *Compliance.* The process of compliance occurs when people yield to a group in order to avoid being punished for nonconformity. An individual who complies may give in publicly but reject the group's opinion privately. Most of the subjects in the Asch study appeared to be complying in order to avoid potential punishment by others in the face-to-face situation (Deutsch and Gerard, 1955). Subjects in the more impersonal context of the Crutchfield experiment may have engaged in less compliance since they had no real contact with the "group." When the friendship of the group is particularly desired, the individual is said to be under *normative pressure* to comply (Kelley, 1952). Under these circumstances, the greater the individual's attraction to the group, the more compliance may be anticipated (Back, 1958). The individual desperately wants to avoid being disliked.

2. *Internalization.* The process of internalization occurs when a person comes to believe that the group is correct. Because the person has incorporated the opinions, preferences, or actions of the group into his or her own value system, there is both public and private acceptance. Internalization probably was a minor influence in the Asch situation, since most subjects experienced difficulty in believing the obviously incorrect judgments of the group. However, internalization may have been a key factor in the Crutchfield situation. Because other group members seemed to be arriving at the erroneous decision independently, subjects might have believed that the others had superior knowledge. Membership in a group that seems to have superior knowledge may place the individ-

ual under *informational pressure* to yield. And the greater the perceived competence of the group, the greater the likelihood that the dissenter will yield (Ettinger et al., 1971; Hollander and Willis, 1967).

3. *Identification.* The process of identification occurs when an individual yields to group pressure because the group has qualities or characteristics that the individual wishes to adopt. Like internalization, the group preference is accepted both publicly and privately. Generally, however, identification effects are less deep or less long-lasting than are internalization effects (Romer, 1979). Identification probably was not the major process that led to conformity in either the Asch or the Crutchfield experiments, since subjects had little opportunity to learn about the personal qualities of the other group members.

Does a conforming personality exist?

A fascinating film, *The Conformist* (directed by Bernardo Bertolucci), tells the story of a man who, as a youth, secretly murdered a adult male who had seduced him. Because of his painful secret, the man feels alienated from the normal social world. To relieve his guilt he resolves to conform absolutely to the rules of the culture. Since he is living in prewar Italy, he becomes a loyal Fascist. The party assigns him the task of assassinating a friend, a philosophy professor who lives in exile in Paris with his beautiful wife. The movie depicts the conflict between the man's obsession with conformity and his deep feelings for the professor and his wife. The film raises important questions about conformity in society. Is there a conforming personality who is likely to give in to the crowd regardless of the issue?

Early researchers believed in the existence of a conforming personality. For example, one researcher reported that 20 percent of subjects exposed to conformity pressures in four separate situations conformed consistently in all four of the situations (Vaughan, 1964). More recently researchers have disagreed with this view (Allen, 1975). Conformity, they argue, usually is a means to some end—for example, Bertolucci's hero tries to reduce his own guilt. Consistent with this reasoning are studies that have shown that men with low self-esteem conform more often than do men who are more self-assured (De Charms and Rosenbaum, 1957; Rosenberg et al., 1960). The less-assured men may be motivated by the need for security. Other researchers have found that people whose need for social approval is high conform more readily than do those whose need for social approval is low. Apparently they are trying to gain other people's liking (Crowne and Liverant, 1963; Strickland and Crowne, 1962). And those who score high on the F Scale of authoritarianism (see Chapter 4) often conform more than do those whose scores are lower. The authoritarian may conform because of an unquestioning respect for convention (Elms and Milgram, 1966).

Conformity, then, seems to be primarily a means for fulfilling a variety of psychological needs. Accepting this assumption, then the existence of a "true conformist" seems unlikely. Probably no one gives in to group pressure *regardless* of circumstance. Conforming behavior in one situation (for example, in the classroom) may not fulfill the same needs as conformity in another situation (for example, in one's friendship group). Thus a person who conforms in order to gain the respect of authority might be expected to conform in the classroom but not when socializing with friends. In contrast, a person who is seeking friendship might conform to pressure from friends but act quite independently in the classroom. Women once were thought to be more conforming than men (Nord, 1969). However, the current stress on feminine assertiveness may encourage women to avoid conforming to the opinion of others.

Modern research does not disclose strong conformity differences between men and women (Eagly, 1978).

Obedience to Authority

We have seen that groups can have a powerful effect on people's actions. In the face of group pressure to conform, people will deny publicly their deepest beliefs and will agree with statements that clearly are false. Such effects are not limited to group situations. Social psychologists have been concerned with authority figures' capacity to obtain obedience. In particular, researchers have tried to understand *destructive obedience*—that is, obedient behavior that aims to punish or destroy property or persons. Many military and police atrocities are committed under orders. Soldiers and police officers might prefer to avoid violence, but they nevertheless act obediently. Many social critics believe that persecution of the Jews in Nazi Germany was due in part to the willingness of a large number of Germans to act obediently. Would obedience be as widespread in the United States or in any other country today? Before answering, put yourself in the place of the adult male subjects in Stanley Milgram's (1965) dramatic experiments on obedience to authority.

You are to be paid $4.50 an hour for participating in a research project at a prestigious educational institution (Yale University). You arrive at the laboratory and are joined by a second participant, a middle-aged man, balding and slightly stout. You are told that the research is concerned with the effects of punishment on learning. In the experiment the two of you are to work together, one as teacher and the other as learner. You draw straws, and you find that luck is on your side: you will serve as the teacher, thus avoiding the learner's punishment—electric shock. You are shown a shock generator—a large panel with a series of thirty buttons, each of which will deliver shock to the learner when-

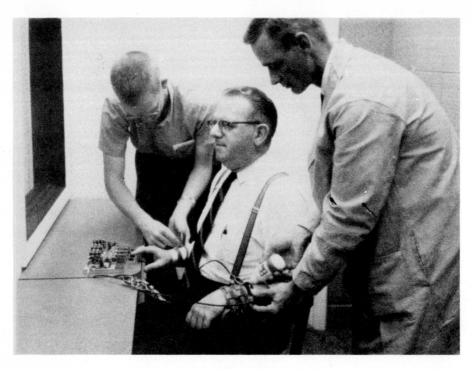

Copyright 1965 by Stanley Milgram. From the film *Obedience,* distributed by the New York University Film Library.

Milgram's learner. What would you do if you were ordered to administer increasing doses of shock to this man? Would you obey, as most subjects did, or might you resist the experimenter's authority? Milgram's research suggests that you would be likely to obey.

---

ever he makes a mistake on the task. Each button delivers an increasing amount of voltage. Thus the button at the extreme left indicates a low 15 volts, and each succeeding button increases the amount of shock by 15 volts, to a maximum of 450 volts. Additional labels offer clues to the meaning of the numbers: the lowest voltage is labeled *slight shock;* one of the highest reads *danger severe shock.* As you test the learner on a memory task, you are supposed to deliver 15 volts to the learner the first time he makes an error, 30 volts on the second error, and so on. To demonstrate the effects of pushing the buttons, you are given a brief and slightly painful

45-volt shock. The learner then is strapped into a chair in an adjoining room, and electrodes are applied to his wrists.

The learner turns out to be rather inept. Soon you find that you have moved from the 15- to the 45-volt button. When you deliver 75 volts, the learner emits a grunt and a moan. As you move toward 150 volts, the learner's pained reactions become increasingly intense, until finally he screams out that he will no longer participate. Soon he stops responding to any questions and begins to pound on the walls when he is shocked. After the 330-volt level is reached, he no longer responds at all. He had complained at an earlier point about a weak heart. Is it possible that he has had a heart attack? Yet every time you express doubts about the procedure, the experimenter insists that you continue. If you resist, the experimenter says that "you have no other choice, you must go on." He persists in his demands until you have passed the button labeled *danger severe shock*.

The "victim" in the experiment was a confederate of Milgram; the "experimenter" was a local school teacher; and the "shock" was not being delivered at all. But if you had been a subject, would you have continued to deliver shocks to the learner, who was obviously tortured by the experience and perhaps even lifeless? The norms of science suggest that a subject should do as the experimenter directs. The experimenter seemed to punish any move to terminate the task. In addition, there was no basis for making a judgment about continuing—no other source of information on which to base a comparison. Milgram says that he originally felt that he would be hard pressed to find a subject who would continue to obey an experimenter until the maximum shock was delivered. Forty psychiatrists agreed. When Milgram asked for their predictions about people's willingness to continue, they predicted that most subjects would not exceed the 150-volt limit. They also suggested that only the rare and possibly neurotic individual would continue until the maximum shock was delivered.

This topic has received so much attention that you may be wiser than the psychiatrists. Their predictions are featured in Figure 10-2 along with the actual behavior of the subjects. You can see that some 62 percent of the subjects were *fully obedient* and continued to deliver shock until they were told they might stop. They did not administer the shock easily. Many subjects displayed great anguish, verbally attacked the experimenter, twitched nervously, or broke out in nervous laughter. Nevertheless, most people continued to obey.

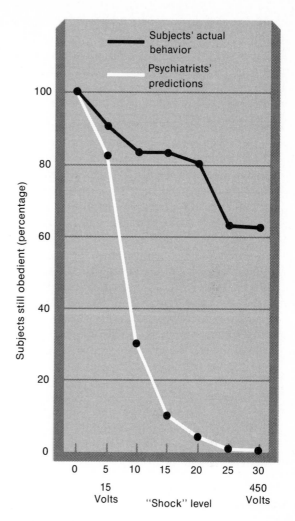

FIGURE **10-2**

Real and estimated levels of obedience

Note that the psychiatrists underestimated the willingness of people to disobey authority. Nearly two-thirds of the subjects delivered maximum available shock to the "unconscious" victim. (Adapted from Milgram, 1974)

Conditions of obedience

Milgram's striking results suggest that in general people are not likely to resist the demands of authority—even when they believe that the authority is wrong. Concern about the potential effects of destructive obedience has caused Milgram and other social psychologists to look for factors that if altered might reduce the tendency to obey blindly. Among their findings are the following:

1. *The legitimacy of the authority.* Milgram suspected that the high level of obedience in the original study was due primarily to the legitimacy that was lent the experimenter's commands by his connection with Yale University. To explore this possibility he established a second laboratory in a rundown office building in Bridgeport, Connecticut. The sponsor of the test was presented as a private commercial research firm. Other conditions of the experiment remained the same. This change in procedure reduced obedience to some extent. Forty-eight percent of the Bridgeport sample delivered the maximum level of shock, compared with 62 percent at Yale. Milgram was struck by the relatively limited reduction in the percentage of subjects who were obedient, and he concluded that high levels of obedience could be obtained even if the institution was not "particularly reputable or distinguished."

2. *The proximity of the victim.* In the original study the victim was in a nearby room, out of the subjects' direct line of sight. However, Milgram's later work showed that when the subject was in the room with the victim and was required to press the victim's hand on a metal plate in order to set off the shock, obedience was reduced markedly (see Table 10-1). The closer the victim, the less the obedience.

3. *The proximity of the authority.* In the original study the experimenter stood near the subject. However, when the experimenter relayed instructions from a nearby room or by telephone, resistance to his commands rose sharply (Rada and Rogers, 1973) (see Table 10-1). When the experimenter gave instructions by phone, many subjects lied about their behavior. They reported that they were administering high levels of shock when actually they were delivering the lowest level of shock possible.

4. *The personal characteristics of the subjects.* Subjects who were obedient were more likely than subjects who were disobedient to see the learner, or victim, as being responsible for what happened to him

TABLE **10-1**

The relationship between physical distance and obedience

Note that the location of both the experimenter and the victim affects subjects' willingness to administer dangerous shocks.

Location arrangements	Subjects who gave the victim extremely dangerous shocks
Experimenter	
At hand	62.5%
Remote	45.0
Victim	
At hand	49.0
Remote	65.0

Source: Adapted from Milgram, 1974

(see the Chapter 7 discussion of the just-world hypothesis). Obedient subjects assigned twice as much responsibility to the learner than did the defiant subjects, and they assigned less responsibility to themselves. Obedient subjects also seemed to have stronger authoritarian characteristics (Elms, 1972) and were less advanced in their level of moral thought (Kohlberg, 1965).

The aftermath of obedience

Milgram's experiments have generated a considerable amount of controversy. Many critics view the research as being fundamentally unethical (Baumrind, 1964). They have questioned Milgram's right as a scientist to subject people to intense pressures, deceive and humiliate them, and cause them to feel guilty about their behavior. Critics also have questioned whether enough has been learned from these studies to justify exposing more than one thousand people to such stress. The same conclusions could have been reached, they argue, by studying the brutal behavior of American troops in Vietnam, the attacks of police officers on demonstrating students, or the otherwise ordinary lives of participants in the murderous Manson cult. Perhaps other less harmful techniques could have been used to demonstrate these ideas (Mixon, 1972).

In his own defense, Milgram cites evidence that shows that 84 percent of the subjects who later were queried indicated that they were glad to have taken part in the study. Less than 2 percent said that they were sorry they had participated. The vast majority of subjects indicated that they had learned something important from their participation. Other psychologists have argued that confronting subjects with moral dilemmas is morally justifiable because people may review their value systems and emerge as better people (Crawford, 1972; Rosnow, 1978). Other defenders argue that a different method would not have been as successful as Milgram's

method was. The major aim of Milgram's work was to show that most people will follow orders and do terrible things to one another. Accounts from the news would probably never provide such convincing evidence. You can see that as in most cases of ethical conflict, no easy resolution exists.

To summarize, we have seen that both groups and individual authority figures can exert powerful pressures on people to behave in ways in which they might not otherwise choose. Conformity to group pressure often occurs because people want to be accepted by other group members and because people turn to others for information that will improve their own decisions. People are especially likely to obey if the authority figure has legitimacy and is close by. People's personal characteristics also contribute to their response to pressures for conformity and obedience.

Unintended Effects of Social Influence

So far we have focused on social influences that produce similarity in people's ideas and actions. However, conforming and obedient reactions are often only the first step in a long chain of social influences. Once an individual's attitudes or behavior has been altered, the individual may in turn influence others in ways that were not considered by the original agent of change. We now will consider processes by which the effects of social influence are spread; and we will look at some of the changes that take place in information as informal networks of social influence operate on it.

The Transmission of Rumor

More than thirty years ago in Matoon, Illinois, a resident reported to the police that a prowler had opened her bedroom window and had sprayed her daughter and herself with a paralyzing gas. The police investigated, and although they could find no evidence, the neighbors reported that a man had been seen leaving the area. The local newspaper reported the incident, using the headline, "Anesthetic Prowler on the Loose." In the next few days dozens of conflicting reports on the prowler were received by the police. As one newspaper reported, "The town's bewildered citizens reeled today under the repeated attack of a mad anesthetist who sprayed deadly nerve gas into 13 homes and knocked out 27 victims. . . . Seventy others, dashing into the area in response to the alarm, fell under the influence of the gas last night. . ." (Quoted in Johnson, 1945, p. 176). The reports soon subsided, leaving many questions. The police never found a single trace of the gas nor any substantial evidence of a prowler. Investigators finally concluded that the phantom anesthetist had never existed (Johnson, 1945).

The informal spread of opinions, ideas, and information can be powerful and quick. For example, when President Kennedy was assassinated, 90 percent of the adult population of the United States knew about the shooting within forty-five minutes of the first news account. Over half heard the news from another person (Greenberg, 1964). Despite the availability of newspapers, magazines, and television, transmission of information depends primarily on *informal communication networks*—that is, groups of people who retain relationships with each other over time and space. So extensive and elaborate are these networks in modern society that one person can communicate without immense effort with virtually any other member of the society. To demonstrate the "small world" of informal communication networks, Stanley Milgram (1977) gave a message to randomly selected people in Wichita, Kansas, and Omaha, Nebraska, and asked them to have it delivered to an unknown target person in Massachusetts (either the wife of a Harvard

divinity student or a Boston stockbroker). Each sender was asked to select one friend or acquaintance who was most likely to know either the target or someone else who would know the target. Milgram found that the message passed among an average of *5.5 persons* before reaching the target. Men were most likely to ask other men to convey the message, and women were most likely to make requests of other women. Thus an Omaha real estate agent might select an investment-broker friend in New York as the person he knew who lived closest to the target. His friend in New York might check with a colleague who once had lived in Boston, and he in turn might know someone who worked in the stockbroker's firm in Boston.

What happens to information as it passes through a communications network? Does it tend to become distorted, as it did in Matoon, Illinois? The first systematic study of the transmission of information in social groups was published in 1932 by the British psychologist, Frederic Bartlett. To explore distortion, Bartlett developed the method of *serial reproduction*. In this procedure, a subject is shown a standard stimulus, such as a drawing or a brief printed story, and after a fifteen- to thirty-minute period the subject is asked to reproduce what he or she has seen or read. A second subject then is shown the first subject's reproduction and after fifteen to thirty minutes is asked to reproduce it as faithfully as possible. This process was continued until the information had been received and reproduced by as many as eighteen people. In general, Bartlett found substantial distortions as the materials moved from person to person.

Distortions that occur in serial reproductions display a characteristic pattern. They tend to change from ambiguous forms to common or conventional patterns. As you can see in Figure 10-3, by the eighth reproduction the rather abstract birdlike form has approximated the form of a cat. By the tenth reproduction it is a clear and realistic cat. This tendency to

Original Drawing

Reproduction 1

Reproduction 2

Reproduction 3

Reproduction 4

Reproduction 5

Reproduction 6

Reproduction 7

Reproduction 8

Reproduction 9

Reproduction 10

FIGURE **10-3** **The transmission of misinformation**

In this classic example of the distortions that can occur as information is transmitted, each subject changed the stimulus passed to him or her, and eventually the owl was transformed into a cat. (From Bartlett, 1932)

twist details to conform to a common, recognizable structure has been called *assimilation* (Allport and Postman, 1947). Assimilation may be achieved in a number of ways. *Leveling* takes place when various elements or details are dropped from the pattern and the story or picture is simplified. For example, the facial features of the birdlike creature in the figure seem to be a cat's ribbon by the ninth reproduction. *Sharpening* takes place when certain important features of the pattern are accentuated or made more apparent. For example, the creature in the figure has sprouted a tail by the eighth reproduction, and the tail is ac-

centuated or clarified for the remainder of the reproductions.

Many distortions that take place in the transmission of information can be traced to poor perception and poor memory. Studies of eye witnesses' testimony have found that sworn statements often are inaccurate (Goldstein, 1977). Witnesses to crimes usually have great difficulty in accurately recalling the criminal's face after several weeks (Buckhout, Figueroa, and Hoff, 1974). Inaccuracies are particularly likely to occur when the person being identified is of another race (Chance, Goldstein, and McBride, 1975; Elliot, Wills, and Goldstein, 1973), when the observer is highly aroused (Johnson and Scott, 1976), or if a suspect resembles common stereotypes of murderers, robbers, and similar types (Shoemaker, South, and Lowe, 1973). Such results are unsettling, given the great reliance that is placed on eye-witness accounts in criminal prosecutions.

Distortions in information may be caused by emotional factors as well as by defects in perception and memory. As we emphasized in our discussion of social comparison, people often are anxious about the meaning of various events. To reduce ambiguity they turn to others for help in deciding what really is

happening (Rosnow and Fine, 1976). From this perspective, communication of unauthenticated information, or rumor, should be more likely to occur if information is ambiguous than if it is clear. To illustrate this argument, researchers have intentionally introduced rumors into various groups and have traced the effects. In one study a student-confederate mentioned in a class discussion that four students had smoked marijuana during a final exam and had been attacked by the teacher for their behavior (Jaeger, Anthony, and Rosnow, 1979). A week later the students were asked whether they had repeated the story to anyone else. Those students who had achieved high scores on tests of anxiety were more likely to transmit the rumor than were students with lower anxiety scores. Apparently the anxious students most needed to reduce ambiguity by assessing other people's reactions to the story.

The MUM Effect: Reluctance to Transmit Bad News

Not all information travels with equal speed and equal impact. People typically are selective in the kind of information they pass to others. For example, people are more likely to tell one another good news than bad news

(Tesser and Rosen, 1975). The tendency to keep quiet about unpleasant matters—termed the *MUM effect*—seems to be based on a fear of arousing other people's hostility. In fact, in early Roman times a messenger who bore news of a defeat in battle often was executed by the emperor. There also is empathic concern—that is, concern that the receiver of the news may be upset by it.

To demonstrate the MUM effect, female students working in groups of three were given an opportunity to communicate good or bad news (Tesser, Rosen, and Conlee, 1972). Two members of each group were confederates of the experimenter; only one member was a naive subject. Before the learning task began one of the confederates (the target) mentioned that she was especially anxious about news from home. Later, when the subject was alone, a messenger arrived and said that the target should call her home. Half of the subjects were told that the target would receive "very good news"; the others were told that the news was "very bad." Later each subject had several opportunities to relay the messenger's news to the target or to the third member of the group.

As you can see in Table 10-2, 85 percent of the subjects told the third member of the group the news—whether it was good news or bad didn't seem to matter. When the news was good, *all* of the subjects relayed the information to the target. However, when the news was bad, only 50 percent of the subjects relayed the information to the target. As additional data showed, the subjects believed that the target was more interested in the news than the third person was and had a greater right to hear it. Yet they did not communicate what they knew. Such findings have been replicated in many other studies (Barnes, 1972; Goethe and Cole, 1969; Rosen and Tesser, 1970). Apparently the person most in need of knowing about a misfortune may be the least likely to be told.

To summarize, conformity and obedience may be only the first in a long chain of reactions to social influence. Information often travels rapidly through informal communication networks. As it is transmitted from one person to another, systematic distortions may take place. Information is leveled and sharpened to fit conventional patterns in the culture. Faulty perception, poor memory, and attempts to reduce anxiety also may contribute to poor transmission. Not all information travels with equal speed across groups. People seem particularly unwilling to communicate bad news, even if they feel that others need to hear it.

TABLE 10-2   No news is bad news

Good news is more likely to be transmitted to a target than is bad news. Note the absence of a difference when the message doesn't matter to the recipient.

Type of recipient	Type of news	
	Good	Bad
Target	100%	50%
Third member of group	85	85

Source: Tesser, Rosen, and Conlee, 1972

Resistance to Influence

For many social psychologists, both conformity and obedience are deeply troubling phenomena. A free society, they argue, cannot exist unless people speak out against the majority, against authority. When people disregard their private feelings and give way to pressure from social groups or from authority figures, the stage is set for tyranny. With such concerns in mind, investigators have set out to study *independent behavior*—that is, behavior in which attempts are made to resist social influence in order to achieve some goal.

A distinction between *independence* and *anticonformity* usually is made (Stricker, Messick, and Jackson, 1970). The latter term refers to behavior in which defiance of the group or the authority figure becomes an end in itself. We will deal with independence rather than with anticonformity. First, we will explore some of the psychological sources of independence. We will consider several psychological capacities that encourage or motivate dissent. We then will look at ways in which social situations can be modified to reduce the effects of social pressure. Finally, we will explore ways in which minorities can influence the majority.

Psychological Wellsprings of Independence

People resist pressures to conform for many reasons—personal beliefs, ethics, and social commitments all may play a part. However, some psychologists believe that resistance may develop from deep psychological needs. Let us consider two such possibilities: the need to feel free and the need to feel unique.

Reactance: the need to be free

When their parents come to visit, many people react with irritation. Children love their parents and want to see them, but unless the visit is brief they often fear that their freedom will be restricted. And they resent the loss of freedom. Some psychologists (Brehm, 1966; Wicklund and Brehm, 1976) believe that such reactions may be highly common in society. They argue that people have a deep and enduring investment in retaining their freedom of choice. Whenever they are threatened by a reduction in freedom, they respond with a negative motivational state, called *reactance*. The individual who experiences reactance will attempt to reduce it by trying to reclaim the lost freedom.

To illustrate reactance, let us consider an interesting study on reactions to censorship (Wicklund and Brehm, 1976). Censorship reduces people's freedom and is likely to produce a state of reactance. A person can reduce this reactance by increasing his or her liking or desire for the censored material. To explore the attitude change that may be produced by censorship, investigators measured junior-high-school students' attitudes toward lowering the voting age (at the time it was twenty-one years). Most students favored such a policy. Later an announcement was made that a speech in favor of this policy would be presented to the student body. Thus the students could look forward to hearing a talk that supported their position strongly. However, on the morning of the scheduled assembly the talk was canceled. Half of the students were told that an official from the county school board had forbidden the speaker to come because the official did not want the students to hear the talk (censorship condition). The rest of the students were told that the speaker was ill. When the students' attitudes toward lowering the voting age were reassessed, the results showed that censorship had backfired. Students who believed that the official was responsible for the cancellation *became increasingly positive toward the censored position*. This result was not found among the students who believed that the speaker had become ill. Similar findings have been demonstrated by other researchers (Ashmore, Ramchandra, and Jones, 1971).

We see that social pressure sometimes can motivate people to resist conformity. Several conditions increase the likelihood of a reactant response.

1. *Reactance increases as the threat to freedom increases.* The greater the threat to one's freedom, the greater the individual's resistance. One study showed, for example, that people who were placed under great pressure to fill out a questionnaire were less likely to comply than were people who received only a mild request

Censorship: high-school style. These boys, youth leaders in a small midwestern city, are participating in a symbolic book burning. Their action was reportedly triggered by the inclusion of *The Exorcist* in a required reading list. Will burning the book make it seem more or less interesting to their fellow students? See the accompanying discussion of reactance for an answer to this question.

(Doob and Zabrack, 1971). Other researchers have found that if one person reveals too much about himself or herself, others may begin to experience reactance and reveal very little about themselves (Archer and Berg, 1978).

2. *Reactance increases as the threatened behavior's importance to the individual increases.* If an individual does not care about a given issue, attacks on the issue will not create much reactance. When an issue is important, the individual may re-

sist the influence attempts even if the source of the pressure is someone to whom he or she is attracted (Brehm and Mann, 1975). One study showed that favors received from others can create reactance. Apparently receiving a favor requires that the favor be returned, and this requirement reduces freedom of choice (Brehm and Cole, 1966). The study also showed that the reduction in freedom may be resented especially when it interferes with an activity that the person feels is important.

3. *Reactance is increased by the belief that one has the right to freedom.* If people feel that they have the right to free speech, they may react with more hostility to government controls on the press than they would if such a right were not assumed in the first place (Wortman and Brehm, 1975). In addition, as the amount of freedom is reduced, reactance increases (Wicklund, 1974). If the government raises the income tax rate by a small amount, people are unlikely to complain. If the increase is large and the freedom to spend is reduced greatly, people may respond by voting the law-makers out of office.

Uniqueness: the need to be different

Think about going to an important party. You spend an afternoon shopping for just the right clothes. You arrive at the party and find that four other people are wearing precisely the same clothing. You might feel irritated or perhaps embarrassed. Some psychologists believe that your reaction expresses a deep and important need—the wish to be *unique*, or different from others (Snyder and Fromkin, 1980).

One reason people want to be unique is because most societies place a high value on scarce entities. For example, a person who is physically strong will receive more attention at a college where good athletes are scarce than at a college where good athletes are plentiful. In addition, feelings of personal identity

BOX 10-2

Is It Better to Be a Man, a Woman, or Both?

Traditional sex-role stereotypes assume that men and women differ in many respects—in behavior, ability, and temperament. As we saw in Chapter 4, the traditional male stereotype includes such traits as autonomy, activity, discipline, logic, courage, hardness, and goal-directedness. In contrast, the traditional female stereotype emphasizes nurturance, emotional expressiveness, dependency, passivity, and relatedness to others. Research has shown that men and women act in ways that are consistent with these stereotypes. For example, in the course of a conversation women look at and gesture to one another more frequently and for longer periods than do men (Ickes and Barnes, 1977). Typically these different patterns of behavior are viewed as part of human nature—that is, as a basic part of men's and women's character.

Recently theorists have begun to question the traditional stereotypes and champion new sex-role options. These theorists argue that the link between traditional sex-role types and biological gender should be severed (Bem, 1974, 1977; Pleck and Sawyer, 1974; Spence and Helmreich, 1977). A person's biological makeup does not demand that he or she be more or less disciplined, courageous, expressive, or nurturant. Rather, they believe, these styles reflect a process of social influence; people adopt the styles in order to fit properly into the culture. If either the requirements of the culture or the needs of the individual were to change, the behavior patterns also could change. Traditional styles are highly restrictive, demanding certain kinds of behavior that may seem to be quite alien to the individual. For example, many men would like to be soft and nurturant and many women would prefer to be active and autonomous. Thus these people probably would welcome a breakdown of the traditional sex-role patterns. This breakdown might facilitate the development of an *androgynous* style of behavior—that is, one in which a person expresses the desirable traits of both sexes as needs and wants dictate (Bakan, 1966).

To demonstrate the strength of these arguments, investigators have developed measures that enable them to single out persons who are committed to traditional sex roles and persons who are androgynous. One of the most popular of these measures is the Bem Sex Role Inventory (BSRI), developed by Sandra Bem (1974, 1977, 1979). The measure is composed of forty personality characteristics. Twenty of them were judged by undergraduate students to be more desirable for men than for women. These include such traits as ambitious, dominant, and self-reliant. The remaining traits were judged to be more desirable for women than for men. These include such traits as affectionate, gentle, and understanding. When completing the inventory, a person evaluates the extent to which each trait is true of him or her. The self-ratings make possible the identification of traditionally masculine, traditionally feminine, or androgynous persons. An individual may achieve a high or a low score on any of the three dimensions regardless of biological gender.

Research using this measure indicates that sex-typed people behave quite differently from androgynous people. For example, in a conformity situation in which the subject has an opportunity to compare his or her judgments with those of others (Crutchfield, 1955), people who score high on feminine traits are more conforming than those who are either masculine or androgynous (Bem, 1975). This finding is true of both men and women.

When given an opportunity to play with a kitten—an activity that is thought to be traditionally feminine—androgynous men spent more time engaged in the activity and enjoyed it more than did men high in masculinity. Androgynous and feminine women were found to give more nurturance to a lonely student who needed counseling (Bem, Martyna, and Watson, 1976). And the behavior of people high in femininity and masculinity differs greatly during conversation. For example, traditionally feminine individuals often smile when they are not speaking, and traditionally masculine individuals change the flow of a conversation. In contrast, androgynous individuals use signals that traditionally are associated with both sexes (LaFrance and Carmen, 1980).

Interestingly, investigators have found that people with traditional sex-typed behavior patterns often experience difficulty in heterosexual relationships because their response styles are incompatible with those of the other sex (Bem and Lenney, 1976). The relatively detached and logical style of the male does not blend with the more sociable and expressive style of the female. The androgynous individual is often able to do whatever is adaptive or compatible in relationships with either sex (Ickes and Barnes, 1978).

As you can see, there are strong value implications in such research. The investigators argue that the traditional patterns of male and female behavior are not functional and should be abandoned. Further, they are attempting to show that the androgynous person is "better" by some criteria. As a result, their work has become controversial (Bem, 1979; Locksley and Colten, 1979; Pedhazur and Tetenbaum, 1979; Spence and Helmreich, 1979). Doubts concerning the measuring instruments and the strength and interpretation of various findings have been expressed. Nevertheless the examination of the society's traditions and the search for alternative ways of behaving do much to sensitize people to possible shortcomings in their own lives.

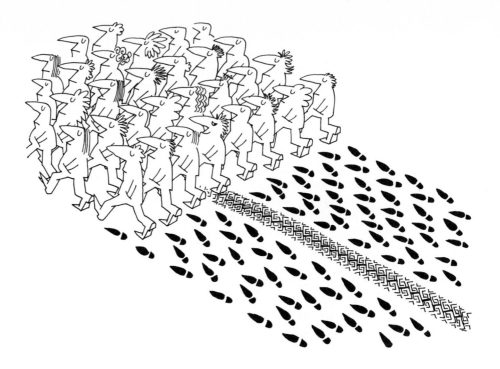

seem to be attached to the ways in which people *differ* from others rather than to the ways in which they are similar. If you write poetry, for example, you may feel that your poetry is an important aspect of your identity. However, you probably don't consider letter writing to be an important aspect of yourself. Virtually everyone writes letters.

To demonstrate the importance of the need for uniqueness, investigators have studied people's reactions to learning that they are highly similar to others. Under these circumstances, most people indicate distress, a lowering in self-esteem, and a lowering in regard for the people whom they are supposed to resemble. When people are given tests of creative thinking, those who believe that they are not unique increase their creativity. They also indicate an increasing willingness to join in unusual or freaky experiences (Fromkin, 1970; Ganster, McCuddy, and Fromkin, 1977). When people try to stress their uniqueness,

they often behave in ways that accentuate their superiority over others (Myers, 1978). People often want to be more than merely different: they also want to be a little better (Myers, Wojcicki, and Aardema, 1977).

Of particular importance to this argument is the fact that if people are told that they are similar to a large number of other people, their conformity may decline markedly. In one study, college students' sense of uniqueness was varied in order to determine the effect of perceived similarity on conformity (Duval, 1972). The students were told that either 5 percent, 50 percent, or 95 percent of ten thousand other college students agreed with their "ten most important attitudes." Each of the students then was placed in a test situation in which he or she had to guess the number of dots that appeared on various slides. Before giving a judgment, each student was allowed to hear estimates that had been made by two other persons. Students who had been told that they were similar to most college students showed the *least* amount of agreement with the other estimates.

We see, then, that people often place a great deal of value on freedom of choice and on being unique. Such values are not always in evidence, however. The early Romans gladly gave up a free democracy for autocracy, and many people would argue that modern Japanese culture places far more value on conformity than it does on uniqueness. Clearly, if conformity and obedience are to be counteracted, people need to know more about the sources of reactance and uniqueness and the conditions that strengthen or weaken these needs. However, many social critics believe that personal resistance to social influence cannot accomplish enough. Attention must be given to the *conditions* under which people give in to influence. Thus we now turn to a discussion of these conditions.

Altering the Conditions for Social Control

As you may recall, the subjects of Milgram's research were far more likely to resist the instructions when the experimenter was not in the room than when he was present. And when the victim was in the room, resistance to the experimenter's commands also increased. In each case, changes in the social situation were being made, and the changes affected the subjects' resistance to pressure. We will consider several kinds of situational factors that must be confronted if social pressure is to be reduced: the characteristics of the influencing agent, the techniques used by the agent, and the presence or absence of surveillance and social support.

Social characteristics: love, honor, and obey

The characteristics of the influencing agent may be extremely important in affecting reactions to pressure. People will try hard to conform to the wishes of some people and will respond negatively to the same requests from others. What personal characteristics increase the likelihood that people will comply with an influencing agent's demands? Personal attractiveness is surely near the top of the list. Physically attractive members of the opposite sex are often more influential than are those who are unattractive—even for people as young as eleven years of age (Dion and Stein, 1978). Friends typically have a stronger effect on people's actions than do strangers. In fact, if people are given a minimal amount of information—if they simply are *told* that they will be attracted to others, their conformity to the group's opinion may increase (Back, 1951).

Prestige and *knowledge* also increase the power of the influencing agent (see Chapter 5). That is, people's willingness to comply with someone's wishes will increase when they believe the person to be an expert in a given area (see McGuire, 1968). In fact, if agents of influence are knowledgeable in one area, they may exert an influence in areas in which they are just as ignorant as everyone else. For example, professionals or wealthy people who serve as jurors are likely to have more influence on other members of the jury than are persons without wealth or a professional title (Strodtbeck, James, and Hawkins, 1957). This effect apparently reflects the other jurors' respect for the influencing agent's prestigious position rather than for his or her superior knowledge.

For people who value independence in society, the finding that the power of an individual or a group may depend on perceived attractiveness or perceived expertise has important social implications. In particular, such findings point up the need for free speech. Free speech and criticism may reduce the importance of attractiveness and allow an expert's wisdom to be refuted. A critical press, extremist political parties, free intellectual debate, irreverent comics, avant garde art, and so forth all operate to reduce the power of influence agents.

Appearance, prestige, and knowledge may increase the effectiveness of influence attempts, but a source's characteristics are only part of the story. You probably can think of some exceptionally influential teachers who do not have these characteristics in great abundance and other teachers whose influence is limited even though they possess all of them. Many social psychologists believe that the personal style and techniques that are employed by the source of influence are as important in producing compliance as are the source's characteristics.

First let us consider the effects of personal style. Harvey London and his colleagues (London, 1973; London, Meldman, and Lanckton, 1971) arranged for pairs of individuals to offer opposing arguments in the discussion of a court case. After the pair had argued, each person in the pair was asked whether the "defendant" was guilty or innocent. Some participants were persuaded easily by their partners; others were the effective persuaders. The task was to find out what made the difference. An analysis of the arguments revealed that the persuaders tended to use words that expressed confidence in their opinions while those who were persuaded tended to express doubt. The effective persuaders registered confidence early in the discussion and then went on to consider other issues. Yet, when a person displayed a high level of confidence throughout the discussion, this tended to make the other person feel inferior or pressured. Too much confidence produced a boomerang effect, with less persuasion resulting (London, McSeveney, and Tropper, 1971). Related research has found that talking fast also can increase one's influence, as long as speed does not interfere with comprehension (Miller et al., 1976).

Influence also may be increased by using special persuasion techniques. One of the most widely studied of these is the *foot-in-the-door technique,* in which the individual first asks for a small favor and then asks for a larger one. To demonstrate the effectiveness of this, investigators varied the kinds of favors they asked of suburban housewives (Freedman and Fraser, 1966). Identifying themselves as members of a safe-driving committee, they first asked the women to do a small favor— display the committee's small sign in the front window of their home. Later the investigators contacted the women again and asked permission to place a large safe-driving sign on their lawn. Women in a control group were not asked to do the initial favor. Of the women who had agreed to the small request, 76 percent also agreed to the larger one. In contrast, only 16 percent of the control group agreed to show the large sign. Although the foot-in-the-door technique does not always work (Foss and Dempsey, 1979), success has been sufficiently frequent to generate much broad interest (Cann, Sherman, and Elkes, 1975; Pliner et al., 1974; Snyder and Cunningham, 1975; Uranowitz, 1975). Many explanations of the effect have been offered, including a suggestion that agreeing to perform a small favor changes people's perceptions of themselves (DeJong, 1979). They come to see themselves as being helpful, and then they act in ways that are consistent with the new view of themselves.

Variations on the foot-in-the-door technique include the *low-ball technique,* in which people are asked for a small favor and after they agree to do it are informed that it will be very costly. This technique is far more successful in gaining ultimate compliance than is a technique in which the people are informed at the outset of the full costs (Cialdini et al., 1975). In the *door-in-the-face* technique people first are asked for an extreme favor (which usually is refused), and then are asked for a smaller favor. Most people agree

Would you buy a new car from this man? The answer depends on what persuasion techniques he uses. Salespersons employ a variety of methods to break down resistance to their messages. Awareness of their techniques is one of the best ways to marshal resistance and maintain independence.

to do the smaller favor (Cialdini et al., 1975). Possibly they feel guilty about not complying with the large request and go along with the smaller one in order to reduce their guilt.

Investigators have been interested in finding out how guilt and other negative feelings affect compliance. In one early study, for example, punishment delivered by subjects in a Milgram-like experiment was varied in order to determine the effect of this variation on subsequent helpfulness (Carlsmith and Gross, 1969). Half of the subjects thought that the punishment they were delivering was a buzzer sound, and the other subjects thought that they were delivering painful electric shock. After the learning task, the learner casually mentioned that he needed volunteers to help save a redwood grove in northern California. Of the subjects who believed that they had shocked the learner, 75 percent agreed to help, while only 25 percent of those who used the buzzer volunteered. Other research shows that people often will comply with requests in order to maintain the public appearance of being a good person (Wallace and Sadalla, 1966), in order to avoid seeming deviant (Kilter and Gross, 1975), and in order to improve their private feelings of goodness (Apsler, 1975). Such motives were discussed in the chapter on positive social behavior (Chapter 7).

We see, then, that there are a variety of techniques that a source of influence may use to reduce independence successfully. Anyone who is concerned with furthering autonomy in society must be prepared to counter such effects. One means of combating the efficacy of such techniques is through documentation of them. Once someone is aware of the un-merited effects produced by another's self-confidence or the foot in the door, for example, the impact of those techniques may be blunted.

Surveillance:
the plight of the watchful eye

In our discussion of research on obedience we reported that the authority's influence was reduced greatly when the authority was not present. When demands for obedience were received by phone, for example, they often were ignored. This finding suggests that the success of social influence attempts often depends on whether the target's activities are under surveillance. People often are compliant when they are under surveillance. If they aren't compliant under such circumstances, they may be punished. Less compliance is likely if surveillance is not possible. Government restrictions, for example, usually fail if the target's behavior cannot be monitored. And laws that govern people's private sexual practices are rarely successful, since in the privacy of their homes people tend to do what they please (Edwards, 1972).

The use of monitoring to increase compliance can have negative consequences for society. In particular, surveillance often increases the monitor's suspicion, and as suspicion increases the amount of monitoring increases further. To illustrate, one investigator looked at the effects that opportunities to monitor people's behavior had on the person doing the monitoring (Strickland, 1958). Subjects were to supervise the work of two assistants. The subjects were told that they could win as much as $10 if the assistants succeeded at the task; if the assistants failed, they would earn nothing. While the assistants were at work the supervisors were allowed to monitor continuously the work of Assistant A, but they could observe the progress of Assistant B only occasionally. The performance of both subjects was the same. However, the supervisors' ratings showed that they perceived the assistants' work much differently. The worker who was monitored was seen as being significantly less trustworthy and less dependable. Supervisors felt that he would not have worked very hard if left unattended. In effect, they believed that Assistant A was working only because he was being observed and that future monitoring of his behavior would be necessary.

Social Support for Nonconformity

Social support for nonconformity is an important factor in fostering independence. To appreciate this argument, let us return to Asch's classic study of conformity. When Asch's subjects were faced with a unanimous but incorrect group opinion they went along with the group approximately 30 percent of the time. In a follow-up study, Asch searched for ways to reduce the conformity. He repeated the experiment, but with one change: *a single confederate spoke out in favor of the correct answer.* Thus the unanimous majority was broken by a single voice of reality. The effects of this minority dissent on the subjects' reactions proved to be powerful. Conformity dropped to approximately 5 percent.

Apparently, if people can find at least *some* social support for their views, they will resist pressure and remain independent. Being isolated seems to be especially difficult.

The evidence that dramatic decreases in conformity can be produced by minimal social support has stimulated much further study. Investigators have wanted to know whether such effects are *general*. That is, was the Asch situation unusual, or are there many other kinds of situations in which minimal social support has the same effects? They have found that social support can decrease conformity in a wide variety of circumstances (Allen, 1965; Edmonds, 1964; Hardy, 1957). This effect takes place in groups of children, in groups of mentally retarded individuals, and in groups of adults (McCool, 1975). In addition, investigators have found that social support is not required continuously and that occasional support can have the same effects. For example, subjects in one study received social support for their opinions during the first half of the experiment (Allen and Bragg, 1965). Then because of a seeming breakdown in the equipment, the supportive partner was no longer able to continue in the experiment. The subject was left isolated. Nevertheless the earlier support had lasting effects: subjects continued to oppose the majority even without the supportive partner being present. Another study showed that the partner in dissent need not agree with the subject in order to encourage the subject's dissent (Bragg, 1972). A dissenter gave wildly incorrect judgments, thereby disagreeing with *both* the majority and the subject. Thus the subjects were free to disagree with the majority. In other words, the presence of another dissenting voice *of any kind* may encourage others to make independent decisions.

The supporter need not always be first in order to reduce conformity. When the supporter gives *post facto* support—that is, when the deviant opinion is given *after* the subject has spoken—the subject can be encouraged to assert independence in the face of group pressure (Boyanowsky and Trueman, 1972). In fact, if a subject receives such support while members of the group are making one kind of judgment (for example, comparing lengths of lines), the subject may be willing to oppose the majority when they later are making another kind of judgment (for example, deciding whether gun control laws should be stronger). That is, a *generalization of opposition* takes place: the independence that is developed in one area carries over to independence in another area (Allen, 1975).

Again, the implications for a free society seem clear. Dissenting opinions must be honored. When dissent is allowed, minorities may feel free to make their opinions clear. More generally, we see that the characteristics of the influencing agent, the availability of monitoring, and the presence of dissent may affect the amount of independence in society. If one wishes to encourage independence from social pressure, factors such as these must be taken into account.

Minority Influence

So far our discussion has treated social influence as if it were a one-way street. The group or the authority figure exerts influence over a target. The target either gives in or resists. However, this view is somewhat oversimplified. The target of influence may be an agent of influence in his or her own right. Minorities may change the majority successfully, a fact that must be studied if minorities are to be encouraged to speak for themselves (Moscovici, 1976).

Many recent political revolutions illustrate the power of minorities to influence majorities. Small but active revolutionary groups have changed the history of Russia, China, Cuba, Chile, and a host of other nations. However, history leaves many ambiguities, and social psychologists have tried to trace minority influence more precisely. Two major questions have been asked: what kinds of influence do minorities have over majorities, and under what conditions are minorities most likely to produce effects that will favor rather than hurt them? Let us consider each of these issues.

Minority Influence: Moving Toward and Away

While many revolutionary minorities are able to influence the majority to move toward the minority position, most revolutions fail. In fact, minority dissent may move the majority *away* from the minority position. Such reversals are called boomerang effects. To demonstrate both positive and negative effects of a minority position, experimenters arranged for groups of subjects to rate their preferences for paintings (Nemeth and Wachtler, 1973). Subjects were shown nineteen pairs of paintings and were asked to select the one in each pair that they liked. They were told that one painting in each pair was by an Italian artist and that the other was painted by a German. The supposed nationalities were assigned at random. Interestingly, preliminary choices by subjects in a control group indicated a preference for the paintings attributed to Italians. Since the national origin had been randomly assigned to each painting, the researchers concluded that these findings reflected a slight prejudice in favor of Italian artists. On the basis of this information the investigators formed other groups of subjects and included a confederate, "Fritz Mueller." As the group members stated their preferences, Mueller took a minority stance that showed a strong and consistent liking for the German works. Mueller's minority position had a strong effect on group preferences. A marked increase was found in the popularity of the German paintings.

In an interesting variation on this theme, the experimenters demonstrated a boomerang effect. In some groups Fritz Mueller was replaced by "Angelo Milano," clearly seen by the group as an Italian. Milano then demonstrated a consistent preference for Italian works. Thus, although Milano represented the general group preference, his consistency furnished an extremist portrayal of the majority view. This extreme expression succeeded in reversing the majority opinion. The group began to express preferences for works attributed to German painters. Not only did the extremist expression fail to win converts, but it backfired.

The boomerang effect seemed to occur because the Italian, who consistently demonstrated preferences for artists from his own country, sensitized the subjects to their own prejudices. Perhaps they came to feel guilty and tried to compensate by showing favor to the German paintings as well. However, this kind of extremism does not always boomerang. When people feel secure in their views, extremist support actually may strengthen their position. To explore this possibility, an experimenter arranged for groups of women to voice their opinions on the issue of women's liberation (Patcheler, 1974). The general opinion among these groups was pro-feminist. When a confederate who took an extreme feminist position was placed in some of the groups, the women in those groups showed marked shifts of opinion in the direction of the confederate's point of view. Similar effects occur at pep rallies, where everyone favors the home team, and among the faithful at religious revivals. In such situations an extreme minority view tends to strengthen preexisting opinions.

When the Minority Speaks Loudest

The position of the minority dissenter is precarious. How can dissenters achieve positive effects and avoid negative effects? How can they best go about converting the secure, satisfied majorities? As with most questions, many answers are possible, and the best solution may change with time and circumstances. One of the most important factors at stake is that which theorist Serge Moscovici (1976) calls the "behavioral style" of the influencing agent. For Moscovici, the successful minority demonstrates (1) *investment* in the issues, (2) *autonomy*, and (3) *consistency*. Thus the minority should appear to have a strong investment in its position. Valuing goals highly and being willing to make sacrifices for their attainment often may impress the majority. The successful collection of signatures for a minority group's petition, for example, seems to depend on how vigorous the petitioner is in his or her appeal and how much he or she seems to believe what is said (Secord, Bevan, and Katz, 1956). Perhaps the broad influence of Gandhi and Luther (Erikson, 1958, 1969) was the result of the courage of conviction that they demonstrated.

Appearing to be an autonomous, free-thinking individual also may have strong impact on the majority. The wide range of minority-support studies discussed earlier in this chapter stands as testimony to this argument. When subjects see an individual stand up against the majority, they are likely to do so themselves. The display of autonomous independence may furnish a personal challenge. Yet this independence should be coupled with a consistency in point of view (Moscovici and Faucheux, 1972; Nunnally and Hussek, 1958). If the minority member gives the impression of being wishy-washy, the majority member may come to doubt the validity of his or her position.

In summary, majorities often are vulnerable to the effects of minority opinion. In response to minority pressure they may change their opinions, values, and modes of behavior. However, to avoid producing a boomerang effect, the minority must choose its behavioral style carefully. Autonomy, consistency, and an investment in the issues may be important first steps in producing positive change.

SUMMARY

1 The conflict between pressures for independence and pressures for fitting into existing society is a central one. Uniformity, conformity, and obedience are three forms of similarity.

2 Uniformity in people's patterns of behavior can derive from several sources. One source is the mastering of the informal rules of a culture in order to function effectively in society. As people begin to follow these rules unthinkingly, uniformity is produced. People also use the behavior of others as a model for effective action. The spread of modeling effects among large numbers of people is called contagion.

3 Uniformity may be increased by the social comparison process. People compare their views with other people's views in order to increase confidence in their own judgments. Muzafir Sherif demonstrated this process in his studies of individual and group responses to the autokinetic effect. When people choose others with whom to compare themselves, they generally chose those who seem to be similar. Uniformity also results from attempts to avoid objective self-awareness, a state produced by self-observation.

4   Conformity occurs when an individual changes his or her personal beliefs or behavior as the result of social pressure. In the most famous study of conformity, Solomon Asch asked subjects to make simple comparisons in the lengths of lines. When a group of confederates unanimously agreed in an obviously incorrect decision, subjects conformed to the incorrect decisions on approximately one-third of the trials. Theorist Herbert Kelman has distinguished among three processes of influence: compliance, in which people conform in order to avoid punishment from the group; internalization, in which people come to believe that the group is correct; and identification, in which people try to adopt the qualities or characteristics of group members. When a person seeks friendship from a group, he or she is said to be under normative pressure to comply. When correct information is desired from the group, the individual is said to be under informational pressure to comply. Because conformity fulfills many different needs for different people, consistent conformists probably are rare.

5   Destructive obedience aims to punish or destroy property or persons. In his demonstration of destructive obedience, Milgram showed that approximately 60 percent of laboratory subjects will deliver shocks to a learner even when the voltage is believed to be dangerously high and the victim of the shocks is screaming in agony or possibly is unconscious. Destructive obedience decreases when the authority figure is not physically present. Milgram's research has stimulated considerable controversy in terms of its ethics.

6   Social influence may have unintended effects. Information often is distorted as it passes through communication networks. The distortion occurs as ambiguous stimuli are assimilated into common, recognizable structures or social beliefs. Information also is distorted in memory and because people often are reluctant to transmit bad news (the MUM effect).

7   A number of psychological sources can promote independence—that is, they can enable people to remain insulated from group pressure or the commands of authority. One source is reactance, a negative emotional state that is evoked when one's freedom of choice is reduced. Reactance increases when the threatened freedom is important and when an individual believes that he or she has a right to the freedom. Censorship also may produce reactance. In addition, people may remain independent because of a need to feel unique.

8   Many social conditions can increase or decrease independence. Persons who are physically attractive or have prestige or knowledge may be particularly effective in influencing others. Also, certain techniques may be used to gain compliance. The expression of a moderate degree of self-confidence may increase compliance. The foot-in-the-door technique often is effective, as are attempts to make the target feel guilty

or lacking in self-esteem. Surveillance often is used effectively to reduce independence. However, all such techniques may fail if the target has social support for nonconformity—that is, if others who are present remain independent in the face of influence attempts.

9 Although majorities often have strong effects on a minority group's behavior, minorities can be effective in moving a majority in their direction. This movement may be especially likely to take place if the minority demonstrates autonomy, consistency over time, and a high investment in the issues.

SUGGESTED READINGS

Milgram, S. *Obedience to authority.* New York: Metheun/Tavistock, 1974.

Moscovici, S. *Social influence and social change* (C. Sherrard & G. Heinz, trans.). London: Academic Press, 1976.

Wheeler, L., Deci, E., Reis, H., & Zuckerman, M. *Interpersonal influence* (2nd ed.). Boston: Allyn and Bacon, 1978.

11: EXCHANGE AND STRATEGY

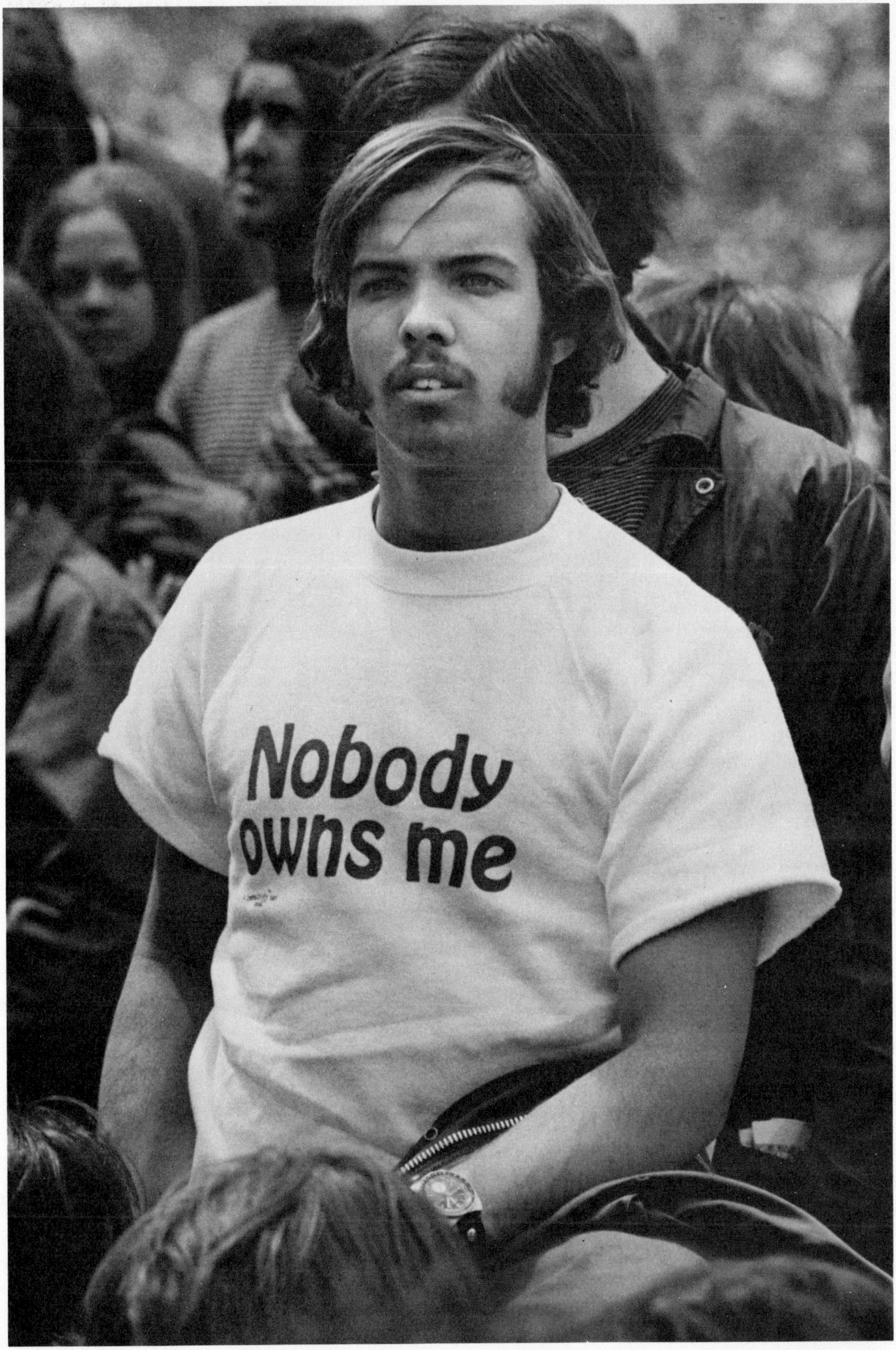
Nobody
owns me

■ *A student we know (we'll call him Brad) recently complained to us about his friend Janet. He finds Janet very attractive and wants to gain her affection. However, Janet is bored by his favorite activities—camping, hiking, hunting, and fishing. She prefers to spend time wandering in interesting areas of the city, trying new restaurants, going to the movies, and talking with friends. Brad finds that whenever he and Janet are in the city, she is very affectionate toward him. When he tries to interest her in outdoor activities, she treats him coolly. As Brad puts it, "I feel like I'm buying her affection. If I do what she wants, she is really nice to me. If I follow my own interests, she just doesn't seem to care about me at all."*

Many social psychologists would agree with Brad's observation that he is buying Janet's affection. What is more, they would argue that in many respects all social relationships operate like a marketplace. People give others certain goods and services, and in return they hope to receive a payoff. At the same time as they are giving, however, they are being rewarded by others, who are hoping to get something in return. No matter what the level of the relationship—romantic attraction or congressional decision making—social life can be conceptualized as a process of giving and taking, buying and selling. In this sense, everyone is bargaining for the best deal possible. You may find this view of human relations to be cynical, and you may wish to adopt a nobler description. Before you reject the notion of social relations as exchange and strategy, however, consider some of the interesting insights that were developed by investigators who have adopted this point of view.

In this chapter we first will examine some of the fundamentals of exchange theory. We then will consider several major lines of investigation that were inspired by the theory. If social life is a process of buying and selling, how do people avoid endless cycles of mutual exploitation? We will see that social harmony is protected by rules of social exchange that govern both the kinds of exchange that are appropriate and the amount of resources to be

exchanged. Despite these rules, exploitation is a major factor in social life. We will look at the factors that contribute to this conflict and consider the question of how destructive conflict can be reduced. Finally we will turn to problems of social strategy. If people are striving continually for greater rewards, they must develop strategies for achieving them. We will look at differences in people's strategic abilities and the way in which various nonverbal signals can be used to achieve one's ends.

Fundamentals of Exchange and Accommodation

Exchange theory rests on four simple assumptions.

1. *Human action is motivated primarily by the desire to gain pleasure and avoid pain.* Regardless of the source of pleasure or pain, virtually all social behavior can be explained in these terms. Even people's most self-sacrificing acts, including martyrdom, can be understood in terms of this essentially hedonistic premise. The self-sacrificing individual may give up physical pleasure, but in so doing he or she may achieve even greater gains such as the imagined blessings of God, esteem from friends, or the like. Within this book the pleasure-pain principle has contributed to

discussions of attraction (Chapter 3), prejudice (Chapter 4), morality (Chapter 6), and positive social behavior (Chapter 7).

2. *The actions of other persons are sources of pleasure and pain.* Most people place a great deal of value on other people's regard, affection, respect, or love, as well as on what others give in the way of time, assistance, guidance, and so forth. Few people find satisfaction in a hermit's isolated life. But just because others are so badly needed, they are an important source of pain. Other people can wound with a chance remark as well as with a physical attack.

3. *By his or her own actions, a person can obtain pleasure-giving actions from others.* This proposition describes social exchange: people trade their own actions for the actions of others. They give pleasure in order to receive pleasure. Brad was acting according to this principle when he joined Janet in the city in order to secure her affection. In the same way, if you want to receive affection from a close friend, a good strategy is to act warmly toward him or her. Your actions are like currency used to buy your friend's behavior.

4. *People try to achieve maximum pleasure at minimum cost.* This proposition assumes that people will expend as little effort as possible to secure maximum rewards. In other words, people use a *minimax strategy* in social life, minimizing pain while maximizing pleasure. If people are trying continuously to cut costs, a tendency toward using fakery or subtle trickery in most relationships may develop. After all, if others learn that someone is out to get as much as possible with as little effort as possible, they may become resentful or hostile. Consider a student who seeks a teacher's praise but wants to reduce the costs of good performance. One strategy might be to include in

term papers quotes or references to obscure works. The teacher may be falsely impressed with the student's extensive "research." This tactic often meets with success. However, if the teacher knows the obscure work, the student may find that the strategy has backfired.

Despite the prevalence of the minimax strategy, all relationships are not exploitative. Because persons depend on each other for pleasure, they tend to seek the forms of exchange that maximize pleasure. They tend to avoid those exploitative exchanges that maximize pain. Thus people will often interact in ways that furnish maximum pleasure, or payoffs, to each other. When people furnish maximum joint payoff to each other, they are engaging in the *accommodation process* (Kelley, 1967).

In one early study of the accommodation process, pairs of subjects were offered an opportunity to work out a mutually satisfying outcome in a potentially painful situation. Male undergraduates were placed in an isolated chamber, and electrodes were attached to their fingers (Sidowski, Wyckoff, and Tabory, 1956). On the table in front of each subject were two buttons and a counter. Each subject was told that he could push either of the two buttons as often as he wished. Depending on which button was pressed at a given time, the subject would either accumulate points on his counter or receive an electric shock. He was told that his task was to accumulate as many points as possible. He then was left alone for twenty-five minutes. Unknown to him, his button pushing was not the source of his points or of the shock. In an adjoining chamber a second subject faced a similar apparatus and received identical instructions. The devices were arranged so that pressing the *right-hand button* in the first chamber would give the second subject a point, while pressing the *left-hand button* in the second chamber would give the first subject a point. Each subject could deliver electric shock to the other unknowingly: the *left-hand button* in the first chamber delivered shock to the second chamber, while the *right-hand button* in the second chamber delivered shock to the first chamber.

Figure 11-1 presents a payoff matrix, a summary of possible payoffs of pleasure and pain. The scoring of points is indicated by a plus (+) sign, and the receiving of shock by a minus (−) sign. Clearly, for mutual accommodation to take place the first subject must press his right-hand button and the second subject must press his left-hand button. Any other combination punishes one or the other or both simultaneously. Mutual accommodation is no simple matter in this situation. Neither subject knows that his outcomes are dependent on the actions of another person, neither knows what pattern of button press-

ing will be rewarding, and no communication is possible. Yet in spite of these obstacles, subjects quickly learn to engage in accommodating exchange.

Figure 11-2 shows the average number of times the point-giving button was pressed in each five-minute period of the experiment. As you can see, the rewards (points) that the subjects give each other increase steadily during the first fifteen minutes and then generally level off. The punishments (shocks) are low at first and decline continuously over the next twenty minutes. The subjects were able to find a mode of relating that afforded great mutual advantage. You may be able to think of many parallels from your daily experiences. Good friends often try to find activities that make both of them happy. Parents and children frequently try to adapt their needs to allow for some degree of family harmony.

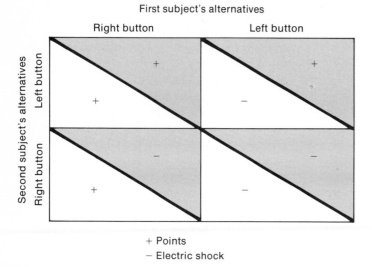

First subject's alternatives

+ Points
− Electric shock

FIGURE **11-1** **A payoff matrix**

Possible payoffs in pleasure and pain are summarized in this diagram. Outcomes for the first subject are shown above the diagonal line in each box, and outcomes for the second subject are shown below it. Thus, if both players press the left button, the first subject gains a point and the second subject receives shock.

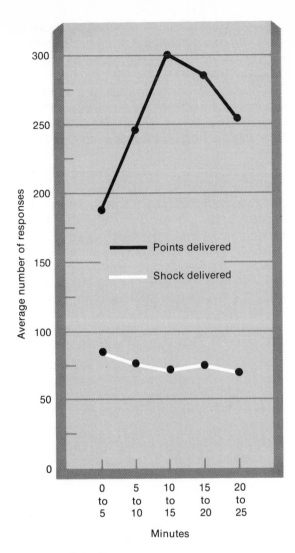

FIGURE **11-2**

The accommodation process in action

Even though the subjects were unaware of each other's presence, they were able to accommodate each other's needs. Note that as time passed they gave each other more pleasure and less pain. (Adapted from Sidowski, Wyckoff, and Tabory, 1956)

Lovers often find themselves trying hard to accommodate each other's needs and wants. Accommodation is everywhere, even in a world in which actions may be based on selfishness.

To summarize, exchange theorists view people as creatures who try at all times to maximize pleasure and minimize pain. All relationships are not exploitative, however. While achieving pleasure from others, people give pleasure to others in return. Accommodation is the process by which people work out relationships that bring mutual pleasure.

Rules of Exchange

Once profitable forms of exchange have been developed, people try to ensure that they are maintained. Thus Brad may mention to Janet that he hopes they can see each other the next weekend, or Janet may express unhappiness if Brad says he will be camping on that weekend. If they are able to develop an expectation that they will spend their leisure time together, their expectations will come to operate as rules. Both of them will feel that they "should" be with the other and that each has a right to punish the other if he or she should decide suddenly to break the pattern.

Rules of exchange govern behavior in society as well as in individual relationships. Such rules are embodied in the social norms of the culture (Homans, 1950). For example, clear norms govern the way people behave in a department store. Customers are expected to pay for merchandise, and merchants are expected to offer merchandise in exchange for money. This pattern of exchange is repeated daily millions of times throughout most of the world. And people are subject to punishment if they do not obey the rules. If the rule is informal (see Chapter 2), failure to comply may result in disapproval or hostility from others. In most stores, dancing in the aisles would be a violation of common norms, and people might frown or treat the dancer as if he or she were an imbecile. If the rule has been formalized through the legal system,

BOX 11-1

What Is the Worth of a Man . . . or a Woman?

According to basic economics, the value of any commodity depends on its scarcity. Diamonds are scarce and thus are valued greatly. Glass is abundant and thus is relatively cheap. According to Marcia Guttentag and Paul Secord (1980), the scarcity or abundance of men and women in society varies over time, and this variation produces widespread social consequences. Men and women need each other for love, pleasure, companionship, procreation, and other purposes. Thus, if either men or women are in scarce supply, their value will increase for members of the opposite sex.

To illustrate their argument and explain differences in social life, Guttentag and Secord have used population data from a variety of cultures and historical periods. Variations in male-female ratios, they believe, account for such social practices as female infanticide, dowries, wife buying, and the women's liberation movement. Let us briefly consider two of Guttentag and Secord's case studies: the rise and fall of courtly love in medieval Europe and the advent of the singles scene in contemporary Western society.

In France and Germany in the twelfth and thirteenth centuries courtly love was practiced among the upper classes. Courtly love emphasized the spiritual adoration of women. To woo the fair maiden, the lover sang ballads that were characterized by restraint, tenderness, and pledges of eternal dedication. Gross physical satisfaction was shunned. The lady remained aloof and unattainable. Although she occasionally granted a suitor her physical favors, she regarded him most approvingly if he behaved in a refined and "courteous" manner. The suitor found the lady's aloofness and high social position to be fascinating. He would undergo considerable self-denial and frustration to gain her passing attention.

Guttentag and Secord suggest that the cause of this passion and denial was related to the social conditions of the times. The need for a large class of armed knights and other personnel to staff newly built castles gave young men of peasant stock the opportunity to become part of the nobility. As these ambitious young men entered the castle social life, they sought women for personal satisfaction and as a means of securing a

failure to comply results in harsher penalties. Taking goods without paying, for example, can lead to arrest. In a major sense, laws represent people's ways of ensuring that accommodating exchanges are maintained throughout the culture and across time.

To illustrate the operation of rules of exchange, experimenters have developed a pleasuring machine. Subjects press a button that delivers pleasant physical vibrations to the buttocks and thighs of another person (Davis, Rainey, and Brock, 1976). Usually these vibrations are delivered in the context of a learning study similar to Milgram's (see the Chapter 10 discussion of obedience research). The pleasure is a reward for correct answers. The individual who delivers the pleasure has a choice of how much pleasure

foothold in the upper classes. The women who might fulfill those needs were few and highly cherished. Later, when the nobility closed its ranks and the ratio of men to women was more equal, courtly love disappeared, and a rough, unbridled antifeminism took its place.

Turning to contemporary society, Guttentag and Secord report that because of fluctuations in the birth rate, the number of marriageable men is lower than the number of marriageable women (Carter and Glick, 1976). Since men are in relatively short supply, they have more social power in relationships than do women. In effect, men have a favorable balance in social exchange and can call the shots. When women are in oversupply men have more alternative relationships from which to choose. Men more readily can have simultaneous or successive multiple relationships. Presumably men marry in order to have a woman as a companion and as a sexual partner and perhaps to have children. With an oversupply of women, most of these ends can be met outside marriage. In fact, the tradition of monogamous marriage may limit the man's alternatives. Considering these facts from the viewpoint of social exchange theory, it might seem that men, rather than women, are reluctant to make a commitment to marriage—because of the high level of satisfaction that can be had in alternative relationships. However, Guttentag and Secord believe that the unequal sex ratio also affects women's behavior in heterosexual exchange. Women become less willing to make commitments to a relationship with a man for several reasons: When women are plentiful the outcomes in relationships with men are relatively poor. Women are more likely than men to have experienced abandonment, desertion, or betrayal. Women are more likely than men to develop a feeling of having been exploited. And they also become more wary of commitments.

As a result of these attitudes the singles scene emerges. Singles activities—in bars, at clubs, on vacations, and so forth—grow in popularity. Women participate because they expect little more than casual relationships. Interestingly, over the next decade the ratio of women to men should begin to favor women. Will romantic love come back into fashion?

he or she wishes to give on each learning trial. Rules of exchange appear to govern how much pleasure the individual gives the learner. For example, informal rules in most Western cultures specify that giving physical pleasure to an intimate friend is appropriate, but giving such pleasure to a stranger is less appropriate. And in fact, when the learner is the subject's date, more physical pleasure is given than when the learner is a stranger of the opposite sex (Davis and Martin, 1978). Another cultural norm specifies that if an intimate acquaintance expresses appreciation for pleasure, giving him or her more pleasure is appropriate. To do the same for a stranger might be understood as inviting intimacy. Again, subjects' behavior is consistent with the rule. When in the laboratory an intimate friend gives signs of great pleasure, subjects tend to give him or her more pleasure in return. However, when the pleasure is expressed by a stranger, increasing expressions of pleasure cause subjects to reduce the amount of pleasure that they give (Davis and Martin, 1978; Davis, Rainey, and Brock, 1976).

Many social psychologists believe that the informal rules that govern exchange in society are of immense consequence in everyday life (Ginsburg, 1979; Harré and Secord, 1972; Thibaut and Kelley, 1959). Such rules ensure that social relationships remain orderly and stable over time (Bales, 1950; Thibaut and Kelley, 1959). Let us look at two broad classes of rules within the society: rules that deal with the kind of resources that may be exchanged and rules that govern the proper amount of exchange.

Resource Theory: Rules of Kind

Many different actions give pleasure to others—from scratching an itchy back to professing eternal devotion. Many theorists feel that trying to describe all of the rules that pertain to all forms of pleasure giving would result simply in endless volumes of dated information. A more fruitful undertaking, it is argued, is the specification of (1) a limited set of classes into which pleasure-giving activities fall and (2) a set of fundamental rules that govern the exchange of activities in the various classes. Uriel and Edna Foa have made the most ambitious attempt to establish the classes of reward and discover the relationships among them (Foa, 1971; Foa and Foa, 1974). On the basis of studies of social exchange in a variety of cultures, the Foas maintain that virtually all the resources that people use to benefit one another fall conveniently into one of six classes: love, services, goods, money, information, and status (see Figure 11-3). Thus, for example, fixing someone's stereo would be giving a service. Telling

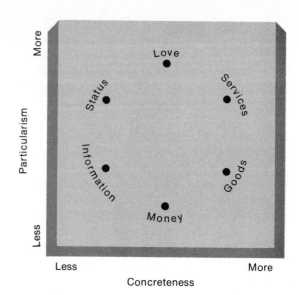

FIGURE **11-3**

How resource classes are related

According to the Foas, the six major resource classes vary in their concreteness and particularism. Cultural rules favor an exchange between similar resources. For example, most people consider exchanging a nonparticular resource, like money, for a particularistic resource, like love, to be inappropriate. (Adapted from Foa, 1971)

someone how to complete a complex assignment would give him or her information, and treating someone with respect would give the person status. You might accept the intellectual challenge offered by the Foas' model: try to locate a way of benefiting another person that does not fall into any of these classes.

The major rules that dictate how resources may be exchanged depend on two major dimensions (Foa and Foa, 1980).

1. *Particularism.* Some resources are given or received only from particular people, while other resources may be exchanged with anyone. Through socialization experiences the young child learns that he or she may exchange affectionate reactions

with, for example, parents, family members, and few others. As older children learn about goods and money, however, they find that these resources can be exchanged with both friends and strangers. They are not particularistic resources.

2. *Concreteness.* Through socialization experiences children also learn that resources vary in their degree of concreteness. Rewards such as goods (candy, toys) and services (the mother's bringing food) are recognized at an early age. They are highly concrete. With the development of skills in abstract reasoning (see Chapter 6), the child comes to recognize less obvious but significant rewards, such as status and information.

The Foas believe that these two dimensions dictate a major rule of exchange: *the closer any two actions are in terms of their degrees of particularism and concreteness, the more appropriate is the exchange between them.* Thus, if someone pats you on the back, the action might be seen as a gesture of love. It is particular to you. The general rule says that you should return the action with a similar action. For example, you might respond by patting or stroking the person. To give him or her a dollar for the pat on the back would be inappropriate. Money is usually not particularistic. Similarly, if the butcher finds a beautiful cut of beef for you, he or she probably would not accept an abstract payment, such as a compliment. The butcher has furnished concrete goods. If you say, "You are really a fine butcher," you have returned the concrete action with an abstract indicator of status. If people do not return the kind of behavior they receive, they may be seen as lacking in responsiveness or concern, and they may generate hostility. (Davis and Perkowitz, 1979).

Many demonstrations of the major principles that underlie resource exchange have been furnished by the Foas (Donnenwerth and Foa, 1974; Foa and Foa, 1974). In one study the Foas had a confederate return resources of varying similarity, and they looked at the effects on subjects (Teichman and Foa, 1975). For some subjects the confederate returned resources that were similar to the subject's original gift in terms of their degrees of particularism and concreteness. In other instances the confederate reacted by giving the subject a resource that was highly dissimilar along both dimensions. Afterward the subjects rated their degree of satisfaction with the exchange. Students generally were more satisfied with exchanges in which the resources resembled each other than they were with those in which the resources were dissimilar. Exceptions occurred, but they are to be expected. The Foas' rules are general, and such rules are broken for many reasons. Other research has analyzed advertisements placed by eight hundred men and women who were using personal columns of magazines to search for a mate (Harrison and Saeed, 1977). Ads placed by women generally emphasized physical attractiveness and a wish for financial security. Men indicated that they were looking for attractive women and that they offered financial security. The proposed exchanges, then, were symmetrical, nonparticular, and concrete.

The Foas' theory provides an interesting account of the kinds of behavior that can be exchanged appropriately. Let us now turn to a second and more extensive line of research, on rules of amount in social exchange.

Equity Theory: Rules of Amount

The Foas' analysis strongly suggests that people prefer to exchange similar resources. Clearly, however, people are not only concerned with the *kinds* of resources that are exchanged, but also with the quantity, or *amount*, of resources in the bargain. People may prefer to receive love in exchange for love, but they pay close attention to *how*

much love is given in return. How strong are these rules? Consider the following cases:

> Your roommate is bringing an intimate friend to visit. Having been busy with a term paper, your roommate has left a mess: cigarette butts, rotten apple cores, and spilled coffee have created a stench. Because you know how important this friend is to your roommate, you spend two hours cleaning. When they arrive they sit down on the couch, and immediately your roommate suggests, "Don't you have to be somewhere now?"

> A young man approaches you on the street and urgently requests money. You are nearly broke but feel sorry for him, so you give him the coins you were going to use to buy chewing gum. He looks at the coins, drops them at your feet, curses you, and walks off.

> During an important exam you observe that the student seated next to you is secretly copying from a notebook. You have been up all night studying for the exam. A week later you find out that the

cheater received a better grade than you did.

Chances are you would feel some discomfort in each of these situations. In the first case you would have given friendship and received polite coolness in return. In the second case you would have given aid and received insults in return. In the third you would have worked hard for a grade that was lower than that of a classmate who did no work. Indeed, we do seem to care about the balance between what is given and what is received.

Many theorists believe that norms that govern the balance between what is given and what is received in an exchange are essential to the well-being of society (Gouldner, 1960). If people tried at all times to gain as much for themselves as possible, social life would be a miserable affair—people would be exploitative, distrustful, and scheming. In our earlier discussion of giving help (Chapter 7) we saw that the norm of reciprocity dictates that people should return good with good and not with evil. The existence of society depends on the development of norms that are concerned with proper, fair, or just forms of exchange. Such norms can be found in virtually all cultures (Benedict, 1946; Gouldner, 1960; Malinowski, 1922; Westermarck, 1908).

One important rule that is concerned with just forms of exchange is the rule of *equity* (Walster, Walster, and Berscheid, 1978). *Equity* occurs when participants in a relationship perceive that the relative rewards and costs are equal for all. The roommate relationship we described was inequitable because one person was receiving all of the rewards and the other was suffering all of the costs. Equity might have been achieved if the roommate had shown affectionate appreciation. The beggar also failed to reward a positive social act. And the cheater experienced great rewards at no cost, while the honest student received less reward and worked harder. In each case the inequity is unpleasant.

As many theorists believe, people often feel distress when they are confronted with inequity in social relationships. They will attempt to rid themselves of the distress by restoring equity. Let us examine reactions to two kinds of inequity: underreward and overreward. We will complete this discussion by considering equality as an alternative to equity.

Underreward: the psychology of getting even

The anguish and anger that are felt when less than a fair share is received usually motivate people to try to restore equity. Demanding more reward is the most obvious way to reestablish equity. For example, when factory workers believe that they are not receiving reasonable pay for their effort, they may strike for higher wages (Marwell, Ratcliff, and Schmitt, 1969; Schmitt and Marwell, 1977). Making the other party in the relationship uncomfortable is a second means of restoring equity. Thus, if workers believe that the balance between rewards and costs is inequitable, they may let productivity fall (Adams, 1965; Clark, 1958; Lawler, 1968). The lower productivity presumably increases the employer's distress.

In an interesting line of research, investigators have traced people's feelings of equity in heterosexual relationships. For example, five hundred undergraduates were asked to evaluate all of the things that they were getting out of an intimate relationship and all that they were putting into it (Walster, Walster, and Traupman, 1979). The students also were asked to evaluate the contentment, happiness, and anger that they derived from the

A happy marriage. Striking a balance between what is given and what is received is a key factor in marital stability. This couple radiates a sense of contentment that suggests that their marital exchange is an equitable one.

relationship. Students who felt that they were putting more into the relationship than they were receiving from it were quite dissatisfied. According to their ratings, they were less content, less happy, and more angry than those who felt that their inputs and outputs were relatively equal. Equity probably is a significant factor in marital stability as well. One study found a relationship between equity and fidelity to one's spouse (Walster, Traupman, and Walster, 1979). Using survey data, the investigators were able to differentiate between married people who felt relatively equal to their partner in general desirability and those who felt that they were more desirable than their partner. The latter, it was reasoned, were feeling relatively unrewarded in comparison with their worth. When measures were taken of the respondents' willingness to engage in extramarital sex (a means of getting even), the researchers found that those who felt that they were more desirable than their mate had extramarital sex sooner after marriage and with more partners than did those who felt equal.

Overreward:
punishment or perceptual change?

In the vignette about the student who cheated, we suggested that people react negatively when someone receives a reward without working for it. This kind of inequity often creates a desire to see the person punished. In this sense, criminal law operates to ensure equity in society. Usually a criminal has taken a reward but hasn't paid the proper cost. Fines and jail sentences are ways of reestablishing equity. Thus, the more the criminal takes, the more severe the penalty. In one research demonstration of this point, subjects were asked to recommend penalties in a rape case (Jones and Aronson, 1973). Subjects in one group were led to believe that the arrest was made before the assailant could consummate the act, while subjects in a second group were told that the act had been completed. In

other words, the second rapist had achieved greater pleasure than the first. When asked to assign prison sentences, subjects recommended a ten-year prison term for the unsuccessful assailant and a sixteen-year prison term for the rapist who completed the act. This particular pleasure proved to be very costly indeed.

In the same way that a criminal's pleasure may yield a stiffer penalty, a criminal's suffering may reduce the penalty for a crime. In one study, subjects were asked to recommend a jail sentence for a purse-snatcher who, they were told, severely beat a female victim, fell while trying to escape, and was paralyzed from the neck down (Austin, Walster, and Utne, 1976). The sentences that were given to the paralyzed criminal were significantly less severe than those given by subjects who were told that the criminal escaped without injury.

Punishing individuals who take too much is relatively easy. But what happens when the overrewarded person is you? If you receive more than your fair share, will you give up some of your rewards or increase your costs in order to achieve equity? Much research indicates that people do feel uncomfortable when overrewarded and may suffer pain as a result (Berscheid, Walster, and Bohrnstedt, 1973; Schmitt and Marwell, 1977). Being rewarded when others are not or receiving a reward without returning it often creates feelings of guilt, cheapness, or indebtedness (Greenberg, 1980).

In one classic illustration of reactions to overreward, researchers hired students to proofread manuscript copy (Adams and Jacobson, 1964). In one condition, subjects were told that although they were unqualified for the job, they would be paid the same amount as professional proofreaders (30¢ per page). In other words, the salary would be *inequitably higher* than they deserved. In the contrasting condition the salary was the same, but the subjects were told that they were receiving the standard student rate. In other words, the pay was fair. An assessment of the quality of the students' work—a count of the errors they found—showed that the overpaid subjects discovered significantly more errors than did those paid equitably. The extra effort seemed to be an attempt to restore equity.

Overreward does not always mean overwork, however. Many researchers find that people do not work harder when overrewarded (Freedman, 1963; Valenzi and Andrews, 1971; Weick, 1966). Instead, they choose means other than self-punishment to restore equity. One way to restore equity is by changing one's perception of the event—recalculating both the rewards and the costs. For example, if you receive more praise than do equally deserving members of your team, you can reassess your contribution and decide that it was superior to theirs. Thus you believe that you merit the extra praise and have no need to feel guilty.

To demonstrate how reassessment can restore equity, Italian and American university students were given rewards of varying degrees of equity in payment for identifying words that were muffled by static (Gergen, Morse, and Bode, 1974). After receiving a description of the work, the students were asked to estimate the difficulty of the task and the wage that would be fair. Payment was decided by a throw of the dice. By design, subjects in one group were to receive the wage they had specified as being fair. Subjects in a second group were to receive approximately 30 percent more than they had asked for, and those in a third group were to receive 80 percent more than the equitable amount. The students then went on to cope with the difficult task. Afterward they were asked to reevaluate the difficulty of the task and the fairness of the pay.

As you can see in Figure 11-4, ratings of task difficulty depended on the level of reward. The greater the amount of overpayment, the more difficult the task was rated

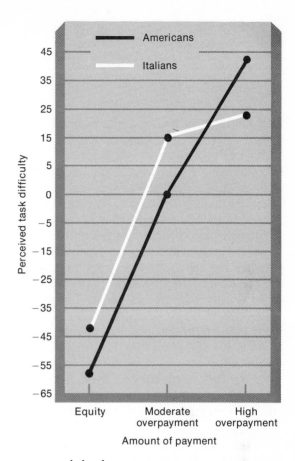

FIGURE 11-4 How much is too much?

Results of this study suggest that overpaying a worker may be impossible—in his or her own eyes. Note that as payment exceeds the subjects' estimates of what is fair, the subjects' perception of task difficulty increases. (Adapted from Gergen, Morse, and Bode, 1974)

by both Italian and American subjects. Reassessments of the fair wage revealed the same pattern. As the overpayment increased, so did the estimates of a fair wage. Interestingly, no differences were found in task performance. Overpaid subjects did not work harder or identify more words correctly. Apparently, as rewards increase, one's idea of what is fair can change. This tactic may be especially likely to occur if no one is around to disagree with the reassessment.

Equity versus Equality: Each According to Performance or Need?

Although equity works to promote a certain degree of fairness in social exchange, many social critics feel that a society that is governed by equity alone would damage many of its members. Equity exchanges are based on an individual's productivity, or contribution, not on an individual's abilities or needs. Distributing rewards on the basis of performance is unfair to people whose abilities are hampered by accident or disease, inadequate training, or various life stresses. Further, people differ greatly in terms of needs. Continuing to reward the excellent performer who already has accumulated a giant fortune, while overlooking the unmet needs of the poor performer also seems to be unfair, especially since people's needs may interfere with their performance and poor performance may ensure that they remain in great need.

On the basis of such arguments, many social theorists propose that equity is only one form of fairness (Leventhal, 1980. They suggest that *equality* in the distribution of resources can be viewed as a preferred alternative to *equity* (Sampson, 1975). Many research studies have documented people's concerns with equality in human relationships and their tendencies to distribute rewards accordingly. For example, people who have greater needs often are felt to deserve greater rewards than those with lesser needs, and such feelings clearly motivate much altruistic, or charitable, giving (Berkowitz, 1972; Schwartz, 1970). When asked to divide a sum of money between themselves and a partner whose need for the money was either great or virtually nonexistent, subjects gave significantly more money to the partner whose needs were great (Leventhal and Weiss, 1969). Lack of ability also is taken into ac-

count by many people. A worker who lacks ability often is rewarded more highly for mediocre work than is a highly competent person whose performance is equal (Lanzetta and Hannah, 1969; Taynor and Deaux, 1973). Needs and abilities sometimes figure into people's calculation of what others deserve.

Given strong arguments for distributing rewards on the basis of equality rather than on the basis of equity, many investigators are interested in the power of socialization in generating a preference for equality. Investigators have found that female subjects tend to select the equality option more often than males do (Benton, 1971; Leventhal and Lane, 1970), suggesting that socialization can make a difference. A study of children also provides support for the assumption that socialization counts. Researchers presented two play situations to over one hundred children between the ages of three and twelve years (Cohen and Sampson, 1975). In one condition the children were told that two dolls had done unequal work, and in the second condition they were told that the dolls had done the same amount of work. The children were asked to divide marshmallows between the dolls. Boys' sensitivity to equity considerations increased with age. By twelve years they strongly preferred to distribute the marshmallows on the basis of production alone. In contrast, girls tended to distribute the marshmallows more equally, regardless of their stage of development.

We have seen that cultures develop rules, or norms, of exchange in order to ensure orderly, predictable, and broadly satisfying patterns of social interaction. The Foas theorize that the range of resources that can be exchanged is limited and that society's rules favor the exchange of resources that are similar in terms of their degrees of particularism and concreteness. Research has focused on rules that govern the amount of resources exchanged and particularly on the equitableness of an exchange. In an equitable exchange each person's relative rewards and costs are equal. Inequity often is uncomfortable, and people often try to restore equity. In situations of underreward, equity may be achieved by increasing the rewards, reducing the costs, or punishing the individuals in the exchange. In situations of overreward, equity may be achieved by working harder or by making sacrifices to restore equity. However, if social circumstances allow, people may alter their perception of fairness, thus using psychological means to restore equity. Critics point out that the equity rule may be unfair and that an equality rule offers many advantages. Preference for equality over equity may be instilled through socialization.

From Exploitation to Cooperation

Exchange theorists assume that people attempt to gain as much as they can at minimum cost. This strategy does not lead to the breakdown of society because people (1) receive satisfaction from mutually pleasureful exchanges and (2) develop rules that ensure the maintenance of these exchanges. Yet exploitation is a central feature of social life, and this is so in part because of the ambiguity of exchange rules. People disagree on what constitutes an equitable exchange—on how much cost or benefit is attached to an action. Convincing others that one is being treated inequitably often is difficult and may depend on a person's skill at manipulating words (Harris and Joyce, 1980). And in close relationships, in which people are supposed to care for each other, people don't always want a careful accounting of what they give and receive (Clark and Mills, 1979). They may avoid keeping a precise account of rewards and costs so that their personal relationships won't seem like business transactions (Pryor and Graburn, 1980). In addition to exploitation that is caused by ambiguous rules, exploitation may result from the establishment of exchanges that benefit some persons but are unfavorable to others. As we saw in our discussion of prejudice (Chapter 4), members of an in-group may work to benefit each other while exploiting members of an out-group.

Equity and equality rules may reduce exploitation, and ambiguity and in-group preferences may increase it. Thus, most exchange situations involve psychological conflicts. Therefore social psychologists have been particularly concerned with a kind of exchange based on mixed motives and in which the desire to cooperate *conflicts* with the desire to exploit. We now will consider research on mixed-motive exchanges and the implications of the findings for the reduction of exploitation.

Exploitation in Mixed-Motive Exchange

Look back at the payoff matrix used by Sidowski, Wyckoff, and Tabory (Figure 11-1). In this situation, the greatest gain was achieved by *both* participants when they pressed a combination of buttons that delivered points to both of them. Although the partners were unaware of each other, they nevertheless worked out a system of cooperation.

Now consider the payoff matrix shown in Figure 11-5. In this situation the participants have a red button and a black button. If both participants press their black button on a given trial, both win $5. If both press their red button, both lose $5. Most important, if one participant selects the red button when the other presses the black one, an uneven division in rewards and punishments occurs. The participant who presses the red button will receive $15, while the one who chooses the black button will receive no money at all. In this situation the advantage of cooperation is not so obvious. Cooperation brings each participant $5. However, if only one participant chooses to cooperate, he or she can be exploited by the other. Exploitation triples

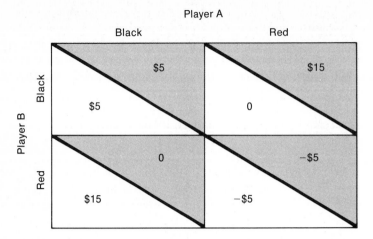

Player A

Black   Red

Player B

Black

$5 $15

$5   0

Red

0   −$5

$15   −$5

FIGURE **11-5** **A mixed-motive matrix**

In this payoff situation, cooperation (pressing the black button) can lead to exploitation. In each box the payoff for player A is above the diagonal line and the payoff for player B is below it.

the other participant's earnings. Suddenly cooperation seems to be less desirable. Yet if both choose to exploit, they both will be penalized. The exploitation alternative is not without danger.

Neither accommodation nor exploitation is the clear-cut choice in the Figure 11-5 payoff situation. This kind of exchange is termed a *mixed-motive* situation. Mixed-motive matrices of this type confront the individual with the *prisoner's dilemma*. This name is based on the following drama (Luce and Raiffa, 1957): Two suspects are taken into custody and separated. The district attorney is certain that they are guilty of a specific crime, but he does not have adequate evidence for convicting them at a trial. He tells the prisoners that they have two alternatives: each may confess or remain silent. The district attorney says that if neither of them confesses, he will book both of them on some minor, trumped-up charge and both will receive minor punishment. If both of them confess, they will be prosecuted, but the district attorney will recommend less than the most

severe sentence. If one confesses and the other remains silent, the confessor will be allowed to turn state's evidence and will go free; the suspect who remains silent will receive the maximum penalty.

Many theorists believe that the prisoner's dilemma represents a situation that is common in daily life. Consider, for example, the difficulties inherent in a typical love relationship. If both partners commit themselves and give generously to each other, their cooperation may yield a fulfilling relationship. However, in making the commitment, each partner runs the risk of being hurt or exploited. If one partner decides to leave, the other can be left desolate. Yet if both play it safe and avoid making themselves vulnerable, the relationship may disappoint both of them. Similar dilemmas occur more generally in social life. For example, Garrett Hardin (1968) has described a society's distribution of its natural resources as a "tragedy of commons." If all herdsmen use the same common pasture and each wants as many cattle as possible, the land will be overgrazed and eroded. All of the herdsmen will lose their cattle. If they cooperate, however, each must limit the size of the herd, which means lower profits and possible exploitation.

When participants in prisoner's dilemma games are faced with choices like those illustrated in Figure 11-5, they generally do not make cooperative choices. Regardless of the number of trials and the amount or type of stake—meaningless points, small change, or dollar bills—subjects usually exploit each other (Christie, Gergen, and Marlowe, 1970; Minas et al., 1960; Rapoport, 1974a). No matter how many people are being exploited as the result of one's choice, cooperation is not likely to be the chosen alternative (Komorita, Sweeney, and Kravitz, 1980). This finding should not be taken to mean that *all* people exploit others at *every* opportunity. As we have pointed out before, vast differences are always found in individuals' behavior. Nevertheless, on the average, subjects faced with this particular kind of choice tend to maximize their own gains rather than cooperate with their peers in the laboratory.

Multiple Paths to Cooperation

In the laboratory setting, people's exploitation of one another is so similar to and consistent with behavior in daily life that many investigators have turned their attention to the problem of reducing exploitation and fostering cooperation in both individual and group relationships. One means of stimulating cooperation is obvious. If payoffs for cooperation are increased and if exploitation is made to be more costly, cooperation should be the more frequently chosen option. Although this option seems to be simple enough, the widespread belief that competition is good may interfere with its application. For example, manufacturers of automobiles might create an effective gasless engine more rapidly if they pooled their resources. However, incentives for such coop-

eration generally do not exist. Other important means of increasing cooperation include the adoption of strategies that elicit a cooperative response, the use of threat, and the improvement of communication. Let us consider each of these in turn.

The strategy of cooperation

Faced with the tragedy-of-commons situation we described, you might decide that total cooperation is the wisest choice. You might reduce the size of your flock or reduce your use of the limited natural resource. Such acts of cooperation should demonstrate your good intentions and furnish a model for others' actions. Indeed, as many experimental demonstrations indicate, a consistently cooperative strategy on the part of one player in the prisoner's dilemma game often has positive effects on the other player (Gruder and Duslak, 1973; Rubin and Brown, 1975). If one player consistently chooses to cooperate for joint maximum gain, the partner typically takes part in this strategy. Such demonstrations of cooperation may be particularly important in the early stages of the exchange (Pilisuk and Skolnick, 1968).

Yet a fully cooperative strategy exposes the player to a certain amount of danger. Unconditional cooperation can be an invitation for exploitation by others (Hamner and Yukl, 1977). Cautious use of a cooperative strategy is advisable when others are *highly competitive* or likely to *suspect one's motives in cooperating.* Under these circumstances cooperativeness may be exploited (Kelley and Stahelski, 1970). Further, when *little likelihood of a long-term trusting relationship exists,* people are likely to take advantage of the one who cooperates (Marlowe, Gergen, and Doob, 1966). Finally, strategies of cooperation may be most effective when the participants have *opportunities to communicate.* When the cooperative individual makes his or her intentions clear or when participants discuss one another's aspirations and needs, a cooperative strategy often may be used to advance the interests of all (Pruitt and Lewis, 1975).

The strategy of playing it tough

For those who find cooperation to be too tender-hearted and instead prefer the John Wayne spirit of courageous toughness, research offers some support for this choice. As game theorists reason, concessions to the opposition raise the level of outcomes to which the opposition aspires (Siegel and Fouraker, 1960). However, taking a tough stand and making few concessions may cause the opposition to lower its aspirations and eventually appreciate the smallest concessions. This position has been demonstrated in the laboratory many times. If a participant in a prisoner's dilemma game takes a tough position, the opponent lowers his or her aspirations for self-gain (Chertkoff and Baird, 1971; Druckman, Solomon, and Zechmeister, 1972; Holmes, Throop, and Strickland, 1971). Such shifts in aspiration level have been demonstrated in numerous studies of college students and in studies of business managers abroad (Harnett, Cummings, and Hamner, 1973).

Yet in spite of its effectiveness, the play-it-tough strategy carries substantial risk. For example, one experiment showed that the tougher the strategy employed by a bargainer, the more disagreeable and the less cooperative the opponent became (Hamner, 1974). Only when the bargainer yielded were profitable agreements reached between the two. The user of a tough strategy was viewed as being "rigid, unreasonable and uncooperative." In other words, the tough strategist may succeed in gaining his or her ends by brute force, but if the opponent has the opportunity to withdraw from the situation, find a better deal elsewhere, or exploit the bargainer, he or she is very likely to do so.

Can some combination of pacifism and toughness best succeed in securing cooperation? Some investigators believe that the answer is yes. The *reformed-sinner* strategy apparently works effectively. In this strategy the bargainer begins by playing it tough but later shifts to a highly agreeable, cooperative orientation. When the "sinner" plays it tough, the opponent also plays it tough. However, when the shift to cooperation takes place, a dramatic increase in the opponent's cooperation usually occurs (Deutsch, 1975).

The strategy of matching: the gritty road to peace

A third major strategy for securing cooperation is based on simple principles of reinforcement: cooperation is rewarded by cooperation, and exploitation is punished by counterexploitation. This approach is termed the *matching* strategy. Results from many laboratory games suggest that it can be an effective strategy across time. If a game requires partners to respond sequentially (first one and then the other), the matching strategy typically produces a high degree of cooperation (see Oskamp's 1971 review).

The matching strategy also creates certain risks. For example, if one party chooses exploitation, the matching may produce a never-ending exchange of blows. In fact, if exploitation were matched strictly, the result would be mutual destruction. Some critics of the current state of international relations feel that many nations of the world are locked into an unending pattern of mutual exploitation. Each nation fears possible attack by another nation, and each distrusts the other's every move. The result is an upward spiral of preparations for aggression.

One strategy for resolving this dilemma has been offered by Charles Osgood (1962). When destructive stalemate is at hand, Osgood argues, a strategy of "graduated reciprocation in tension reduction" (GRIT) should be invoked. First, one participant must take the initiative and make a cooperative gesture (however small). At the outset a nation might not wish to reduce its defensive capacity, but

GRIT in action. Egyptian President Anwar Sadat, U.S. President Jimmy Carter, and Israeli Prime Minister Manachem Begin are shown celebrating the signing of the May 1979 treaty between Egypt and Israel. Although many issues in this conflict remain unresolved, the negotiations stand as the first positive steps in tension reduction—a strategy that may pave the way to further exchanges and ultimately to the end of the conflict.

other moves toward cooperation are possible—for example, cultural exchanges, mutual scientific exploration, or increased trade. If such minimally cooperative gestures meet with success, then more offers of cooperation can be made. Such offers may be reciprocated eventually, producing a steady reduction in international tension. As the tension level declines, reduced defense spending begins to be plausible. One could argue that in U.S.-Soviet relations, the shift from cold war to minimal cooperation during the past thirty years reflects a GRIT strategy.

Theorists believe that for the GRIT strategy to succeed the participant who is seeking peace should (1) announce the cooperative gestures at the outset and invite reciprocation; (2) carry out the cooperative gestures in ways that are clear and invite verification;

and (3) leave sufficient vulnerability so that the cooperative plans seem to be credible but not so much vulnerability that defense is impossible (Lindskold, 1979). The peace-seeking participant must be prepared to carry out these steps even if the adversary does not reciprocate. Experimental evidence suggests that the GRIT strategy can work (Pilisuk and Skolnick, 1968). International relations might well benefit from this work.

Researchers have realized over the years that no single strategy will meet with consistent success (Hamner and Yukl, 1977). A given strategy may be successful with certain kinds of people and not with others, or it may succeed at certain times and not at other times (Yukl et al., 1976). Further, once the opponents become aware of the strategy, they may adopt a counterstrategy that reduces its

effectiveness. In light of these problems, the best overall approach to increasing cooperation may be *flexible rigidity* (Pruitt and Lewis, 1975). That is, people should maintain their *goals* rigidly while being highly flexible in their choices of *means* to the goals. Thus if you belong to a club and want to see the membership criteria changed, you should stick to your goal but be willing to consider many different ways of reaching it.

Threat and Cooperation

We have seen that increasing payoffs and employing various payoff strategies may improve cooperation. If these methods don't work, cooperation sometimes can be obtained by the use of *threat*. That is, reward or punishment does not have to be employed directly. The *promise* of reward or punishment may be enough. One can threaten to walk out of an unsatisfactory relationship, cancel payment for defective merchandise, or curtail economic aid to a rebellious nation.

Is threat an effective way to produce cooperation? To answer this question, let us first consider the early work by Morton Deutsch and Robert Krauss (1960). These investigators devised a bargaining game in which profits were based on the speed with which a task was completed. Each participant was to imagine himself or herself in charge of a trucking company (either Acme or Bolt). The company was supposed to carry merchandise over a road depicted on a board that was in front of the participants. For each trip completed, the participants were to be paid 60¢ minus their *operating expenses* (1¢ for each second the merchandise was in transit). As you can see in Figure 11-6, both Acme and Bolt begin each trial from a separate position, face separate destinations, and have the choice of a long route or a short one. Conflict arises when the participants realize that the quicker route, which allows them to make the most money, is only *one lane wide*. If both participants select this lane, they will be unable to pass each other and may sit immobile while they both lose money. Their other option is to take turns using the short route and alternately accept the minor (10¢) penalty incurred for going the longer way.

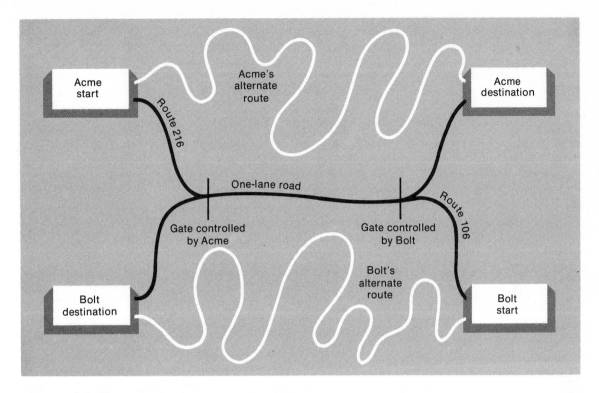

FIGURE 11-6 **Deutsch and Krauss's trucking game**

In this version of the game, note the presence of two gates. Each opponent can threaten the other by blocking his or her access to the one-lane road that leads to the goal most directly. (Adapted from Deutsch and Krauss, 1960)

Once the options were established, Deutsch and Krauss furnished the participants with various threat capabilities. In the *bilateral-threat* condition, Acme and Bolt each have a gate that can be used to block the other's transit (this is the condition illustrated in Figure 11-6). In the *unilateral-threat* condition, only Acme has a gate. This capability effectively deprives Bolt of the shortest route because Acme can use the gate to penalize Bolt and Bolt has no means of defense. In the *no-threat* condition, neither participant has a gate. All pairs of participants played the game twenty times. All were instructed to make as much money as possible. No communication was permitted.

The effects of threat capacity on the participants' ability to cooperate is shown in Table 11-1. Note that both participants are better off when they can't threaten each other. If threat is available to one or both participants, both of them *lose* money. In fact, the greater the threat potential, the more money is lost. Participants in the bilateral-threat condition manage to lose jointly on the average of almost $9. They lose only half of this amount when Acme alone has threat capability. They earn money only when neither has threat capability.

Taken by itself, this research suggests that threat not only stands in the way of cooperation, but actually reduces benefits for every-

TABLE 11-1 **When threatening fails**

These findings from the trucking game reveal that the only condition under which players actually can win money is when neither player can threaten the other. Note that maximum loss is sustained when both players have a threat capability.

Player	Payoffs under various conditions of threat		
	None	Unilateral	Bilateral
Acme	$1.22	− $1.19	− $4.07
Bolt	.81	− 2.87	− 4.69
TOTAL	2.03	− 4.06	− 8.75

Source: Adapted from Deutsch and Krauss, 1960

one concerned. Yet threat often works effectively, both in daily relations and on the international scene. Under what conditions is threat likely to meet with success?

Some researchers feel that when *important outcomes* are at stake people are likely to give in to threat (Gallo, 1966; McClintock and McNeel, 1966). In the trucking game players who backed down in the face of threat may have felt that they would *lose face*—seem weak and foolish. Since very little money was at stake, their pride may have come first. In international relations more may be at stake—such as the lives of many people. Under these circumstances, saving face may seem trivial, and people may cooperate with a threatening agent.

In the original experiment, communication between Acme and Bolt was forbidden. However, if people are allowed to *communicate* and encouraged to negotiate with each other, threat does not pose an insurmountable barrier to cooperation (Deutsch and Krauss, 1962; Krauss and Deutsch, 1966). And if the demands that are made are reasonable, possession of threat may increase cooperation (Bonoma and Tedeschi, 1973; Michelini and Messe, 1974; Schlenker et al., 1970). Anger apparently is the issue. If the threatened person isn't angered, the threat actually can in-

crease mutual cooperation (Heilman, 1974; Rubin, Lewicki, and Dunn, 1973).

Communication, Trust, and Cooperation

The importance of communication in increasing cooperation will be familiar to you from previous discussions. We have seen that with increased communication, the negative effects of threat can be overcome and the development of cooperative strategies can be enhanced. Recall also the discussions of prejudice (Chapter 4) in which we noted that intergroup strife could be reduced by bringing various groups into contact. Similarly, in the discussion of destructive obedience (Chapter 10) we found that people were less willing to hurt a victim they had to confront face to face than one they did not confront directly.

Studies of the prisoner's dilemma and similar situations also show that when participants are not allowed to communicate with each other the amount of exploitation usually increases (Voissem and Sistrunk, 1971; Wichman, 1970). Other research shows that seeing someone on a video screen is enough to reduce the amount of exploitation (Gardin et al., 1973; Kleinke and Pohlen, 1971). And even if direct communication is impossible, the more information people have about one

An ineffective strategy. Threat sometimes elicits cooperation, but this response occurs only under special circumstances. If the target of the threat responds with anger (as the young woman here seems to be doing), the likelihood of cooperation is greatly reduced.

in one's community requires a major act of faith. An individual must feel free to carry out any action—from walking down the street to going to bed at night—without fear that others want to take advantage or exploit him or her. As trust increases, people typically become more cooperative in mixed-motive exchanges (Deutsch, 1960; Kimmel et al., 1980; Wrightsman, 1966; Zand, 1972). Distrust increases exploitation (Rubin and Brown, 1975). Because trust often develops slowly and is broken easily (Worchel, 1979), communication often is critical in its maintenance. Communication allows participants to discuss their intentions and their vulnerabilities, both of which are important in assessing trustworthiness (Schlenker, Helm, and Tedeschi, 1973; Swinth, 1967). Communication may enable participants to dispel myths that have developed about them, and this also contributes to increased trust (Kelley and Stahelski, 1970).

To summarize, when cooperation and self-interest conflict, a mixed-motive exchange takes place. In experiments with the prisoner's dilemma game (a mixed-motive situation), most people make exploitative choices. Their exploitation may be reduced if (1) the reward placed on cooperation is greater than that placed on exploitation and (2) strategies of pure cooperation, playing it tough, and matching are employed properly. Each strategy has advantages and shortcomings. Threat also is a means of securing cooperation, but it may backfire if the threatening agent is not cooperative and communicative. The most promising means of increasing cooperation may be the improvement of communication.

another's rewards and costs, the less exploitative they are (Felsenthal, 1977; Komorita and Kravitz, 1979). In fact, heated communication may be better than no communication at all. Research on marital conflict shows that couples who confront their problems directly often show increased agreement in their opinions. Couples who avoid conflict often remain in mutual ignorance of each other's opinions (Knudson, Sommers, and Golding, 1980).

Why is communication beneficial? One major reason is that it can build trust. Without trust, positive exchanges are unlikely to take place (Deutsch, 1973). Feeling at home

The Strategic Management of Relationships

Let us return to the problem of poor Brad, who is smitten with Janet but faces a quandary. If Brad wants Janet's affection, he must go out with her in the city, yet he really prefers the country and would love to spend his weekends there. If our analysis thus far is correct, Brad probably will choose to accommodate his needs to Janet's. They both enjoy going out together in the city; they both are miserable when alone. However, if Brad were clever, he might be able to change Janet's preferences. Maintaining their pleasurable exchange does not mean that Brad is doomed to city life. By strategically managing the relationship—inviting city friends to go camping with them, introducing his camping friends to her, or camping in beautiful locations—Brad might be able to change Janet's preferences and thus enjoy both her company and the out-of-doors. It is to such techniques of management that we now turn. We will look at the process of selecting strategies, and we will consider individual differences in strategy management. We then will focus on nonverbal techniques for relationship management, and we will examine the effects of facial expressions and body movements.

Self-presentation, Scripts, and Negotiation

In his popular volume, *The Presentation of Self in Everyday Life* (1959), Erving Goffman furnishes the following novelistic account of Preedy, an Englishman who is making his first appearance on the beach by his summer hotel:

> But in any case he took care to avoid catching anyone's eye. First of all, he had to make it clear to those potential companions of his holiday that they were of no concern to him whatsoever. He stared through them, round them, over them—eyes lost in space. The beach might have been empty. If by chance a ball was thrown his way, he looked surprised; then let a smile of amusement lighten his face (Kindly Preedy), looked round dazed to see that there *were* people on the beach, tossed it back with a smile to himself and not a smile *at* the peo-

ple, and then resumed carelessly his nonchalant survey of space.

> But it was time to institute a little parade, the parade of the Ideal Preedy. By devious handlings he gave any who wanted to look a chance to see the title of his book—a Spanish translation of Homer, classic thus, but not daring, cosmopolitan too—and then gathered together his beach-wrap and bag into a neat sand-resistant pile (Methodical and Sensible Preedy), rolled slowly to stretch at ease his huge frame (Big-Cat Preedy), and tossed aside his sandals (Carefree Preedy, after all). (Sansom, quoted in Goffman, 1959, p. 6)

As Goffman argues, every movement and every action can be used to create impressions. In shaping these impressions the individual also is influencing the way in which others will respond to him or her. Thus all behavior can serve the function of controlling others (Carson, 1979; Powers, 1973). This argument can be extended beyond action to include one's possessions—clothing, books, records, and so forth. For example, well-selected art in a person's home informs visitors that the home belongs to a person of education and taste and that the owner should be treated with deference (Csikszentmihalyi and Rochberg-Halton, 1980).

From the rule-role viewpoint, one's actions and objects shape others' conduct because people have expectations about the sequences of behavior that are appropriate in various situations (Schank and Abelson, 1977). These sequences, or *psychological scripts*, are learned through direct observation, through listening to others' accounts, through watching television and movies, through reading books, and so forth. For example, a variety of scripts govern a culture's sexual relations (Gagnon, 1973; Simon, 1973). One of the most popular scripts requires that each person in the relationship first get to know the other's personality, likes, tastes, and values. Positive sentiments then develop, and in the consolidation stage, sexual intercourse occurs. Finally, in the commitment

Who shall I be today? Hairstyles, makeup, clothing—all shape others' impressions of the self. Rule-role theorists argue that such nonverbal cues provide information necessary for the effective management of social relationships. The more explicit the cue, the less flexible the sequence of behavior that is likely to follow.

stage interdependency and sexual exclusiveness are specified (Scanzoni, 1972). Other scripts offer prescriptions for such varied sexual exchanges as one-night stands, shipboard romances, and education by a prostitute. Most of these scripts are familiar to people who have been socialized in the culture, and they all specify the particular time in the sequence at which sexual intercourse is to take place.

Given the wide availability of scripts, effective management begins when one person

furnishes a cue that motivates the other to begin acting out a desired script. Thus, for example, displaying an attractive appearance may trigger others' fantasies and romantic scripts, or scripts of adoration may be called forth. Doing various favors for the attractive person also may trigger an appropriate sequence. Indeed, attractive people often find themselves the target of helpful favors, wanted or unwanted (Sroufe et al., 1977). Being agreeable also is appropriate in a romantic script. In one powerful demonstration of the impact of attractiveness cues on agreeable behavior, researchers varied the appearance and attitudes of a male confederate in order to observe the kind of script the variations elicited (Zanna and Pack, 1975). Female subjects were asked to describe themselves. The male who listened was either attractive and interested in a relationship or unattractive and uninterested in a relationship, and he professed one of two views about women. The subjects in one group heard that his ideal woman is subordinate to her husband, passive, and home-oriented. Subjects in a second group heard that his ideal woman is independent, ambitious, and competitive. The researchers wanted to know whether the women would alter the descriptions of themselves to suit the romantic script initiated by the man. When the man was unattractive and uninterested in a relationship, the women's self-descriptions did not reflect his preferences. When he was attractive and available, the women's descriptions fit his views. If he preferred a traditional woman, they displayed traditional qualities; if he valued feminist characteristics, so did they.

Of course, no one *makes* someone engage in a particular script. People may or may not accept the invitation furnished by the cue. As communication theorist Paul Watzlawick (1976) has pointed out, a bank robber cannot do his job successfully unless tellers follow the script for being robbed. A teller might foil the robbery by saying to the robber, "You've

got to be kidding," or, "I don't have a bag for the money, I'll have to get one." More important, most cues are ambiguous and can signal the start of a variety of scripts. When a man and a woman strike up a lively conversation in a singles bar, for example, willingness to talk may be a cue for a brief-conversation script or a one-night-stand script. The conversation may even cue the beginning of a deep and committed relationship (Cavan, 1966). This ambiguity allows individuals to *negotiate scripts*—that is, to probe each other's intentions and furnish the desired script with additional cues (Cicourel, 1972; Rommetveit, 1976). If the partner in the barroom conversation suggests going out to dinner, he or she is attempting to secure the other's agreement that they are not engaged in a brief-conversation script. However, many options remain open. Theoretically scripts may be renegotiated at any point during the relationship. However, once participants

reach agreement on a given script, shifting to an alternative script may create embarrassment (Cronen and Pearce, in press). If two men agree that they are going to fight, one of them can hardly say "I thought it was all a joke" when he sees the other rolling up his sleeves.

Self-monitoring: Toward Improved Strategy

Some people seem to manage their relationships effectively, while others seem to be clumsy and ineffective in doing so. One reason for such differences may be the variations that exist in people's ability to read others' cues. Many studies show, for example, that women often are superior to men in their sensitivity to other people's body and facial cues. The superiority is found regardless of the subjects' age or the gender of the people being judged (Buck, 1976; Hall, 1978; Zaidel and Mehrabian, 1969). When women misjudge a cue, their errors usually reflect a failure to recognize possible deception (Rosenthal and DePaulo, 1979). People who read cues accurately usually are more effective in their interpersonal relationships than are those who misinterpret cues (Hall et al., 1978; Rosenthal et al., 1979).

A number of different factors influence individuals' abilities to manage relationships. To tap such differences, Mark Snyder (1979) has developed a scale that is composed of twenty-five descriptive statements. Analysis of responses to the questionnaire has highlighted a number of ingredients that are crucial to success in managing relationships. Among the most important of the ingredients are the following (Briggs, Cheek, and Buss, 1980):

1. *Paying attention to others as sources of appropriate actions.* Effective people should indicate that they would look to other people for cues of how to act in situations of uncertainty.

2. *The ability to control and modify one's presentation.* Effective people should indicate that they are able to make spontaneous speeches or unflinchingly tell lies when necessary.

3. *Willingness or desire to tailor one's actions to the social situation.* Effective people should be able to describe themselves as having little difficulty in changing their behavior to suit different people.

People who describe themselves as having these three capabilities are said to be high in *self-monitoring.* They tend to differ from those who are low in self-monitoring characteristics. For example, investigators have found that compared with those who are low in self-monitoring, individuals who are high in self-monitoring are more accurate in judging other people's emotional states (Geizer,

Rarick, and Soldow, 1977; Krauss, Geller, and Olson, 1976), and others rate them as being more friendly and outgoing and less worried, anxious, and nervous in relationships (Lippa, 1976, 1978). Further, when observing someone whom they expect to date, both men and women who are high in self-monitoring are more likely than those who are low in self-monitoring to notice and remember accurately information about the person (Berscheid et al., 1976). When they are observed in conversation, individuals high in self-monitoring manifest less shyness than do those who are low in self-monitoring, (Ickes and Barnes, 1977; Pilkonis, 1977). Further, those who are high in self-monitoring, as opposed to those who are low, are more likely to initiate conversation with a stranger and guide the course of the conversation (Ickes and Barnes, 1977). And the individual who is high in self-monitoring is more likely than the one who is low to be the leader of a group (Garland and Beard, 1978).

Yet the person who is high in self-monitoring may face special problems in close, long-term relations. Persons high in self-monitoring move from situation to situation in chameleonlike fashion, adopting whatever guise is necessary for success (Snyder and Monson, 1975). Little correspondence may exist between their public opinions and their privately held attitudes (Snyder and Swann, 1976). Knowing what they "truly" believe does not help much in predicting their future actions (Snyder and Tanke, 1976). Thus the intimate friends of an individual high in self-monitoring may find him or her to be untrustworthy and unreliable, lacking any deep or enduring character (Gergen, 1977a).

In summary, we see that people use a wide variety of cues as they attempt to manage one another in relationships. These cues typically stimulate a relatively stereotyped sequence of actions that is based on a psychological script. Many cues do not specify clearly the script

BOX 11-2

The Machiavellian Personality

In a world in which people gain or lose in interpersonal relationships, some people gain more than others do. One factor that separates the winners from the losers is motivation. Some people simply don't care whether they win or lose; they are content to let matters take their course. Other people care deeply about winning in almost every situation they encounter. These people take pleasure in the process of social manipulation. Differences between winners and losers have captured the interest of investigators Richard Christie and Florence Geis (1970). They believe that social manipulation is a way of life for certain people. These individuals (1) lack *true affect* in their relationships, since winners must think coolly and rationally about strategy, (2) lack *concern for conventional morality,* since moral rules often stand in the way of successful manipulation, and (3) have *low ideological commitment,* since long-range ideological goals lend themselves to inflexibility of action.

Such individuals, argue Christie and Geis, approximate the stereotype of Nicolò Machiavelli, a philosopher who counseled Italian nobility during the Renaissance. Christie and Geis used material from Machiavelli's treatise *The Prince* to develop indicators of the Machiavellian personality type. Subjects who take this test are asked whether they agree or disagree with a wide variety of statements drawn from the work. The following are several sample items:

1. The best way to handle people is to tell them what they want to hear.

2. Anyone who completely trusts anyone else is asking for trouble.

3. Most people who get ahead in the world lead clean, moral lives. (p. 17–18)

As you can see, a person who agrees with the first two items and disagrees with the third would be displaying Machiavellian tendencies.

Do people with high Machiavellian scores behave differently from those with low Machiavellian scores? This question has prompted a variety of studies, and the answer clearly is yes. In one interesting study the bargaining behavior of high Machiavellians was compared with that of those who were less manipulative. Groups of three students were asked to play a game in which the participants could bargain for money. The experimenter paid out ten one-dollar bills in front of the students and instructed them as follows:

The money will belong to any two of you who can agree with each other as to how you will divide the $10 between you. (You will not be allowed to divide the money among all three of you.) The two prospective partners can divide the $10 any way they choose. For example, they might split it 5 and 5, 8 and 2, or any other split. Of course, the third man, who at the time is being left out of the agreement, can also make offers to either of the two bargainers, and try to win one of them over to making the agreement with him. The game is over when any two players have made an agreement which the third player cannot get them to break. The money belongs to the two who have made the agreement and is divided accordingly between them. (p. 162)

The question was whether those with high Machiavellian scores would be more successful in their bargaining attempts than those with low scores. The amounts won by subjects who were high scorers exceeded the amounts won by those who were medium and low scorers. High-scorers averaged $5.57, medium-scorers averaged $3.14, and low-scorers averaged $1.29. Clearly the sentiments expressed on the questionnaire were related to actions in this bargaining situation.

How did Machiavellians accomplish their goal? Observations of the bargainers revealed that the major strategy of the Machiavellian was to structure the game for the other two players. Typically this type of subject would open the game with a comment like "OK, who wants to make the first offer?" In effect, the Machiavellian controlled the social reality of the situation. Much additional research supports this picture of the Machiavellian as a person who often sets out to manipulate the social world (Bogart et al., 1970; Christie and Boehm, 1970; Durkin, 1970; Exline et al., 1970; Lubinsky, 1977; Milord and Perry, 1977). Apparently Machiavellians also take special pleasure in their ability to manipulate others (Geis, 1964).

Yet lest it be concluded that the Machiavellians among us are always on top, we should note that people often see through the Machiavellians' manipulations and react negatively. In one study of leadership, medium-scorers on the test—not high-scorers—were rated highest in leadership capabilities (Gleason, Seaman, and Hollander, 1978). And a study of student teachers indicated that low-scorers had teaching skills that were superior to those of high-scorers (Biggers, 1977).

Thus we see that one who believes in the philosophy of manipulation also acts on it. However, the Machiavellian's skills may vary, and the results of the manipulation sometimes may backfire.

that they are meant to elicit. As a result, people can carry out subtle negotiations regarding the scripts they will follow together. Some people are better than others in managing relations over time. For example, women often are better than men in reading various body and facial cues. People who say they (1) pay attention to cues from others, (2) have control over their own presentation of cues, and (3) are willing to tailor their actions to fit situations are said to be high in self-monitoring. In many studies such individuals are found to relate easily and confidently to others and guide the direction of conversation. Over time, however, such people may prove to be unsatisfactory partners in intimate relationships.

Nonverbal Cues in Social Relationships

Many of the cues that initiate or sustain a given script are nonverbal. For example, folding one's arms across one's chest and staring into the distance may indicate that one is closed to others' invitations to interact (Argyle, 1975). Or if the person who is speaking during a conversation turns to look directly at the listener, this may signal that the listener's turn is about to begin (Duncan, Brunner, and Fiske, 1979). Similarly, by smiling during a conversation, one person can induce another to smile (Duncan and Fiske, 1977; Rosenfeld, 1967). The subtlety and power of such nonverbal signals have provoked keen interest in social psychology. Let us briefly consider investigations into the effects of facial expressions and body movement.

Facial expression: a universal code?

From Darwin to the present, theorists have suggested that the face is the primary vehicle for the expression of emotion (Tomkins, 1962). People who have disfigured faces often experience painful isolation, not only because they lack beauty, but also because others cannot use facial cues to read their emotions. As a result, some theorists believe that facial cues, unlike most cues for social control, may have a genetic origin—that is, knowledge of emotional expression may be built in biologically. If this were true, facial expressions would be a form of universal communication.

One of the most intensive inquiries into the possibility that facial expressions are universal has been carried out by Paul Ekman and his colleagues (Ekman, 1978; Ekman, Friesen, and Ellsworth, 1972). Thousands of subjects throughout the world were shown photographs that depict various emotions. For example, adults in the United States, Brazil, Chile, Argentina, and Japan were asked to select representations of six different emotions from a group of photographs (Ekman, 1972; Ekman, Sorenson, and Friesen, 1969). The emotions were happiness, sadness, anger, fear, surprise, and disgust. Given the photographs opposite, which of these emotions do you think each expresses? People in diverse cultures show extremely high agreement as to the particular facial expressions that are represented. Of course, individuals in these cultures watch television, read newspapers, and encounter visitors from other cultures. Therefore, the ability to decode facial expressions might have been learned through cross-cultural exposure. To offset the effect of social learning, additional experiments were carried out in the preliterate cultures of Borneo and New Guinea (Ekman and Friesen, 1971). These studies demonstrated that at least for the expressions of fear, happiness, and anger, people in isolated tribes also showed high agreement with each other and with samples in the literate cultures, suggesting that some genetic basis for recognizing emotions does exist.

Despite these primitive agreements about the meaning of facial expressions, such expressions clearly can mean different things to different people. Social and individual factors

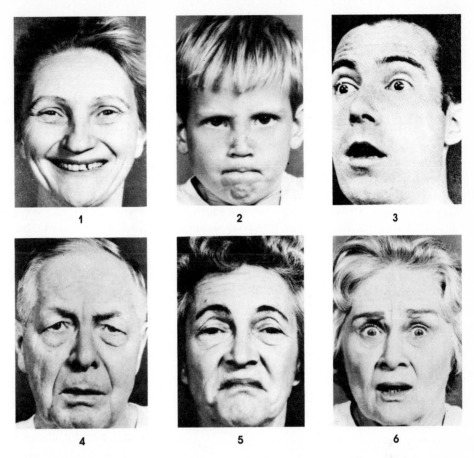

What are these people feeling? It's not very hard to guess. The emotions represented are (1) happiness, (2) anger, (3) surprise, (4) sadness, (5) disgust, and (6) fear.

introduce variations in both the production and the interpretation of facial expressions. These variations can reduce communication in the following ways:

1. *Display rules.* Cultures differ in their rules that govern how an emotion is to be expressed—that is, on what an occasion and with what intensity it is to be shown. In one demonstration of this difference, Japanese and American subjects were filmed by a hidden television camera while they watched a highly stressful film (Ekman and Friesen, 1969). Thinking that they were unobserved, the subjects demonstrated similar grimaces and other forms of facial stress. In contrast, when similar groups of subjects watched the film in the presence of an interviewer, the Japanese showed few signs of stress. In fact, many positive expressions were recorded. These findings suggest that Japanese men and women provide few cues to their feelings when they are in public situations. Similar differences may be found when comparing other cultures (Argyle, 1975).

2. *Deception.* People can use facial cues in trying to deceive one another. Investigators have been particularly interested in discovering ways of unmasking the deceiver. They have tried to find cues that might give away the deceiver's underlying emotional state—for example, movements or gestures that might have served as *leakage signals*. People often engage in more self-manipulations, such as touching the face with the hand, when they are lying (Ekman and Friesen, 1974; Knapp, Hart, and Dennis, 1974; McClintock and Hunt, 1975), or they may gesture less than usual (Mehrabian, 1971). A person's voice often becomes higher in pitch when he or she is lying (Ekman, Friesen, and Scherer, 1976; Krauss, Geller, and Olson, 1976). Although some people shift their eyes away from the target when they are lying and other people will smile frequently, such cues do not always prove to be reliable (McClintock and Hunt, 1975; Exline et al., 1970).

3. *Decoding categories.* Cultures differ in the categories or labels they use to interpret emotions (see Chapter 2). The Japanese, for example, make a clear distinction between sadness, which they view as a possible reaction to a tragedy, and depression, which is viewed as an irrational state (Argyle, 1975). Other cultures don't make a strong distinction between the two emotions and people in those cultures might fail to read the cues correctly.

4. *Expressive capacity.* People differ in their expressive capacity (Buck et al., 1972; Lanzetta and Kleck, 1970). Some people's face remains relatively composed regardless of circumstances, while other people wear all their emotions on their face.

We see, then, that under restricted conditions people in all cultures can understand one another's facial expressions. However,

the accuracy of interpretation across and within cultures may be reduced by a number of social and individual factors.

Body signals: the power in posture

Although the face furnishes immensely important cues to other people's emotional states, postures and gestures also play a significant role in social management. Much of the early research on body cues was inspired by psychiatrists and psychotherapists who wanted to know more about their patients than their patients were willing or able to disclose. For example, on the basis of clinical observation, these workers argued that uncrossing the legs is a signal of flirtation, drooping shoulders are an indication of helplessness or a request for help, folded arms are an indication of self-protection or withdrawal, and snuggling into a chair is an expression of sexual arousal (Mahl, 1967; Scheflen and Scheflen, 1972). Although these body cues may provide a therapist with important information about a single patient, they are unreliable indicators of the cues used more broadly in the society.

Social psychologists have turned to controlled studies in order to find clusters of behaviors, including posture and body movements, that provide reliable cues to social behavior. In one line of research, investigators have tried to isolate the various cues that indicate that an actor is to be viewed as powerful and that the observer is supposed to adopt the script of a subordinate. To explore dominance cues, subjects have been filmed from behind a one-way mirror while playing the role of a person who is interacting with someone of higher or lower status (Mehrabian, 1972). When they were "interacting" with someone of lower status, subjects tended to adopt more relaxed postures than when the other person was higher in status than they. The most important aspect of relaxation is an asymmetry in body position—for example,

each arm may be placed in a different position. In contrast, when interacting with a person of higher status, a person's hands may be clasped together or both arms may hang at his or her sides. The higher-status person may lean forward or backward, while the lower-status person will tend to remain upright.

Postural cues may be accompanied by various other body indicators. Touch may be an important signal (LaFrance and Mayo, 1978). When a high-status person and a low-status person are interacting, the high-status person usually feels free to touch the low-status person, while the low-status person seldom attempts to touch the high-status person. (Henley, 1973, 1977). Interestingly, this research shows also that in heterosexual relationships, males touch females with greater frequency than females touch males. Gaze also may be an important cue to dominance (Exline and Fehr, 1978). In one study, a confederate of the experimenters gazed at subjects during a conversation for various lengths of time (Argyle, Lefebvre, and Cook, 1974). In one condition he never let his gaze fall on the subjects; in other conditions he looked at them only while they were talking or only while they were listening; and in a final condition he gazed at them continuously. As the subjects' ratings of the confederate showed, he was seen as being most powerful when he gazed continuously; he was seen as being moderately powerful when his gazes were periodic; and he was seen as being least powerful when he avoided eye contact. Interestingly, the subjects' evaluations showed that liking for the confederate was greatest when he gazed periodically. Other research has shown that a steady gaze can cause people to move away— apparently out of fear (Ellsworth, Carlsmith, and Henson, 1972)—or avoid approaching (Kurtz, 1972).

1 Exchange theory rests on four assumptions: (1) human behavior is motivated primarily by pleasure and pain, (2) other people's actions are primary sources of pleasure and pain, (3) a person's actions may be used to secure pleasure-giving actions from others, and (4) people attempt to achieve maximum pleasure at minimum cost. When people make choices that maximize joint pleasure, they are said to be engaged in accommodation.

2 When exchange patterns furnish rewards, people try to sustain the pleasurable exchange by developing rules. The rules often are incorporated into cultural norms regarding proper action. Uriel and Edna Foa have proposed a model of the kinds of resources that may be exchanged. They argue that resources may be placed along two dimensions: (1) particularism, which refers to the degree to which a resource may be exchanged with a particular individual, and (2) concreteness, which refers to the extent to which a resource is physical or symbolic. People exchange resources that are similarly placed along these two dimensions. The exchange of love (a particularistic resource) for money (a nonparticularistic resource) is a violation of the rule that governs exchanges of kind. Rules also govern the proper amount of exchange. The equity rule specifies that the rewards and costs for each member of a relationship should be in proportion. Thus people will respond negatively to both underreward and overreward, and they will attempt to restore equity. Equity also may be restored by altering one's perception of what is fair. Many social theorists believe that society would be enhanced if the equity principle, which takes account of people's inputs, were replaced by an equality principle, which takes account of people's needs.

3 Often the pattern of available rewards does not favor accommodation. Rather, people are faced with mixed-motive situations in which the desire to cooperate for a joint gain of moderate size conflicts with the desire to exploit another person for a large gain. In the prisoner's dilemma game (a mixed-motive situation) people usually choose to exploit each other. Because mixed-motive situations are common in society, many social psychologists have sought ways of reducing exploitation. Strategies such as steady cooperation, playing it tough, or matching behavior can reduce exploitation, as can threat, but each has dangers as well as advantages. The development of communication probably is the most promising route to the reduction of exploitation.

4 In order to manage relationships successfully, people supply each other with both verbal and nonverbal cues for sequences of behavior, or scripts, that they wish to follow. Because cues often are ambiguous, people tend to negotiate for the scripts they will follow.

5 Some people are more successful at managing their relationships than are others. Women often are more accurate than men in judging the

cues that are provided by others. Mark Snyder has developed a scale on which skills that may contribute to effective management of other persons may be assessed. Persons who possess such skills are said to be high in *self-monitoring*. Such individuals usually are highly successful in many interpersonal settings. However, their behavioral instability may make them seem to be untrustworthy.

6 Some of the most interesting cues to other peoples' intentions are nonverbal. The face is believed to be the primary vehicle for the transmission of signals of emotion. Certain facial expressions communicate the same messages across cultural boundaries. However, emotional expressions are not fully reliable indicators of emotion because rules for emotional display differ across cultures and because people often deceive one another, use different decoding categories, and differ in their expressive capacities.

7 Body movements, posture, and gestures also may serve as important cues in social relationships. People who wish to communicate their power in a relationship may adopt a relaxed posture, with their limbs placed in asymmetrical positions. They also may touch other people more frequently and gaze at them for longer periods of time than is usual.

SUGGESTED READINGS

Argyle, M. *Bodily communication.* New York: International Universities Press, 1975.

Chadwick-Jones, J. K. *Social exchange theory: Its structure and influence in social psychology.* London: Academic Press, 1976.

Gergen, K. J. *The psychology of behavior exchange.* Reading, Mass.: Addison-Wesley, 1969.

Goffman, E. *The presentation of self in everyday life.* New York: Doubleday/Anchor, 1959.

Homans, G. C. *Social behavior: Its elementary forms.* New York: Harcourt Brace Jovanovich, 1974.

LaFrance, M., & Mayo, C. A. W. *Moving bodies: Nonverbal communication in social relationships.* Monterey, Calif.: Brooks/Cole, 1978.

Walster, E., Walster, G. W., & Berscheid, E. *Equity: Theory and research.* Boston: Allyn and Bacon, 1978.

INTERACTION IN GROUPS

418

■ *"The Delta Gamma sorority was so alive that year. We led the campus in academic performance, yet we still had time to paint the sacred lions in front of the SAE House a brilliant red, dance at the campus carnival, play touch football against the Thetas, throw water balloons at Phi Delt invaders, and do charity work besides. Somehow, the house was a nest for all of us, and we felt a sense of closeness that seemed permanent and unbreakable. Few of us, I think, looked forward to leaving at graduation. Yet, Judy, the chapter president, went off to New York where she was turned on to the tough-minded philosophy of Ayn Rand and worked her way into the publishing world. Sandy, who had also served as a chapter president, later joined a Republican campaign group, and became one of Ronald Reagan's first active supporters. Joanie married a political science major, and the two of them went off to work in radical politics. Sal also went to New York, but she wanted to become an actress. Gail went to California to learn about sun and surfers. I hear from each of them from time to time, but you know, it might be a disaster if we all got together again. We are all so different now."* (Anonymous, Delta Gamma, University of Minnesota)

This account of college friends is not unusual. You probably can think of various groups to which you once were deeply attached, which were vital to your life at some point, but to which you no longer can return comfortably. And as this woman suggests, group membership has probably influenced your beliefs, your sentiments, and your activities. Experiences such as those she describes are part of most people's lives. As sorority members, the women adopted a pattern of behavior that changed radically as each moved into another group. Once they were energetic friends; now they face insurmountable barriers to a satisfactory relationship. So powerful are the effects of groups on people's lives that over a dozen governments now use informal groups to generate grass-roots support for their regimes (Chu, Rahim, and Kincaid, 1976; Whyte, 1974).

In this chapter we will explore people's experiences in groups—in families, in friendship and work circles, and in other organizations. For the purpose of our discussion, a *group* can be defined as *consisting of two or more people who interact or communicate* (Shaw, 1976). Typically this interaction takes

place on a *face-to-face basis* (Homans, 1950). Groups are composed of people who perceive themselves as *forming a unit that endures through time and space* (Campbell, 1958). Members of a group typically *share at least one common goal* (Hare, 1976). In fact, most groups are organized to achieve something—win an election, decide the fate of a criminal, create and sell a new product, and so forth.

In previous chapters we have been concerned primarily with *dyadic interaction*—that is, relations between two people, a minimal group. As the number of persons in a group increases, new processes and problems emerge. The social theorist George Simmel (1903) pointed out that simply adding one more person creates problems that are never experienced in dyads. For example, two people can form a coalition against a third person. As Simmel argued, three-person groups are inherently unstable. Persons in a threesome may find themselves engaged in continuous bargaining—no member wants to be forced into minority status. In this chapter we will be particularly concerned with the quality of life in groups of three persons or more. Our discussion will be organized around some of the major questions that social psychologists have asked about group life. The first questions deal with formation and functioning of groups: the barriers that prevent group formation and the factors that draw groups together. We will be especially interested in the effects of tightly knit, or *cohesive*, groups on their members' attitudes and behavior and on the decision-making abilities of the groups as a whole. We then will consider the effects of group membership on individual members' freedom of thought and behavior. In particular, we will address the question of how groups deal with deviance. Finally, we will turn to the question of group effectiveness. As we have noted, most groups are organized for a purpose. We will ask how group membership influences an individual member's performance and what happens to the performance of the group as a whole as more members are added.

Attraction in Groups: The Question of Cohesiveness

People often join groups because they believe that membership will provide them with warmth and support. A person may join a sorority or a fraternity, for example, because the other members seem to like one another, or someone may take a particular job because the other employees seem to be friendly. Yet all groups do not provide positive experiences. Antagonism and hostility often characterize the relationships that exist among members of work and family groups. Groups may provide their members with good times or bad times. The key question is, what factors contribute to positive sentiments among group members, and what factors cause antagonism to prevail? Or in practical terms, what can one do to ensure that family members or co-workers accept and support one another?

Social psychologists who have studied these questions have developed a concept that identifies attraction among group members. This concept, which usually is termed *cohesiveness* (Festinger, 1951), refers to the degree to which members of a group are attracted to one another and to the group as a whole. If attraction is intense and a high value is placed on membership, the group is said to be cohesive (Collins and Raven, 1968). Cohesiveness can be measured in several ways. For example, each member of a group can be asked to evaluate his or her feelings toward each of the other members, and these evaluations can be added together. Group members can also be asked to evaluate the group as a whole. For example, they can be asked whether they believe that their group is better at sticking together than are other groups (Mann and Baumgartel, 1952). Or they can be asked about their "sense of belonging" (Indik, 1965). The concept of cohesiveness is useful in examining factors that may enhance or diminish attraction among group members as well as factors that may influence the functioning of groups.

Impediments to Cohesiveness: Hierarchy and Subgroups

The presence of increased numbers of people in groups creates barriers to cohesiveness. One such barrier stems from the requirement that various functions be distributed among group members (see Chapter 9). Some people inevitably take on decision-making tasks for the group and act as coordinators, facilitators, or heads. Other people take care of minor details. Still others may have no function at all. And when functions are distributed among group members, so is power. As a result, groups tend to become hierarchical, and high-ranking members are able to control or influence events.

As hierarchies develop, attraction patterns among members are altered. Open expressions of affection between senior and junior members of a hierarchy are not usually permitted. Senior members of a group fear that they will be unable to carry out their tasks if they become involved emotionally with junior members (Blau, 1964). For the same reason, military organizations discourage officers from "fraternizing" with enlisted personnel, and universities frown on intimate relationships between faculty members and students. In addition, senior members distrust signals of attraction from junior members, perceiving the overtures as flattery or subtle manipulation (see Chapter 9). Finally, the use of coercive power by senior members may cause junior members to become resentful (Zander, 1971). As we saw in Chapter 8, parents' use of coercive power, for example, may be a major source of antagonism within a family.

A second barrier to cohesiveness in groups stems from differences in people's liking for one another. Group members inevitably prefer certain individuals and care less about others. Persons who are particularly attracted to each other may form subgroups within the larger group. Cliques within fraternities and sororities are good examples of such subgroups. And as we mentioned in our discussion of prejudice (Chapter 4), members of in-groups tend to see one another as being superior to members of the out-group, and they tend to discriminate against them. The existence of power differences also may contribute to the development of subgroups. People at various levels in a hierarchy may form subgroups because they share similar experiences or because a coalition can increase their power (Caplow, 1956; Gamson, 1964; Vinacke and Arkoff, 1957). The larger the group, the more likely that subgroups will develop. Relating to large numbers of people is difficult, and subgroups provide members with secure, close relationships (Becker et al., 1973; Castore, 1962). Thus the larger the group, the more likely that cohesiveness will be reduced (Gerard and Hoyt, 1974; Kinney, 1953; Porter and Lawler, 1968).

Subgroups are often hidden, and sometimes even members of high-school classes aren't aware of the friendship cliques that silently influence their social life. Social psychologists have developed measures that reveal the existence of these groups. The most widely used measure was developed by J. G. Moreno in 1943. Moreno coined the term *sociometry* to refer to his method of studying group structure by assessing individual members' preferences. In this technique the investigator typically asks each group member to indicate which other member of the group he or she would prefer to have as an associate in various activities. The indicators then are organized into a visual representation, called a *sociogram*. Figure 12-1 presents sociograms for two hypothetical groups. In the pattern on the left, attraction is distributed equally among the group members. Each member has named someone else as his or her most preferred associate, and in turn each member is preferred by at least one other member of the group. This group should be highly cohesive. In the pattern on the right, attraction is unequally distributed. The group is composed of two distinct subgroups. Members of one subgroup receive no preference rankings from members of the other subgroup. In-group versus out-group hostility should be prevalent in such a group, and overall cohesiveness should be low.

As theorist Alvin Zander (1977) has pointed out, the existence of both hierarchies and subgroups also fosters secrecy in groups. Members at one level of the hierarchy do not wish to disclose their knowledge or observations to members at other levels. Similarly, members of subgroups often gossip behind the backs of other group members. Secrets may be necessary to reduce friction within the group, but at the same time they are derogatory toward those from whom they are kept (Keller and Brown, 1974). As a result, secrets often lower the cohesiveness of a group. Hierarchies and subgroups can thus be

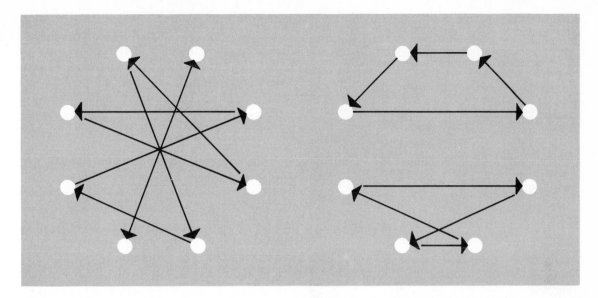

FIGURE **12-1** **The sociometric structure of two groups**

In this diagram each arrow shows a friendship choice. Note the potential for cohesiveness in the group on the left. The group on the right should be low in cohesiveness. (Based on Moreno, 1943)

more negative in their ultimate effects on group life than are the problems they were supposed to solve in the first place.

We see, then, that the development of hierarchies and subgroups can interfere with cohesiveness in social groups. Strong ties of attraction are difficult to maintain when group members have different amounts of power. And overall cohesiveness may break down when some group members select other group members as their closest friends or allies. However, many factors can overcome obstacles to cohesiveness. Let us consider several of these.

Building Group Cohesiveness

In his early theorizing, Leon Festinger (1951) proposed that cohesiveness can be increased by *any* factor that enhances the value of a group to an individual member. Thus success in achieving goals should make groups more cohesive. Apparently the members value one

another more when they realize that each member's gains depend on the input of all (Blanchard, Adelman, and Cook, 1975; Lott and Lott, 1965). As we saw in our discussion of prejudice (Chapter 4), when racially integrated groups achieve their goals, the barriers to friendship that were created by prejudice tend to disappear. Similarly, when a sports team is on a winning streak, cohesiveness increases (Lott and Lott, 1965). However, losing may promote attraction if group members can blame their loss on environmental conditions (Worchel and Norvell, 1980).

Threats from the outside may increase group members' value to one another and thus improve cohesiveness (Stein, 1976). For example, researchers have found that small-town merchants who anticipate competition from a large chain store demonstrate increased cohesiveness (Mulder and Stemerding, 1963). Cohesiveness also increases in communities that experience natural disasters (Quarentelli and Dynes, 1972) and in civilian populations

Winning is love. Members of the New York Yankees are shown celebrating their victory over Kansas City in the 1978 pennant race. The cohesiveness displayed in their moment of triumph reflects a common experience in groups: success in achieving a goal often increases the attraction of group members to one another.

the group may suffer a loss or be destroyed. Thus cohesiveness increases in groups that are engaging in competition (Sherif and Sherif, 1953). For an illustration, you may wish to return to the Chapter 4 description of Sherif's study of group competition at boys' summer camps. In that highly competitive situation the boys' groups became fully—even dangerously—united.

Although competition from outside may increase cohesiveness, competition from within a group often has the reverse effect. In one early attempt to demonstrate the effects of within-group competition, reward structures were varied for groups whose members were working on problems in human relations (Deutsch, 1949). Some groups faced a *cooperative* reward structure, in which the weekly grade was based on the average overall performance of the group. Other groups faced a *competitive* reward structure, in which the weekly grade was based on individual performance. Thus, if someone contributed good ideas in the cooperative group, the entire group benefited. In the competitive group an individual alone would benefit from his or her own performance. The differing reward structures had marked effects on the group members' behavior. Members of the cooperative groups demonstrated an avid interest in one another's ideas. They were anxious to work together and contribute to the group goal. They were friendly, they encouraged one another, and they were rarely critical of one another's contributions. The opposite pattern prevailed in the competitive groups. Members of those groups tried to excel and they tried to outdo one another. They did not seem to care for one another, and they were inclined to be critical of one another. Interestingly, the cooperative groups were more productive—they solved the human relations problems more quickly than did the competitive groups.

On the basis of these and other findings, many social psychologists have been critical

that are subjected to bombing (Janis, 1951). Political leaders often use the threat of outside invasion to generate national cohesiveness. This technique has been used recently in Iran in order to maintain an otherwise shaky regime, and it was effective in the United States and Great Britain during the Second World War.

Competition from outside a group operates much like threat—it raises the possibility that

of competitive reward structures (Blau, 1959; Haythorn, 1953; Shaw, 1958; Willis and Joseph, 1959; Zander and Wolfe, 1964). Some researchers have shown how cooperative-learning groups can be established—with each member responsible for teaching part of a day's assignment to the other members (Aronson and Geffner, 1978; Aronson and Osherow, 1980). The establishment of this kind of cooperative education (a stark contrast to the usual competitive approach) usually results in the formation of cohesive groups and the breakdown of traditional ethnic and racial barriers to friendship. Despite these demonstrations, debate over the effects of cooperative versus competitive reward structures continues (Rosenbaum, 1980). For example, investigators have shown that competition within a group can increase productivity (Deutsch, 1949; Sherif, 1979).

Clearly, many other factors can increase cohesiveness in groups. If group members have similar tastes and interests, cohesiveness may be enhanced (Good and Nelson, 1971). And if initiation into a group is difficult, membership may seem to be more valuable (Aronson and Mills, 1959). We see, then, that a variety of factors—including group success, outside threat, and competition—may overcome the barriers to group cohesiveness.

The Fruits of Cohesiveness: The Sweet and the Bitter

In a cohesive group, members come to feel affectionate regard for one another. The consequences of such regard for other aspects of group life are not always favorable, however. Let us consider both the positive and the negative effects of cohesiveness on the attitudes and behavior of the individual group members and on the functioning of the group itself.

Cohesion and contentment

During the early 1900s the goal of most psychological research in the work setting was the improvement of workers' efficiency and discipline. This orientation was termed *scientific management* (Taylor, 1911). By the late 1930s, however, psychologists recognized that the focus on productivity was too limited. Workers are not machines and cannot be tuned to work at peak efficiency. The work place is a social setting, and in order to improve efficiency account must be taken of an individual worker's relationships with others. With these concerns in mind, research on group cohesiveness gained a good deal of practical significance.

Investigation of this issue suggests that cohesiveness can be beneficial in work groups. Investigators have found that workers in cohesive groups generally display high levels of morale or general feelings of satisfaction with their job (Exline, 1957; Gross, 1954; Marquis, Guetzkow, and Heyns, 1951). Cohesiveness in work groups also increases members' sense of security and their self-regard—perhaps because the members give one another mutual support. Workers in highly cohesive groups feel less nervous and jumpy on the job (Seashore, 1954). Compared with workers in less cohesive groups, they tend to score higher on measures of self-esteem and feel freer to report embarrassing events to others in the group (Julian, Bishop, and Fiedler, 1966) and express their emotions (French, 1941; Pepitone and Reichling, 1955).

In addition to having high morale and feelings of self-confidence, members of cohesive work groups demonstrate less absenteeism and less job turnover (Fox and Scott, 1943; Mayo and Lombard, 1944).

Does increased morale, self-esteem, and commitment to the job result in higher levels of productivity? Often production does rise. Apparently people do better work in the positive atmosphere of a cohesive group because they expect their colleagues to give them approval for their efforts (Sacks, 1952). Studies of job proficiency indicate that people do better work when they are surrounded by close

BOX 12-1

Groups for Human Potential

Groups can work in a variety of ways to aid people. The use of groups to stimulate human potential began with the work of several well-known psychologists. Kurt Lewin (1948) conducted workshops to aid community leaders in reducing racial tensions. Group members found that their most profound insights occurred not when they discussed incidents in the community, but rather when they focused the group on itself and dealt with tensions within and among the members. Lewin's pioneering work led to the formation of the National Training Laboratory (NTL), which continues to hold summer workshops that center on the T-group ("T" for training). The therapists Carl Rogers and Fritz Perls have also made substantial contributions to the human potential movement. For Rogers (1967), the "encounter group" is a way of teaching people how exchanges of positive regard can increase trust and openness (see Chapter 3). Rogers believes that participants in encounter groups emerge with a new sense of self and new capacities for dealing with others. In contrast, Fritz Perls—founder of the Gestalt therapy movement (Perls, Hefferline, and Goodman, 1965)—believes that the culture is too clever with words. That is, people use words to avoid the real problems of relating. For Perls, groups break down people's verbal defenses, making possible the experience of "true feelings." In effect Perls is arguing that groups may be used to improve one's implicit knowledge (see Chapter 1)—that is, one's nonverbal know-how.

In recent years, group techniques for aiding people in a variety of ways have been developed. For example, groups are used to reduce drug dependence and cigarette smoking, build community spirit, increase sexual contentment, develop coping strategies, enhance self-esteem, and promote racial integration. In addition, many specialized techniques have been created to develop, change, or stimulate individuals (Schutz, 1967). With its increasing popularity, the human potential movement has also generated considerable controversy (Back, 1972). Critics have pointed to the absence of ethical and legal limits to what a group leader might do, and they have suggested that limits should be set on who may conduct such groups. While thousands of people can testify to the positive effects of the groups, stories of suicides, broken homes, psychotic breakdowns, and lawsuits against trainers are told. Clearly, research on the benefits of group participation has been badly needed.

Lieberman, Yalom, and Miles (1973) have carried out the most significant test to date on the impact of the encounter-group experience on participants. In the study, students were placed at random in each of ten different groups. Each group met for thirty hours over a period of ten weeks. The researchers found that according to all accounts—the subjects', the friends', and the leaders'—the group experience did produce marked changes. The changes were evident six months after completion of the program, suggesting that the experience had real carry-over into everyday life. Unfortunately, not all changes were favorable. In fact, many casualties resulted from the group experience. For many people, emotional distress increased, and their adaptive abilities and ways of relating were hurt by participation in the groups. Three potent factors were found to distinguish between group members who changed positively and members who changed negatively.

1. *Positive changers and casualties were different from each other when they entered the encounter experience.* Both types of group member wanted to experience self-change. However, positive changers accepted the idea that there might be some pain, some disorientation, and some effort required to produce change. In contrast, casualties seemed to expect the groups to work miracles. They believed that they had little to do but sit back and wait.

2. *The group process differed in successful and unsuccessful groups.* In particular, it was found that self-disclosure and emotional expressiveness were not in themselves beneficial and that they produced positive changes primarily when they were invested with meaning by the leader. In other words, telling all or breaking down in tears doesn't produce positive change unless someone explains why such a thing happens and what it means.

3. *Leadership style differed in successful and unsuccessful groups.* If a leader let things take their course or was highly impersonal and distant, the casualty rate was high. On the other hand, too much control of the group also was detrimental. Groups need continued interest and input from the leader, but if the leader exerts too much control, his or her efforts may be in vain.

Thus, if you are interested in selecting a group, you should ask several important questions. First, what are the leader's qualifications, and what kinds of techniques does he or she employ? You also might want to pay special attention to the level and style of the leader's input. Finally, you might ask yourself what kind of effort you are willing to make. If you have the right qualities and you choose a group carefully, you may find that the experience is valuable.

A positive encounter. Participating in encounter groups has become a popular activity for people interested in personal development. This kind of group experience can have profound positive effects and also can generate serious negative consequences.

friends rather than strangers (Husband, 1940). Army units are more efficient at reconnaissance tasks when they are high in cohesiveness than when they are low (Goodacre, 1951). In part, high performance may result from the increased cooperation (Haythorn, 1953) and high levels of communication (Lott and Lott, 1961) that characterize cohesive groups.

There is one important exception to the high level of performance that often is found in cohesive groups. It has long been observed that members of many working groups establish norms of proper performance (Homans, 1950). Such performance norms may be at a low level, particularly if a group is hostile toward management. Group members who break the norms by performing at a high level—"rate-busters," as they are called—may be punished informally by the group. Cohesive groups are especially effective in enforcing these norms.

Cohesion and catastrophe: groupthink

It is Saturday night and you and a group of close friends have driven to a neighboring town to have a few beers. Someone proposes a game. The loser of each round of the game will have to gulp down a pint of beer. The suggestion is greeted by hearty cheers. However, you remember the devastating results of your last experience with this game, and you begin to think about the ride home and how dangerous it will be. Perhaps you make a joke about the ride, but you are ignored. Again the cheers go up. A new round of beers is ordered, and the game is about to begin. How do you think you might respond? Would you suggest doing something else? Would you mention the dangers of the drive again? Would you ask the driver of the car not to play? Chances are you would not. In fact, you probably would not do anything. Essentially you would have been victimized by what Irving Janis has called *groupthink*—that is, a way of thinking in which a cohesive group's need for unanimity overwhelms the members' realistic appraisal of alternative courses of action.

Janis (1968) argues that decision making in cohesive groups is impaired by the members' tendency to engage in groupthink. Members of cohesive groups are usually close friends, and they put strong pressure for consensus on one another (Dion, Miller, and Magnan, 1971; Festinger, Pepitone, and Newcomb, 1952; Wyer, 1966). Group members don't want to criticize their friends' ideas and point out their flaws—this would violate the friendship. People want to fit in with the group and keep the good feelings flowing through conformity (Brandstätter, 1978; Schuler and Pelzer, 1978). As Janis argues, the desire for consensus among highly cohesive groups can lead to disaster. Janis's analysis of government policy-making groups, including those responsible for decisions made during the Korean and Vietnam wars and before the Bay of Pigs invasion, suggests that groupthink may have paved the way for many fiascoes (Tetlock, 1979).

Groupthink often distorts decision making in the following ways:

1. Discussions are limited to a minimum number of alternatives. Members typically avoid creating alternatives to the group's initial preference.

2. The group fails to examine either the course of action that initially was preferred by the majority or any alternative courses of action. Group members do not wish to cast one another in a negative light.

3. The group avoids seeking expert opinion. If expert opinion is sought, the group selectively supports the opinion that favors its initial position. The group thus remains homogeneous and unified in its sentiment.

Yet Janis is not saying that cohesion *must* give rise to inferior decisions. Nor does he propose that better decisions are necessarily generated by groups in which the members are hostile to one another. Rather, Janis proposes that cohesive groups can make constructive decisions if steps are taken to reduce the threat of groupthink. For example, various individuals can be assigned the role of critical evaluator, a high priority can be placed on airing doubts and uncertainties, and the agenda can be arranged so that members pay less attention to initial preferences than to competing alternatives. Further, if the group leader openly welcomes new ideas, groupthink effects may be countered (Flowers, 1977).

To explore the effects of encouraging conflicting ideas, researchers gave management trainees a highly complex task of determining what equipment would be necessary for survival on the moon (Hall and Watson, 1970).

After working alone on the problem, the trainees were asked to work on it in either a cohesive or a conflict-oriented group. The cohesive groups were instructed to reach a collective solution. The conflict-oriented groups were asked to (1) avoid changing positions for the purpose of creating harmony, (2) prohibit majority votes and other conflict-reducing tendencies, and (3) view differences in opinion as being natural and helpful rather than oppositional.

After the decisions were collected the researchers compared them with a series of expert answers provided by the Research Section of the NASA Manned Spaceflight Center. It was found that the conflict-oriented groups produced better quality decisions and demonstrated a higher level of creativity than did the standard groups. In addition, comparisons of the group decisions and the individual decisions revealed that the conflict-oriented groups developed better solutions than did even their most skilled individual members. Among the conflict-oriented groups, 75 percent achieved higher scores than did their most competent member. This figure dropped to 25 percent for the cohesive groups. Thus cohesiveness may be highly valued among group members, but it may be hazardous to the group's success if special precautions are not taken.

To summarize, cohesiveness can be impeded by power differences within groups and by the development of friendship subgroups, or cliques. Sociograms may be used to detect the existence of cliques in informal groups. Yet despite these barriers to cohesiveness, group members usually develop strong friendships. Cohesiveness among group members is enhanced when the group is (1) successful in fulfilling its goals, (2) threatened from outside, (3) in competition with other groups, or (4) operating on the basis of a cooperative as opposed to a competitive reward structure. Cohesiveness can have positive and negative effects. In work groups, cohesiveness increases morale and self-esteem and often improves work performance. However, when group members are engaged in decision making, high cohesiveness can lead to groupthink—the tendency to let unanimity prevail and overlook alternatives. The disasters produced by groupthink can often be avoided by introducing conflict strategies into group discussion.

Freedom in Groups: The Question of Deviance

A boy (we'll call him Tommy) moved to a new neighborhood. Tommy is small for his age, and because of his stature and his newness to the neighborhood, he became a target of much vicious teasing. One older boy particularly enjoyed tormenting him. He pounded on Tommy, tore his clothes, and broke his glasses. Finally Tommy was afraid to go outside, and so after school he stayed inside and watched television. A remarkable change occurred recently, however. At school Tommy became the favorite of a group of slightly older boys. These boys included him in their activities, and they made certain that no further bullying took place. Tommy is much happier now.

This story illustrates a phenomenon that is of vast importance in social life. Groups offer safety and power. People often seek out groups in order to gain freedom from various threats. Indeed, the increased feeling of potency that is experienced in a group may lead people to overestimate the true gain in power that is produced by the group (Janssens and Nuttin, 1976). Primitive tribes, teenage gangs, college cliques, business organizations, unions, and, indeed, entire nations are formed to ward off threat. Yet the freedom that groups furnish their members may be diminished by the simultaneous demands for obedience to the group itself. While groups protect certain freedoms, they can destroy

Communes: experiments in group living. Communal living arrangements offer their members a kind of intimacy and a sense of sharing that often stands in marked contrast to patterns prevailing in society at large. The subsequent breakup of many of these groups reflects in part their immense demands on individual members for commitment to group values and compliance with group rules.

others. For example, Tommy is free now to wander his neighborhood in safety, but he is not free to choose his afternoon activities. He must stay with his group. Similarly, a union may protect a worker from management, but a union member is not free to decide whether to work during a strike.

Given this ironic conflict over freedoms lost and found, two important questions arise: why is individual freedom lost within a group, and what factors increase a group's control over its members? We will deal with each question in turn.

Rejection of the Deviant

Two reasons for the reduction of freedom in groups will be familiar. First, as we mentioned in our discussion of social exchange (Chapter 11), when people establish rewarding forms of interaction they usually attempt to maintain them. The patterns become *rules of operation* for the participants, and deviations from the rules usually are punished (Mikula and Schwinger, 1978). If you are a member of an informal card-playing group, for example, your failure to show up for a game may reduce the other members' pleasure. In fact, if all of the members were unreliable, there would be no group. Thus groups demand obedience from their members so that a reliable supply of rewards will be maintained.

The second reason why freedom in groups is lost will be familiar from our discussion of *social comparison theory* (Chapter 10). As we mentioned, most people try to develop a sense of the adequacy of their opinions and abilities. They accomplish this by comparing themselves with other people. When these other people are members of a given group, a consensus about what is adequate and what is not is often achieved. The consensus forms a *social reality*—a socially supported understanding of the world. To deviate from the consensus is to threaten the group's sense of reality.

Leon Festinger (1950) has suggested a third reason for the reduction of freedom in groups. Festinger argues that group members seek consensus in order to *move toward group goals*. As we have noted, many groups are organized to accomplish some end—they try to earn money, win games, protect a nation, and so forth. In order to achieve these goals,

standard operating rules are required. A military unit would be destroyed quickly if any private could decide to be commander-for-a-day and dish out orders to the officers. In other words, rules are required in order to fulfill *system needs*—that is, the needs that enable the group, as a system of related entities, to fulfill its functions. Thus system needs also interfere with autonomous action.

To demonstrate these various pressures toward uniform behavior in groups, consider a classic study of group conformity (Schachter, 1951). This study is particularly dramatic because groups were composed of relative strangers who would be expected to have little objection to one another's deviancy. In the study, groups of eight to ten college students (including three confederates of the investigator) were asked to decide the fate of a juvenile delinquent. Each member's opinion was announced to the group. During this procedure one confederate gave an opinion that *deviated* from that of the majority. The second confederate gave an opinion that was *modal* for the group. The third confederate was a *slider:* his initial opinion was extreme, but he allowed himself to be influenced during the discussion so that by the end of the discussion his opinion was modal. The case was discussed for forty-five minutes, during which time the first two confederates maintained their opinions.

TABLE 12-1 **People pay attention to a person who is deviant**

Note the discrepancy between the large number of communications addressed to the deviant and the relatively limited amount of attention paid to the other confederates.

Type of subject	Average number of communications per ten-minute interval			
	5 to 15 min.	*15 to 25 min.*	*25 to 35 min.*	*35 to 45 min.*
Deviant	3.81	7.15	9.46	5.21
Slider	0.53	0.55	0.21	0.17
Modal	0.13	0.06	0.06	0.10

Source: Adapted from Schachter, 1951

Table 12-1 shows the average number of communications addressed to the deviant, the modal confederate, and the slider during the discussion. As you can see, communication to the deviant increases and far exceeds that directed to the others. Group members appear to be making an active effort to bring the deviant's opinion into line with the group. During the last ten minutes, however, communications directed toward the deviant drop off. At this point the group seems to be rejecting him. He is no longer treated as a member of the group, and, in fact, evaluations that were taken later showed that group members were hostile to him. Group members liked the modal confederate the most, although the least amount of communication was addressed to him.

This pattern of increases in pressure on and hostility toward deviants has been demonstrated in numerous studies (Levine, 1980). When the group is cohesive, the pressure on the deviant is likely to be particularly intense. Apparently both the group itself and its success mean a lot to members of cohesive groups, and so members of cohesive groups have less tolerance for deviants than do members of groups that are not cohesive (Gerard, 1954). Also, pressures against deviance may be strong when the group members depend on each other for obtaining the group's goals (Lauderdale, 1976; Wiggins, Dill, and Schwartz, 1965). When success is within the group's grasp, members may find a deviant voice to be particularly irritating. The amount of pressure that is placed on the deviant increases as the magnitude of his or her deviance increases (Suchner and Jackson,

Total interdependence. This circle, seemingly a magicians doing, illustrates an important feature of group life: if people are willing to depend on each other, they may accomplish goals that none can reach alone. At the same time, in reaching such goals no deviant behavior may be allowed.

1976). Group members may tolerate small departures from the group norm, but large differences are more threatening. As Schachter found, of course, the deviant can go too far—at which point he or she is treated as an outsider. In fact, when a group can redefine its boundaries easily—when it can exclude a deviant member without difficulty—then deviants may be under less pressure to conform to group norms (Festinger and Thibaut, 1951).

We see, then, that groups reduce their members' freedom of action in order to (1) ensure pleasureful exchanges within the group, (2) support shared notions about social reality, and (3) ensure that the group attains its goals. In effect, group members are under constant pressure to conform to group norms. The pressure may be particularly strong if the group is cohesive or likely to attain its goal.

The Group Confronts the Individual: Social-Impact Theory

Groups may try to shape their members to specifications, but such efforts are not always successful. In previous chapters we discussed two ways in which a group member may hold on to personal freedom. As we saw in our discussion of leadership processes (Chapter 9), groups offer the freedom to deviate to those who furnish the group with rewards. And in our discussion of social influence (Chapter 10), we described minority influences on the majority. A deviant can gain freedom by moving the group in a new direction.

Social-impact theory offers additional insights into how individual freedom may be retained in a group setting. This theory, developed by Bibb Latané and his colleagues (Latané, 1978; Latané and Nida, 1980), is concerned with people's impact on one another in a wide range of situations. Let us see how this applies to the problem of the group's impact on the deviant.

According to social-impact theory, three factors determine a group's impact:

1. *The number of influence sources (in this case, group members).* The larger the group, the greater its capacity to influence the deviant. This assumption is supported by laboratory research. When there is an increase in the number of persons with opinions different from those of an individual, the likelihood that the individual will alter the opinion in the direction of the group's opinion also increases (Shaw, 1976).

2. *Strength of the influence sources.* The stronger the group, the greater its capacity to influence the deviant. *Strength* refers to all those characteristics of group members that might attract the deviant. When group members can protect, nurture, help, give status, or otherwise furnish pleasure, their strength is increased. Again, many laboratory demonstrations lend support to this view. For example, people who actually secure pleasure through others, or believe that they will, are likely to shift their views in an effort to be agreeable and are more likely to agree to group goals (Festinger, Schachter, and Back, 1950; Zander, 1971).

3. *Immediacy.* The greater the immediacy of a source, the greater the impact on the deviant. *Immediacy* refers to the source's closeness to the deviant in space or time. Thus, if the members of a group gather in the same room, immediacy would be high. If the deviant leaves the group, the longer he or she remains away the lower the group's immediacy. An illustration of immediacy is furnished by Milgram's work on obedience (Chapter 10). When the experimenter was in the room with the subjects they were far more likely to obey his commands than they were when he was absent and delivered the commands by phone.

In practical terms, social-impact theory suggests that the greatest possibility for freedom is offered by small groups. Small groups consist of fewer sources of influence, and so the deviant may be able to influence the group's actions. From this point of view, a group of two persons offers maximum freedom. The theory also suggests that the more the deviant needs or wants the group, the more limited is his or her freedom. In effect, the group's power to control rests on its possession of resources that are needed by the deviant. As the Japanese Zen masters say, pure freedom is achieved when one wants nothing. Finally, the theory suggests that freedom is likely to be available in groups that are characterized by physical or social distance: a neighborhood in which houses are not close by or a friendship group that meets only at designated times.

In summary, we find that people often join groups in order to enhance their freedom. At the same time, becoming a group member limits one's freedom in important ways. The group may require the member to obey those rules of exchange that traditionally have given the members pleasure. Most groups also demand that members conform to the group's view of social reality and to rules that are set up to enable the group to achieve its goals. The pressure to conform that is placed on deviants may increase if the group is cohesive and if it has a high probability of attaining its goals. Social-impact theory suggests that the group's ability to keep its members in line depends on the size of the group, the power or attractiveness of the group members, and the geographical and temporal closeness of the group members. Groups can provide freedom, but only if they are chosen carefully.

Group Influence on Individuals: Social Facilitation Effects

If you have ever played on a team or acted in a play or participated in any kind of public performance, you know what a special thrill

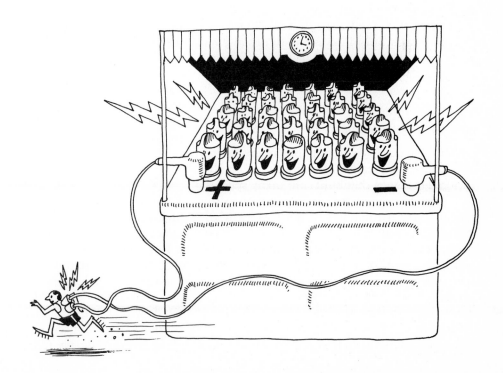

this kind of activity can provide. You may have felt that your performance under such circumstances surpassed anything you could have done in private. In fact, the common experience of improved performance furnished the basis for the Triplett experiment that was discussed in Chapter 1. Triplett's early work demonstrated that bicyclists who raced alone against time were significantly slower than bicyclists who raced against other bicyclists. This improved performance was duplicated so often that by 1920 Floyd Allport termed the superior performance that was elicited by the presence of the group the *social facilitation effect*. Over the years researchers have carried out additional social facilitation research with animals and humans, both in the laboratory and in the field and in dozens of situations. Social facilitation has been found to be a robust social phenomenon (Begum and Lehr, 1963; Connolly, 1968; Hunt and Hillery, 1973; Rosenquist, 1972; Zajonc, Heingartner, and Herman, 1969). As researchers have piled up evidence for the existence of social facilitation, their findings have generated lively controversy. Two questions are especially interesting to social psychologists: why does social facilitation occur, and what factors are responsible for its failure to occur?

Arousal or Apprehension?

Robert Zajonc (1965, 1980b) has offered a biologically based explanation for social facilitation. He argues that built into many species of organism is a genetic predisposition to respond to other members of the species with *generalized physiological arousal*. Thus, when others form an audience their presence enhances arousal, which then is channeled into task performance, improving the performance. Studies of both animals and humans support this position. Lower animals, such as rats and cockroaches, often respond to other members of their species with an ele-

vated level of arousal or with generalized activity (Larsson, 1956; Latané and Cappell, 1972). And when humans perform before others, they show evidence of increased arousal—palmar sweating and changes in muscle potential and respiration rate, for example (Burtt, 1921; Chapman, 1974; Geen, 1977; Martens, 1969).

Other theorists have not been fully satisfied with Zajonc's explanation of social facilitation effects. They argue that the mere presence of others is not the relevant influence, but rather what the presence means to the individual. In particular, the critics argue, when other people are present an individual often feels *evaluation apprehension*—that is, concern with the possibility of receiving a positive or negative reaction to the quality of one's performance (Cottrell, 1972; Henchy and Glass, 1968; Weiss and Miller, 1971). Thus an audience that consists of blindfolded persons would have little effect on task performance. However, if the audience could watch the proceedings with active interest, performance most likely would be facilitated (Cottrell et al., 1968). An audience that is perceived as a potential evaluator causes more arousal in the performer than does an audience that "merely" is present (Gore and Taylor, 1973; Paulus and Murdoch, 1971; Sasfy and Okun, 1974). These findings suggest that in humans at least, evaluation apprehension may play an important role in social facilitation.

When Social Facilitation Fails

You may have some objections to both of the preceding explanations of social facilitation effects. Like most people, you may recollect a few masterful performances of your own that were inspired by the presence of others and many instances in which an audience had just the reverse effect. The perfectly memorized poem or the mathematical proof that sounded like nonsense when delivered in class or the flawless tennis serve that failed as others were watching—experiences like these are familiar to everyone. In fact, such effects have long been documented in social psychology (Allport, 1924; Dashiell, 1935; Pessin, 1933). How can such debilitating effects be explained by the social facilitation theories?

Arousal theorists and apprehension theorists both offer a similar answer to this question. They argue that the arousal—whether general or specific to evaluation—activates an organism's *dominant response*—that is, the response that has been learned most thoroughly. However, the most thoroughly learned response is not necessarily the best response. Thus, for the average tennis player whose serve generally is mediocre but occasionally is excellent, the dominant response is a mediocre serve. And the presence of others may be a hindrance to an average or below-average player. However, for a skilled player whose serve generally is excellent, the presence of others will be facilitating. The dominant response is the good serve. Consider the data featured in Table 12-2. They indicate, first, the accuracy with which human beings were able to find their way through a maze that is simple enough to require the use of normal (dominant) thinking skills. As you can see, the presence of others

reduces the errors made while solving the simple maze. Note, however, that the presence of others increases the errors made while solving a maze that is complex enough to require the use of higher-level thinking skills.

Both biological arousal and evaluation apprehension offer similar explanations of performance decrement, and at this point neither theory seems to be superior to the other (Geen, 1980). Certain findings favor biological theory, other findings favor apprehension theory. To appreciate this, look again at Table 12-2 and consider the behavior of cockroaches. When cockroaches, either alone or in the presence of other roaches, run either simple or complex mazes, the pattern of their performance is identical to that of humans. That is, when cockroaches run a difficult maze they perform less well in the presence of other cockroaches. This finding is consistent with Zajonc's theory of biologically based arousal. Accounting for such findings on the basis of evaluation apprehension is difficult, however—unless one argues that the roaches are worried about being judged by other roaches.

Evaluation apprehension theorists also have evidence for their arguments, however. First, many animal studies indicate that the presence of another animal is not arousing,

TABLE **12-2** **Audiences: help or hindrance?**

Note the differential effect of an audience on humans and insects. When a task is easy, an audience facilitates performance. When a task is difficult, an audience makes it harder.

Experimental condition	Human subjects: errors made while solving problems	Cockroaches: time required to run maze
Simple maze		
Alone	44.7	40.5
Others present	36.2	33.0
Complex maze		
Alone	184.9	110.5
Others present	220.3	129.5

Source: Adapted from Zajonc, 1980b

Have you ever felt shy? If you are a typical college student, chances are the answer is yes. Of a large group of students surveyed in California, 99 percent indicated that they had experienced shyness, and 42 percent of that group said that shyness was a basic part of their personality (Zimbardo, Pilkonis, and Norwood, 1974). Of those who labeled themselves as basically shy, 63 percent said that shyness posed a real problem for them. Further, surveys of the population as a whole reveal that shyness is not just a teenage problem. A similar proportion of the adult population reports the same experience (Pilkonis and Zimbardo, 1979). Men and women have not been found to differ in the intensity of the problem.

Under what conditions do people experience the most intense shyness? Being in a large group and being the focus of attention seem to create the most intense discomfort for young people, with strangers or members of the opposite sex posing particular difficulties (Zimbardo, Pilkonis, and Norwood, 1974). Groups pose equal or possibly greater difficulties for adults. One sample of three thousand adults reported that "speaking before a group" was the primary fear in life (Wallace et al., 1977). This fear outranked anxiety about sickness and death.

Shyness can produce both physical and emotional consequences. Typically the shy person experiences elevated heart rate, perspiration, and feelings of nausea (Zimbardo, 1977). Intellectual performance and memory may be impaired (Hatvany and Zimbardo, 1977; Liebling and Shaver, 1973). Laboratory studies show that shy people differ behaviorally from those who are not shy. During heterosexual interaction they speak less frequently and for a smaller percentage of the time. They allow more silences to develop, and they break fewer silences (Pilkonis, 1977a). In addition, shy people feel less comfortable about heterosexual encounters than do those who are not shy. Others see shy people as being less friendly, assertive, and relaxed.

but rather is calming (Davitz and Mason, 1955; Eckman, Meltzer, and Latané, 1969; Morrison and Hill, 1967). Studies of humans have found variations in performance that seem to depend on the *meaning* of another person's presence. Specifically, if another's presence signifies that one may be evaluated negatively, a reduction in performance often takes place. If someone's presence has no negative connotation—if the person just happens to be present but is not watching, does not

want to help, or expects to see a good performance—the performance decrements are not found (Clark and Fouts, 1973; Geen, 1977; Good, 1973). Research on social embarrassment and on forms of stage fright has produced similar findings (Borden, 1980). In one experiment, people were asked to sing "Love Is a Many Splendored Thing" in front of an audience (Garland and Brown, 1972). The extent to which the subjects engaged in various face-saving activities depended importantly

Shyness may reflect the kind of apprehension about evaluation that we discuss in this chapter. An individual may feel especially shy when he or she is apprehensive about failing in the view of others (Pilkonis, 1977b). Newcomers to groups may be especially vulnerable while other group members are making decisions about their acceptability. One fascinating line of research has looked at the behavior of persons who are newcomers to high judicial bodies, such as the Supreme Court. Although recently appointed justices have had long years of experience in public service, the courts that they served on have usually been relatively low in status. Thus, even a Supreme Court justice may experience evaluation apprehension. An assessment of members of the Washington State Supreme Court revealed that new members were significantly more likely to vote with the majority and to avoid registering a dissenting opinion than were those who were well-established (Walker, 1973). Similarly, new members of the United States Supreme Court have tended to join the strongest clique, or subgroup. Only after several years of service have they shifted to minority cliques or become independent (Snyder, 1958). Apparently, then, the evaluation apprehension that is so common to the shy person may be present also in members of the most august ruling bodies. In their conformity, the justices resemble the shy subject in a laboratory experiment (Maslach and Solomon, 1977; Souza and Silva, 1977).

Can anything be done to help persons plagued by shyness? Many psychologists believe that specialized training in social skills may be useful (Argyle, Trower, and Bryant, 1974; Pilkonis and Zimbardo, 1979). Such training often encourages the individual to try various techniques for getting along more effectively with others. Self-help techniques also have been proposed for the chronically shy (Zimbardo, 1977). People can take matters into their own hands. A person who has taken a risk several times and has spoken up finds typically that shyness begins to recede. The initial try often is the most difficult.

on the subjects' expectations of the audience's negative reaction.

Clearly, variations in the meaning of the presence of others do have important effects on deterioration in performance. Such findings are not easily explained by the biological arousal position. Thus each explanation sensitizes us to certain possibilities. Each one furnishes a different insight into how the presence of other people influences performance, and therefore each is useful.

Diffusion of Responsibility in Groups

Social facilitation effects may be offset by the diffusion of responsibility that often takes place in groups. To appreciate this argument, let us examine findings from an intriguing early study. The investigator, Ringelmann, asked young male subjects to exert as much force as possible on a rope (Dashiell, 1935). He found that a single individual could exert an average force of 63 kilograms. Thus two persons pulling together ought to exert double that, or 126 kilograms. And eight persons should produce a combined force of 504 kilograms. Further, social facilitation processes should result in a combined force that exceeds the simple sum of forces that are produced by the individuals alone.

Yet, if you will examine the data presented in the second column of Table 12-3, you will see that two people did not exert twice as much force as each had exerted alone. Their output was slightly *lower* than expected (118 kilograms). Also, individual output decreased as the size of the group increased. Eight persons exerted a force of only 256 kilograms—approximately half the expected total. As group size increased, the amount of work contributed by each person declined. Such results have been termed *social loafing*, suggesting that people do not put as much effort into a task when their contribution is submerged in

TABLE 12-3

Potential and actual productivity

Note that as group size grows, so does the discrepancy between what is actually produced and what is potentially possible. The more people working in a group, the less effort each individual contributes.

Group size	Potential productivity	Actual productivity	Process losses
1	63	63	
2	126	118	8
3	189	160	29
8	504	248	256

Source: Adapted from Dashiell, 1935

the total group output (Latané, Williams, and Harkins, 1979).

Ringelmann's results indicate that social facilitation effects can be limited by diffusion

A social dimension of religion. The support and security offered by membership in fundamentalist religious groups has attracted large numbers of young people to their ranks. Social critics see the increased interest in fundamentalist groups as a reflection of dissatisfaction with current social alternatives.

of responsibility. In discussing bystander intervention studies (Chapter 7) we talked about the effect of the group on the individual's feelings of responsibility. When people witness an emergency, their sense of responsibility may be decreased as the number of available helpers is increased. For example, in a study of chivalry in elevators, a female confederate of the investigators "accidentally" dropped a handful of pencils or coins in elevators in three large cities on fifteen hundred separate occasions (Latané and Dabbs, 1975). The number of people in the elevator varied from one to six. Approximately 40 percent of the passengers who were alone with the confederate helped her. This figure dropped to 15 percent when six passengers were present. Similarly, a study of tipping in restaurants found that individuals who dine alone leave an average tip of 19 percent. However, people dining in groups of five or six leave average tips of only 13 percent per person (Freeman et al., 1975). Apparently this reduction in the individual's feelings of personal responsibility affects group performance as well as individual positive social action.

The Group at Work: Produce or Perish

The fate of society rests in the hands of groups. Key decisions on which people's lives depend are made by cabinets, legislatures, and committees. The goods people buy, the foods they eat, and even the entertainment they enjoy—all are group products. Concern with the power that is inherent in groups has led many social psychologists to look at the question of how groups work—how they go about the process of making decisions. In this section we will consider the factors and processes that operate to reduce the effectiveness of group performance. Then we will look at various means of improving group performance.

Biases in Group Decision-Making

The quality of group performance is often undermined by various biasing agents—factors or processes that reduce people's capacities to process information in a rational manner. Let us consider three such biases.

Individual predispositions

People bring with them to any group various attitudes and opinions, and these views typically influence group decisions. In an ideal decision-making group individual predispositions would be discussed and evaluated openly. Individual members would try to understand one another's opinions, and they would try to reach some kind of balanced outcome. Often, however, this process of opinion exchange and readjustment does not occur. Individuals cling to their initial biases, distorting the final group decision.

To illustrate, James Davis and his colleagues (Davis, 1980; Davis, Bray, and Holt, 1977) have carried out extensive research on decision making in juries. In one study, more than eight hundred students were asked about their general belief in the guilt or innocence of defendants in rape trials (Davis et al., 1978). From their responses, three different types of predisposition were isolated: proprosecution, moderate, and prodefense. Then groups of students with each kind of bias were shown a videotape in which a defendant was accused of rape. The defendant admitted that the rape had taken place. However, he argued that the woman had not only consented, but had initiated the affair. The woman argued that the man had misrepresented himself as a police officer and subsequently had raped her. Witnesses on both sides gave testimony, both lawyers made summary statements, and the judge charged the jury. The students then were asked to give their opinion as to the defendant's guilt.

The students' preliminary biases had a strong effect in their evaluation of the case.

BOX 12-3

Social Psychology Faces the Jury

The jury trial is one arena for group decision-making that has attracted a considerable amount of attention from social psychologists. One important line of research on juries considered the effect of the selection of jurors on the outcome of trials. Social psychologists have actually become involved in the process of jury selection. This involvement has been possible because in the United States prospective jurors are often interviewed by both the prosecution and the defense. This procedure is supposed to prevent biased individuals from serving on a jury and thus ensure a fair trial. However, lawyers tend to look for specific prejudices and overlook the possibility that a juror may harbor certain psychological dispositions that will influence his or her reaction to the evidence. Detecting such psychological factors can allow jurors with unfavorable predispositions to be screened out. Social psychologists who study the psychological predispositions of jurors may thus be able to furnish lawyers with information that can help them win their cases.

The first demonstration of the power of social psychology in the courtroom took place in Harrisburg, Pennsylvania, in the early 1970s. The U.S. government was attempting to convict a group of activists who opposed the Vietnam War. The group, known in the press as the Harrisburg Seven, was led by Catholic priests Philip and Daniel Berrigan. They were accused of having committed crimes against the state, including theft of government records, conspiracy, and sabotage. A number of social psychologists, also political activists, assisted the defense (Schulman et al., 1973). They wanted to use their professional skills to increase the probability of acquittal. To do so, they set out to determine which groups in the Harrisburg community had the most positive attitude toward the liberal political position that was represented by the defendants. Using a public opinion survey, they were able to determine the various age, economic, religious, racial, and gender groups that would be sympathetic to the Harrisburg Seven. These criteria were then used in selecting a jury that ultimately voted ten to two for acquittal.

Does this mean that the psychologists had successfully influenced the outcome of the trial? There is no way to answer such a question directly since we cannot know how a jury chosen by another method would have voted. Yet additional information strongly suggests that the screening methods were effective. Consider, for example, the two jurors who did not vote for acquittal. One was a fifty-four-year-old Republican businessman. He was not acceptable according to the psychological analysis, but the defense lawyers had decided to include him anyway. The other was a woman who was influenced strongly by the businessman's religious convictions. If the businessman had been rejected, as was suggested by the psychologists, the jury might have voted unanimously for acquittal. In addition, the researchers showed that some 54 percent of Harrisburg residents polled during the trial thought that the defendants were guilty. In contrast, only 17 percent of the jurors believed in their guilt. As one recent reviewer has concluded, "virtually no one who has used scientific jury selection has lost a case" (Saks and Hastie, 1978, p. 62).

Spurred by such results, social psychologists have made an effort to locate general factors that might predict jurors' decisions. Among their findings are the following: Jurors who are under thirty years of age tend to be more lenient than older jurors (Sealy and Cornish, 1973). Jurors who are high in authoritarianism (see Chapter 4) are often more punitive than jurors who are low in authoritarianism (Vidmar and Crinkla, 1973). And people who believe that crime is primarily a product of "bad people" are more likely to vote to convict a defendant than are people who believe that crime is the result of social conditions (Saks, 1976). Finally, people with more education tend to be more lenient than people with less education (Simon, 1967). Other psychologists have concentrated on the effects that jury composition has on the verdict. For example, socially undesirable jurors cause other jurors to take an opposite stand (Fischoff, 1979). Thus, if you were a lawyer, selecting a socially disreputable juror who was sure to vote against your client would be fruitful.

Does this mean that social psychologists are in a position to determine the results of all jury trials? It does not. For most cases that reach a jury the evidence is so powerful that there is little likelihood of personal values influencing the conclusion (Saks and Hastie, 1978; Saks, Werner, and Ostrom, 1975). One study of several thousand cases revealed that 78 percent of the time judges and juries agreed in their verdicts (Kalven and Zeisel, 1971). In addition, most jurors try to shed their prejudices and make impartial decisions. As Michael Saks concludes, "Through learning outside of court, and by the court atmosphere, the judges' charges, and the rules of the game, jurors adopt a role of 'fairness' and 'objectivity' which may be as extreme as they ever have had or will in their lives" (1978, p. 70).

When the case is ambiguous, however, a social psychologist's participation in jury selection seems to count. Does the psychologist's activity represent a corruption of justice? This issue has been debated widely. In their own defense, social psychologists argue that all jurors have biases of some kind and that impartial judgment is impossible in principle. Lawyers add that they are charged with making the most positive case possible. Each side can and should do likewise. Considering these arguments, do you think that jury selection is a proper activity for social psychologists?

Proprosecution subjects were more likely to render a guilty verdict than were subjects whose preliminary biases favored the defense. The students then were organized into six-person juries, whose members all shared one of the three preliminary dispositions. Although the groups discussed the case for approximately thirty minutes, the discussion did little to alter individual biases. Proprosecution juries were more likely to recommend conviction than were prodefense juries. Further, in a follow-up test of the students' beliefs about the case, the same biases—either pro or con—persisted. Similar biases that stem from jurors' initial dispositions have been reported by other researchers (Berg and Vidmar, 1975; Bray and Noble, 1978; Mitchell and Byrne, 1973).

Minimally acceptable solutions: the case is closed

In addition to the detrimental effects that personal biases have on group decisions, the character of a discussion also can influence final outcomes. According to Richard Hoffman and his colleagues (Hoffman, 1979), when a group reaches a conclusion that is minimally acceptable, its members may develop a bias in favor of the solution. They will insulate themselves against criticism and will fail to consider new ideas.

The discovery of this type of bias was made during a study of how small groups solve complex problems in industrial management. Specifically, groups of students were asked to find answers to such questions as, how can a seven-person group best assemble a carburetor? While the groups were working out their answers, observers noted their proposed solutions, justifications of solutions, expression of agreement, questions, and criticisms. On the basis of these observations, Hoffman and his colleagues propose that groups follow a typical pattern when they are solving complex problems. First, ideas are put forward until a given solution meets with a minimally positive response from the more talkative group members. Once this minimal accord has been reached, a shift takes place in the quality of the group discussion. Rather than criticizing the solution or giving serious thought to new alternatives, members begin to search for a justification for the minimally acceptable solution. If new solutions are offered, members usually focus on the short-comings of the solution. Thus, if a minimally acceptable solution were offered early in the discussion, the solution might remain relatively unchallenged and undefeated for the remainder of the discussion (Hoffman and Maier, 1979). After a solution has passed a minimal threshold for adoption, other solutions tend to be overlooked (Hoffman, Friend, and Bond, 1979). Interestingly, the members who are most satisfied with the group process and most committed to the minimally acceptable solutions have the most influence in the group discussions. In demonstrating their power in the group, these members seem to become self-satisfied and convinced they are correct.

Choice shifts: risky and tame

Hoffman and his collaborators suggest that group members often fasten on to a solution and then close their minds to competing possibilities. This does not explain, however, why one decision rather than another is reached. Much research in recent years has dealt with this issue, and the work offers insight into some of the processes that produce group decisions. To appreciate what these researchers have been studying, consider the following situation: "A man with a severe heart ailment must seriously curtail his customary way of life if he does not undergo a delicate medical operation which might cure him completely or might prove fatal" (Stoner, 1961, p. 58). Given the problems of living unhappily and the prospects of death, what would you advise? Should the man have the

operation if the chances of his dying are one in ten? What if the chances are three in ten? five in ten? seven in ten? or nine in ten? As you can see, the higher the probability of fatality, the riskier the venture. Essentially you are advising on the level of acceptable risk.

In the initial research, subjects were asked first to respond privately to twelve dilemmas such as this one, and then they were asked to meet in groups to discuss the problems and reach a solution (Stoner, 1961). The groups' decisions tended to be far riskier than those made by the individuals. After group discussion the group members became less conservative and more risky than they had been when working alone. This phenomenon, termed the *risky shift*, excited instant attention. Do such results mean that decision-making groups all over the world reach far riskier decisions than any group member would reach alone? Have group processes led to the use of the atom bomb at Hiroshima, the Bay of Pigs invasion, or the Russian invasion of Afghanistan?

Subsequent research on the risky shift has shown that after a group reaches a risky decision, the individual members *remain privately committed* to this new decision (Wallach, Kogan, and Bem, 1962). Subjects stick by their group's decision for as long as two weeks. Further, participation in a group is not a prerequisite for occurrence of the risky shift. Exposing a person to a group's arguments is often enough to increase the riskiness of the person's recommendation (Lamm, 1967).

Why does this shift occur? Several possible explanations seem to be reasonable.

1. *Cultural values favor risk.* Because young people want to seem "cool," they are inclined to shift in the risky direction when they are interacting with their peers (Brown, 1965). Research suggests that this process may operate in many cases (Wallach and Wing, 1968) and that people often like those who take risky positions (Jellison and Riskind, 1970).

2. *Groups diffuse responsibility.* We have noted that people in group situations feel relatively little personal responsibility for outcomes. If people feel that they cannot be blamed for failure, they may feel free to recommend riskier decisions (Wallach, Kogan, and Bem, 1964).

3. *Groups release their members' inhibitions.* Although caution is often considered proper, it does not eliminate people's longing for the adventure of risk. Thus finding that another group member is arguing for risk may release common constraints (Higbee, 1971; Pruitt, 1971).

Continued research on this topic has shown that group decisions are not always riskier than individual decisions. Group decisions can be more cautious than the decision favored by any single individual. For example, the degree of risk may depend on the dilemmas that are confronted. Although people shift in a riskier direction in some cases, they become more conservative in other cases (Fraser, Gouge, and Billig, 1971; Lambert, 1978; Rabow et al., 1966). Researchers also have shown that when groups bet on horse races, they tend to be more cautious than individuals (Knox and Safford, 1976).

We see, then, that group discussion can move a group of individuals to make a collective decision that none of them would have endorsed before the discussion. However, the movement may be toward either greater risk or more conservatism. Group discussion *polarizes* the group (Myers and Lamm, 1976), but which extreme is polarization likely to favor? Many researchers believe that the direction will be toward that favored by the majority of members when they first enter the group (Doise, 1969; Macaulay, 1970; Zaleska, 1978). That is, if the majority slightly favors a risky decision, the group will undergo a risky shift. If the majority tends to be conservative when discussion begins, it will become even more conservative during discus-

sion. These effects take place because group members begin to think of various arguments that will demonstrate the validity of their position. With arguments increasing on one side and criticism mounting on the other, the shift toward the extreme will appear to be the only "rational" solution (Burnstein and Vinokur, 1977). In support of this position, one study found that the direction of shift can be predicted by the *number* of arguments. That is, if there are more conservative arguments brought out in the discussion, the shift will be toward the conservative position—and the same process characterizes risk (Burnstein, Vinokur, and Trope, 1973).

In summary, the outcome of group discussion can be influenced by several kinds of bias. First, people enter groups with individual biases. And not only do they fail to take account of alternative perspectives, but they push the group in the direction of their biases. Second, group members often seize upon the first decision that seems to be minimally acceptable, and thereafter they fail to give serious attention to possible alternatives. Third, discussion may cause a group to take a more extreme stand—either riskier or more conservative—than that favored privately by any member before the discussion.

Toward Improving Group Decisions

Groups do not always make worse decisions than individuals. Consider, for example, the results of an early study of group decision-making. Subjects watched the first part of a film, *Twelve Angry Men*, which depicted a deadlocked jury trying to reach a verdict in a murder case (Hall, Mouton, and Blake, 1963). Each subject predicted the film's outcome and then met in groups to discuss his or her views and again predict the film's outcome. When the two sets of predictions were compared, the group discussion proved to be superior. Apparently, by contrasting and comparing their views, the group members were able to discard inferior predictions and retain the better ones. Within the group setting members may also learn from one another or be reminded of facts they have forgotten (Doise, 1978; Laughlin and Adamopoulos, 1980). Such processes may characterize real jury proceedings. As early research demonstrated, juries compare views and develop a consensus, and usually they come up with a far more accurate picture of the event in question than does any individual juror (Dashiell, 1935). Also, jury discussion sometimes reduces individual jurors' biases (Izzett and Leginski, 1974).

Thus we have evidence that group decisions can be superior to individual decisions. The major question, then, is locating the various conditions that favor successful group decision-making. Let us consider four key factors: the task, the communications structure, the membership, and the strategy.

Selecting the task

The success or failure of a group decision may be related to the type of task or problem being solved. Groups may be superior at solving some kinds of task, while individuals may be better at other kinds. Ivan Steiner (1972) has proposed that the success, or productivity, of a group depends on the way in which individual contributions combine to form a final "product." He distinguishes among four types of task, each with different requirements:

1. *Additive tasks.* For the additive task, each member's product can be added together to yield the total group product. Collecting campaign funds, shoveling snow, or cheering for a favorite team are examples of additive tasks. The amount of funds collected or snow shoveled represents the simple sum of each individual's contribution. For most additive tasks, the more people available to work, the greater the productivity. However, decision-making groups are usually not confronted with additive tasks.

2. *Conjunctive tasks.* For conjunctive tasks, each member of a group performs roughly the same function, but each member depends on the other members. A column of marchers or a team of mountain climbers are performing a conjunctive task. All of the members perform similar activities, and all depend on one another for group success. Adding the individual member's output does not usually increase group productivity. In fact, a group engaged in a conjunctive task can be only as effective as its least proficient member (Steiner and Rajaratnam, 1961). For example, a column of marchers or a team of mountain climbers can move no faster than its slowest member. Decision-making tasks can be conjunctive when each group member must provide the group with information and the group product depends on all of the information that is submitted. Under these circumstances, the group can be only as successful as its least reliable source of information.

3. *Disjunctive tasks.* For disjunctive tasks there is no division of labor, and the group product does not depend on the summed efforts of individuals. Solving a complex problem is an example of a disjunctive task. Each member works on the solution, but the group's success is not a simple sum of the work that each member contributes. Group productivity on a disjunctive task usually depends on the proficiency of the most competent member (Marquart, 1955). If a group is working on a complex mathematical problem, for example, the presence of a single member who is proficient in mathematics would ensure group success. Two members who are both skilled may further increase the efficiency of the group (Laughlin et al., 1975; Laughlin and Adamopoulos, in press).

4. *Discretionary tasks.* For discretionary tasks, members can combine their efforts in any way they wish, and the group product depends importantly on the manner in which the efforts are coordinated. Committees, policy-making groups, and families are frequently faced with discretionary tasks. The offerings of any individual may be accepted or rejected, and the skills of various members may be combined in a variety of ways to yield a product. The success of the group does not necessarily depend on whether the group possesses an expert. Much depends on how the members' efforts are balanced and coordinated. Adding or subtracting members does not necessarily influence the group product. If the group develops effective operating procedures, success will remain constant even if there is fluctuation in the number of members.

Steiner (1972) argues that for each kind of task, productivity also depends on *process gain* and *process loss.* That is, certain benefits and costs usually result from bringing people together. Productivity is gained from the benefits, while the costs cause a loss in productivity. Thus, for example, if social facilitation effects occur and people are more energized, process gain would be achieved. However, if evaluation apprehension develops, then the group would suffer process loss. Process loss poses a special problem in the case of discretionary tasks. If people must decide how a group is to function, the effort that is devoted to the decision must be viewed as process loss. The long hours that faculty members spend participating in university committee meetings may be viewed as a form of process loss. The work must be done in order for education to take place, but the committees themselves are not engaged in education. In general, Steiner argues, *group productivity* equals *individual productivity* plus *process gain* minus *process loss.*

Selecting the communications structure

The effectiveness of a group depends not only on the task, but also on the *structure of communication*—that is, the typical pattern of communication that is adopted by the group in order to accomplish the task. Consider the communication strategies of two hypothetical football coaches. Head coaches often have several assistants: one for backs who carry the ball, another for the linemen who block for the backs, another for the ends who catch the balls thrown by the backs, and so forth. The "Bulldogs'" head coach is very independent. He collects information from each of his assistants, but then he uses the information in making the major decisions by himself. The "Panthers'" head coach believes in staff meetings. Major decisions are made during discussions among the entire coaching staff. The two head coaches differ in the structure of communication they employ. The Bulldogs' communication is a one-way process, primarily directed toward the head coach, with little significant communication taking place among the assistants. The Panthers' communication, however, can travel from one assistant coach to another and to the head coach. Which kind of structure is more likely to meet with success?

Research on communications structures began more than twenty-five years ago. In one classic study, experimental subjects were placed randomly in individual cubicles from which they could communicate only by written note (Leavitt, 1951). Restrictions also were placed on the participants to whom the communications could be sent. Thus, in some groups one member could communicate with each of the other members, but the others could communicate only with the one member. (See the wheel pattern in Figure 12-2.) The Bulldogs' coaching staff has this type of structure. Other patterns are shown in Figure 12-2. The circular structure of communication resembles that used by the Panthers'

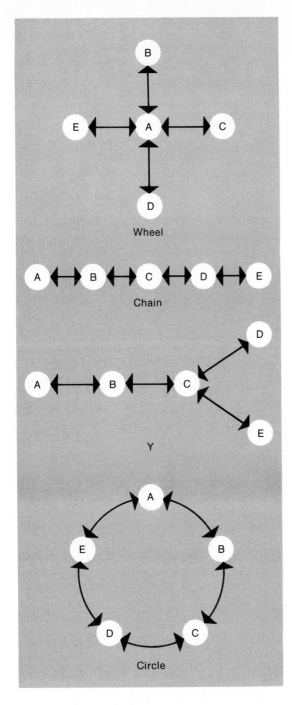

Wheel

Chain

Y

Circle

FIGURE **12-2**

Types of communications structures

Note that the wheel is the most centralized pattern and that the circle is the least centralized. Often a more centralized structure enables groups to solve problems effectively, but with a cost in morale. (Adapted from Leavitt, 1951)

and the Y) are moderate in their degree of centralization.

How do the various types of groups compare in their productivity? For many simple tasks, groups with centralized communications structures perform better than groups with other structures (Leavitt, 1951; Morrisetti, 1966; Mulder, 1963). The central individual is in a position to piece together the information that is furnished by the peripheral members, and a correct decision can be reached with dispatch. This structure is particularly useful when the number of people in the centralized structure is great, since the problems in sharing information become immense (Mulder, 1963). However, as tasks become increasingly complex, a centralized structure may be less useful. If the task is highly complex, a single individual may be overwhelmed with information and by the responsibilities of the position. Details that might be worked out on the lower levels may never receive attention. On complex tasks, then, the decentralized group often performs better than do groups with other structures (Shaw and Blum, 1965).

However, Steiner's concepts of process gain and loss are relevant in considering communications structures. Group members' satisfaction varies with the type of structure. Members in centralized structures generally experience a lower degree of satisfaction than do members in decentralized structures (Shaw, 1955; Collins and Raven, 1968; Harshberger, 1971). This finding is consistent with results of early studies of democratic versus autocratic forms of governance (Lippitt and

coaching staff. These two structures differ in their *degree of centralization:* the wheel is highly centralized; the circle is decentralized. The two additional structures (the chain

White, 1943). Many people show more signs of interest, motivation to work, and general satisfaction when they can discuss group policies with each other than when a single individual has all the decision-making power. To the extent that centralization of decision making reduces satisfaction, process loss is generated. Ultimately this process loss should lower a group's effectiveness. In the case of the Bulldogs' coaching staff, for example, the centralization may enable the team to win temporarily. However, if the assistant coaches become increasingly dissatisfied with their jobs, they may be less motivated to do well and eventually may move to other jobs.

Ultimately the maximum advantage would seem to result from flexible communications structures. Groups confront a variety of tasks that differ in many ways over time (Glanzer and Glaser, 1961). The efficiency of the group may depend on its adaptability. For football coaches, a decentralized structure may be useful in deciding overall strategy before a game. The complexity of the task and the available time lend themselves to such communication. During a game, however, when immediate decisions must be made a centralized structure probably would be superior. Group decisions would only yield confusion. Thus an effective group must remain flexible in its communications structure and change the structure as the demands of the situation are altered (Faucheux and Moscovici, 1967; Roby, 1968).

Selecting the membership

The effectiveness of a group also depends on its selection of members. In government, business, athletics, and many other enterprises, people are selected on the basis of their contribution to the group's success. Many researchers believe that membership selection is the single most powerful point of leverage in group effectiveness (Hackman and Morris, 1975). The group leader is probably the single most important member to be selected. In Chapter 9 we discussed the way in which various leadership styles influence group productivity and morale. Now we will consider the selection of the ordinary group member. The process of selecting members on the basis of clearly required skills, such as shooting baskets or solving computer problems, raises few interesting problems for the social psychologist. More challenging is the search for the subtle characteristics of group members that can aid or impede the group's progress. Let us consider one of these searches.

Anyone who works closely with groups soon becomes aware that group performance often depends on the particular styles of interaction that people bring to the group. A skillful athletic team may fail dismally if its star is totally self-centered and attacks other teammates for their inferior play. A decision-making group can waste countless hours if a single member is aggressive. In effect, such persons contribute to process loss. Group researcher R. F. Bales (1950, 1970; Bales and Cohen, 1979) believes that people can be classified according to their particular styles of relating to others and that knowing what styles various group members possess can tell one a great deal about the outcomes of their interaction.

Bales's classification system emerges from long experience with discussion groups. As Bales reasons, certain actions occur in discussion groups with relative frequency, and these actions can be recorded by trained observers (Couch, 1960). Based on the number of times a person engages in each of these actions, one can characterize his or her preferred style of relating to others. The forms of action are as follows:

1. Seems Friendly	7. Asks for Information
2. Dramatizes	8. Asks for Opinion
3. Agrees	9. Asks for Suggestions
4. Gives Suggestions	10. Disagrees
5. Gives Opinion	11. Shows Tension
6. Gives Information	12. Seems Unfriendly

(Bales and Cohen, 1979, p. 96)

Bales suggests that people's personality styles vary on three central dimensions:

1. *Upward versus downward.* People vary in their activity level within a group. Some people will be active, outgoing, and opinionated, while others will be shy or retiring. A group member who frequently gives information to others, dramatizes the situation, or gives suggestions would fall on the upward end of the dimension. Someone who asks for opinions and information would be at the downward end.

2. *Positive versus negative.* People also differ in their friendliness and sociability. Some are friendly, while others seem to be cold and isolated. A person who frequently shows unfriendliness or disagreement or asks for other people's opinions would be placed toward the negative end of the dimension. Someone who agrees and seems friendly would be at the positive end.

3. *Forward versus backward.* Some people seem to take their group participation seriously and are interested in working toward group goals. Others seem to reject group goals and are more interested in themselves. People whose concerns are with group productivity are placed on the forward end of the dimension. Such people would give opinions, frequently ask for suggestions, or show tension.

Bales argues that full appreciation of personal style requires ratings on all three dimensions. Thus the person who is upward, positive, and forward is one who takes a great deal of initiative, is friendly, and is interested in group goals. He or she might be an ideal member of many decision-making groups. In contrast, a person who is downward, negative, and backward is one who is inactive, unfriendly, and antagonistic to group goals. Usually such a person would create problems in a group.

Should a group that desires high productivity select only upward, positive, forward members? Not necessarily. It is important, argues Bales, to take into account the task to be accomplished. For example, if faced with an additive task, in which each member's activity lends itself to group achievement, then a full complement of upward, positive, forward members might be desirable. However, in discretionary tasks, where the group must reach complex decisions about how it should function, having some members who are less upward would be an advantage. Active, striving members often clash (Bales and Cohen, 1979). Not everyone can talk at once. And to avoid the phenomenon of groupthink, someone who is less positive and who will challenge the group is needed. Thus the membership style needed for group success depends on the task to be confronted.

Selecting the strategy

The effectiveness of a group also depends on the way in which decisions are reached. Investigators have found that most groups share a norm that inhibits discussion about the decision-making process itself (Hackman and Morris, 1975; Shure et al., 1962; Weick, 1969). Perhaps this reluctance explains one investigator's finding that logically connected arguments in 124 discussion groups lasted an average of fifty-eight seconds (Berg, 1967). Group members generally interjected into the discussion comments that were only remotely relevant to the question being considered. Can discussion about decision-making strategies aid a group? In one exploration of this issue, investigators analyzed transcripts of one hundred separate discussion groups that were working on a wide variety of tasks (Hackman and Morris, 1975). They were particularly interested in the relationship between the attention that was directed to strategies of decision making and the creativeness of the group product (as judged independently). The results of this assessment are shown in Figure 12-3. You can see that the greater the number of statements of strategy, the higher the group's creativity.

Are certain strategies more likely to pay off than others? Irving Janis and Leon Mann (1977) believe that the answer is yes. Based on their extensive analysis of group problem-solving, Janis and Mann recommend the following strategies for effective problem solving in groups:

1. *Challenge time-worn decisions.* If a group has been in existence for a long time, its decision-making habits and the kinds of decisions it typically makes should be questioned.

2. *Develop a balance sheet.* When a complex decision is at stake, a group should develop lists of positive and negative factors before making a final decision. This task should be carried out impartially. The list should not be developed with the aim of proving whether a decision is good or bad. The group should try simply to generate as many ideas, pro and con, as possible.

3. *Role play the decision outcome.* Once a group decision seems to be reasonable, the group should think through the consequences. Group members should imagine themselves acting on the basis of the decision.

4. *Obtain decision counseling.* Particularly when a group has a history of poor decision-making or finds the process difficult, an outside counselor may be called in. This counselor might observe the group impartially and furnish new insights.

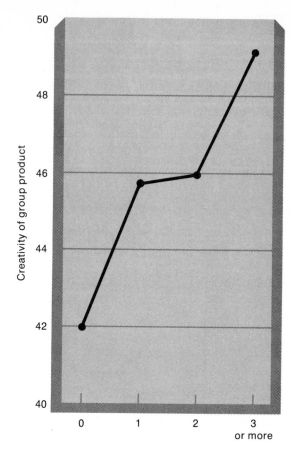

Number of strategy comments made during the first third of the work period

FIGURE 12-3

Planning can improve group effectiveness

When group members plan strategy—when they explicitly discuss the way in which they will go about working on a task—the group's performance improves. Note that as the number of comments increases, so does creativity. (Adapted from Hackman and Morris, 1975)

1   Groups may be defined as consisting of two or more people who interact on a face-to-face basis, who perceive themselves as forming a unit that endures across time and space, and who share at least one common goal.

2 Cohesiveness refers to the degree to which group members are attracted to each other and to the group as a whole. Cohesiveness may be impeded by the tendency of group members to form hierarchies and subgroups, or cliques. Subgroups may be detected by the use of the sociogram. Cohesiveness may be increased by group success, by threats from outside the group, and by competition with other groups. Cohesive work groups display higher levels of morale, job satisfaction, self-confidence, and commitment to the job. Highly cohesive groups may be especially vulnerable to groupthink, the tendency to search for high levels of agreement while sacrificing realistic appraisals of alternatives.

3 Group membership often limits individual freedom because groups may require their members to obey rules that guarantee other members' satisfaction. Groups also develop and protect a sense of social reality, and they require obedience to rules that are set up to enable the group to reach its goals. Highly cohesive groups may be especially punitive toward the deviant. Social impact theory suggests that a group's success in reducing tendencies to deviate will depend on the number of group members, the power or attractiveness of the group, and the geographical and temporal closeness of the group members.

4 When an individual's level of performance increases as a result of the presence of a group, the improvement is called the social facilitation effect. Social facilitation may have both biological and social origins. The effect may not occur if others are present, if tasks are difficult, or if responsibility for the group product is diffused.

5 Group performance may be affected by a variety of factors. Group decisions may be biased by members' personal predispositions, by the group's tendency to fasten on minimally acceptable solutions, and by their tendency to develop more polarized decisions. To improve the quality of group performance, tasks that are suited to the group should be selected, communications systems should be used as needed, members who are appropriate for the task should be chosen, and specialized strategies for improving group decisions should be employed.

SUGGESTED READINGS

Davis, J. H. *Group performance.* Reading, Mass.: Addison-Wesley, 1969.

Doise, W. (Douglas Graham, trans.) *Groups and individuals: Explanations in social psychology.* Cambridge, England: Cambridge University Press, 1978.

Lakin, M. *Interpersonal encounter: Theory and practice in sensitivity training.* New York: McGraw-Hill, 1972.

Shaw, M. E. *Group dynamics: The psychology of small group behavior* (2nd ed.). New York: McGraw-Hill, 1975.

Wheeler, D. D., & Janis, I. L. *A practical guide for making decisions.* New York: Free Press, 1980.

13:

THE PHYSICAL AND SOCIAL ENVIRONMENT

■ *The supersonic transport plane has become a commercial possibility in the past decade. The plane can be built (witness the Concorde); but if it is flown over land, everything below its path will be exposed to a supersonic boom as the aircraft breaks the sound barrier. Will people tolerate this intrusion into their lives? Will they accept the sonic boom as they accept traffic noise, or will they reject the boom as being intolerable?*

■ *A community health center that offers low-cost medical care to the poor was built recently in a ghetto section of a major city. Excellent services were made available at considerable cost to the state. Unfortunately, few persons make use of the center, and the investment seems to have been wasted. Why don't people use the center? Can anything be done to remedy this wasteful situation? Should other cities cancel plans to build similar centers?*

■ *The rate of oil consumption in the United States is now a matter of grave concern. Not only are the world's oil deposits being depleted rapidly, but inflation is getting worse as the price of foreign oil increases. Reducing oil consumption requires that individual citizens rely less on the automobile, increase their use of mass transportation, and lower the temperature in their homes. How can such personal decisions be encouraged? What can be done to both raise public awareness of the energy crisis and increase voluntary reduction in energy use?*

These examples are typical of problems that occur in our society every day. Many social psychologists believe that members of their discipline should devote themselves to solving such problems. Kurt Lewin (1951) argued that social psychologists should take an active interest in society's problems and strive to use the discipline for social betterment. As we mentioned in Chapter 1, during the Second World War many social psychologists devoted their research efforts to aiding the nation. Lewin, for example, developed techniques for convincing housewives to change their food-buying habits so that national resources could be used more effectively. Other psychologists helped to select and train undercover agents, searched for ways to reduce battle fatigue, and developed means for increasing morale among members of the armed forces. A concern with social problems was revived in the United States during the 1960s. Protests against the nation's oppression of its black citizens and opposition to the Vietnam War were at a peak, prompting social scientists to think more carefully about the possible fate of American society. Psychologists began to ask whether their work might change the culture in significant ways. This committtment to helping solve practical problems has continued to the present day.

Yet most of the work described in this volume does not attempt to solve specific social problems. Most social psychological theory and research is highly abstract. Of major concern are the factors *in general* that influence people's attitudes and behavior, rather than the specific problems that people encounter in unique situations. For example, the general notion that reward influences social behavior provides no insight into what is rewarding in any specific situation or how influential the reward will be compared with all competing influences. At this point you might ask why psychologists bother with ab-

stract statements if these statements don't offer concrete solutions to practical problems. The answer is that in order to solve a practical problem one must know where to look for solutions. Abstract theories suggest important factors or processes that the problem-solver should consider in working out the solution.

To illustrate, a researcher who is interested in how people would react to the supersonic boom has much to learn from general theory. Theoretical work on social comparison (Chapter 10) suggests that reactions to the boom might depend not only on the loudness of the sound, but also on how people perceive others reacting. If they see their friends responding negatively, the sound may seem to be irritating to them as well. This is not to say that social comparison would definitely have an effect on people's reaction to the boom. However, the theoretical work (along with its empirical illustrations) does point to important possibilities for the prob-lem-solver to consider. This example illustrates the *sensitizing* function of theory, discussed in Chapter 1. As Kurt Lewin said, "There is nothing so practical as a good theory."

In this chapter we will look at social psychological research in practical settings. We first will focus on the relationship between human beings and their physical surroundings. As sensitivity to environmental problems has increased, social psychologists have become particularly interested in how human relations are influenced by the physical environment. We will turn to the social environment, looking at the effect that people have on one another. In particular, we will consider the effects of stress, crowding, and family size. Understanding the effects of the physical and the social environment on contemporary life does not take us far enough, however. If social change is to take place, then planning and measuring change are necessary, and social psychology can aid in this undertaking. We therefore will pay particular attention to research that measures the continuing change in the quality of people's lives and to research that evaluates the impact of programs of social change.

The Physical Environment for Good or Ill

Stop reading for a moment and look around. Look at the colors that surround you, the shapes of the furniture, or the view from your window. Listen to the sounds, perhaps the voices of your friends, the traffic noise, or music from your radio. Try to feel the temperature and the moisture in the air, sense whatever smells reach your nose, and touch the furniture, the walls, and the floor. How do these various inputs from the environment make you feel? Do your surroundings help you to feel comfortable, secure, happy, and alive? Or do they seem to be depressing, cold, sterile, or distracting? These questions are important for human well-being. Often people take their surroundings for granted. Yet most of what people see, hear, feel, and smell has been created by human hands and can be altered or removed. Social psychologists have been deeply interested in the physical environment because environmental influences on feelings and thoughts carry over to social relationships as well (Cone and Hayes, 1977). For example, as we saw in our discussion of aggression (Chapter 8), the amount of heat in the environment can have an impact on aggressive behavior. We cannot discuss the full range of environmental concerns that interest social psychologists. However, an understanding of the importance of environmental effects and the way social psychologists go about studying them can be gained by concentrating on three separate issues: the effects of architectural design, the influence of environmental sound, and techniques for forming optimal relationships between people and their environments.

Architecture and Human Relations: Public and Private Space

A student came to the counseling center at our college in a state of great distress. He felt that he was on the verge of emotional collapse. He had watched anxiously as both his brother and sister entered mental institutions, and he was afraid that his time had come. A recurrent theme, as he tried to understand his emotional state, was the family home, which was an architectural gem that had been featured in many leading magazines. The student attributed his difficulties and those of his brother and sister to their home. The house had been designed so that the children's activities could be monitored constantly. The children had no private spaces, no place where they could be out of earshot or away from their parents' watchful eyes.

The relationship between the problems of the children and the design of the house must remain a matter of conjecture. However, the question of how architecture affects people's lives has increasingly demanded the attention of social psychologists, architects, and city planners (Golledge, 1977; Korte, 1978; Parsons, 1976; Wohlwill, 1976). City-dwellers have begun to complain about the problems that are created by the "renewal" of their neighborhoods. Housing projects that were designed for better living have become battlefields for teenagers. Critics speak of the sterility of suburban housing developments. Clearly, architects cannot assume that economics, engineering, and aesthetics are the only issues that must be considered in the designing of new housing. When creating human living space, the architect also designs human relations.

Let us consider an early study of the impact of housing on people (Yancey, 1972). The

Pruitt-Igoe housing project, built in 1954, consisted of more than forty eleven-story buildings and contained almost three thousand dwelling units. Most of the residents were black; many were living on some form of public assistance. The project originally was praised by *Architectural Forum* for its unique design and the absence of wasted space between apartments. But what was the impact of the housing project on its residents' lives? Consider one visitor's description:

Walking into the project, one is struck by the mosaic of glass that covers what were grassy areas and playgrounds. The barren dirt, or mud when it rains, is constantly tracked into the apartments. Windows, particularly those on the lower floors, are broken out. Many of them are covered with plywood. Streets and parking lots are littered with trash, bottles, and tin cans. Derelict cars provide an attractive source of entertainment for children. Fences around "tot-lots" are torn; swings, sliding boards, and merry-go-rounds are noticeably unpainted, rusted, and broken.

Within the buildings themselves, the neglect is more apparent . . . one is struck with the stale air and the stench of urine, trash, and garbage on the floors. . . . Open garbage is often found on the floor next to the incinerator. The laundry rooms, located off the gallery, are sometimes used as lavatories. . . . Residents of Pruitt-Igoe continually expressed concern with being assaulted, beaten, or raped. We were frequently warned of such dangers and were told never to enter buildings alone and to stay out of the elevators, especially after dark. We were told stories of people being cut by bottles thrown from the buildings and were warned

The death of Pruitt-Igoe. In less than twenty years this housing project was so badly vandalized by its tenants that it had to be torn down. Social scientists, exploring the question of why, have uncovered facts about the importance of a sense of community in maintaining the quality of life in multifamily dwellings. Such findings have led to changes in the planning and design of housing projects.

never to stand immediately outside of a building. (Yancey, 1972, p. 130)

Why had the expensive and well-intentioned complex become virtually uninhabitable? As Yancey (1972) and others believed, the culprit was the design of the complex. Many of the social problems that were experienced by residents of the project could be traced to the lack of semipublic space or facilities around which informal networks of friends or acquaintances might have developed. The absence of common terraces, porches, recreation rooms, and lobbies made informal socializing impossible. The structure's design prevented the development of a sense of community, which could have mo-

tivated the residents to cooperate for the common good. As one woman described her neighbors in the project:

> They are selfish, I've got no friends here. There's none of this door-to-door coffee business of being friends here or anything like that. Down here if you are sick you just go to the hospital. There are no friends to help you. I don't think my neighbors would help me and I wouldn't ask them anyway. I don't have trouble with my neighbors because I never visit them. The rule of the game down here is go for yourself. (quoted in Yancey, 1972, p. 132)

The importance of a sense of community is supported in other research as well. For example, slum residents in the West End neighborhood of Boston were found to be far more positive about the neighborhood if they had close friends or kin who also resided there than if they were relatively isolated (Fried and Gleicher, 1972). Measures of neighborhood satisfaction also are found to be correlated with the number of friends residing nearby (Michelson, 1970; Zehner, 1972). The architectural features of Pruitt-Igoe simply did not facilitate the development of close relationships. Would another design have been more successful? A study of housing developments in Baltimore indicates that common space and facilities may lead to an increasing amount of neighboring, visiting, and mutual helping among residents (Winer et al., 1962).

While the need for community space that encourages informal meeting is clear, all living spaces need not maximize social interchange. Recall the emotionally disturbed student whose home offered no privacy. The young man believed that lack of privacy was the cause of his and his brother's and sister's deep psychological damage. Perhaps people need structures that *simultaneously encourage social relations and allow privacy.*

In a demonstration of this possibility, researchers studied the behavior of patients living in hospital psychiatric wards (Ittelson, Proshansky, and Rivlin, 1970). If you were designing a psychiatric hospital, how many patients would you assign to a room? Argu-

ments can be made for multipatient rooms and for relative privacy. Multiple-occupancy bedrooms may enable patients to learn to live with others and might counteract the patients' tendency to slip into depression. In contrast, people often require privacy and need to feel unobserved and in control of their surroundings.

To answer the question of optimum room size, the investigators observed the activities of patients in rooms of various sizes. Particular attention was paid to the difference between smaller rooms (with three or less patients) and larger rooms (with four or more patients). Observers circulated throughout the ward at thirty-six specified intervals and made note of where each patient was and what he or she was doing. Was behavior *social* (talking with others, playing games, and so forth), *isolated but active* (reading, arts and crafts, personal hygiene, and so forth), or *isolated and passive* (lying in bed awake or asleep, sitting alone, staring into space, and so forth)? Once behavioral observations had been collected, the relationship between the number of patients in a bedroom and the activities that took place in the bedroom could be determined. Socializing was thought to be the most therapeutic behavior, and isolated passive activities were the least favorable. As you can see in Table 13-1, patients in the small rooms were more likely than those in

TABLE **13-1**   **Three is company; four can be a crowd**

The fewer roommates a mental patient has, the more sociable he or she is likely to be. Sharing space with many roommates seems to encourage passive and isolated behavior.

Number of patients per bedroom	Percentage of time devoted to each behavior		
	Social	Active	Isolated/passive
1–3	17	25	56
4–12	9	19	71

Source: Adapted from Ittelson, Proshansky, and Rivlin, 1970

more populated rooms to be involved in active social interchange. The percentage of patients who were isolated but active also was higher among those in small bedrooms rather than in large bedrooms. In contrast, more patients in the large bedrooms than in the small ones were lying in bed asleep, passively staring into space, and so forth. The study suggests that for psychiatric hospitals, rooms with few patients are preferable to multipatient rooms.

What about the space inhabited by college students? How does the typical dormitory room in a modern university affect the quality of a student's life? Many students live in dormitories in which the rooms open onto

One room, many interpretations. This chapter has discussed a number of ways in which the physical environment can have an impact on its inhabitants. But what about the opposite possibility? What kind of impact do people have on their environment? To explore this question, photographer Barbara Pfeffer visited a series of apartments with identical floor plans. As you can see, the tenants created widely different environments for themselves.

long corridors. Figure 13-1 presents a diagram of a corridor at the State University of New York at Stony Brook. This design is duplicated roughly at many universities throughout the country. Other dormitory designs provide students with suites in which rooms adjoin a common space. And, of course, many students live in houses, private rooms in the

community, or at home. Do these various facilities make a difference in a student's sense of well-being?

Research carried out by Baum and Valins (1977) suggests that design features may have far-reaching consequences for a student's life. The study first compared students' comments on the quality of life on long corridors versus

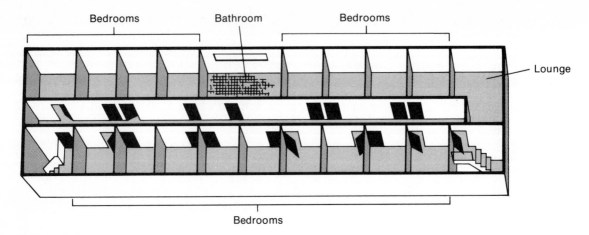

Bedrooms   Bathroom   Bedrooms

Lounge

Bedrooms

FIGURE **13-1**   **The stress of dormitory life**

This plan represents the dormitory wing studied by Baum and Valins. The corridors were found to produce greater sociability than suites, but much of it was unwanted. Students characterized this kind of living space as being crowded, unpredictable, and uncontrollable. (From Baum and Valins, 1977)

that in suites or on short corridors. The researchers found that although corridor life is highly sociable, much of the sociability is unwanted. Students find that they are visited at any time of the day or night, often by people they don't particularly care to see and often when they are busy. As a result, they see their living spaces as being more crowded, unpredictable, and uncontrollable than do students in suites or on short corridors.

At the end of their freshman year, students who lived in the different environments were compared in a laboratory study that assessed their attitudes and actions toward other people. The question was whether the presence or absence of privacy would affect their lives outside the dormitory. To explore this issue, groups of randomly selected students who lived on long corridors, on short corridors, and in suites were asked to wait *alone* or *with a second person* (a confederate of the experimenters) for the experiment to begin. While waiting, each subject was observed through an unobtrusive mirror. The students did not differ in behavior while waiting alone. But in the presence of the confederate, the long-corridor students were unsociable. They sat further from the confederate than did the short-corridor and suite students. They also initiated fewer verbal interchanges with the confederate and gazed in his direction for a briefer duration. The long-corridor students later reported that they felt significantly more stress and significantly more negative feelings toward the confederate while they were waiting than did the short-corridor and suite students. Life outside the dormitory seemed to have been influenced strongly by life inside the dormitory.

In summary, we see that the design of living spaces may have important consequences for social relationships. In high-rise apartment buildings, for example, spaces that invite interaction may foster a useful sense of community. However, private space also seems to be essential for optimal feelings of well-being. Studies of mental institutions and college dormitories indicate that spaces that expose people to large amounts of public contact can create feelings of discomfort.

Environmental Noise: Does It Matter?

If you ever have been in Paris, you know the kind of traffic sounds that can be heard through any window there. Parisian drivers are noted for their expressiveness; they use their automobile horns to communicate their feelings. Motorcycles also are popular, and occasionally the clatter of hoofs signals the passing of mounted police. Among the traffic sounds, one can hear the heated voices of angry lovers, the shouting of schoolchildren, and sometimes the chanting of striking mobs. The visitor endures, occasionally feeling amused, and sometimes, when it becomes still, may feel uneasy. What are the effects of exposure to such noise? Does the noise disturb people's sleep, interrupt their work, or affect their relationships with one another? Should noise be considered a pollutant, as much a hazard as air pollution or street crime?

Before exploring these questions let us first consider what loudness is and what physical effects it can produce. The loudness of a sound is related to the *amplitude*, or volume, of sound waves, which typically is represented by a decibel (db) scale. High decibel levels can create extreme discomfort and also can result in permanent hearing loss. Even two hours of exposure to a rock group playing at 110 db can produce a serious impairment in auditory acuity (Lebo and Oliphant, 1968). Of course, most people rarely are exposed to sounds that literally are deafening. The important question thus is whether sounds of lesser intensity may have other kinds of detrimental effects.

Various field studies suggest that unwanted sound may be a treacherous intruder. Frequent exposure to noise often is correlated with reports of chronic illness (Cameron, Robertson, and Zaks, 1972), increased need for physicians' services (Grandjean et al., 1973), and a higher than usual rate of heart disease, allergies, sore throats, and digestive disorders (Cohen, 1973; Jansen, 1973). Infants born to mothers who were exposed to aircraft noise suffer a higher infant mortality rate than do those whose mothers were not exposed to such noise (Ando and Hattori, 1973). Exposure to high-intensity noise in industry has been found to be associated with the presence of headaches, nausea, instability, argumentativeness, anxiety, and sexual impotence (Cohen, Glass, and Phillips, 1977; Miller, 1974). Research in the area near London's Heathrow Airport shows that psychiatric-hospital admission rates are higher for more noisy as opposed to less noisy areas (Herridge, 1974; Herridge and Low-Beer, 1973). Researchers have entered schools and homes to examine the effects of noise on children's studies and on their cognitive abilities (Heft, 1979). Children who live on lower floors of apartment buildings—the floors close to high-density traffic—have been found to suffer more hearing problems and have poorer reading skills than children who live on the upper floors of the same building

BOX
13-1

**Black Rooms:
Breaking the
Barriers of
Light**

Would you believe that spending less than one hour in a particular environment could cause you to change patterns of social behavior that you had held for many years? Before you reject that possibility, put yourself in the place of a subject in one of our studies.

You are intrigued by a sign that asks for volunteers to participate in a research project in environmental psychology. You decide to volunteer. You travel to a nearby college and are taken to a small cubicle and asked to complete several rather uninteresting questionnaires. You then are given the following account of what is to come and what will be expected of you: You will be taken to a room that is completely dark. You will be expected to remain in the room with some other people for about an hour. There is nothing special that you must do; the researchers simply are interested in people's reactions to various kinds of environments. You will *never* see or have an opportunity to meet the other participants in the study. Each of you will enter and leave the room individually, and you will be sent home at different intervals.

After this briefing your shoes are removed, your valuables are locked away, and you are led to the room that is completely dark. You hear voices and soon find that more than a half-dozen men and women are present. How will you behave in this unusual environment?

Along with a colleague we set up this situation for some fifty people, ranging in age from seventeen to twenty-two years (Gergen, Gergen, and Barton, 1973). We wanted to know whether common norms of intimacy would prevail in a situation in which people could not be held accountable for their behavior. We used tape recordings, subjects' descriptions, and questionnaires administered after the session to find out what happened in the black room. The findings proved to be interesting. For each group that entered the room, explorations of the space and lively chatter dominated the first quarter of the hour, but soon discussion turned to matters that group members later indicated were "extremely important" to

(Cohen, Glass, and Singer, 1973). Further, when the reading skills of children whose classrooms are adjacent to elevated railroad tracks are compared with the skills of children on the quiet side of the same building, the children on the quiet side demonstrate superior skills (Crook and Langdon, 1974).

Although the implications of such research are alarming, the entire blame should not necessarily be placed on noise levels. All of this research is correlational and does not allow us to rule out other possible factors. For

example, industrial workers who choose to work in high-intensity noise areas may be different kinds of people from those workers who do not choose such environments. The worker who chooses to work with a jackhammer may be already more vulnerable to physical and psychological difficulties than the worker who chooses to wire electronic computers. Differences in the noise to which they later are exposed may not be the cause of their problems. Similarly, children who live on lower floors of apartment buildings may

them. After approximately forty minutes, conversation began to fade, and members of the group began to engage in physical interaction. Some 90 percent of the participants indicated that they touched each other on purpose. Almost 50 percent engaged in hugging, and only 20 percent tried to prevent another person from touching them. The touching was far more than casual gesturing. Some 80 percent of the subjects indicated that they were aroused sexually. The following description was written by one of the male participants:

> As I was sitting, Beth came up and we started to play touchy face and touchy body and started to neck. We expressed it as showing "love" to each other. Shortly before I was taken out, we decided to pass our love on, to share it with other people. So we split up and Laurie took her place. We had just started touchy face and touchy body and kissed a few times before I was tapped to leave.

In contrast, control subjects who were participating in the same experiment but with the lights on behaved "normally." They sedately sat at a distance of several feet from one another and talked politely for the full hour.

Why did intimacy develop so rapidly in the dark room? It is difficult to be certain, but undoubtedly the environment, which ensured a degree of anonymity, contributed strongly to the breakdown of formality. Paradoxically, freedom from social responsibility led the subjects to pleasureful sharing and to caring experiences. The dark-room subjects were much more involved with one another than were those who could see. The experience of deindividuation (discussed in Chapter 8) need not produce aggression. If proper circumstances are arranged, deindividuation can be liberating (Johnson and Downing, 1979). It is interesting to consider whether our daily norms inhibit people from relating to one another as they might truly wish.

have parents who place less value on education than do those parents who live in the more expensive apartments on upper floors. To overcome some of these difficulties, investigators have arranged laboratory experiments that enable them to trace more precisely the effects of noise. Let us consider some of this work.

Because of the obvious implications of noise on work performance, much laboratory research has explored the effects of noise on the ability to carry out various tasks. Early research on this issue indicated that as long as noise remains under 110 db, people can work undisturbed on simple motor or mental tasks (Kryter, 1970). However, interest in the effect of noise on performance was heightened when David Glass and Jerome Singer (1972) published their work on the aftereffects of noise. Is it possible, they asked, that the detrimental effects of noise do not occur while the noise is present, but afterward? After all, during a noisy period people can defend themselves against effects of the noise by concentrating a little more carefully and by trying to be a little more patient than usual. Glass and Singer reasoned that these defenses require an expenditure of effort and that the stress may take its toll in the period following the noise.

In one demonstration of this point, Glass and Singer asked subjects to work on various cognitive tasks while exposing them to twenty-three bursts of loud (100 db) or softer (56 db) noise. Following the noise condition, subjects were given a drawing task to perform in a quiet room. Portions of this task were unsolvable, and the researchers wanted to know how fast subjects would give up. The more rapidly they gave up, it was reasoned, the less their *tolerance for frustration*. The subjects also were given a proofreading task. Here, the greater the number of errors they found in the copy, the higher the *quality of their performance*. In Figure 13-2 you can see that the subjects who heard soft sounds in the initial session later performed more effectively than did those who heard loud sounds: they gave up less easily on the drawing task and found more errors on the proofreading task.

Further research on noise has concentrated on the effects of predictability. As Glass and Singer (1972) reasoned, unpredictable noise may be particularly stressful because it *cannot be controlled* by the individual. As we noted in our discussion of power (Chapter 9), when people feel helpless about their condition, they may become depressed and listless. To demonstrate the helplessness effect, investigators exposed subjects to noise and varied the extent to which the subjects believed that they had control over the onset and termination of the noise. When people believed that they could control the noise, their later performance deteriorated little. When they didn't believe that they could control the noise, their later performance declined (Sherrod et al., 1977). Even being able

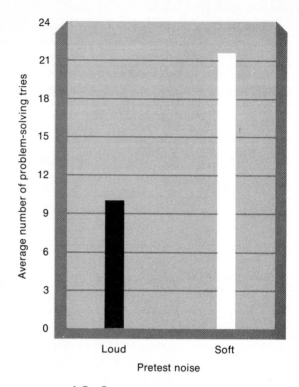

FIGURE 13-2   **The aftermath of noise**

Note the discrepancy in effort between subjects who were exposed to loud noise before they started the problem-solving task and subjects who were exposed to a lower-volume noise. (Adapted from Glass and Singer, 1972)

to drown out bothersome noise may produce a valuable feeling of security. Thus in a noisy dormitory a record player may increase one's success in studying rather than serve as a distraction.

What is the effect of noise on relationships with other people? Does the discomfort go beyond interrupting task performance and have a negative effect on social life? Research suggests that it does (Bell, Fisher, and Loomis, 1978). For example, noise can affect aggression. In one study of this issue, investigators exposed students to either 55-db or 95-db bursts of noise while the students were delivering electric shocks to a confederate of the experimenters (Donnerstein and Wilson, 1976). Subjects who were exposed to high-intensity noise delivered more shock to the confederate than did subjects who were exposed to low-intensity noise. The investigators then explored the effect of uncontrollable noise on aggressive behavior. Half of the subjects were told that they could control the 95-db noise, and the other subjects were told that they could not control it. The subjects who felt that they had control over the noise used lower levels of shock on the confederate than did subjects who felt that they had no control.

Noise also can reduce positive social behavior. Because attention is constricted by environmental noise, people may not notice that help is needed, or they may have no psychological resources at their disposal (Cohen, 1978). In an interesting demonstration of this possibility, investigators varied environmental noise levels as a confederate, armed with a large load of books, got out of a car that was parked by a busy sidewalk and then dropped the books (Mathews and Canon, 1975). Noise was varied by having a second confederate in a nearby yard turn on a power lawnmower that didn't have a muffler. In the low-noise condition the mower was not running; in the high-noise condition the mower emitted a roar of approximately 87 db. The confederate's need of help was varied by sometimes putting a cast on his arm. As you can see in Figure 13-3, the noise had powerful effects on pedestrians' helpfulness. When the victim wore no cast, twice as many people helped him in the quiet condition as in the noise condition. When the victim was wearing a cast and so needed more help, a full 80 percent of the pedestrians offered assistance in the quiet condition. When the lawnmower was running, however, only 15 percent of the passers-by offered help.

In summary, we see that concern about noise pollution is justified. Noise—particu-

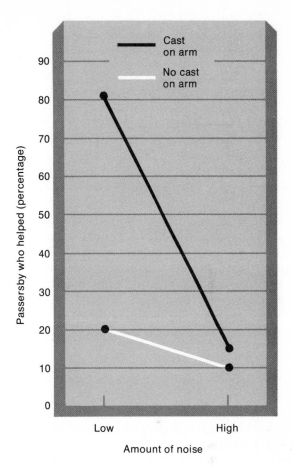

FIGURE **13-3**

The effect of noise on helpfulness

This study found that the loud buzzing of a lawn-mower was stressful enough to reduce markedly people's helpfulness when a student was in distress. (Adapted from Mathews and Canon, 1975)

larly unpredictable and seemingly uncontrollable noise—may have negative consequences on people's feelings, thoughts, and actions. Performance on various tasks may deteriorate, and people may be more irritated with and less helpful toward others. Prolonged exposure to noise also may cause damage to one's physical system.

The Ecological Approach to Environmental Issues

So far our sampling of research on the relationship between the environment and social behavior has focused on the effects of the environment on people. A contrasting viewpoint taken by many social psychologists is termed the *ecological approach.* Concern here is with the relationship between the environment and behavior (Stokols and Shumaker, 1980). Influenced by ecological study in biology, these psychologists have shifted away from viewing the individual as a passive recipient of environmental inputs. Rather, they view people as active organisms who seek harmonious relationships with the environment and with each other. The achievement of optimal relations is the central concern in the ecological approach (Wicker, 1979).

Special interest in the ecological approach was generated by Barker and Wright's 1951 publication, *One Boy's Day.* At the time, most research took place during a brief period in the laboratory. Barker and Wright, however, were curious about what people did for an entire day in real-life settings. They observed the activities of a young boy from the time he arose in the morning until he retired. The chief outcome of this research was a highlighting of the immense importance of *social situations* in dictating what the child did. When at the family dining table, for example, the boy adopted an entire pattern of social behavior that was virtually absent when he was with his friends on the playground or in a math class at school.

From these dramatic differences emerged the concept of the *behavior setting*, which may be defined as a self-regulated sequence of interpersonal events that occur within a bounded environment. To illustrate a behavior setting, consider a family dinner. The event is bounded in time and space. Dinner in North America typically occurs in a spe-

cific room of a house between the evening hours of six and eight. The event is self-regulated, inasmuch as family members usually carry out tasks without having any formal program or specific orders. Family members all know what is expected of them, and if any member deviates, other members usually will act to bring him or her back into line. If a family member is late for dinner, takes more than his or her share of the food, or sits sullenly, others in the family usually will respond with criticism or corrective comments in order to restore the usual series of events.

The results of one survey of behavior settings in two contrasting towns drew attention to the relationship between population size and the number of available behavior settings (Barker and Schoggen, 1973). Town A had a small population and a large number of behavior settings; town B had a larger population but fewer behavior settings. The researchers conceptualized a balance in the population–behavior-setting relationship as reflecting *optimal manning.* Optimal manning exists when the number of people that is demanded by the behavior setting is equal to the number of essential tasks to be carried out. When the number of available persons is below the number of essential tasks, the setting is *undermanned;* when they exceed the number of tasks, it is *overmanned.* In general, optimally manned settings lend themselves to greater proficiency of task performance (Clark, 1978; Wicker, 1973).

In Barker and Schoggen's opinion, the difference in manning requirements in the two communities had a substantial impact on the character of the people. They reasoned that people will make adjustments in order to maintain harmony in an undermanned setting. Since the community cannot afford the loss of a member, less well equipped people may be asked to fulfill functions, and lower standards may be used to judge performance. People in undermanned communities will work harder and participate in a greater variety of settings. Thus a woman in the undermanned environment of town A might work at the court house, sing in the choir, play in a bridge group, serve on a school committee, and raise a family. All of these activities become possible because the environment is undermanned. The investigators believe that the response to undermanning may shape the character of the people in the community. And they found that in contrast with the people in town B, town A residents "on the average are more important people, have greater responsibilities, have lower standards of adequate performance, value concrete accomplishments more and personal qualities less, are more insecure, are more versatile, and work harder" (1973, p. 401).

Although optimal manning may mean that various tasks are accomplished more efficiently and more effectively, many psychologists believe that undermanning can have important advantages for certain groups. Consider the high-school experience. In large

high schools many students are available for each extracurricular activity. Smaller high schools usually do not have enough students to distribute among the various activities. As a result, large high schools usually can field better athletic teams or publish better newspapers. However, only a small percentage of the student body can participate in such activities. As a result, those students from smaller schools may experience a richer life. An illustration of the positive effect of undermanning appears in Table 13-2. When students from large and small high schools were asked about the responsible positions they held in school, students from small schools excelled in almost every category (Wicker, 1968). The same study showed that students from small schools, when compared with students from large schools, had developed more skills while in high school, felt more self-confidence, felt more needed, worked harder, were more concerned with being successful at their activities, and were able to work more closely with

TABLE **13-2** **Undermanning: the relationship between population and participation**

Students from small high schools were more likely to help with various school activities than were students from large high schools. Note, for example, that putting on a home basketball game required the help of 71 percent of those attending the small schools, while only 9 percent of the large-school students were needed.

	Proportion of those attending who help with the activity		
Type of setting	Small schools	Large schools	Small minus large
Basketball game at home school	.71	.09	.62
Class or organization business meeting	.37	.21	.16
School play or musical production	.77	.15	.62
Informal dance at night	.32	.18	.14
Class or club money-raising project	.99	.80	.19
School-sponsored trip away from school	.20	.40	−.20

Source: Adapted from Wicker, 1968

others. Responses from a national sample of students indicate that students from small high schools, as opposed to students from large high schools, demonstrate significantly greater achievements in writing, leadership, music, and the dramatic arts (Baird, 1969). Clearly, undermanning may have important advantages for high-school students.

To summarize, the ecological approach to environmental issues is concerned with the relationship between the environment and social interaction. As early studies indicated, people engage in markedly different patterns of behavior as they move from one behavior setting to another. Behavior settings are optimally manned when the number of persons in the setting is equal to the number of tasks to be carried out. Under optimally manned conditions, tasks often are accomplished efficiently and effectively. However, in undermanned settings, such as communities or schools, people often engage in a richer range of activity than they do in overmanned settings.

The Environment of Others

Houses, streets, offices, and apartment buildings; noise, space, and color—all of these make up our physical environment. And as we have just seen, the features of the physical environment often influence people's psychological states and their relationships with one another. Yet physical surroundings are only part of the environment. The environment also is made up of people, and people create a host of complex problems. Consider, for example, the issue of sheer numbers of people. Today overpopulation threatens entire societies. Housing is difficult to find in large cities. Public transportation is overburdened. People often live in crowded conditions. Further, and as we indicated in Chapter 3, people have definite rules about social distance. When others come too close, a person may feel less

comfortable and less secure. The environment of others has marked effects on an individual's sense of well-being and must be given the same close attention that is given the physical environment.

Social psychologists have devoted much attention to problems that are created by the environment of others. To gain an appreciation of this work, let us sample three of the most interesting and most important areas of study: the problem of stress, the experience of crowding, and the influence of family size on intelligence.

Stress: The Secret Strangler

People grow old and die. That is neither new nor interesting. People with weak hearts or diseased livers may die at a younger than usual age. These seem to be problems for medical science. Or are they? Everyone has heard stories of people who died suddenly at a relatively early age after lives that were relatively free of sickness and were both productive and stable. Often the only event of major consequence that precedes the final illness is retirement. Can illness be influenced by retirement? In recent years an increasing number of investigators have come to believe that the answer is yes—life stresses can have an important effect on physical well-being. Death may be hastened or postponed by the quality of one's social life.

In the 1940s Adolf Meyer, a physician, began to explore the relationship between people's medical and social histories. Rather than viewing the physical system as one that is isolated and autonomous, Meyer believed that physical functioning is related intimately to an individual's relationships with others (Lief, 1948). Influenced by Meyer's work, other investigators began to explore the nature of stress, how it was produced, and its effects on the individual (Selye, 1956; Wolf, 1965). A *stressful reaction* was defined as one in which (1) an attitude of defense is adopted and (2) there is a speedup in functions that are controlled by the autonomic nervous system—such as heart rate, breathing, and adrenaline secretion (Selye, 1956). In some of the most impressive research on physical reactions to stress, Holmes, Rahe, and their colleagues explored the stress and medical histories of individuals with a variety of careers, from football players to physicians. To appreciate the flavor of the research, consider the various life events in Table 13-3. Forty-three common events are listed. You first might ask

yourself how much adjustment you would require if you faced each of these events. In fact, Holmes and Rahe used such a procedure in developing their indicators of stress. As they reasoned, the greater readjustment, the greater the stress. They asked people from a variety of age groups and cultural backgrounds to evaluate the readjustmen. that would be required by each event. Analysis of the ratings resulted in the scale values that are shown in the right-hand columns of Table 13-3. Death of a spouse was judged by the

TABLE **13-3** **The impact of life changes**

The Life Change Scale provides a measure of the relative stressfulness of common events. The change units are additive. Thus a person who was fired from a job at the same time that he or she was getting a divorce is assumed to be under more stress than a person whose husband or wife has just died.

Event	Scale of impact	Event	Scale of impact
Death of spouse	100	Son or daughter leaving home	29
Divorce	73	Trouble with in-laws	29
Marital separation	65	Outstanding personal achievement	28
Jail term	63	Spouse begins or stops work	26
Death of close family member	63	Begin or end school	26
Personal injury or illness	53	Change in living conditions	25
Marriage	50	Revision of personal habits	24
Fired at work	47	Trouble with boss	23
Marital reconciliation	45	Change in work hours or conditions	20
Retirement	45	Change in residence	20
Change in health of family member	44	Change in schools	10
Pregnancy	40	Change in recreation	19
Sex difficulties	39	Change in church activities	19
Gain of new family member	39	Change in social activities	19
Business readjustment	39	Mortgage or loan less than $10,000	17
Change in financial state	38	Change in sleeping habits	16
Death of close friend	37	Change in number of family get-	
Change to different line of work	36	togethers	15
Change in number of arguments		Change in eating habits	15
with spouse	35	Vacation	13
Mortgage over $10,000	31	Christmas	12
Foreclosure of mortgage or loan	30	Minor violations of the law	11
Change in responsibilities at work	29		

Source: Holmes and Rahe, 1967

BOX
13-2

**The Loss
Effect:
Surviving
the Death of
a Loved One**

Grandma Bell died while she was in California visiting her daughter. On the first anniversary of her death, Grandpa Bell, dressed in his best suit, appeared at his son's door. He told his son that he was going to the airport to pick up Grandma. His memory had deteriorated since Grandma's death, and he often seemed to forget that she would never return. A few weeks later, Grandpa Bell died. Afterward the family said that he really had died on the same day as his wife. The rest was just marking time.

You probably are familiar with stories of this kind. The death of a husband or wife frequently is followed closely by the partner's death. Look again at the ranking of the life change events (Table 13-3) and you will see that "death of spouse" is ranked highest in stressfulness, leading the next highest event by a considerable margin. Note also that marital or familial loss is implicated in all of the leading stress-producing events except "jail term." What happens to a person after his or her spouse's death? Research suggests that, like Grandpa Bell, the mourner may confront a reduction in life expectancy (Kastenbaum and Costa, 1977; Rowland, 1977; Schulz, 1978; Stroebe et al., in press). This response is not limited to aged people. As you can see in the table below, widowed people of every age are more vulnerable to death than are those who are married—and this is true for individuals living in many different nations. The table shows the death ratios of widowed to married people during one year. A ratio of 1.00 would mean that the probability of death is equal for widowed and married people. A ratio of 2.00 means that twice the proportion of widowed

majority of the people sampled to require the greatest amount of readjustment and is given a score of 100 *life-change units.* Divorce generally is the second most stressful event, but it seems to require a considerably less amount of readjustment than the death of a spouse. Marital separation is just a little less stressful than divorce, and so on through minor violations of the law, which require the least readjustment of all the items on the measure.

Given these values, the amount of stress to which a person has been exposed in any given period can be estimated. For example, if one of your parents had died recently, the other had become ill, your family's financial status had declined rapidly, you were having sexual difficulties, you had just entered school and changed your residence, your social activities had been disrupted, the frequency of family get-togethers had declined, and you had received a speeding ticket, you would have a high score on the test. In fact, your score would be 275, a figure obtained by totaling the life-change units for each of the various events. You would, according to this measure, be in a state of high stress. On the other hand, if your life had continued pretty much as usual and the only event on the scale that was relevant was having begun school, you would receive the low score of 26. You would be experiencing a low state of stress.

Once the investigators were able to identify the kinds of normal life events that produce high stress and the people who were experiencing various amounts of stress, the next question was, what are the consequences of high stress for the individual? In particular, is the person under high stress more likely

persons died as did married persons. Note that males seem to be more affected by the loss of a spouse than do females. Younger people seem to be more affected than older people. And the loss effect seems to be more powerful in cultures where women assume more traditional roles. These data suggest that special programs of therapy may be necessary to help persons who survive the death of their mate.

Country	Sex	Death ratios by age		
		35–44	45–54	55–64
United States	Males	2.9	2.0	1.5
	Females	1.8	1.4	1.2
England	Males	2.8	1.9	1.6
	Females	2.3	1.5	1.4
Germany	Males	4.2	2.5	1.8
	Females	2.2	1.6	1.3
Japan	Males	4.5	2.9	2.0
	Females	1.6	1.4	1.3

Source: Adapted from Stroebe et al., in press

than one under low stress to suffer bodily deterioration? To explore this issue the investigators carried out a variety of studies, comparing individuals who achieved high and low scores on the stress measure. The results of such comparisons are dramatic. In one early study, some two hundred doctors rated their exposure to stress over a ten-year period and provided a history of their illnesses during the period (Holmes, 1970). When the group was divided into those individuals who had experienced mild, moderate, and severe stress during the ten-year period, important health differences were found. Only 37 percent of the mild-life-crisis group had experienced important changes in health. This figure jumps to 51 percent in the moderate-life-crisis group and to 79 percent for the group experiencing the greatest amount of stress.

Given correlational findings such as these the next question is whether the stress measure can be used to *predict* health problems. If a person's score is high, does he or she run a high risk of illness? The answer to this question appears to be yes. A comparison of stress levels and illness for twenty-five hundred officers and enlisted men aboard three cruisers revealed that the high-stress group reported almost 90 percent more illness than did the low-stress group (Rahe, 1968). Further, the stress scale also predicts minor difficulties, such as cuts, bruises, headaches, stomachaches, backaches, and colds (Holmes and Holmes, 1970). In addition, more than 50 percent of a group of football players with high stress scores were injured during the football season. Approximately 25 percent of the players in the medium-stress group sustained injuries, and only 9 percent of those in a low-stress group were later injured (Holmes, 1970).

These latter findings suggest that stress may lead not only to bodily deterioration, but also to the likelihood of accidents. People under stress may be less careful, less cautious, or less thoughtful about the future. Supporting this view are findings that show an association between high stress and bone fractures, pregnancy, and imprisonment (see Holmes and Masuda's 1974 review). Educational performance also may be affected by stress. Students' grades are correlated highly with stressful life experiences: the greater the stress, the poorer the grades (Harris, 1972).

Do these findings suggest that if you recently have experienced great stress you are doomed to illness, injury, or other discomfort? Not necessarily. People differ greatly in their *coping strategies*, or methods of defending against stressful events. Some individuals may be able to turn their attention elsewhere, rationalize their problems, or concentrate on more optimistic pursuits (Rahe, 1974). Other individuals defend themselves against stress by failing to acknowledge their problems. They may display an unemotional reaction to life's important occurrences (Hinkle, 1974). If a friend dies or if a spouse or lover leaves, they may deny the significance of the relationship. Such individuals also seem to show more than average concern with their own well-being. In effect, their style of living has a self-centered, "sociopathic" flavor. Being totally without stress may not be so desirable.

The Experience and Effects of Crowding

Cities offer their residents many benefits. City-dwellers can live near their place of work, saving both travel time and money. Centrally located work places—stores, warehouses, restaurants, and offices—are less costly to operate. Nearby services and leisure activities are convenient to use and likely to be profitable. The proximity of large numbers of people, then, results in gains in efficiency and profit. Despite these benefits, densely populated cities create psychological and social problems for their residents. Social psychologists have been especially interested in the problems that are created by crowding.

Early research on this topic was stimulated by investigation of *population density* among animals. Population density—the ratio of the number of animals to the available space—was shown to have a variety of debilitating effects in animal colonies. For example, if rats are allowed to breed naturally in a fixed physical space and with adequate food and water, a severe disruption occurs eventually in sexual patterns and in the female's care of the young (Calhoun, 1962). In many animal species increased population density also produces high rates of aggressive activity (Marsden, 1972) and indications of physical deterioration, particularly in those physiological systems most vulnerable to stress (Christian, Lloyd, and Davis, 1965). Density also produces breakdowns in dominance hierarchies, or pecking orders (Wynne-Edwards, 1962, 1965). Such findings have stimulated researchers to begin examining the relationship between population density and various indicators of social, physical, and mental breakdowns in humans. Studies have found that population density often is associated positively with indicators of crime and mental illness (Booth, 1975; Galle, Gove, and McPherson, 1972; Winsborough, 1965).

Yet neither the animal nor the human studies have proved fully convincing to social psychologists (Stokols, 1978). First, generalizations from animal to human populations are very hazardous in this context (Loo, 1975) because humans are more adaptable than animals and can learn to respond flexibly to complex or stressful circumstances (Dubos, 1965). Second, city-dwellers differ in hundreds of ways—for example, in ethnicity, occupation, family composition, motives, and values—from people who live in less populated areas. Thus many factors other than density may produce the positive association between density and pathology (Freedman, Klevansky, Ehrlich, 1971). Third, the results of density studies often depend on the measure of density that is used. The many ways of measuring density include number of persons per room, number of families per dwelling, and amount of physical space per person (Day and Day, 1973; Webb, 1975). Because the measures are so varied, one study that uses a given measure of density may fail to confirm or even reverse the results of other density studies (Booth and Cowell, 1974; Mitchell, 1971).

As a result of the existence of these problems, social psychologists have turned from density studies to research on the experience of crowding. Although the experience of crowding can be influenced by the number of people who are present in a given space, it is not wholly dependent on it. Three people can be experienced as a crowd, while larger groups at times can be pleasureful. Researchers now focus on the factors that give rise to the negative experience of crowding and the behavioral results of the experience.

The negative experience of crowding has a number of different sources:

1. *Loss of freedom.* As the number of people increases, freedom of action tends to decrease (Esser, 1971; Proshansky, Ittelson, and Rivlin, 1970; Schopler and Stockdale, 1977; Zlutnick and Altman, 1972). For example, if reaching decisions depends on a group, the larger the group, the less chance for an individual to realize his or her particular wants. Or the more crowded a subway car, the less likely that an individual will be able to move around. The result is a feeling of being crowded. However, the presence of even a single individual can produce a feeling of crowding. When a person wishes to be left alone to think, write, or study, even a single person's presence can be oppressive.

2. *Increase in stimulation.* As the number of people increases, the *immediacy*, or the amount of stimulation furnished by the people's presence, also tends to increase. For example, eye contact and physical contact, loudness of voices, intensity of odors, intimacy of conversation—all of these sources of stimulation may become more intense. Such increases often arouse people or place them under stress (Aiello, Epstein, and Karlin, 1975; Desor, 1972; Nicosia et al., 1979; Schaeffer and Patterson, 1980; Sundstrom, 1978). As Milgram (1970) has argued, people who live in cities must learn strategies for coping with the stimulus overload, which is created by large numbers of people. The increased stimulation with which city-dwellers must cope may increase other people's capacities for influencing their activities (see Chapter 12). As you can see, one reason parents separate themselves from their children in their living spaces is to reduce the immediacy of the stimulation produced by their children. Parents who can tolerate a child's crying in another room may find the crying to be intolerable if the child is immediately present.

3. *Loss of privacy.* The presence of other people interferes with the *valued state of privacy.* As Irwin Altman (1975, 1978) has proposed, people strive for a sense of self-identity. They want to know where the self begins and where it ends and what their capacities and limitations are. To maintain a sense of self, people exercise *boundary controls*—that is, they manage the amount of contact they have with the outside environment. A person typically

In this chapter we have emphasized the stress that is generated by various environmental inputs, such as crowds or noise or the death of a loved one or the loss of a job. However, stress does not always originate outside the person. Some people are *stress prone*—that is, they choose lifestyles that place them under great stress. And they often suffer the consequences of the lifestyle. The most extensive research on the stress-prone person distinguishes between the *Type A personality* and the *Type B personality* (Friedman, 1969; Glass, 1977; Rosenman, 1969). The Type A personality is "engaged in a relatively chronic struggle to obtain an unlimited number of poorly defined things from the environment in the shortest period of time and, if necessary, against the opposing effects of other things or persons . . ." (Friedman, 1969, p. 84). This struggle is manifested in three ways: (1) competitive striving for achievement, (2) an exaggerated sense of urgency, and (3) aggressiveness and hostility (Zyzanski and Jenkins, 1970). The Type B personality does not display these characteristics. To determine who fits the patterns, respondents are asked such questions as whether they ever have been told that they eat too fast and whether a spouse or a close friend would rate them as being hard driving and competitive or would say that they are too active and should slow down. Positive answers to such questions would indicate a Type A lifestyle.

The origin of Type A and Type B behaviors is unclear. However, data from a study that assessed people's experiences in high school and college indicates that these patterns are discernible at an early age (Glass, 1977). In contrast to Type A students, Type B high-school students participate in more sports and social activities and Type A college students participate in more nonathletic extracurricular activities and win more academic honors. This evidence suggests that the Type A person strives for high achievement, while the Type B person seems to be more social.

In order to gain a better understanding of the Type A and B personalities, investigators have examined reactions in various

maintains a state of balance between the need for privacy and the need for public contact. Too much public contact threatens privacy. The individual experiences crowding.

4. *Environmental threats.* As the number of people in a small space grows, heat and noise levels may increase as well, and feelings of crowding may be produced (Freedman et al., 1972; Griffitt and Veitch, 1971). Also, as the number of people increases, rules for personal space may be broken (see Chapter 3), and this makes people feel uncomfortable (Ross et al., 1973; Sundstrom, 1975; Worchel and Teddlie, 1976). Increased numbers also threaten the order and predictability that typically are found in small groups (Chandler, Koch, and Paget, 1976; Evans and Eichelman, 1976; Schopler, McCallum, and Rusbult, 1977).

What are the effects of the experience of crowding on the individual or on social relationships? Research indicates that feeling crowded may be accompanied by increased

experimental situations. For example, when given various tasks that require different amounts of effort, Type As tend to work at maximum speed regardless of instruction. Type Bs tend to work at whatever speed is required by the instruction (Glass, 1977). When their task performance is threatened in various ways, Type As continue to strive without paying attention to environmental inputs while Type Bs vary their activities according to their experience (Lovallo and Pishkin, 1980). If interrupted during work on a decision-making task, Type As show greater irritation than do Type Bs (Glass, 1977). When placed in a stressful situation, Type As are more likely to evaluate their progress by comparing themselves with others (Dembroski and MacDougall, 1978). One researcher, who placed subjects on a treadmill for many hours, found that Type As were less willing to admit fatigue than were Type Bs (Glass, 1977). And the presence of others stimulates Type As to increase their efforts on a task, while Type Bs are less affected (Gastorf, Suls, and Sanders, 1980).

What are the physical effects of these differences in lifestyle? Laboratory research shows that Type As respond to many tasks with a greater increase in blood pressure and heart rate than do Type Bs—this effect is particularly noticeable when challenges are great (Dembroski et al., 1979; Manuk, Craft, and Gold, 1978). Also, sympathetic nervous system reactions of the kind that damage the cardiovascular system are more frequent in Type As than in Type Bs (Herd, 1978; Williams et al., 1978). Perhaps most telling are studies that examine the incidence of coronary disease and recurring heart attack. Type As' risk of contracting these ailments is substantially greater than is Type Bs' (Brand et al., 1976; Haynes, Feinleib, and Kannel, 1978; Jenkins, Zyzanski, and Rosenman, 1976).

We see, then, that the individual may generate his or her own chronic stress, and the results may be deadly. The immediate question for Type A personalities is whether they can voluntarily alter their life patterns.

feelings of anger, unhappiness, personal discomfort, fear, and depression (Baum and Greenberg, 1975; Nogami, 1976; Paulus et al., 1975). People also may attribute their feelings of nervousness and aggressiveness to others when they feel crowded (Worchel and Teddlie, 1976). Other responses to crowding include trying to stand farther away from other people (Nesbitt and Steven, 1974), avoiding eye contact (Sundstrom, 1975), and selecting isolated seats in a room (Baum and Koman, 1976). An individual may use these actions in an attempt to regain a state of uncrowdedness or privacy (Altman, 1978). Performance on complicated tasks may deteriorate as crowding increases (Evans, 1974; McClelland, 1974; Saegert, 1974). Such results are quite consistent with findings on the negative effects that group size has on complex task performance, as discussed in Chapter 12. Related research has shown that even when negative effects on task performance are not immediate, performance may suffer *after* a person has been in a crowd (Dooley, 1974; Evans, 1975; Sherrod, 1974). In addition, aggressive actions may increase when people feel crowded. For ex-

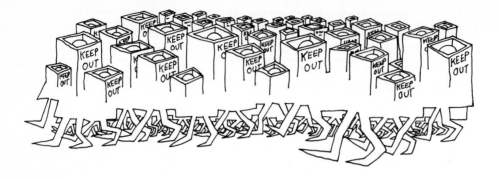

ample, when the number of toys is limited and more children are added to a given space, aggressive activity increases (Hutt and Vaizey, 1966; Rohe and Patterson, 1974). And men—but not women—become increasingly competitive and give harsher sentences in mock jury deliberations as the environment becomes crowded (Freedman et al., 1972). Finally, helpfulness tends to decline as the number of people increases (Bickman et al., 1973).

Studies of crowded family conditions demonstrate similar negative effects on the person and on social relationships. Children rather than adults often bear the brunt of crowded conditions. Children, to a greater extent than adults, may become isolated in family relationships as the conditions become crowded (Mitchell, 1971; Suttles, 1968). And children may blame other family members for household problems (Clausen and Clausen, 1973), show increased nervousness (Gasparini, 1973), and demonstrate lowered physical and intellectual development (Booth and Johnson, 1975).

Yet although the experience of crowding *can* have a variety of negative consequences, these responses are not inevitable. Learning can influence reactions to crowded conditions. For example, subways in Japan are so crowded during rush hours that public servants are hired to push as many people as possible into the cars. The riders have learned to cope with the conditions and remain unper-

turbed, even jolly. Such learning may not require a lifetime of experience (Baron and Rodin, 1978). For example, a crowded market can be an adventure to the senses. And theoretical enlightenment regarding the effects of crowding may reduce its negative effects (Langer and Saegert, 1977). The development of strategies of cooperative organization also may reduce the impact of crowding (Stokols, 1976, 1978). Finally, environmental changes can reduce the experience of crowding even under conditions of high population density. For example, making rules concerning noise and movement or reducing the number of complex tasks to be performed may be helpful in certain circumstances.

Intelligence:
The Benefits of Small Families

The social environment can have intellectual as well as emotional consequences for the individual. Living with others not only can affect one's physical well-being, but can improve or decrease one's general intelligence. The notion that intelligence is influenced by the social environment is relatively new. For many years scores on IQ tests were believed to represent the underlying genetic capacities of an individual. This view now seems to be misleading. To be sure, genetics may make a contribution to a person's score on such tests. However, test performance can be influenced by a host of other factors: motivation to perform, familiarity with the test materials, fear of failure, practice, and so forth. In a broad sense, performing well on intelligence tests may be like doing well at baseball, skiing, or card games. Some people are naturally gifted; others are unable to succeed under any circumstances. With proper training and motivation, however, most people can learn to improve their performance.

The view that intelligence is not fixed has led investigators to look for ways in which the social environment can influence IQ-test scores. After all, motivation, fears, and opportunity for practice all may be related to social experience. In other words, high or low intelligence may be influenced systematically by the social environment. One challenging line of inquiry into the influence of social factors has been that of Zajonc and his colleagues on the effects of family size on intelligence (Zajonc, 1976; Zajonc, Markus, and Markus, 1979).

The researchers wanted to explain findings from a study of the IQ scores of four hundred thousand nineteen-year-old Dutch men (Belmont and Marolla, 1973). The study showed that men from large families scored lower on the intelligence measure than did men from small families. Since there is little reason to believe that genes "wear out" as parents have more children, the researchers reasoned that the IQ differences may be due to the different social environments in small and large families. As they argued, each family member contributes to the family's intellectual climate. Younger children have less well developed mental abilities and tend to reduce the intellectual climate. In a family with a great many children, the overall level of conversation, play, exploration, and other forms of interaction will be lower. As each additional child is born, he or she has fewer opportunities to enjoy intellectually stimulating interaction with the parents and more opportunities to interact with less stimulating siblings.

In light of this reasoning the researchers compared the average IQ scores for children from two-children families with IQs for children from six-children and nine-children families. As they found, the average IQ score for the first child in a family of two was over 100. In a family of six children the firstborn performs less well, and if the firstborn is in a family of nine children, his performance drops again. The same pattern characterizes the IQs of second-born children. As the families grow larger, each successive child tends to obtain a lower score. The most disadvantaged of the lot is the child born ninth in a family of nine.

Do these findings suggest that everyone from a large family is intellectually disadvantaged? Not at all. Many factors may offset the effect of family size. For example, if two or more years separate each child, the number of siblings may have little or no effect on intelligence. In fact, a young child whose brothers and sisters are in middle childhood or older may benefit from a relatively high intellectual climate. Finally, the good or bad effects on one's family environment may be offset by various experiences within and outside the home (Moffitt, 1976). Children themselves sometimes may experience intellectual gains by teaching their younger siblings (Zajonc, Markus, and Markus, 1979). Further, having a large family does not rule out parents' setting high standards of performance. And, children need not spend all of their time at home. If a child spends a considerable amount of time playing and working with peers and teachers, the effects of family environment may be relatively unimportant. Still, the findings do serve notice to parents of large families: pressing children to participate in activities outside the home may be especially important for an optimum level of development.

We have seen that other people form a significant part of the surrounding environment and are as potent in their effects as are

Family size: an environmental issue. Research suggests that the environment in large families may be somewhat less intellectually stimulating than the environment of small families. The issue is a complex one, however, because of the economic pressures that often complicate life in large families.

physical surroundings. Other people are a principal source of stress. Research indicates that as exposure to stressful experiences increases, so does the probability of physical illness and accidents. Coping strategies may be useful in offsetting the effects of stress. The social environment can create the experience of feeling crowded, and crowding can cause feelings of stress, loss of control, and loss of privacy. Crowding also can have negative effects on people's emotional and social life. The number of people that is in an environment also can influence intellectual performance. In particular, children who grow up

in large families often experience a poorer intellectual environment than do children who live in small families. As a result, performance on intelligence tests may suffer.

Building for the Future

We have sampled from social psychological studies of the physical and social environment. Most of this work has focused on the problems of today: how people respond to the structures they build, the noise they create, the emotional and intellectual environment in which they live, and so forth. Yet many social psychologists are concerned not only with today, but also with transforming society and developing new ways of living, loving, and working. New policies are needed for the aged, the poor, the handicapped, and others. Can social psychologists contribute to planning and building the future? Over the past decade the possibility for such a contribution has become increasingly real. Many investigators now see a prominent role for social psychology in the building of a more humane society.

Planning for the future can be *reactive* or *proactive*. In reactive planning the question is, where is society headed? If the direction seems to be undesirable, programs or policies can be put in motion to change the direction. In proactive planning the questions are, where should society be headed and how can the vision be put into effect? Let us first consider the contribution of social psychology to reactive planning. Then we will examine the proactive case.

Social Indicators: Reactive Planning

How does one go about assessing the direction that the future will take? Perhaps the most important technique is the establishment of *trend lines*. A trend line is an indicator of changes in the character of a given phenomenon across time. A trend line usually is based on several assessments of a given phenomenon. These data make possible the determination of whether a phenomenon is becoming more or less prevalent, abundant, powerful, or significant. For example, if we know that violent crimes totaled approximately 150 incidents for every 100,000 people in the United States in 1960, we have an interesting fact. However, if we know that by 1965 the number jumped to 250 per 100,000 and that by 1970 it reached 400 per 100,000 (which was the case), we have discovered a dramatic trend. A tripling in the crime rate

demands close attention. Such trends indicate the direction of change and in this sense offer a significant estimate of the future of society—unless new policies are developed.

Assessing social trends has a long and honorable history in the social sciences. Economists have long made use of such economic indicators as the gross national product (GNP), the inflation rate, and the balance of trade. Likewise, population experts have used birth-rate statistics in important ways. For example, studies of the birth rate over the years increased awareness of the "population explosion." This trend line made clear that if a change did not take place, society would be confronted with catastrophic problems in a mere twenty years. As a result, various programs—including the establishment of free family-planning clinics—were undertaken. These programs, along with other factors, caused a decline in the birth rate.

The assessment of *indicators of social life* is a relatively recent development. In 1967, Raymond Bauer pointed out:

> Only the armchair philosophers dare to formulate the trends in quality of life . . . and there are always dire warnings that we are going to the dogs. . . . For many of the important topics on which social critics blithely pass judgment, and on which policies are made, there are no yardsticks by which to know if things are getting better or worse. (p. 20)

The concern with the quality of life was embodied in the concept of *social systems accounting*. As a technique, social systems accounting was designed to operate in a fashion similar to cost accounting in economics: it was meant to assess the social costs and benefits of various policies over time (Gross, 1966). The federal government has since established a Committee on National Goals. This committee has been charged specifically with assessing the extent to which the character of life in the United States makes possible the achievement of such goals as ade-

A satisfying time of life. The effect of the environment on people can be assessed by cross-sectional studies that explore differences across the life span. Research of this type has found that the later years seem to provide people with the most life satisfaction. This finding may be especially true of people who can remain actively involved in their work. Ellen Cotton is one such person. Now in her 60s she maintains her own cattle ranch.

quate education, equality of opportunity, and so forth (Bauer, 1967).

The range of possible social assessments is unlimited. Some investigators have been interested in admission rates to mental hospitals, the murder rate, and people's allocation of time, feelings of safety or security, and so on (Mann, 1977; Wholey, 1979). For example, the changing status of women has been of central concern. One indicator of increased social and economic opportunity is the number of women who are obtaining advanced education. Data show that in comparison with the 1940s, an increasing number of women in the United States are being awarded bachelor's degrees. However, because male graduates are also increasing in number, *no relative gain* in equality has taken place. In fact, compared with the 1940s, proportionately more men than women received bachelor's degrees in the 1970s. The same pattern characterizes acquisition of master's degrees. Women have obtained an increasing number, but so have men. And once again in comparison with the 1940s, recent trends favor men. Men show an increase in doctorates obtained since the 1960s. No increase is found for women. Thus, if education is an indicator of social progress, women have made fewer gains than have men during the past thirty years.

Of special relevance to psychology, investigators have begun to develop an overall index of the *quality of life* (Andrews and Witney, 1976; Campbell, Converse, and Rodgers, 1976). They are interested in working out a simple summary measure of people's general feelings of happiness or satisfaction. They also want to know which segments of society are experiencing increases or decreases in the quality of life. Finally, if life has changed for particular groups, which factors are responsible, and can they be changed?

In one of the first attempts to document overall quality of life, investigators surveyed a national sample of adults and asked them the following question: "Taking all things together, how would you say things are these days—would you say you are very happy, pretty happy, or not too happy?" (Gurin et al., 1960). Approximately one-third (35 percent) of the respondents said they were "very happy." Over half (54 percent) felt that they were "pretty happy," and 11 percent were "not too happy." During the next fifteen years the same question appeared on other surveys. A continuous decline was found in the percentage of the population willing to describe themselves as very happy. By 1972 the figure had dropped to only 22 percent (Campbell, Converse, and Rodgers, 1976). This is not to

imply that the size of the not-too-happy group has grown continuously. In fact, its percentage remains relatively constant over the fifteen-year span.

Investigators have not been entirely satisfied with the information obtained from this kind of single-item measure. They have wanted to differentiate among the various aspects of life satisfaction in order to get a more precise picture of the state of society. In an ambitious attempt to develop a more precise indicator of the quality of life, twelve different domains of life satisfaction have been isolated (Campbell, Converse, and Rodgers, 1976). Each domain was rated in importance by a national sample of respondents. In order of importance, the domains are as follows:

1. Health
2. Marriage
3. Family life
4. National government
5. Friendship
6. Housing
7. Job
8. Community
9. Religious faith
10. Leisure activities
11. Financial situation
12. Organizations

National-survey respondents then were asked to rate their satisfaction in each domain on a seven-point scale (ranging from "completely satisfied" to "completely dissatisfied"). This more detailed kind of measure was expected to provide a more exact profile of the sources of satisfaction or dissatisfaction for various groups.

Because the twelve domains have been rated by only a single national sample, trend lines across time do not yet exist. However, by comparing changes in life satisfaction among various age groups, a kind of trend line across the life cycle can be established. Interestingly, when the various domains of satisfaction are considered together, the responses of aged individuals contradict the common view that life becomes grim as one ages. The greatest life satisfaction is experienced by individuals who are approximately seventy years old. Although satisfaction declines after the age of seventy, it never reaches the low experienced by people in their twenties and thirties. In fact, in virtually every domain except health, seventy-year-olds experience an increase in satisfaction.

One final matter worth noting is that life satisfaction tends to decline during the decade after college. Satisfaction with health, marriage, family, and savings all are relatively low for twenty- to thirty-year-old individuals. The decrease in satisfaction with marriage and family may seem to be familiar (see the Chapter 3 discussion of the sad fate of romantic love in most marriages during the first ten years). Building a career and a family may threaten life satisfaction during this period.

In summary, we find that one major way in which social psychologists can aid in building the future is by establishing indicators of the effect of the social environment on individuals and measuring these indicators across time. By establishing trend lines, investigators can chart society's progress and can increase people's awareness of problems that are developing. Social scientists then can inquire more specifically about the factors that are creating the problems. These inquiries may provide information on how the problems can be combated.

Evaluation Research: Proactive Planning

Locating trends in human behavior makes reaction possible, and thereby the future can be changed. However, change also can result from the development of alternatives to the status quo. Planning can take place *proactively*. That is, people can try to put into effect new plans—for treating schizophrenics,

teaching junior-high-school students, controlling highway speeds, and so forth. Proactive planning needs no precedents, previous trends, or relevant data. Nevertheless, it can be facilitated by *evaluation research*. Evaluation research measures the results of implemented programs or policies. Is a new treatment of schizophrenics any more successful than available alternatives? Do students learn more by using a new curriculum rather than more traditional techniques? Is highway safety improved under a speed regulation? Evaluation research can find answers to such questions. Using the results of the evaluation, decisions can be made as to whether the innovation should be continued, altered, or abandoned (Wholey, 1979).

One evaluation research project was inspired by government officials in Cincinnati, Ohio, who were concerned about the high crime rate in their city and the social distance between police officers and the people in the neighborhoods in which they worked (Schwartz and Clarren, 1977). City officials believed that matters might improve if the police force were decentralized—that is, if neighborhood police teams were established. The teams would work within given communities on a continuous basis and would be given a considerable amount of authority in making decisions within the communities. To determine objectively whether the innovation was successful and whether other cities might find such a program valuable, city officials selected an independent group to evaluate the plan.

The first step in evaluation research is the *formalization*, or spelling out, of specific goals. The goals must be clear enough so that researchers can develop concrete *criterion measures*—measures of behavior against which progress toward the goals can be assessed. For example, a program goal in Cincinnati was to increase neighborhood residents' feelings of security. Thus a survey of the residents' awareness of the presence of police officers in their neighborhood was a criterion measure of security. A second program goal was to increase police officers' knowledge of the community to which they were assigned. Progress toward this goal was measured by asking businessmen whether they recognized the officer who patrolled their neighborhood. Recognition, it was reasoned, would facilitate interaction.

Armed with a set of program goals and a set of measures for each goal, evaluation researchers set out to collect relevant data (Schwartz and Clarren, 1977). Their first surveys took place prior to the implementation of the program. These surveys allowed the researchers to establish a *base line* against which later findings could be compared. Then, after the decentralization program had been in operation for six months, the researchers asked random samples from the community the same questions. To make sure that the gain was not a temporary phenomenon, the same surveys were conducted a year after the program had begun. As the results showed, residents' awareness of the presence of police officers in their neighborhood increased steadily from the base line to the final evaluation. Before the program began, approximately 20 percent of the residents were aware of the police officers patrolling their neighborhood. A year after the program, this figure had risen to 60 percent. Similarly,

an increasing percentage of businessmen recognized the officers on patrol. A year after the program began, recognition had increased by 30 percent. Results such as these, collected by independent researchers, can help a great deal in evaluating a program's effects. With such reliable evidence at hand, other city officials can consider more confidently changes in their own police organizations.

Evaluation research can be used in many different settings. For example, at the national level such research has tested the effects of increased educational spending (Ribich and Murphy, 1975), specialized taxation (Burtless and Hausman, 1980), antipoverty incentive programs (Haveman and Watts, 1975), gun control laws (Zimring, 1976), energy regulations (Mead, 1980), drinking and driving legislation (Ross, 1975), and school integration (Coleman, 1975). At the state and local levels, investigators have explored such topics as the effects of regional mental health centers (Bigelow, 1975), water scarcity programs (Berk et al., 1980), municipal service programs (Millar, Hatry, and Koss, 1977), aid programs for released prisoners (Lenihan, 1976), programs for new careers (Grant and Grant, 1975), and early education intervention for culturally disadvantaged children (Bronfenbrenner, 1979). A full treatment of such research is contained in the *Handbook of Evaluation Research* (Struening and Guttentag, 1975).

SUMMARY

1   Social psychologists have been greatly concerned with finding solutions to practical problems in society. General theory does much to sensitize people to the possible influences and processes that operate in social life, and thus it has practical consequences. However, research also must focus on specific problems if solutions are to be found.

2   The physical environment can create important social problems. In the design of buildings, for example, the failure to furnish space for both public interaction and privacy can result in a breakdown in social

relations and feelings of well-being. Noise also may have negative effects on social life. People who live in a noisy environment often suffer from a variety of physical and emotional problems. The noise can cause immediate and delayed deterioration in performance. Uncontrollable noise may be particularly debilitating.

3 Some social psychologists are concerned with the relationship between the physical world and the social world. This ecological research looks at behavior settings—the self-regulated sequences of interpersonal events that occur in various environmental settings. In undermanned settings the number of available people is insufficient for the available tasks. Productivity may be low in such settings, but people's activities often gain in richness.

4 Other people form part of one's environment, and the presence of others may create problems no less powerful than those created by the physical environment. Other people are important sources of stress. Research on stress indicates that the greater the number of stressful events to which one is exposed, the more vulnerable one is to physical deterioration and accidents. Coping strategies may combat the effects of stress. Crowding also may have negative consequences. Although there is little indication that population density is in itself detrimental, an increased number of people often can contribute to the experience of being crowded. This experience in turn may lead to emotional discomfort and behavioral difficulties. An increased number of people within the family setting may have a negative effect on measures of intelligence.

5 Much social psychological research on practical problems is used to guide policies for the future. Such research can be reactive or proactive. Reactive research attempts to determine the direction in which the society is going so that necessary adjustments can be made. For example, research that uses social indicators attempts to determine the rise and fall of the crime rate, the educational level of the population, the equality of opportunity, and other characteristics of society. Proactive studies often employ evaluation research—that is, investigation of the results of various programs or policies. Such evaluations often furnish valuable information that can be used either in changing the programs or policies or in demonstrating their benefits.

SUGGESTED READINGS

Altman, I. *The environment and social behavior: Privacy, personal space, territory, crowding.* Monterey, Calif.: Brooks/Cole, 1975.

Bell, P. A., Fisher, J. D., & Loomis, R. J. *Environmental psychology.* Philadelphia: W. B. Saunders, 1978.

Freedman, J. L. *Crowding and behavior.* New York: Viking Press, 1975.

McGrath, J. E. (Ed.). *Social and psychological factors in stress.* New York: Holt, Rinehart & Winston, 1970.

Proshansky, H. M., Ittelson, W. H., & Rivlin, L. G. *Environmental psychology: Man and his physical setting.* New York: Holt, Rinehart & Winston, 1970.

Shontz, F. C. *The psychological aspects of physical illness and disability.* New York: Macmillan, 1975.

Selye, H. *The stress of life.* New York: McGraw-Hill, 1956.

Wicker, A. W. *An introduction to ecological psychology.* Monterey, Calif.: Brooks/Cole, 1979.

GLOSSARY

A

accommodation process in social exchange
The tendency to engage in relationships so as to provide maximum pleasure and minimal pain.

accomplice An experimenter's associate who responds in a preplanned manner as part of an experiment. Also called **confederate.**

additive task A task in which each group member's output can be added together to yield the total group product. See also **conjunctive task, discretionary task, disjunctive task.**

affective component of attitudes The feelings a person has about an object, ranging from positive to negative.

affiliation need The basic social need to be with other people.

aggression Behavior designed to produce negative outcomes (for example, pain, sorrow, or death) in other people.

altruism Behavior that benefits other people and is carried out with no expectation of external reward.

Anderson's impression formation model A method of forming impressions whereby people integrate various pieces of information by averaging and weighting the information in terms of its importance.

androgyny The state of possessing both traditionally masculine and traditionally feminine traits.

anticonformity Behavior in which defiance of a group or an authority is an end in itself. See also **independence.**

anti-Semitism Prejudice and/or discrimination against Jews.

antisocial action Behavior that harms other people (for example, aggression, destruction, or selfishness). See also **positive social action.**

anxiety Apprehension or uneasiness that stems from a concern about what may happen in the future.

archival method A research procedure that depends on historical documents and records for data. This method is particularly useful in studying the unfolding of social patterns over a period of time or the effects of particular historical conditions.

arousal A state of generalized physiological activation that produces changes in bodily states (for example, increased heart rate and sweating palms).

Asch's theory of social perception The notion that in the perception of another person the meaning of each concept used in labeling the person is influenced by the surrounding context. The overall impression is therefore qualitatively different from the simple sum of the person's traits.

assimilation The tendency to twist the details of an ambiguous stimulus in order to produce a more recognizable structure. In Sherif and Hovland's attitude research, a distortion of judgment in which messages are believed to be more supportive than they actually are.

associative learning   Learning that one event is likely to occur in the presence of another event.

attitude   A readiness to respond to a particular person or object or a set of people or objects in a favorable or an unfavorable manner. Attitudes have an object and are judgmental and relatively long-lasting. See also **affective component, cognitive component, conative component.**

attraction   A positive sentiment about or an emotional feeling toward other people.

attribution theory   A theory concerned with the way in which people perceive the causes of events or actions. See also **causal source, consistency rule, consensus rule, distinctiveness rule.**

authoritarianism   A personality style characterized by identification with and submission to authority, denial of feelings, and cynicism.

autistic hostility   The strong dislike felt by one group for another. This feeling develops in the absence of communication and contact.

autokinetic effect   An optical illusion in which a stationary pinpoint of light that is viewed in an otherwise dark room appears to be moving.

autonomic nervous system   The division of the nervous system that controls the functioning of internal organs, smooth muscles, and glands.

B

backlash   A coerced group's attempt to punish the coercing agent in retaliation.

balance theory   A cognitive attitude theory assuming that people prefer consistency to inconsistency in their beliefs and that they will make choices that restore balance.

base-rate   The general probability that an event will occur over time. More broadly, the frequency with which an event takes place in the general population.

behaviorist orientation   One of the three major theoretical perspectives in social psychology. The behaviorist orientation emphasizes the exploration of reliable relationships between environmental conditions and social behavior. See also **cognitive orientation, rule-role orientation.**

behavior setting   Barker's term referring to self-regulated sequences of interpersonal events that occur within bounded environments. Behavior setting refers to both activities and the environment in which the activities occur.

biased memory scanning   The process of reviewing one's memories and selecting from them only those that support one's arguments; a self-generated form of attitude change.

biasing agent   A factor or process that reduces a person's capacity to process information in a rational manner. See also **choice shift.**

bogus pipeline procedure   A technique for measuring attitudes. Subjects are led to believe that their true reactions will be revealed by a device that measures physiological responses.

boomerang effect   The reaction of an audience; this reaction is the opposite of that which is advocated by a message.

bystander effect   The tendency for response to an emergency situation to take place more slowly as the number of members in the group of bystanders increases.

C

calculus of positive social action   The process by which a person estimates the gains and losses involved in helping other people.

case study   A field study that is limited to the comprehensive examination of a single individual, group, or event.

catharsis   The reduction of an emotion through its expression. See also **frustration-aggression hypothesis.**

causal source   The person or event that is viewed as the instigator of an action or a series of actions. *Internal attribution* places the causal source in the actor; *external attribution* places the causal source in the situation.

central organizing traits   The personality traits (for example, warm versus cold) that are of major importance when one person is organizing his or her impression of another. See also **Asch's theory of social perception, trait.**

choice shift   The tendency of a group to choose either a far riskier or a far more conservative solution to a dilemma than any one group member would choose. This tendency is due to the influence of the group situation. See also **risky shift, tame shift.**

coercion   A type of power that typically produces only compliance and therefore does not produce psychological change. See also **expert power, information power, legitimate power, referent power, reward and coercive power.**

cognition   Knowing in the broadest sense, including thoughts, judgment, knowledge, perception, and memory.

cognitive component of attitudes The concepts and perceptions that a person has about an object or a class of objects.

cognitive conservatism The tendency of a person to resist altering his or her impressions once they are formed.

cognitive consistency theory The assumption that most people want agreement or harmony in their thoughts about the world. See also **balance theory, cognitive dissonance.**

cognitive consonance A satisfying psychological state that a person experiences when two or more cognitions (ideas about the world) are consistent with one another.

cognitive dissonance Festinger's term for an uncomfortable psychological state accompanied by a physical state of arousal that is produced by the awareness of two or more simultaneously existing ideas that are in conflict or are inconsistent.

cognitive orientation One of the three major theoretical perspectives in social psychology. Cognitive orientation emphasizes those thought processes that organize and interpret the properties of the environment. See also **behaviorist orientation, rule-role orientation.**

cohesiveness The degree to which members of a group are attracted to one another and to the group as a whole.

communication structure The pattern of communication networks that exists among members of a group. Typical structures are *centralized* (having one coordinator) or *decentralized* (having many lines of interaction).

communicator credibility The degree to which a communicator is a trustworthy, informed, and unbiased source of information.

complementarity in attraction The tendency of people to be attracted to those whose traits and capacities complement their own and maximize rewards.

compliance The tendency to yield to group pressure in order to avoid punishment for nonconformity. The outward change is not necessarily accompanied by inward change. See also **identification, internalization.**

conative component of attitudes A person's action orientation toward an object or a class of objects.

concepts The properties that are common to an object or to a class of objects or ideas. In *conceptualization*, stimuli are grouped together on the basis of common properties. See also **hypothesis testing, natural categories.**

conceptual bias The overlooking of differences due to oversimplification in categorizing. Also, a general experiential limitation due to the misuse of categorization.

concrete dimension in resource theory In the Foas' model, a dimension that refers to the extent to which a resource is physical. See also **particularistic dimension, resource theory.**

concrete operational stage Piaget's third stage of cognitive development in which a child learns to classify and mentally manipulate objects. See also **formal operational stage, preoperational stage, sensorimotor stage.**

confederate See **accomplice.**

conformity A change in belief or behavior as the result of real or imagined social pressure.

conjunctive task A task in which each member of a group performs roughly the same function but depends on the other group members. See also **additive task, discretionary task, disjunctive task.**

consciousness raising A technique that aims to sensitize group members to oppressive influences on their lives and develop a sense of solidarity and a means of collective defense within the group.

consensus rule in causal attribution Kelley's proposal that the greater the consensus in other people's response to a stimulus, the greater the attribution of causality to that stimulus.

consistency A person's tendency to organize his or her perceptions of others so that all the elements fit together in a coherent, logical pattern. This is a major principle underlying perceptual organization.

consistency rule in causal attribution Kelley's proposal that the greater the consistency of a stimulus in creating a response across diverse situations, the greater the attribution of causality to that stimulus.

contagion The spreading of a behavior pattern through a large number of people. Contagion is a modeling effect.

context The range of social and physical circumstances in which a person's actions are encountered.

control group In an experiment, the subjects who are not exposed to the stimulus being studied. See also **experimental group.**

conventional morality Kohlberg's second level of moral development, in which the individual begins to attend to social rules and expectations. See also **postconventional morality, pre-conventional morality.**

coping strategies Methods of thinking and behaving that are developed in order to deal with a difficulty (such as stress, depression, or learned helplessness).

correlation coefficient The numerical indicator of the degree of relationship between two variables. The coefficient varies between -1 (negative correlation) and $+1$ (positive correlation). A correlation of zero means that there is no relationship between the variables.

covariation in attribution theory Kelley's rule that an effect (an outcome) will be attributed to the condition that is present when the effect is present and absent when the effect is absent. See also **consensus rule, consistency rule, distinctiveness rule.**

criterion measures Measures of behavior against which progress toward given goals can be assessed.

cross-cultural research A research method in which the responses of people in different societies are compared.

cross-sectional research Research that assesses patterns of conduct in a population at a given time.

crowding A stress-related psychological state that may be produced by a perceived high-population density.

cultural truism A statement of belief that people in a culture have been socialized into accepting without question. Cultural truisms represent common areas of agreement, make people intelligible to one another, and provide a common ground from which relationships may be developed.

D

debrief To inform subjects of the true design and purpose of an experiment following their participation in it when partial or deceptive information may have been provided beforehand.

defensive avoidance The tendency to become increasingly resistant to a persuasive appeal as fear-inducing communications increase.

deindividuation The process of reducing the markers that distinguish a person's personal identity.

demand characteristic A cue that makes clear to subjects what the experimenter is attempting to investigate, enabling the subjects to behave in ways that confirm the experimenter's hypotheses. See also **experimenter bias.**

dependent variable(s) In experimental research, the group of responses that are expected to change due to changes in the independent variable(s). The dependent variable is the measured response. See also **independent variable(s).**

desensitization Lowered arousal due to frequent exposure.

destructive obedience Obedient behavior that aims to punish or destroy people or property. See also **obedience.**

dialectic thinking The practice of examining ideas by considering opposing forces and the change that is likely to be produced by those forces.

discretionary task A task in which group members can combine their joint efforts in any way they wish. The product depends on how the efforts are coordinated. See also **additive task, conjunctive task, disjunctive task.**

discrimination The behavioral component of prejudice. Discrimination is an action that reflects an unfavorable attitude toward a person based solely on his or her class or category membership. See also **prejudice.**

disjunctive task A task in which there is no division of labor. The group product does not depend on the summed efforts of the group members. See also **additive task, conjunctive task, discretionary task.**

distinctiveness rule in causal attribution Kelley's proposal that the more distinctive the response to a stimulus, the greater the attribution of causality to that stimulus.

dominant response The response that is learned most thoroughly.

door-in-the-face technique A technique of social influence in which an extreme favor is requested first in order to increase compliance with a lesser request.

drive reducer A condition or set of conditions that acts to lessen physiological arousal or need state.

dyad A two-person group.

E

ecology The study of the relationship between an environment and the social behavior of organisms in the environment.

empathy The capacity to imagine oneself in the place of another person; the ability to experience the feelings of another person.

encounter group A term used to describe a group that is organized in order to bring people together for the purpose of learning more about their behavior in social relationships. Also called **T-group.**

enlightenment effect The change in a person's activities due to a knowledge of theoretical predictions about his or her behavior. Such effects may threaten accurate prediction of behavior.

equality rule A principle of social exchange in which each participant perceives that the relative rewards and costs are equal. Equality rule takes into account each participant's abilities or needs.

equity rule A principle of social exchange in which each participant perceives that the relative rewards and costs are equal. Equity rule takes into account each participant's productivity.

equity theory A theory that specifies the way in which costs and rewards are to be distributed in society.

Eros One of Freud's proposed primary motives. Eros is the motive for pleasure. See also **Thanatos.**

ethnocentrism The belief that a person's own group is superior to all other groups. The result of this belief is the rejection of all out-groups.

ethology The study of the characteristic behavior patterns that are common to an animal species in a particular natural environment.

evaluation apprehension A person's concern with the possibility that other people will react (either positively or negatively) to the quality of his or her performance.

evaluation research Programs of research that attempt to measure rigorously the results of implemented social programs. Such research can form the basis fo changes in social policy.

exchange theory A theory of interpersonal behavior that is based on four major assumptions: human behavior is motivated primarily by pleasure and pain; the actions of other people are primary sources of pleasure and pain; a person's actions may be used to secure pleasure-giving actions from others; people attempt to gain maximum pleasure at minimum cost.

excitation transfer A process in which arousal that was generated by one stimulus can intensify unrelated activity.

experimental group In an experiment, the subjects who are exposed to the stimulus under study. See also **control group.**

experimental method A method of investigation in which one or more independent variables are manipulated, extraneous variables are controlled, and one or more dependent variables are observed. This method often, but not necessarily, is carried out in a laboratory.

experimenter bias The distortions in the outcome of a study that are produced when the investigator communicates subtly and perhaps unconsciously how a subject should behave. See also **demand characteristic.**

expert power The capacity to alter the actions of others based on the actor's skill at carrying out valued activities.

explicit knowledge Understanding the social and physical worlds in terms of concepts rather than in terms of intuitions lodged in continuing experience. See also **implicit knowledge.**

extrinsic reward Reward that is received from an external source as the result of one's action. See also **intrinsic reward.**

F

Fiedler's theory of leadership A perspective that considers the interaction between a leader's personal style and the leadership situation. *Task-oriented leaders* are most effective when a situation clearly favors success or failure. *Relationship-oriented leaders* are successful when a situation is moderately favorable.

field study A method of psychological research that requires the ongoing activities of people in their natural environment to be recorded precisely and systematically.

field theory Lewin's theory that the way in which people represent their world psychologically is the primary determinant of their actions and that social behavior is a function of both intrapersonal factors and the environment. See also **life space.**

foot-in-the-door technique A technique of social influence in which a small favor is requested first in order to increase later compliance with a more extreme request.

formal operational stage Piaget's fourth stage of cognitive development in which a child can construct a belief system, think abstractly, and think reflexively about himself or herself. See also **concrete operational stage, preoperational stage, sensorimotor stage.**

frustration-aggression hypothesis Dollard and his colleagues' proposal that frustration always leads to some kind of aggression and that aggression is always the result of frustration.

F-scale A method of measuring personality in which a questionnaire is used to assess the tendency to be subservient to authority. *F* stands for Fascist. See also **authoritarianism.**

fundamental attribution error The tendency to disregard the effects that situations have on people's actions and to focus instead on people's personal dispositions.

G

gender ratio The proportion of one sex to the other in any particular societal subgroup.

generative theory A theory that challenges the beliefs or assumptions that are common to a culture and in doing so develops alternatives to the status quo and furnishes a choice in the place of dogmatic belief.

Gestalt The German term meaning "form." In Gestalt psychology the term refers to an integrated perceptual unit.

Gestalt psychology An area of psychology that emphasizes the way in which a person's internal processes impose form on the external world.

GRIT strategy (graduated reciprocation in tension reduction) Osgood's proposal for the deescalation of patterns of mutual exploitation in social exchange.

group Two or more people who interact or communicate, perceive themselves as forming a unit, and typically share at least one common goal.

groupthink A set of behavior patterns (including the delimiting of alternatives, the reduction of critical examination, and the stifling of expert opinion) that often undermines the decision-making process in group situations.

H

halo effect The tendency to see individuals as possessing only positive (and therefore no negative) characteristics. The halo effect often leads to inaccurate judgments.

hedonism In psychology, the theory that people's actions are driven by the search for pleasure and the avoidance of pain.

hierarchy The ranking of group members according to status and/or ability to control or influence events. More generally, a group of persons or things arranged in order of rank, grade, and so forth.

hypothesis A theoretical proposition used to predict behavior that is yet to be observed.

hypothesis testing A form of learning in which tentative concepts are formed and are tested against experiences. See also **concept**.

I

identification The tendency to yield to group pressures because the group has attractive qualities. More generally, the process by which people pattern themselves on others and thus learn social roles. See also **compliance, internalization**.

idiosyncracy credit In Hollander's interactionist model of leadership, the accumulation of benefits provided by a leader to his or her group, allowing the leader the freedom to deviate from expectation without fear of retaliation.

imitation Tarde's proposal that the innate tendency to imitate other people is the key to the understanding of social life. More generally, copying the behavior of other people. See also **contagion, modeling**.

immediacy In Latané's social impact theory, the closeness of the influence sources to the target in space or time. See also **social impact theory**. With respect to crowding, immediacy refers to the amount of stimulation (eye contact, touching, smelling, and so forth) that is furnished by people in a given setting.

implicit knowledge Understanding the social and physical worlds in terms of continuing experience rather than in terms of concepts. See also **explicit knowledge**.

implicit personality theory A person's assumptions about the way personality traits are clustered together (for example, assuming that honesty and sincerity go together).

impression management The process by which a person shapes other people's impressions of himself or herself. See also **self-monitoring**.

independence Isolation from group pressure or the commands of authority. See also **anticonformity, conformity, obedience**.

independent variable(s) The factor that is systematically varied or controlled by an investigator in order to determine its effects on behavior. See also **dependent variable(s)**.

informational pressure A type of social influence in which a group produces conformity by providing the target person with needed information. See also **normative pressure**.

information power The capacity to alter other people's actions based on the possession of useful information.

ingratiation The strategy of manipulating another person by furnishing benefits.

instinct An inborn behavioral predisposition.

interactionist view of leadership The belief that personality factors and situational factors determine whether a person will achieve a position of power; the right-person-for-the-right-time perspective. See also **Fiedler's theory.**

internalization The tendency to yield to group expectations because of a belief that the group is correct. More generally, the incorporation of another person's beliefs into one's own system of values. See also **compliance, identification.**

interview A method of psychological research in which people are asked questions about their behavior, motives, ideas, preferences, and so forth.

intrinsic reward Personal reward that is derived from the process of carrying out an action. See also **extrinsic reward.**

J

just-world hypothesis The belief that people get what they deserve or that they deserve what they get in life.

L

leakage signals Movements or gestures that give cues to a person's underlying emotional state.

learned association A mental connection; an idea or memory that is elicited by something that usually is in close temporal proximity to it (in everyday speech, for example, "mother" might elicit the response "father").

learned helplessness A condition of apathy that is produced when animals (and humans) learn that they have no control over what happens to them.

legitimate power The capacity to alter other people's actions based on social agreement about who has the right to direct behavior.

leveling A method of stimulus assimilation in which various elements or details are dropped from a pattern so that the stimulus is simplified and thus is easier to identify or classify. See also **assimilation, sharpening.**

levels of intimacy Levinger's model of the course of development in deep relationships.

liberating function of theory A characteristic function of theory in which the awareness of shortcomings in people's activities is increased, more fruitful alternatives become apparent, and liberation from existing constraints in everyday life takes place.

life-change units In Holmes and Rahe's Life Change Scale, the measure of stress.

life space In Lewin's field theory, the person and the psychological environment; all the related influences that affect a given behavior when it takes place.

locus of control A person's characteristic sense of control over his or her life. The locus of control may be attributed to internal causes or external causes.

loneliness An emotional state that can be said to exist when a person's network of social relationships is smaller or less satisfying than he or she wishes it to be.

longitudinal research Studies that examine the responses or characteristics of one population over a period of time.

looking-glass self The theoretical notion that a person's self-concept depends on the reflected opinions that are communicated to him or her by significant others.

low-ball technique A technique of social influence in which compliance with a small favor is obtained and then the target is informed that the favor will actually be costly.

M

Machiavellianism A style of behavior in which a person manipulates others in order to gain his or her own ends.

matching hypothesis in social attraction The proposal that people select for romantic relationships those persons who are approximately equivalent to themselves in terms of physical attractiveness.

maximum joint payoff In social exchange theory, the tendency to make choices that provide each person with maximum pleasure; the goal of social relationships. See also **accommodation process.**

mean The sum of scores divided by the number of scores; the arithmetic average.

mere exposure effect The increase in attraction toward an object or a person as a result of frequent observation.

minimax strategy in social exchange The strategy in which people try to reduce the costs that are necessary to achieve their ends, therefore minimizing their pain while maximizing their pleasure.

mirror-image phenomenon in intergroup prejudice A term describing the process by which prejudice is increased. Group members see themselves as well-intentioned and right thinking and their enemy as mistaken and threatening.

mixed-motive exchange In the prisoner's dilemma game, a type of interaction in which the desire to cooperate conflicts with the desire to exploit and the best outcome for each partner is also the most risky.

modeling The process by which a person acquires social behaviors by copying, or imitating, the actions, attitudes, and emotional responses of others. Also called **observational learning.** See also **social learning theory.**

moral career Goffman's term referring to the fact that every person's social life is judged constantly by others. Thus social life can be seen as a moral career.

moral development As studied by Piaget, Kohlberg, and others, a child's acquisition of ideas about right and wrong.

morality The quality of being in accord with those rules of right and wrong that are established by a culture to ensure its continuation.

motivated perception The conceptualization of people or events in self-gratifying ways.

motivation A general term referring to the forces (needs, drives, and so forth) that move an organism to act.

MUM effect The tendency to remain silent about bad news.

N

natural categories Certain basic concepts that may result from the natural impact of the physical world on the sense receptors. See also **concept.**

negative reinforcement Punishment that is designed to reduce the frequency of a given response. See also **positive reinforcement.**

neobehaviorism A behaviorist orientation that emphasizes the relationship between environmental events and social behavior but recognizes that the internal properties of the organism are also important in determining this relationship. See also **behaviorist orientation.**

nonverbal communication Relating information about oneself by means of conscious and unconscious bodily gestures or signals.

norm A widely shared expectation about the appropriateness of a given behavior in a given situation.

normative pressure A type of social influence in which a group produces conformity by providing the target person with needed friendship. See also **informational pressure.**

O

obedience The change in a belief or behavior in response to pressure from an authority figure.

objective self-awareness See **self-consciousness.**

operant conditioning The use of rewards and punishment in molding behavior.

optimal manning A condition that occurs when the number of people that is demanded by a behavior setting is equal to the number of essential tasks to be carried out. See also **overmanning, undermanning.**

overjustification effect The tendency to cease believing that an activity is justified in itself when external reasons can be found for carrying it out.

overmanning A condition that occurs when the number of available persons exceeds the number of essential tasks to be carried out in a given behavior setting. See also **optimal manning, undermanning.**

P

particularistic dimension in resource theory In the Foas' model, the degree to which resources may be exchanged with a particular individual as opposed to any member of society.

payoff matrix In social exchange theory, a table summarizing outcomes in terms of pleasure and pain received from the various options that are available.

perception The process by which a person becomes aware of objects, situations, and so forth by means of the senses. Perception is an active cognitive process.

personality The distinctive individual characteristics of a person that constitute his or her way of dealing with others.

personal space The area around a person's body inside which other people are neither expected nor welcome unless they are invited by the individual.

person perception The way in which people develop and use conceptions or impressions of other people and themselves. Person perception is based primarily on a set of preestablished concepts that are popular within a culture.

persuasion The use of argument, reasoning, or entreaty in trying to cause someone to do or believe something.

polarization in attitude change The process by which attitudes or feelings become more extreme, such that a positive attitude will become more favorable and a negative attitude will become less favorable.

population In psychological research, the designation for all people in a particular category (for example, infants, college sophomores, or registered voters) used as a base for statistical measurement.

positive bias in attitude change The tendency to agree with any persuasive message.

positive reinforcement Reward that is designed to increase the frequency of a given response. See also **negative reinforcement.**

positive social action A type of behavior in which one person does something to benefit another. Also called **prosocial behavior.** See also **antisocial behavior.**

postconventional morality Kohlberg's third and highest level of moral development, in which one places reliance on his or her own conception or symbolic understanding of morality. See also **conventional morality, preconventional morality.**

power The capacity to alter other people's actions. See also **expert power, information power, legitimate power, referent power, reward and coercive power.**

preconventional morality Kohlberg's first level of moral development, in which rules are followed out of a fear of punishment or an expectation of reward. See also **conventional morality, postconventional morality.**

prejudice A readiness to respond to a person in an unfavorable manner solely on the basis of his or her class or category membership. Prejudice is an attitude. See also **discrimination.**

preoperational stage Piaget's second stage of cognitive development during which a child is able to perceive the external world in terms of internal symbols and begins to take a perspective that is different from his or her own. See also **concrete operational stage, formal operational stage, sensorimotor stage.**

primacy effect In attitude change or impression formation, the tendency for information that is received first to be most important in determining a person's overall judgment or impression of objects, issues, or other people. See also **recency effect.**

prisoner's dilemma game A laboratory situation designed to facilitate the study of social exchange, especially exchange in which motives for cooperation and exploitation are simultaneously aroused.

privacy The valued state of having selective control over the access that others have to one's self or one's group.

proactive planning A type of social planning for the future in which a researcher asks questions about where society should be heading and how visions of the future can be put into effect. See also **reactive planning.**

process gain and loss In a group situation, the benefits and costs that either increase or decrease the group's productivity.

propinquity Nearness. Attraction research has shown that as geographical distance decreases, attraction-based relationships are likely to increase.

proposition A general statement concerning relationships among entities.

prosocial behavior See **positive social action.**

prototype A trait clustering that is used as a convenient way of categorizing people in their daily relationships.

proxemics The study of interpersonal distance and spatial behavior (as in, for example, crowding).

public opinion survey A research method in which large, representative samples of people are interviewed. This is the best method available for documenting the broad characteristics that exist in a culture at any given time.

Pygmalion effect The tendency to use subtle or deliberate communications or actions to create in others that which one expects to find.

R

radical behaviorism A behaviorist orientation that assumes that human behavior can be understood *entirely* in terms of the environment and that internal processes need not be taken into account. See also **behaviorist orientation, neobehaviorism.**

reactance A negative emotional state that may result when a person's freedom of choice is reduced. Reactance can be a psychological source of independence.

reactive planning A type of social planning for the future in which predictions are made about where society is heading. See also **proactive planning.**

recency effect In attitude change or impression formation, the tendency for the most recently received information to be most important in shaping a person's overall impressions of objects, issues, or other people. See also **primacy effect.**

reciprocity norm The expectation that good, and

not harm, will be returned to those who have furnished benefit.

referent power The capacity to alter another person's actions based on his or her identification with the agent of power.

reinforcement effect A principle in psychology stating that behavior that is followed by reward is likely to recur and behavior that is followed by punishment is not likely to recur. See also **negative reinforcement, positive reinforcement.**

reinforcement schedule The rate with which a given action is rewarded or punished.

relative deprivation Davies's notion that revolutionary activity is most likely to occur when an extended period of rising expectations is followed by a reversal or a leveling of outcomes. More generally, a person's perception of his or her status in comparison with his or her expectations.

reliability The repeatability of statistical findings. If a measurement procedure assigns the same value to a characteristic each time it is measured under essentially the same circumstances, it can be said to be reliable.

replication Repetition of an experiment often using widely diverse populations in order to reassess the reliability or validity of its results.

resource theory The Foas' model of social exchange. Resource theory suggests that the set of classes into which the sources of all pleasure-giving activities fall may be limited and that there may be a set of fundamental rules that govern the exchange of activities in the various classes. See also **concrete dimension, particularistic dimension.**

response Any behavior that results from stimulation. See also **stimulus.**

reward and coercive power The capacity to alter the actions of others based on the ability of the agent to reward or punish others for their actions.

risky shift The tendency for group discussion to lead to far more daring decisions than would be made by individual members prior to the discussion. Shifts toward caution also may occur. See also **tame shift.**

role playing A method of research or therapy in which people are asked to assume a part, or a role. Also, an experimental method that has been suggested as an alternative to the use of deception.

rule-role orientation One of the three major theoretical perspectives in social psychology. Rule-role orientation emphasizes the way in which shared rules or role prescriptions influence patterns of conduct across time.

rumor Unauthenticated information; hearsay.

S

salience The quality of being noticeable. An attitude is salient to the degree to which it is called to a person's attention.

scapegoating The process of casting blame on undeserving and less powerful targets because the source of frustration is unavailable or cannot be attacked.

scientific management Taylor's term for the attempt to maximize worker productivity by managing workers like they were machines.

script In rule-role theory, people's expectation about the sequences of behavior that are appropriate in a situation.

selective exposure A way of obtaining information. A person attends to data that support his or her choice and overlooks data that refute it.

self-concept The impression a person forms about himself or herself. A self-concept consists of ideas, attitudes, and beliefs and often is influenced by comparison with others.

self-consciousness Awareness of oneself as a social object. Also called **objective self-awareness.**

self-fulfilling prophecy Merton's term for a belief so strong that an attitude or a behavior is influenced by it, causing the belief to come true.

self-handicapping The process by which people who are threatened with failure make tasks more difficult in order to have an excuse for failing.

self-monitoring Snyder's concept summarizing the key factors that are influential in a person's ability to manage social relationships.

self-perception theory Bem's proposal that people use observations of their own behavior to judge their own attitudes.

self-reinforcement The process of rewarding or punishing oneself psychologically for various actions.

self-serving bias in causal attribution The tendency to see oneself as the cause of one's successes but to attribute failure to external sources.

sensitizing function of theory A characteristic function of theory in which possible factors that influence people's daily lives become apparent along with an awareness of the possible consequences of an action.

sensorimotor stage Piaget's first stage of cognitive development in which a child relies on incoming sensory experience for a perception and knowledge of the world. See also **concrete operational stage, formal operational stage, preoperational stage.**

serial reproduction An experimental task used to test whether information remains accurate as it passes through a communication network.

sex-role stereotype A cluster of social beliefs regarding the supposed characteristics and "proper" behavior of the two sexes.

sharpening A method of stimulus assimilation in which certain features of a stimulus are accentuated or made more apparent so that they may be used in identification or classification. See also **assimilation, leveling.**

similarity in attraction The finding that people are attracted to those persons whose interests, traits, and capacities are similar to their own.

simple and sovereign theories Theoretical formulations developed mainly during the nineteenth century. Such theories often rely on a single, guiding principle to explain social behavior.

sleeper effect in attitude change The increased power of a low credibility source in influencing an audience after a period of time has elapsed.

social comparison The process by which people compare themselves with others and in doing so discover the "proper" labels for themselves.

social distinctiveness The way in which people differ from one another.

social exchange theory See **exchange theory.**

social facilitation The improvement of a person's performance as a result of the presence of others.

social impact theory Latané's proposal that the impact people have on one another in a wide range of situations is determined by three major factors: the number of influence sources, the strength of the sources, and the closeness of the sources to the target.

social influence Pressure that changes behavior or attitudes in the direction of the prevailing patterns in a culture or subculture. See also **compliance, conformity, obedience.**

socialization The process by which the behavior of members of a given society is shaped by other members of the society. More specifically, the way in which children acquire a knowledge

of the standards and rules that are required to function in society.

social learning theory A theory proposing that social development occurs through observing other people's behavior and modeling oneself on this behavior.

social psychology A discipline that is devoted to the systematic study of human interaction and its psychological basis.

social reality A socially supported understanding of the world.

social systems accounting A technique similar to cost accounting in economics. Social systems accounting is designed to assess the social costs and benefits of various policies over time.

sociogram A visual representation of group members' individual social preferences.

sociometry A method of studying group structure by assessing individual members' social preferences.

stereotype A socially derived category into which people are placed solely on the basis of their group identification.

stimulus A situation or event that may elicit changes in an organism. See also **response.**

stress A physical and psychological reaction to a threat of some kind. An attitude of defense is adopted and there is a speedup in the functions controlled by the autonomic nervous system. See also **autonomic nervous system.**

superego The Freudian term for conscience.

sustaining mechanism in prejudice An influence that supports and maintains prejudice within social groups (for example, shared values and awareness of group membership).

system needs The needs of a group, as a system of related entities, for fulfillment of its functions. System needs may interfere with the personal need for free and autonomous action.

T

tame shift The tendency for decisions that are made after group discussion has taken place to be more conservative than those made by the individual group members prior to the discussion. Shifts toward risk also may occur. See also **risky shift.**

tension of obligation An uncomfortable psychological state that occurs when a person benefits from the actions of another and experiences indebtedness or the obligation to reciprocate.

Thanatos One of Freud's proposed primary motives. Thanatos is the instinct for death and destruction in humans. See also **Eros.**

Thematic Apperception Test (TAT) Murray's task in which a person is shown an ambiguous picture and is asked to make up a story about the picture. It is assumed that the subject will project into the story his or her deepest concerns.

theory A set of logically related propositions that describe and explain a domain of observation. In social psychology, theory may improve the understanding of and communications about social life; it may increase sensitivity to various processes that affect people's lives; and it may offer alternative forms of action.

trait A characteristic of personality.

trend line An indicator of changes in the character of a given phenomenon across time.

two-factor theory of emotions Schachter's proposal that a person's emotional experience requires generalized physical arousal followed by a cognitive label for the arousal.

Type A and Type B Categories used to describe patterns of adjustment. In contrast to Type Bs, Type As are extremely competitive and achievement-oriented and are more prone to coronary disease.

U

undermanning A condition that occurs when the number of persons available is below the number of essential tasks to be carried out in a given behavior setting. See also **optimal manning, overmanning.**

unobtrusive measure A method of obtaining information about a subject's behavior without his or her awareness. Unobtrusive measures do not change the behavior being studied.

V

variable That which is systematically varied or measured in an experiment. See also **dependent variable(s), independent variable(s).**

W

warm-glow effect The tendency for a person who has just been made to feel good about himself or herself to act in a more generous, or altruistic, manner.

weapons effect A situation in which the mere presence of weapons tends to increase the likelihood of aggressive behavior.

REFERENCE LIST

A

Abel, E. L. The relationship between cannabis and violence: A review. *Psychological Bulletin*, 1977, *84*, 193–211.

Abelson, R. P. Script processing, attitude formation, and decision making. In J. S. Carrol & J. W. Payne (Eds.), *Cognition and social behavior*. Hillsdale, N.J.: Lawrence Erlbaum, 1976.

Abelson, R. P., Aronson, E., McGuire, W. J., Newcomb, T. M., Rosenberg, M. J., & Tannenbaum, P. H. (Eds.). *Theories of cognitive consistency: A sourcebook*. Skokie, Ill.: Rand McNally, 1968.

Aberbach, J. D., & Walker, J. L. The meanings of black power. *American Political Science Review*. 1970, *64*, 367–388.

Abramson, L. Y., Seligman, M. E. P., & Teasdale, J. D. Learned helplessness in humans: Critique and reformulation. *Journal of Abnormal Psychology*, 1978, *87*, 49–74.

Adams, G. R. Physical attractiveness research: Toward a developmental social psychology of beauty. *Human Development*, 1977, *20*, 217–239.

Adams, J. S. Inequality in social exchange. In L. Berkowitz (Ed.), *Advances in experimental social psychology* (Vol. 2). New York: Academic Press, 1965.

Adams, J. S., & Jacobson, P. R. Effects of wage inequities on work quality. *Journal of Abnormal and Social Psychology*, 1964, *69*, 19–25.

Adler, A. *The practice and theory of individual personality*. New York: Harcourt Brace Jovanovich, 1929.

Adorno, T. W., Frenkel-Brunswick, E., Levinson, D. J., & Sanford, R. N. *The authoritarian personality*. New York: Harper & Row, 1950.

Aebischer, V. *Les femmes et le bavardage: Observations en psychologie sociale*. Unpublished doctoral dissertation, Ecole des Hautes Etudes en Science Sociales, Paris, 1979.

Aiello, J. R., Epstein, Y. M., & Karlin, R. A. Effects of crowding on electro dermal activity. *Sociological Symposium*, 1975, *14*, 42–57.

Ajzen, I. Intuitive theories of events and the effects of base-rate information on prediction. *Journal of Personality and Social Psychology*, 1977, *35*, 303–314.

Ajzen, I., & Fishbein, M. Attitude-behavior relations: A theoretical analysis and review of empirical research. *Psychological Bulletin*, 1977, *84*, 888–918.

Ajzen, I., & Fishbein, M. *Understanding attitudes and predicting social behavior*. Englewood Cliffs, N. J.: Prentice-Hall, 1980.

Albert, S., & Kessler, S. Ending social encounters. *Journal of Experimental Social Psychology*, 1978, *14*, 541–553.

Allen, V. L. Uncertainty of outcome and post-decision dissonance. In L. Festinger et al., *Conflict, decision, and dissonance*. Stanford, Calif.: Stanford University Press, 1964.

Allen, V. L. Situational factors in conformity. In L. Berkowitz (Ed.), *Advances in experimental social psychology* (Vol. 2). New York: Academic Press, 1965.

Allen, V. L. Social support for nonconformity. In L. Berkowitz (Ed.), *Advances in experimental social psychology* (Vol. 8). New York: Academic Press, 1975.

Allen, V. L., & Bragg, B. W. E. *The generalization of nonconformity within a homogeneous content dimension*. Unpublished manuscript, University of Wisconsin, Madison, 1965.

Allgeier, E. R., Byrne, D., Brooks, B., & Revnes, D. The waffle phenomenon: Negative evaluations of those who shift attitudinally. *Journal of Applied Social Psychology*, 1979, *9*, 170–182.

Allinsmith, W. The learning of moral standards. In D. R. Miller & G. E. Swanson (Eds.), *Inner conflict and defense*. New York: Holt, Rinehart & Winston, 1960.

Alloy, L. B., & Abramson, L. Y. Judgment of contingency in depressed and nondepressed college students: A nondepressive distortion. *Journal of Experimental Psychology: General*, 1979, *108*, 441–485.

Allport, F. H. The influence of the group upon association and thought. *Journal of Experimental Psychology*. 1920, *3*, 159–182.

Allport, F. H. *Social psychology*. Boston: Houghton Mifflin, 1924.

Allport, G. W. Attitudes. In C. Murchison (Ed.), *Handbook of social psychology*. Worcester, Mass.: Clark University Press, 1935.

Allport, G. W. *The Nature of Prejudice*. Reading, Mass.: Addison-Wesley, 1954.

Allport, G. W. The historical background of modern social psychology. In G. Lindzey & E. Aronson (Eds.), *The handbook of social psychology* (Vol. 1). Reading, Mass.: Addison-Wesley, 1968.

Allport, G. W., & Postman, L. *The psychology of rumor*. New York: Holt, Rinehart & Winston, 1947.

Allyn, J., & Festinger, L. The effectiveness of

unanticipated persuasive communication. *Journal of Abnormal and Social Psychology*, 1961, *62*, 35–40.

Almond, G. A., & Verba, S. *The civic culture.* Princeton, N.J.: Princeton University Press, 1963.

Alper, T. P., & Korchin, S. S. Memory for socially relevant material. *Journal of Abnormal and Social Psychology*, 1952, *47*, 25–38.

Alpert, R. *Power tactics used in intimate relations.* Unpublished manuscript, Temple University, Philadelphia, 1978.

Altman, I. *Environment and social behavior: Privacy, personal space, territory, and crowding.* Monterey, Calif.: Brooks/Cole, 1975.

Altman, I. Crowding: Historical and contemporary trends in crowding research. In A. Baum & Y. M. Epstein (Eds.), *Human response to crowding.* Hillsdale, N.J.: Lawrence Erlbaum, 1978.

Altman, I., & Gauvain, M. A cross-cultural and dialectic analysis of homes. In L. Liben, N. Newcombe, & A. Patterson (Eds.), *Spatial representation and behavior across the life span: Theory and application.* New York : Academic Press, in press.

Altman, I., & Haythorn, W. W. The ecology of isolated groups. *Behavioral Science,* 1967, *12,* 169–182.

Altman, I., & Taylor, D. A. *Social penetration: The development of interpersonal relationships.* New York: Holt, Rinehart & Winston, 1973.

Altman, I., Taylor, D. A., & Wheeler, L. Ecological aspects of group behavior in social isolation. *Journal of Applied Social Psychology,* 1971, *1,* 76–100.

Altus, W. D. Birth order and its sequelae. *Science,* 1966, *151,* 44–49.

Amir, M. *Patterns in forcible rape.* Chicago: University of Chicago Press, 1971.

Amir, Y. The role of intergroup contact in change of prejudice and ethnic relations. In P. A. Katz (Ed.), *Toward the elimination of racism.* Elmsford, N.Y.: Pergamon Press, 1976.

Anderson, E. A., & Burgess, R. L. *Interaction patterns between same-and-opposite gender parents and children in abusive and non-abusive families.* Paper presented at the 11th Annual Meeting of the Association for the Advancement of Behavior Therapy, Atlanta, December 1977.

Anderson, N. H. Averaging versus adding as a stimulus combination rule in impression formation. *Journal of Experimental Psychology,* 1965, *70,* 394–400.

Anderson, N. H. Component ratings in impression formation. *Psychonomic Science,* 1966, *6,* 279–280.

Anderson, N. H. Cognitive algebra: Integration theory applied to social attribution. In L. Berkowitz (Ed.), *Cognitive theories in social psychology.* New York: Academic Press, 1978.

Anderson, N. H., & Hubert, S. Effects of concomitant verbal recall on order effects in personality impression formation. *Journal of Verbal Learning and Verbal Behavior,* 1963, *2,* 379–391.

Anderson, R., Manoogian, S. T., & Reznick, J. S. The undermining and enhancing of intrinsic motivation in preschool children. *Journal of Personality and Social Psychology,* 1976, *34,* 915–922.

Ando, Y., & Hattori, H. Statistical studies on the effects of intense noise during human fetal life. *Journal of Sound and Vibration,* 1973, *27,* 101–110.

Andreas, C. R. To receive from kings: An examination of government-to-government aid and its unintended consequences. *Journal of Social Issues,* 1969, *25,* 167–180.

Andrews, F. M., & Witney, S. B. *Social indicators of well-being: Americans' perceptions of life quality.* New York: Plenum, 1976.

Apfelbaum, E. *Prolegomena for a history of social psychology: Some hypotheses concerning its emergence in the 20th century and its raison d'etre.* Paper presented at the Cheiron Society, 1978.

Apfelbaum, E., & Lubek, I. Resolution vs. revolution? The theory of conflicts in question. In L. Strickland, F. Aboud, & K. J. Gergen (Eds.), *Social psychology in transition.* New York: Plenum, 1976.

Apsler, R. Effects of embarrassment on behavior toward others. *Journal of Personality and Social Psychology,* 1975, *32,* 145–153.

Apsler, R., & Friedman, H. Chance outcomes and a just world: A comparison of observers and recipients. *Journal of Personality and Social Psychology,* 1975, *31,* 887–894.

Archer, R. L., & Berg, J. H. Disclosure reciprocity and its limits: A reactance analysis. *Journal of Experimental Social Psychology,* 1978, *14,* 527–540.

Archer, R. L., & Burleson, J. A. The effects of timing of self-disclosure on attraction and reciprocity. *Journal of Personality and Social Psychology,* 1980, *38,* 120–130.

Argyle, M. *Bodily communication.* New York: International Universities Press, 1975.

Argyle, M., Lefebvre, L., & Cook, M. The meaning of five patterns of gaze. *European Journal of Social Psychology,* 1974, *4,* 125–136.

Argyle, M., & McHenry, R. Do spectacles really affect judgments of intelligence? *British Journal of Social and Clinical Psychology,* 1971, *10,* 27–29.

Argyle, M., Trower, P. E., & Bryant, B. M. Explorations in the treatment of personality disorders and neuroses by social skills training. *British Journal of Medical Psychology,* 1974, *47,* 63–72.

Arkin, R. M., Appelman, A. J., & Burger, J. M. Social anxiety, self-presentation and the self-serving bias in causal attribution. *Journal of Personality and Social Psychology,* 1980, *38,* 23–35.

Armor, D. J. The evidence on busing. *Public Interest,* 1972, *28,* 90–126.

Armor, D. J. *Measuring the effects of television on aggressive behavior.* Santa Monica, Calif.: Rand Corporation, 1976.

Aronfreed, J. M. The effects of experimental socialization paradigms upon two moral responses to transgression. *Journal of Abnormal and Social Psychology,* 1963, *66,* 437–448.

Aronfreed, J. M. *Conduct and conscience: The socialization of internalized control over behavior.* New York: Academic Press, 1968.

Aronfreed, J. M., & Leff, R. *The effects of intensity of punishment and complexity of discrimination upon the learning of internalized suppression.* Unpublished manuscript, University of Pennsylvania, Philadelphia, 1963.

Aronfreed, J. M., & Reber, A. Internalized behavioral suppression and the timing of social punishment. *Journal of Personality and Social Psychology,* 1965, *1,* 3–16.

Aronson, E., & Geffner, R. The effects of a cooperative classroom structure on students' behavior and attitudes. In D. Bar-Tal & L. Saxe (Eds.), *Social psychology of education: Theory and research.* Washington, D.C.: Hemisphere, 1978.

Aronson, E., & Golden, B. The effect of relevant and irrelevant aspects of communicator credibility on opinion change. *Journal of Personality,* 1962, *30,* 135–146.

Aronson, E., & Mills, T. Effects of severity of initiation on liking for a group. *Journal of Abnormal and Social Psychology,* 1959, *59,* 177–181.

Aronson, E., & Osherow, N. Cooperation, prosocial behavior, and academic performance: Experiments in the desegregated classroom. In L. Bickman (Ed.), *Applied social psychology annual* (Vol. 1). Beverly Hills, Calif.: Sage Publications, 1980.

Aronson, E., & Worchel, P. Similarity vs. liking as determinants of interpersonal attractiveness. *Psychonomic Science,* 1966, *5,* 157–158.

Arrowood, J., & Short, J. A. Agreement, attraction, and self-esteem. *Canadian Journal of Behavioral Science,* 1973, *5,* 242–252.

Asch, S. E. Forming impressions of personality. *Journal of Abnormal and Social Psychology,* 1946, *41,* 258–290.

Asch, S. E. *Social psychology.* Englewood Cliffs, N.J.: Prentice-Hall, 1952.

Asch, S. E. Studies of independence and conformity: A minority of one against a unanimous majority. *Psychological Monographs,* 1956, *70* (Whole No. 416).

Asher, S., & Allen, V. L. Racial preference and social comparison processes. *Journal of Social Issues,* 1969, *25,* 157–165.

Ashmore, R. D. Prejudice: Causes and cures. In B. E. Collins, *Social psychology.* Reading, Mass.: Addison-Wesley, 1970.

Ashmore, R. D., & Butsch, R. J. *Perceived threat and the perception of violence in biracial settings: Toward an experimental paradigm.* Paper presented at the meeting of the Eastern Psychological Association, Boston, April 1972.

Ashmore, R. D., Ramchandra, V., & Jones, R. A. *Censorship as an attitude change induction.* Paper presented at the meeting of the Eastern Psychological Association, New York, April 1971.

Austin, W. Sex differences in bystander intervention in a theft. *Journal of Personality and Social Psychology,* 1979, 37, 2110–2120.

Austin, W., Walster, E., & Utne, M. K. Equity and the law: The effect of a harm-doer's "suffering in the act" on liking and assigned punishment. In L. Berkowitz & E. Walster (Eds.), *Advances in experimental social psychology* (Vol. 9). New York: Academic Press, 1976.

Averill, J. R. A constructivist view of emotion. In R. Plutchik & H. Kellerman (Eds.), *Emotion: Theory, research and experience.* New York: Academic Press, 1980.

Ax, A. F. The physiological differentiation between fear and anger in humans. *Psychosomatic Medicine,* 1953, 15, 433–442.

B

Back, K. W. Influence through social communication. *Journal of Abnormal and Social Psychology,* 1951, 46, 9–23.

Back, K. W. Influence through social communication. In E. Maccoby, T. Newcomb, & E. Hartley (Eds.), *Readings in social psychology.* New York: Holt, Rinehart & Winston, 1958.

Back, K. W. *Beyond words.* New York: Russell Sage Foundation, 1972.

Back, K. W., & Gergen, K. J. Apocalyptic and serial time orientation and the structure of opinions. *Public Opinion Quarterly,* 1963, 27, 427–442.

Backman, C., & Secord, P. F. The effect of perceived liking on interpersonal attraction. *Human Relations,* 1959, 12, 379–384.

Bagehot, W. *Physics and Politics.* New York: D. Appleton, 1875.

Baird, L. L. Big school, small school: A critical examination of the hypothesis. *Journal of Educational Psychology,* 1969, 60, 253–260.

Bakan, D. *The duality of human existence.* Skokie, Ill.: Rand McNally, 1966.

Baker, J. W., & Schaie, K. W. Effects of aggressing "alone" or "with another" on physiological and psychological arousal. *Journal of Personality and Social Psychology,* 1969, 12, 80–86.

Baldwin, J. M. *Mental development in the child and in the race.* New York: Macmillan, 1895.

Bales, R. F. *Interaction process analysis: A method for the study of small groups.* Reading, Mass.: Addison-Wesley, 1950.

Bales, R. F. *Personality and interpersonal behavior.* New York: Holt, Rinehart & Winston, 1970.

Bales R. F., & Cohen, S. P. *SYMLOG: A system for the multiple level observation of groups.* New York: Free Press, 1979.

Bandura, A. *Relationship of family patterns to child behavior disorders.* Progress Report, Stanford University, Stanford, Calif., Project No. M-1734, U.S. Public Health Service, 1960.

Bandura, A. Vicarious and self-reinforcement processes. In R. Glaser (Ed.), *The nature of reinforcement.* New York: Academic Press, 1971.

Bandura, A. *Aggression: A social learning analysis.* Englewood Cliffs, N.J.: Prentice-Hall, 1973.

Bandura, A. *Social learning theory.* Englewood Cliffs, N.J.: Prentice-Hall, 1977.

Bandura, A., & Kupers, C. J. The transmission of patterns of self-reinforcement through modeling. *Journal of Abnormal and Social Psychology,* 1964, 69, 1–9.

Bandura, A., & MacDonald, F. J. The influence of social reinforcement and the behavior of models in shaping children's moral judgments. *Journal of Abnormal and Social Psychology,* 1963, 67, 274–281.

Bandura, A., Ross, O., & Ross, S. A. Transmission of aggression through imitation of aggressive models. *Journal of Abnormal and Social Psychology,* 1961, 63, 575–582.

Bandura, A., & Walters, R. H. *Social learning and personality development.* New York: Holt, Rinehart & Winston, 1963.

Barash, D. P. *Sociobiology and behavior.* New York: Elsevier, North Holland, 1977.

Barefoot, J. C., & Girodo, M. The misattribution of smoking cessation symptoms. *Canadian Journal of Behavior Science,* 1972, 4, 358–363.

Baritz, L. *The servants of power: A history of the use of social science in American industry.* Middletown, Conn.: Wesleyan University Press, 1980.

Barker, R. G., & Schoggen, P. *Qualities of community life.* San Francisco: Jossey-Bass, 1973.

Barker, R. G., & Wright, H. F. *One boy's day.* New York: Harper & Row, 1951.

Barker, R. G., & Wright, H. F. *Midwest and its children: The psychological ecology of an American town.* New York: Harper & Row, 1955.

Barnes, S. F. *The transmission of positive and negative romantic messages using the lost-letter technique.* Unpublished paper, Wright State University, Dayton, Ohio, 1972.

Baron, R. A. The aggression-inhibiting influence of heightened sexual arousal. *Journal of Personality and Social Psychology,* 1974, 30, 318–322.

Baron, R. A. *Human aggression.* New York: Plenum, 1977.

Baron, R. A. The aggression-inhibiting influence of sexual humor. *Journal of Personality and Social Psychology,* 1978, 36, 189–197.

Baron, R. A., & Bell, P. A. Aggression and heat: Mediating effects of prior provocation and exposure to an aggressive model. *Journal of Personality and Social Psychology,* 1975, 31, 825–832.

Baron, R. A., & Bell, P. A. Sexual arousal and aggression by males: Effects of type of erotic stimuli and prior provocation. *Journal of Personality and Social Psychology,* 1977, 35, 79–87.

Baron, R. A., & Lawton, S. F. Environmental influences on aggression: The facilitation of modeling effects by high ambient temperatures. *Psychonomic Science,* 1972, 26, 80–83.

Baron, R. A., & Ransberger, V. M. Ambient temperature and the occurrence of collective violence: The "long, hot summer" revisited. *Journal of Personality and Social Psychology,* 1978, 36, 351–360.

Baron, R. M., & Rodin, J. Personal control as a mediator of crowding. In A. Baum, J. E. Singer, & S. Valins (Eds.), *Advances in experimental psychology* (Vol. 1). Hillsdale, N.J.: Lawrence Erlbaum, 1978.

Baron, R. S., Baron, P., & Miller, N. The relation between distraction and persuasion. *Psychological Bulletin,* 1973, 80, 310–323.

Bar-Tal, D. *Prosocial behavior: Theory and research.* Washington, D.C.: Hemisphere, 1976.

Bar-Tal, D. Interactions of teachers and pupils. In I. H. Frieze, D. Bar-Tal, & J. Carroll (Eds.), *New approaches to social problems.* San Francisco: Jossey-Bass, 1979.

Bar-Tal, D., & Frieze, I. H. Achievement motivation for males and females as a determinant for attributions for success and failure. *Sex Roles,* 1977, 3, 301–313.

Bar-Tal, D., & Saxe, L. Perceptions of similarly and dissimilarly attractive couples. *Journal of Personality and Social Psychology,* 1976, 33, 772–781.

Bartlett, F. C. *Remembering.* Cambridge, England: Cambridge University Press, 1932.

Barton, E. M., Baltes, M. M., & Orzech, M. J. Etiology of dependence in older nursing home residents during morning care: The role of staff behavior. *Journal of Personality and Social Psychology,* 1980, 38, 423–431.

Bass, B. M. The leaderless group discussion. *Psychological Bulletin,* 1954, 51, 465–492.

Bass, B. M. Effects on the subsequent performance of negotiators of studying issues or planning strategies alone or in groups. *Psychological Monographs,* 1966, 80 (Whole No. 614).

Basseches, M. Dialectical schemata: A

framework for the empirical study of the development of dialectical thinking. *Human Development*, in press.

Bateson, N. Familiarization, group discussion, and risk taking. *Journal of Experimental Social Psychology*, 1966, *2*, 119–129.

Batson, D. C., Pate, S., Lawless, H., Sparkman, P., Lambers, S., & Worman, B. Helping under conditions of common threat: Increased "we-feeling" or ensuring reciprocity. *Social Psychology Quarterly*, 1979, *42*, 410–414.

Bauer, R. A. (Ed.). *Social indicators*. Cambridge, Mass.: M.I.T. Press, 1967.

Bauer, R. A. The obstinate audience: The influence process from the point of view of social communication. *American Psychologist*, 1964, *19*, 319–328.

Baum, A., & Greenberg, C. I. Waiting for a crowd: The behavioral and perceptual effects of anticipated crowding. *Journal of Personality and Social Psychology*, 1975, *32*, 671–679.

Baum, A., & Koman, S. K. Differential response to anticipated crowding: Psychological effects of social and spatial density. *Journal of Personality and Social Psychology*, 1976, *34*, 526–536.

Baum, A., & Valins, S. *Architecture and social behavior: Psychological studies of social density*. Hillsdale, N.J.: Lawrence Erlbaum, 1977.

Baumrind, D. Some thoughts on the ethics of research: After reading Milgram's "Behavior study of obedience." *American Psychologist*, 1964, *19*, 421–423.

Baumrind, D. IRB's and social science research: The costs of deception. *IRB: A Review of Human Subjects Research*, 1979, *1*, 1–4.

Bayton, J. A., McAlister, L. B., & Hammer, J. R. Race-class stereotypes. *Journal of Negro Education*, Winter 1956, 75–78.

Beaman, A. L., Klentz, B., Diener, E., & Svanum, S. Self-awareness and transgression in children: Two field studies. *Journal of Personality and Social Psychology*, 1979, *37*, 1835–1846.

Becker, E. *The structure of evil*. New York: George Braziller, 1968.

Becker, F. D., Sommer, R., Bee, J., & Oxley, B. College classroom ecology. *Sociometry*, 1973, *36*, 514–525.

Begum, B. O., & Lehr, D. J. Effects of authoritarianism on vigilance performance. *Journal of Applied Psychology*, 1963, *47*, 75–77.

Bell, P. A., & Baron, R. A. Aggression and heat: The influence of ambient temperature, negative affect and a cooling drink on physical aggression. *Journal of Personality and Social Psychology*, 1976, *33*, 245–255.

Bell, P. A., Fisher, J. D., & Loomis, R. T. *Environmental psychology*. Philadelphia: W. B. Saunders, 1978.

Belmont, L., & Marolla, F. A. Birth order, family size, and intelligence. *Science*, 1973, *182*, 1096–1101.

Beloff, H. Two forms of social conformity: Acquiescence and conventionality. *Journal of Abnormal and Social Psychology*, 1958, *56*, 99–104.

Bem, D. J. Self-perception theory. In L. Berkowitz (Ed.), *Advances in experimental social psychology* (Vol. 6). New York: Academic Press, 1972.

Bem, D. J., & Allen, A. On predicting some of the people some of the time: The search for cross-situational consistencies in behavior. *Psychological Review*, 1974, *81*, 506–520.

Bem, S. L. The measurement of psychological androgyny. *Journal of Consulting and Clinical Psychology*, 1974, *42*, 115–162.

Bem, S. L. Sex role adaptability: One consequence of psychological androgyny. *Journal of Personality and Social Psychology*, 1975, *31*, 634–643.

Bem, S. L. On the utility of alternative procedures for assessing psychological androgyny. *Journal of Consulting and Clinical Psychology*, 1977, *45*, 196–205.

Bem, S. L. Theory and measurement of androgyny: A reply to the Pedhazur-Tetenbaum and Locksley-Colten critiques. *Journal of Personality and Social Psychology*, 1979, *37*, 1047–1054.

Bem, S. L., & Lenney, E. Sex typing and the avoidance of cross-sex behavior. *Journal of Personality and Social Psychology*, 1976, *33*, 48–54.

Bem, S. L., Martyna, W., & Watson, C. Sex typing and androgyny: Further explorations of the expressive domain. *Journal of Personality and Social Psychology*, 1976, *34*, 1016–1023.

Benassi, V. A., Sweeney, P. D., & Drevno, G. E. Mind over matter: Perceived success at psychokinesis. *Journal of Personality and Social Psychology*, 1979, *37*, 1377–1386.

Benedict, R. *The chrysanthemum and the sword*. Boston: Houghton Mifflin, 1946.

Bennett, R. M., Buss, A. H., & Carpenter, J. A. Alcohol and human physical aggression. *Quarterly Journal of Studies on Alcohol*, 1969, *30*, 870–877.

Benton, A. A. Productivity, distributive justice, and bargaining among children. *Journal of Personality and Social Psychology*, 1971, *18*, 68–78.

Berelson, B., Lazarsfeld, P. F., & McPhee, W. N. *Voting*. Chicago: University of Chicago Press, 1954.

Berg, D. A descriptive analysis of the distribution and duration of themes discussed by task-oriented small groups. *Speech Monographs*, 1967, *34*, 172–175.

Berg, K. S., & Vidmar, N. Authoritarianism and recall of evidence about criminal behavior. *Journal of Research in Personality*, 1975, *9*, 147–157.

Berger, P., & Luckmann, T. *The social construction of reality*. New York: Doubleday/Anchor, 1966.

Berger, S. M. Conditioning through vicarious instigation. *Psychological Review*, 1962, *69*, 450–466.

Bergin, A. E. The effects of dissonant persuasive communications upon changes in self-referring attitudes. *Journal of Personality*, 1962, *30*, 423–438.

Berglas, S., & Jones, E. E. Drug choice as a self-handicapping strategy in response to noncontigent success. *Journal of Personality and Social Psychology*, 1978, *36*, 410–417.

Bergman, B. A. The effects of group size, personal space, and success-failure on physiological arousal, test performance and questionnaire response. Unpublished doctoral dissertation, Temple University, Philadelphia, 1971.

Berk, R. A., Cooley, T. F., Lacivita, C. J., Parker, S., Sredl, K., & Brewer, M. Reducing consumption in periods of acute scarcity: The case of water. In E. W. Stromsdorfer & G. Farkas (Eds.), *Evaluation studies: Review annual* (Vol. 5). Beverly Hills, Calif.: Sage Publications, 1980.

Berkowitz, L. Effects of perceived dependency relationships upon conformity to group expectations. *Journal of Abnormal and Social Psychology*, 1957, *55*, 350–354.

Berkowitz, L. *Roots of aggression: A re-examination of the frustration-aggression hypothesis*. New York: Atherton Press, 1969.

Berkowitz, L. The self, selfishness and altruism. In J. M. Macaulay & L. Berkowitz (Eds.), *Altruism and helping behavior*. New York: Academic Press, 1970.

Berkowitz, L. Social norms, feelings, and other factors affecting helping and altruism. In L. Berkowitz (Ed.), *Advances in experimental social psychology* (Vol. 6). New York: Academic Press, 1972.

Berkowitz, L. Reactance and the unwillingness to help others. *Psychological Bulletin*, 1973, *79*, 310–317.

Berkowitz, L. Decreased helpfulness with increased group size through lessening the effects of the needy individuals' dependency. *Journal of Personality*, 1978, *46*, 299–310.

Berkowitz, L., & Alioto, J. T. The meaning of an observed event as a determinant of its aggressive consequences. *Journal of Personality and Social Psychology*, 1973, *28*, 206–217.

Berkowitz, L., & Daniels, L. R. Responsibility and dependency. *Journal of Abnormal and Social Psychology*, 1963, *66*, 429–436.

Berkowitz, L., & Geen, R. G. Stimulus qualities of the target of aggression: A further study. *Journal of Personality and Social Psychology*, 1967, *5*, 364–368.

Berkowitz, L., Green, J. A., & Macaulay, J. R. Hostility catharsis as the reduction of emotional tension. *Psychiatry*, 1962, *25*, 23–31.

Berkowitz, L., & Lepage, A. Weapons as aggression-eliciting stimuli. *Journal of*

Personality and Social Psychology, 1967, 7, 202–207.

Berle, A. *Power*. New York: Harcourt Brace Jovanovich, 1967.

Bernard, J. *The future of marriage*. New York: World, 1972.

Bernard, L. L. *Instinct: A study in social psychology*. New York: Holt, Rinehart & Winston, 1926.

Bernard, L. L. Social psychology. In *Encyclopedia of Social Science* (Vol. 14). New York: Macmillan, 1934.

Bernstein, A. M., Stephan, W. G., & Davis, M. H. Explaining attribution for achievement: A path analytic approach. *Journal of Personality and Social Psychology*, 1979, 37, 1810–1821.

Berscheid, E. Opinion change and communicator-communicatee similarity and dissimilarity. *Journal of Personality and Social Psychology*, 1966, 4, 670–680.

Berscheid, E., & Graziano, W. The initiation of social relationships and interpersonal attraction. In R. L. Burgess & T. L. Huston (Eds.), *Social exchange in developing relationships*. New York: Academic Press, 1979.

Berscheid, E., Graziano, W., Munson, M., & Dermer, M. Outcome dependency: Attention, attribution, and attraction. *Journal of Personality and Social Psychology*, 1976, 34, 978–989.

Berscheid, E., & Walster, E. *Interpersonal attraction*. Reading, Mass.: Addison-Wesley, 1969.

Berscheid, E., & Walster, E. A little bit about love. In T. L. Huston (Ed.), *Foundations of interpersonal attraction*. New York: Academic Press, 1974.

Berscheid, E., Walster, E., & Bohrnstedt, G. The body image report. *Psychology Today*, 1973, 7, 119–131.

Bickman, L. Social influence and diffusion of responsibility in an emergency. *Journal of Experimental Social Psychology*, 1972, 8, 438–445.

Bickman, L. The social power of a uniform. *Journal of Applied Social Psychology*, 1974, 1, 47–61.

Bickman, L., Teger, A., Gabriele, T., McLaughlin, C., Berger, M., & Sunaday, E. Dormitory density and helping behavior. *Environment and behavior*, 1973, 5, 465–490.

Bigelow, D., & Carlo, D. The impact of therapeutic effectiveness data on community mental health center management: The systems evaluation project. *Community Mental Health Journal*, 1975, 11, 64–73.

Biggers, J. L. Machiavellianism in a prospective teacher group. *Education*, 1977, 98, 91–96.

Billig, M., & Tajfel, H. Social categorization and similarity in intergroup behavior. *European Journal of Social Psychology*, 1973, 3, 27–52.

Birnbaum, M. H., & Mellers, B. A. Stimulus recognition may mediate exposure effects. *Journal of Personality and Social Psychology*, 1979, 37, 391–394.

Birnbaum, M. H., & Stegner, S. E. Source credibility in social judgment: Bias, expertise and the judge's point of view. *Journal of Personality and Social Psychology*, 1979, 37, 48–74.

Blake, R. R., & Mouton, S. Competition, communication and conformity. In I. A. Berg & B. M. Bass (Eds.), *Conformity and deviation*. New York: Harper & Row, 1961.

Blanchard, F. A., Adelman, L., & Cook, S. W. Effect of group success and failure upon interpersonal attraction in cooperating interracial groups. *Journal of Personality and Social Psychology*, 1975, 31, 1020–1030.

Blau, P. M. Social integration, social rank and the process of interaction. *Human Relations*, 1959, 18, 152–157.

Blau, P. M. *Exchange and power in social life*. New York: John Wiley & Sons, 1964.

Bleda, P. Toward a clarification of the role of cognitive and affective processes in the similarity-attraction relationship. *Journal of Personality and Social Psychology*, 1974, 29, 368–373.

Block, J. Advancing the psychology of personality: Paradigmatic shift or improving the quality of research. In D. Magnusson & N. S. Endler (Eds.), *Personality at the crossroads: Current issues in interactional psychology*. Hillsdale, N.J.: Lawrence Erlbaum, 1977.

Blood, R. O., Jr. *Love match and arranged marriage*. New York: Free Press, 1967.

Blood, R. O., Jr., & Wolfe, D. M. *Husbands and wives: The dynamics of married living*. New York: Free Press, 1960.

Blum, E. R., & Kennedy, W. A. Modification of dominant behavior in school children. *Journal of Personality and Social Psychology*, 1967, 7, 275–281.

Blumenthal, A. L. A reappraisal of Wilhelm Wundt. *American Psychologist*, 1975, 30, 1081–1086.

Blumenthal, A. L. Wilhelm Wundt and early American psychology: A clash of two cultures. *Annals of the New York Academy of Sciences*, 1977, 291, 13–20.

Blumenthal, M. D., Chadiha, L. B., Cole, G. A., & Jayaratne, T. E. *More about justifying violence: Methodological studies of attitudes and behavior*. Ann Arbor: University of Michigan Press, 1975.

Blumenthal, M. D., Kahn, R. L., Andrews, F. M., & Head, K. B. *Justifying violence: Attitudes of American men*. Ann Arbor, Mich.: Institute for Social Research, 1972.

Bogart, K., Geis, F., Levy, M., & Zimbardo, P. No dissonance for Machiavellians. In R. Christie & F. L. Geis (Eds.), *Studies in Machiavellianism*. New York: Academic Press, 1970.

Bohmer, C., & Blumberg, A. Twice traumatized: The rape victim and the court. *Judicature*, 1975, 58, 390–399.

Bonoma, T. D., & Tedeschi, J. T. Some effects of source behavior on targets' compliance to threats. *Behavioral Science*, 1973, 18, 34–41.

Booth, A., & Cowell, J. *The effects of crowding upon health*. Paper presented at the meeting of the American Population Association, New York, 1974.

Booth, A., & Johnson, D. R. The effect of crowding on child health and development. *American Behavioral Scientist*, 1975, 18, 736–749.

Borden, R. J. Audience influence. In P. B. Paulus (Ed.), *Psychology of social influence*. Hillsdale, N.J.: Lawrence Erlbaum, 1980.

Borgida, E., & Nisbett, R. E. The differential impact of abstract vs. concrete information on decisions. *Journal of Applied Social Psychology*, 1977, 7, 258–271.

Bourne, L. E., Dominowski, R. L., & Loftus, E. F. *Cognitive processes*. Englewood Cliffs, N.J.: Prentice-Hall, 1979.

Boutilier, R. G., Roed, J. C., & Svendsen, A. C. Crisis in the two social psychologies: A critical comparison. *Social Psychology Quarterly*, 1980, 43, 5–17.

Bowers, K. S. Situationism in psychology: An analysis and a critique. *Psychological Review*, 1973, 80, 307–336.

Bowman, C. H., & Fishbein, M. Understanding public reaction to energy proposals: An application of the Fishbein model. *Journal of Applied Social Psychology*, 1978, 8, 319–340.

Boyanowsky, E. O., & Trueman, M. *Generalization of independence mediated by self-role congruence*. Unpublished manuscript, 1972.

Bradburn, N. *The structure of psychological well-being*. Chicago: Aldine, 1969.

Bradley, G. W. Self-serving biases in the attribution process: A re-examination of the fact or fiction question. *Journal of Personality and Social Psychology*, 1978, 36, 56–71.

Bragg, B. W. E. *The effect of variable social support on within-content generalization of nonconformity*. Unpublished manuscript, 1972.

Braginsky, B. M., Braginsky, D. D., & Ring, K. *Methods of Madness: The mental hospital as a last resort*. New York: Holt, Rinehart & Winston, 1969.

Braginsky, D. D., & Braginsky, B. M. Surplus people: Their lost faith in self and system. *Psychology Today*, 1975, 9, 68–72.

Braiker, H. B., & Kelley, H. H. Conflict in the development of close relationships. In R. L. Burgess & T. L. Huston (Eds.), *Social exchange in developing relationships*. New York: Academic Press, 1979.

Brain, R. *Friends and lovers*. New York: Basic Books, 1976.

Brand, R. J., Rosenman, R. H., Sholtz, R. I., & Friedman, M. Multivariate prediction of coronary heart disease in the Western Collaborative Group Study compared to the findings of the Framingham Study. *Circulation*, 1976, *53*, 348–355.

Brandstätter, H. Social emotions in discussion groups. In H. Brandstätter, J. H. Davis, & H. Schuler (Eds.), *Dynamics of group decisions.* Beverly Hills, Calif.: Sage Publications, 1978.

Brannon, R., Cyphers, G., Hesse, S., Hesselbart, S., Keane, R., Schuman, H., Vicarro, T., & Wright, D. Attitude action: A field experiment joined to a general population survey. *American Sociological Review*, 1973, *38*, 625–636.

Bray, R. M., & Noble, A. M. Authoritarianism and decisions of mock juries: Evidence of jury bias and group polarization. *Journal of Personality and Social Psychology*, 1978, *36*, 1424–1430.

Brehm, J. W. Post-decision changes in the desirability of alternatives. *Journal of Abnormal and Social Psychology*, 1956, *52*, 384–389.

Brehm, J. W. Attitudinal consequences of commitment to unpleasant behavior. *Journal of Abnormal and Social Psychology*, 1960, *60*, 379–383.

Brehm, J. W. *A theory of psychological reactance.* New York: Academic Press, 1966.

Brehm, J. W., & Cole, A. Effect of a favor which reduces freedom. *Journal of Personality and Social Psychology*, 1966, *3*, 420–426.

Brehm, J. W., & Crocker, J. C. An experiment on hunger. In J. W. Brehm & A. R. Cohen, *Explorations in cognitive dissonance.* New York: John Wiley & Sons, 1962.

Brehm, J. W., Gatz, G., Goethals, G., McCrommon, J., & Ward, L. *Psychological arousal and interpersonal attraction.* Mimeographed, 1970.

Brehm, J. W., & Mann, M. Effect of importance of freedom and attraction to group members on influence produced by group pressure. *Journal of Personality and Social Psychology*, 1975, *31*, 816–828.

Breland, H. M. Birth order effects: A reply to Schooler. *Psychological Bulletin*, 1973, *80*, 210–212.

Brewer, M. B. *Cognitive differentiation and intergroup bias: Cross-cultural studies.* Paper presented at the Symposium on the Development and Maintenance of Intergroup Bias, Annual Meeting of the American Psychological Association, New Orleans, 1974.

Brewer, M. B. In-group bias in the minimal group situation: A cognitive motivational analysis. *Psychological Bulletin*, 1979, *86*, 307–324.

Brickman, P., Rabinowitz, V. C., Coates, D., Cohn, E., Kidder, L., & Karuza, J. *Helping.* Unpublished manuscript, University of Michigan, Ann Arbor, 1979.

Brickman, P., Ryan, K., & Wortman, C. Causal chains: Attribution of responsibility as a function of immediate and prior causes. *Journal of Personality and Social Psychology*, 1975, *32*, 1060–1067.

Briggs, S. R., Cheek, J. M., & Buss, A. H. An analysis of the self-monitoring scale. *Journal of Personality and Social Psychology*, 1980, *38*, 679–686.

Brigham, J. C. *Views of white and black schoolchildren concerning racial differences.* Paper presented at the meeting of the Midwestern Psychological Association, Detroit, 1971.

Brinberg, D. An examination of the determinants of intention and behavior: A comparison of two models. *Journal of Applied Social Psychology*, 1979, *9*, 560–575.

Brink, J. R. Effect of interpersonal communication on attraction. *Journal of Personality and Social Psychology*, 1977, *35*, 783–790.

Brock, T. Communicator-recipient similarity and decision change. *Journal of Personality and Social Psychology*, 1965, *1*, 650–654.

Broll, L., Gross, A., & Piliavin, I. Effects of offered and requested help on help seeking and reactions to being helped. *Journal of Applied Social Psychology*, 1974, *4*, 244–258.

Bronfenbrenner, U. Freudian theories of identification and their derivatives. *Child Development*, 1960, *31*, 15–40.

Bronfenbrenner, U. *The ecology of human development: Experiments by nature and design.* Cambridge, Mass.: Harvard University Press, 1979.

Broverman, I. K., Broverman, D. M., Clarkson, F. E., Rosenkrantz, P. S., & Vogel, S. R. Sex-role stereotypes and clinical judgments of mental health. *Journal of Consulting and Clinical Psychology*, 1970, *34*, 1–7.

Broverman, I. K., Vogel, S. R., Broverman, D. M., Clarkson, F. E., & Rosenkrantz, P. S. Sex-role stereotypes: A current appraisal. *Journal of Social Issues*, 1972, *28*, 59–78.

Brown, B. R. The effects of need to maintain face on interpersonal bargaining. *Journal of Experimental Social Psychology*, 1968, *4*, 107–122.

Brown, D. G. Sex role development in a changing culture. *Psychological Bulletin*, 1958, *55*, 232–242.

Brown, H. *Brain and behavior.* New York: Oxford University Press, 1976.

Brown, I. J. Learned helplessness through modeling: Self-efficacy and social comparison processes. In L. C. Perlmutter & R. A. Monty (Eds.), *Choice and perceived control.* Hillsdale, N.J.: Lawrence Erlbaum, 1979.

Brown, I. J., & Inouye, D. K. Learned helplessness through modeling: The role of perceived similarity in competence. *Journal of Personality and Social Psychology*, 1978, *36*, 900–908.

Brown, M., & Amoroso, D. M. Attitudes toward homosexuality among West Indian male and female college students. *Journal of Social Psychology*, 1975, *97*, 163–168.

Brown, P., & Elliott, R. Control of aggression in a nursery school class. *Journal of Experimental Child Psychology*, 1965, *2*, 103–107.

Brown, R. W. *Words and things.* New York: Free Press, 1958.

Brown, R. W. *Social psychology.* New York: Free Press, 1965.

Brownmiller, S. *Against our will: Men, women, and rape.* New York: Bantam Books, 1975.

Bryan, J. H. Model affect and children's imitative behavior. *Child Development*, 1971, *42*, 2061–2065.

Bryan, J. H., & Test, M. Models and helping: Naturalistic studies in aiding behavior. *Journal of Personality and Social Psychology*, 1967, *6*, 400–407.

Bryan, J. H., & Walbek, N. Preaching and practicing generosity: Children's actions and reactions. *Child Development*, 1970, *41*, 329–353.

Buck, R. W. A test of non-verbal receiving ability: Preliminary studies. *Human Communication Research*, 1976, *2*, 162–171.

Buck, R. W., & Parke, R. D. Behavioral and physiological response to the presence of a friendly or neutral person in two types of stressful situations. *Journal of Personality and Social Psychology*, 1972, *24*, 143–153.

Buck, R. W., Savin, V. J., Miller, R. E., & Caul, W. F. Communication of affect through facial expressions in humans. *Journal of Personality and Social Psychology*, 1972, *23*, 362–371.

Buckhout, R., Figueroa, D., & Hoff, E. *Eyewitness identification: Effects of suggestion and bias in identifications from photographs* (Report No. CR-11). Center for Responsive Psychology, Brooklyn College, New York, May 1974.

Bunker, B. B., & Seashore, E. W. Power; collusion; intimacy-sexuality; support. In A. G. Sargent (Ed.), *Beyond sex roles.* St. Paul: West, 1977.

Burgess, E. W., & Wallin, P. *Engagement and marriage.* Chicago: J. B. Lippincott, 1953.

Burgess, T. O. G., II, & Sales S. M. Attitudinal effects of "mere exposure": A re-evaluation. *Journal of Experimental Social Psychology*, 1971, *7*, 461–462.

Burnstein, E. Sources of cognitive bias in the representation of simple social structures: Balance, minimal change, reciprocity, and the respondent's own attitude. *Journal of Personality and Social Psychology*, 1967, *7*, 36–48.

Burnstein, E., Miller, H., Vinokur, A., Katz, S., & Crowley, J. Risky shift is eminently rational. *Journal of Personality and Social Psychology*, 1971, *20*, 462–467.

Burnstein, E., & Vinokur, A. Persuasive argumentation and social comparison as determinants of attitude polarization. *Journal of Experimental Social Psychology*, 1977, *13*, 315–330.

Burnstein, E., Vinokur, A., & Trope, Y. Interpersonal comparison versus persuasive argumentation: A more direct test of alternative explanations for group-induced shifts in individual choice. *Journal of Experimental Social Psychology*, 1973, 9, 236–245.

Burt, M. R. Cultural myths and supports for rape. *Journal of Personality and Social Psychology*, 1980, 38, 217–230.

Burtless, G., & Hausman, J. A. The effect of taxation on labor supply: Evaluating the Gary Negative Income Tax Experiment. In E. W. Stromsdorfer & G. Farkas (Eds.), *Evaluation studies: Annual review* (Vol. 5). Beverly Hills, Calif.: Sage Publications, 1980.

Burton, R. V. Generality of honesty reconsidered. *Psychological Review*, 1963, 70, 481–499.

Burtt, H. E. The inspiration-expiration ratio during truth and falsehood. *Journal of Experimental Psychology*, 1921, 4, 1–23.

Buss, A. H. *A dialectical psychology*. New York: Halsted Press, 1979.

Buss, A. H., Booker, A., & Buss, E. Firing a weapon and aggression. *Journal of Personality and Social Psychology*, 1972, 22, 196–302.

Byrne, D. Parental antecedents of authoritarianism. *Journal of Personality and Social Psychology*, 1965, 1, 369–373.

Byrne, D., Cherry, F., Lamberth, J., & Mitchell, H. E. Husband-wife similarity in response to erotic stimuli. *Journal of Personality*, 1973, 41, 384–394.

Byrne, D., & Clore, G. L. A reinforcement model of evaluative responses. *Personality: An International Journal*, 1970, 2, 103–128.

Byrne, D., & Griffitt, W. Interpersonal attraction. *Annual Review of Psychology*, 1973, 24, 317–336.

Byrne, D., & Lamberth, J. Reinforcement theories and cognitive theories as complementary approaches to the study of attraction. In B. I. Murstein (Ed.), *Theories of love and attraction*. New York: Springer, 1971.

Byrne, D., & Rhamey, R. Magnitude of positive and negative reinforcements as a determinant of attraction. *Journal of Personality and Social Psychology*, 1965, 2, 884–889.

Byrne, D., & Wong, T. J. Racial prejudice, interpersonal attraction and assumed dissimilarity of attitudes. *Journal of Abnormal and Social Psychology*, 1962, 65, 246–253.

C

Cacioppo, J. T. Effects of exogenous changes in heart rate on facilitation of thought and resistance to persuasion. *Journal of Personality and Social Psychology*, 1979, 37, 489–498.

Cacioppo, J. T., & Petty, R. E. Attitudes and cognitive response: An electrophysiological approach. *Journal of Personality and Social Psychology*, 1979, 37, 2181–2199.

Calder, B. J., Insko, C. A., & Yandell, B. The relation of cognitive and memorial processes to persuasion in simulated jury trial. *Journal of Applied Social Psychology*, 1974, 4, 62–93.

Calder, B. J., & Staw, B. M. Self-perception or intrinsic and extrinsic motivation. *Journal of Personality and Social Psychology*, 1975, 31, 599–605.

Calhoun, J. B. A behavioral sink. In E. L. Bliss (Ed.), *Roots of behavior*. New York: Harper & Row, 1962.

Callahan-Levy, C. M., & Messé, L. A. Sex differences in the allocation of pay. *Journal of Personality and Social Psychology*, 1979, 37, 433–446.

Calvert-Boyanowsky, J., & Leventhal, H. The role of information in attenuating behavioral responses to stress: A reinterpretation of the misattribution phenomenon. *Journal of Personality and Social Psychology*, 1975, 32, 214–221.

Cameron, P., Robertson, D., & Zaks, J. Sound pollution, noise pollution, and health: Community parameters. *Journal of Applied Psychology*, 1972, 56, 67–74.

Campbell, A., Converse, P. E., & Rodgers, W. L. *The quality of American life: Perceptions, evaluations, and satisfactions*. New York: Russell Sage Foundation, 1976.

Campbell, A., Gurin, G., & Miller, W. E. *The voter decides*. New York: Harper & Row, 1954.

Campbell, A. A. Factors associated with attitudes toward Jews. In T. Newcomb & E. Hartley (Eds.), *Readings in social psychology*. New York: Holt, Rinehart & Winston, 1947.

Campbell, A. A. *White attitudes toward black people*. Ann Arbor, Mich.: Institute for Social Research, 1971.

Campbell, D. T. Common fate, similarity and other indices of the status of aggregates of persons as social entities. *Behavioral Science*, 1958, 3, 14–25.

Campbell, D. T. Social attitudes and other acquired behavioral dispositions. In S. Koch (Ed.), *Psychology: A study of a science* (Vol. 6). New York: McGraw-Hill, 1963.

Campbell, D. T. Stereotypes and the perception of group differences. *American Psychologist*, 1967, 22, 812–829.

Campbell, D. T. On the genetics of altruism and the counterhedonic components in human culture. In L. Wispé (Ed.), *Altruism, sympathy, and helping*. New York: Academic Press, 1978.

Campbell, E. Q. *The attitude effects of educational desegregation in a Southern community*. Unpublished doctoral dissertation, Vanderbilt University, Nashville, 1956.

Campbell, E. Q. Some social psychological correlates of direction in attitude change. *Social Forces*, 1958, 36, 335–340.

Cann, A. A., Sherman, S. J., & Elkes, R. Effects of initial request size and timing of second request on compliance: The foot in the door and the foot in the face. *Journal of Personality and Social Psychology*, 1975, 32, 774–882.

Canon, L. K. Self-confidence and selective exposure to information. In L. Festinger et al., *Conflict, decision, and dissonance*. Stanford, Calif.: Stanford University Press, 1964.

Cantor, N., & Mischel, W. Prototypes in person perception. In L. Berkowitz (Ed.), *Advances in Experimental Social Psychology* (Vol.12). New York: Academic Press, 1979.

Caplow, T. A theory of coalitions in the triad. *American Sociological Review*, 1956, 21, 489–493.

Carducci, B. J., Cozby, P. C., & Ward, C. D. Sexual arousal and interpersonal evaluations. *Journal of Experimental Social Psychology*, 1978, 14, 449–457.

Carlsmith, J. M., & Anderson, C. A. Ambient temperature and the occurrence of collective violence: A new analysis. *Journal of Personality and Social Psychology*, 1979, 37, 337–344.

Carlsmith, J. M., & Gross, A. E. Some effects of guilt on compliance. *Journal of Personality and Social Psychology*, 1969, 11, 240–244.

Carroll, J. S. A psychological approach to deterrence: The evaluation of crime opportunities. *Journal of Personality and Social Psychology*, 1978, 36, 1512–1520.

Carter, H., & Glick, P. C. *Marriage and divorce: A social and economic study* (Rev. ed.). Cambridge, Mass.: Harvard University Press, 1976.

Cartwright, D. Determinants of scientific progress: The case of research on the risky shift. *American Psychologist*, 1973, 28, 222–231.

Cartwright, D. (Ed.). *Field theory: Selected theoretical papers in social science*. New York: Harper & Row, 1951.

Cartwright, D., & Harary, F. Structural balance: A generalization of Heider's theory. *Psychological Review*, 1956, 63, 277–293.

Cartwright, D., & Zander, A. (Eds.). *Group dynamics* (3rd ed.). New York: Harper & Row, 1968.

Carver, C. S. Facilitation of physical aggression through objective self-awareness. *Journal of Experimental Social Psychology*, 1974, 10, 365–370.

Carver, C. S., Blaney, P. H., & Scheier, M. F. Reassertion and giving up: The interactive role of self-directed attention and outcome expectancy. *Journal of Personality and Social Psychology*, 1979, 37, 1859–1870.

Castore, C. H., & DeNinno, J. *Role of relevance in the selection of comparison others*. Paper presented at the meeting of the American Psychological Association, Honolulu, August 1972.

Castore, G. F. Number of verbal interrelationships as a determinant of group size.

Journal of Abnormal and Social Psychology, 1962, 64, 456–458.

Castro, M. A. Reactions to receiving aid as a function of cost to donor and opportunity to aid. Journal of Applied Social Psychology, 1974, 4, 194–209.

Cattell, R. B., & Nesselroade, J. Likeness and completeness theories examined by sixteen personality factor measures on stably and unstably married couples. Journal of Personality and Social Psychology, 1967, 7, 351–361.

Cattell, R. B., & Stice, G. F. Four formulae for selecting leaders on the basis of personality. Human Relations, 1954, 7, 493–507.

Cavan, S. Liquor license: An ethnography of bar behavior. Chicago: Aldine, 1966.

Cavior, N. Physical attractiveness, perceived attitude similarity and interpersonal attraction among fifth and eleventh grade boys and girls. Unpublished doctoral dissertation, University of Houston, Texas, 1970.

Centers, R. Sexual attraction and love. Springfield, Ill.: Charles C. Thomas, 1975.

Certner, B. Exchange of self-disclosures in same sexed groups of strangers. Journal of Consulting and Clinical Psychology, 1973, 40, 292–297.

Chaiken, S. Communicator physical attractiveness and persuasion. Journal of Personality and Social Psychology, 1979, 37, 1387–1397.

Chaiken, S., & Eagly, A. H. Communication modality as a determinant of message persuasiveness and message comprehensibility. Journal of Personality and Social Psychology, 1976, 34, 605–614.

Chaikin, A. L., Sigler, E., & Derlega, V. J. Nonverbal mediators of teacher expectancy effects. Journal of Personality and Social Psychology, 1974, 30, 144–149.

Chance, J., Goldstein, A. G., & McBride, L. Differential experience and recognition memory for faces. Journal of Social Psychology, 1975, 97, 243–253.

Chandler, M. J., Koch, D., & Paget, K. F. Developmental changes in the response of children to conditions of crowding and congestion. In H. McGurk (Ed.), Ecological factors in human development. Amsterdam: North Holland, 1976.

Chapman, A. J. An electro-myographic study of social facilitation: A test of the 'mere presence' hypothesis. British Journal of Psychology, 1974, 65, 123–128.

Charters, W. W., & Newcomb, T. M. Some attitudinal effects of experimentally increased salience of a membership group. In E. Maccoby, T. Newcomb, & E. Hartley (Eds.), Readings in social psychology (3rd ed.). New York: Holt, Rinehart & Winston, 1958.

Chemers, M. M., & Skrzypek, G. J. An experimental test of the contingency model of leadership effectiveness. Journal of Personality and Social Psychology, 1972, 24, 172–177.

Cherlin, A. Work life and marital dissolution. In G. Levinger & O. C. Moles (Eds.), Divorce and separation. New York: Basic Books, 1979.

Cherniss, C. Personality and ideology: A personalogical study of women's liberation. Psychiatry, 1972, 35, 113–114.

Cherry, F., & Byrne, D. Authoritarianism. In T. Blass (Ed.), Personality variables in social behavior. Hillsdale, N.J.: Lawrence Erlbaum, 1977.

Chertkoff, J. M., & Baird, S. L. Applicability of the big lie technique and the last clear chance doctrine to bargaining. Journal of Personality and Social Psychology, 1971, 20, 298–303.

Christian, J. J., Lloyd, J. A., & Davis, D. E. The role of endocrines in the self-regulation of mammalian populations. Recent Progress in Hormone Research, 1965, 21, 501–578.

Chowdhry, K., & Newcomb, T. M. The relative abilities of leaders and non-leaders to estimate opinions of their own groups. Journal of Applied Social Psychology, 1952, 47, 51–57.

Christie, R., & Boehm, V. Machiavellians meet Miss Rheingold. In R. Christie & F. L. Geis (Eds.), Studies in Machiavellianism. New York: Academic Press, 1970.

Christie, R., & Geis, F. L. Some consequences of taking Machiavelli seriously. In E. F. Borgatta & W. W. Lambert (Eds.), Handbook of personality theory and research. Chicago: Rand McNally, 1968.

Christie, R., & Geis, F. Studies in Machiavellianism. New York: Academic Press, 1970.

Christie, R., Gergen, K. J., & Marlowe, D. The penny-dollar caper. In R. Christie & F. L. Geis, (Eds.), Studies in Machiavellianism. New York: Academic Press, 1970.

Christie, R., & Merton, R. K. Procedures for the sociological study of the values climate of medical schools. In H. H. Gee & R. J. Seaser (Eds.), The ecology of the medical student. Evanston, Ill.: American Association of Medical Colleges, 1958.

Christy, P. R., Gelfand, D. M., & Hartmann, D. P. Effects of competition-induced frustration in two classes of modeled behavior. Developmental Psychology, 1971, 5, 104–111.

Chu, G. C., Rahim, S. A., Kincaid, D. L. (Eds.), Communication for group transformation in development. Honolulu: University Press of Hawaii/East-West Center, 1976.

Churchill, W. Homosexual behavior among males. New York: Hawthorn Books, 1967.

Cialdini, R. B., Cacioppo, J. T., Bassett, R., & Miller, J. A. Low-ball procedure for producing compliance: Commitment then cost. Journal of Personality and Social Psychology, 1978, 36, 463–476.

Cialdini, R. B., Levy, A., Herman, C. P., Kozkowski, L. T., & Petty, R. E. Elastic shifts of opinion: Determinants of direction and durability. Journal of Personality and Social Psychology, 1976, 34, 633–672.

Cialdini, R. B., Vincent, J. E., Lewis, S. K., Catalan, J., Wheeler, D., & Darby, B. L. Reciprocal concessions procedure for inducing compliance: The door-in-the-face technique. Journal of Personality and Social Psychology, 1975, 31, 206–215.

Cicourel, A. V. Basic and normative rules in the negotiation of status and role. In D. Sudnow (Ed.), Studies in social interaction. New York: Free Press, 1972.

Clark, J. V. A preliminary investigation of some unconscious assumptions affecting labor efficiency in eight supermarkets. Unpublished doctoral dissertation, Graduate School of Business Administration, Harvard University, Cambridge, Mass., 1958.

Clark, K. B. Dark ghetto: Dilemmas of social power. New York: Harper & Row, 1965.

Clark, K. B., & Clark, M. P. Racial identification and preference in Negro children. In T. M. Newcomb & E. L. Hartley (Eds.), Readings in social psychology. New York: Holt, Rinehart & Winston, 1947.

Clark, K. B., & Clark, M. P. Emotional factors in racial identification and preference in Negro children. Journal of Negro Education, 1950, 19, 341–350.

Clark, L. P. Effects of social density and manning on group performance. Paper presented at the annual meeting of the American Psychological Association, Toronto, 1978.

Clark, M. S., Gotay, C. C., & Wills, J. Acceptance of help as a function of similarity of the potential helper and opportunity to repay. Journal of Applied Social Psychology, 1974, 4, 224–229.

Clark, M. S., & Mills, J. Interpersonal attraction in exchange and communal relationships. Journal of Personality and Social Psychology, 1979, 37, 12–24.

Clark, N., & Fouts, G. T. Effects of positive, neutral, and negative experiences with an audience on social facilitation in children. Perceptual and Motor Skills, 1973, 37, 1008–1010.

Clark, R. D., & Word, L. E. Where is the apathetic bystander? Situational characteristics of the emergency. Journal of Personality and Social Psychology, 1974, 29, 279–287.

Clausen, J. A., & Clausen, S. The effects of family size on parents and children. In J. Fawcett (Ed.), Psychological perspectives on population. New York: Basic Books, 1973.

Cline, V. B., Croft, R. G., & Courrier, S. Desensitization of children to television violence. Journal of Personality and Social Psychology, 1973, 27, 360–365.

Clore, G. L., Bray, R. M., Itkin, S. M., & Murphy, P. Interracial attitudes and behavior at a summer camp. Journal of Personality and Social Psychology, 1978, 36, 107–116.

Clore, G. L., & Byrne, D. A reinforcement-affect model of attraction. In T. L. Huston (Ed.), *Foundations of interpersonal attraction*. New York: Academic Press, 1974.

Coan, R. W. Personality variables associated with cigarette smoking. *Journal of Personality and Social Psychology*, 1973, 26, 86–104.

Coch, L., & French, J. R. P., Jr. Overcoming resistance to change. In D. Cartwright & A. Zander (Eds.), *Group dynamics: Research and theory* (2nd ed.). Evanston, Ill.: Row, Peterson, 1962.

Cohen, A. Industrial noise and medical absence, and accident record data on exposed workers. In W. D. Ward (Ed.), *Proceedings of the International Congress on Noise as a Public Health Problem*. Washington, D.C.: U.S. Government Printing Office, 1973.

Cohen, A. R. Communication discrepancy and attitude change: A dissonance theory approach. *Journal of Personality*, 1959, 27, 386–396.

Cohen, A. R. A "forced-compliance" experiment on repeated dissonances. In J. W. Brehm & A. R. Cohen (Eds.), *Explorations in cognitive dissonance*. New York: John Wiley & Sons, 1962.

Cohen, E., & Sampson, E. E. *Distributive justice: A preliminary study of children's equal and equitable allocations of rewards using the doll play technique*. Paper presented at the meeting of the Eastern Psychological Association, New York, April 1975.

Cohen, E. G., & Roper, S. S. Modification of interracial disability: An application of status characteristic theory. *American Sociological Review*, 1972, 37, 643–657.

Cohen, R. Altruism: Human, cultural, or what? In L. Wispé (Ed.), *Altruism, sympathy and helping*. New York: Academic Press, 1978.

Cohen, S. Environmental load and the allocation of attention. In A. Baum & S. Valins (Eds.), *Advances in environmental research*. Hillsdale, N.J.: Lawrence Erlbaum, 1977.

Cohen, S., Glass, D. C., & Phillips, S. Environment and health. In H. E. Freeman, S. Levine, & L. G. Reeder (Eds.), *Handbook of medical sociology*. Englewood Cliffs, N.J.: Prentice-Hall, 1977.

Cohen, S., Glass, D., & Singer, J. Apartment noise, auditory discrimination, and reading ability in children. *Journal of Experimental Social Psychology*, 1973, 4, 407–422.

Coke, J. S., Batson, C. D., & McDavis, K. Empathic mediation of helping: A two-stage model. *Journal of Personality and Social Psychology*, 1978, 36, 752–766.

Coleman, J. Recent trends in school integration. *Educational Researcher*, 1975, 4, 3–12.

Collins, B. E., & Raven, B. H. Group structure: Attractions, coalitions, communication, and power. In G. Lindzey & E. Aronson (Eds.), *Handbook of social psychology* (Vol. 4). Reading, Mass.: Addison-Wesley, 1968.

Comstock, G., Chaffee, S., Katzman, N., McCombs, M., & Roberts, D. *Television and human behavior*. New York: Columbia University Press, 1978.

Condry, J., & Dyer, S. Fear of success: Attribution of cause to the victim. *Journal of Social Issues*, 1976, 32, 63–71.

Cone, J. D., & Hayes, S. C. Applied behavior analysis and the solution of environmental problems. In I. Altman & J. F. Wohlwill (Eds.), *Human behavior and environment* (Vol. 2). New York: Plenum, 1977.

Conner, R. L. Hormones, biogenic amines and aggression. In S. Levine (Ed.), *Hormones and behavior*. New York: Academic Press, 1972.

Connolly, K. The social facilitation of preening behavior in Drosophila Melanogaster. *Animal Behavior*, 1968, 16, 385–391.

Conot, R. *Rivers of blood, years of darkness*. New York: Bantam Books, 1967.

Cook, S. W. *The effect of unintended interracial contact upon racial interaction and attitude change*. Final Report, University of Colorado, Boulder, Contract OEC-4-7-051320-0273, U.S. Dept. of Health, Education, & Welfare, August 1971.

Cook, T. D., & Flay, B. R. The persistence of experimentally induced attitude change. In L. Berkowitz (Ed.), *Advances in experimental social psychology* (Vol. 11). New York: Academic Press, 1978.

Cook, T. D., Gruder, C. L., Hennigan, K. M., & Flay, B. R. History of the sleeper effect: Some logical pitfalls in accepting the null hypothesis. Psychological Bulletin, 1979, 86, 662–679.

Cooper, E., & Dinerman, H. Analysis of the film "Don't Be a Sucker": A study of communication. *Public Opinion Quarterly*, 1951, 15, 243–264.

Cooper, H. M., & Lowe, C. A. Task, information and attributions for academic performance by professional teachers and roleplayers. *Journal of Personality*, 1977, 45, 469–483.

Cooper, J. Personal responsibility and dissonance: The role of foreseen consequences. *Journal of Personality and Social Psychology*, 1971, 18, 354–363.

Cooper, J., & Fazio, R. H. The formation and persistence of attitudes that support intergroup conflict. In W. G. Austin & S. Worchel (Eds.), *The social psychology of intergroup relations*. Monterey, Calif.: Brooks/Cole, 1979.

Cooper, J., Zanna, M., & Goethals, G. Mistreatment of an esteemed other as a consequence affecting dissonance reduction. *Journal of Experimental Social Psychology*, 1974, 10, 224–233.

Costa, P. T., McCrae, R. R., & Avenberg, D. Enduring dispositions in adult males. *Journal of Personality and Social Psychology*, 1980, 38, 793–800.

Costantini, E., & Craik, K. H. Personality and politicians: California party leaders, 1960–1976. *Journal of Personality and Social Psychology*, 1980, 38, 641–661.

Costanzo, P. R., Coie, J. D., Grument, J. F., & Farnell, D. A re-examination of the effects of intent and consequences on children's moral judgment. *Child Development*, 1973, 44, 154–161.

Cottrell, N. B. Social facilitation. In C. G. McClintock (Ed.), *Experimental social psychology*. New York: Holt, Rinehart & Winston, 1972.

Cottrell, N. B., Wack, D. L., Sekerak, G. J., & Rittle, R. H. Social facilitation of dominant responses by the presence of an audience and the mere presence of others. *Journal of Personality and Social Psychology*, 1968, 9, 245–250.

Couch, A. S. *Psychological determinants of interpersonal behavior*. Unpublished doctoral dissertation, Harvard University, Cambridge, Mass., 1960.

Craig, G., & Duck, S. W. Similarity, interpersonal attitudes and attraction: The evaluative-descriptive distinction. *British Journal of Social and Clinical Psychology*, 1977, 16, 15–21.

Crandall, V. J., Preston, A., & Rabson, A. Maternal reactions and the development of independence and achievement behavior in young children. *Child Development*, 1960, 31, 243–251.

Crawford, T. In defense of obedience research: An extension of the Kelman ethic. In A. G. Miller (Ed.), *The social psychology of psychological research*. New York: Free Press, 1972.

Cromwell, R. L., Butterfield, E. C., Brayfield, F. M., & Curry, J. L. *Acute myocardial infarction: Reaction and recovery*. St. Louis: C. V. Mosby, 1977.

Cronbach, L. Beyond the two disciplines of scientific psychology. *American Psychologist*, 1975, 30. 116–127.

Cronen, B. E., & Pearce, W. B. Logical force in interpersonal communication: A new concept of the necessity in social behavior. *Communication*, in press.

Crook, M., & Langdon, F. The effects of aircraft noise in schools around London airport. *Journal of Sound and Vibration*, 1974, 34, 221–232.

Crosby, F. A model of egotistical relative deprivation. *Psychological Review*, 1976, 83, 85–113.

Cross, H. A., Halcomb, C. G., & Matter, W. W. Imprinting or exposure learning in rats given early auditory stimulation. *Psychonomic Science*, 1967, 10, 223–234.

Crowne, D. P., & Liverant, S. Conformity under varying conditions of personal commitment. *Journal of Abnormal and Social Psychology*, 1963, 66, 547–555.

Crutchfield, R. S. Conformity and character. *American Psychologist*, 1955, 10, 191–198.

Csikszentmihalyi, M. *Beyond boredom and anxiety.* San Francisco: Jossey-Bass, 1975.

Csikszentmihalyi, M., & Rochberg-Halton, E. *The meaning of things: A study of household symbols,* unpublished manuscript, University of Chicago, 1980.

Culbertson, F. The modification of an emotionally held attitude through role playing. *Journal of Abnormal and Social Psychology,* 1957, *54,* 230–233.

Cunningham, M. R. Weather, mood, and helping behavior: Quasi experiments with the sunshine Samaritan. *Journal of Personality and Social Psychology,* 1979, *37,* 1947–1956.

Cunningham, M. R., Steinberg, J., & Greu, R. Wanting to and having to help: Separate motivations for positive mood and guilt-induced helping. *Journal of Personality and Social Psychology,* 1980, *38,* 181–192.

Cvetkovich, G. Dialectical perspectives on empirical research. *Personality and Social Psychology Bulletin,* 1977, *30,* 688–696.

D

Dabbs, J. M., Jr. Self-esteem, communicator characteristics, and attitude change. *Journal of Abnormal and Social Psychology,* 1964, *69,* 173–181.

Dabbs, J. M., Jr., & Leventhal, H. Effects of varying the recommendations in fear arousing communication. *Journal of Personality and Social Psychology,* 1966, *4,* 525–531.

Daher, D., & Banikiotes, P. Impersonal attraction and rewarding aspects of disclosure content and level. *Journal of Personality and Social Psychology,* 1976, *33,* 492–496.

Damon, W. *The social world of the child.* San Francisco: Jossey-Bass, 1977.

Daniels, L. R., & Berkowitz, L. Liking and response to dependency relationships. *Human Relations,* 1963, *16,* 141–148.

Darley, J. M., & Batson, C. D. "From Jerusalem to Jericho": A study of situational and dispositional variables in helping behavior. *Journal of Personality and Social Psychology,* 1973, *27,* 100–108.

Dashiell, J. F. Experimental studies of the influence of social situations on the behavior of individual human adults. In C. Murchison (Ed.), *Handbook of social psychology.* Worcester, Mass.: Clark University Press, 1935.

D'Augelli, J. F., & D'Augelli, A. R. Sexual involvement and relationship development. In R. L. Burgess & T. L. Huston (Eds.), *Social exchange in developing relationships.* New York: Academic Press, 1979.

Davidson, A. R., & Jaccard, J. J. Variables that moderate the attitude-behavior relation: Results of a longitudinal survey. *Journal of Personality and Social Psychology,* 1979, *37,* 1364–1376.

Davidson, J., & Kiesler, S. Cognitive behavior before and after decisions. In L. Festinger, *Conflict, decision, and dissonance.* Stanford, Calif.: Stanford University Press, 1964.

Davies, J. C. Toward a theory of revolution. *American Sociological Review,* 1962, *27,* 5–19.

Davies, J. C. The J-curve of rising and declining satisfactions as a cause of great revolutions and a contained rebellion. In H. D. Graham & T. R. Gurr (Eds.), *Violence in America.* New York: New American Library, 1969.

Davis, D., & Martin, H. J. When pleasure begets pleasure: Recipient responsiveness as a determinant of physical pleasuring between heterosexual dating couples and strangers. *Journal of Personality and Social Psychology,* 1978, *36,* 767–777.

Davis, D., & Perkowitz, W. T. Consequences of responsiveness in dyadic interaction: Effects of probability of response and proportion of content-related responses on interpersonal attraction. *Journal of Personality and Social Psychology,* 1979, *37,* 534–550.

Davis, D., Rainey, H. G., & Brock, T. C. Interpersonal physical pleasuring: Effects of sex combinations, recipient attributes, and anticipated future interaction. *Journal of Personality and Social Psychology,* 1976, *33,* 89–106.

Davis, J. H. Group decision and procedural justice. In M. Fishbein (Ed.), *Progress in social psychology* (Vol. 1). Hillsdale, N.J.: Lawrence Erlbaum, 1980.

Davis, J. H., Bray, R. M., & Holt, R. W. The empirical study of decision processes in juries: A critical review. In J. Tapp & F. Levine (Eds.), *Law, justice, and the individual in society: Psychological and legal issues.* New York: Holt, Rinehart & Winston, 1977.

Davis, J. H., Laughlin, P. R., & Komorita, S. S. The social psychology of small groups: Cooperative and mixed motive interaction. In M. P. Rosenzweig & L. W. Porter (Eds.), *Annual review of psychology* (Vol. 27). Palo Alto, Calif.: Annual Reviews, 1976.

Davis, J. H., Spitzer, C. E., Nagao, D. H., & Stasser, G. Bias in social decisions by individuals and groups: An example from mock juries. In H. Brandstatter, J. H. Davis, & H. Schuler (Eds.), *Dynamics of group decisions.* Beverly Hills, Calif.: Sage Publications, 1978.

Davitz, J. R., & Mason, D. J. Socially facilitated reduction of fear response in rats. *Journal of Comparative and Physiological Psychology,* 1955, *48,* 149–151.

Dawes, R. M., Singer, D., & Lamons, F. An experimental analysis of the contrast effect and its implications for intergroup communication and the indirect assessment of attitude. *Journal of Personality and Social Psychology,* 1972, *21,* 281–295.

Day, A., & Day, L. H. Cross-national comparison of population density. *Science,* 1973, *181,* 1016–1023.

de Ajuriaguerra, J. M. D. (Ed.). *Handbook of child psychiatry and psychology.* New York: Masson, 1980.

Deaux, K., & Taynor, J. Evaluation of male and female ability: Bias works two ways. *Psychological Reports,* 1973, *32,* 261–262.

De Charms, R. Personal causation and perceived control. In L. C. Perlmutter & R. A. Monty (Eds.), *Choice and perceived control.* Hillsdale, N.J.: Lawrence Erlbaum, 1979.

De Charms, R., & Rosenbaum, M. E. The problem of vicarious experience. In D. Willner (Ed.), *Decisions, values, and groups.* Elmsford, N.Y.: Pergamon Press, 1957.

Deci, E. L. *Intrinsic motivation.* New York: Plenum, 1975.

Deci, E. L., & Porac, J. Cognitive evaluation theory and the study of human motivation. In M. Lepper & D. Greene (Eds.), *The hidden costs of reward: New perspectives on the psychology of human motivation.* Hillsdale, N.J.: Lawrence Erlbaum, 1978.

DeGré, G. Freedom and social structure. In M. E. Olsen (Ed.), *Power in societies.* London: Macmillan, 1970.

DeJong, W. An examination of self-perception mediation of the foot-in-the-door effect. *Journal of Personality and Social Psychology,* 1979, *37,* 2221–2239.

Dembroski, T. M., Lasater, T. M., & Ramirez, A. Communicator similarity, fear arousing communications, and compliance with health care recommendations. *Journal of Applied Social Psychology,* 1978, *8,* 254–269.

Dembroski, T. M., & MacDougall, J. M. Stress effects on affiliation preferences among subjects possessing the Type A coronary-prone behavior. *Journal of Personality and Social Psychology,* 1978, *36,* 23–33.

Dembroski, T. M., MacDougall, J. M., Herd, J. A., & Shields, J. L. Effect of level of challenge on pressor and heart rate responses in Type A and B subjects. *Journal of Applied Social Psychology,* 1979, *9,* 209–228.

Dembroski, T. M., Weiss, S. M., Shields, J. L., & Haynes, S. G. (Eds.). *Coronary-prone behavior.* Bethesda, Md.: National Institutes of Health, 1978.

Dengerink, H. A., Schnedler, R. W., & Covey, M. K. Role of avoidance in aggressive responses to attack and no attack. *Journal of Personality and Social Psychology,* 1978, *36,* 1044–1053.

Dentan, R. K. *The Semai: a nonviolent people of Malaya.* New York: Holt, Reinhart, and Winston, 1968.

De Paulo, B. M., & Fisher, J. D. The cost of asking for help. *Basic and Applied Social Psychology,* 1980, *1,* 23–35.

Derlega, V. J., & Chaikin, A. L. Privacy and

self-disclosure in social relationships. *Journal of Social Issues*, 1977, *33*, 102–115.

Derlega, V. J., & Grzelak, J. Appropriateness of self-disclosure. In G. J. Cheleene (Ed.), *Self-disclosure*. San Francisco: Jossey-Bass, 1979.

Dermer, M., & Thiel, D. J. When beauty may fail. *Journal of Personality and Social Psychology*, 1975, *31*, 1168–1176.

Desor, J. A. Toward a psychological theory of crowding. *Journal of Personality and Social Psychology*, 1972, *21*, 79–83.

Deur, J. D., & Parke, R. P. Effects of inconsistent punishment on aggression in children. *Developmental Psychology*, 1970, *2*, 403–411.

Deutsch, M. An experimental study of the effects of cooperation and competition among group processes. *Human Relations*, 1949, *2*, 199–232.

Deutsch, M. The effect of motivational orientation upon trust and suspicion. *Human Relations*, 1960, *13*, 123–139.

Deutsch, M. The disadvantaged child and the learning process. In A. H. Passow (Ed.), *Education in depressed areas*. New York: Teachers College Press, 1963.

Deutsch, M. *The resolution of conflict*. New Haven, Conn.: Yale University Press, 1973.

Deutsch, M. Equity, equality, and need: What determines which value will be used as the basis for distributive justice. *Journal of Social Issues*, 1975, *31*, 137–149.

Deutsch, M., & Collins, M. *Interracial housing*. Minneapolis: University of Minnesota Press, 1951.

Deutsch, M., & Gerard, H. A study of normative and informational social influences on individual judgment. *Journal of Abnormal and Social Psychology*, 1955, *51*, 629–636.

Deutsch, M., & Krauss, R. M. The effect of threat on interpersonal bargaining. *Journal of Abnormal and Social Psychology*, 1960, *16*, 181–189.

Deutsch, M., & Krauss, R. M. Studies of interpersonal bargaining. *Journal of Conflict Resolution*, 1962, *6*, 52–76.

Deutsch, M., Krauss, R. M., & Rosenau, N. Dissonance or defensiveness? *Journal of Personality*, 1962, *30*, 28–37.

Deutsch, M., & Solomon, L. Reactions to evaluations by others as influenced by self evaluation. *Sociometry*, 1959, *22*, 93–112.

Deutscher, I. *Why do they say one thing, do another?* Morristown, N.J.: Silver Burdett/General Learning Press, 1973.

De Vellis, R. F., De Vellis, B. M., & Mc-Cauley, C. Vicarious acquisition of learned helplessness. *Journal of Personality and Social Psychology*, 1978, *36*, 894–899.

DeWaele, J., & Harré, R. The personality of individuals. In R. Harré (Ed.), *Personality*. Totowa, N.J.: Littlefield, Adams/Rowman & Littlefield, 1976.

Dewards, J. N. (Ed.), *Sex and society*. Skokie,

Ill.: Rand McNally/Markham, 1972.

Diener, C. I., & Dweck, C. S. An analysis of learned helplessness: Continuous changes in performance, strategy and achievement cognitions following failure. *Journal of Personality and Social Psychology*, 1978, *36*, 451–462.

Diener, E., & Defour, D. Does television violence enhance program popularity? *Journal of Personality and Social Psychology*, 1978, *36*, 333–342.

Diener, E., Fraser, S. C., Beaman, A. L., & Kelem, R. T. Effects of deindividuation variables on stealing among Halloween trick-or-treaters. *Journal of Personality and Social Psychology*, 1976, *33*, 178–183.

Diener, E., & Srull, T. K. Self-awareness, psychological perspective, and self-reinforcement in relation to personal and social standards. *Journal of Personality and Social Psychology*, 1979, *37*, 413–423.

Dienstbier, R. A. The role of anxiety and arousal attribution in cheating. *Journal of Experimental Social Psychology*, 1972, *8*, 168–179.

Diggory, J. C. *Self-evaluation concepts and studies*. New York: John Wiley & Sons, 1966.

Dillehay, R. C. On the irrelevance of the classical negative evidence concerning the effect of attitudes on behavior. *American Psychologist*, 1973, *28*, 887–891.

Dillon, W. S. *Gifts and nations*. Paris: Editions Mouton and Ecole Pintique des Hautes Etudes, 1968.

Dion, K. K. Physical attractiveness and evaluations of children's transgressions. *Journal of Personality and Social Psychology*, 1972, *24*, 207–213.

Dion, K. K. Young children's stereotyping of facial attractiveness. *Developmental Psychology*, 1973, *9*, 183–188.

Dion, K. K. The incentive value of physical attractiveness. *Personality and Social Psychology Bulletin*, 1977, *3*, 67–70.

Dion, K. K., & Berscheid, E. Physical attractiveness and peer perception among children. *Sociometry*, 1974, *37*, 1–12.

Dion, K. K., Berscheid, E., & Walster, E. What's beautiful is good. *Journal of Personality and Social Psychology*, 1972, *24*, 285–290.

Dion, K. K., & Stein, S. Physical attractiveness and interpersonal influence. *Journal of Experimental Social Psychology*, 1978, *14*, 97–108.

Dion, K. L., Miller, N., & Magnan, M. A. Cohesiveness and social responsibility as determinants of group risk taking. *Journal of Personality and Social Psychology*, 1971, *20*, 400–406.

Doherty, W. J., & Ryder, R. G. Locus of control, interpersonal trust and assertive behavior among newlyweds. *Journal of Personality and Social Psychology*, 1979, *37*, 2212–2220.

Doise, W. Intergroup relations and polarization of individual and collective judg-

ments. *Journal of Personality and Social Psychology*, 1969, *12*, 136–143.

Doise, W. *Groups and individuals: Explanations in social psychology*. Cambridge, England: Cambridge University Press, 1978.

Dollard, J., Doob, L. W., Miller, N. E., Mowrer, O. H., & Sears, R. R. *Frustration and aggression*. New Haven, Conn.: Yale University Press, 1939.

Dollinger, S. J., & Thelen, M. H. Overjustification and children's intrinsic motivation: Comparative effects of four rewards. *Journal of Personality and Social Psychology*, 1978, *36*, 1259–1269.

Donnenwerth, G. V., & Foa, U. G. Effect of resource class on retaliation to injustice in interpersonal exchange. *Journal of Personality and Social Psychology*, 1974, *29*, 785–793.

Donnerstein, E., & Donnerstein, M. The effect of attitudinal similarity on interracial aggression. *Journal of Personality*, 1975, *43*, 485–502.

Donnerstein, E., & Wilson, D. W. Effects of noise and perceived control on ongoing and subsequent aggressive behavior. *Journal of Personality and Social Psychology*, 1976, *34*, 774–781.

Donnerstein, M., & Donnerstein, E. Modeling in the control of interracial aggression: The problem of generality. *Journal of Personality*, 1977, *45*, 100–116.

Doob, A. N., & Wood, L. E. Catharsis and aggression: Effects of annoyance and retaliation on aggressive behavior. *Journal of Personality and Social Psychology*, 1972, *22*, 156–162.

Doob, A. N., & Zabrack, M. The effects of freedom-threatening instructions and monetary inducements on compliance. *Canadian Journal of Behavioral Science*, 1971, *3*, 408–412.

Dooley, B. B. *Crowding stress: The effects of social density on men with "close" or "far" personal space*. Unpublished doctoral dissertation, University of California, 1974.

Dorris, J. W. *Persuasion as a function of distraction and counter-arguing*. Unpublished manuscript, University of California, Los Angeles, 1967.

Dorse, W. Actions and judgments: Collective and individual structuring. In H. Brandstätter, J. H. Davis, & H. Schuler (Eds.), *Dynamics of group decisions*. Beverly Hills, Calif.: Sage Publications, 1978.

Drabman, R. S., & Thomas, M. H. Does media violence increase children's tolerance of real-life aggression? *Developmental Psychology*, 1974, *10*, 418–421.

Drabman, R. S., & Thomas, M. H. Does watching violence on television cause apathy? *Pediatrics*, 1976, *57*, 329–331.

Drachman, D., DeCarufel, A., & Insko, C. A. The extra credit effect in interpersonal attraction. *Journal of Experimental Social Psychology*, 1978, *14*, 458–465.

Druckman, D. Ethnocentrism in the internation simulation. *Journal of Conflict Resolution*, 1968, *12*, 45–68.

Druckman, D., Solomon, D., & Zechmeister, K. Effects of representational role obligations on the process of children's distribution of resources. *Sociometry*, 1972, *35*, 387–410.

Dubos, R. *Man adapting*. New Haven, Conn.: Yale University Press, 1965.

Dudycha, G. J. An objective study of punctuality in relation to personality and achievement. *Archives of Psychology*, 1936, *204*, 1–319.

Dunbar, J., Brown, M., & Amoroso, D. M. Some correlates of attitudes toward homosexuality. *Journal of Social Psychology*, 1973, *89*, 271–279.

Duncan, S., Jr., Brunner, L. J., & Fiske, D. W. Strategy signals in face-to-face interaction. *Journal of Personality and Social Psychology*, 1979, *37*, 301–313.

Duncan, S., Jr., & Fiske, D. W. *Face-to-face interaction: Research, methods, and theory*. Hillsdale, N.J.: Lawrence Erlbaum, 1977.

Durkheim, E. *The division of labor in society*. Glencoe, Ill.: Free Press, 1949.

Durkheim, E. *The elementary forms of the religious life*. London: George Allen & Unwin, 1954. (Originally published, 1895.)

Durkin, J. E. Encountering: What low Machs do. In R. Christie & F. L. Geis (Eds.), *Studies in Machiavellianism*. New York: Academic Press, 1970.

Dutton, D., & Aron, A. Some evidence for heightened sexual attraction under conditions of high anxiety. *Journal of Personality and Social Psychology*, 1974, *30*, 510–517.

Duval, S. *Conformity as a function of perceived level of personal uniqueness and being reminded of the object status of self*. Unpublished doctoral dissertation, University of Texas, Austin, 1972.

Duval, S., Duval, V. H., & Neely, R. Self-focus, felt responsibility, and helping behavior. *Journal of Personality and Social Psychology*, 1979, *37*, 1769–1778.

Duval, S., & Wicklund, R. A. *A theory of objective self-awareness*. New York: Academic Press, 1972.

Dweck, C. S. The role of expectations and attributions in the alleviation of learned helplessness. *Journal of Personality and Social Psychology*, 1975, *31*, 674–685.

Dweck, C. S., Goetz, T. E., & Strauss, N. L. Sex differences in learned helplessness: IV. An experimental and naturalistic study of failure generalization and its mediators. *Journal of Personality and Social Psychology*, 1980, *38*, 441–452.

E

Eagly, A. H. The comprehensibility of persuasive arguments as a determinant of opinion change. *Journal of Personality and Social Psychology*, 1974, *29*, 758–773.

Eagly, A. H. Sex differences in influenceability. *Psychological Bulletin*, 1978, *85*, 86–116.

Eagly, A. H., & Chaiken, S. An attribution analysis of the effect of communicator characteristics on opinion change: The case of communicator attractiveness. *Journal of Personality and Social Psychology*, 1975, *32*, 136–144.

Eagly, A. H., & Jelaak, K. Width of the latitude of acceptance as a determinant of attitude change. *Journal of Personality and Social Psychology*, 1972, *23*, 383–397.

Eagly, A. H., Wood, W., & Chaiken, S. Causal inferences about communicators and their effect on opinion change. *Journal of Personality and Social Psychology*, 1978, *36*, 424–435.

Eastman, P. Consciousness-raising as a resocialization process for women. *Smith College Studies in Social Work*, 1973, *43*, 180–181.

Eaton, W. O., & Clore, G. L. Interracial imitation at a summer camp. *Journal of Personality and Social Psychology*, 1975, *32*, 1099–1105.

Ebbeson, E. B., & Allen, R. B. Cognitive processes in implicit personality trait inferences. *Journal of Personality and Social Psychology*, 1979, *37*, 471–488.

Eckman, J., Meltzer, J. D., & Latané, B. Gregariousness in rats as a function of familiarity of environment. *Journal of Personality and Social Psychology*, 1969, *11*, 107–114.

Edmonds, V. Logical error as a function of group consensus: An experimental study of the effect of erroneous group consensus upon the logical judgments of graduate students. *Social Forces*, 1964, *43*, 33–38.

Edwards, D. W. Blacks vs. whites: When is race a relevant variable? *Journal of Personality and Social Psychology*, 1974, *29*, 39–49.

Egan, G. *Encounter: Group processes for interpersonal growth*. Monterey, Calif.: Brooks/Cole, 1970.

Ehrenkranz, J., Bliss, E., & Sheard, M. Plasma testosterone: Correlation with aggressive behavior and social dominance in man. *Psychosomatic Medicine*, 1974, *36*, 469–475.

Eisen, S. V. Actor-observer differences in information inference and causal attribution. *Journal of Personality and Social Psychology*, 1979, *37*, 261–272.

Eisenberger, R., Kaplan, R. M., & Singer, R. D. Decremental and nondecremental effects of noncontingent social behavior. *Journal of Personality and Social Psychology*, 1974, *30*, 716–722.

Eiser, J. R. *Cognitive social psychology: A guidebook to theory and research*. New York: McGraw-Hill, 1980.

Eiser, J. R., & Stroebe, W. *Categorization and social judgment*. London: Academic Press, 1972.

Ekman, P. Universals and cultural differences in facial expressions of emotion. In J. K. Cole (Ed.), *Nebraska Symposium on Motivation* (Vol. 19). Lincoln: University of Nebraska Press, 1972.

Ekman, P. Facial expression. In A. W. Siegman & S. Feldstein (Eds.), *Nonverbal behavior and communication*. Hillsdale, N.J.: Lawrence Erlbaum, 1978.

Ekman, P., & Friesen, W. V. Nonverbal leakage and clues to deception. *Psychiatry*, 1969, *32*, 88–106.

Ekman, P., & Friesen, W. V. Constants across cultures in the face and emotion. *Journal of Personality and Social Psychology*, 1971, *17*, 124–129.

Ekman, P., & Friesen, W. V. Detecting deception from the body or face. *Journal of Personality and Social Psychology*, 1974, *29*, 288–298.

Ekman, P., Friesen, W. V., & Ellsworth, P. *Emotion in the human face*. Elmsford, N.Y.: Pergamon Press, 1972.

Ekman, P., Friesen, W. V., O'Sullivan, M., & Scherer, K. Relative importance of face, body and speech in judgments of personality and affect. *Journal of Personality and Social Psychology*, 1980, *38*, 270–277.

Ekman, P., Friesen, W. V., & Scherer, K. R. Body movement and voice pitch in deceptive interaction. *Semiotica*, 1976, *16*, 23–27.

Ekman, P., Sorenson, E. R., & Friesen, W. V. Pan-cultural elements in facial displays of emotion. *Science*, 1969, *164*, 86–88.

Ekstein, R. Psychoanalysis, sympathy, and altruism. In L. Wispé (Ed.), *Altruism, sympathy, and helping*. New York: Academic Press, 1978.

Elliott, E. S., Wills, E. J., & Goldstein, A. G. The effects of discrimination training on the recognition of white and Oriental faces. *Bulletin of the Psychonomic Society*, 1973, *2*, 71–73.

Ellsworth, P. C., Carlsmith, J. M., & Henson, A. The stare as a stimulus to flight in human subjects: A series of field experiments. *Journal of Personality and Social Psychology*, 1972, *21*, 302–311.

Elman, J. B., Press, A., & Rosenkrantz, P. S. *Sex roles and self-concepts: Real and ideal*. Paper presented at the meeting of the American Psychological Association, Miami, Fla., August 1970.

Elms, A. C. *Social psychology and social relevance*. Boston: Little, Brown, 1972.

Elms, A. C., & Janis, I. L. Counter-norm attitudes induced by consonant versus dissonant conditions of role playing. *Journal of Experimental Research in Personality*, 1965, *1*, 50–60.

Elms, A. C., & Milgram, S. Personality characteristics associated with obedience and defiance toward authoritative command. *Journal of Experimental Research in Personality*, 1966, *1*, 282–289.

Emmet, D. *Rules, roles, and relations*. Boston: Beacon Press, 1966.

Epley, S. W. Reduction of the behavioral effects of aversive stimulation by the presence of companions. *Psychological Bulletin*, 1974, *81*, 271–283.

Epps, E. G. The impact of school desegregation on aspirations, self-concepts and other aspects of personality. *Law and Contemporary Problems*, 1975, *39*, 300–313.

Epstein, S. The self-concept: A review and the proposal of an integrated theory of personality. In E. Staub (Ed.), *Personality: Basic issues and current research*. Englewood Cliffs, N.J.: Prentice-Hall, 1980.

Erickson, B., Lind, E. A., Johnson, B. C., & O'Barr, W. M. Speech style and impression formation in a court setting: The effects of "powerful" and "powerless" speech. *Journal of Experimental Social Psychology*, 1978, *14*, 266–279.

Erikson, E. H. *Young man Luther: A study in psychoanalysis and history*. New York: W. W. Norton, 1958.

Erikson, E. H. *Gandhi's truth: On the origins of militant nonviolence*. New York: W. W. Norton, 1969.

Erlanger, H. B. Social class and corporal punishment in child rearing: A reassessment. *American Sociological Review*, 1974, *39*, 68–85.

Eron, L. D. Prescription for reduction of aggression. *American Psychologist*, 1980, *35*, 244–252.

Eron, L. D., Huesmann, L. R., Lefkowitz, M. M., & Walder, L. O. Does television violence cause aggression? *American Psychologist*, 72, *27*, 253–263.

Esser, A. *Behavior and environment: The use of space by animals and men*. New York: Plenum, 1971.

Ettinger, R., Marino, C., Endler, N., Geller, S., & Natziuk, T. Effects of agreement and correctness on relative competence and conformity. *Journal of Personality and Social Psychology*, 1971, *19*, 204–212.

Evans, G. W. *Behavioral and physiological consequences of crowding in humans*. Unpublished doctoral dissertation, University of Massachusetts, Amherst, 1975.

Evans, G. W., & Eichelman, W. Preliminary models of conceptual linkages among proxemic variables. *Environment and Behavior*, 1976, *8*, 87–116.

Evans, R. I. Behavioral medicine: A new applied challenge to social psychologists. In L. Bickman (Ed.), *Applied social psychology annual* (Vol. 1). Beverly Hills, Calif.: Sage Publications, 1980.

Exline, R. V. Group climate as a factor in the relevance and accuracy of social perception. *Journal of Abnormal and Social Psychology*, 1957, *55*, 382–388.

Exline, R. V., & Fehr, B. J. Applications of semiosis to the study of visual interaction. In A. W. Siegman & S. Feldstein (Eds.), *Nonverbal behavior and communication*. Hillsdale, N.J.: Lawrence Erlbaum, 1978.

Exline, R. V., Thibaut, J., Hickey, C. B., & Gumpert, P. Visual interaction in relation to Machiavellianism and an unethical act. In R. Christie & F. L. Geis (Eds.), *Studies in Machiavellianism*. New York: Academic Press, 1970.

Eysenck, H. J. *Crime and personality* (2nd ed.). London: Granada, 1970.

F

Falbo, T. Multidimensional scaling of power strategies. *Journal of Personality and Social Psychology*, 1977, *35*, 537–548.

Falbo, T., & Peplau, L. A. Power strategies in intimate relationships. *Journal of Personality and Social Psychology*, 1980, *38*, 618–628.

Fanon, F. *The wretched of the earth*. New York: Grove Press, 1965.

Farb, P. *Man's rise to civilization as shown by the Indians of North America from primeval times to the coming of the industrial state*. New York: E. P. Dutton, 1968.

Faucheux, C., & Moscovici, S. Le style de comportement d'une minorité et son influence sur les rèsponses d'une majorité. *Bulletin du C.E.R.P.*, 1967, *16*, 337–360.

Fazio, R. H., & Zanna, M. P. Direct experience and attitude-behavior consistency. In L. Berkowitz (Ed.), *Advances in experimental social psychology* (Vol. 13). New York: Academic Press, 1980.

Fehrenbach, P. A., Miller, D. J., & Thelen, M. H. The importance of consistency of modeling behavior upon imitation: A comparison of single and multiple models. *Journal of Personality and Social Psychology*, 1979, *37*, 1412–1417.

Feierbend, I. K., Feierbend, R. L., & Hesvold, B. A. Social change and political violence: Cross-national patterns. In H. D. Graham & T. R. Gurr (Eds.), *Violence in America: Historical and comparative perspectives*. Washington, D.C.: National Commission on the Causes & Prevention of Violence, 1969.

Feild, H. S. Attitudes toward rape: A comparative analysis of police, rapists, crisis counselors and citizens. *Journal of Personality and Social Psychology*, 1978, *36*, 156.

Fellner, C. H., & Marshall, J. R. Kidney donors. In J. R. Macauley & L. Berkowitz (Eds.), *Altruism and helping behavior*. New York: Academic Press, 1970.

Felsenthal, D. S. Bargaining behavior when profits are unequal and losses are equal. *Behavioral Science*, 1977, *22*, 334–340.

Felson, R. P., & Bohrnstedt, G. W. "Are the good beautiful or the beautiful good?" The relationship between children's perceptions of ability and perceptions of physical attractiveness. *Social Psychology Quarterly*, 1979, *42*, 386–392.

Felton, B., & Kahana, E. Adjustment and situationally-bound locus of control among the institutionally aged. *Journal of Gerontology*, 1974, *29*, 295–301.

Fenigstein, A. Does aggression cause a preference for viewing media violence? *Journal of Personality and Social Psychology*, 1979, *37*, 2307–2317.

Ference, T. P. Feedback and conflict as determinants of influence. *Journal of Experimental Social Psychology*, 1971, *7*, 1–16.

Ferguson, C. K., & Kelley, H. H. Significant factors in overevaluation of own-group's product. *Journal of Abnormal and Social Psychology*, 1964, *69*, 223–228.

Ferguson, T. J., & Wells, G. L. Priming of mediators in causal attribution. *Journal of Personality and Social Psychology*, 1980, *38*, 461–470.

Fernberger, S. W. Persistence of stereotypes concerning sex differences. *Journal of Abnormal and Social Psychology*, 1948, *43*, 97–101.

Feshbach, S. The role of fantasy in the response to television. *Journal of Social Issues*, 1976, *32*, 71–80.

Feshbach, S., & Singer, R. D. *Television and aggression: An experimental field study*. San Francisco: Jossey-Bass, 1971.

Festinger, L. Informal social communication. *Psychological Review*, 1950, *57*, 271–282.

Festinger, L. Informal communications in small groups. In H. Guetzkow (Ed.), *Groups, leadership and men: Research in human relations*. Pittsburgh: Carnegie Press, 1951.

Festinger, L. A theory of social comparison processes. *Human Relations*, 1954, *7*, 117–140.

Festinger, L. *A theory of cognitive dissonance*. Stanford, Calif.: Stanford University Press, 1957.

Festinger, L., & Carlsmith, J. M. Cognitive consequences of forced compliance. *Journal of Abnormal and Social Psychology*, 1959, *58*, 203–210.

Festinger, L., & Maccoby, N. On resistance to persuasive communications. *Journal of Abnormal and Social Psychology*, 1964, *68*, 359–366.

Festinger, L., Pepitone, A., & Newcomb, T. Some consequences of de-individuation in a group. *Journal of Abnormal and Social Psychology*, 1952, *47*, 382–389.

Festinger, L., Schachter, S., & Back, K. *Social pressures in informal groups: A study of human factors in housing*. New York: Harper & Row, 1950.

Festinger, L., Schachter, S., & Reicken, H. *When prophecy fails*. Minneapolis: University of Minnesota Press, 1956.

Festinger, L., Thibaut, J. Interpersonal communication in small groups. *Journal of Abnormal and Social Psychology*, 1951, *46*, 92–99.

Fiedler, F. E., Chemers, M. M., & Mahan, L. *Improving leadership effectiveness: The leader match concept*. New York: John Wiley & Sons, 1976.

Fiedler, F. E., O'Brien, G. E., & Ilgen, D. R. The effect of leadership style upon the performance and adjustment of volunteer teams operating in a stressful foreign environment. *Human Relations*, 1969, *22*,

503–514.

Findley, J. D., & Brady, J. V. Facilitation of large ratio performance by use of conditioned reinforcement. *Journal of the Experimental Analysis of Behavior*, 1965, *8*, 125–129.

Firestone, I. J., Kaplan, K. J., & Russell, J. C. Anxiety, fear and affiliation with similar-state versus dissimilar-state others: Misery sometimes loves nonmiserable company. *Journal of Personality and Social Psychology*, 1973, *26*, 409–414.

Fischer, W. F. Sharing in pre-school children as a function of amount and type of reinforcement. *Genetic Psychology Monographs*, 1963, *68*, 215–245.

Fischoff, S. "Recipe for a jury" revisited: A balance theory prediction. *Journal of Applied Social Psychology*, 1979, *9*, 335–349.

Fishbein, M. The relationships between beliefs, attitudes, and behavior. In S. Feldman (Ed.), *Cognitive consistency: Motivational antecedents and behavioral consequents*. New York: Academic Press, 1966.

Fishbein, M. Toward an understanding of family planning behaviors. *Journal of Applied Social Psychology*, 1972, *2*, 214–227.

Fishbein, M. (Ed.). *Readings in attitude theory and measurement*. New York: John Wiley & Sons, 1967.

Fishbein, M., & Ajzen, I. Attitudes toward objects as predictors of single and multiple behavioral criteria. *Psychological Review*, 1974, *81*, 59–74.

Fishbein, M., & Ajzen, I. *Belief, attitude, intention and behavior: An introduction to theory and research*. Reading, Mass.: Addison-Wesley, 1975.

Fisher, J. D., & Nadler, A. Effect of donor resources on recipient self-esteem and self-help. *Journal of Experimental Social Psychology*, 1976, *12*, 139–150.

Fisher, J. D., Nadler, A., & Whitcher, S. J. *Recipient reactions to aid: A conceptual review and a new theoretical framework*. Unpublished manuscript, University of Connecticut, Storrs, 1980.

Fishkin, J., Keniston, K., & Mackinnon, C. Moral reasoning and political ideology. *Journal of Personality and Social Psychology*, 1973, *27*, 109–119.

Flanders, J. P., & Thistlethwaite, D. L. Effects of familiarization and group discussion on risk taking. *Journal of Personality and Social Psychology*, 1967, *5*, 91–97.

Flapan, D. *Children's understanding of social interaction*. New York: Teachers College Press, 1968.

Flavell, J. H. *Cognitive development*. Englewood Cliffs, N.J.: Prentice-Hall, 1977.

Flavell, J. H., Botkin, P., Fry, C., Wright, J., & Jarvis, P. *The development of role-taking and communication skills in children*. New York: John Wiley & Sons, 1968.

Fleishman, J. A. Collective action as helping behavior: Effects of responsibility diffusion on contributions to a public good.

Journal of Personality and Social Psychology, 1980, *38*, 629–640.

Flowers, M. L. A laboratory test of some implications of Janis' group-think hypothesis. *Journal of Personality and Social Psychology*, 1977, *35*, 888–896.

Foa, E. B. Frustration-aggression as exchange of resources. *Dissertation Abstracts International*, 1971, *31*, 5518.

Foa, E. B., & Foa, U. G. *Societal structures of the mind*. Springfield, Ill.: Charles C Thomas, 1974.

Foa, E. B., & Foa, U. G. Resource theory: Interpersonal behavior as exchange. In K. J. Gergen, M. S. Greenberg, & R. H. Willis (Eds.), *Social exchange: Advances in theory and research*. New York: Plenum, 1980.

Foa, U. G. Interpersonal and economic resources. *Science*, 1971, *345*–351.

Fodor, E. M., & Farrow, D. L. The power motive as an influence on use of power. *Journal of Personality and Social Psychology*, 1979, *37*, 2091–2097.

Foley, L. A. Personality and situational influences on changes in prejudice: A replication of Cook's railroad game in a prison setting. *Journal of Personality and Social Psychology*, 1976, *34*, 848–856.

Fontana, A. F., & Noel, B. Moral reasoning in the university. *Journal of Personality and Social Psychology*, 1973, *27*, 419–429.

Ford, C. S., & Beach, F. A. *Patterns of sexual behavior*. New York: Harper & Row, 1951.

Foss, R. D., & Dempsey, C. B. Blood donation and the foot-in-the-door technique: A limiting case. *Journal of Personality and Social Psychology*, 1979, *37*, 580–590.

Fox, J. B., & Scott, J. F. *Absenteeism: Management's problem*. Boston: Harvard University Division of Research, 1943.

Frandsen, K. D. Effects of threat appeals and media of transmission. *Speech Monographs*, 1963, *30*, 101–104.

Fraser, S., Gouge, C., & Billig, M. Risky shifts, cautious shifts and group polarization. *European Journal of Social Psychology*, 1971, *1*, 7–29.

Freedman, J. L. Attitudinal effects of inadequate justification. *Journal of Personality*, 1963, *31*, 371–385.

Freedman, J. L., & Fraser, S. Compliance without pressure: The foot-in-the-door technique. *Journal of Personality and Social Psychology*, 1966, *4*, 195–202.

Freedman, J. L., Heshka, S., & Levy, A. Population density and pathology: Is there a relationship? *Journal of Experimental Social Psychology*, 1975, *11*, 539–552.

Freedman, J. L., Klevansky, S., & Ehrlich, P. R. The effect of crowding on human task performance. *Journal of Applied Social Psychology*, 1971, *1*, 7–25.

Freedman, J. L., Levy, A. S., Buchanan, R. W., & Price, J. Crowding and human aggressiveness. *Journal of Experimental Social Psychology*, 1972, *8*, 528–548.

Freedman, J. L., & Sears, D. O. Warning, dis-

traction, and resistance to influence. *Journal of Personality and Social Psychology*, 1965, *1*, 262–266.

Freeman, S., Walker, M., Borden, R., & Latané, B. Diffusion of responsibility and restaurant tipping: Cheaper by the bunch. *Personality and Social Psychology Bulletin*, 1975, *1*, 584–587.

French, J. R. P., Jr. The disruption and cohesion of groups. *Journal of Abnormal and Social Psychology*, 1941, *36*, 361–377.

French, J. R. P., Jr., & Raven, B. H. The bases of social power. In D. Cartwright (Ed.), *Studies in social power*. Ann Arbor: University of Michigan Press, 1959.

Frenkel-Brunswick, E. Further exploration by a contributor to "the authoritarian personality." In R. Christie & M. Jahoda (Eds.), *Studies in the scope and method of "the authoritarian personality."* New York: Free Press, 1954.

Freud, S. *Civilization and its discontents* (Joan Riviere, trans.). London: Hogarth Press, 1930.

Freud, S. Why war? In L. Bramson & G. Goethals (Eds.), *War: Studies from psychology, sociology, anthropology*. New York: Basic Books, 1964.

Fried, M., & Gleicher, P. Some sources of residential satisfaction in an urban slum. In J. F. Wohlwill & D. H. Carson (Eds.), *Environment and the social sciences: Perspectives and applications*. Washington, D.C.: American Psychological Association, 1972.

Fried, R., & Berkowitz, L. Music hath charms . . . and can influence helpfulness. *Journal of Applied Social Psychology*, 1979, *9*, 199–209.

Friedman, H. S. Effects of self-esteem and expected duration of interaction on liking for a highly rewarding partner. *Journal of Personality and Social Psychology*, 1976, *33*, 686–690.

Friedman, M. *Pathogenesis of coronary artery disease*. New York: McGraw-Hill, 1969.

Friedrich, W. N., & Boriskin, J. A. The role of the child in abuse: A review of the literature. *American Journal of Orthopsychiatry*, 1976, *46*, 580–590.

Frieze, I. H. The role of information processing in making causal attributions for success and failure. In J. Carroll & J. Payne (Eds.), *Cognition and social behavior*. New York: John Wiley & Sons, 1976.

Frieze, I. H., & Weiner, B. Cue utilization and attributional judgments for success and failure. *Journal of Personality*, 1971, *39*, 559–605.

Frijda, N. H. Emotion and recognition of emotion. In M. B. Arnold (Ed.), *Feelings and emotions*. New York: Academic Press, 1970.

Frodi, A. The effect of exposure to weapons on aggressive behavior from a cross-cultural perspective. *International Journal of Psychology*, 1975, *10*, 283–292.

Frodi, A. Sexual arousal, situational restrictiveness and aggressive behavior from a cross-cultural perspective. *Journal of Research in Personality*, 1977, *11*, 48–58.

Frodi, A., Macauley, J., & Thome, P. R. Are women always less aggressive than men? A review of the experimental literature. *Psychological Bulletin*, 1977, *84*, 634–660.

G

Gadlin, H. *Child discipline and the pursuit of the self: an historical interpretation*. Advances in child development and behavior. (Vol. 12). New York: Academic Press, 1978.

Gaebelein, J. W. Sex differences in instigative aggression. *Journal of Research in Personality*, 1977, *11*, 466–474.

Gaebelein, J. W., & Hay, W. M. Third-party instigation of aggression as a function of attack and vulnerability. *Journal of Research in Personality*, 1974, *7*, 324–333.

Gaertner, S. L., & Dovidio, J. F. The subtlety of white racism, arousal and helping behavior. *Journal of Personality and Social Psychology*, 1977, *35*, 691–707.

Gagnon, J. H. Scripts and the coordination of sexual conduct. In J. K. Cole & R. Dienstbier (Eds.), *Nebraska Symposium on Motivation, 1973* (Vol. 21). Lincoln: University of Nebraska Press, 1973.

Gagnon, J. H., & Simon, W. *The sexual scene*. Chicago: Aldine, 1970.

Galle, O. R., Gove, W. R., & McPherson, J. M. Population density and pathology: What are the relationships for man? *Science*, 1972, *176*, 23–30.

Gallo, P. S. Effects of increased incentives upon the use of threat in bargaining. *Journal of Personality and Social Psychology*, 1966, *4*, 14–20.

Gallup, G. *Gallup poll*. Princeton, N.J.: Audience Research, 1955.

Gallup, G. *Gallup poll*. Princeton, N.J.: Audience Research, 1977.

Galton, E. Police processing of rape complaints: A case study. *Journal of Criminal Law*, 1976, *4*, 15–30.

Gamson, W. A. Experimental studies of coalition formation. In L. Berkowitz (Ed.), *Advances in experimental social psychology* (Vol. 1). New York: Academic Press, 1964.

Gamson, W. A., & McEvoy, J. Police violence and its public support. *Annals of the American Academy of Political and Social Science*, 1970, *391*, 97–110.

Ganster, D., McCuddy, M., & Fromkin, H. L. *Similarity and undistinctiveness as determinants of favorable and unfavorable changes in self esteem*. Paper presented at the meeting of the Midwestern Psychological Association, Chicago, 1977.

Garbarino, J. A. A preliminary study of some ecological correlates of child abuse: The impact of socioeconomic stress on mothers. *Child Development*, 1976, *47*, 178–185.

Garbarino, J. A., & Bronfenbrenner, U. The socialization of moral judgment and behavior in cross-cultural perspective. In T. Lickona (Ed.), *Moral development and behavior*. New York: Holt, Rinehart & Winston, 1976.

Gardin, H., Kaplan, K. J., Firestone, I. J., & Cowan, G. A. Proxemic effects on cooperation, attitude, and approach-avoidance in a prisoner's dilemma game. *Journal of Personality and Social Psychology*, 1973, *27*, 13–18.

Garfinkel, H. *Studies in ethnomethodology*. Englewood Cliffs, N.J.: Prentice-Hall, 1967.

Garland, H., & Beard, J. F. *The relationship between self-monitoring and leader emergence across two task situations*. Unpublished manuscript, College of Business Administration, University of Texas, Arlington, 1978.

Garland, H., & Brown, B. R. Face-saving as affected by subject's sex, audience's sex and audience expertise. *Sociometry*, 1972, *35*, 280–289.

Gaskell, G., & Pearton, R. Aggression and sport. In J. H. Goldstein (Ed.), *Sports, games, and play: Social and psychological viewpoints*. Hillsdale, N.J.: Lawrence Erlbaum, 1979.

Gasparini, A. Influence of the dwelling on family. *Ekistics*, 1973, *216*, 344–348.

Gastorf, J. W., Suls, J., & Sanders, G. S. Type A coronary-prone behavior pattern and social facilitation. *Journal of Personality and Social Psychology*, 1980, *38*, 773–780.

Geen, R. G. Effects of frustration attack and prior training in aggressiveness upon aggressive behavior. *Journal of Personality and Social Psychology*, 1968, *9*, 316–321.

Geen, R. G. Some effects of observing violence upon the behavior of the observer. In B. A. Maher (Ed.), *Progress in experimental personality research*. New York: Academic Press, 1978.

Geen, R. G. The effects of anticipation of positive and negative outcomes on audience anxiety. *Journal of Consulting and Clinical Psychology*, 1977, *45*, 715–716.

Geen, R. G. The effects of being observed on performance. In P. B. Paulus (Ed.), *Psychology of group influence*. Hillsdale, N.J.: Lawrence Erlbaum, 1980.

Geen, R. G., & Quanty, M. B. The catharsis of aggression: An evaluation of a hypothesis. In L. Berkowitz (Ed.), *Advances in experimental social psychology* (Vol. 10). New York: Academic Press, 1977.

Geer, J., & Jamecky, L. The effect of being responsible for reducing another's pain on subjects' response and arousal. *Journal of Personality and Social Psychology*, 1973, *26*, 232.

Geis, F. L. *Machiavellianism and success in a three-person game*. Unpublished doctoral dissertation, Columbia University, New York, 1964.

Geizer, R. S., Rarick, D. L., & Soldow, G. F. Deception and judgment accuracy: A study in person perception. *Personality and Social Psychology Bulletin*, 1977, *3*, 446–449.

Gelfand, D. M., Hartman, D. F., Cromer, C. C., Smith, C. L., & Page, B. C. The effects of institutional prompts and praise on children's donation rates. *Child Development*, 1975, *46*, 980–983.

Gelfand, D. M., Hartman, D. P., Walder, P., & Page, B. Who reports shoplifters? A field-experimental study. *Journal of Personality and Social Psychology*, 1973, *25*, 276–285.

Geller, D. M., Goodstein, L., Silver, M., & Sternberg, W. C. On being ignored: The effects of the violation of implicit rules of social interaction. *Sociometry*, 1974, *37*, 541–556.

Gelles, R. J. *The violent home: A study of physical aggression between husbands and wives*. Beverly Hills, Calif.: Sage Publications, 1974.

Gelles, R. J., & Straus, M. A. Determinants of violence in the family: Toward a theoretical integration. In W. Burr, R. Hill, F. I. Nye, & I. Reiss (Eds.), *Contemporary theories about the family*. New York: Free Press, 1979.

Gerard, H. B. The anchorage of opinions in face-to-face groups. *Human Relations*, 1954, *7*, 313–325.

Gerard, H. B., Conolley, E. S., & Wilhelmy, R. A. Compliance, justification, and cognitive change. In L. Berkowitz (Ed.), *Advances in experimental social psychology* (Vol. 7). New York: Academic Press, 1974.

Gerard, H. B., & Hoyt, M. F. Distinctiveness of social categorization and attitude toward ingroup members. *Journal of Personality and Social Psychology*, 1974, *29*, 836–842.

Gerard, H. B., & Miller, N. *Desegregation: A longitudinal study*. New York: Plenum, in press.

Gerard, H. B., & Rabbie, J. M. Fear and social comparison. *Journal of Abnormal and Social Psychology*, 1961, *62*, 586–592.

Gerbner, G., & Gross, L. The scary world of TV's heavy viewer. *Psychology Today*, 1976, *89*, 41–45.

Gergen, K. J. The effects of interaction goals and personalistic feedback on presentation of self. *Journal of Personality and Social Psychology*, 1965, *1*, 413–425.

Gergen, K. J. Social psychology as history. *Journal of Personality and Social Psychology*, 1973, *26*, 309–320.

Gergen, K. J. The decline of character: Socialization and self-consistency. In G. DiRenzo (Ed.), *We, the people: American character and social change*. Westport, Conn.: Greenwood Press, 1977.

Gergen, K. J. Toward generative theory. *Journal of Personality and Social Psychology*, 1978, *36*, 1344–1360.

Gergen, K. J. *Social psychology and the phoenix of unreality*. Paper presented at the meeting of the American Psychological Association, New York, 1979.

Gergen, K. J. The function and foibles of negotiating self-conception. In M. Lynch, A. Norem-Hebeisen, & K. J. Gergen (Eds.), *Self concept: Advances in theory and research.* Cambridge, Mass.: Ballinger, in press.

Gergen, K. J., Ellsworth, P., Maslach, C., & Siepel, M. Obligation, donor resources and reactions to aid in three-nation study. *Journal of Personality and Social Psychology,* 1975, *31,* 390–400.

Gergen, K. J., & Gergen, M. M. International assistance from a psychological perspective. In *Yearbook of world affairs, 1971* (Vol. 25). London: Institute of World Affairs, 1972.

Gergen, K. J., & Gergen, M. M. Understanding foreign assistance through public opinion. In *Yearbook of world affairs, 1974* (Vol. 28). London: Stevens & Sons, 1974.

Gergen, K. J., & Gergen, M. M. *Form and function in social explanation.* Paper presented at the Houston Symposium on Philosophy and Behavioral Science, Houston, Tex., 1980.

Gergen, K. J., Gergen, M. M., & Barton, W. Deviance in the dark. *Psychology Today,* 1973, *7,* 129–130.

Gergen, K. J., Gergen, M. M., & Meter, K. Individual orientations to prosocial behavior. *Journal of Social Issues,* 1972, *28,* 105–130.

Gergen, K. J., Morse, S. J., & Bode, K. A. Overpaid or overworked? Cognitive and behavioral reactions to inequitable rewards. *Journal of Applied Social Psychology,* 1974, *4,* 259–274.

Gergen, K. J., & Taylor, M. G. Social expectancy and self-presentation in a status heirarchy. *Journal of Experimental Social Psychology,* 1969, *5,* 79–92.

Gergen, M. M. *The effects of age and type of residence on forms of social explanation.* Unpublished doctoral dissertation, Temple University, Philadelphia, 1980.

Gibb, C. A. Leadership. In G. Lindzey & E. Aronson (Eds.), *The handbook of social psychology* (Vol. 4). Reading, Mass: Addison-Wesley, 1969.

Gibbins, K. Communication aspects of women's clothes and their relation to fashion ability. *British Journal of Social and Clinical Psychology,* 1969, *8,* 301–312.

Gil, D. G. *Violence against children: Physical child abuse in the U.S.* Cambridge, Mass.: Harvard University Press, 1970.

Gil, D. G. A socio-cultural perspective on physical child abuse. *Child Welfare,* 1971, *50,* 389–395.

Gil, D. G. Unraveling child abuse. *American Journal of Orthopsychiatry,* 1975, *45,* 346–356.

Gillig, P. M., & Greenwald, A. G. Is it time to lay the sleeper effect to rest? *Journal of Personality and Social Psychology,* 1974, *29,* 132–139.

Gilligan, C. In a different voice: Woman's conception of the self and of morality. *Harvard Educational Review,* 1977, *4,* 481–517.

Gilligan, C. Woman's place in man's life cycle. *Harvard Educational Review,* 1979, *49,* 431–446.

Gilligan, C. *Do the social sciences have an adequate theory of moral development?* Unpublished manuscript, Harvard University, Cambridge, Mass., 1980.

Ginsburg, G. P. Situated action: An emergent paradigm in social psychological research. In L. Wheeler (Ed.), *Review of personality and social psychology.* Beverly Hills, Calif.: Sage Publications, in press.

Ginsburg, G. P. (Ed.). *Emerging strategies in social psychological research.* New York: John Wiley & Sons, 1979.

Gintner, G., & Lindskold, S. Rate of participation and expertise as factors influencing leader choice. *Journal of Personality and Social Psychology,* 1975, *32,* 1085–1089.

Glanzer, M., & Glaser, R. Techniques for the study of group structure and behavior: II. Empirical studies of the effects of structure in small groups. *Psychological Bulletin,* 1961, *58,* 1–27.

Glass, D. C. *Behavior patterns, stress and coronary disease.* Hillsdale, N.J.: Lawrence Erlbaum, 1977.

Glass, D. C., & Singer, J. E. *Urban stress.* New York: Academic Press, 1972.

Gleason, J. M., Seaman, F. J., & Hollander, E. P. Emergent leadership processes as a function of task structure and Machiavellianism. *Social Behavior and Personality,* 1978, *6,* 33–36.

Goethals, G. R., Allison, S. J., & Frost, M. Perceptions of the magnitude and diversity of social support. *Journal of Experimental Social Psychology,* 1979, *15,* 570–581.

Goethals, G. R., Cooper, J., & Naficy, A. Role of foreseen, foreseeable and unforeseeable behavioral consequences in the arousal of cognitive dissonance. *Journal of Personality and Social Psychology,* 1979, *37,* 1179–1185.

Goethals, G. R., & Nelson, R. E. Similarity in the influence process: The belief-value distinction. *Journal of Personality and Social Psychology,* 1973, *25,* 117–122.

Goethe, J., & Cole, C. *On reluctance to transmit negative information.* Unpublished term paper, University of Georgia, Athens, December 1969.

Goffman, E. *The presentation of self in everyday life.* Garden City, N.Y.: Doubleday, 1959.

Goffman, E. *Asylums.* New York: Doubleday/Anchor, 1961.

Goffman, E. *Stigma: Notes on the management of spoiled identity.* Englewood Cliffs, N.J.: Prentice-Hall, 1963.

Goffman, E. *Gender advertising.* New York: Harper & Row, 1979.

Goldschmidt, J., Gergen, M. M., Quigley, K., & Gergen, K. J. The women's liberation movement: Attitudes and action. *Journal of Personality,* 1974, *42,* 601–617.

Goldstein, A. G. The fallibility of the eyewitness: Psychological evidence. In B. D. Sales (Ed.), *Psychology in the legal process.* New York: Spectrum Publications, 1977.

Goldstein, J. H., & Arms, R. L. Effects of observing athletic contests on hostility. *Sociometry,* 1971, *34,* 83–90.

Goldstein, M. J., & Davis, E. E. Race and belief: A further analysis of the social determinants of behavioral intentions. *Journal of Personality and Social Psychology,* 1972, *22,* 346–355.

Goldstein, M. J., Kant, H. S., & Hartman, J. J. *Pornography and sexual deviance.* Berkeley: University of California Press, 1974.

Golledge, R. G. Multidimensional analysis in the study of environmental behavior and environmental design. In I. Altman & J. F. Wohlwill (Eds.), *Human behavior and environment* (Vol. 2). New York: Plenum, 1977.

Gollin, E. Forming impressions of personality. *Journal of Personality,* 1954, *23,* 65–76.

Gollob, H. F. The subject-verb-object approach to social cognition. *Psychological Review,* 1974, *81,* 286–321.

Good, K. J. Social facilitation: Effects of performance anticipation, evaluation and response competition on free associations. *Journal of Personality and Social Psychology,* 1973, *28,* 270–275.

Good, L. R., & Nelson, D. A. Effects of person-group and intergroup attitude similarity on perceived group attractiveness and cohesiveness. *Psychonomic Science,* 1971, *25,* 215–217.

Goodacre, D. M. The use of a sociometric test as a predictor of combat unit effectiveness. *Sociometry,* 1951, *14,* 148–152.

Goodman, M. E. *Race awareness in young children.* Reading, Mass.: Addison-Wesley, 1952.

Goodstadt, B., & Hjelle, L. A. Power to the powerless: Locus of control and the use of power. *Journal of Personality and Social Psychology,* 1973, *27,* 190–196.

Goranson, R., & Berkowitz, L. Reciprocity and responsibility reactions to prior help. *Journal of Personality and Social Psychology,* 1966, *3,* 227–232.

Goranson, R., & King, D. *Rioting and daily temperature: Analysis of the U.S. riots in 1967.* Unpublished manuscript, York University, Toronto, 1970.

Gordon, S. *Lonely in America.* New York: Simon & Schuster, 1976.

Gore, P. M., & Rotter, J. B. A personality correlate of social action. *Journal of Personality,* 1963, *31,* 58–64.

Gore, W. V., & Taylor, D. M. The nature of the audience as it affects social inhibition. *Representative Research in Social Psychology,* 1973, *4,* 18–27.

Gormly, J. A comparison of predictions from

consistency and affect theories for arousal during interpersonal agreement. *Journal of Personality and Social Psychology*, 1974, *30*, 658–663.

Gottlieb, D. E., Taylor, S. E., & Ruderman, A. Cognitive bases of children's moral judgments. *Developmental Psychology*, 1977, *13*, 547–556.

Gottman, T. M. *Experimental investigation of marital interaction.* New York: Academic Press, 1979.

Gough, H. G. *Manual for the California Psychological Inventory* (Rev. ed.). Palo Alto, Calif.: Consulting Psychologists Press, 1969.

Gough, H. G., & Peterson, D. R. The identification and measurement of predispositional factors in crime and delinquency. *Journal of Consulting Psychology*, 1952, *16*, 207–212.

Gouldner, A. W. A norm of reciprocity: A preliminary statement. *American Sociological Review*, 1960, *25*, 161–178.

Graf, R. C., & Riddell, L. C. Helping behavior as a function of interpersonal perception. *Journal of Social Psychology*, 1972, *86*, 227–231.

Graham, B. Loneliness: How it can be cured. *Reader's Digest*, October 1969, pp. 135–138.

Grandjean, E., Graf, P., Lauber, A., Meier, H. P., & Müller, R. A survey on aircraft noise in Switzerland. In W. D. Ward (Ed.), *Proceedings of the International Congress on Noise as a Public Health Problem.* Washington, D.C.: U.S. Government Printing Office, 1973.

Grant, J., & Grant, D. Evaluation of new career programs. In M. Guttentag & E. L. Struening (Eds.), *Handbook of evaluation research* (Vol. 2). Beverly Hills, Calif.: Sage Publications, 1975.

Gray, J. E., Cutler, C. A., Dean, J. G., & Kempe, C. H. Prediction and prevention of child abuse and neglect. *Journal of Social Issues*, 1979, *35*, 127–139.

Green, A. H., Gaines, R. W., & Sandgrund, A. Child abuse: Pathological syndrome of family interaction. *American Journal of Psychiatry*, 1974, *131*, 882–886.

Greenberg, B. S. Diffusion of news of the Kennedy assassination. *Public Opinion Quarterly*, 1964, *28*, 225–232.

Greenberg, M. S. A theory of indebtedness. In K. J. Gergen, M. S. Greenberg, & R. H. Willis (Eds.), *Social exchange: Advances in theory and research.* New York: Plenum, 1980.

Greenberg, M. S., Ruback, R. B., Wilson, C. E., & Mills, M. K. Theft victims' decision to call the police: An experimental approach. In G. Cooke, (Ed.), *The role of the forensic psychologist.* Springfield, Ill.: Charles C. Thomas, 1980.

Greenberg, M. S., & Shapiro, S. Indebtedness: An adverse aspect of asking for or receiving help. *Sociometry*, 1971, *34*, 290–301.

Greenberg, M. S., Wilson, C. E., & Mills, M. K. An experimental approach to victim decision making. In V. J. Konečni & E. B. Ebbeson (Eds.), *Social psychological analysis of legal processes.* San Francisco: W. H. Freeman, in press.

Greenberg, M. S., Wilson, C. E., Ruback, R. B., & Mills, M. K. Social and emotional determinants of victim crime reporting. *Social Psychology Quarterly*, 1979, *42*, 364–372.

Greenwald, A. G. When does role playing produce attitude change? Toward an answer. *Journal of Personality and Social Psychology*, 1970, *16*, 214–219.

Greenwald, A. G. The totalitarian ego: Fabrication and revision of personal history. *American Psychologist*, 1980, *35*, 603–618.

Gregory, W. L., Chartier, G. M., & Wright, M. H. Learned helplessness and learned effectiveness: Effects of explicit response cues on individuals differing in personal control expectancies. *Journal of Personality and Social Psychology*, 1979, *37*, 1982–1992.

Greydanus, A. Matters of the heart. *Saturday Review*, April 3, 1976.

Griffitt, W. Environmental effects on interpersonal affective behavior: Ambient effective temperature and attraction. *Journal of Personality and Social Psychology*, 1970, *15*, 240–244.

Griffitt, W. Response to erotica and the projection of response to erotica to the opposite sex. *Journal of Experimental Research in Personality*, 1973, *6*, 330–338.

Griffitt, W., & Garcia, L. Reversing authoritarian punitiveness: The impact of verbal conditioning. *Social Psychological Quarterly*, 1979, *42*, 55–61.

Griffitt, W., & Veitch, R. Influences of population density on interpersonal affective behavior. *Journal of Personality and Social Psychology*, 1971, *17*, 92–98.

Griffitt, W., & Veitch, R. Preacquaintance attitude similarity and attraction revisited: Ten days in a fallout shelter. *Sociometry*, 1974, *37*, 163–173.

Grim, P., Kohlberg, L., & White, S. Some relationships between conscience and attentional processes. *Journal of Personality and Social Psychology*, 1968, *8*, 239–252.

Gross, A. E., & Crofton, C. What is good is beautiful. *Sociometry*, 1977, *40*, 85–90.

Gross, A. E., & Latané, J. G. Some effects of receiving and giving help. Unpublished manuscript, University of Maryland, College Park, 1973.

Gross, A. E., & Latané, J. G. Receiving help, reciprocation and interpersonal attraction. *Journal of Applied Social Psychology*, 1974, *4*, 210–223.

Gross, B. M. Let's have a real State of the Union message. *Challenge*, 1966, *3*, 15–21.

Gross, E. Primary functions of the small group. *American Journal of Sociology*, 1954, *60*, 24–30.

Grossman, J. C., & Eisenman, R. Experimental manipulation of authoritarianism and its effect on creativity. *Journal of Consulting and Clinical Psychology*, 1971, *34*, 238–244.

Gruder, C. L. Determinants of social comparison choices. *Journal of Experimental Social Psychology*, 1971, *7*, 473–489.

Gruder, C. L., & Duslak, R. J. Elicitation of cooperation by retaliatory and nonretaliatory strategies in a mixed motive game. *Journal of Conflict Resolution*, 1973, *17*, 162–174.

Gruder, C. L., Romer, D., & Korth, B. Dependency and fault as determinants of helping. *Journal of Experimental Social Psychology*, 1978, *14*, 227–235.

Grusec, J. E. Power and the internalization of self-denial. *Child Development*, 1971, *42*, 93–105.

Grush, J. E. Impact of candidate expenditures, regionality, and prior outcomes on the 1976 Democratic presidential primaries. *Journal of Personality and Social Psychology*, 1980, *38*, 337–347.

Grush, J. E., Clore, G., & Costin, F. Dissimilarity and attraction: When difference makes a difference. *Journal of Personality and Social Psychology*, 1975, *32*, 783–789.

Grush, J. E., McKeough, K. L., & Ahlering, R. F. Extrapolating laboratory exposure research to actual political elections. *Journal of Personality and Social Psychology*, 1978, *36*, 257–270.

Grush, J. E., & Yehl, J. G. Marital roles, sex differences, and interpersonal attraction. *Journal of Personality and Social Psychology*, 1979, *37*, 116–123.

Gumpert, P., Deutsch, M., & Epstein, Y. Effect of incentive magnitude on cooperation in the prisoner's dilemma game. *Journal of Personality and Social Psychology*, 1969, *11*, 66–69.

Gunzburger, D. W., Wegner, D. M., & Anooshian, L. Moral judgment and distributive justice. *Human Development*, 1977, *20*, 160–170.

Gurin, G., Veroff, J., & Feld, S. *Americans view their mental health.* New York: Basic Books, 1960.

Gurr, T. R. Psychological factors in civil violence. *World Politics*, 1968, *20*, 245–278.

Gurr, T. R. A comparative survey of civil strive. In H. D. Graham & T. R. Gurr (Eds.), *Violence in America: Historical and comparative perspectives.* New York: Praeger, 1969.

Gurr, T. R. *Why men rebel.* Princeton, N.J.: Princeton University Press, 1970.

Gurwitz, S. B., & Dodge, K. A. Effects of confirmations and disconfirmations on stereotype-based attributions. *Journal of Personality and Social Psychology*, 1977, *35*, 495–500.

Guttentag, M. Special characteristics of social intervention programs: Evaluation of social intervention programs. *Annals of* the New York Academy of Sciences, 1973, 218, 6.

Guttentag, M., & Secord, P. F. *Too many women.* Unpublished manuscript, University of Houston, Tex., 1980.

H

Haan, N. Two moralities in action contexts: Relationships to thought, ego regulation, and development. *Journal of Personality and Social Psychology*, 1978, 36, 286–305.

Hackman, J. R., & Morris, C. G. Group tasks, group interaction process, and group performance effectiveness: A review and proposed integration. In L. Berkowitz (Ed.), *Advances in experimental social psychology* (Vol. 8). New York: Academic Press, 1975.

Halfner, D. P. Arousing fear in dental health education. *Journal of Public Health Dentistry*, 1965, 25, 140–146.

Hall, E. J., Mouton, J. S., & Blake, R. R. Group problem solving effectiveness under conditions of pooling versus interaction. *Journal of Social Psychology*, 1963, 59, 147–157.

Hall, E. T. *The silent language.* New York: Doubleday, 1959.

Hall, E. T. *The hidden dimension.* New York: Doubleday, 1966.

Hall, J., & Watson, W. H. The effects of normative intervention on group decision-making performance. *Human Relations*, 1970, 23, 299–317.

Hall, J. A. Gender effects in decoding nonverbal cues. *Psychological Bulletin*, 1978, 85, 845–857.

Hall, J. A. Voice tone and persuasion. *Journal of Personality and Social Psychology*, 1980, 38, 924–940.

Hall, J. A., Rosenthal, R., Archer, D., DiMatteo, M. R., & Rogers, P. L. The profile of nonverbal sensitivity. In P. McReynolds (Ed.), *Advances in psychological assessment* (Vol. 4). San Francisco: Jossey-Bass, 1978.

Hamilton, D. L., & Bishop, G. D. Attitudinal and behavioral effects of initial integration of white suburban neighborhoods. *Journal of Social Issues*, 1976, 32, 47–56.

Hamilton, D. L., Katz, L. B., & Leirer, V. O. Organizational processes in impression formation. In R. Hastie, T. M. Ostrom, E. B. Ebbeson, R. S. Wyer, D. L. Hamilton, & D. E. Carlston (Eds.), *Person memory*. Hillsdale, N.J.: Lawrence Erlbaum, 1980.

Hamner, W. C. Effects of bargaining strategy and pressure to reach agreement in a stalemated negotiation. *Journal of Personality and Social Psychology*, 1974, 30, 458–467.

Hamner, W. C., & Yukl, G. A. The effectiveness of different offer strategies in bargaining. In D. Druckman (Ed.), *Negotiations: Social-psychological perspectives*. London: Sage Publications, 1977.

Haney, C., Banks, C., & Zimbardo, P. G. Interpersonal dynamics in a simulated prison. *International Journal of Criminology and Penology*, 1973, 1, 69–97.

Harackiewicz, J. M. The effects of reward contingency and performance feedback on intrinsic motivation. *Journal of Personality and Social Psychology*, 1979, 37, 1352–1363.

Hardin, G. The tragedy of the commons. *Science*, 1968, 162, 1243–1248.

Harding, J., & Hogrefe, R. Attitudes of white department store employees toward Negro co-workers. *Journal of Social Issues*, 1952, 8, 18–28.

Hardy, K. R. Determinants of conformity and attitude change. *Journal of Abnormal and Social Psychology*, 1957, 54, 289–294.

Hardyck, J. A., & Braden, M. When prophecy fails again: A report of failure to replicate. *Journal of Abnormal and Social Psychology*, 1962, 65, 136–141.

Hare, A. P. *Handbook of small group research*. New York: Free Press, 1976.

Harnett, D. L., Cummings, L. L., & Hamner, W. C. Personality, bargaining style, and payoff in bilateral monopoly bargaining among European managers. *Sociometry*, 1973, 36, 325–345.

Harré, R., Morgan, J., & O'Neill, L. *Nicknames: Their origins and social consequences*. London: Routledge & Kegan Paul, 1979.

Harré, R., & Secord, P. F. *The explanation of social behavior*. Totowa, N.J.: Littlefield, Adams/Rowman & Littlefield, 1973. (Originally published, Oxford: Blackwell, 1972.)

Harrell, W. A., & Hartnagel, T. The impact of Machiavellianism and the trustfulness of the victim on laboratory theft. *Sociometry*, 1976, 39, 157–165.

Harris, M., & Meyer, F. Dependency, threat, and helping. *Journal of Social Psychology*, 1973, 90, 239–242.

Harris, M. B. Mediators between frustration and aggression in a field experiment. *Journal of Experimental Social Psychology*, 1974, 10, 561–571.

Harris, P. W. *The relationship of life change to academic performance among selected college freshmen at varying levels of college readiness*. Unpublished doctoral dissertation, East Texas State University, Commerce, 1972.

Harris, R. J., & Joyce, M. A. What's fair? It depends on how you phrase the question. *Journal of Personality and Social Psychology*, 1980, 38, 165–179.

Harrison, A. A. Mere exposure. In L. Berkowitz (Ed.), *Advances in experimental social psychology* (Vol. 10). New York: Academic Press, 1977.

Harrison, A. A., & Saeed, L. Let's make a deal: An analysis of revelations and stipulations in lonely hearts advertisements. *Journal of Personality and Social Psychology*, 1977, 35, 257–264.

Harshberger, D. An investigation of a structural model of small group problem solving. *Human Relations*, 1971, 24, 43–63.

Hart, R. J. Crime and punishment in the army. *Journal of Personality and Social Psychology*, 1978, 36, 1456–1471.

Hartley, E. L. *Problems in prejudice*. New York: Columbia University Press/King's Crown Press, 1946.

Hartman, D. P., Gelfand, D. M., Smith, C. L., Payl, S. C., Cromer, C. S., Page, B. C., & Lebenta, D. V. Factors affecting the acquisition and elimination of children's altruistic behavior. *Journal of Experimental Child Psychology*, 1976, 21, 328–338.

Hartshorne, H., & May, M. A. *Studies in the nature of character* (Vol. 1). New York: Macmillan, 1928.

Hartup, W. W., & Coates, B. Imitation of a peer as a function of reinforcement from the peer group and rewardingness of the model. *Child Development*, 1967, 38, 1003–1016.

Harvey, J. H., Yarkin, K. L., Lightner, J. M., & Tolin, J. P. Unsolicited interpretation and recall of interpersonal events. *Journal of Personality and Social Psychology*, 1980, 38, 551–568.

Hass, R. G. Persuasion or moderation? Two experiments on anticipatory belief change. *Journal of Personality and Social Psychology*, 1975, 31, 1155–1162.

Hass, R. G., & Linder, D. E. Counterargument availability and the effects of message structure on persuasion. *Journal of Personality and Social Psychology*, 1972, 23, 319–333.

Hass, R. G., & Mann, R. W. Anticipatory belief change: Persuasion or impression management? *Journal of Personality and Social Psychology*, 1976, 34, 105–111.

Hastorf, A. H. The "reinforcement" of individual actions in a group situation. In L. Krasner & L. P. Ullmann (Eds.), *Research in behavior modification: New developments and implications*. New York: Holt, Rinehart & Winston, 1965.

Hastorf, A. H., & Cantril, H. They saw a game: A case study. *Journal of Abnormal and Social Psychology*, 1954, 49, 129–134.

Hatfield, E., & Traupman, J. Intimate relationships: A perspective from equity theory. In S. Duck & R. Gilmore (Eds.), *Personal relationships*. London: Academic Press, 1981.

Hatfield, E., Utne, M. K., & Traupman, J. Equity theory and intimate relationships. In R. L. Burgess & T. L. Huston (Eds.), *Social exchange in developing relationships*. New York: Academic Press, 1979.

Hatfield, E., & Walster, G. W., & Piliavin, J. A. Equity theory and helping relationships. In L. Wispé (Ed.), *Altruism, sympathy, and helping*. New York: Academic Press, 1978.

Hatvany, N., & Zimbardo, P. G. *Shyness, arousal, and memory: The path from discomfort to distraction to recall deficits*. Unpublished manuscript, Stanford University, Stanford, Calif., 1977.

Haveman, R. H., & Watts, H. W. *Social experimentation as policy research: Review of negative income tax experiments.* Unpublished manuscript, University of Wisconsin, Madison, 1975.

Haynes, S. G., Feinleib, M., & Kannel, W. B. The relationship of psychological factors and coronary heart disease in Framingham. *American Journal of Epidemiology,* 1978, *108,* 229.

Haythorn, W. W. The influence of individual members on the characteristics of small groups. *Journal of Abnormal and Social Psychology,* 1953, *48,* 276–284.

Hebelein, T., & Black, J. Attitudinal specificity and the prediction of behavior in a field setting. *Journal of Personality and Social Psychology,* 1976, *33,* 474–479.

Heft, H. Background and focal environment conditions of the home and attention in young children. *Journal of Applied Social Psychology,* 1979, *9,* 47–69.

Heider, F. Attitudes and cognitive organization. *Journal of Personality,* 1946, *21,* 107–112.

Heider, F. *The psychology of interpersonal relations.* New York: John Wiley & Sons, 1958.

Heilman, M. E. Threats and promises: Reputational consequences and transfer of credibility. *Journal of Experimental Social Psychology,* 1974, *10,* 310–324.

Heingartner, A., & Hall, J. V. Affective consequences in adults and children of repeated exposure to auditory stimuli. *Journal of Personality and Social Psychology,* 1974, *29,* 719–723.

Heisler, W. J., & Gemmill, G. R. Machiavellianism, job satisfaction, job strain, and upward mobility: Some cross-organizational evidence. *Psychological Reports,* 1977, *41,* 592–594.

Helfer, R. E., & Kempe, C. H. *Helping the battered child and his family.* Philadelphia: J. B. Lippincott, 1972.

Henchy, T., & Glass, D. C. Evaluation apprehension and social facilitation of dominant and subordinate responses. *Journal of Personality and Social Psychology,* 1968, *10,* 446–454.

Hendrick, C. Social psychology's quest for new methods: May a thousand flowers bloom (Review of *Emerging strategies in social psychological research,* edited by G. P. Ginsburg). *Contemporary Psychology,* 1980, *25,* 533–534.

Hendrick, C., & Bukoff, A. Assessing the reassessment of the validity of laboratory-produced attitude change. *Journal of Personality and Social Psychology,* 1976, *34,* 1068–1077.

Henley, N. M. Status and sex: Some touching observations. *Bulletin of the Psychonomic Society,* 1973, *2,* 91–93.

Henley, N. M. *Body politics: Power, sex, and nonverbal communication.* Englewood Cliffs, N.J.: Prentice-Hall, 1977.

Hensley, V., & Duval, S. Some perceptual determinants of perceived similarity, liking, and correctness. *Journal of Personality and Social Psychology,* 1976, *34,* 159–168.

Hepburn, R. A., Gonzales, V., & deBurciaga, C. P. The Chicana as feminist. In A. G. Sargent (Ed.), *Beyond sex roles.* St. Paul: West, 1977.

Herd, J. A. Physiological correlates of coronary-prone behavior. In T. M. Dembroski, S. Weiss, J. Shields, S. G. Haynes, & F. Feinleib (Eds.), *Coronary-prone behavior.* New York: Springer-Verlag New York, 1978.

Herridge, C. F. Aircraft noise and mental health. *Journal of Psychosomatic Research,* 1974, *18,* 239–243.

Herridge, C. F., & Low-Beer, L. Observations of the effects of aircraft noise near Heathrow Airport on mental health. In W. D. Ward (Ed.), *Proceedings of the International Congress on Noise as a Public Health Problem.* Washington, D.C.: U.S. Government Printing Office, 1973.

Herzberg, J. Self-excoriation by young women. *American Journal of Psychology,* 1977, *134,* 320–321.

Heslin, R., & Blake, B. Performance as a function of payment, commitment and task interest. *Psychonomic Science,* 1969, *15,* 323–324.

Hess, R., & Torney, J. *The development of political attitudes in children.* Chicago: Aldine, 1967.

Higbee, K. L. Expression of "Walter-Mittyness" in actual behavior. *Journal of Personality and Social Psychology,* 1971, *20,* 416–422.

Higgins, E. T., Rhodewalt, F., & Zanna, M. P. Dissonance motivation: Its nature, persistence and reinstatement. *Journal of Experimental Social Psychology,* 1979, *15,* 16–34.

Hill, C. T., Rubin, Z., & Peplau, L. A. Break-ups before marriage: The end of 103 affairs. *Journal of Social Issues,* 1976, *32,* 147–167.

Hinkle, L. E., Jr. The effect of exposure to culture change, social change, and changes in interpersonal relationships on health. In B. S. Dohrenwend & B. P. Dohrenwend (Eds.), *Stressful life events: Their nature and effects.* New York: John Wiley & Sons, 1974.

Hinkle, S., & Schopler, J. Ethnocentrism in the evaluation of group products. In W. G. Austin & S. Worchel, (Eds.), *The social psychology of intergroup relations.* Monterey, Calif.: Brooks/Cole, 1979.

Hitler, A. *Mein Kampf* (Ralph Manheim, trans.). Boston: Houghton Mifflin, 1943.

Hobbes, T. *Leviathan.* New York: Bobbs-Merrill, 1958. (Originally published, 1651.)

Hochschild, A. R. Emotion work, feeling rules and social structure. *American Journal of Sociology,* 1979, *85,* 551–575.

Hoffman, L. R. (Ed.). *The group problem solving process: Studies of a valence model.* New York: Praeger, 1979.

Hoffman, L. R., Friend, K. E., & Bond, G. R. Problem differences and the process of adopting group solutions. In L. R. Hoffman (Ed.), *The group problem solving process: Studies of a valence model.* New York: Praeger, 1979.

Hoffman, L. R., & Maier, N. R. F. Valence in the adoption of solutions by problem-solving groups: Concept, method, and results. In L. R. Hoffman (Ed.), *The group problem-solving process: Studies of a valence model.* New York: Praeger, 1979.

Hoffman, M. L. Altruistic behavior and the parent-child relationship. *Journal of Personality and Social Psychology,* 1975, *31,* 937–943.

Hoffman, M. L. Moral internalization: Current theory and research. In L. Berkowitz (Ed.), *Advances in experimental social psychology* (Vol. 10). New York: Academic Press, 1977.

Hoffman, M. L., & Saltzstein, H. D. Parent discipline and the child's moral development. *Journal of Personality and Social Psychology,* 1967, *5,* 45–57.

Hogan, R. Development of an empathy scale. *Journal of Counseling and Clinical Psychology,* 1969, *33,* 307–316.

Hogan, R. A dimension of moral judgment. *Journal of Counseling and Clinical Psychology,* 1970, *35,* 205–212.

Hogan, R. Moral conduct and moral character: A psychological perspective. *Psychological Bulletin,* 1973, *80,* 217–232.

Hogan, R. Moral development and the structure of personality. In D. DePalma & J. Foley (Eds.), *Moral development: Current theory and research.* Hillsdale, N.J.: Lawrence Erlbaum, 1975.

Hogan, R., & Dickstein, E. Moral judgment and perceptions of injustice. *Journal of Personality and Social Psychology,* 1972, *23,* 409–413.

Hogan, R., & Henley, N. Nomotics: The science of human rule systems. *Law and Society Review,* 1970, *5,* 135–146.

Hogan, R., Mankin, D., Conway, J., & Fox, S. Personality correlates of undergraduate marijuana use. *Journal of Counseling and Clinical Psychology,* 1970, *35,* 58–63.

Hokanson, J. E., & Burgess, M. The effects of status, type of frustration, and aggression on vascular processes. *Journal of Abnormal and Social Psychology,* 1962, *65,* 232–237.

Hokanson, J. E., & Shetler, S. The effect of overt aggression on physiological arousal. *Journal of Abnormal and Social Psychology,* 1961, *63,* 446–448.

Hollander, E. P. Competence and conformity in the acceptance of influence. *Journal of Abnormal and Social Psychology,* 1960, *61,* 365–369.

Hollander, E. P. Competence, status, and idiosyncrasy credit. *Psychological Review,* 1958, *65,* 117–127.

Hollander, E. P. Leadership and social exchange processes. In K. J. Gergen, M.

Greenberg, & R. Willis (Eds.), *Social exchange: Advances in theory and research.* New York: Plenum, 1980.

Hollander, E. P., & Julian, J. W. A further look at leader legitimacy, influence, and innovation. In L. Berkowitz (Ed.), *Group processes.* New York: Academic Press, 1978.

Hollander, E. P., & Willis, R. Some current issues in the psychology of conformity and nonconformity. *Psychological Bulletin,* 1967, *68,* 62–76.

Hollenberg, E., & Sperry, M. Some antecedents of aggression and effects of frustration in doll play. *Personality: Topical Symposia,* 1951, *1,* 32–43.

Hollis, M. *Models of man.* London: Cambridge University Press, 1977.

Holmes, D. S., & Jackson, T. H. Influence of locus of control in interpersonal attraction and affective reactions in situations involving reward and punishment. *Journal of Personality and Social Psychology,* 1975, *31,* 132–136.

Holmes, J. G., Throop, W., & Strickland, L. H. The effects of prenegotiation expectations on the distributive bargaining process. *Journal of Experimental Social Psychology,* 1971, *7,* 582–589.

Holmes, T. H. Psychologic screening. In *Football injuries: Papers presented at a workshop.* Washington, D.C.: National Academy of Sciences, 1970.

Holmes, T. H., & Masuda, M. Life change and illness susceptibility. In B. S. Dohrenwend & B. P. Dohrenwend (Eds.), *Stressful life events: Their nature and effects.* New York: John Wiley & Sons, 1974.

Holmes, T. H., & Rahe, R. H. The social readjustment rating scale. *Journal of Psychosomatic Research,* 1967, *11,* 213–218.

Holmes, T. S. *Adaptive behavior and health change.* Unpublished medical thesis, University of Washington, Seattle, 1970.

Holmes, T. S., & Holmes, T. H. Short-term intrusions into the life style routine. *Journal of Psychosomatic Research,* 1970, *14,* 121–132.

Holstein, C. B. Irreversible stepwise sequence in the development of moral judgment: A longitudinal study of males and females. *Child Development,* 1976, *47,* 51–61.

Holsti, O. R., & North, R. C. History of human conflict. In E. B. McNeil (Ed.), *Social science and human conflict.* Englewood Cliffs, N.J.: Prentice-Hall, 1965.

Homans, G. C. *The human group.* New York: Harcourt Brace Jovanovich, 1950.

Homans, G. C. *Social behavior in its elementary forms* (Rev. ed.). New York: Harcourt Brace Jovanovich, 1974.

Horai, J., Naccar, N., & Fatoullah, E. The effects of expertise and physical attractiveness upon opinion agreement and liking. *Sociometry,* 1974, *37,* 601–606.

Hornberger, R. H. The differential reduction of aggressive responses as a function of interpolated activities. *American Psychol-*

ogist, 1959, *14,* 354.

Horner, M. S. Femininity and successful achievement: A basic inconsistency. In J. Bardwick, E. Douvan, M. S. Horner, & D. Gutmann (Eds.), *Feminine personality and conflict.* Monterey, Calif.: Brooks/Cole, 1970.

Horner, M. S. Toward an understanding of achievement related conflicts in women. *Journal of Social Issues,* 1972, *28,* 157–176.

Horner, M. S., & Rhoem, W. *The motive to avoid success as a function of age, occupation and progress in school.* Unpublished manuscript, University of Michigan, Ann Arbor, 1968.

Hornstein, H. A. *Cruelty and kindness.* Englewood Cliffs, N.J.: Prentice-Hall, 1976.

Hornstein, H. A., Fisch, E., & Holmes, M. Influence of a model's feeling about his behavior and his revelance as a comparison of other observers' helping behavior. *Journal of Personality and Social Psychology,* 1968, *10,* 222–226.

Hornstein, H. A., Lakind, E., Frankel, G., & Manne, S. Effects of knowledge about remote social events on pro-social behavior, social conception, and mood. *Journal of Personality and Social Psychology,* 1976, *32,* 1038–1046.

Horowitz, E. L. The development of attitude toward Negroes. *Archives of Psychology,* 1936, *194.*

Hovland, C. I., Harvey, O. J., & Sherif, H. Assimilation of contrast effects in reactions to communication and attitude change. *Journal of Abnormal and Social Psychology,* 1957, *55,* 244–252.

Hovland, C. I., & Janis, I. L. (Eds.). *Personality and persuasibility.* New Haven: Yale University Press, 1959.

Hovland, C. I., Janis, I. L., & Kelley, H. *Communication and persuasion.* New Haven, Conn.: Yale University Press, 1953.

Hovland, C. I., Lumsdaine, A. A., & Sheffield, F. D. *Experiments on mass communication.* Princeton, N.J.: Princeton University Press, 1949.

Hovland, C. I., & Mandell, W. An experimental comparison of conclusion-drawing by the communicator and by the audience. *Journal of Abnormal and Social Psychology,* 1952, *47,* 581–588.

Hovland, C. I., & Sears, R. R. Minor studies in aggression: VI. Correlation of lynchings with economic indices. *Journal of Psychology,* 1940, *9,* 301–310.

Hovland, C. I., & Weiss, W. The influence of source credibility on communication effectiveness. *Public Opinion Quarterly,* 1951, *15,* 635–650.

Howard, J. *Please touch: A guided tour of the human potential movement.* New York: McGraw-Hill, 1970.

Howard, J. W., & Rothbart, M. Social categorization and memory for in-group and out-group behavior. *Journal of Personality and Social Psychology,* 1980, *38,* 301–310.

Howard, W., & Crano, W. D. Effects of sex, conversation, location, and size of observer group on bystander intervention in a high risk situation. *Sociometry,* 1974, *37,* 491–507.

Hoyt, M. F., Henley, M., & Collins, B. Studies in forced compliance: Confluence of choice and consequence on attitude change. *Journal of Personality and Social Psychology,* 1972, *23,* 205–210.

Hoyt, M. F., & Raven, B. H. Birth order and the 1971 Los Angeles earthquake. *Journal of Personality and Social Psychology,* 1973, *28,* 123–130.

Hraba, J., & Grant, G. Black is beautiful: A re-examination of racial preference and identification. *Journal of Personality and Social Psychology,* 1970, *16,* 398–402.

Hunt, M. *The natural history of love.* New York: Alfred A. Knopf, 1959.

Hunt, P. J., & Hillery, J. M. Social facilitation in a coaction setting: An examination of the effects of over-learning trials. *Journal of Experimental Social Psychology,* 1973, *9,* 563–571.

Husband, R. W. Cooperative versus solitary problem solution. *Journal of Social Psychology,* 1940, *11,* 405–409.

Huston, T. L. Ambiguity of acceptance, social desirability, and dating choice. *Journal of Experimental Social Psychology,* 1973, *9,* 32–42.

Huston, T. L., & Burgess, R. L. Social exchange in developing relationships: An overview. In R. L. Burgess & T. L. Huston (Eds.), *Social exchange in developing relationships.* New York: Academic Press, 1979.

Huston, T. L., & Levinger, G. Interpersonal attraction and relationships. *Annual Review of Psychology,* 1978, *29,* 115–156.

Hutt, C., & Vaizey, M. J. Differential effects of group density on social behavior. *Nature,* 1966, *209,* 1371–1372.

Huttenlocher, J., & Presson, C. C. Mental rotation and the perspective problem. *Cognitive Psychology,* 1973, *4,* 277–299.

I

Ickes, W. J., & Barnes, R. D. The role of sex and self-monitoring in unstructured dyadic interactions. *Journal of Personality and Social Psychology,* 1977, *35,* 315–330.

Ickes, W. J., & Barnes, R. D. Boys and girls together—and alienated: On enacting stereotyped sex roles in mixed-sex dyads. *Journal of Personality and Social Psychology,* 1978, *36,* 669–683.

Ickes, W. J., Wicklund, R. A., & Ferris, C. B. Objective self-awareness and self-esteem. *Journal of Experimental Social Psychology,* 1973, *9,* 202–219.

Indik, B. Organization size and member participation: Some empirical tests of alternative explanations. *Human Relations,* 1965, *18,* 339–350.

Ingham, A. G., Levinger, G., Graves, J., & Peckham, V. The Ringelmann effect: Studies of group size and group performance. *Journal of Experimental Social Psychology*, 1974, *10*, 371–384.

Inn, A., Wheeler, A. C., & Sparling, C. L. Interactions between jurors as a function of majority vs. unanimity decision rule. *Journal of Applied Social Psychology*, 1977, *7*, 27–37.

Insko, C. A., Arkoff, A., & Insko, V. M. Effects of high and low fear-arousing communications upon opinions toward smoking. *Journal of Experimental Social Psychology*, 1965, *1*, 256–266.

Insko, C. A., & Robinson, J. E. Belief similarity versus race as determinants of reactions to Negroes by Southern white adolescents: A further test of Rokeach's theory. *Journal of Personality and Social Psychology*, 1967, *7*, 216–221.

Insko, C. A., Turnbull, W., & Yandell, B. Facilitating and inhibiting effects of distraction on attitude change. *Sociometry*, 1975, *4*, 508–528.

Insko, C. A., Worchel, S., Folger, R., & Kutkus, A. A balance theory interpretation of dissonance. *Psychological Review*, 1975, *82*, 169–183.

Isen, A. M. Success, failure, attention and reaction to others: The warm glow of success. *Journal of Personality and Social Psychology*, 1970, *15*, 294–301.

Isen, A. M., Clark, M., & Schwartz, M. Duration of the effect of good mood on helping: "Footprints in the sands of time." *Journal of Personality and Social Psychology*, 1976, *34*, 385–393.

Isen, A. M., Horn, N., & Rosenhan, D. L. Effects of success and failure on children's generosity. *Journal of Personality and Social Psychology*, 1973, *27*, 239–248.

Isen, A. M., & Levin, P. F. Effects of feeling good on helping: Cookies and kindness. *Journal of Personality and Social Psychology*, 1972, *21*, 384–388.

Isen, A. M., Shalker, T. E., Clark, M., & Karp, L. Affect, accessibility of material in memory, and behavior: A cognitive loop? *Journal of Personality and Social Psychology*, 1978, *36*, 1–12.

Isen, A. M., & Simmonds, S. F. The effect of feeling good on a helping task that is incompatible with good mood. *Social Psychology*, 1978, *41*, 346–349.

Ittelson, W. H., Proshansky, H. M., & Rivlin, L. G. Bedroom size and social interaction on the psychiatric ward. In J. F. Wohlwill & D. H. Carson (Eds.), *Environment and the social sciences: Perspectives and applications*. Washington, D.C.: American Psychological Association, 1972.

Ittelson, W. H., Proshansky, H. M. & Rivlin, L. G. The environmental psychology of the psychiatric ward. In H. M. Proshansky, W. H. Ittelson, & L. G. Rivlin (Eds.), *Environmental Psychology: Man and his physical setting*. New York: Holt, Rinehart & Winston, 1970.

Izard, C. E. *Human emotions*. New York: Plenum, 1977.

Izzett, R. R., & Leginski, W. Group discussion and the influence of defendant characteristics in a simulated jury setting. *Journal of Social Psychology*, 1974, *93*, 271–279.

J

Jacobs, R. C., & Campbell, D. T. The perpetuation of an arbitrary tradition through several generations of a laboratory microculture. *Journal of Abnormal and Social Psychology*, 1961, *62*, 649–658.

Jaeger, M. J., Anthony, S., & Rosnow, R. L. *Some determining factors in the transmission of a rumor*. Unpublished study, London School of Economics, London, and Temple University, Philadelphia, 1979.

Jaffee, Y., Malamuth, N., Feingold, J., & Feshbach, S. Sexual arousal and behavioral aggression. *Journal of Personality and Social Psychology*, 1974, *30*, 759–764.

Janis, I. L. *Air war and emotional stress: Psychological studies of bombing and civilian defense*. New York: McGraw-Hill, 1951.

Janis, I. L. Group identification under conditions of external danger. In D. Cartwright & A. Zander (Eds.), *Group dynamics: Research and theory*. New York: Harper & Row, 1968.

Janis, I. L., & Feshbach, S. Effects of fear-arousing communications. *Journal of Abnormal and Social Psychology*, 1953, *48*, 78–92.

Janis, I. L., & Field, P. B. Sex differences and personality factors related to persuasibility. In I. L. Janis et al., *Personality and persuasibility*. New Haven, Conn.: Yale University Press, 1959.

Janis, I. L., & Gilmore, I. The influence of incentive conditions on the success of role-playing in modifying attitudes. *Journal of Personality and Social Psychology*, 1965, *1*, 17–27.

Janis, I. L., Kaye, D., & Kirschner, P. Facilitating effects of "eating while reading" on responsiveness to persuasive communications. *Journal of Personality and Social Psychology*, 1965, *1*, 181–186.

Janis, I. L., & King, B. The influence of role-playing on opinion change. *Journal of Abnormal and Social Psychology*, 1954, *49*, 211–218.

Janis, I. L., & Mann, L. Effectiveness of emotional role-playing in modifying smoking habits and attitudes. *Journal of Experimental Research in Personality*, 1965, *1*, 84–90.

Janis, I. L., & Mann, L. *Decision making: A psychological analysis of conflict, choice and commitment*. New York: Free Press, 1977.

Janis, I. L., et al. *Personality and persuasibility*. New Haven, Conn.: Yale University Press, 1959.

Janov, A. *The primal scream: Primal therapy: The cure for neurosis*. New York: G. P. Putnam's Sons, 1970.

Jansen, G. Non-auditory effects of noise: Physiological and psychological reactions in man. In W. D. Ward (Ed.), *Proceedings of the International Congress on Noise as a Public Health Problem*. Washington, D.C.: U.S. Government Printing Office, 1973.

Janssens, L., & Nuttin, J. R. Frequency perception of individual and group success as a function of competition, coaction and isolation. *Journal of Personality and Social Psychology*, 1976, *34*, 830–836.

Jay, M. *The dialectical imagination*. London: William Heinemann, 1973.

Jellison, J. M., & Riskind, J. A social comparison of abilities interpretation of risk-taking behavior. *Journal of Personality and Social Psychology*, 1970, *15*, 375–390.

Jenkins, C. D., Zyzanski, S. J., & Rosenman, R. H. Risk of new myocardial infarction in middle-aged men with manifest coronary artery disease. *Circulation*, 1976, *53*, 342–347.

Jennings, H. H. *Leadership and isolation*. New York: Longmans, Green, 1950.

Jennings, M. K., & Zeigler, L. H. *Political expressionism among high school teachers: The intersection of community and occupational values*. Unpublished manuscript, 1968.

Jennings, R. *Television station employment practices: The status of minorities and women*. New York: Office of Communication, United Church of Christ, 1972.

Jennings (Walstedt), J., Geis, F. L., & Brown, V. Difference of television commercials on women's self-confidence and independent judgment. *Journal of Personality and Social Psychology*, 1980, *38*, 203–210.

Jensen, A. How much can we boost IQ and scholastic achievement? *Harvard Educational Review*, 1969, *39*, 1–125.

Johnson, C., & Scott, B. *Eyewitness testimony and suspect identification as a function of arousal, sex of witness, and scheduling of interrogation*. Paper presented at the meeting of the American Psychological Association, Washington, D.C., September 1976.

Johnson, D. M. The "phantom anesthetist" of Mattoon: A field study of mass hysteria. *Journal of Abnormal and Social Psychology*, 1945, *40*, 175–186.

Johnson, P. Women and interpersonal power. In I. Frieze, J. Parsons, P. Johnson, D. Ruble, & G. Zellman, *Women and sex roles: A social psychological perspective*. New York: W. W. Norton, 1978.

Johnson, R. D., & Downing, L. L. Deindividuation and valence of cues: Effects in prosocial and antisocial behavior. *Journal of Personality and Social Psychology*, 1979, *37*, 1532–1538.

Johnson, T. J., Feigenbaum, R., & Weiby, M. Some determinants and consequences of the teacher's perception of causality. *Journal of Educational Psychology*, 1964, *55*, 237–246.

Jones, C., & Aronson, E. Attribution of fault to a rape victim as a function of respectability of the victim. *Journal of Personality and Social Psychology*, 1973, *26*, 415–419.

Jones, E. E., & Davis, K. E. From acts to dispositions. In L. Berkowitz (Ed.), *Advances in experimental social psychology* (Vol. 2). New York: Academic Press, 1965.

Jones, E. E., Gergen, K. J., & Davis, K. E. Some determinants of reactions to being approved or disapproved as a person. *Psychological Monographs*, 1962, *76* (2, Whole No. 521).

Jones, E. E., Gergen, K. J., & Davis, K. E. Some determinants of reactions to being approved or disapproved as a person. *Psychological Monographs*, 1962, *76*, (2, Whole No. 521).

Jones, E. E., Gergen, K. J., Gumpert, P., & Thibaut, J. Some conditions affecting the use of ingratiation to influence performance evaluation. *Journal of Personality and Social Psychology*, 1965, *1*, 613–625.

Jones, E. E., & Goethals, G. Order effects in impression formation: Attribution context and the nature of the entity. In E. E. Jones et al. (Eds.), *Attribution: Perceiving the causes of behavior*. Morristown, N.J.: Silver Burdett/General Learning Press, 1972.

Jones, E. E., Jones, R. G., & Gergen, K. J. Tactics of ingratiation among leaders and subordinates in a status hierarchy. *Psychological Monographs*, 1963, *77* (3, Whole No. 566).

Jones, E. E., & Nisbett, R. E. *The actor and the observer: Divergent perceptions of the cause of behavior*. Morristown, N.J.: Silver Burdett/General Learning Press, 1971.

Jones, E. E., & Pittman, T. S. Toward a general theory of strategic self presentation. In J. Suls (Ed.), *Psychological perspectives on the self*. Hillsdale, N.J.: Lawrence Erlbaum, in press.

Jones, E. E., & Sigall, H. The bogus pipeline: A new paradigm for measuring affect and attitude. *Psychological Bulletin*, 1971, *76*, 349–364.

Jones, E. E., & Thibaut, J. W. Interaction goals as bases of inference in interpersonal perception. In R. Tagiuri & L. Petrullo (Eds.), *Person perception and interpersonal behavior*. Stanford, Calif.: Stanford University Press, 1958.

Jones, J. M., & Williamson, S. A. Athletic Profile Inventory (API): Assessment of athletes' attitudes and values. In J. H. Goldstein (Ed.), *Sports, games, and play: Social and psychological viewpoints*. Hillsdale, N.J.: Lawrence Erlbaum, 1979.

Jones, R., Linder, D., Kiesler, C., Zanna, M., & Brehm, J. Internal states or external stimuli: Observers' attitude judgments and the dissonance theory–self-persuasion controversy. *Journal of Experimental Social Psychology*, 1968, *4*, 247–269.

Jones, R. A. *Self-fulfilling prophecies*. Hillsdale, N.J.: Lawrence Erlbaum, 1977.

Jones, S. C. Self and interpersonal evaluations: Esteem theories versus consistency theories. *Psychological Bulletin*, 1973, *79*, 185–199.

Jones, S. C., & Panitch, D. The self-fulfilling prophecy and interpersonal attraction. *Journal of Experimental Social Psychology*, 1971, *7*, 356–366.

Jones, S. C., & Regan, D. T. Ability evaluation through social comparison. *Journal of Experimental Social Psychology*, 1974, *10*, 133–146.

Jordan, N. Behavioral forces that are a function of attitudes and of cognitive organization. *Human Relations*, 1953, *6*, 273–288.

Jourard, S. M. Self disclosure and other-cathexis. *Journal of Abnormal and Social Psychology*, 1959, *59*, 428–439.

Jourard, S. M. *The transparent self*. New York: Van Nostrand Reinhold, 1971.

Judd, C. M., & Harackiewicz, J. M. Contrast effects in attitude judgment: An examination of the accentuation hypothesis. *Journal of Personality and Social Psychology*, 1980, *38*, 390–398.

Judd, C. M., & Kulik, J. A. Schematic effects of social attitudes on information processing and recall. *Journal of Personality and Social Psychology*, 1980, *38*, 569–578.

Julian, J. W., Bishop, D. W., & Fiedler, F. E. Quasi-therapeutic effects of intergroup competition. *Journal of Personality and Social Psychology*, 1966, *3*, 321–327.

K

Kagan, J., & Moss, H. A. *Birth to maturity*. New York: John Wiley & Sons, 1962.

Kahle, L. R. Stimulus condition self-selection by males in the interaction of locus of control and skill-chance situations. *Journal of Personality and Social Psychology*, 1980, *38*, 50–56.

Kahle, L. R., & Berman, J. J. Attitudes cause behaviors: A cross-lagged panel analysis. *Journal of Personality and Social Psychology*, 1979, *37*, 315–321.

Kahneman, D., & Tversky, A. On the psychology of prediction. *Psychological Review*, 1973, *80*, 237–251.

Kalven, H., & Zeisel, H. *The American jur*. Boston: Little, Brown, 1966.

Kandel, D. B. Similarity in real-life adolescent friendship pairs. *Journal of Personality and Social Psychology*, 1978, *36*, 306–312.

Kane, T. R., Joseph, J. M., & Tedeschi, J. T. Person perception and the Berkowitz paradigm for the study of aggression. *Journal of Personality and Social Psychology*, 1976, *33*, 663–673.

Kanfer, F. H., & Marston, A. R. Human reinforcement: Vicarious and direct. *Journal of Experimental Psychology*, 1963, *66*, 245–254.

Kaplan, M. F. Context effects in impression formation: The weighted average versus the meaning-change formulation. *Journal of Personality and Social Psychology*, 1971, *19*, 92–99.

Kaplan, M. F. Stimulus inconsistency and response dispositions in forming judgments of other persons. *Journal of Personality and Social Psychology*, 1973, *25*, 58–64.

Kaplan, M. F. Context induced shifts in personality trait evaluations: A comment on the evaluative halo effect and the meaning change interpretations. *Psychological Bulletin*, 1974, *81*, 891–895.

Kaplan, M. F. Evaluative judgments are based on evaluative information: Evidence against meaning change in evaluative context effects. *Memory and Cognition*, 1975, *3*, 378–380.

Kaplan, R. M., & Singer, R. D. TV violence and viewer aggression. *Journal of Social Issues*, 1976, *32*, 35–70.

Kaplowitz, S. A. Toward a systematic theory of power attribution. *Social Psychology*, 1978, *41*, 131–148.

Kardiner, A., & Ovesey, L. *The mark of oppression*. New York: W. W. Norton, 1951.

Karlins, M., Coffman, T., & Walters, G. On the fading of social stereotypes: Studies in three generations of college students. *Journal of Personality and Social Psychology*, 1969, *13*, 1–16.

Karnoil, R. Children's use of intention cues in evaluating behavior. *Psychological Bulletin*, 1978, *85*, 76–86.

Karr, R. G. *Homosexual labeling: An experimental analysis*. Unpublished doctoral dissertation, University of Washington, Seattle, 1975.

Karr, R. G. Homosexual labeling and the male role. *Journal of Social Issues*, 1978, *34*, 73–83.

Karylowski, J. Self-esteem, similarity liking and helping. *Personality and Social Psychology Bulletin*, 1976, *2*, 71–74.

Kastenbaum, R., & Costa, P. T. Psychological perspectives on death. *Annual Review of Psychology*, 1977, *28*, 225–249.

Katz, A. M., & Hill, R. Residential propinquity and marital selection: A review of theory, method, and fact. *Marriage and Family Living*, 1958, *20*, 27–35.

Katz, D., & Braly, K. W. Racial stereotypes of 100 college students. *Journal of Abnormal and Social Psychology*, 1933, *28*, 280–290.

Katz, D., & Stotland, E. A preliminary statement of a theory of attitude structure and change. In S. Koch (Ed.), *Psychology: A study of science* (Vol. 3). New York: McGraw-Hill, 1959.

Katz, I., Cohen, S., & Glass, D. C. Some determinants of cross-racial helping behavior. *Journal of Personality and Social Psychology*, 1975, *32*, 964–970.

Katz, I., & Glass, D. C. An ambivalence-amplification theory of behavior toward the stigmatized. In W. G. Austin & S. Worchel (Eds.), *The social psychology of intergroup relations.* Monterey, Calif.: Brooks/Cole, 1979.

Katz, P. A., & Zalk, S. R. Doll preferences: An index of racial attitudes? *Journal of Educational Psychology,* 1974, *66,* 663–668.

Keasey, C. B. Experimentally induced changes in moral opinions and reasoning. *Journal of Personality and Social Psychology,* 1973, *26,* 30–38.

Keasey, C. B., & Tomlinson-Keasey, C. Petition signing in a naturalistic setting. *Journal of Social Psychology,* 1973, *89,* 313–314.

Keefe, M., & O'Reilly, H. Changing perspectives in sex crimes investigation. In M. Walker & S. Brodsky (Eds.), *Sexual assault.* Lexington, Mass.: Lexington Books, 1976.

Keller, P., & Brown, C. T. An interpersonal ethic for communication. In J. M. Civilky (Ed.), *Messages: A reader in communication.* New York: Random House, 1974.

Kelley, H. H. Two functions of reference groups. In G. Swanson, T. Newcomb, & E. Hartley (Eds.), *Readings in social psychology* (2nd ed.). New York: Holt, Rinehart & Winston, 1952.

Kelley, H. H. Attribution theory in social psychology. In D. Levine (Ed.), *Nebraska Symposium on Motivation* (Vol. 15). Lincoln: University of Nebraska Press, 1967.

Kelley, H. H. Interpersonal accommodation. *American Psychologist,* 1968, *23,* 399–410.

Kelley, H. H. *Causal schemata and the attribution process.* Morristown, N.J.: Silver Burdett/General Learning Press, 1972.

Kelley, H. H. The processes of causal attribution. *American Psychologist,* 1973, *28,* 107–128.

Kelley, H. H. *Personal relationships.* Hillsdale, N.J.: Lawrence Erlbaum, 1979.

Kelley, H. H., & Michela, S. L. Attribution theory and research. *Annual Review of Psychology,* 1980, *31,* 457–502.

Kelley, H. H., & Stahelski, A. J. Social interaction basis of cooperators' and competitors' beliefs about others. *Journal of Personality and Social Psychology,* 1970, *16,* 66–91.

Kelley, H. H., & Thibaut, J. W. *Interpersonal relations: A theory of interdependence.* New York: John Wiley & Sons, 1978.

Kellogg, R., & Baron, R. S. Attribution theory, insomnia and the reverse placebo effect: A reversal of Storm's and Nisbett's findings. *Journal of Personality and Social Psychology,* 1975, *32,* 231–236.

Kelman, H. C. Compliance, identification and internalization: Three processes of opinion change. *Journal of Conflict Resolution,* 1958, *2,* 51–60.

Kelman, H. C. Processes of opinion change. *Public Opinion Quarterly,* 1961, *25,* 57–78.

Kelman, H. C. *A time to speak: On human values and social research.* San Francisco: Jossey-Bass, 1968.

Kelman, H. C. Attitudes are alive and well and gainfully employed in the sphere of action. *American Psychologist,* 1974, *29,* 310–335.

Kelman, H. C. Privacy and research with human beings. *Journal of Social Issues,* 1977, *33,* 169–195.

Kelman, H. C., & Cohen, S. P. Reduction of international conflict: An international approach. In W. G. Austin & S. Worchel (Eds.), *The social psychology of intergroup relations.* Monterey, Calif.: Brooks/Cole, 1979.

Kelman, H. C., & Hovland, C. I. "Reinstatement" of the communicator in delayed measurement of opinion change. *Journal of Abnormal and Social Psychology,* 1953, *48,* 327–335.

Kenrick, D. T., Bauman, D. J., & Cialdini, R. B. A step in the socialization of altruism as hedonism: Effects of negative mood on children's generosity under public and private conditions. *Journal of Personality and Social Psychology,* 1979, *37,* 747–755.

Kenrick, D. T., & Gutierres, S. E. Contrast effects and judgments of physical attractiveness: When beauty becomes a social problem. *Journal of Personality and Social Psychology,* 1980, *38,* 131–140.

Kerckhoff, A. C. The social context of interpersonal attraction. In T. Huston (Ed.), *Foundations of interpersonal attraction.* New York: Academic Press, 1974.

Kerckhoff, A. C., & Back, K. W. *The June bug: A study of hysterical contagion.* New York: Appleton-Century-Crofts, 1968.

Kerckhoff, A. C., & Davis, K. Values consensus and need complimentarity in mate selection. *American Sociological Review,* 1962, *27,* 295–303.

Kerr, N. L. Severity of prescribed penalty and mock jurors' verdicts. *Journal of Personality and Social Psychology,* 1978, *36,* 1431–1442.

Kessler, S., & McKenna, W. *Gender.* New York: John Wiley & Sons, 1979.

Keyes, R. The height report. *Esquire,* November 1979, pp. 31–36; 41–43.

Keyes, R. *The height of your life.* Boston: Little, Brown, 1980.

Kidd, R. F., & Berkowitz, L. Effect of dissonance arousal on helpfulness. *Journal of Personality and Social Psychology,* 1976, *33,* 613–622.

Kidder, L. H., & Cohn, E. S. Public views of crime and crime prevention. In I. Frieze, D. Bar-Tal, & J. Carroll (Eds.), *New approaches to social problems.* San Francisco: Jossey-Bass, 1979.

Kiesler, C. A. *The psychology of commitment.* New York: Academic Press, 1971.

Kiesler, C. A., & DeSalvo, J. The group as an influencing agent in a forced compliance paradigm. *Journal of Experimental Social Psychology,* 1967, *3,* 160–171.

Kiesler, C. A., & Pallak, M. S. Arousal properties of dissonance manipulations. *Psychological Bulletin,* 1976, *83,* 1014–1025.

Kiesler, S., & Baral, R. The search for a romantic partner: The effects of self-esteem and physical attractiveness on romantic behavior. In K. J. Gergen & D. Marlowe (Eds.), *Personality and social behavior.* Reading, Mass.: Addison-Wesley, 1970.

Kilter, T. A., & Gross, A. E. Effects of public and private deviancy on compliance with a request. *Journal of Experimental Social Psychology,* 1975, *11,* 553–559.

King, B., & Janis, I. L. Comparison of the effectiveness of improvised vs. nonimprovised role-playing in producing opinion changes. *Human Relations,* 1956, *9,* 177–186.

King, M. L. The role of the behavioral scientist in the civil rights movement. *American Psychologist,* 1968, *23,* 180–186.

Kinney, E. E. A study of peer group social acceptability at the fifth-grade level at a public school. *Journal of Educational Research,* 1953, *47,* 57–64.

Kipnis, D. Does power corrupt? *Journal of Personality and Social Psychology,* 1972, *24,* 33–41.

Kipnis, D. *The powerholder.* Chicago: University of Chicago Press, 1976.

Kipnis, D., Castell, P., Gergen, M. M., & Mauch, D. Metamorphic effects of power. *Journal of Applied Psychology,* 1976, *61,* 127–135.

Kipnis, D., & Cosentino, J. Use of leadership powers in industry. *Journal of Applied Psychology,* 1969, *53,* 460–466.

Kissel, S. Stress reducing properties of social stimuli. *Journal of Personality and Social Psychology,* 1965, *2,* 378–384.

Klapper, J. T. *The effects of the mass media.* New York: Columbia University, Bureau of Applied Social Research, 1949.

Kleinke, C. L. Effects of personal evaluations. In G. J. Chelune (Ed.), *Self-disclosure.* San Francisco: Jossey-Bass, 1979.

Kleinke, C. L., & Pohlen, P. D. Affective and emotional responses as a function of other person's gaze and cooperativeness in a two-person game. *Journal of Personality and Social Psychology,* 1971, *17,* 308–313.

Knapp, M. L., Hart, R. P., & Dennis, H. S. An exploration of deception as a communication construct. *Human Communication Research,* 1974, *1,* 15–29.

Kniveton, B. H. The effect of rehearsal delay on long-term imitation of filmed aggression. *British Journal of Psychology,* 1973, *64,* 259–265.

Know, R. E., & Douglas, R. L. Trivial incentives, marginal comprehension and dubious generalizations from prisoner's dilemma studies. *Journal of Personality and Social Psychology,* 1971, *20,* 160–165.

Knox, R. E., & Safford, R. K. Group caution at the racetrack. *Journal of Experimental Social Psychology,* 1976, *12,* 317–324.

Knudson, R. M., Sommers, A. A., & Golding

S. L. Interpersonal perception and mode of resolution in marital conflict. *Journal of Personality and Social Psychology,* 1980, *38,* 751–763.

Kobasa, S. C. Stressful life events, personality and health: An inquiry into hardiness. *Journal of Personality and Social Psychology,* 1979, 37, 1–11.

Koeske, G. F., & Crano, W. D. The effects of congruous and incongruous source-statement combinations upon the judged credibility of a communication. *Journal of Experimental Social Psychology,* 1968, *4,* 384–399.

Koeske, G. F., & Koeske, R. K. Deviance and a generalized disposition toward internality: An attributional approach. *Journal of Personality,* 1975, *43,* 634–646.

Koffka, K. *Principles of Gestalt psychology.* New York: Harcourt Brace Jovanovich, 1935.

Kohlberg, L. *Relationships between the development of moral judgment and moral conduct.* Paper presented at the Symposium for Research in Child Development, Minneapolis, 1965.

Kohlberg, L. The child as a moral philosopher. *Psychology Today,* 1968, *2,* 24–30.

Kohlberg, L. Stage and sequences: The cognitive-developmental approach to socialization. In D. A. Goslin (Ed.), *Handbook of socialization theory and research.* Chicago: Rand McNally, 1969.

Kohlberg, L., & Kramer, R. Continuities and discontinuities in childhood and adult moral development. *Human Development,* 1969, *12,* 93–120.

Kohlberg, L., & Turiel, E. Moral development and moral education. In G. Lesser (Ed.), *Psychology and educational practice.* Chicago: Scott, Foresman, 1971.

Kohler, W. *Gestalt psychology: An introduction to new concepts in modern psychology.* New York: Liveright, 1947.

Koller, P. S., & Kaplan, R. M. A two-process theory of learned helplessness. *Journal of Personality and Social Psychology,* 1978, *36,* 1177–1183.

Komorita, S. S., & Kravitz, D. A. The effects of alternatives in bargaining. *Journal of Experimental Social Psychology,* 1979, *15,* 147–157.

Komorita, S. S., Sweeney, J., & Kravitz, D. A. Cooperative choice in the N-person dilemma situation. *Journal of Personality and Social Psychology,* 1980, *38,* 504–516.

Konečni, V. J. Some effects of guilt on compliance: A field replication. *Journal of Personality and Social Psychology,* 1972, *23,* 30–32.

Konečni, V. J. The mediation of aggressive behavior: Arousal level versus anger and cognitive labelling. *Journal of Personality and Social Psychology,* 1975, *32,* 706–712.

Konečni, V. J. The role of adversive events in the development of intergroup conflict. In W. G. Austin & S. Worchel (Eds.), *The social psychology of intergroup relations.*

Monterey, Calif.: Brooks/Cole, 1979.

Konečni, V. J., & Ebbeson, E. B. Disinhibition versus the cathartic effect: Artifact and substance. *Journal of Personality and Social Psychology,* 1976, *34,* 352–365.

Koretzky, M. B., Kohn, M., & Jeger, A. M. Cross-situational consistency among problem adolescents: An application of the two-factor model. *Journal of Personality and Social Psychology,* 1978, *36,* 1054–1059.

Korte, C. Helpfulness in the urban environment. In A. Baum, J. E. Singer, & S. Valins (Eds.), *Advances in experimental psychology* (Vol. 1). Hillsdale, N.J.: Lawrence Erlbaum, 1978.

Koslin, S., Amarel, M., & Ames, N. A distance measure of racial attitudes in primary grade children: An explanatory study. *Psychology in the Schools,* 1969, *6,* 382–385.

Kothandapani, V. Validation of feeling, belief and intention to act as three components of attitude and their contribution to prediction of contraceptive behavior. *Journal of Personality and Social Psychology,* 1971, *19,* 321–333.

Kramer, B. M. *Residential contact as a determinant of attitudes towards Negroes.* Unpublished doctoral dissertation, Harvard University, Cambridge, Mass., 1950.

Krantz, D. S., Glass, D. C., & Snyder, M. L. Helplessness, stress level and the coronary-prone behavior pattern. *Journal of Experimental Social Psychology,* 1974, *10,* 284–300.

Krauss, R. M., & Deutsch, M. Communication in interpersonal bargaining. *Journal of Personality and Social Psychology,* 1966, *4,* 572–577.

Krauss, R. M., Geller, V., & Olson, C. *Modalities and cues in perceiving deception.* Washington, D.C.: American Psychological Association, 1976.

Kravetz, D., & Sargent, A. G. Consciousness raising groups: A resocialization process for personal and social change. In A. G. Sargent (Ed.), *Beyond sex roles.* St. Paul: West, 1977.

Krebs, D. Empathy and altruism. *Journal of Personality and Social Psychology,* 1975, *32,* 1134–1146.

Krebs, D., & Adinolfi, A. Physical attractiveness, social relations, and personality style. *Journal of Personality and Social Psychology,* 1975, *31,* 245–253.

Krisher, H. P., III, Darley, S. A., & Darley, J. M. Fear-provoking recommendations, intentions to take preventative actions, and actual preventative actions. *Journal of Personality and Social Psychology,* 1973, *26,* 301–308.

Kriss, M., Indenbaum, E., & Tesch, F. Message type and status of interactants as determinants of telephone helping behavior. *Journal of Personality and Social Psychology,* 1974, *30,* 856–859.

Krulewitz, J. E., & Nash, J. E. Effects of sex

role attitudes and similarity on men's rejection of male homosexuals. *Journal of Personality and Social Psychology,* 1980, *38,* 67–74.

Kryter, K. *The effects of noise on man.* New York: Academic Press, 1970.

Kuhn, D., Langer, J., Kohlberg, L., & Haan, N. The development of formal operations in logical and moral judgment. *Genetic Psychology Monographs,* 1977, *95,* 97–188.

Kulka, R. A., & Weingarten, H. *The long-term effects of parental divorce in childhood on adult adjustment: A twenty year perspective.* Paper presented at the annual meeting of the American Sociological Association, Boston, August 1979.

Kurdek, L. Perspective taking as the cognitive basis of children's moral development: A review of the literature. *Merrill-Palmer Quarterly,* 1978, *24,* 3–28.

Kurtz, J. *Antagonistic signaling and territorial defense.* Unpublished master's thesis, University of Delaware, Newark, 1972.

L

LaFrance, M., & Carmen, B. The nonverbal display of psychological androgyny. *Journal of Personality and Social Psychology,* 1980, *38,* 36–49.

LaFrance, M., & Mayo, C. *Moving bodies: Nonverbal communication in social relationships.* Monterey, Calif.: Brooks/Cole, 1978.

Lakin, M. *Interpersonal encounter: Theory and practice in sensitivity training.* New York: McGraw-Hill, 1972.

Lambert, R. Situations of uncertainty: Social influence and decision processes. In H. Brandstätter, J. H. Davis, H. Schuler (Eds.), *Dynamics of group decisions.* Beverly Hills, Calif.: Sage Publications, 1978.

Lamm, H. Will an observer advise higher risk taking after hearing a discussion of the decision problem? *Journal of Personality and Social Psychology,* 1967, *6,* 467–471.

Lana, R. E. Three theoretical interpretations of order effects in persuasive communications. *Psychological Bulletin,* 1964, *61,* 314–320.

Landis, C. The interpretation of facial expression in emotion. *Journal of General Psychology,* 1929, *2,* 59–72.

Landy, D., & Aronson, E. The influence of the character of the criminal and his victim on the decisions of simulated jurors. *Journal of Experimental Social Psychology,* 1969, *5,* 141–152.

Landy, D., & Sigall, H. Beauty is talent: Task evaluation as a function of the performer's physical attractiveness. *Journal of Personality and Social Psychology,* 1974, *29,* 299–304.

Lane, R. The need to be liked and the anxious college liberal. *Annals,* 1965, *361,* 71–80.

Lane, R. Criminal violence in America: The

first hundred years. *Annals of the American Academy of Political and Social Science,* 1976, *423,* 1–13.

Langer, E., & Abelson, R. P. The semantics of asking for a favor: How to succeed in getting help without really dying. *Journal of Personality and Social Psychology,* 1972, *24,* 26–32.

Langer, E., & Saegert, S. Crowding and cognitive control. *Journal of Personality and Social Psychology,* 1977, *35,* 175–182.

Langer, E., Taylor, S. E., Fiske, S., & Chanowitz, B. Stigma, staring, and discomfort: A novel-stimulus hypothesis. *Journal of Experimental Social Psychology,* 1976, *12,* 451–463.

Langner, T. S., Herson, J. H., Greene, E. L., Jameson, J. D., & Goff, J. A. Children of the city: Affluence, poverty, and mental health. In V. Allen (Ed.), *Psychological factors in poverty.* Skokie, Ill.: Rand McNally/Markham, 1970.

Lanzetta, J. T., & Hannah, T. E. Reinforcing behavior of "naive" trainers. *Journal of Personality and Social Psychology,* 1969, *11,* 245–252.

Lanzetta, J. T., & Kleck, R. Encoding and decoding of facial affect in humans. *Journal of Personality and Social Psychology,* 1970, *16,* 12–19.

LaPiere, R. T. Attitudes vs. actions. *Social Forces,* 1934, *13,* 230–237.

L'Armand, K., & Pepitone, A. Helping to reward another person: A cross-cultural analysis. *Journal of Personality and Social Psychology,* 1975, *31,* 189–198.

Larsen, K. S. Authoritarianism and attitudes toward police. *Psychological Reports,* 1968, *23,* 349–350.

Larsson, K. *Conditioning and sexual behavior in the male albino rat.* Stockholm: Almqvist & Wiksell, 1956.

Latané, B. Field studies of altruistic compliance. *Representative Research in Social Psychology,* 1970, *1,* 49–62.

Latané, B. *The psychology of social impact.* Presidential address, Society for Personality and Social Psychology, at the meeting of the American Psychological Association, Toronto, 1978.

Latané, B., & Cappell, H. The effects of togetherness on heart rate in rats. *Psychonomic Science,* 1972, *29,* 177–179.

Latané, B., & Dabbs, J. Sex, group size, and helping in three cities. *Sociometry,* 1975, *38,* 180–194.

Latané, B., & Darley, J. M. Group inhibition of bystander intervention in emergencies. *Journal of Personality and Social Psychology,* 1968, *10,* 215–221.

Latané, B., & Darley, J. M. *The unresponsive bystander: Why doesn't he help?* New York: Appleton-Century-Crofts, 1970.

Latané, B., & Nida, S. Social impact theory and group influence: A social engineering perspective. In P. B. Paulus (Ed.), *Psychology of group influence.* Hillsdale, N.J.: Lawrence Erlbaum, 1980.

Latané, B., & Rodin, J. A lady in distress: Inhibiting effects of friends and strangers on bystander intervention. *Journal of Experimental Social Psychology,* 1969, *5,* 189–202.

Latané, B., Williams, K., & Harkins, S. Many hands make light the work: The causes and consequences of social loafing. *Journal of Personality and Social Psychology,* 1979, *37,* 822–832.

Lauderdale, P. Deviance and moral boundaries. *American Sociological Review,* 1976, *41,* 660–676.

Laughlin, P. R., & Adamopoulos, J. Social combination process and individual learning for six-person cooperative groups on an intellective task. *Journal of Personality and Social Psychology,* 1980, *38,* 941–947.

Laughlin, P. R., & Adamopoulos, J. Social decision schemes on intellective tasks. In H. Brandstätter, J. H. Davis, & G. Stocker-Kreichgauer (Eds.), *Contemporary problems in group decision making.* New York: Academic Press, in press.

Laughlin, P. R., Kerr, N. L., Davis, J. H., Haff, H. M., & Marciniak, K. A. Group size, member ability, and social decision schemes on an intellective task. *Journal of Personality and Social Psychology,* 1975, *31,* 522–535.

Law Enforcement Assistance Administration. *Criminal victimization in the United States: A comparison of 1974 and 1975 findings.* Washington, D.C.: National Criminal Justice Information & Statistics Service, 1977.

Lawler, E. E. Effects of hourly overpayment on productivity and work quality. *Journal of Personality and Social Psychology,* 1968, *10,* 306–314.

Lazarus, R. S. The self-regulation of emotion. In L. Levi (Ed.), *Emotions: Their parameters and measurement.* New York: Raven Press, 1975.

Lazarus, R. S., Kanner, A. D., & Folkman, S. Emotions: A cognitive-phenomenological analysis. In R. Plutchik & H. Kellerman (Eds.), *Emotion: Theory, research, and experience.* New York: Academic Press, 1980.

Lazarus, R. S., & Launier, R. Stress-related transactions between person and environment. In A. Pervim & M. Lewis (Eds.), *Interaction between internal and external determinants of behavior.* New York: Plenum, 1977.

Leavitt, H. J. Some effects of certain communication patterns on group performance. *Journal of Abnormal and Social Psychology,* 1951, *46,* 38–50.

Lebo, C., & Oliphant, K. Music as a source of acoustic trauma. *Laryngoscope,* 1968, *78,* 1211–1218.

Lefcourt, H. M. *Locus of control: Current trends in theory and research.* Hillsdale, N.J.: Lawrence Erlbaum, 1976.

Lefcourt, H. M., & Wine, J. Internal versus external control of reinforcement and the development of attention in experimental situations. *Canadian Journal of Behavioral Science,* 1969, *1,* 167–181.

Lefkowitz, M., Blake, R. R., & Mouton, J. S. Status factors in pedestrian violation of traffic signals. *Journal of Abnormal and Social Psychology,* 1955, *51,* 704–706.

Lehne, G. K. Homophobia among men. In D. David & R. Brannon (Eds.), *The forty-nine percent majority: The male sex role.* Reading, Mass.: Addison-Wesley, 1976.

Leik, R., & Leik, S. A. Transition in interpersonal commitment. In R. L. Hamblin & J. H. Kunkel (Eds.), *Behavioral theory in sociology.* New Brunswick, N.J.: Transaction Books, 1977.

Leister, A. F., Borden, D., & Fiedler, F. E. The effect of contingency model leadership training on the performance of navy leaders. *Academy of Management Journal,* 1977, *20,* 464–470.

Lenihan, K. J. *When money counts: An experimental study of providing financial aid and job placement services to released prisoners.* Washington, D.C.: Bureau of Social Science Research, 1976.

Lenrow, P. B. Studies in sympathy. In S. S. Tomkins & C. E. Izard (Eds.), *Affect, cognition, and personality.* New York: Springer, 1965.

Lenrow, P. B. Dilemmas of professional helping: Continuities and discontinuities with folk helping roles. In L. Wispé (Ed.), *Altruism, sympathy and helping.* New York: Academic Press, 1978.

Leon, M., Oden, G. C., & Anderson, N. H. Functional measurement of social values. *Journal of Personality and Social Psychology,* 1973, *27,* 301–310.

Leonard, R. Self-concept and attraction for similar and dissimilar others. *Journal of Personality and Social Psychology,* 1975, *31,* 926–929.

Lepper, M. R., & Greene, D. Overjustification research and beyond: Toward a means-ends analysis of intrinsic and extrinsic motivation. In M. R. Lepper & D. Greene (Eds.), *The hidden costs of reward.* Hillsdale, N.J.: Lawrence Erlbaum, 1978.

Lepper, M. R., Greene, D., & Nisbett, R. E. Undermining children's intrinsic interest with extrinsic reward: A test of the "overjustification" hypothesis. *Journal of Personality and Social Psychology,* 1973, *28,* 129–137.

Lerner, M. J. Evaluation of performance as a function of performer's reward and attractiveness. *Journal of Personality and Social Psychology,* 1965, *1,* 355–360.

Lerner, M. J. The desire for justice and reactions to victims. In J. R. Macaulay & L. Berkowitz (Eds.), *Altruism and helping behavior.* New York: Academic Press, 1970.

Lerner, M. J., & Agar, E. The consequences of perceived similarity: Attraction and rejection, approach and avoidance. *Journal of Experimental Research in Personality,* 1972, *6,* 69–75.

Lerner, R. Concepts of individual and social relationship development. In R. L. Burgess & T. L. Huston (Eds.), *Social exchange in developing relationships.* New York: Academic Press, 1979.

Leshner, A. I. *An introduction to behavioral endocrinology.* New York: Oxford University Press, 1978.

Lesser, G. S., & Abelson, R. P. Personality correlates of persuasibility in children. In I. L. Janis & C. I. Hovland (Eds.), *Personality and persuasibility.* New Haven, Conn.: Yale University Press, 1959.

Lessing, E. E., & Zagorin, S. W. Black power ideology and college students' attitudes toward their own and other racial groups. *Journal of Personality and Social Psychology,* 1972, *21,* 61–73.

Leventhal, G. W. What should be done with equity theory? New approaches to the study of fairness in social relationships. In K. J. Gergen, M. S. Greenberg, & R. H. Willis (Eds.), *Social exchange: Advances in theory and research.* New York: Plenum, 1980.

Leventhal, G. W., & Lane, D. W. Sex, age, and equity behavior. *Journal of Personality and Social Psychology,* 1970, *15,* 312–316.

Leventhal, G. W., & Weiss, T., & Long, G. Equity, reciprocity, and reallocating the rewards in the dyad. *Journal of Personality and Social Psychology,* 1969, *13,* 300–305.

Leventhal, H. Findings and theory in the study of fear communications. In L. Berkowitz (Ed.), *Advances in experimental social psychology* (Vol. 5). New York: Academic Press, 1970.

Leventhal, H. Emotions: A basic problem for social psychology. In C. Nemeth (Ed.), *Social psychology: Classic and contemporary integrations.* Chicago: Rand McNally, 1974.

Leventhal, H., & Niles, P. Persistence of influence for varying durations of exposure to threat stimuli. *Psychological Reports,* 1965, *16,* 223–233.

Leventhal, H., & Perloe, S. A relationship between self-esteem and persuasibility. *Journal of Abnormal and Social Psychology,* 1962, *64,* 385–388.

Leventhal, H., & Singer, R. P. Affect arousal and positioning of recommendations in persuasive communications. *Journal of Personality and Social Psychology,* 1966, *4,* 137–146.

Leventhal, H., Watts, J. C., & Pagano, F. Effects of fear and instructions on how to cope with danger. *Journal of Personality and Social Psychology,* 1967, *6,* 313–321.

Levine, C. Role-taking standpoint and adolescent usage of Kohlberg's conventional stages of moral reasoning. *Journal of Personality and Social Psychology,* 1976, *34,* 41–53.

Levine, J. M. Reaction to opinion deviance in small groups. In P. B. Paulus (Ed.), *Psychology of group influence.* Hillsdale, N.J.: Lawrence Erlbaum, 1980.

Levine, M. *A cognitive theory of learning.* Hillsdale, N.J.: Lawrence Erlbaum, 1975.

Levine, S. M., & Murphy, G. The learning and forgetting of controversial material. *Journal of Abnormal and Social Psychology,* 1943, *38,* 507–517.

Levinger, G. A three-level approach to attraction: Toward an understanding of pair relatedness. In T. L. Huston (Ed.), *Foundations of interpersonal attraction.* New York: Academic Press, 1974.

Levinger, G. A social psychological perspective on marital dissolution. *Journal of Social Issues,* 1976, *32,* 21–47.

Levinger, G., & Huesmann, L. R. An "incremental exchange" perspective on the pair relationship. In K. J. Gergen, M. Greenberg, & R. H. Willis (Eds.), *Social exchange: Advances in theory and research.* New York: Plenum, 1980.

Levinger, G., & Snoek, J. D. *Attraction in relationships: A new look at interpersonal attraction.* Morristown, N.J.: Silver Burdett/General Learning Press, 1972.

Levinson, D. J., & Huffman, P. E. Traditional family ideology and its relation to personality. *Journal of Personality,* 1955, *23,* 251–273.

Levitt, E. E., & Klassen, A. D. Public attitudes toward homosexuality. *Journal of Homosexuality,* 1974, *1,* 29–43.

Levy, P., Lundgren, D., Ansel, M., Fell, D., Fink, B., & McGrath, J. E. Bystander effect in a demand-without-threat situation. *Journal of Personality and Social Psychology,* 1972, *24,* 166–171.

Lewin, K. Self hatred among Jews. *Contemporary Jewish Record,* 1941, *4,* 219–232.

Lewin, K. *Resolving social conflicts: Selected papers on group dynamics.* G. W. Lewin (Ed.). New York: Harper & Row, 1948.

Lewin, K. *Field theory in social sciences.* New York: Harper & Row, 1951.

Lewis, H. R., & Streitfeld, H. S. *Growth games: How to tune in yourself, your family, your friends.* New York: Harcourt Brace Jovanovich, 1970.

Lewis, W. H. Feuding and social change in Morocco. *Journal of Conflict Resolution,* 1961, *5,* 43–54.

Leyens, J. P., & Parke, R. E. Aggressive slides can induce a weapons effect. *European Journal of Social Psychology,* 1975, *5,* 229–236.

Lieberman, M. A., Yalom, I. D., & Miles, M. B. *Encounter groups: First facts.* New York: Basic Books, 1973.

Liebling, B. A., & Shaver, P. Evaluation, self-awareness and task performance. *Journal of Experimental Social Psychology,* 1973, *9,* 297–306.

Lief, A. (Ed.). *The commonsense psychiatry of Dr. Adolf Meyer.* New York: McGraw-Hill, 1948.

Lindskold, S. Managing conflict through announced conciliatory initiatives backed with retaliatory capability. In W. Austin

& S. Worchel, *The social psychology of intergroup relations.* Monterey, Calif.: Brooks/Cole, 1979.

Lingle, J. H., Geva, N., Ostrom, T. M., Leippe, M. R., & Baumgardner, M. H. Thematic effects of person judgments on impression organization. *Journal of Personality and Social Psychology,* 1979, *37,* 674–687.

Linsenmeier, J. A. W., & Wortman, C. Attitudes toward workers and toward their work: More evidence that sex makes a difference. *Journal of Applied Social Psychology,* 1979, *9,* 326–334.

Linville, P. W., & Jones, E. E. Polarized appraisals of outgroup members. *Journal of Personality and Social Psychology,* 1980, *38,* 689–703.

Lipitz, M. E., Cohen, I. H., Dworkin, J., & Rogers, L. S. Need complementarity, marital stability and mental satisfaction. In K. J. Gergen & D. Marlowe (Eds.), *Personality and social behavior.* Reading, Mass.: Addison-Wesley, 1970.

Lippa, R. Expressive control and the leakage of dispositional introversion-extroversion during role-played teaching. *Journal of Personality,* 1976, *44,* 541–559.

Lippa, R. The effect of expressive control on expressive consistency and on the relation between expressive behavior and personality. *Journal of Personality,* 1978, *46,* 438–461.

Lippitt, R., & White, R. The "social climate" of children's groups. In R. G. Baker, J. Kounin, & H. Wright (Eds.), *Child behavior and development.* New York: McGraw-Hill, 1943.

Lippmann, W. *Public-opinion.* New York: Harcourt Brace Jovanovich, 1922.

Livesley, W., & Bromley, D. *Person perception in childhood and adolescence.* London: John Wiley & Sons, 1973.

Locksley, A., & Colten, M. E. Psychological androgyny: A case of mistaken identity. *Journal of Personality and Social Psychology,* 1979, *37,* 1017–1031.

Loftis, J., & Ross, L. Retrospective misattribution of a conditioned emotional response. *Journal of Personality and Social Psychology,* 1974, *30,* 683–687.

Lombardo, J. P., Weiss, R. F., & Stich, M. H. Effectance reduction through speaking in reply and its relation to attraction. *Journal of Personality and Social Psychology,* 1973, *28,* 325–332.

London, H. *Psychology of the persuader.* Morristown, N.J.: Silver Burdett/General Learning Press, 1973.

London, H., McSeveney, D., & Tropper, R. Confidence, overconfidence, and persuasion. *Human Relations,* 1971, *24,* 359–369.

London, H., Meldman, P., & Lanckton, A. V. The jury method: How the persuader persuades. *Public Opinion Quarterly,* 1971, *34,* 171–183.

London, P. The rescuers: Motivational hypothesis about Christians who saved Jews from the Nazis. In J. R. Macaulay & L. Berkowitz (Eds.), *Altruism and helping behavior.* New York: Academic Press, 1970.

Longstretch, L. E. Distance to goal and reinforcement schedule as determinants of human instrumental behavior. *Proceedings of the 74th Annual Convention of the American Psychological Association,* 1966, 39–40.

Loo, C. The psychological study of crowding. *American Behavioral Scientist,* 1975, *18,* 826–842.

Lord, C. G. Schemas and images as memory aids: Two modes of processing social information. *Journal of Personality and Social Psychology,* 1980, *38,* 257–269.

Lord, C. G., Ross, L., & Lepper, M. R. Biased assimilation and attitude polarization: The effects of prior theories on subsequently considered evidence. *Journal of Personality and Social Psychology,* 1979, *37,* 2098–2109.

Lorenz, K. *On aggression* (Marjorie Kerr Wilson, trans.). New York: Harcourt Brace Jovanovich, 1966.

Lorenz, K. *Studies in animal and human behavior* (Vol. 1). (R. Martin, trans.). Cambridge, Mass.: Harvard University Press, 1970.

Lott, A. J., & Lott, B. E. Group cohesiveness, communication level, and conformity. *Journal of Abnormal and Social Psychology,* 1961, *62,* 408–412.

Lott, A. J., & Lott, B. E. Group cohesiveness as interpersonal attraction: A review of relationships with antecedent and consequent variables. *Psychological Bulletin,* 1965, *64,* 259–309.

Lott, A. J., & Lott, B. E. The role of reward in the formation of positive interpersonal attitudes. In T. L. Huston (Ed.), *Foundations of interpersonal attraction.* New York: Academic Press, 1974.

Lovaas, O. I. Effect of exposure to symbolic aggression on aggressive behavior. *Child Development,* 1961, *32,* 37–44.

Lovallo, W. R., & Pishkin, V. Performance of Type A (coronary-prone) men during and after exposure to uncontrollable noise and task failure. *Journal of Personality and Social Psychology,* 1980, *38,* 963–971.

Lubek, I. Aggression. In A. R. Buss (Ed.), *Psychology in social context.* New York: Irvington, 1979.

Lubinsky, R. Machiavellianism, values, administrative effectiveness, and self-reported vs. colleague-reported perceptions of public school principals. *Dissertation Abstracts International,* 1977, *37,* 4754 (8A).

Luce, R. D., & Raiffa, H. *Games and decisions.* New York: John Wiley & Sons, 1957.

Luchins, A. S. Experimental attempts to minimize the impact of first impressions. In C. E. Hovland (Ed.), *The order of presentation in persuasion.* New Haven,

Conn.: Yale University Press, 1957.

Lynch, J. G., & Cohen, J. L. The use of subjective expected utility theory as an aid to understanding variables that influence helping behavior. *Journal of Personality and Social Psychology,* 1978, *36,* 1138–1151.

Lynn, D. B. A note on sex differences in the development of masculine and feminine identification. *Psychological Review,* 1959, *66,* 126–135.

M

McArthur, L. Z. The how and what of why: Some determinants and consequences of causal attribution. *Journal of Personality and Social Psychology,* 1972, *22,* 171–193.

McArthur, L. Z., & Resko, B. G. The portrayal of men and women in American television commercials. *Journal of Social Psychology,* 1975, *97,* 209–220.

McCall, C. A psychology professor gives evidence that bad Samaritans are a thief's best friends. *People Weekly,* August 18, 1980, pp. 70–71.

Macaulay, J. R. A shill for charity. In J. R. Macaulay & L. Berkowitz (Eds.), *Altruism and helping behavior.* New York: Academic Press, 1970.

McClelland, D. C. *Power: The inner experience.* New York: Irvington, 1975.

McClelland, D. C., & Winter, D. G. *Motivating economic achievement.* New York: Free Press, 1969.

McClelland, L. A. *Crowding and social stress.* Unpublished doctoral dissertation, University of Michigan, Ann Arbor, 1974.

McClintock, C. G., & Hunt, R. C. Nonverbal indicators of affect and deception in an interview setting. *Journal of Applied Social Psychology,* 1975, *5,* 54–67.

McClintock, C. G., & McNeel, S. P. Reward and score feedback as determinants of cooperative and competitive game behavior. *Journal of Personality and Social Psychology,* 1966, *14,* 606–613.

Maccoby, E. *Social development: Psychological growth and the parent-child relationship.* New York: Harcourt Brace Jovanovich, 1980.

McConaghy, N. Penile response conditioning and its relationship to aversion training in homosexuals. *Behavior Therapy,* 1970, *1,* 213–222.

McCool, R. *The effect of group pressure and social support on educably mentally retarded children.* Unpublished doctoral dissertation, University of Wisconsin, Madison, 1975.

McCord, J. Some child-rearing antecedents to criminal behavior in adult men. *Journal of Personality and Social Psychology,* 1979, *37,* 1477–1486.

MacDonald, A. P. Anxiety, affiliation, and social isolation. *Developmental Psychology,* 1970, *3,* 242–254.

MacDonald, A. P. Homophobia: Its roots and

meaning. *Homosexual Counseling Journal,* 1976, *3,* 23–33.

MacDonald, A. P., & Games, R. G. Some characteristics of those who hold positive and negative attitudes toward homosexuals. *Journal of Homosexuality,* 1974, *1,* 9–27.

McDougall, W. *Introduction to social psychology.* London: Methuen, 1908.

McFatter, R. M. Sentencing strategies and justice: Effects of punishment philosophy on sentencing decisions. *Journal of Personality and Social Psychology,* 1978, *36,* 1490–1500.

McGinnies, E., & Ward, C. Persuasibility and locus of control: Five cross-cultural experiments. *Journal of Personality,* 1974, *42,* 360–371.

McGovern, L. Dispositional social anxiety and helping behavior under three conditions of threat. *Journal of Personality,* 1976, *44,* 84–97.

McGuire, W. J. The effectiveness of supportive and refutational defenses in immunizing and restoring beliefs against persuasion. *Sociometry,* 1961, *24,* 184–197.

McGuire, W. J. The nature of attitudes and attitude change. In G. Lindzey & E. Aronson (Eds.), *The handbook of social psychology* (Vol. 3). Reading, Mass.: Addison-Wesley, 1968.

McGuire, W. J., McGuire, C. V., Child, P., & Fujioka, T. Salience of ethnicity in the spontaneous self-concept as a function of one's ethnic distinctiveness in the social environment. *Journal of Personality and Social Psychology,* 1978, *36,* 511–520.

McGuire, W. J., McGuire, C. V., & Winton, W. Effects of household sex composition on the salience of one's gender in the spontaneous self-concept. *Journal of Experimental Social Psychology,* 1979, *15,* 77–90.

McGuire, W. J., & Papageorgis, D. The relative efficacy of various types of prior belief-defense in producing immunity against persuasion. *Journal of Abnormal and Social Psychology,* 1961, *62,* 327–337.

Maden, M. F., & Wrench, D. F. Significant findings in child abuse research. *Victimology,* 1977, *2,* 196–224.

Magnusson, D., & Endler, N. S. (Eds.), *Personality at the crossroads: Current issues in interactional psychology.* Hillsdale, N.J.: Lawrence Erlbaum, 1977.

Mahl, G. F. Some clinical observations on nonverbal behavior in interviews. *Journal of Nervous and Mental Disease,* 1967, *144,* 492–505.

Maisel, R. *Report of the continuing audit of public attitudes and concerns.* Unpublished paper, Harvard Medical Laboratory of Community Psychiatry, Cambridge, Mass., 1969.

Malinowski, B. *Argonauts of the western Pacific.* New York: E. P. Dutton, 1922.

Maloney, W. E. *The worst of everything.* New York: Grosset & Dunlap, 1975.

Manis, M., Dovalina, I., Avis, N. E., & Cardoze, S. Base rates can affect individual predictions. *Journal of Personality and Social Psychology,* 1980, *38,* 231–248.

Mann, F., & Baumgartel, H. *Absences and employee attitudes in an electric power company.* Ann Arbor, Mich.: Institute for Social Research, 1952.

Mann, R. D. A review of the relationship between personality and performance in small groups. *Psychological Bulletin,* 1959, *56,* 241–270.

Mann, S. H. The use of social indicators in environmental planning. In I. Altman & J. F. Wohlwill (Eds.), *Human behavior and environment* (Vol. 2). New York: Plenum, 1977.

Manuck, S. B., Craft, S. A., & Gold, K. J. Coronary-prone behavior pattern and cardiovascular response. *Psychophysiology,* 1978, *15,* 403–411.

Markus, H. Self-schemata and processing information about the self. *Journal of Personality and Social Psychology,* 1977, *35,* 63–78.

Marlowe, D., Gergen, K. J., & Doob, A. N. Opponent's personality, expectation of social interaction, and interpersonal bargaining. *Journal of Personality and Social Psychology,* 1966, *3,* 206–213.

Marquart, D. I. Group problem solving. *Journal of Social Psychology,* 1955, *41,* 103–113.

Marquis, D. G., Guetzkow, H., & Heyns, R. W. A social psychological study of the decision-making conference. In H. Guetzkow (Ed.), *Groups, leadership, and men: Research in human relations.* Pittsburgh: Carnegie Press, 1951.

Marrow, A. J. *The practical theorist: The life and work of Kurt Lewin.* New York: Basic Books, 1969.

Marsden, H. M. Crowding and animal behavior. In J. F. Wohlwill & D. H. Carson (Eds.), *Environment and the social sciences: Perspectives and applications.* Washington, D.C.: American Psychological Association, 1972.

Marsh, P., Rosser, E., & Harré, R. *The rules of disorder.* London: Routledge & Kegan Paul, 1978.

Marshall, G. *The affective consequences of "inadequately explained" physiological arousal.* Unpublished doctoral dissertation, Stanford University, Stanford, Calif., 1976.

Martens, R. Palmar sweating and the presence of an audience. *Journal of Experimental Social Psychology,* 1969, *5,* 371–374.

Martindale, C. *The romantic progression: Psychology of literary history.* New York: Halsted Press, 1975.

Marwell, F., & Schmitt, D. R. Cooperation and interpersonal risk: Cross-cultural and cross-procedural generalizations. *Journal of Experimental Social Psychology,* 1972, *8,* 494–499.

Marwell, G., & Hage, J. The organization of role relationships: A systematic description. *American Sociological Review,* 1970, *35,* 884–900.

Marwell, G., Ratcliff, K., & Schmitt, D. R. Minimizing differences in a maximizing difference game. *Journal of Personality and Social Psychology,* 1969, *12,* 158–163.

Marx, T. *Protest and prejudice: A study of belief in a black community.* New York: Harper & Row, 1969.

Maslach, C. Negative emotional biasing of unexplained arousal. *Journal of Personality and Social Psychology,* 1979, *37,* 953–969.

Maslach, C., & Solomon, T. Pressures toward dehumanization from within and without. Unpublished manuscript, University of California, Berkeley, 1977.

Mathews, K. E., & Canon, L. K. Environmental noise level as a determinant of helping behavior. *Journal of Personality and Social Psychology,* 1975, *32,* 571–577.

Maykovich, M. K. Correlates of racial prejudice. *Journal of Personality and Social Psychology,* 1975, *32,* 1014–1020.

Mayo, E., & Lombard, G. F. F. *Teamwork and labor turnover in the aircraft industry in southern California.* Boston: Harvard University Division of Research, 1944.

Mayo, G. D., & Kinzer, J. R. A comparison of the "racial" attitudes of white and Negro high school students in 1940 and 1948. *Journal of Psychology,* 1950, *29,* 397–405.

Mazen, R., & Leventhal, H. The influence of communicator-recipient similarity upon the beliefs and behavior of pregnant women. *Journal of Experimental Social Psychology,* 1972, *8,* 289–302.

Mead, G. H. *Mind, self, and society.* Chicago: University of Chicago Press, 1934.

Mead, M. Warfare is only an invention—not a biological necessity. *Asia,* 1940, *40,* 402–405.

Mead, W. J. The performance of government in energy regulations. In E. W. Stromsdorfer & G. Farkas (Eds.), *Evaluation studies: Review annual* (Vol. 5). Beverly Hills, Calif.: Sage Publications, 1980.

Mednick, M. Social change and sex-role inertia: The case of the kibbutz. In M. Mednick, S. Tangri, & L. Hoffman (Eds.), *Women and achievement: Social and motivational analyses.* New York: John Wiley & Sons, 1975.

Mehrabian, A. Verbal and nonverbal interaction of strangers in a waiting situation. *Journal of Experimental Research in Personality,* 1971, *5,* 127–138.

Mehrabian, A. *Nonverbal communication.* Chicago: Aldine-Atherton, 1972.

Mehrabian, A., & Ksionsky, S. Anticipated compatability as a function of attitude or status similarity. *Journal of Personality,* 1971, *39,* 225–241.

Mettee, D. R., & Smith, G. Social comparison and personal attraction: The case for dissimilarity. In J. M. Suls & R. L. Miller (Eds.), *Social comparison processes:*

Theoretical and empirical perspectives. Washington, D.C.: Hemisphere, 1977.

Mewborn, C. R., & Rogers, R. W. Effects of threatening and reassuring components of fear appeals on physiological and verbal measures of emotion and attitudes. *Journal of Experimental Social Psychology,* 1979, *15,* 242–253.

Meyer, J. P. Causal attribution for success and failure: A multivariate investigation of dimensionality, formation and consequences. *Journal of Personality and Social Psychology,* 1980, *38,* 704–718.

Meyer, T. P. The effects of sexually arousing and violent films on aggressive behavior. *Journal of Sex Research,* 1972, *8,* 324–333.

Michelini, R. L., & Messé, L. A. Reactions to threat as a function of equity. *Sociometry,* 1974, *37,* 432–439.

Michelson, W. *Man and his urban environment: A sociological approach.* Reading, Mass.: Addison-Wesley, 1970.

Midlarsky, E., & Bryan, J. H. Training charity in children. *Journal of Personality and Social Psychology,* 1967, *5,* 408–415.

Midlarsky, E., Bryan, J. H., & Brickman, P. Aversive approval: Interactive effects of modeling and reinforcement on altruistic behavior. *Child Development,* 1973, *44,* 321–328.

Midlarsky, M., & Midlarsky, E. Status inconsistency, aggressive attitude and helping behavior. *Journal of Personality,* 1976, *44,* 379–391.

Mikula, G., & Schwinger, T. Intermember relations and reward allocation: Theoretical considerations of affects. In H. Brandstätter, J. H. Davis, & H. Schuler (Eds.), *Dynamics of group decisions.* Beverly Hills, Calif.: Sage Publications, 1978.

Milgram, S. Issues in the study of obedience: A reply to Baumrind. *American Psychologist,* 1964, *19,* 848–852.

Milgram, S. Some conditions of obedience and disobedience. *Human Relations,* 1965, *18,* 57–76.

Milgram, S. The experience of living in cities. *Science,* 1970, *167,* 1461–1468.

Milgram, S. *Obedience to authority.* New York: Harper & Row, 1974.

Milgram, S. *The individual in a social world.* Reading, Mass.: Addison-Wesley, 1977.

Milgram, S., & Shotland, R. L. *Television and antisocial behavior: Field experiments.* New York: Academic Press, 1973.

Millar, A., Hatry, H. P., & Koss, M. *Monitoring the outcomes of social services* (2 vols.). Washington, D.C.: Urban Institute, 1977.

Miller, C. E. A test of four theories of coalition formation: Effects of payoffs and resources. *Journal of Personality and Social Psychology,* 1980, *38,* 153–164.

Miller, D., & Ross, M. Self-serving biases in the attribution of causality: Fact or fiction? *Psychological Bulletin,* 1975, *82,* 213–225.

Miller, I. W., III, & Norman, W. H. Learned

helplessness in humans: A review and attribution-theory model. *Psychological Bulletin*, 1979, 86, 93–118.

Miller, J. Effects of noise on people. *Journal of the Acoustical Society of America*, 1974, 56, 729–764.

Miller, N., & Campbell, D. Recency and primacy in persuasion as a function of the timing of speeches and measurements. *Journal of Abnormal and Social Psychology*, 1959, 59, 1–9.

Miller, N., Maruyama, G., Beaber, R. J., & Valone, K. Speed of speech and persuasion. *Journal of Personality and Social Psychology*, 1976, 34, 615–624.

Miller, N. E. The frustration-aggression hypothesis. *Psychological Review*, 1941, 48, 337–342.

Miller, R. L. *However, what is good is not always beautiful.* Unpublished manuscript, General Research Corporation, McLean, Va., 1976.

Mills, J., & Aronson, E. Opinion change as a function of communicator's attractiveness and desire to influence. *Journal of Personality and Social Psychology*, 1965, 1, 173–177.

Mills, J., & Jellison, J. M. Effect on opinion change of similarity between communicator and the audience he addressed. *Journal of Personality and Social Psychology*, 1967, 6, 98–101.

Milord, J., & Perry, R. P. Traits and performance of automobile salesmen. *Journal of Social Psychology*, 1977, 103, 163–164.

Milton, G. A. The effects of sex-role identification upon problem solving skills. *Journal of Abnormal and Social Psychology*, 1957, 55, 208–212.

Minard, R. D. Race relationships in the Pocahontas coal field. *Journal of Social Issues*, 1952, 8, 29–44.

Minas, J. S., Scodel, A., Marlowe, D., & Rawson, H. Some descriptive aspects of two-person non-zero-sum games. *Journal of Conflict Resolution*, 1960, 4, 193–197.

Minnigerode, F. A. Attitudes toward homosexuality: Feminist attitudes and sexual conservatism. *Sex Roles*, 1976, 2, 347–352.

Mischel, W. *Personality and assessment.* New York: John Wiley & Sons, 1968.

Mitchell, H. E. *Authoritarian punitiveness in simulated jury decision-making: The good guys don't always wear white hats.* Paper presented at the meeting of the Midwestern Psychological Association, Chicago, May 1973.

Mitchell, H. E., & Byrne, D. The defendant's dilemma: Effects of jurors' attitudes and authoritarianism on judicial decisions. *Journal of Personality and Social Psychology*, 1973, 25, 123–129.

Mitchell, R. E. Some social implications of high-density housing. *American Sociological Review*, 1971, 36, 18–29.

Mixon, D. Instead of deception. *Journal of the Theory of Social Behavior*, 1972, 2, 146–177.

Moffitt, A. Critique: Zajonc and science: A case study. In L. Strickland, F. Aboud, & K. J. Gergen (Eds.), *Social psychology in transition.* New York: Plenum, 1976.

Moore, H. T. The comparative influence of majority and expert opinion. *American Journal of Psychology*, 1921, 32, 16–20.

Morawski, J. G. The structure of social psychological communities: A framework for examining the sociology of social psychology. In L. Strickland (Ed.), *Soviet and Western perspectives in social psychology.* Elmsford, N.Y.: Pergamon Press, 1979.

Moreland, R. L., & Zajonc, R. B. Exposure effects may not depend on stimulus recognition. *Journal of Personality and Social Psychology*, 1979, 37, 1085–1096.

Moreno, J. L. Sociometry and the cultural order. *Sociometry*, 1943, 6, 299–344.

Morgan, C. J. Bystander intervention: Experimental test of a formal model. *Journal of Personality and Social Psychology*, 1978, 36, 43–55.

Morgan, W. G. Situational specificity in altruistic behavior. *Representative Research in Social Psychology*, 1973, 4, 56–66.

Moriarty, T. Crime, commitment and the responsive bystander: Two field experiments. *Journal of Personality and Social Psychology*, 1975, 31, 370–376.

Morin, S. F. Educational programs as a means of changing attitudes toward gay people. *Homosexual Counseling Journal*, 1974, 1, 160–165.

Morin, S. F., & Garfinkel, E. M. Male homophobia. *Journal of Social Issues*, 1978, 34, 29–47.

Morris, D., Collett, P., Marsh, P., & O'Shaughnessy, M. *Gestures.* Briarcliff Manor, N.Y.: Stein & Day, 1979.

Morris, L. A., & O'Neal E. C. Drug name familiarity and the placebo effect. *Journal of Clinical Psychology*, 1974, 7, 280–282.

Morris, S. C., III, & Rosen, S. Effects of felt adequacy and opportunity to reciprocate on help-seeking. *Journal of Experimental Social Psychology*, 1973, 9, 265–276.

Morris, W. N., Worchel, S., Bois, J. L., Pearson, J. A., Rountree, C. A., Samaha, G. M., Wachtler, J., & Wright, S. L. Collective coping with stress: Group reactions to fear, anxiety and ambiguity. *Journal of Personality and Social Psychology*, 1976, 33, 674–679.

Morrisette, J. O. Group performance as a function of task difficulty and size and structure of group: II. *Journal of Personality and Social Psychology*, 1966, 3, 357–359.

Morrison, B. J., & Hill, W. F. Socially facilitated reduction of the fear response in rats raised in groups or in isolation. *Journal of Comparative and Physiological Psychology*, 1967, 63, 71–76.

Morse, S. J. Help, likeability and social influence. *Journal of Applied Social Psychology*, 1972, 2, 34–46.

Morse, S. J., & Gergen, K. J. Social comparison, self-consistency and the concept of self. *Journal of Personality and Social Psychology*, 1970, 16, 149–156.

Moscovici, S. Society and theory in social psychology. In J. Israel & H. Tajfel (Eds.), *The context of social psychology: A critical assessment.* New York: Academic Press, 1972.

Moscovici, S. *Social influence and social change.* New York: Academic Press, 1976.

Moscovici, S., & Faucheux, C. Social influence, conformity bias, and the study of active minorities. In L. Berkowitz (Ed.), *Advances in experimental social psychology* (Vol. 6). New York: Academic Press, 1972.

Moscovici, S., & Lage, E. Studies in social influence: III. Majority vs. minority in a group. *European Journal of Social Psychology*, 1976, 6, 149–174.

Mouton, J., Blake, R. P., & Olmstead, J. A. The relationship between frequency of yielding and the disclosure of personal identity. *Journal of Personality*, 1956, 24, 339–347.

Moyer, K. E. *The physiology of hostility.* Skokie, Ill.: Rand McNally/Markham, 1971.

Muir, D., & Weinstein, E. The social debt: An investigation of lower-class and middle-class norms of social obligation. *American Sociological Review*, 1962, 27, 532–539.

Mulder, M. *Group structure, motivation and group performance.* The Hague and Paris: Mouton, 1963.

Mulder, M., & Stemerding, A. D. Threat, attraction to group, and need for strong leadership. *Human Relations*, 1963, 16, 317–334.

Mulder, M., Veen, P., Hijzen, T., & Jansen, P. On power equalization: A behavioral example of power-distance reduction. *Journal of Personality and Social Psychology*, 1973, 26, 151–157.

Munn, N. The effect of knowledge of the situation upon judgment of emotion from facial expressions. *Journal of Abnormal and Social Psychology*, 1940, 35, 324–338.

Murphy, G., & Likert, R. *Public opinion and the individual: A psychological study of student attitudes on public questions, with a retest five years later.* New York: Harper & Row, 1938.

Murray, H. A. *Explorations in personality: A clinical and experimental study of fifty men of college age.* New York: Oxford University Press, 1938.

Myers, D. G. Polarizing effects of social comparison. *Journal of Experimental Social Psychology*, 1978, 14, 554–563.

Myers, D. G., & Kaplan, M. F. Group-induced polarization in simulated juries. *Personality and Social Psychology Bulletin*, 1976, 2, 63–66.

Myers, D. G., & Lamm, H. The group polarization phenomenon. *Psychological Bulletin*, 1976, 83, 602–627.

Myers, D. G., Wojcicki, S. G., & Aardema, B.

Attitude comparison: Is there ever a bandwagon effect? *Journal of Applied Social Psychology*, 1977, 7, 341–347.

N

Naditch, M. P. Locus of control, relative discontent and hypertension. *Social Psychiatry*, 1974, 9, 111–117.

Naditch, M. P., Gargan, M., & Michael, L. B. Denial, anxiety, locus of control and the discrepancy between aspirations and achievements as components of depression. *Journal of Abnormal Psychology*, 1975, 84, 1–9.

Nadler, A., Altman, A., & Fisher, J. D. Helping is not enough: Recipient's reactions to aid as a function of positive and negative information about the self. *Journal of Personality*, 1979, 47, 615–628.

Nadler, A., Fisher, J. D., & Streufert, S. The donor's dilemma: Recipient's reactions to aid from friend or foe. *Journal of Applied Social Psychology*, 1974, 4, 275–285.

Nadler, A., & Porat, I. Names do not help: Effects of anonymity and focus of need attribution on help-seeking behavior. *Personality and Social Psychology Bulletin*, 1978, 4, 624–626.

Nadler, E. B. Yielding, authoritarianism, and authoritarian ideology regarding groups. *Journal of Abnormal and Social Psychology*, 1959, 58, 408–410.

Nahir, H. T., & Yussen, S. R. The performance of kibbutz and city reared Israeli children on two role-taking tests. *Developmental Psychology*, 1977, 13, 450–455.

National Center for Education Statistics. *Salaries and tenure of full-time instructional faculty 1974–1975*. Washington, D.C.: U.S. Dept. of Health, Education, & Welfare, 1975.

Nelson, E. A., Grinder, R. E., & Mutterer, M. L. Sources of variance in behavioral measures of honesty in temptation situations: Methodological analysis. *Developmental Psychology*, 1969, 1, 265–279.

Nemeth, C. The role of an active minority in intergroup relations. In W. Austin & S. Worchel (Eds.), *The social psychology of intergroup relations*. Monterey, Calif.: Brooks/Cole, 1979.

Nemeth, C., & Wachtler, J. Consistency and modification of judgment. *Journal of Experimental Social Psychology*, 1973, 9, 65–79.

Nesbitt, P. D., & Steven, G. Personal space and stimulus intensity at a southern California amusement park. *Sociometry*, 1974, 37, 105–115.

Nesdale, A. R., & Rule, B. G. The effects of an aggressor's characteristics and an observer's accountability on judgments of aggression. *Canadian Journal of Behavioral Science*, 1974, 6, 342–350.

Newcomb, T. M. *Consistency of certain extrovert-introvert behavior patterns in 51 problem boys*. New York: Teachers College, Columbia University, Bureau of Publications, 1929.

Newcomb, T. M. *Personality and social change: Attitude formation in a social community*. New York: Holt, Rinehart & Winston/Dryden Press, 1943.

Newcomb, T. M. Autistic hostility and social reality. *Human Relations*, 1947, 1, 69–86.

Newcomb, T. M. An approach to the study of communicative acts. *Psychological Review*, 1953, 60, 393–404.

Newcomb, T. M. *The acquaintance process*. New York: Holt, Rinehart & Winston, 1961.

Newcomb, T. M. Reciprocity of interpersonal attraction: A nonconfirmation of a plausible hypothesis. *Social Psychology Quarterly*, 1979, 42, 299–306.

Newcomb, T. M., Koenig, K. E., Flacks, R., & Warwick, D. P. *Persistence and change: Bennington College and its students after twenty-five years*. New York: John Wiley & Sons, 1967.

Newtson, D. Attribution and the unit of perception of ongoing behavior. *Journal of Personality and Social Psychology*, 1973, 28, 28–38.

Newtson, D., Enquist, G., & Boris, J. The objective basis of behavior units. *Journal of Personality and Social Psychology*, 1977, 35, 847–862.

Nicosia, G. J., Hyman, D., Kavlin, R. A., Epstein, Y. M., & Aiello, J. R. Effects of body contact on reactions to crowding. *Journal of Applied Social Psychology*, 1979, 9, 508–523.

Nisbett, R. E., & Bellows, N. Verbal reports about causal influences as social judgments: Private access versus public theories. *Journal of Personality and Social Psychology*, 1975, 35, 613–624.

Nisbett, R. E., Borgida, E., Crandall, R., & Reed, H. Popular induction: Information is not necessarily informative. In J. S. Carroll & J. W. Payne (Eds.), *Cognition and social behavior*. Hillsdale, N.J.: Lawrence Erlbaum, 1976.

Nisbett, R. E., & Ross, L. *Human inference*. Englewood Cliffs, N.J.: Prentice-Hall, 1980.

Nisbett, R. E., & Schachter, S. Cognitive manipulation of pain. *Journal of Experimental Social Psychology*, 1966, 2, 227–236.

Nisbett, R. E., & Wilson, T. D. Telling more than we can know: Verbal reports on mental processes. *Psychological Review*, 1977, 84, 231–259.

Noble, W. W. Psychological research and Black self-concept: A critical review. *Journal of Social Issues*, 1973, 29, 11–31.

Nogami, G. Y. Crowding: Effects of group size, room size, or density? *Journal of Applied Social Psychology*, 1976, 6, 105–125.

Nord, W. R. Social exchange theory: An integrative approach to social conformity. *Psychological Bulletin*, 1969, 71, 173–208.

Norton, A. J., & Glick, P. C. Marital instability: Past, present and future. *Journal of Social Issues*, 1976, 32, 5–20.

Novak, D. E., & Lerner, M. J. Rejection as a consequence of perceived similarity. *Journal of Personality and Social Psychology*, 1968, 9, 147–152.

Nowicki, S., & Roundtree, J. Correlates of locus of control in secondary school-age students. *Developmental Psychology*, 1971, 4, 479–488.

Nunn, C. Z., Crockett, H. J., & Williams, J. A. *Tolerance for nonconformity*. San Francisco: Jossey-Bass, 1978.

Nunnally, J. C. *Popular conceptions of mental health: Their development and change*. New York: Holt, Rinehart & Winston, 1961.

Nunnally, J. C., & Hussek, T. R. The phony language examination: An approach to the measurement of response bias. *Educational and Psychological Measurement*, 1958, 18, 275–282.

O

Oakley, A. *The sociology of housework*. New York: Pantheon Books, 1974.

O'Connor, J. *Developmental changes in abstractness and moral reasoning*. Unpublished doctoral dissertation, George Peabody College for Teachers, Nashville, 1971.

O'Neal, E. C., & Kaufman, L. The influence of attack, arousal, and information about one's arousal upon interpersonal aggression. *Psychonomic Science*, 1972, 26, 211–214.

Orne, M. T. On the social psychology of the psychological experiment: With particular reference to demand characteristics and their implications. *American Psychologist*, 1962, 17, 776–783.

Osgood, C. E. *An alternative to war or surrender*. Urbana: University of Illinois Press, 1962.

Osgood, C. E., & Tannenbaum, P. H. The principle of congruence in the prediction of attitude change. *Psychological Review*, 1955, 62, 44–55.

Oskamp, S. Effects of programmed strategies on cooperation in the prisoner's dilemma and other mixed motive games. *Journal of Conflict Resolution*, 1971, 15, 225–259.

Oskamp, S. *Attitudes and opinions*. Englewood Cliffs, N.J.: Prentice-Hall, 1977.

Ostrom, T. M. Between-theory and within-theory conflict in explaining context effects on impression formation. *Journal of Experimental Social Psychology*, 1977, 13, 492–503.

Ostrom, T. M., Werner, C., & Saks, M. J. An integration theory analysis of "jurors" presumptions of guilt or innocence. *Journal of Personality and Social Psychology*, 1978, 36, 436–450.

P

Page, M. M. Post-experimental assessment of awareness in attitude conditioning. *Educational and Psychological Measurement*, 1971, *31*, 891–906.

Pancer, S. M., McMullen, L. M., Kabatoff, R. A., Johnson, K. G., & Pond, C. A. Conflict and avoidance in the helping situation. *Journal of Personality and Social Psychology*, 1979, *37*, 1406–1411.

Parsons, H. M. Work environments. In I. Altman & J. F. Wohlwill (Eds.), *Human behavior and environment* (Vol. 1). New York: Plenum, 1976.

Partridge, E. D. Leadership among adolescent boys. *Teachers College Contribution to Education*, 1934, No. 608.

Patcheler, G. *Normes et changement d'attitudes: De la modification des attitudes envers les femmes*. These de Zeme cycle, Universite de Paris, mimeographed, 1974.

Patcheler, G., & Bouchet, Y. Attitude polarisation, familiarisation, and group process. *European Journal of Social Psychology*, 1973, *3*, 83–90.

Patterson, A. H. *Hostility catharsis: A naturalistic quasi-experiment*. Paper presented at the annual meeting of the American Psychological Association, New Orleans, 1974.

Pattison, E. M. Confusing concepts about the concept of homosexuality. *Psychiatry*, 1974, *47*, 340–349.

Paulus, P. B., Annis, A. B., Seta, J. L., Schkade, J. K., & Matthews, R. W. Density does affect task performance. *Journal of Personality and Social Psychology*, 1976, *34*, 641–647.

Paulus, P. B., Cox, V., McCain, G., & Chandler, J. Some effects of crowding in a prison environment. *Journal of Applied Social Psychology*, 1975, *5*, 86–91.

Paulus, P. B., & Murdock, P. Anticipated evaluation and audience presence in the enhancement of dominant responses. *Journal of Experimental Social Psychology*, 1971, *7*, 280–291.

Pavlov, J. P. *Conditioned reflexes* (G. V. Anrep, trans.). London: Oxford University Press, 1927.

Pawlicki, R. E., & Almquist, C. Authoritarianism, locus of control and tolerance of ambiguity as reflected in membership and nonmembership in the women's liberation group. *Psychological Reports*, 1973, *32*, 1331–1337.

Peabody, D. Group judgment in the Philippines: Evaluative and descriptive aspects. *Journal of Personality and Social Psychology*, 1968, *10*, 290–300.

Peabody, D. *National characteristics*. Unpublished manuscript, Swarthmore College, Swarthmore, Pa., 1980.

Peevers, B. H., & Secord, P. F. Developmental changes in attribution of descriptive concepts to persons. *Journal of Personality and Social Psychology*, 1973, *27*, 120–128.

Penhazur, E. J., & Tetenbaum, T. J. Bem Sex Role Inventory: A theoretical and methodological critique. *Journal of Personality and Social Psychology*, 1979, *37*, 996–1016.

Penner, L. A., Summers, L. S., Brookmire, D. A., & Dertke, M. C. The lost dollar: Situational and personality determinants of a pro and antisocial behavior. *Journal of Personality*, 1976, *44*, 280–293.

Pepitone, A. Motivation effects in social perception. *Human Relations*, 1949, *3*, 57–76.

Pepitone, A., & Reichling, G. Group cohesiveness and the expression of hostility. *Human Relations*, 1955, *8*, 327–337.

Peplau, L. A. Power in dating relationships. In J. Freeman (Ed.), *Women: A feminist perspective* (2nd ed.). Palo Alto, Calif.: Mayfield, 1979.

Perlman, D., & Peplau, L. A. Toward a social psychology of loneliness. In R. Gilmore & S. Duck (Eds.), *Personal relationships in disorder*. London: Academic Press, in press.

Perls, F. S., Hefferline, R. F., & Goodman, P. *Gestalt therapy*. New York: Dell, 1965.

Pessin, J. The comparative effects of social and mechanical stimulation on memorizing. *American Journal of Psychology*, 1933, *45*, 263–270.

Peterson, P. D., & Thurstone, L. L. *Motion pictures and the social attitudes of children*. New York: Macmillan, 1933.

Pettigrew, T. F. Racially separate or together? *Journal of Social Issues*, 1969, *25*, 43–69.

Petty, R. E., & Cacioppo, J. T. Issue involvement can increase or decrease persuasion by enhancing message-relevant cognitive responses. *Journal of Personality and Social Psychology*, 1979, *37*, 1915–1926.

Petty, R. E., Harkins, S. G., & Williams, K. D. The effects of group diffusion of cognitive effort on attitudes: An information-processing view. *Journal of Personality and Social Psychology*, 1980, *38*, 81–92.

Petty, R. E., Wells, G. L., & Brock, T. C. Distraction can enhance or reduce yielding to propaganda: Thought disruption versus effort justification. *Journal of Personality and Social Psychology*, 1976, *34*, 874–884.

Petty, R. E., Williams, K. D., Karlins, S. G., & Latané, B. Social inhibition of helping yourself: Bystander response to a cheeseburger. *Personality and Social Psychology Bulletin*, 1977, *3*, 571–574.

Phares, E. J. Internal-external control as a determinant of amount of social influence exerted. *Journal of Personality and Social Psychology*, 1965, *2*, 642–647.

Phares, E. J. *Locus of control in personality*. Morristown, N.J.: Silver Burdett/General Learning Press, 1976.

Philadelphia Bulletin, *Income of blacks remains half of whites*, April 2, 1978.

Piaget, J., & Inhelder, B. *The psychology of the child*. New York: Basic Books, 1958.

Piaget, J. *The moral judgment of the child*.

Glencoe, Ill.: Free Press, 1965.

Piliavin, I. M., Hardyck, J. A., & Vadom, A. *Reactions to the victim in a just or non-just world*. Paper presented at a meeting of the Society of Experimental Social Psychology, Bethesda, Md., August 1967.

Piliavin, I. M., Piliavin, J. A., & Rodin, J. Costs diffusion and the stigmatized victim. *Journal of Personality and Social Psychology*, 1975, *32*, 429–438.

Piliavin, I. M., Rodin, J., & Piliavin, J. A. Good Samaritanism: An underground phenomenon? *Journal of Personality and Social Psychology*, 1969, *14*, 289–299.

Piliavin, J. A., & Piliavin, I. M. Effect of blood on reactions to a victim. *Journal of Personality and Social Psychology*, 1972, *23*, 353–362.

Pilisuk, M., & Skolnick, P. Inducing trust: A test of the Osgood proposal. *Journal of Personality and Social Psychology*, 1968, *8*, 121–133.

Pilkonis, P. A. The behavioral consequences of shyness. *Journal of Personality*, 1977, *45*, 596–611. (a)

Pilkonis, P. A. Shyness, public and private, and its relationship to other measures of social behavior. *Journal of Personality*, 1977, *45*, 585–595. (b)

Pilkonis, P. A., & Zimbardo, P. G. The personal and social dynamics of shyness. In C. E. Izard (Ed.), *Emotions in personality and psychopathology*. New York: Plenum, 1979.

Pineo, P. C. Disenchantment in the later years of marriage. *Marriage and Family Living*, 1961, *23*, 3–11.

Pines, H. A., & Julian, J. W. Effects of task and social demands on locus of control differences in information processing. *Journal of Personality*, 1972, *40*, 407–416.

Pittman, T. S., Cooper, E. E., & Smith, T. W. Attribution of causality and the overjustification effect. *Personality and Social Psychology Bulletin*, 1977, *3*, 280–283.

Pleck, J. H. Man to man: Is brotherhood possible? In N. Glazer-Malbin (Ed.), *Old family/new family: Interpersonal relationships*. New York: Van Nostrand Reinhold, 1975.

Pleck, J. H., & Sawyer, J. (Eds.). *Men and masculinity*. Englewood Cliffs, N.J.: Prentice-Hall, 1974.

Pliner, P., Hart, H., Kohl, J., & Saari, D. Compliance without pressure: Some further data on the foot-in-the-door technique. *Journal of Experimental Social Psychology*. 1974, *10*, 17–22.

Plutchik, R., & Ax, A. F. A critique of "Determinants of emotional state" by Schachter and Singer. *Psychophysiology*, 1967, *4*, 79–82.

Polanyi, M. *The tacit dimension*. London: Routledge & Kegan Paul, 1967.

Pomazal, R. J. *Attitudes, normative beliefs, and altruism: Helping for helping behavior*. Unpublished doctoral dissertation, University of Illinois, Urbana, 1974.

Pomazal, R. J., & Jaccard, J. J. An informational approach to altruistic behavior. *Journal of Personality and Social Psychology*, 1976, *33*, 317–326.

Porter, L. W., & Lawler, E. E. *Managerial attitudes and performance.* Homewood, Ill.: Richard D. Irwin, 1968.

President's Commission on Law Enforcement and the Administration of Justice. *Task force report: Narcotics and Drug abuse.* Washington, D.C.: U.S. Government Printing Office, 1967.

Price, R., & Bouffard D. Behavioral appropriateness and situational constraint as dimensions of social behavior. *Journal of Personality and Social Psychology*, 1974, *30*, 579–586.

Pritchard, R. D., Dunnette, M. D., & Jorgenson, D. O. Effects of perceptions of equity and inequity on worker performance and satisfaction. *Journal of Applied Psychology*, 1972, *56*, 75–94.

Proshansky, H. M., Ittleson, W. H., & Rivlin, L. G. Freedom of choice and behavior in a physical setting. In H. M. Proshansky, W. H. Ittleson, & L. G. Rivlin (Eds.), *Environmental psychology: Man and his physical setting.* New York: Holt, Rinehart & Winston, 1970.

Proshansky, H. M., Ittleson, W. H., & Rivlin, L. G. *Environmental psychology: People and their settings.* New York: Holt, Rinehart & Winston, 1976.

Pruitt, D. G. Reciprocity and credit building in a laboratory dyad. *Journal of Personality and Social Psychology*, 1968, *8*, 143–147.

Pruitt, D. G. Conclusions: Toward an understanding of choice shifts in group discussions. *Journal of Personality and Social Psychology*, 1971, *20*, 495–510.

Pruitt, D. G., & Lewis, S. A. Development of integrative solutions in bilateral negotiations. *Journal of Personality and Social Psychology*, 1975, *31*, 621–633.

Pryor, F. L., & Graburn, N. H. The myth of reciprocity. In K. J. Gergen, M. Greenberg, & R. Willis (Eds.), *Behavior exchange: Advances in theory and research.* New York: John Wiley & Sons, 1980.

Q

Quarantelli, E. L., & Dynes, R. R. When disaster strikes. *Psychology Today*, 1972, *5*, 66–70.

Quattrone, G. A., & Jones, E. E. The perception of variability with in-groups and out-groups: Implications for the law of small numbers. *Journal of Personality and Social Psychology*, 1980, *38*, 141–152.

Quay, H. C. (Ed.), *Juvenile delinquency: Research and theory.* New York: Van Nostrand Reinhold, 1965.

Quigley-Fernandez, B., & Tedeschi, J. T. The bogus pipeline as a lie detector: Two validity studies. *Journal of Personality and Social Psychology*, 1978, *36*, 247–256.

R

Rabbie, J. M., Brehm, J. W., & Cohen, R. A. Verbalization and reactions to cognitive dissonance. *Journal of Personality*, 1959, *27*, 407–417.

Rabow, J., Fowler, F. J., Jr., Bradford, D. L., Hofeller, M. A., & Shibuya, Y. The role of social norms and leadership in risk-taking. *Sociometry*, 1966, *29*, 16–27.

Rada, J. B., & Rogers, R. W. *Obedience to authority: Presence of authority and command strength.* Paper presented at the meeting of the Southeastern Psychological Association, New Orleans, April 1973.

Radke, M., & Trager, H. G. Children's perceptions of the serial roles of Negroes and whites. *Journal of Psychology*, 1950, *29*, 3–33.

Radloff, R. Opinion evaluation and affiliation. *Journal of Abnormal and Social Psychology*, 1961, *62*, 578–585.

Rahe, R. H. Life-change measurement as a predictor of illness. *Proceedings of the Royal Society of Medicine*, 1968, *61*, 1124–1126.

Rahe, R. H. The pathway between subjects' recent life changes and their near-future illness reports: Representative results and methodological issues. In B. S. Dohrenwend & B. P. Dohrenwend (Eds.), *Stressful life events: Their nature and effects.* New York: John Wiley & Sons, 1974.

Rahe, R. H., & Holmes, T. H. *Life crises and disease onset: Qualitative and quantitative definition of the life crisis and its association with health change.* Unpublished manuscript, University of Washington, Seattle, 1964.

Rajecki, D. W., Nerenz, D. R., Freedenberg, T. G., & McCarthy, P. J. Components of aggression in chickens and conceptualizations of aggression in general. *Journal of Personality and Social Psychology*, 1979, *37*, 1902–1914.

Rands, M., & Levinger, G. Implicit theories of relationship: An intergenerational study. *Journal of Personality and Social Psychology*, 1979, *37*, 645–661.

Ransford, H. E. Isolation, powerlessness and violence: A study of attitudes and participation in the Watts riots. *American Journal of Sociology*, 1968, *73*, 581–591.

Rapoport, A. (Ed.). *Game theory as a theory of conflict resolution.* Dordrecht, The Netherlands: D. Reidel, 1974.

Rappoport, L. On praxis and quasi-rationality. *Human Development*, 1975, *18*, 194–204.

Raven, B. H. The comparative analysis of power and power preference. In J. Tedeschi (Ed.), *Perspectives on social power.* Chicago: Aldine, 1974.

Raven, B. H., & Kruglanski, A. Conflict and power. In P. G. Swingle (Ed.), *The nature of conflict.* New York: Academic Press, 1970.

Raven, B. H., & Rubin, J. Z. Interpersonal influence and social power. In B. H. Raven & J. Z. Rubin (Eds.), *Social psychology: People in groups.* New York: John Wiley & Sons, 1976.

Rawlings, E. J. Reactive guilt and anticipatory guilt in altruistic behavior. In J. R. Macaulay & L. Berkowitz (Eds.), *Altruism and helping behavior.* New York: Academic Press, 1970.

Reese, E. P. *Human behavior, analysis and application.* Dubuque, Ia.: Wm. C. Brown, 1978.

Regan, D. T. Effects of a favor and liking on compliance. *Journal of Experimental and Social Psychology*, 1971, *7*, 627–639.

Regan, D. T., Straus, E., & Fazio, R. Liking and the attribution process. *Journal of Experimental Social Psychology*, 1974, *10*, 385–397.

Regan, D. T., & Totten, J. Empathy and attribution: Turning observers into actors. *Journal of Personality and Social Psychology*, 1975, *32*, 850–856.

Regan, J. W. Guilt, perceived injustice, and altruistic behavior. *Journal of Personality and Social Psychology*, 1971, *18*, 124–132.

Reis, H. T., Nezlek, J., & Wheeler, L. Physical attractiveness in social interaction. *Journal of Personality and Social Psychology*, 1980, *38*, 604–617.

Resick, P. A., & Sweet, J. J. Child maltreatment intervention: Directions and issues. *Journal of Social Issues*, 1979, *35*, 140–160.

Rest, J., Cooper, D., Coder, R., Masanz, J., & Anderson, D. Judging the important issues in moral dilemmas—an objective measure of development. *Developmental Psychology*, 1974, *10*, 491–501.

Rettig, S. An exploratory study of altruism. *Dissertation Abstracts*, 1956, *16*, 2229–2230.

Ribich, T. I., & Murphy, J. L. The economic returns to increased educational spending. *Journal of Human Resources*, 1975, *10*, 56–77.

Richardson, D. C., & Campbell, J. L. Alcohol and wife abuse: The effect of alcohol on attributions of blame for wife abuse. *Personality and Social Psychology Bulletin*, 1980, *6*, 51–56.

Riegel, K. The dialectics of human development. *American Psychologist*, 1976, *31*, 689–700.

Ring, K., Lipinski, C. E., & Braginsky, D. D. The relationship of birth order to self-evaluation, anxiety reduction and susceptibility to emotional contagion. *Psychological Monographs*, 1965, *79*, (10, Whole No. 603).

Robbins, L., & Robbins, E. Comment on: Toward an understanding of achievement-related conflicts in women. *Journal of Social Issues*, 1973, *29*, 133–137.

Robinson, D., & Rhode, S. Two experiments with an anti-Semitism poll. *Journal of Abnormal and Social Psychology*, 1946, *41*, 136–144.

Roby, T. B. *Small group performance.* Chicago: Rand McNally, 1968.

Rodin, J., & Langer, E. Long-term effects of a control-relevant intervention with the institutionalized aged. *Journal of Personality and Social Psychology,* 1977, *35,* 897–902.

Rodrigues, A. The biasing effect of agreement in balanced and unbalanced triads. *Journal of Personality,* 1968, *36,* 138–153.

Roethlishberger, F. J., & Dickson, W. J. *Management and the worker.* Cambridge, Mass.: Harvard University Press, 1939.

Rogers, C. R. *On becoming a person.* Boston: Houghton Mifflin, 1961.

Rogers, C. R. The process of the basic encounter group. In J. F. G. Bugental (Ed.), *Challenges of humanistic psychology.* New York: McGraw-Hill, 1967.

Rogers, C. R. *Carl Rogers on encounter groups.* New York: Harper & Row/Harrow Books, 1970.

Rogers, R. W. Expressions of aggression: Aggression-inhibiting effects of anonymity to authority and threatened retaliation. *Personality and Social Psychology Bulletin,* 1980, *6,* 315–320.

Rogers, R. W., & Mewborn, C. R. Fear appeals and attitude change: Effects of a threat's noxiousness, probability of occurrence, and the efficacy of coping responses. *Journal of Personality and Social Psychology,* 1976, *34,* 54–61.

Rogers, T. Self-reference in memory: Recognition of personality items. *Journal of Research in Personality,* 1977, *11,* 295–305.

Rohe, W., & Patterson, A. H. The effects of varied levels of resources and density on behavior in a day care center. In D. H. Carson (Ed.), *EDRA: 5 man-environment interactions.* Milwaukee: Environmental Design Research Association, 1974.

Rohrer, J. H., Baron, S. H., Hoffman, E. L., & Swander, D. V. The stability of autokinetic judgments. *Journal of Abnormal and Social Psychology,* 1954, *49,* 595–597.

Rokeach, M. Generalized mental rigidity as a factor in ethnocentrism. *Journal of Abnormal and Social Psychology,* 1948, *43,* 259–278.

Rokeach, M. *The open and closed mind.* New York: Basic Books, 1960.

Rokeach, M., & Mezei, L. Race and shared belief as factors in social choice. *Science,* 1966, *151,* 167–172.

Romer, D. Internalization versus identification in the laboratory: A causal analysis of attitude change. *Journal of Personality and Social Psychology,* 1979, *37,* 2171–2180.

Rommetveit, R. On the architecture of intersubjectivity. In L. H. Strickland, F. E. Aboud, & K. J. Gergen (Eds.), *Social psychology in transition.* New York: Plenum, 1976.

Rosch, E. Principles of categorization. In E. Rosch & B. B. Lloyd (Eds.), *Cognition and categorization.* Hillsdale, N.J.: Lawrence Erlbaum, 1978.

Rosen, B., & D'Andrade, R. G. The psychosocial origins of achievement motivation. *Sociometry,* 1959, *22,* 185–218.

Rosen, S., & Tesser, A. On reluctance to communicate undesirable information: The MUM effect. *Sociometry,* 1970, *33,* 253–263.

Rosenbaum, M. E. Cooperation and competition. In P. B. Paulus (Ed.), *Psychology of group influence.* Hillsdale, N.J.: Lawrence Erlbaum, 1980.

Rosenberg, M. *Conceiving the self.* New York: Basic Books, 1979.

Rosenberg, M., & Simmons, R. G. *Black and white self-esteem: The urban school child.* Washington, D.C.: American Sociological Association, 1971.

Rosenberg, M. J., & Abelson, R. P. An analysis of cognitive balancing. In M. J. Rosenberg, C. I. Hovland, W. J. McGuire, R. P. Abelson, & J. W. Brehm, *Attitude organization and change.* New Haven, Conn.: Yale University Press, 1960.

Rosenberg, S. V., Nelson, C., & Vivekanathan, P. S. A multidimensional approach to the structure of personality impression. *Journal of Personality and Social Psychology,* 1968, *9,* 283–294.

Rosenberg, S. V., & Sedlak, A. Structural representations of implicit personality theory. In L. Berkowitz (Ed.), *Advances in experimental social psychology* (Vol. 6). New York: Academic Press, 1972.

Rosenfeld, H. M. Nonverbal reciprocation of approval: An experimental analysis. *Journal of Experimental Social Psychology,* 1967, *3,* 102–111.

Rosenhan, D. L. The natural socialization of altruistic autonomy. In J. R. Macaulay & L. Berkowitz (Eds.), *Altruism and helping behavior.* New York: Academic Press, 1970.

Rosenhan, D. L. Toward resolving the altruism paradox: Affect, self-reinforcement, and cognition. In L. Wispé (Ed.), *Altruism, sympathy, and helping.* New York: Academic Press, 1978.

Rosenhan, D. L., Frederick, F., & Burrowes, A. Preaching and practicing and effects of channel discrepancy on norm internalization. *Child Development,* 1968, *39,* 291–301.

Rosenhan, D. L., Underwood, B., & Moore, B. Affect moderates self-gratification and altruism. *Journal of Personality and Social Psychology,* 1974, *30,* 546–552.

Rosenkoetter, L. I. Resistance to temptation: Inhibitory and disinhibitory effects of models. *Developmental Psychology,* 1973, *8,* 80–84.

Rosenkrantz, P. S., Vogel, S. R., Bee, H., Broverman, I. K., & Broverman, D. M. Sex-role stereotypes and self-concepts in college students. *Journal of Consulting and Clinical Psychology,* 1968, *32,* 287–295.

Rosenman, R. H. *Type A behavior pattern— pro and con.* Unpublished manuscript,

Harold Brunn Institute, Mount Zion Hospital and Medical Center, San Francisco, 1975.

Rosenquist, H. S. *Social facilitation in rotary pursuit tracking.* Paper presented at the meeting of the Midwestern Psychological Association, Cleveland, May 1972.

Rosenthal, R. *Experimenter effects in behavioral research.* New York: Appleton-Century-Crofts, 1966.

Rosenthal, R. The Pygmalian effect lives. *Psychology Today,* 1973, *7,* 56–63.

Rosenthal, R., & DePaulo, B. M. Sex differences in eavesdropping on nonverbal cues. *Journal of Personality and Social Psychology,* 1979, *37,* 273–285.

Rosenthal, R., Hall, J. A., DiMatteo, M. R., Rogers, P. L., & Archer, D. *Sensitivity to nonverbal communication: The PONS test.* Baltimore: Johns Hopkins University Press, 1979.

Rosenthal, R., & Jacobson, L. F. Teacher expectations for the disadvantaged. *Scientific American,* 1968, *4,* 19–23.

Rosenthal, R., & Rosnow, R. L. The volunteer subject. In R. Rosenthal & R. L. Rosnow (Eds.), *Artifact in behavioral research.* New York: Academic Press, 1969.

Rosenthal, T. L., & Zimmerman, B. J. *Social learning and cognition.* New York: Academic Press, 1977.

Rosnow, R. L. The prophetic vision of Grambattista Vico: Implications for the state of social psychological theory. *Journal of Personality and Social Psychology,* 1978, *36,* 1322–1331.

Rosnow, R. L., & Fine, G. A. *Rumor and gossip: The social psychology of hearsay.* New York: Elsevier North Holland, 1976.

Rosnow, R. L., Gitler, A. G., & Holz, R. F. Some determinants of post decisional information preferences. *Journal of Social Psychology,* 1969, *79,* 235–245.

Ross, A. S. The effect of observing a helpful model on helping behavior. *Journal of Social Psychology,* 1970, *81,* 131–132.

Ross, A. S. The effect of increased responsibility on bystander intervention: The presence of children. *Journal of Personality and Social Psychology,* 1971, *19,* 306–310.

Ross, H. L. The Scandinavian myth: The effectiveness of drinking-and-driving legislation in Sweden and Norway. *Journal of Legal Studies,* 1975, *4,* 285–310.

Ross, L. The intuitive psychologist and his shortcomings: Distortions in the attribution process. In L. Berkowitz (Ed.), *Advances in experimental social psychology* (Vol. 10). New York: Academic Press, 1977.

Ross, L. Afterthoughts on the intuitive psychologist. In L. Berkowitz (Ed.), *Cognitive theories in social psychology.* New York: Academic Press, 1978.

Ross, L., Greene, S., & House, P. The "false consensus effect": An egocentric bias in social preception and attribution processes. *Journal of Experimental Social Psy-*

chology, 1977, *13*, 279–301.

Ross, L., Rodin, J., & Zimbardo, P. G. Toward an attribution therapy: The reduction of fear through induced cognitive-emotional misattribution. *Journal of Personality and Social Psychology*, 1969, *12*, 279–288.

Ross, M., Layton, B., Erickson, B., & Schopler, J. Affect, facial regard, and reactions to crowding. *Journal of Personality and Social Psychology*, 1973, *28*, 69–76.

Rossman, B. B., & Gollob, H. F. Social influence and pleasantness judgments involving people and issues. *Journal of Experimental Social Psychology*, 1976, *12*, 374–391.

Roth, S., & Bootzin, R. B. The effects of experimentally induced expectancies of learned helplessness. *Journal of Personality and Social Psychology*, 1974, *29*, 253–264.

Rothbart, M., Evans, M., & Fulero, S. Recall for confirming events: Memory processes and the maintenance of social stereotypes. *Journal of Experimental Social Psychology*, 1979, *15*, 343–355.

Rotter, J. B. Generalized expectancies for internal versus external control of reinforcement. *Psychological Monographs*, 1966, *80* (1, Whole No. 609).

Rotter, J. B. Some implications of a social learning theory for the practice of psychotherapy. In D. J. Levis (Ed.), *Learning approaches to therapeutic behavior change*. Chicago: Aldine, 1970.

Rotter, J. B. Generalized expectancies for problem solving and psychotherapy. *Cognitive Therapy and Research*, 1978, *2*, 1–10.

Rotter, J. B., Liverant, S., & Crowne, D. P. The growth and extinction of expectancies in chance controlled and skilled tasks. *Journal of Psychology*, 1961, *52*, 161–177.

Rowland, K. F. Environmental events predicting death for the elderly. *Psychological Bulletin*, 1977, *84*, 349–372.

Rubenstein, E. A. Warning: The Surgeon General's research program may be dangerous to preconceived notions. *Journal of Social Issues*, 1976, *32*, 18–34.

Rubin, J. Z., & Brown, B. R. *The social psychology of bargaining and negotiation*. New York: Academic Press, 1975.

Rubin, J. Z., Lewicki, R. J., & Dunn, L. Perception of promisors and threateners. *Proceedings of the 81st Annual Convention of the American Psychological Association*, 1973, *8*, 141–142.

Rubin, K. H., & Schneider, F. W. The relationship between moral judgment, egocentrism and altruistic behavior. *Child Development*, 1973, *44*, 661–665.

Rubin, Z. Measurement of romantic love. *Journal of Personality and Social Psychology*, 1970, *16*, 265–273.

Rubin, Z. *Liking and loving*. New York: Holt, Rinehart & Winston, 1973.

Rubin, Z. Disclosing oneself to a stranger: Reciprocity and its limits. *Journal of Ex-*

perimental Social Psychology, 1975, *11*, 233–260.

Rubinstein, C. M., & Shaver, P. Loneliness in two northeastern cities. In T. Hartog & R. Audy (Eds.), *The anatomy of loneliness*. New York: International Universities Press, 1980.

Rubinstein, C. M., Shaver, P., & Peplau, L. A. Loneliness. *Human Nature*, 1979, *2*, 59–65.

Ruble, D., & Feldman, N. Order of consensus, distinctiveness and consistency information and causal attribution. *Journal of Personality and Social Psychology*, 1976, *34*, 930–937.

Rubovits, P., & Maehr, M. Pygmalion analyzed: Toward an explanation of the Rosenthal-Jacobson findings. *Journal of Personality and Social Psychology*, 1971, *19*, 197–203.

Ruddick, S., & Daniels, P. *Working it out*. New York: Pantheon Books, 1977.

Rufus, P. Interaction of personality and political systems in decisions to run for office. *Journal of Social Issues*, 1968, *24*, 93–109.

Rule, B. G., Dyck, R., McAra, M., & Nesdale, A. R. Judgments of aggression serving personal versus prosocial purposes. *Social Behavior and Personality: An International Journal*, 1975, *3*, 55–63.

Rule, B. G., & Nesdale, A. R. Moral judgment of aggressive behavior. In R. G. Geen & E. C. O'Neal (Eds.), *Perspectives on aggression*. New York: Academic Press, 1976.

Runyon, W. M. A stage-state analysis of the life course. *Journal of Personality and Social Psychology*, 1980, *38*, 951–962.

Rushton, J. P. Generosity in children: Immediate and long-term effects of modeling, preaching and moral judgment. *Journal of Personality and Social Psychology*, 1975, *31*, 459–466.

Russ, R. C., Gold, J. A., & Stone, W. F. Attraction to a dissimilar stranger as a function of level of effectance arousal. *Journal of Experimental Social Psychology*, 1979, *15*, 481–492.

Ryan, E. D. The cathartic effect of vigorous motor activity on aggressive behavior. *Research Quarterly*, 1970, *41*, 542–551.

Ryan, W. *Blaming the victim*. New York: Pantheon Books, 1971.

S

Sacks, E. L. Intelligence scores as a function of experimentally established social relationships between child and examiner. *Journal of Abnormal and Social Psychology*, 1952, *47*, 354–358.

Saegert, S. C. *Effects of spatial and social density on arousal, mood, and social orientation*. Unpublished doctoral disserta-

tion, University of Michigan, Ann Arbor, 1974.

Saegert, S. C., Swap, W., & Zajonc, R. B. Exposure context and interpersonal attraction. *Journal of Personality and Social Psychology*, 1973, *25*, 234–242.

St. Jean, R. Reformulation of the value hypothesis in group risk taking. *Proceedings of the 78th Annual Convention of the American Psychological Association*, 1970, *5*, 339–340.

St. John, N. *School desegregation: Outcomes for children*. New York: John Wiley & Sons, 1975.

Saks, M. J. The limits of scientific jury selection: Ethical and empirical. *Jurimetrics Journal*, 1976, *17*, 3–22.

Saks, M. J., & Hastie, R. *Social psychology in court*. New York: Van Nostrand Reinhold, 1978.

Saks, M. J., Werner, C. M., & Ostrom, T. M. The persumption of innocence and the American juror. *Journal of Contemporary Law*, 1975, *2*, 46–54.

Saltzstein, H. D., Deamond, R. M., & Belenky, M. Moral judgment level and conformity behavior. *Developmental Psychology*, 1972, *7*, 327–336.

Samelson, F. History, origin, myth, and ideology: Comte's "discovery" of social psychology. *Journal for the Theory of Social Behavior*, 1974, *4*, 217–231.

Samelson, F. From "race psychology" to "studies in prejudices": Some observations in the thematic reversal in social psychology. *Journal of the History of the Behavioral Sciences*, 1978, *14*, 265–278.

Sampson, E. E. On justice as equality. *Journal of Social Issues*, 1975, *31*, 45–64.

Sampson, E. E. Psychology and the American ideal. *Journal of Personality and Social Psychology*, 1977, *35*, 767–780.

Sampson, E. E. *Cognitive psychology as ideology*. Unpublished manuscript, Clark University, Worcester, Mass., 1980.

Sandell, R. *Linguistic style and persuasion*. London: Academic Press, 1977.

SanMiguel, C. L., & Millham, J. The role of cognitive and situational variables in aggression toward homosexuals. *Journal of Homosexuality*, 1976, *2*, 11–27.

Sappington, A., & Grizzard, R. Self-discrimination responses in black school children. *Journal of Personality and Social Psychology*, 1975, *31*, 224–231.

Sarnoff, I. Identification with the aggressor: Some personality correlates of anti-Semitism among Jews. Unpublished doctoral dissertation, University of Michigan, Ann Arbor, 1951.

Sasfy, J., & Okun, M. Form of evaluation and audience expertness as joint determinants of audience effects. *Journal of Experimental Social Psychology*, 1974, *10*, 461–467.

Sattin, D. B., & Miller, J. K. The ecology of child abuse within a military community. *American Journal of Orthopsychiatry*, 1971, *41*, 675–678.

Savage, R. E., Perlmutter, L. C., & Monty, R. A. Effect of reduction in the amount of choice and the perception of control on learning. In L. C. Perlmutter & R. A. Monty (Eds.), *Choice and perceived control.* Hillsdale, N.J.: Lawrence Erlbaum, 1979.

Scanzoni, J. *Sexual bargaining: Power politics in the American marriage.* Englewood Cliffs, N.J.: Prentice-Hall, 1972.

Scanzoni, J. Social exchange and behavioral interdependence. In R. L. Burgess & T. L. Huston (Eds.), *Social exchange in developing relationships.* New York: Academic Press, 1979.

Schachter, S. Deviation, rejection and communication. *Journal of Abnormal and Social Psychology,* 1951, *46,* 190–207.

Schachter, S. *The psychology of affiliation.* Stanford, Calif.: Stanford University Press, 1959.

Schachter, S. The interaction of cognitive and physiological determinants of emotional state. In L. Berkowitz (Ed.), *Advances in experimental social psychology* (Vol. 1). New York: Academic Press, 1964.

Schachter, S., & Singer, J. L. Cognitive, social and physiological determinants of emotional state. *Psychological Review,* 1962, *65,* 121–128.

Schaeffer, G. H., & Patterson, M. L. Intimacy, arousal, and small group crowding. *Journal of Personality and Social Psychology,* 1980, *38,* 283–290.

Schaffer, D. R. Some effects of consonant and dissonant attitudinal advocacy on initial attitude salience and attitude change. *Journal of Personality and Social Psychology,* 1975, *32,* 160–168.

Schank, R. C., & Abelson, R. P. *Scripts, plans, goals, and understanding: An inquiry into human knowledge structures.* Hillsdale, N.J.: Lawrence Erlbaum, 1977.

Scheflen, A. E., & Scheflen, A. *Body language and the social order.* Englewood Cliffs, N.J.: Prentice-Hall, 1972.

Scheibe, K. E. *Minors, masks, lies and secrets: The limits of human predictability.* New York: Praeger, 1979.

Schill, T. R. Aggression and blood pressure responses of high- and low-guilt subjects following frustration. *Journal of Consulting and Clinical Psychology,* 1972, *38,* 461.

Schiltz, M. E. *Public attitudes toward social security, 1935–1956.* Washington, D.C.: U.S. Government Printing Office, 1970.

Schlenker, B. R., Bonoma, T., Tedeschi, J. T., & Pivnick, W. P. Compliance to threats as a function of the wording of the threat and the exploitativeness of the threatener. *Sociometry,* 1970, *33,* 394–408.

Schlenker, B. R., Helm, B., & Tedeschi, J. T. The effects of personality and situational variables on behavioral trust. *Journal of Personality and Social Psychology,* 1973, *25,* 419–427.

Schmitt, D. R., & Marwell, G. Cooperation and the human group. In R. Hamblin & J. Kunkel (Eds.), *Behavior theory in sociology.* New Brunswick, N.J.: Transaction Books, 1977.

Schneider, D. J. Implicit personality theory: A review. *Psychological Bulletin,* 1973, *79,* 294–309.

Schneider, D. J. Traits of dispositions: Some phenomenological evidence. Unpublished manuscript, University of Texas, San Antonio, 1978.

Schneider, D. J., Hastorf, A. H., & Ellsworth, P. C. *Person perception.* Reading, Mass.: Addison-Wesley, 1979.

Schneider, K. S. Personality correlates of altruistic behavior under four experimental conditions. *Journal of Social Psychology,* 1977, *102,* 113–116.

Schopler, J. Social power. In L. Berkowitz (Ed.), *Advances in experimental social psychology* (Vol. 2). New York: Academic Press, 1965.

Schopler, J., & Bateson, N. The power of dependence. *Journal of Personality and Social Psychology,* 1965, *2,* 247–254.

Schopler, J., & Layton, B. D. Determinants of the self-attribution of having influenced another person. *Journal of Personality and Social Psychology,* 1972, *22,* 326–332.

Schopler, J., McCallum, R., & Rusbult, C. E. Behavioral interference and internality-externality as determinants of subject crowding. Unpublished paper, University of North Carolina, Chapel Hill, 1977.

Schopler, J., & Stockdale, J. E. An interference analysis of crowding. *Environmental Psychology and Non-Verbal Behavior,* 1977, *1,* 81–88.

Schopler, J., & Thompson, V. The role of attribution processes in mediating amount of reciprocity for a favor. *Journal of Personality and Social Psychology,* 1968, *10,* 243–250.

Schuler, H., & Peltzer, U. Friendly versus unfriendly non-verbal behavior: The effects on partners' decision-making preferences. In H. Brandstätter, J. H. Davis, & H. Schuler (Eds.), *Dynamics of group decisions.* Beverly Hills, Calif.: Sage Publications, 1978.

Schulman, J., Shaver, P., Colman, R., Emrich, B., & Christie, R. Recipe for a jury. *Psychology Today,* 1973, *7,* 77–84.

Schulz, R. Control, predictability and the institutionalized aged. *Journal of Personality and Social Psychology,* 1976, *33,* 563–573.

Schulz, R. *The psychology of death, dying and bereavement.* Reading, Mass.: Addison-Wesley, 1978.

Schulz, R., & Aderman, D. Effect of residential change on the temporal distance of death of terminal cancer patients. *Omega: Journal of Death and Dying,* 1973, *4,* 157–162.

Schulz, R., & Hanusa, B. H. Long-term effects of control and predictability-enhancing interventions: Findings and ethical issues. *Journal of Personality and Social Psychology,* 1978, *36,* 1194–1201.

Schulz, R., & Hanusa, B. H. Environmental influences on the effectiveness of control- and competence-enhancing interventions. In L. C. Perlmutter & R. A. Monty (Eds.), *Choice and perceived control.* Hillsdale, N.J.: Lawrence Erlbaum, 1979.

Schutz, A. *Collected papers: I. The problem of social reality.* The Hague: Martinus Nijhoff, 1962.

Schutz, W. C. *Joy.* New York: Grove Press, 1967.

Schwartz, A. J., & Clarren, S. N. *The Cincinnati team policing experiment: A summary report.* Washington, D.C.: Police Foundation, 1977.

Schwartz, B. New developments in operant conditioning and their implications. In K. J. Gergen, M. S. Greenberg, & R. H. Willis (Eds.), *Social exchange: Advances in theory and research.* New York: Plenum, 1980.

Schwartz, B., Lacey, H., & Schuldenfrei, R. Operant psychology as factory psychology. *Behaviorism,* 1978, *6,* 229–254.

Schwartz, G., & Merten, D. *Love and commitment.* Beverly Hills, Calif.: Sage Publications, 1980.

Schwartz, S. H. Moral decision making and behavior. In J. R. Macaulay & L. Berkowitz (Eds.), *Altruism and helping behavior.* New York: Academic Press, 1970.

Schwartz, S. H. Awareness of interpersonal consequences, responsibility denial and volunteering. *Journal of Personality and Social Psychology,* 1974, *30,* 57–63.

Schwartz, S. H. Normative influences on altruism. In L. Berkowitz (Ed.), *Advances in experimental social psychology* (Vol. 10). New York: Academic Press, 1977.

Schwartz, S. H. Temporal instability as a moderator of the attitude-behavior relationship. *Journal of Personality and Social Psychology,* 1978, *36,* 715–724.

Schwartz, S. H., & Clausen, G. Responsibility, norms, and helping in an emergency. *Journal of Personality and Social Psychology,* 1970, *16,* 299–310.

Schwartz, S. H., & Fleishman, J. A. Personal norms and the mediation of legitimacy effects on helping. *Social Psychology,* 1978, *41,* 306–315.

Schwartz, S. H., & Tessler, R. A test of a model for reducing measured attitude-behavior discrepancies. *Journal of Personality and Social Psychology,* 1972, *24,* 225–236.

Schwendinger, J., & Schwendinger, H. Rape myths: In legal, theoretical, and everyday practice. *Crime and Social Justice,* 1974, *1,* 18–26.

Schwenn, M. *Arousal of the motive to avoid success.* Unpublished junior honors thesis, Harvard University, Cambridge, Mass., 1970.

Scott, M., & Lyman, S. Accounts. *American Sociological Review,* 1968, *33,* 46–62.

Scroggs, J. Penalties for rape as a function of

victim provocativeness, damage, and resistance. *Journal of Applied Social Psychology*, 1976, *6*, 360–368.

Sealy, A. P., & Cornish, W. R. Jurors and their verdicts. *Modern Law Review*, 1973, *36*, 496–508.

Sears, D. O. Selective exposure. In R. P. Abelson, E. Aronson, W. J. McGuire, T. M. Newcomb, M. J. Rosenberg, & P. H. Tannenbaum (Eds.), *Theories of cognitive consistency: A sourcebook*. Chicago: Rand McNally, 1965.

Sears, D. O., Freedman, J. L., & O'Connor, E. F. The effects of anticipated debate and commitment on the polarization of audience opinion. *Public Opinion Quarterly*, 1964, *28*, 615–627.

Sears, D. O., & McConahay, J. B. Racial socialization, comparison levels and the Watts riot. *Journal of Social Issues*, 1970, *26*, 121–140.

Sears, D. O., & Riley, R. J. Positivity biases in evaluations of political candidates. Unpublished manuscript, University of California, Los Angeles, 1969.

Sears, D. O., & Whitney, R. E. *Political persuasion*. Morristown, N.J.: Silver Burdett/ General Learning Press, 1973.

Sears, R. R., Maccoby, E. E., & Levin, H. *Patterns of child rearing*. Evanston, Ill.: Row Peterson, 1957.

Seashore, S. E. *Group cohesiveness in the industrial work group*. Ann Arbor, Mich.: Institute for Social Research, 1954.

Secord, P. F., & Backman, C. W. *Social psychology*. New York: McGraw-Hill, 1964.

Secord, P. F., Bevan, W., & Katz, B. The Negro stereotype and perceptual accentuation. *Journal of Abnormal and Social Psychology*, 1956, *53*, 78–83.

Seeman, M. The urban alienations: Some dubious theses from Marx to Marcuse. *Journal of Personality and Social Psychology*, 1971, *19*, 135–143.

Segal, S., & DuCette, J. Locus of control and pre-marital high school pregnancy. *Psychological Reports*, 1973, *33*, 887–890.

Segall, M. H. *Cross-cultural psychology: Human behavior in global perspective*. Monterey, Calif.: Brooks/Cole, 1979.

Seligman, C., Fazio, R. H., & Zanna, M. P. Effects of salience of extrinsic rewards on liking and loving. *Journal of Personality and Social Psychology*, 1980, *38*, 453–460.

Seligman, C., Kriss, M., Darley, J. M., Fazio, R. H., Becker, L. G., & Pryor, J. B. Predicting summer energy consumption from homeowners' attitudes. *Journal of Applied Social Psychology*, 1979, *9*, 70–90.

Seligman, M. E. P. *Helplessness*. San Francisco: W. H. Freeman, 1975.

Seligman, M. E. P., & Maier, S. F. Failure to escape traumatic shock. *Journal of Experimental Psychology*, 1967, *74*, 1–9.

Seligman, M. E. P., Maier, S. F., & Solomon, R. L. Unpredictable and uncontrollable aversive events. In F. R. Brush (Ed.), *Aversive conditioning and learning*. New York:

Academic Press, 1971.

Selltiz, C., Wrightsman, L. S., & Cook, S. W. *Research methods in social relations* (3rd ed.). New York: Holt, Rinehart & Winston, 1976.

Selman, R. L. Social-cognitive understanding: A guide to educational and clinical practice. In T. Lickona (Ed.), *Moral development and behavior*. New York: Holt, Rinehart & Winston, 1976.

Selye, H. *The stress of life*. New York: McGraw-Hill, 1976.

Selznick, G. J., & Steinberg, S. *The tenacity of prejudice*. New York: Harper & Row, 1969.

Senn, D. J. Attraction as a function of similarity-dissimilarity in task performance. *Journal of Personality and Social Psychology*, 1971, *18*, 120–123.

Serbin, L. A., Tonnick, I. J., & Sternglanz, S. H. Shaping cooperative cross-sex play. *Child Development*, 1977, *48*, 924–929.

Sermat, V. Some situational and personality correlates of loneliness. Unpublished paper, York University, Toronto, 1974.

Shaffer, D. R., Rogel, M., & Hendrick, C. Intervention in the library: The effect of increased responsibility on bystander willingness to prevent a theft. *Journal of Applied Social Psychology*, 1975, *5*, 309–319.

Shanteau, J., & Nagy, F. Probability of acceptance in dating choice. *Journal of Personality and Social Psychology*, 1979, *37*, 522–533.

Shantz, C. U. The development of social cognition. In E. M. Hetherington (Ed.), *Review of child development research* (Vol. 5). Chicago: University of Chicago Press, 1975.

Shantz, C. U., & Watson, T. S. Spatial abilities and spatial egocentrism in the young child. *Child Development*, 1971, *42*, 171–181.

Sharabany, R. *The development of intimacy among children in the kibbutz*. Paper presented at the biennial meeting of the International Society for the Study of Behavioral Development, Ann Arbor, Mich., August 1973.

Sharabany, R. *Intimate friendships among kibbutz and city children and its measurement*. Unpublished doctoral dissertation, Cornell University, Ithaca, N.Y., 1974. (University Microfilms No. 74–17, 682)

Shaver, K. G. *Principles of social psychology*. Cambridge, Mass.: Winthrop, 1977.

Shaver, P. Questions concerning fear of success and its conceptual relatives. *Sex Roles*, 1976, *2*, 305–320.

Shaver, P., & Rubinstein, C. M. *Living alone, loneliness and health*. Paper presented at the 87th Annual Convention of the American Psychological Association, New York, September 1979.

Shaver, P., & Rubinstein, C. M. Childhood attachment experience and adult loneliness. In L. Wheeler (Ed.), *The review of*

personality and social psychology, Beverly Hills, Calif.: Sage Publications, 1980.

Shaw, M. E. A comparison of two types of leadership in various communication nets. *Journal of Abnormal and Social Psychology*, 1955, *50*, 127–134.

Shaw, M. E. Some effects of irrelevant information upon problem solving by small groups. *Journal of Social Psychology*, 1958, *47*, 33–37.

Shaw, M. E. *Group dynamics: The psychology of small group behavior* (2nd ed.). New York: McGraw-Hill, 1976.

Shaw, M. E., & Blum, J. M. Group performance as a function of task difficulty and the group's awareness of member satisfaction. *Journal of Applied Psychology*, 1965, *49*, 151–154.

Shepherd, J. W., & Bagley, A. The effects of biographical information and order of presentation on the judgment of an aggressive action. *Journal of Social and Clinical Psychology*, 1970, *9*, 177–179.

Sherif, C. W., Sherif, M., & Nebergall, R. E. *Attitude and attitude change: The social judgment-involvement approach*. Philadelphia: W. B. Saunders, 1965.

Sherif, M. A study of some social factors in perception. *Archives of Psychology*, 1935, *27*, no. 187.

Sherif, M. Superordinate goals in the reduction of intergroup conflicts. *American Journal of Sociology*, 1958, *63*, 349–356.

Sherif, M. Superordinate goals in the reduction of intergroup conflict: An experimental evaluation. In W. G. Austin & S. Worchel (Eds.), *The social psychology of intergroup relations*. Monterey, Calif.: Brooks/Cole, 1979.

Sherif, M., Harvey, O. J., White, B. J., Hood, W. R., & Sherif, C. W. *Intergroup cooperation and competition: The Robbers Cave experiment*. Norman, Okla.: University Book Exchange, 1961.

Sherif, M., & Hovland, C. I. *Social judgment: Assimilation and contrast effects in communication and attitude change*. New Haven, Conn.: Yale University Press, 1961.

Sherif, M., & Sherif, C. W. *Groups in harmony and tension*. New York: Harper & Row, 1953.

Sherif, M., & Sherif, C. W. Research on intergroup relations. In W. G. Austin & S. Worchel (Eds.), *The social psychology of intergroup relations*. Monterey, Calif.: Brooks/Cole, 1979.

Sherif, M., White, B. J., & Harvey, O. J. Status in experimentally produced groups. *American Journal of Sociology*, 1955, *60*, 370–379.

Sherman, S. J., Ahlm, K., Berman, L., & Lynn, S. Contrast effects and their relationship to subsequent behavior. *Journal of Experimental Social Psychology*, 1978, *14*, 340–350.

Sherrod, D. R. Crowding, perceived control, and behavioral after-effects. *Journal of Ap-*

plied Social Psychology, 1974, 4, 171–186.

Sherrod, D. R., Hage, J., Halpern, P., & Moone, B. Effects of personal causation and perceived control on responses to an aversive environment: The more control, the better. Journal of Experimental Social Psychology, 1977, 13, 14–27.

Shiflett, S. C., & Nealey, S. M. The effects of changing leader power: A test of situational engineering. Organizational Behavior and Human Performance, 1972, 7, 371–382.

Shoemaker, J. D., South, D. R., & Lowe, J. Facial stereotypes of deviants and judgments of guilt or innocence. Social Forces, 1973, 51, 427–433.

Shortell, J., Epstein, S., & Taylor, S. P. Instigation to aggression as a function of degree of defeat and the capacity for massive retaliation. Journal of Personality, 1970, 38, 313–328.

Shotter, J. Images of man in psychological research. London: Methuen, 1977.

Shotter, J. Action, joint action and intentionality. In M. Brenner (Ed.), The structure of action. Oxford: Blackwell, 1980.

Shrauger, J. S., & Jones, S. C. Social validation and interpersonal evaluations. Journal of Experimental Social Psychology, 1968, 4, 315–323.

Shure, G. H., Rogers, M. S., Larsen, I. M., & Tassone, J. Group planning and task effectiveness. Sociometry, 1962, 25, 263–282.

Shweder, R. How relevant is an individual difference theory of personality? Journal of Personality, 1975, 43, 455–485.

Shweder, R. Illusory correlations and the MMPI controversy. Journal of Consulting and Clinical Psychology, 1977, 45, 917–924.

Sicoly, F., & Ross, M. The facilitation of ego-biased attributions by means of self-serving observer feedback. Journal of Personality and Social Psychology, 1977, 35, 734–741.

Sidowski, J. B., Wyckoff, L. B., & Tabory, L. The influence of reinforcement and punishment in a minimal social situation. Journal of Abnormal and Social Psychology, 1956, 52, 115–119.

Siegel, S., & Fouraker, L. E. Bargaining and group decision making. New York: McGraw-Hill, 1960.

Siegman, A. W. The telltale voice: Nonverbal messages of verbal communication. In A. W. Siegman & S. Feldstein (Eds.), Nonverbal behavior and communication. Hillsdale, N.J.: Lawrence Erlbaum, 1978.

Sigall, H., & Landy, D. Radiating beauty: Effects of having a physically attractive partner on person perception. Journal of Personality and Social Psychology, 1973, 28, 218–224.

Sigall, H., & Ostrove, N. Beautiful but dangerous: Effects of offender attractiveness and nature of the crime on juridic judgment. Journal of Personality and Social

Psychology, 1975, 31, 410–414.

Silver, L. B., Dublin, C. C., & Lourie, R. S. Does violence breed violence? Contributions from a study of the child abuse syndrome. American Journal of Psychiatry, 1969, 126, 404–407.

Silverman, I., & Shaw, M. E. Effects of sudden mass school desegregation on interracial interaction and attitudes in one Southern city. Journal of Social Issues, 1973, 29, 133–142.

Simmel, G. The number of members as determining the sociological form of the group. American Journal of Sociology, 1903, 8, 1–46; 158–196.

Simon, J. G., & Feather, N. T. Causal attributions for success and failure at university examinations. Journal of Educational Psychology, 1973, 64, 46–56.

Simon, R. J. The jury and the defense of insanity. Boston: Little, Brown, 1967.

Simon, W. The social, the erotic, and the sensual: The complexities of sexual scripts. In J. K. Cole & R. Dienstbier (Eds.), Nebraska Symposium on Motivation (Vol. 21). Lincoln: University of Nebraska Press, 1973.

Simons, C., & Piliavin, J. The effect of deception on reactions to a victim. Journal of Personality and Social Psychology, 1972, 21, 56–60.

Simonton, D. K. Eminence, creativity, and geographic marginality: A recursive structural equation model. Journal of Personality and Social Psychology, 1977, 35, 805–816.

Simonton, D. K. Thematic fame, melodic originality, and musical Zeitgeist: A biographical and trans-historical content analysis. Journal of Personality and Social Psychology, 1980, 38, 972–983.

Simpson, M. A. Brought in dead. Omega: Journal on Death and Dying, 1976, 7, 243–248.

Sipes, R. G. War, sports and aggression: An empirical test of two rival theories. American Anthropologist, 1973, 75, 64–86.

Sistrunk, F., & McDavid, J. W. Sex variable in conforming behavior. Journal of Personality and Social Psychology, 1971, 17, 200–207.

Skinner, B. F. Walden two. New York: Macmillan, 1948.

Skinner, B. F. Beyond freedom and dignity. New York: Alfred A. Knopf, 1971.

Sloan, L. R. The function and impact of sports for fans: A review of theory and contemporary research. In J. H. Goldstein (Ed.), Sports, games and play: Social and psychological viewpoints. Hillsdale, N.J.: Lawrence Erlbaum, 1979.

Sloan, L. R., Love, R., & Ostrom, T. M. Political heckling: Who really loses? Journal of Personality and Social Psychology, 1974, 30, 518–525.

Smedley, J. W., & Bayton, J. A. Evaluative race-class stereotypes by race and perceived class of subjects. Journal of Person-

ality and Social Psychology, 1978, 36, 530–536.

Smith, G. F., & Dorfman, D. D. The effect of stimulus uncertainty on the relationship between frequency of exposure and liking. Journal of Personality and Social Psychology, 1975, 31, 150–155.

Smith, M. Percy Forman: Defense Counselor. Life, 1966, pp. 94–97.

Smith, M., Gabriel, R., Schott, J., & Padia, W. Evaluation of the effects of Outward Bound. Unpublished manuscript, University of Colorado, Boulder, 1975.

Smith, M. B. Humanizing social psychology. San Francisco: Jossey-Bass, 1974.

Smith, S. M. The battered child syndrome. London: Butterworth, 1973.

Smith, W. F. The effects of social and monetary rewards on intrinsic motivation. Unpublished doctoral dissertation, Cornell University, Ithaca, N.Y., 1976.

Snow, R. E. Unfinished Pygmalion. Contemporary Psychology, 1969, 14, 197–200.

Snyder, C. R., & Fromkin, H. L. Uniqueness: The human pursuit of difference. New York: Plenum, 1980.

Snyder, E. C. The Supreme Court as a small group. Social Forces, 1958, 36, 232–239.

Snyder, M. L. Self-monitoring processes. In L. Berkowitz (Ed.), Advances in experimental social psychology (Vol. 12). New York: Academic Press, 1979.

Snyder, M. L., & Cunningham, M. R. To comply or not to comply: Testing the self-perception explanation of the foot-in-the-door phenomenon. Journal of Personality and Social Psychology, 1975, 31, 64–67.

Snyder, M. L., & Monson, T. C. Persons, situations, and control of social behavior. Journal of Personality and Social Psychology, 1975, 32, 637–644.

Snyder, M. L., Stephan, W. G., & Rosenfield, D. Egotism and attribution. Journal of Personality and Social Psychology, 1976, 33, 435–441.

Snyder, M. L., & Swann, W. B., Jr. When actions reflect attitudes: The policies of impression management. Journal of Personality and Social Psychology, 1976, 34, 1034–1042.

Snyder, M. L., & Tanke, E. D. Behavior and attitude: Some people are more consistent than others. Journal of Personality, 1976, 44, 510–517.

Snyder, M. L., Tanke, E. D., & Berscheid, E. Social perception and interpersonal behavior: On the self-fulfilling nature of social stereotypes. Journal of Personality and Social Psychology, 1977, 35, 656–666.

Snyder, M. L., & Uranowitz, S. W. Reconstructing the past: Some cognitive consequences of person perception. Journal of Personality and Social Psychology, 1978, 36, 941–950.

Sokal, M. James McKeen Cattell and American psychology in the 1920's. Unpublished manuscript, Worcester Polytechnic Institute, Worcester, Mass., 1978.

Sommer, J. G. The rich, the poor and American private philanthropy. In R. Eells (Ed.), *International business philanthropy*. New York: Macmillan, 1979.

Sommers, R. *Personal space: The behavioral analysis of design*. Englewood Cliffs, N.J.: Prentice-Hall, 1969.

Souza, E., & Silva, M. C. *Social and cognitive dynamics of shyness*. Unpublished master's thesis, Stanford University, Stanford, Calif., 1977.

Spence, J. T. Verbal and nonverbal rewards and punishments in the discrimination learning of children of varying socio-economic status. *Developmental Psychology*, 1972, *6*, 381–384.

Spence, J. T., & Helmreich, R. L. *Masculinity and femininity*. Austin: University of Texas Press, 1977.

Sroufe, R., Chaikin, A., Cook, R., & Freeman, V. The effects of physical attractiveness on honesty. *Personality and Social Psychology Bulletin*, 1977, *3*, 59–62.

Stang, D. J. Methodological factors in mere exposure research. *Psychological Bulletin*, 1974, *81*, 1014–1025.

Stark, R., & McEvoy, J. Middle class violence. *Psychology Today*, 1970, *4*, 52–65.

Staub, E. A child in distress: The influence of age and number of witnesses on children's attempts to help. *Journal of Personality and Social Psychology*, 1970, *14*, 130–140.

Staub, E. The use of role playing and induction in children's learning of helping and sharing behavior. *Child Development*, 1971, *42*, 805–817.

Staub, E. *The development of prosocial behavior in children*. Morristown, N.J.: Silver Burdett/General Learning Press, 1975.

Staub, E. *Positive forms of social behavior*. New York: Academic Press, 1978.

Staub, E., & Sherk, L. Need for approval: Child's sharing behavior. *Child Development*, 1970, *14*, 243–253.

Steele, C. M. Name-calling and compliance. *Journal of Personality and Social Psychology*, 1975, *31*, 361–369.

Steffensmeier, D., & Steffensmeier, R. Sex differences in reactions to homosexuals: Research continuities and further developments. *Journal of Sex Research*, 1974, *10*, 52–67.

Stein, A. Conflict and cohesion: A review of the literature. *Journal of Conflict Resolution*, 1976, *20*, 143–172.

Stein, A. H. Imitation of resistance to temptation. *Child Development*, 1967, *38*, 157–169.

Stein, R. T., & Heller, T. An empirical analysis of the correlations between leadership status and participation rates reported in the literature. *Journal of Personality and Social Psychology*, 1979, *37*, 1993–2002.

Steiner, I. D. *Group process and productivity*. New York: Academic Press, 1972.

Steiner, I. D. Attribution of choice. In M. Fishbein (Ed.), *Progress in social psychology* (Vol. 1). Hillsdale, N.J.: Lawrence Erlbaum, 1980.

Steiner, I. D., & Rajaratnam, N. A model for the comparison of individual and group performance scores. *Behavioral Science*, 1961, *6*, 142–147.

Stephan, W. G. School desegregation: An evaluation of predictions made in Brown vs. the Board of Education. *Psychological Bulletin*, 1978, *85*, 217–238.

Stephan, W. G., & Rosenfield, D. Effects of desegregation on racial attitudes. *Journal of Personality and Social Psychology*, 1978, *36*, 795–799.

Sternglanz, S. H., & Serbin, L. Sex role stereotyping in children's television programs. *Developmental Psychology*, 1974, *10*, 710–715.

Stevenson, H. W., & Stewart, E. C. A developmental study of racial awareness in young children. *Child Development*, 1958, *29*, 339–409.

Stewart, A. J., & Rubin, Z. The power motive in the dating couple. *Journal of Personality and Social Psychology*, 1976, *34*, 305–309.

Stewart, R. Effects of continuous responding on the order effect in personality impression formation. *Journal of Personality and Social Psychology*, 1965, *1*, 161–165.

Stockdale, J. E., Wittman, L. S., Jones, L. E., & Greaves, D. A. *A multi-dimensional analysis of subjective crowding*. Paper presented at Human Consequences of Crowding Symposium, Antalya, Turkey, 1977.

Stokols, D. The experience of crowding in primary and secondary environments. *Environment and Behavior*, 1976, *8*, 49–86.

Stokols, D. In defense of the crowding construct. In A. Baum, J. E. Singer, & S. Valins (Eds.), *Advances in experimental psychology* (Vol. 1). Hillsdale, N.J.: Lawrence Erlbaum, 1978.

Stokols, D., & Shumaker, S. A. People in places: A transactional view of settings. In T. Harvey (Ed.), *Cognition, social behavior and the environment*. Hillsdale, N.J.: Lawrence Erlbaum, 1980.

Stone, L. J., & Hokanson, J. E. Arousal reduction via self-punitive behavior. *Journal of Personality and Social Psychology*, 1969, *12*, 72–79.

Stone, W. F. Patterns of conformity in couples varying in intimacy. *Journal of Personality and Social Psychology*, 1973, *27*, 413–418.

Stoner, J. A. F. *A comparison of individuals and group decisions involving risk*. Unpublished master's thesis, Massachusetts Institute of Technology, Cambridge, 1961.

Storms, M. D., Denney, D. R., McCaul, K. D., & Lowery, C. R. Treating insomnia. In I. Frieze, D. Bar-Tal, & T. Carrol (Eds.), *New approaches to social psychology*. San Francisco: Jossey-Bass, 1979.

Stotland, E., Zander, A., & Natsoulas, T. Generalization of interpersonal similarity. *Journal of Abnormal and Social Psychology*, 1961, *62*, 250–256.

Strassberg, D. S. Relationships among locus of control, anxiety and valued goal expectations. *Journal of Consulting and Clinical Psychology*, 1973, *2*, 319–328.

Streufert, S., & Streufert, S. C. Effects of conceptual structure, failure and success on attribution of causality and interpersonal attitudes. *Journal of Personality and Social Psychology*, 1969, *11*, 138–147.

Streufert, S., & Streufert, S. C. *Behavior in the complex environment*. Washington, D.C.: V. H. Winston & Sons, 1978.

Stricker, L. J., Messick, S., & Jackson, D. N. Conformity, anticonformity and independence: Their dimensionality and generality. *Journal of Personality and Social Psychology*, 1970, *16*, 494–507.

Strickland, B. R. *Locus of control and health-related behaviors*. Paper presented at the meeting of the Inter-American Congress of Psychology, Bogotá, Colombia, December 1974.

Strickland, B. R. Internal-external control of reinforcement. In T. Blass (Ed.), *Personality variables in social behavior*. Hillsdale, N.J.: Lawrence Erlbaum, 1977.

Strickland, B. R., & Crowne, D. P. Conformity under conditions of simulated group pressure as a function of the need for social approval. *Journal of Social Psychology*, 1962, *58*, 171–181.

Strickland, L. Surveillance and trust. *Journal of Personality*, 1958, *26*, 200–215.

Strodtbeck, F. L., James, R. M., & Hawkins, D. Social status in jury deliberations. *American Sociological Review*, 1957, *22*, 713–719.

Stroebe, W., Insko, C. A., Thompson, V. D., & Layton, B. D. Effects of physical attractiveness, attitude similarity, and sex on various aspects of interpersonal attraction. *Journal of Personality and Social Psychology*, 1971, *18*, 79–91.

Stroebe, W., Stroebe, M., Gergen, K. J., & Gergen, M. M. The effects of bereavement on mortality: A social psychological analysis. In J. R. Eiser (Ed.), *Social psychology and behavioral medicine*. London: John Wiley & Sons, in press.

Struening, E. L., & Guttentag, M. (Eds.). *Handbook of evaluation research*. Beverly Hills, Calif.: Sage Publications, 1975.

Suchner, R. W., & Jackson, D. Responsibility and status: A causal or only a spurious relationship? *Sociometry*, 1976, *39*, 243–256.

Sudnow, D. Dead on arrival. *Interaction*, November 1973, 23–31.

Suedfeld, P., Bochner, S., & Matas, C. Petitioner's attire and petition signing by peace demonstrators: A field experiment. *Journal of Applied Social Psychology*, 1971, *1*, 278–283.

Sullivan, E. V. A study of Kohlberg's structural theory of moral development: A critique of liberal social science ideology. *Human Development*, 1977, *20*, 352–376.

Sundstrom, E. An experimental study of

crowding: Effects of room size, intrusion, and goal blocking of non-verbal behavior, self-disclosure, and self-reported stress. *Journal of Personality and Social Psychology*, 1975, *35*, 645–654.

Sundstrom, E. Crowding as a sequential process: Review of research on the effects of population density on humans. In A. Baum & Y. M. Epstein (Eds.), *Human response to crowding*. Hillsdale, N.J.: Lawrence Erlbaum, 1978.

Sussmann, M., & Davis, T. Balance theory and the negative interpersonal relationship: Attraction and agreement in dyads and triads. *Journal of Personality*, 1975, *43*, 560–581.

Sutherland, E. *Principles of criminology*. Philadelphia: J. B. Lippincott, 1966.

Suttles, G. D. *The social order of the slum*. Chicago: University of Chicago Press, 1968.

Sweeney, M. A., & Cottle, W. C. Nonverbal acuity: A comparison of counselors and noncounselors. *Journal of Counseling Psychology*, 1976, *23*, 394–397.

Swinth, R. L. The establishment of the trust relationship. *Journal of Conflict Resolution*, 1967, *11*, 335–344.

Szasz, T. S. The myth of mental illness. *American Psychologist*, 1960, *15*, 113–118.

T

Taft, R. Selective recall and memory distinction of favorable and unfavorable material. *Journal of Abnormal and Social Psychology*, 1954, *49*, 23–29.

Tajfel, H. Value and the perceptual judgment of magnitude. *Psychological Review*, 1957, *64*, 192–204.

Tajfel, H. The roots of prejudice: Cognitive aspects. In P. Watson (Ed.), *Psychology and race*. Chicago: Aldine, 1973.

Tajfel, H., & Turner, J. An integrative theory of intergroup conflict. In W. G. Austin & S. Worchel (Eds.), *The social psychology of intergroup relations*. Monterey, Calif.: Brooks/Cole, 1979.

Taleporos, E. Motivational patterns in attitudes towards the women's liberation movement. *Journal of Personality*, 1977, *45*, 484–500.

Tapp, J. L., & Kohlberg, L. Developing senses of law and legal justice. *Journal of Social Issues*, 1971, *27*, 65–92.

Tavris, C., & Offir, C. *The longest war: The psychology of sex differences*. New York: Harcourt Brace Jovanovich, 1977.

Taylor, D. A. The development of interpersonal relationships: Social penetration processes. *Journal of Social Psychology*, 1968, *75*, 79–90.

Taylor, F. W. *The principles of scientific management*. New York: Harper & Row, 1911.

Taylor, M. C. Race, sex and the expression of self-fulfilling prophecies in a laboratory teaching situation. *Journal of Personality and Social Psychology*, 1979, *37*, 897–912.

Taylor, R. B., DeSoto, C. B., & Lieb, R. Sharing secrets: Disclosure and discretion in dyads and triads. *Journal of Personality and Social Psychology*, 1979, *37*, 1196–1203.

Taylor, S. E. A categorization approach to stereotyping. In D. L. Hamilton (Ed.), *Cognitive processes in stereotyping and intergroup behavior*. Hillsdale, N.J.: Lawrence Erlbaum, in press.

Taylor, S. E., Crocker, J., Fiske, S. T., Sprinzen, M., & Winkler, J. D. The generalizability of salience effects. *Journal of Personality and Social Psychology*, 1979, *37*, 357–368.

Taylor, S. E., & Fiske, S. T. Point of view and perception of causality. *Journal of Personality and Social Psychology*, 1975, *32*, 439–445.

Taylor, S. E., & Mettee, D. R. When similarity breeds contempt. *Journal of Personality and Social Psychology*, 1971, *20*, 175–181.

Taylor, S. P., Vardaris, R. M., Rawitch, A. B., Gammon, C. B., Cranston, J. W., & Lubetkin, A. I. The effects of alcohol and delta-9-tetra hydrocannabinal on human physical aggression. *Aggressive Behavior*, 1976, *2*, 153–161.

Taynor, J., & Deaux, K. When women are more deserving than men: Equity, attribution and perceived sex differences. *Journal of Personality and Social Psychology*, 1973, *28*, 360–367).

Tedeschi, J. T. (Ed.). *The social influence process*. Chicago: Aldine-Atherton, 1972.

Tedeschi, J. T., Smith, R. B., & Brown, R. C. A reinterpretation of research on aggression. *Psychological Bulletin*, 1974, *81*, 540–562.

Teger, A., & Pruitt, D. Components of group risk taking. *Journal of Experimental Social Psychology*, 1967, *3*, 189–205.

Teichman, M., & Foa, U. G. Effect of resources similarity on satisfaction with exchange. *Social Behavior and Personality*, 1975, *3*, 213–224.

Terman, L. M. *Psychological factors in marital happiness*. New York: McGraw-Hill, 1938.

Tesser, A. Self-generated attitude change. In L. Berkowitz (Ed.), *Advances in experimental social psychology* (Vol. 11). New York: Academic Press, 1978.

Tesser, A., & Conlee, M. C. Some effects of time and thought on attitude polarization. *Journal of Personality and Social Psychology*, 1975, *31*, 262–270.

Tesser, A., & Rosen, S. The reluctance to transmit bad news. In L. Berkowitz (Ed.), *Advances in experimental social psychology* (Vol. 8). New York: Academic Press, 1975.

Tesser, A., Rosen, S., & Conlee, M. C. News valence and available recipient as determinants of news transmission. *Sociometry*, 1972, *35*, 619–628.

Tetlock, P. E. Identifying victims of group

think from public statements of decision makers. *Journal of Personality and Social Psychology*, 1979, *37*, 1314–1324.

Thelan, M. H., Dollinger, S. J., & Roberts, M. C. On being imitated: Its effects on attraction and reciprocal imitation. *Journal of Personality and Social Psychology*, 1975, *31*, 467–472.

Thibaut, J. W., & Kelley, H. H. *The social psychology of groups*. New York: John Wiley & Sons, 1959.

Thistlethwaite, D. L. Impact of disruptive external events on student attitudes. *Journal of Personality and Social Psychology*, 1974, *30*, 228–242.

Thomas, M. H., & Drabman, R. S. Effects of television violence on expectations of others' aggression. *Personality and Social Psychology Bulletin*, 1978, *4*, 73–76.

Thomas, M. H., Horton, R. W., Lippincott, E. C., & Drabman, R. S. Desensitization to portrayals of real-life aggression as a function of exposure to television violence. *Journal of Personality and Social Psychology*, 1977, *35*, 450–458.

Thompson, E. G., Gard, J. W., & Phillips, J. L. Trait dimensionality and "balance" in subject-verb-object judgments. *Journal of Personality and Social Psychology*, 1980, *38*, 57–66.

Thompson, W. C., Lowan, C. L., & Rosenhan, D. L. Focus of attention mediates the impact of negative affect on altruism. *Journal of Personality and Social Psychology*, 1980, *38*, 291–300.

Thorndike, E. L. A constant error in psychological ratings. *Journal of Applied Psychology*, 1920, *4*, 25–29.

Thorndike, E. L. *The fundamentals of learning*. New York: Teachers College Press, 1932.

Thorndike, R. L. Review of Pygmalion in the classroom. *American Educational Research Journal*, 1966, *5*, 708–711.

Tjosvold, D. Commitment to justice in conflict between unequal status persons. *Journal of Applied Social Psychology*, 1977, *7*, 149–162.

Tjosvold, D., & Sagaria, S. D. Effects of relative power on cognitive perspective-taking. *Personality and Social Psychology Bulletin*, 1978, *4*, 256–259.

Tönnies, F. *Community and society*. East Lansing: Michigan State University Press, 1957.

Tomkins, S. S. *Affect, imagery, consciousness* (Vol. 1). New York: Springer, 1962.

Touhey, J. C. Comparison of two dimensions of attitude similarity on heterosexual attraction. *Journal of Personality and Social Psychology*, 1972, *23*, 8–10.

Tracy, J., & Clark, E. Treatment for child abusers. *Social Work*, 1974, *19*, 338–342.

Traynham, R. N. *The effects of modifying color meaning concepts on racial attitudes in five- and eight-year-old children*. Unpublished master's thesis, University of Arkansas, Fayetteville, 1974.

Triandis, H. C. *Interpersonal behavior.* Monterey, Calif.: Brooks/Cole, 1976.

Triandis, H. C., & Brislin, R. W. (Eds.). *Handbook of cross-cultural psychology: Social psychology* (Vol. 5). Boston: Allyn & Bacon, 1980.

Triandis, H. C. & Davis, E. E. Race and belief as determinants of behavioral intentions. *Journal of Personality and Social Psychology,* 1965, *2,* 715–725.

Trimble, J. E. *An index of the social indicators of the American Indian in Oklahoma.* Oklahoma City: Oklahoma Indian Affairs Commission, 1972.

Triplett, N. The dynamogenic factors in pace making and competition. *American Journal of Psychology,* 1897, *9,* 507–533.

Tuchman, G. The symbolic annihilation of women by the mass media. In G. Tuchman, A. K. Daniels, & J. Benet (Eds.), *Hearth and home: Images of women in the mass media.* New York: Oxford University Press, 1978.

Tuddenham, R. D., & McBride, P. The yielding experiment from the subject's point of view. *Journal of Personality,* 1959, *27,* 259–271.

Tumes, J. *The contingency theory of leadership: A behavioral investigation.* Paper presented at the meetings of the Eastern Academy of Management, Boston, May 1972.

Turiel, E. An experimental test of the sequentiality of developmental stages in the child's moral judgements. *Journal of Personality and Social Psychology,* 1966, *3,* 611–618.

Turnbull, C. M. *The mountain people.* New York: Simon & Schuster, 1972.

Turner, C. W., & Simons, L. S. Effects of subject sophistication and evaluation apprehension on aggressive responses to weapons. *Journal of Personality and Social Psychology,* 1974, *30,* 341–348.

Turner, E. A., & Wright, J. Effects of severity of threat and perceived availability on the attractiveness of objects. *Journal of Personality and Social Psychology,* 1965, *2,* 128–132.

Tversky, A., & Kahneman, D. Causal schemas in judgments under uncertainty. In M. Fishbein (Ed.), *Progress in social psychology* (Vol. 1). Hillsdale, N.J.: Lawrence Erlbaum, 1980.

U

Ugwuegbu, D. C. Racial and evidential factors in juror attribution of legal responsibility. *Journal of Experimental Social Psychology,* 1979, *15,* 133–146.

Unger, R. K. Toward a redefinition of sex and gender. *American Psychologist,* 1979, *34,* 1085–1094.

U.S. Riot Commission. *Report of the National Advisory Commission on Civil Disorders.* New York: Bantam Books, 1968.

U.S. Senate, Committee on Labor and Public Welfare, Subcommittee on Children and Youth. *Child Abuse Prevention and Treatment Act: Hearing on S. 1191,* 93rd Cong., 1st sess., 1973.

Upshaw, H. S. The personal reference scale: An approach to social judgment. In L. Berkowitz (Ed.), *Advances in experimental social psychology* (Vol. 4). New York: Academic Press, 1969.

Uranowitz, S. W. Helping and self-attribution: A field experiment. *Journal of Personality and Social Psychology,* 1975, *31,* 852–854.

U'ren, M. B. The image of women in textbooks. In V. Gomick & B. K. Moran (Eds.), *Woman in sexist society: Studies in power and powerlessness.* New York: New American Library, 1971.

V

Valenzi, E. R., & Andrews, I. R. Effects of hourly overpay and underpay inequity when tested with a new induction procedure. *Journal of Applied Psychology,* 1971, *55,* 22–27.

Van Kirk, M. *Response time analysis: Executive summary.* Washington, D.C.: Law Enforcement Assistance Administration, 1978.

Vaughan, G. M. Concept formation and the development of ethnic awareness. *Journal of Genetic Psychology,* 1963, *103,* 93–103.

Vaughan, G. M. Ethnic awareness in relation to minority group membership. *Journal of Genetic Psychology,* 1964, *105,* 119–130. (a)

Vaughan, G. M. The trans-situational aspect of conforming behavior. *Journal of Personality,* 1964, *32,* 335–354. (b)

Vaughan, K. B., & Lanzetta, J. T. Vicarious instigation and conditioning of facial expressive and autonomic responses to a model's expressive display of pain. *Journal of Personality and Social Psychology,* 1980, *38,* 909–923.

Verplanck, W. S. The control of the content of conversation: Reinforcement of statements of opinion. *Journal of Abnormal and Social Psychology,* 1955, *51,* 668–676.

Vidmar, N., & Crinkla, L. *Retribution and utility as motives in sanctioning behavior.* Paper presented at the meeting of the Midwestern Psychological Association, Chicago, May 1973.

Vinacke, W. E., & Arkoff, A. Experimental study of coalitions in the triad. *American Sociological Review,* 1957, *22,* 406–415.

Vinokur, A. Distribution of initial risk levels and group decisions involving risk. *Journal of Personality and Social Psychology,* 1969, *13,* 207–214.

Vockell, E. L., Felker, D. W., & Miley, C. H. Birth order literature 1967–1971: Bibliography and index. *Journal of Individual Psychology,* 1973, *29,* 39–53.

Vohs, J. L., & Garret, R. L. Resistance to persuasion: An integrative framework. *Public Opinion Quarterly,* 1968, *32,* 445–452.

Voissem, N. H., & Sistrunk, F. Communication schedule and cooperative game behavior. *Journal of Personality and Social Psychology,* 1971, *19,* 160–167.

W

Wagner, C., & Wheeler, L. Model need and cost effects in helping behavior. *Journal of Personality and Social Psychology,* 1969, *12,* 111–116.

Wagner, R. V. Complementary needs, role expectations, interpersonal attraction and the stability of working relationships. *Journal of Personality and Social Psychology,* 1975, *32,* 116–124.

Wahrman, R., & Pugh, M. D. Competence and conformity: Another look at Hollander's study. *Sociometry,* 1972, *35,* 376–386.

Wahrman, R., & Pugh, M. D. Sex, nonconformity and influence. *Sociometry,* 1974, *37,* 137–147.

Walker, T. G. Behavior of temporary members in small groups. *Journal of Applied Psychology,* 1973, *58,* 144–146.

Wallace, I., Wallechinsky, D., & Wallace, A. *The people's almanac presents the book of lists.* New York: William Morrow, 1977.

Wallace, J., & Sadalla, E. Behavioral consequences of transgression: I. The effects of social recognition. *Journal of Experimental Social Psychology,* 1966, *1,* 187–194.

Wallach, M. A., Kogan, N., & Bem, D. J. Group influence on individual risk taking. *Journal of Abnormal and Social Psychology,* 1962, *65,* 75–86.

Wallach, M. A., Kogan, N., & Bem, D. J. Diffusion of responsibility and level of risk taking in groups. *Journal of Abnormal and Social Psychology,* 1964, *68,* 263–274.

Wallach, M. A., & Wing, C. Is risk a value? *Journal of Personality and Social Psychology,* 1968, *9,* 101–106.

Walster, E. Did you ever see a beautiful conservative? A note. (Mimeographed.) University of Wisconsin, Madison, 1971.

Walster, E. The effect of self-esteem on romantic liking. *Journal of Experimental Social Psychology,* 1965, *1,* 184–197.

Walster, E. The temporal sequence of postdecision processes. In L. Festinger et al., *Conflict, decision, and dissonance.* Stanford, Calif.: Stanford University Press, 1964.

Walster, E., Aronson, V., Abrahams, D., & Rottman, L. Importance of physical attractiveness in dating behavior. *Journal of Personality and Social Psychology,* 1966, *4,* 508–516.

Walster, E., Traupman, J., & Walster, G. W. Equity and extramarital sex. *The Archives of Sexual Behavior,* 1979.

Walster, E., Walster, G. W., & Berscheid, E. *Equity, theory and research.* Boston: Allyn & Bacon, 1978.

Walster, E., Walster, G. W., Piliavin, J., & Schmidt, L. "Playing hard to get": Understanding an elusive phenomenon. *Journal of Personality and Social Psychology*, 1973, *26*, 113–121.

Walster, E., Walster, G. W., & Traupman, J. Equity and premarital sex. *Journal of Personality and Social Psychology*, 1979, *36*, 82–92.

Walters, G. C., & Grusec, J. E. *Punishment.* San Francisco: W. H. Freeman, 1977.

Walters, R. H. Implications of laboratory studies of aggression for the control and regulation of violence. *Annals of the American Academy of Political and Social Science*, 1966, *364*, 60–72.

Ward, C. D. Attitude and involvement in the absolute judgment of attitude statements. *Journal of Personality and Social Psychology*, 1966, *4*, 465–476.

Waterman, C. K., & Katkin, E. S. The energizing (dynamogenic) effect of cognitive dissonance on task performance. *Journal of Personality and Social Psychology*, 1967, *6*, 126–131.

Watson, J. B. *Psychology from the standpoint of a behaviorist.* New York: J. B. Lippincott, 1919.

Watts, W. A., & Holt, L. E. Persistence of opinion change induced under conditions of forewarning and distraction. *Journal of Personality and Social Psychology*, 1979, *37*, 778–789.

Watzlawick, P. *How real is real? Confusion, disinformation, communication.* New York: Random House, 1976.

Weary, G. Examination of affect and egotism as mediators of bias in causal attributions. *Journal of Personality and Social Psychology*, 1980, *38*, 348–357.

Webb, E. J., Campbell, D. T., Schwartz, R. D., & Sechrest, L. *Unobtrusive measures: Nonreactive research in the social sciences.* Chicago: Rand McNally, 1966.

Webb, S. D. The meaning, measurement and interchangeability of density and crowding indices. *Australian and New Zealand Journal of Sociology*, 1975, *11*, 60–62.

Webster, S. W. The influence of interracial contact on social acceptance in a newly integrated school. *Journal of Educational Psychology*, 1961, *52*, 292–296.

Wegner, D. M., & Shaefer, D. The concentration of responsibility: An objective self-awareness analysis of group size effects in helping situations. *Journal of Personality and Social Psychology*, 1978, *36*, 147–155.

Weick, K. E. Reduction of cognitive dissonance through task enhancement and effort expenditure. *Journal of Abnormal and Social Psychology*, 1964, *68*, 533–539.

Weick, K. E. The concept of equity in the perception of pay. *Administrative Science Quarterly*, 1966, *11*, 414–439.

Weick, K. E. *The social psychology of organizing.* Reading, Mass.: Addison-Wesley, 1969.

Weigel, R. H., & Cook, S. W. Participation in decision-making: A determinant of interpersonal attraction in cooperating interra-

cial groups. *International Journal of Group Tension*, 1975, *5*, 179–195.

Weigel, R. H., & Newman, L. S. Increasing attitude-behavior correspondence by broadening the scope of the behavioral measure. *Journal of Personality and Social Psychology*, 1976, *33*, 793–802.

Weigel, R. H., Vernon, D. T. A., & Tognacci, L. N. The specificity of the attitude as a determinant of attitude-behavior congruence. *Journal of Personality and Social Psychology*, 1974, *30*, 724–728.

Weigel, R. H., Wiser, P. L., & Cook, S. W. The impact of cooperative learning experiences on cross-ethnic relations and attitudes. *Journal of Social Issues*, 1975, *31*, 219–244.

Weiner, B., Frieze, I., Kukla, A., Reed, L., Rest, S., & Rosenbaum, R. M. *Perceiving the causes of success and failure.* Morristown, N.J.: Silver Burdett/General Learning Press, 1971.

Weiner, B., Russell, D., & Lerman, D. Affective consequences of causal ascriptions. In T. H. Harvey, W. Ickes, & R. F. Kidd (Eds.), *New directions in attribution research* (Vol. 2). Hillsdale, N.J.: Lawrence Erlbaum, 1978.

Weiner, B., Russell, D., & Lerman, D. The cognition-emotion process in achievement-related contexts. *Journal of Personality and Social Psychology*, 1979, *37*, 1211–1220.

Weiss, L., & Lowenthal, M. F. Life course perspectives on friendship. In M. F. Lowenthal, M. Thurnher, & D. Chiriboga (Eds.), *Four stages of life.* San Francisco: Jossey-Bass, 1975.

Weiss, R. F., Buchanan, W., Altstatt, L., & Lombardo, J. P. Altruism is rewarding. *Science*, 1971, *171*, 1262–1263.

Weiss, R. F., & Miller, F. G. The drive theory of social facilitation. *Psychological Review*, 1971, *78*, 44–57.

Weiss, R. S. *Loneliness: The experience of emotional and social isolation.* Cambridge, Mass.: M.I.T. Press, 1973.

Weissbrod, C. Noncontingent warmth induction, cognitive style and children's imitative donation and rescue effort behaviors. *Journal of Personality and Social Psychology*, 1976, *34*, 274–281.

Wellens, A. R., & Thistlethwaite, D. L. Comparison of three theories of cognitive balance. *Journal of Personality and Social Psychology*, 1971, *20*, 82–92.

Wells, G. L. Asymmetric attributions for compliance: Reward vs. punishment. *Journal of Experimental Social Psychology*, 1980, *16*, 47–60.

Wells, G. L., & Harvey, J. Do people use consensus information in making causal attributions? *Journal of Personality and Social Psychology*, 1978, *35*, 279–293.

Werner, C., & Parmalee, P. Similarity of activity preferences among friends: Those who play together stay together. *Social Psychology Quarterly*, 1979, *42*, 62–66.

Werner, P. D. Personality and attitude-activism correspondence. *Journal of Personality and Social Psychology*, 1978, *36*, 1375–1390.

Werner, P. D., & Middlestadt, S. E. Factors in the use of oral contraceptives by young women. *Journal of Applied Social Psychology*, 1979, *9*, 537–547.

West, S. G., & Brown, T. J. Physical attractiveness, the severity of the emergency and helping: A field experiment and interpersonal simulations. *Journal of Experimental Social Psychology*, 1975, *11*, 531–538.

West, S. G., Gunn, S. P., & Chernicky, P. Ubiquitous Watergate: An attributional analysis. *Journal of Personality and Social Psychology*, 1975, *32*, 55–65.

West, S. G., Whitney, G., & Schnedler, R. Helping a motorist in distress: The effects of sex, race, and neighborhood. *Journal of Personality and Social Psychology*, 1975, *31*, 691–698.

Westermarck, E. *The origins and development of the moral ideas.* (Vol. 2). London: Macmillan, 1908.

Weyant, J. M. Effects of mood states, costs and benefits on helping. *Journal of Personality and Social Psychology*, 1978, *36*, 1169–1176.

Wheeler, D. D., & Janis, I. L. *A practical guide for making decisions.* New York: Free Press, 1980.

Wheeler, L., & Nezlek, T. Sex differences in social participation. *Journal of Personality and Social Psychology*, 1977, *35*, 742–754.

Wheeler, L., Shaver, K. G., Jones, R. A., Goethals, G. R., Cooper, J., Robinson, J. E., Gruder, C. L., & Butzine, K. W. Factors determining the choice of a comparison other. *Journal of Experimental Social Psychology*, 1969, *5*, 219–232.

White, C. B. Moral development in Bahamian school children: A cross-cultural examination of Kohlberg's stages of moral reasoning. *Developmental Psychology*, 1975, *11*, 535–536.

White, C. B., Bushnell, N., & Regnemer, J. L. Moral development in Bahamian school children: A 3-year examination of Kohlberg's stages of moral development. *Developmental Psychology*, 1978, *14*, 58–65.

White, L. A. Erotica and aggression: The influence of sexual arousal, positive affect, and negative affect on aggressive behavior. *Journal of Personality and Social Psychology*, 1979, *37*, 591–601.

Whitney, R. E. Agreement and positivity in pleasantness ratings of balanced and unbalanced social situations: A cross-cultural study. *Journal of Personality and Social Psychology*, 1971, *17*, 11–14.

Wholey, J. S. *Evaluation: Promise and performance.* Washington, D.C.: Urban Institute, 1979.

Whyte, M. K. *Small groups and political rituals in China.* Berkeley: University of California Press, 1974.

Whyte, W. F. *Streetcorner society*. Chicago: University of Chicago Press, 1943.

Wichman, H. Effects of isolation and communication on cooperation in a two-person game. *Journal of Personality and Social Psychology*, 1970, *16*, 114–120.

Wicker, A. W. Attitudes versus actions: The relationship of verbal and overt behavioral responses to attitude objects. *Journal of Social Issues*, 1969, *25*, 41–78.

Wicker, A. W. An examination of the "other variables" explanation of attitude-behavior inconsistency. *Journal of Personality and Social Psychology*, 1971, *19*, 18–30.

Wicker, A. W. Undermanning, performances and students' subjective experiences in behavior settings in large and small high schools. *Journal of Personality and Social Psychology*, 1968, *10*, 255–261.

Wicker, A. W. Undermanning theory and research: Implications for the psychological and behavioral effects of excess populations. *Representative Research in Social Psychology*, 1973, *4*, 185–206.

Wicker, A. W. *An introduction to ecological psychology*. Monterey, Calif.: Brooks/Cole, 1979.

Wicklund, R. A. *Freedom and reactance*. Potomac, Md.: Lawrence Erlbaum, 1974.

Wicklund, R. A. Objective self-awareness. In L. Berkowitz (Ed.), *Advances in experimental social psychology* (Vol. 9). New York: Academic Press, 1975.

Wicklund, R. A., & Brehm, J. W. *Perspectives on cognitive dissonance*. Hillsdale, N.J.: Lawrence Erlbaum, 1976.

Widom, C. S. Toward an understanding of female criminality. In B. A. Maher (Ed.), *Progress in experimental personality research*. New York: Academic Press, 1978.

Wiggins, J. A., Dill, F., & Schwartz, R. D. A status liability. *Sociometry*, 1965, *28*, 197–209.

Wilder, D. A. Reduction of intergroup discrimination through individuation of the outgroup. *Journal of Personality and Social Psychology*, 1978, *36*, 1361–1374.

Wilder, D. A., & Thompson, J. E. Intergroup contact with independent manipulations of in-group and out-group interaction. *Journal of Personality and Social Psychology*, 1980, *38*, 589–603.

Wilke, H., & Lanzetta, J. T. The obligation to help: The effects of amount of prior help on subsequent helping behavior. *Journal of Experimental Social Psychology*, 1970, *6*, 488–493.

Wilkinson, J., & Kipnis, D. Interfirm use of power. *Journal of Applied Psychology*, 1978, *63*, 315–320.

Williams, A. F. Factors associated with seat belt use in families. *Journal of Safety Research*, 1972, *4*, 133–138.

Williams, E. Medium or message: Communications medium as a determinant of interpersonal evaluation. *Sociometry*, 1975, *38*, 119–130.

Williams, J. E., & Bennett, S. M. The definition of sex stereotypes via the objective check list. *Sex Roles*, 1975, *1*, 327–337.

Williams, J. E., Best, D. L., & Boswell, D. A. The measurement of children's racial attitudes in the early school years. *Child Development*, 1975, *46*, 501–508.

Williams, R. B., Friedman, M., Glass, D. C., Herd, J. A., & Schneiderman, N. Section summary: Mechanics linking behavioral and pathophysiological processes. In T. M. Dembroski, S. Weiss, J. Shields, S. G. Haynes, & M. Feinleib (Eds.), *Coronary-prone behavior*. New York: Springer-Verlag New York, 1978.

Willis, R. H., & Joseph, M. L. Bargaining behavior: I. "Prominence" as a predictor of the outcome of games of agreement. *Journal of Conflict Resolution*, 1959, *3*, 102–113.

Wilson, E. O. *On human nature*. Cambridge, Mass.: Harvard University Press, 1978.

Wilson, L., & Rogers, R. W. The fire this time: Effects of race of target, insult and potential retaliation in black aggression. *Journal of Personality and Social Psychology*, 1975, *32*, 857–864.

Wilson, W. C. Development of ethnic attitudes in adolescence. *Child Development*, 1963, *34*, 247–256.

Wilson, W. R. Feeling more than we can know: Exposure effects without learning. *Journal of Personality and Social Psychology*, 1979, *37*, 811–821.

Winch, R. F. *Mate-selection: A study of complementary needs*. New York: Harper & Row, 1958.

Winch, R. F., Ktsanes, T., & Ktsanes, V. The theory of complementary needs in mate selection: An analytic and descriptive study. *American Sociological Review*, 1954, *19*, 241–249.

Winer, D. M., Walkley, R. P., Pinkerton, T. C., & Tayback, M. *The housing environment and family life*. Baltimore: Johns Hopkins University Press, 1962.

Winsborough, H. The social consequences of high population density. *Law and Contemporary Problems*, 1965, *30*, 120–126.

Winter, D. G. *The power motive*. New York: Free Press, 1973.

Winter, D. G., & Green, D. L. Motives, involvements, and leadership among black college students. *Journal of Personality*, 1971, *39*, 319–332.

Wish, M., Deutsch, M., & Kaplan, S. J. Perceived dimensions of interpersonal relations. *Journal of Personality and Social Psychology*, 1976, *33*, 409–420.

Wishner, T. Reanalysis of "impressions of personality." *Psychological Review*, 1960, *67*, 96–112.

Wohlwill, J. F. Environmental aesthetics: The environment as a source of affect. In I. Altman & J. F. Wohlwill (Eds.), *Human behavior and environment* (Vol. 1). New York: Plenum, 1976.

Wolf, S. *The stomach*. New York: Oxford University Press, 1965.

Wolf, T. M., & Cheyne, T. A. Persistence of effects of live behavioral, televised behavioral and live verbal models on resistance to deviation. *Child Development*, 1972, *43*, 1429–1436.

Wolfgang, A., & Wolfgang, J. Exploration of attitudes via physical interpersonal distance toward the obese, drug users, homosexuals, police and other marginal figures. *Journal of Clinical Psychology*, 1971, *27*, 510–512.

Women on Words and Images. *Dick and Jane as victims: Sex stereotyping in children's reading*. Princeton, N.J.: Women on Words and Images, 1972.

Worchel, P. Trust and distrust. In W. G. Austin, & S. Worchel, *The social psychology of intergroup relations*. Monterey, Calif.: Brooks/Cole, 1979.

Worchel, S. The effect of three types of arbitrary thwarting on the instigation to aggression. *Journal of Personality*, 1974, *42*, 301–318.

Worchel, S., & Andreoli, V. A. Attribution of causality as a means of restoring behavioral freedom. *Journal of Personality and Social Psychology*, 1974, *29*, 237–245.

Worchel, S., Andreoli, V. A., & Folger, R. Intergroup cooperation and intergroup attraction: The effect of previous interaction and outcome of combined effort. *Journal of Experimental Social Psychology*, 1977, *13*, 131–140.

Worchel, S., Arnold, S., & Harrison, W. Aggression and power restoration: The effects of identifiability and timing on aggressive behavior. *Journal of Experimental Social Psychology*, 1978, *14*, 43–52.

Worchel, S., Lind, E., & Kaufman, K. Evaluations of group products as a function of expectations of group longevity, outcome of competition, and publicity of evaluations. *Journal of Personality and Social Psychology*, 1975, *31*, 1089–1097.

Worchel, S., & Norvell, N. Effect of perceived environmental conditions during cooperation on intergroup attraction. *Journal of Personality and Social Psychology*, 1980, *38*, 764–772.

Worchel, S., & Teddlie, C. The experience of crowding: A two-factor theory. *Journal of Personality and Social Psychology*, 1976, *34*, 30–40.

Word, C. O., Zanna, M. P., & Cooper, J. The nonverbal mediation of self-fulfilling prophecies in interracial interaction. *Journal of Experimental Social Psychology*, 1974, *10*, 109–120.

Worthy, M., Gary, A., & Kahn, G. Self disclosure as an exchange process. *Journal of Personality and Social Psychology*, 1969, *13*, 59–63.

Wortman, C. B., Adesman, P., Herman, E., & Greenberg, R. Self disclosure: An attributional perspective. *Journal of Personality and Social Psychology*, 1976, *33*, 184–191.

Wortman, C. B., & Brehm, J. W. Responses

to uncontrollable outcomes: An integration of reactance theory and the learned helplessness model. In L. Berkowitz (Ed.), *Advances in experimental social psychology* (Vol. 8). New York: Academic Press, 1975.

Wortman, C. B., Costanza, P. R., & Witt, T. R. Effect of anticipated performance on the attributions of causality to self and others. *Journal of Personality and Social Psychology*, 1973, *27*, 372–381.

Wrightsman, L. S. Effects of waiting with others on changes in level of felt anxiety. *Journal of Abnormal and Social Psychology*, 1960, *61*, 216–222.

Wrightsman, L. S. Personality and attitudinal correlates of trusting and trustworthy behaviors in a two-person game. *Journal of Personality and Social Psychology*, 1966, *4*, 328–332.

Wyer, R. S. Effects of incentive to perform well, group attraction and group acceptance on conformity in a judgmental task. *Journal of Personality and Social Psychology*, 1966, *4*, 21–27.

Wyer, R. S. Changes in meaning and halo effects in personality impression formation. *Journal of Personality and Social Psychology*, 1974, *29*, 829–835.

Wyer, R. S., & Srull, T. K. The processing of social stimulus information: A conceptual integration. In R. Hastie, T. M. Ostrom, E. B. Ebbeson, R. S. Wyer, D. L. Hamilton, & D. E. Carlston (Eds.), *Personal memory: The cognitive basis of social perception*. Hillsdale, N.J.: Lawrence Erlbaum, 1980.

Wynne-Edwards, V. C. *Animal dispersion in relation to social behavior*. Edinburgh: Oliver & Boyd, 1962.

Wynne-Edwards, V. C. Self-regulating systems in populations of animals. *Science*, 1965, *147*, 1543–1548.

Y

Yancy, W. Architecture, interaction and social control: The case of a large-scale housing project. In J. F. Wohlwill & D. H. Carson (Eds.), *Environment and the social sciences: Perspectives and applications*. Washington, D.C.: American Psychological Association, 1972.

Yukl, G. A., Malone, M. P., Hayslip, B., & Pamin, T. A. The effects of time pressure and issue settlement order on integrative bargaining. *Sociometry*, 1976, *39*, 277–281.

Z

Zaidel, S. F., & Mehrabian, A. The ability to communicate and infer positive and negative attitudes facially and vocally. *Journal of Experimental Research in Personality*, 1969, *3*, 233–241.

Zajonc, R. B. *Structure and cognitive field*. Unpublished doctoral dissertation, University of Michigan, Ann Arbor, 1954.

Summarized in The process of cognitive tuning in communication. *Journal of Abnormal and Social Psychology*, 1960, *61*, 159–167.

Zajonc, R. B. Social facilitation. *Science*, 1965, *149*, 269–274.

Zajonc, R. B. Family configuration and intelligence. *Science*, 1976, *192*, 227–236.

Zajonc, R. B. Feeling and thinking: Preferences need no inferences. *American Psychologist*, 1980, *35*, 151–175. (a)

Zajonc, R. B. Compresence. In P. B. Paulus (Ed.), *Psychology of group influence*. Hillsdale, N.J.: Lawrence Erlbaum, 1980. (b)

Zajonc, R. B., Crandall, R., Kail, R. B., & Swap, W. C. Effect of extreme exposure frequencies on different affective ratings of stimuli. *Perceptual and Motor Skills*, 1974, *38*, 667–678.

Zajonc, R. B., Heingartner, A., & Herman, E. M. Social enhancement and impairment of performance in the cockroach. *Journal of Personality and Social Psychology*, 1969, *13*, 83–92.

Zajonc, R. B., Markus, H. M., & Markus, G. B. The birth order puzzle. *Journal of Personality and Social Psychology*, 1979, *37*, 1325–1341.

Zajonc, R. B., Markus, H. M., & Wilson, W. R. Exposure effects and associative learning. *Journal of Experimental Social Psychology*, 1974, *10*, 248–263.

Zajonc, R. B., Shaver, P., Tavris, C., & Van Kreveld, D. Exposure, satiation and stimulus discriminability. *Journal of Personality and Social Psychology*, 1972, *21*, 270–280.

Zajonc, R. B., Swap, W. C., Harrison, A., & Roberts, P. Limiting conditions of the exposure effect: Satiation and relativity. *Journal of Personality and Social Psychology*, 1971, *18*, 384–391.

Zalba, S. R. The abused child: A typology for classification and treatment. *Social Work*, 1967, *12*, 70–79.

Zaleska, M. Some experimental results: Majority influence on group decisions. In H. Brandstätter, J. H. Davis, & H. Schuler (Eds.), *Dynamics of group decisions*. Beverly Hills, Calif.: Sage Publications, 1978.

Zand, D. E. Trust and managerial problem-solving. *Administrative Science Quarterly*, 1972, *17*, 229–239.

Zander, A. *Motives and goals in groups*. New York: Academic Press, 1971.

Zander, A. *Groups at work*. San Francisco: Jossey-Bass, 1977.

Zander, A., & Havelin, A. Social comparison and interpersonal attraction. *Human Relations*, 1960, *13*, 21–32.

Zander, A., & Wolfe, D. Administrative rewards and coordination among committee members. *Administrative Science Quarterly*, 1964, *9*, 50–69.

Zanna, M. P., & Hamilton, D. L. Attribute dimension and patterns of trait inferences. *Psychonomic Science*, 1972, *27*, 353–354.

Zanna, M. P., Higgins, E. T., & Taves, P. A.

Is dissonance phenomenologically aversive? *Journal of Experimental Social Psychology*, 1976, *12*, 530–538.

Zanna, M. P., Kiesler, C. A., & Pilkonis, P. A. Positive and negative attitudinal affect established by classical conditioning. *Journal of Personality and Social Psychology*, 1970, *14*, 321–328.

Zanna, M. P., Olson, J. M., & Fazio, R. H. Attitude behavior consistency: An individual difference perspective. *Journal of Personality and Social Psychology*, 1980, *38*, 432–440.

Zanna, M. P., & Pack, S. J. On the self-fulfilling nature of apparent sex differences in behavior. *Journal of Experimental Social Psychology*, 1975, *11*, 583–591.

Zavalloni, M., & Cook, S. W. Influence of judge's attitudes on ratings of favorableness of statements about a social group. *Journal of Personality and Social Psychology*, 1965, *1*, 43–54.

Zborowski, M., & Herzog, E. *Life is with people*. New York: International Universities Press, 1952.

Zehner, R. Neighborhood and community satisfaction: A report on new towns and less planned suburbs. In J. F. Wohlwill & D. H. Carson (Eds.), *Environment and the social sciences: Perspectives and applications*. Washington, D.C.: American Psychological Association, 1972.

Ziller, R. C. Group dialectics: The dynamics of groups over time. *Human Development*, 1977, *20*, 293–308.

Zillmann, D. *Hostility and aggression*. Hillsdale, N.J.: Lawrence Erlbaum, 1978.

Zillmann, D., Johnson, R. C., & Day, K. D. Attribution of apparent arousal and proficiency of recovery from sympathetic activation affecting activation transfer to aggressive behavior. *Journal of Experimental Social Psychology*, 1974, *10*, 503–515.

Zillmann, D., Katcher, A. H., & Milavsky, B. Excitation transfer from physical exercise to subsequent aggressive behavior. *Journal of Experimental Social Psychology*, 1972, *8*, 247–259.

Zillmann, D., & Sapolsky, B. S. What mediates the effect of mild erotica on hostile behavior by males? *Journal of Personality and Social Psychology*, 1977, *35*, 587–596.

Zimbardo, P. G. The human choice: Individuation, reason and order versus deindividuation, impulse and chaos. In W. J. Arnold & D. Levine (Eds.), *Nebraska Symposium on Motivation* (Vol. 16). Lincoln: University of Nebraska Press, 1969.

Zimbardo, P. G. *Shyness: What it is, what to do about it*. Reading, Mass.: Addison-Wesley, 1977.

Zimbardo, P. G., & Ebbeson, E. B. *Influencing attitudes and changing behavior*. Reading, Mass.: Addison-Wesley, 1969.

Zimbardo, P. G., & Formica, R. Emotional comparison and self-esteem as determinants of affiliation. *Journal of Personality*, 1963, *31*, 141–162.

Zimbardo, P. G., Pilkonis, P. A., & Norwood, R. M. *The silent prison of shyness.* Office of Naval Research Technical Report (No. Z-17). Stanford University, Stanford, Calif., November 1974.

Zimring, F. E. Firearms and federal law: The Gun Control Act of 1968. In G. V. Glass (Ed.), *Evaluation studies review annual* (Vol. 1). Beverly Hills, Calif.: Sage Publications, 1976.

Zipf, S. G. Resistance and conformity under reward and punishment. *Journal of Abnormal and Social Psychology,* 1960, *61,* 102–109.

Zlutnick, S., & Altman, I. Crowding and human behavior. In J. F. Wohlwill & D. H. Carson (Eds.), *Environment and the social sciences: Perspectives and applications.* Washington, D.C.: American Psychological Association, 1972.

Zuckerman, M. Belief in a just world and altruistic behavior. *Journal of Personality and Social Psychology,* 1975, *31,* 972–976.

Zuckerman, M. Actions and occurrences in Kelley's cube. *Journal of Personality and Social Psychology,* 1978, *36,* 647–656.

Zuckerman, M. Attribution of success and failure revisited, or: The motivational bias is alive and well in attribution theory. *Journal of Personality,* 1979, *47,* 245–287.

Zuckerman, M., Porac, J., Lathin, D., Smith, R., & Deci, E. On the importance of self-determination for intrinsically motivated behavior. *Personality and Social Psychology Bulletin,* 1978, *4,* 443–451.

Zuckerman, M., & Reis, H. T. Comparison of three models for predicting altruistic behavior. *Journal of Personality and Social Psychology,* 1978, *36,* 498–510.

Zuroff, D. C. Learned helplessness in humans: An analysis of learning processes and the roles of individual and situational differences. *Journal of Personality and Social Psychology,* 1980, *30,* 130–146.

Zyzanski, S. J., & Jenkins, C. D. Basic dimensions within the coronary-prone behavior pattern. *Journal of Chronic Diseases,* 1970, *22,* 781–795.

COPYRIGHTS AND ACKNOWLEDGMENTS

Tables

Box 2-1 Ross, L., Greene, D., & House, P. The "false consensus effect": an egocentric bias in social perception and attribution processes. *Journal of Experimental Social Psychology*, 1977, *13*, 273–301. **Box 2-2** Kelley, H. H. The warm-cold variable in first impressions of persons. *Journal of Personality*, 1950, *18*, 431–439. Copyright 1950 by Duke University Press. **Box 2-3** Schiltz, M. E. *Public Attitudes toward Social Security 1935-1956*. Reprinted by permission of the Social Security Administration.

3-1 Wilson, W. R. Feeling more than we can know: exposure effects without learning. *Journal of Personality and Social Psychology*, 1979, *37*, 811–821. Copyright 1979 by the American Psychological Association. Reprinted by permission. **3-2** Hoyt, M., & Raven, B. H. Birth order and the 1971 earthquake. *Journal of Personality and Social Psychology*, 1973, *38*, 123–130. Copyright 1973 by the American Psychological Association. Reprinted by permission. **3-3** Rands, M., & Levinger, G. Implicit theories of relationship: an intergenerational study. *Journal of Personality and Social Psychology*, 1979, *37*, 645–661. Copyright 1979 by the American Psychological Association. Reprinted by permission. **Box 3-1** Gross, A. E., & Crofton, C. What is good is beautiful. *Sociometry*, 1977, *40*, 89. Reprinted by permission of the authors and the American Sociological Association. **Box 3-3** Rubin, Z. Measurement of romantic love. *Journal of Personality and Social Psychology*, 1970, *16*, 265–273. Copyright 1970 by the American Psychological Association. Reprinted by permission.

4-1 Rosenkrantz, P., Vogel, S., Bee, H., Broverman, I., & Broverman, D. M. Sex-role stereotypes and self-concepts in college students. *Journal of Personality and Social Psychology*, 1968, *32*, 287–295. Copyright 1968 by the American Psychological Association. Reprinted by permission. **4-2** From *Readings in Social Psychology* edited by Theodore M. Newcomb & Eugene L. Hartley. Copyright 1947 by Henry Holt and Company, Inc. Renewed © 1975 by Theodore M. Newcomb and Eugene L. Hartley. Adapted by permission of Holt, Rinehart and Winston. **4-3** Karlins, M., Coffman, T. L., & Walters, G. On the fading of social stereotypes: studies in three generations of college students. *Journal of Personality and Social Psychology*, 1969, *13*, 1–16. Copyright 1969 by the American Psychological Association. Reprinted by permission. **4-4** Based on data from Peabody, D. Reprinted by permission of the author. **4-5** From Deutsch, M., & Collins, M. *Interracial Housing*, the University of Minnesota Press, Minneapolis. Copyright © 1951 by the University of Minnesota.

6-1 Hoffman, M. L., & Saltzstein, H. D. Parent discipline and the child's moral development. *Journal of Personality and Social Psychology*, 1967, *5*, 45–47. Copyright 1967 by the American Psychological Association. Reprinted by permission. **6-3** Adapted from *Studies in the Nature of Character* by Hugh Hartshorne & Mark A. May. Reprinted by Arno Press Inc., 1975. **6-4** Bem, D. J., & Allen, A. On predicting some of the people some of the time: the search for cross-situational consistencies in behavior. *Psychological Review*, 1974, *81*, 506-520. Copyright 1974 by the American Psychological Association. Reprinted by permission.

7-1 Gergen, K. J., & Gergen, M. M. International assistance from the psychological perspective. *Yearbook of World Affairs 1971*, 1972, *25*, 87–103. Reprinted by permission of the authors.

8-1 Brown, P., & Elliott, R. Control of aggression in a nursery school class. *Journal of Experimental Child Psychology*, 1965, *2*, 103–107. **8-2** Taylor, S. P., Lubetkia, A. T., Gammon, C. B., Cranston, J. W., Vardares, R. M., & Rawitch, A. B. The effects of alcohol and delta-9-tetra hydrocannabinal on human physical aggression. *Aggressive Behavior*, 1976, *2*, 153–161.

9-2 Keyes, R. *The Height of Your Life.* Copyright © 1980 by Ralph Keyes. Reprinted by permission of Little, Brown and Company and The Sterling Lord Agency. **9-3** Schulz, R. Control, predictability and the institutionalized aged. *Journal of Personality and Social Psychology*, 1976, *33*, 563–573. Copyright 1976 by the American Psychological Association. Reprinted by permission. **9-4** Kipnis, D. Does power corrupt? *Journal of Personality and Social Psychology*, 1972, *24*, 33–41. Copyright 1972 by the American Psychological Association. Reprinted by permission.

10-1 Milgram, S. *Obedience to Authority*, 1974, 35–36 and 60–61. Copyright © 1974 by Stanley Milgram. Reprinted by permission of Harper & Row, Publishers, Inc. and Tavistock Publications Ltd. **10-2** Tesser, A., Rosen, S., & Conlee, M. News valence and available recipient as determinants of news transmission. *Sociometry*, 1972, *35*, 619–628. Reprinted by permission of the authors and the American Sociological Association. **Box 10-1** From *Personality and Social Change* by Theodore M. Newcomb. Copyright 1943 by Theodore M. Newcomb. Renewed © 1971 by Theodore M. Newcomb. Adapted by permission of Holt, Rinehart and Winston.

11-1 Deutsch, M., & Krauss, R. M. The effect of threat upon interpersonal bargaining. *Journal of Personality and Social Psychology*, 1960, *61*, 181–189. Copyright 1960 by the American Psychological Association. Reprinted by permission.

12-2 Zajonc, R. B. Social facilitation. *Science*, 1965, *149*, 269–274. Copyright 1965 by the American Association for the Advancement of Science. Reprinted by permission. **12-3** Dashiell, D. F. Experimental studies of the influence of social situations on the behavior of individual human adults. *The Handbook of Social Psychology*, Ed. by C. Murchison, 1935. Reprinted by permission of Clark University Press.

13-1 From *Environmental Psychology: Man and His Physical Setting* edited by Harold M. Proshansky, William H. Ittelson, & Leanne G. Rivlin. Copyright © 1970 by Holt, Rinehart and Winston, Inc. Adapted by permission of Holt, Rinehart and Winston. **13-2** Wicker, A. W. Undermanning performance and students' subjective experiences in behavior settings of large and small high schools. *Journal of Personality and Social Psychology*, 1968, *10*, 255–261. Copyright 1968 by the American Psychological Association. Reprinted by permission. **13-3** Reprinted with permission from *Journal of Psychosomatic Research*, 1967, *11*, 213–218, Holmes, T. H., & Rahe, R. H. The social readjustment rating scale. Copyright 1967, Pergamon Press, Ltd. **Box 13-2** Stroebe, W., Stroebe, M., Gergen, K. J., and Gergen, M. M. The effects of bereavement on mortality, a social psychological analysis. In J. R. Eiser (Ed.), *Social Psychology and Behavioral Medicine.* Reprinted by permission of John Wiley & Sons, Ltd.

Figures

1-1 Berglas, S., & Jones, E. E. Drug choice as a self-handicapping strategy in response to noncontingent success. *Journal of Personality and Social Psychology*, 1978, *36*, 405–417. Copyright 1978 by the American Psychological Association. Reprinted by permission.

2-1 Pepitone, A. Motivation effects in social perception. *Human Relations*, 1949, *3*, 57–76. Copyright 1949 by the Plenum Publishing Corporation. **2-2** Rosenberg, S., Nelson, G., & Vivekanathan, P. S. A multidimensional approach to the structure of personality impressions. *Journal of Personality and Social Psychology*, 1968, *9*, 282–294. Copyright 1968 by the American Psychological Association. Reprinted by permission. **2-3** Gergen, K. J. The effects of interaction goals and personalistic feedback on presentation of self. *Journal of Personality and Social Psychology*, 1965, *1*, 413–425. Copyright 1965 by the American Psychological Association. Reprinted by permission. **2-4** Schachter, S., & Singer, J. L. Cognitive, social and physiological determinants of emotional state. *Psychological Review*, 1962, *65*, 121–128. Copyright 1962 by the American Psychological Association. Reprinted by permission.

3-1 Sommers, R. *Personal Space: The Behavioral Analysis of Design.* © 1969, p. 33. Reprinted by permission of Prentice-Hall, Inc., Englewood Cliffs, New Jersey. **3-2** Kiesler, S. B., & Baral, R. The search for a romantic partner: The effects of self-esteem and physical attractiveness on romantic behavior. In K. J. Gergen & D. Marlow (Eds.) *Personality and Social Behavior.* Reading, Massachusetts: Addison-Wesley, 1970, 155–166. Reprinted by permission of the authors. **3-3** Levinger, G., & Snoek, J. D. *Attraction in Relationships.* New York: General Learning Press, 1972. Copyright to authors, 1978. **3-4** Blood, R. O. *Love Match and Arranged Marriages.* Copyright © 1967 by the Free Press, a division of Macmillan Publishing Co., Inc.

4-1 From Teacher expectations for the disadvantaged by R. Rosenthal and L. F. Jacobson. Copyright © 1968 by Scientific American, Inc. All rights reserved. **4-3** Campbell, A. *White Attitudes toward Black People.* Ann Arbor: Institute for Social Research, the University of Michigan, 1971. **4-4** Mednick, M. Social change and sex-role inertia: The case of the kibbutz. In M. Mednick, S. Tangri, & L. Hoffman (Eds.) *Women and Achievement.* Washington, D.C.: Hemisphere Publishing Corporation.

5-1 Hovland, C., & Weiss, W. The influence of source credibility on communication effectiveness. *Public Opinion Quarterly*, 1951, *15*, 635–650. **5-2** McGuire, W. J., & Papageorgis, D. The relative effect of various types of prior belief-defense in producing immunity against persuasion. *Journal of Abnormal and Social Psychology*, 1961, *62*, 327–337. Copyright 1961 by the American Psychological Association. Reprinted by permission. **5-3** Brehm, J. W. Post-decision change in the desirability of alternatives. *Journal of Abnormal and Social Psychology*, 1956, *52*, 384–389. Copyright 1956 by the American Psychological Association. Reprinted by permission. **5-4** Calder, B. J., Insko, C. A., & Yandell, M., The relation of cognitive and memorial processes to persuasion in simulated jury trial. *Journal of Applied Psychology*, 1974, *4*, 62–93. Copyright 1974 by the American Psychological Association. Reprinted by permission. **5-5** Tesser, A., & Conlee, M. C. Some effects of time and thought on attitude polarization. *Journal of Personality and Social Psychology*, 1975, *31*, 262–270. Copyright 1975 by the American Psychological Association. Reprinted by permission.

6-1 Bandura, A., & McDonald, F. J. Shaping children's moral judgments. *Journal of Abnormal and Social Psychology*, 1963, *67*, 274–281. Copyright 1963 by the American Psychological Association. Reprinted by permission.

7-1 Krebs, D. Empathy and altruism. *Journal of Personality and Social Psychology*, 1975, *32*, 1134–1146. Copyright 1975 by the American Psychological Association. Reprinted by permission. **7-2** From *Popular Conceptions of Mental Health: Their Development and Change* by Jum C. Nunnally, Jr. Copyright © 1961 by Holt, Rinehart and Winston, Inc. Reprinted by permission of Holt, Rinehart and Winston. **7-3** Bibb Latané & John M. Darley. *The Unresponsive Bystander: Why Doesn't He Help?* © 1970, p. 97. Reprinted by permission of Prentice-Hall, Inc., Englewood Cliffs, N.J. **7-4** Gergen, K. J., Ellsworth, P., Maslach, C., & Siepel, M. Obligation, donor resources and reactions to aid in a three-nation study. *Journal of Personality and Social Psychology*, 1975, *31*, 390-400. Copyright 1975 by the American Psychological Association. Reprinted by permission.

8-1 Donnerstein, M., & Donnerstein, E. Modeling in the control of interracial aggression: The problem of generality. *Journal of Personality*, 1977, *45*, 100–116. Copyright 1977 by Duke University Press. **8-2** Eron, L. D., Huesmann, L. R., Lefkowitz, M., & Walder, L. O. Does television violence cause aggression? *American Psychologist*, 1972, *27*, 253–263. Copyright 1972 by the American Psychological Association. Reprinted by permission. **8-3** Harris, M. B. Mediators between frustration and aggression in a field experiment. *Journal of Experimental Social Psychology*, 1974, *10*, 561–571. **8-4** Zillmann, D., Johnson, R. C., & Day, K. D. Attribution of apparent arousal and proficiency of recovery from sympathetic activation affecting excitation transfer to aggressive behavior. *Journal of Experimental Social Psychology*, 1974, *10*, 503–515.

9-1 From *Research in Behavior Modification, New Developments and Implications* by L. Krasner & L. P. Ullmann (Eds.). Copyright © 1965 by Holt, Rinehart and Winston, Inc. Reprinted by permission of the author. **9-2** Fiedler, F. E. The contingency model and the dynamics of the leadership process. In L. Berkowitz (Ed.) *Advances in Experimental Social Psychology.* New York: Academic Press, 1978, 59–112. **9-3** Davies, J. C. Toward a theory of revolution. *American Sociological Review*, 1962, *27*, 5–19. Reprinted by permission of the author and the American Sociological Association.

10-2 Milgram, S. *Obedience to Authority*, 1974, 30, 35. Copyright © 1974 by Stanley Milgram. Reprinted by permission of Harper & Row Publishers, Inc. and Tavistock Publications Ltd. **10-3** Bartlett, F. C. *Remembering: A Study in Experimental and Social Psychology.* Cambridge University Press, 1932.

11-2 Sidowski, J. B., Wykoff, L. B., & Tabory, L. The influence of reinforcement and punishment in a minimal social situation. *Journal of Abnormal and Social Psychology*, 1956, *52*, 115–119. Copyright 1956 by the American Psychological Association. Reprinted by permission. **11-3** Foa, U. G., Interpersonal and economic resources. *Science*, 1971, *171*, 345–351, 29, January 1971. Copyright 1971 by the American Association for the Advancement of Science. Reprinted by permission. **11-4** Gergen, K. J., Morse, S. J., & Bode, K. A. Over-paid or over-worked? Cognitive and behavioral reactions to inequitable rewards. *Journal of Applied Social Psychology*, 1974, *4*, 259–274. Copyright 1974 by the American Psychological Association. Reprinted by permission. **11-6** Deutsch, M., & Krauss, R. M. The effect of threat upon interpersonal bargaining. *Journal of Abnormal and Social Psychology*, 1960, *61*, 181–189. Copyright 1960 by the American Psychological Association. Reprinted by permission.

12-2 Leavitt, J. J. Some effects of certain communications patterns on group performance. *Journal of Abnormal and Social Psychology*, 1951, *46*, 38–50. Copyright 1951 by the American Psychological Association. Reprinted by permission. **12-3** Hackman, J. R., & Morris, C. G. Group tasks, group interaction process, and group performance effectiveness: A review and proposed integration. In L. Berkowitz (Ed.) *Advances in Experimental Social Psychology.* New York: Academic Press, 1975.

13-1 Baum, A., & Valins, S. *Architecture and Social Behavior: Psychological Studies of Social Density.* Hillsdale, New Jersey: Lawrence Erlbaum, 1977. **13-2** Glass, D. C., & Singer, J. E. *Urban Stress.* New York: Academic Press, 1972. **13-3** Matthews, Jr., K. E., & Cannon, L. K. Environmental noise levels as a determinant of helping behavior. *Journal of Personality and Social Psychology*, 1975, *32*, 571–577. Copyright 1975 by the American Psychological Association. Reprinted by permission.

Pictures

Page 3 Ken Karp. **11** Clara Spain. **14** George Gardner. **16** Richard Amick. **22** Fritz Heider. **39** Susie Fitzhugh. **42** (4) courtesy Robert Karpen, (7) courtesy Debra Kase, (9) courtesy Dodie Shaw. **44** The National Gallery of Canada, Ottawa. **49, 50** left, UPI; right, Jim Anderson/Black Star. **71** George Gardner © 1979. **81, 83** Joel Gordon © 1980. **87** © Allan L. Price, Rapho/Photo Researchers, Inc. **89** Museo del Prado. **115** Mary Gergen. **119** Jim Holland/Stock, Boston. **122** Bettmann Archive. **132** © Hella Hammid, Rapho/Photo Researchers, Inc. **143** National Archives. **148** Charleen Bacigalupo. **152** Marlis Muller. **161** Paul Seder. **165** Skoogfors/Liaison/Gamma. **169** National Archives. **182** Wide World Photos. **186** UPI. **193** Lochon/Liaison/Gamma. **201** Girl Scouts USA. **205** Paul Seder. **208** Suzanne Szasz/Photo Researchers, Inc. **213** Roger Malloch © 1969, Magnum Photos. **223** Suzanne Szasz. **231** UPI. **241** Hugh Rogers/Monkmeyer Press Photo. **245** Paul Seder. **258** Michael Abramson. **260** Kenneth Siegel © 1980. **266** courtesy Children, Inc. **268** Gloria Karlson from Portogallo. **277** Richard Lawrence Stack/Black Star. **286** © 1976 Marjorie Pickens. **292** Joel Gordon. **296** De Sazo/Rapho/Photo Researchers, Inc. **306** George Gardner. **311** Owen Franken/Stock, Boston. **314** UPI. **316** Sipa Press from Black Star. **332** David M. Grossman. **336** Philip G. Zimbardo. **347, 350** Ellis Herwig/Stock, Boston. **356** FPG. **360** Stanley Milgram. **369** Wide World Photos. **375** Burt Glinn/Magnum. **383** Fred Lombardy. **393** © Chester Higgins/Rapho/Photo Researchers, Inc. **401** Wide World Photos. **405** Jean Boughton/Stock, Boston. **407** Joel Gordon. **413** Ed Gallob. **419** Harvey Stein. **424** Mitchell B. Reibel/Focus on Sports. **428** Bonnie Freer © 1978. **431** J. Martin Natvig. **433** John Timbers. **440** Bonnie Freer © 1978. **454** Skoogfors/Gamma/Liaison. **460** Wide World Photos. **462, 463** Barbara Pfeffer. **482** Peter Menzel/Stock, Boston. **484** Barbara Pfeffer.

NAME INDEX

Baron, P., 176
Baron, R. A., 176, 279, 280, 300, 303, 307, 490
Baron, R. S., 77
Bar-Tal, D., 91, 127, 242, 249, 275
Bartlett, F. C., 364, 365
Barton, E. M., 306, 331
Barton, W., 466
Bass, B. M., 321
Basseches, M., 227
Bateson, N., 315
Batson, D. C., 247
Bauer, R. A., 170, 483, 484
Baum, A., 463, 464, 479
Bauman, D. J., 249
Baumrind, D., 34, 363
Bayton, J. A., 138
Beach, F. A., 109
Beaman, A. L., 216
Beard, J. F., 409
Becker, E., 99
Becker, F. D., 422
Begum, B. O., 436
Belenky, M., 225
Bell, P. A., 307, 468, 489
Bellows, N., 70
Belmont, L., 481
Bem, D. J., 190, 191, 210, 235, 236, 288, 445, 446
Bem, S. L., 370, 371
Benassi, V. A., 334
Benedict, R., 393
Bennett, R. M., 300
Bennett, S., 125
Benton, A. A., 396
Berelson, B., 170
Berg, J. H., 370
Berg, K. S., 444, 451
Berger, P., 147
Berger, S. M., 245
Bergin, A. E., 72
Berglas, S., 17
Berk, R. A., 487
Berkowitz, L., 248, 249, 250, 252, 253, 258, 263, 264, 290, 291, 295, 297, 303, 306, 307, 315, 396
Berle, A., 339
Berman, J. J., 194
Bernard, L. L., 249
Bernstein, A. M., 69
Berscheid, E., 90, 91, 92, 94, 107, 114, 117, 167, 393, 394, 409, 417
Best, D. L., 131

Bevan, W., 379
Bickman, L., 194, 314, 480
Bigelow, D., 487
Biggers, J. L., 411
Billig, M., 138, 446
Birnbaum, M. H., 86, 163, 165
Bishop, D. W., 153, 425
Black, J., 264
Blake, R. R., 214, 446
Blanchard, F. A., 154, 423
Blau, P. M., 422, 425
Bliss, E., 281
Block, J., 236
Blood, R. O., 113–14
Blum, E. R., 205
Blum, J. M., 449
Blumberg, A., 194
Blumenthal, A. L., 21, 293
Bochner, S., 147
Bode, K. A., 395
Boehm, V., 411
Bogart, K., 411
Bohmer, C., 194
Bohrnsteadt, G. W., 92, 114, 394
Bond, J. R., 444
Bonoma, T. D., 404
Booker, A., 307
Booth, A., 476, 477, 480
Bootzin, R. B., 333
Borden, D., 327
Borgida, E., 49
Boris, J., 45
Boswell, D. A., 131
Bouffard, D., 49
Bourne, L. F., 45
Boutilier, R. G., 20
Bowers, K. S., 235
Bowman, C. H., 197
Boyanowsky, E. O., 377
Bradborn, N., 102
Braden, M., 181
Bradley, G. W., 68
Brady, J. V., 207
Bragg, B. W. E., 377
Braginsky, B., 25, 101, 103
Braginsky, D., 25, 103
Braiker, H. B., 108
Brain, R., 110
Braly, K. W., 145
Brand, R. J., 479
Brandstätter, H., 429
Brannon, R., 194
Bray, R. M., 132, 138, 441, 444
Brehm, J. W., 112, 168, 179, 183, 184, 185, 191, 192, 368, 370

Brewer, M. B., 136, 137, 138
Brickman, P., 70, 265, 269
Briggs, S. R., 409
Brigham, J. C., 135
Brinberg, D., 197
Brink, J. R., 98
Brislin, R. W., 6, 34
Brock, T. C., 167, 176, 199, 303, 388, 390
Brody, G. H., 123
Broll, L., 270
Bronfenbrenner, U., 151, 212, 487
Brookmire, D. A., 245
Broverman, I. K., 126
Brown, B. R., 399, 405, 438
Brown, C. T., 422
Brown, D. G., 124
Brown, H., 281
Brown, I. J., 129, 331, 333
Brown, M., 140
Brown, P., 283, 445
Brown, R. G., 317
Brown, R. W., 45
Brown, T. J., 253
Brown, V., 134, 170
Brownmiller, S., 194
Bryan, J. H., 204, 265
Bryant, B. M., 439
Buck, R. W., 101, 408, 414
Buckhout, R., 366
Bukoff, A., 167
Bunker, B. B., 129
Burger, J. M., 69
Burgess, E. W., 98, 109
Burgess, M., 302
Burgess, R. L., 107, 288
Burgess, T. O. G., 86
Burleson, J. A., 107
Burnstein, E., 189, 446
Burrowes, A., 215
Burtless, G., 487
Burton, R. V., 235
Burtt, H. E., 436
Bushnell, N., 225
Buss, A. H., 300, 307, 409
Buss, A. R., 225
Buss, E., 307
Butsch, R. J., 136
Byrne, D., 59, 95, 96, 132, 138, 444

C

Cacioppo, J. T., 166, 174
Calder, B. J., 187, 193, 211
Calhoun, J. B., 476

Krisher, H. P., 170
Kriss, M., 253
Kruglanski, A., 313
Krulewitz, J. E., 140, 141
Kryter, K., 467
Ksionsky, S., 96
Ktsanes, T., 97
Ktsanes, V., 97
Kuhn, D., 224
Kukla, R. A., 103
Kulik, J. A., 41
Kupers, C. J., 215
Kurtz, J., 415

L
Lacey, H., 7, 211
LaFrance, M., 371, 415, 417
Lakin, M., 453
Lambert, R., 446
Lamberth, J., 95, 132
Lamm, H., 445, 446
Lana, R. E., 37, 61
Lanckton, A. V., 374
Landis, C., 48
Landreth, C., 123
Landy, D., 91, 93, 295
Lane, R., 136, 171, 396
Langdon, F., 466
Langer, E., 249, 333, 480
Lanzetta, J. H., 247, 263, 396, 414
LaPiere, R. T., 139
L'Armand, K., 247
Larsen, K. S., 132
Larsson, K., 436
Lasater, T. M., 170
Latané, B., 255, 258, 259, 260, 261, 262, 271, 434, 436, 438, 440, 441
Latané, J. G., 63
Lauderdale, P., 433
Laughlin, P. R., 447
Lawler, E. E., 393, 422
Lawton, S. F., 307
Layton, B. D., 69
Lazarsfeld, P., 170
Lazarus, R. S., 74
Leavitt, H. J., 448, 449
Lefcourt, H. M., 334, 335
Lefebvre, L., 415
Leff, R., 206
Lefkowitz, M., 214
Leginsky, W., 447
Lehne, G. K., 140
Lehr, D. J., 436

Leik, R., 116
Leik, S. A., 116
Leister, A. F., 327
Lenihan, K. J., 487
Lenney, E., 371
Lenrow, B. B., 245, 267
Leon, M., 59
Leonard, R., 98
Lepage, A., 306
Lepper, M. R., 185, 206, 210
Lerman, D., 102
Lerner, M. J., 98, 252
Leshner, A. I., 281
Lessing, E. E., 130
Leventhal, G. W., 396
Leventhal, H., 76, 77, 167, 169
Levin, H., 136, 288
Levin, P. F., 248
Levine, C., 229
Levine, J. M., 185
Levine, M., 45
Levinger, G., 98, 106, 107, 108, 109, 112, 114
Levinson, D. J., 132
Levitt, E. E., 141
Levy, A. S., 261
Lewin, K., 21–24, 123, 188, 426, 456, 457
Lewin, M., 37
Lewis, S., 402
Lewis, W. H., 136
Leyens, J. P., 307
Lieb, R., 108
Lieberman, M. A., 426
Liebling, B. A., 438
Lief, A., 422
Likert, R., 142
Linder, D. E., 168
Lindskold, S., 327, 401
Linsenmeir, J. A. W., 125
Linville, P. W., 148, 149
Lipetz, M. E., 98
Lipinski, C. E., 101
Lippa, R., 409
Lippitt, R., 449–50
Lippmann, W., 146
Liverant, S., 334, 359
Livesley, W., 55
Lloyd, J. A., 476
Locksley, A., 371
Loftis, J., 77
Loftus, E. F., 45
Lombard, G. F. F., 425
Lombardo, J. P., 98

London, H., 244, 374
Loo, C., 476
Loomis, R. T., 468, 489
Lord, C. G., 41, 185
Lorenz, K., 280, 281, 308
Lott, A. J., 423, 428
Lott, B. E., 423, 428
Lourie, R. S., 285
Love, R., 176
Lowan, C. L., 246
Low-Beer, L., 465
Lowe, C. A., 69
Lowe, J., 366
Lowenthal, M. S., 112
Lubek, I., 280, 340
Lubinsky, R., 411
Luce, R. D., 398
Luchins, A. S., 61
Luckman, T., 147
Lumsdaine, A. A., 167
Lyman, S., 70
Lynch, J. G., 243
Lynne, D. B., 123

M
McAlister, L. B., 138
McArthur, L. A., 64
McArthur, L. Z., 134
McBride, L., 366
McBride, P., 357
McCallum, R., 478
Macaulay, J., 288, 303, 446
McCauley, C., 331
McClelland, D. C., 193, 345
McClelland, L. A., 479
McClintock, C. G., 404, 414
Maccoby, E. E., 136
Maccoby, N., 176, 203, 239, 288
McConaghy, N., 141
McConahay, J. B., 136
McCool, R., 377
McCord, J., 216
McCrae, R. R., 236
McCuddy, M., 372
McDavis, K., 247
MacDonald, A. P., 101, 140, 141
McDonald, F. J., 228, 229
MacDougall, J. M., 280
McDougall, W., 249, 479
McEvoy, J., 14, 285
McFatter, R. M., 209
McGain, G., 479
McGinnies, E., 164
McGovern, L., 245

SUBJECT INDEX

A

Accommodation process, 385

Aggression, 278–309; active suppression, 279; androgens and, 281; animal, 281; biological basis, 280–82; condemnation of, 294–95; cross-cultural differences, 281–82; definition, 279–80; desensitization to, 291–92; displacement of 284–85; drugs and, 299–301; emotion and, 279, 293–94, 301, 303–04; environment and, 304–07; Freud's theory of, 280–81; frustration and, 294–99; indirect and direct, 279; learned, 282–93; Lorenz's theory of, 280–81; noise and, 468–69; norms of, 292–93; passive, 279; reduction of, 287, 291–92, 301–05; reward and punishment of, 282–89, 303–04; sex and, 299–301; and television violence, 289–92; weapons and, 306–07

Affect defined, 82

Affective component of attitudes, 121

Affiliation needs in leaders, 320; sources of, 100–01

Aging: learned helplessness and, 332–33; life satisfaction and, 485–86

Agreement bias in attitudes, 189

Altruism, 242, 266. *See also* Positive social action

Androgens and aggression, 281

Anonymity: and deindividuation, 305–06; and positive social action, 266

Androgyny, 370–71

Antisocial action, 242

Applications of social psychology, 5, 456–58, 482–87

Architecture, 458–64; behavior settings, 470; dormitories, 462–64; ecological approach, 470; noise and, 465–69; sense of community, 460–61, 464; space, 458–64. *See also* Environment; Physical environment

Archival research, 29

Arousal: aggression and reduction of, 302; generalized, 75; labeling, 75–77

Assimilation in attitude change, 172–73; of information, 365–66

Association, 55–57

Attitudes: components of, 121; definition, 121; intentions and, 195–97; salience in prejudice, 141–45; similarity and attraction, 95–96; survey, 30–31

Attitude change: audience characteristics, 171–76; and behavior, 193–97; Bem's model, 190–91; channel of communication, 170–71; cognitive dissonance, 178–86; commitment, 184–85; communicator's characteristics, 163–67; communicator's environment, 176–77; conformity and, 355–56; Festinger's model, 178; Fishbein's model, 195–97; information processing, 186–93; message, 167, 170; persuasibility and, 165–66; reactance and, 368–69

Attraction: complementarity, 97–99; costs and rewards, 82–84; deep relations, 105–16; familiarity, 85–86; Hall's model, 86–88; Homan's model, 86–88; information and, 100; ingratiation, 99–100; matching process, 90–91; physical beauty, 89–95; positive regard, 99–100; proximity and, 84–85, 86–89; rules of distance and, 86–89; and scripts, 407–08; similarity, 95–99; social influence and, 373. *See also* Physical attraction

Attribution: actor and audience, 67–68; biases in,

68; causality, 63–70; criticisms of theory, 69–70; of emotions, 74–77; error, 66–67; internal and external, 63; Kelley's model, 63–65; of responsibility, 251–52; rules of, 64–65; self-serving bias, 68–69. *See also* Social perception

Audiences: and attitude change, 171–76; effect on performance, 8, 435–41

Authoritarian personality, 131–33; conformity and, 359

Authority, obedience and, 362

Autokinetic effect, 351–52

Availability bias, 52

Availability heuristic, 52

Averaging model of impression formation, 59–61

B

Balance theory, 188–89

Base-rate information, 49–51

Battered children, 284–85

Behavior, attitude change and, 193–97; setting, 470

Behaviorism, 18–19, 26; human values and, 25–28; moral actions, 203–12

Bennington study, 354–55

Bias: in attitude change, 85–86; conceptual, 41–44; experimenter, 33–34; in group decisions, 441–46; in social perception, 65–68

Birth-order: affiliation and, 101; intelligence and, 481; power and, 319

Bogus pipeline procedure, 142, 144

Bystander intervention, 255–62; crime and, 256–57; diffusion of responsibility, 258–59, 262, 441; norms of, 262–64; number of bystanders, 258–60, 262; probability of action, 262–63

C

Case study method, 29–30

Catharsis, 301–03

Causal chains, 70

Causality, 69–70

Cognitive balance, 188

Cognitive component of attitudes, 121

Cognitive development: Kohlberg's theory, 221–30; natural morality, 221–22; Piaget's theory, 218–20

Cognitive dissonance theory, 178–86; criticisms of, 190–91

Cognitive label, 75

Cognitive theory, 20–24, 27; dissonance theory, 178–86, 190–91; human values and, 25–28; moral development, 218–30

Cohesiveness of groups, 421–30; attraction in, 421–22; benefits of, 425–28; competition, 424–25; disadvantages of, 429–30; hierarchies, im-

pediment to, 421–23; human potential and, 426–27; performance and, 425, 428–29; threats to, 423–24. *See also* Decision-making in groups, Group

Commitment, attitude change and, 184–85

Communication: and attitude change, 164–76; in groups, 448–50; nonverbal, 412–14; and prejudice reduction, 151–54

Competition, intergroup, 136–38

Complementarity, attraction and, 97–99

Compliance, 338, 358

Conative component of attitudes, 121

Concepts: learning, 45; problems associated with, 41–44; usefulness of, 41

Conceptualizing, 40–46

Conceptual biases, 41–44

Conformity: Asch's studies of, 353, 356–57; 376–77; compliance and, 358; definition, 348, 354–59; internalization and, 358; personality and, 358–59; understanding of, 357–58

Conscience, 202–03

Consciousness raising, 156–58

Consensus in attributions, 64–65

Consistency: attitude change and, 178, 186; attributions and, 65; emotional, 59; logical, 59; perception and, 57–61

Contagion, 350–51

Cooperation, 399–405; communication and, 404–05; GRIT strategy of, 400–01; and matching strategy, 400; and threat, 402–04; and trust, 405

Coping strategies, 333, 476

Correlation: coefficient, 31–32; definition, 31

Costs in interpersonal attraction, 83. *See also* Exchange theory

Counterexploitation, 400–01

Crime, 256–57; and equity, 394; witness to, 366

Cross-cultural research: on aggressive behavior, 281–82; concept learning, 45–46; facial expressions, 412–14; impression formation, 46–51; methods, 6; moral development, 225, 228; norms of intimacy, 109–11; 112–13; physical beauty, 89; social exchange, 390

Crowding, 476–80

D

Death: instinct, 280; social status and rescue from, 250–51; of spouse, 474–75

Debriefing, 34

Deception, ethics of, 35, 363

Decision-making: attitude change and, 183–84; contribution of social psychologists to, 482–87; marriage and, 115–16

Decision-making in groups, 441–52; Bales's classification system, 450–51; biases in, 441–46;

Human values and social psychological theory, 25–28

Hypothesis, 9

Hypothesis testing, 45

I

Identification, 313–14, 358

Identity, aggression and, 305–06

Idiosyncrasy credits, 328

I-E scale, 333–35

Imitation, 7. *See also* Modeling

Implicit knowledge, 44; theories, 51, 56

Impression formation: and attribution, 63–70; base-rate, 49–51; central traits in, 51–54; primacy and recency effects, 61–63; rules of, 46–47; of self, 47–48; social influences on, 46–51

Impression management, 406–08

Independence, 368, 368–73, 377–79

Independent variable, 32–33

Information, attraction and, 100–01, 104–05

Information distortion, 363–67

Information processing: attitude change and, 186–93; and person perception, 57–63; in stereotype formation, 146–49

Ingratiation, attraction and, 99–100

Instinct: and aggression, 280–81; and altruism, 245; of imitation, 349

Intelligence: family size and, 481–82; leadership and, 321

Interactionism: definition, 236; leadership and, 325–28; morality and, 235–36

Intentions: behavior and, 192–97; beliefs and, 195–97

Intergroup: conflict and competition, 136–38; dissimilarity, 138–39

Internal control, 333–35

Internalization, 358

Interpersonal attraction. *See* Attraction

Interpersonal transaction, 327–29

Interpersonal sensitivity, leadership and, 321–22

Interview method, 30–32

Intimacy: development of, 105–09; norms of, 109–16. *See also* Deep relations

J

"June-bug" epidemic, 350–51

Juries, 442–43

Just-world hypothesis, 251–52

K

Knowledge, explicit versus implicit, 44

L

Labeling, 43; formation of, 46–51; self-gratifying, 47

Leadership: Fiedler's approach, 325–29; interactionism and, 325–28; interpersonal transactions and, 327–29; personality of, 320–23; physical features, 320; situation and, 323–25; task-and-relationship oriented, 325–26

Learned helplessness, 330–35; control and, 333–35; environment and, 330–31; patients and, 330

Life change scale, 473–76

Life space, 23

Locus of control, 333–35

Loneliness, 102–03

Longitudinal research, 231–33

Love, 105–16; duration, 113–16; measurement of, 110–11; norms of, 112–13

Low-ball technique, 374

M

Machiavellian personality, 410–11

Manning, 470–72

Marriage, 113–16; communication in, 114; decision-making and, 115–16; division of labor, 114–15; happiness and, 113–14, 89–91; similarity and, 92, 98–99; success in, 114–16; Winch's complementarity theory, 98–99

Matching strategy, 400–01

Maximum joint payoff, 385–87

Media, prejudice and, 133–34

Memory, 62–63; and attitude change, 185–86, 191–93; attribution and, 62–63; biased scanning, 194; negative memory bias, 148; polarizing effect, 192; recency and primacy effects, 61–36

Mere exposure effect, 85–86

Milgram's obedience experiments, 359–63

Minority influence, 377–79

Mirror-image phenomenon, 151

Mixed-motive situations, 398–99

Modeling: aggression, 286–89; helping behavior, 264–65; moral development, 212–15; prejudice, 131–33; uniform behavior 350–51

Models, 212, 215–16; aggression and, 286, 289; helping behavior and, 265; positive social action, 264–66; prejudice and, 131–33

Motives: affiliation, 100–01, 320; and intentions, 195–97; and moral action, 210–11; and resistance to conformity, 368–73; in social exchange, 384–87; and social perception, 47–48

Morality: behaviorist theory, 203–12; cognitive theory, 218–30; dialectic thinking and, 226–27; disciplinary techniques, 217–18; psychoanalytic theory, 203; rule-role perspective, 232–33; social learning theory, 212-18; socialization versus situationism, 230–36

MUM effect, 366–67

Mutuality in relationships, 107

Reward, 208–12; aggression and, 282–89, 303–04; cooperation and, 400–04; equity and, 391–97; extrinsic and intrinsic, 210–11; moral behavior and, 204–12; power and, 316–17; relationships and, 82–83

Risky shift, 444–46

Ritual, 30

Role-playing: attitude change and, 179–80; as research method, 35

Roles, 24–25

Rule-role theory, 24–25, 27, human values and, 25–28; morality and, 232–33; relationships and, 406–15

Rules, 24–25; attribution, 64–65; exchange, 387–97; groups and, 431; and morality, 203; 222–24; morality of subordination, 232–33; nonverbal behavior and, 412–14; physical distance and, 87; social influence and, 349–50; of violence, 292–93

Rumor, 363–66

S

Scapegoats, 135

Scientific management, 425

Scripts, 406–12

Self-concept. *See* Self-perception

Self-confidence: leadership and, 321; social comparison and, 352

Self-esteem, 72–74; group membership and, 425; power and, 339; prejudice and, 123–26; reaction to help and, 270; similarity, attraction and, 96–97

Self-fulfilling expectations, 127–29; control and, 335

Self-disclosure, intimacy and, 108

Self-handicapping strategies, 17–18

Self-monitoring, 408–09

Self-perception, 70–77; attitude change and, 187–91; construction of self-concept and, 71–74; definition, 70; distinctiveness and, 74; and emotions, 74–77; Festinger's theory, 72–74; Mead's model, 71–72; self-esteem and, 72; Schachter's theory, 75–77; social comparison and, 72–74

Self-reinforcement, 215–16

Self-serving bias, 68–69

Serial reproduction, 364–65

Sex and aggression, 299–301

Sex bias, in media, 133–34

Sex differences: bias in media, 133–34, 232; in conformity, 359; in education, 484–85; effects of physical beauty, 90–92; in intimacy, 111–12; moral decisions, 232–33; and power strategies,

340–41; in prejudice toward women, 125, 130–31; in self-images, 125, 130–31, 134; in self-perceptions of success, 126–27, 130–31; stereotypes of, 123–25

Sex roles, 370–71; stereotypes, 123–26

Shyness, 438–39

Similarity: attraction and, 95–99; social comparison and, 351–52, 372–73

Situational control, 325–26

Situationism: definition, 235; leadership and, 323–25; morality and, 230–36

Sleeper effect on attitudes, 164

Social change: and distribution of power, 339–43; effect of social theory on, 12–13; evaluation research and, 486–87; minority influence on, 337–39; reactive planning and, 483–86; social prediction and, 15–16

Social comparison, 72, 74, 351–52; conformity and, 357; groups and, 431

Social distance, power and, 339

Social distinctiveness, 74

Social Exchange. *See* Exchange

Social facilitation, 8, 435–41

Socal impact theory, 434–35

Social indicators, 483–86

Social influence, 349–79; Asch's studies, 253, 356–57; authority and, 362; compliance and, 358; contagion, 350–51; internalization, 358; modeling, 350–51; obedience and, 359–62; and personality, 358; rule following, 349–50; social comparison and, 351–52; uniformity, 348, 349–53

Social learning theory: equity versus equality, 396; moral development and, 212

Social loafing, 440

Social perception, 40–77; actor and audience, 67; Asch's theory, 51–55; attribution of causality, 63–70; base rate and, 49–50; consistency in, 57–61; context and, 48–51; concepts, 41–46; conceptual biases, 41–44; implicit personality theory and, 56–57; impression formation, 46–51; judgment biases and, 52–53; Kelley's model, 63–65; labeling and, 46–51; memory and, 62–63; natural categories and, 44–45; objectification of rules, 46–47; organization of, 51–63; recency and primacy effects, 61–63; self and, 70–77; self-gratifying labels and, 46–47; self-serving bias, 68–69

Social psychology: application, 7–8; definition, 5–6; goals of research, 15–18; history of, 6–8, 20–21; human values and, 25–28; research methods, 28–35; theoretical orientations, 18–25; theory, 5–6, 9–15

Social reality, 431

Social systems accounting, 483–84
Sociogram, 422
Sociometry, 422
Stanford prison experiment, 335–37
Stereotypes: biases in, 149–50; definition, 145–47; functions of, 149; in-group and out-group, 147–49; sex role, 370–71
Stress, 478–79; environment and, 472–76
Subordination, rules of, 232–33
Surveillance, 376; and power, 313–16

T
Tension of obligation, 270–71
Thanatos, 280
Thematic apperception test, 318–19
Theory: definition, 9; enlightenment effects, 12; generative, 13; goals of, 10–15; logical coherence, 9–10; propositions in, 9; simple and sovereign, 7; in social psychology, 5–6
Threat, 402–04
Traits: descriptions, 54–55; and social perception, 54–55. *See also* Personality

Trucking game, 402–03
Two-factor theory of emotion, 75–77
Type A personality, 478–79
Type B personality, 478–79

U
Uniformity, 348, 349–53
Uniqueness, 369, 372–73
Unit relationship, 272

V
Victim blaming, 252
Value bias: in defining aggression, 279–80; sex-role research and, 371
Violence and television programs, 32. *See also* Aggression

W
War, 280, 281–82
Weapons effect, 306–07
Women, prejudice toward, 123–27, 133–34. *See also* Sex differences; Gender

B
C   3
D   4
E   5
F   6
G   7
H   8
I   9
J   0